Lecture Notes in Computer Science 3006

Commenced Publication in 1973
Founding and Former Series Editors:
Gerhard Goos, Juris Hartmanis, and Jan van Leeuwen

Springer
Berlin
Heidelberg
New York
Hong Kong
London
Milan
Paris
Tokyo

Mitsuru Matsui   Robert Zuccherato (Eds.)

Selected Areas in Cryptography

10th Annual International Workshop, SAC 2003
Ottawa, Canada, August 14-15, 2003
Revised Papers

Springer

Volume Editors

Mitsuru Matsui
Mitsubishi Electric Corporation
5-1-1 Ofuna, Kamakura, Kanagawa, 247-8501 Japan
E-mail: matsui@iss.isl.melco.co.jp

Robert Zuccherato
Entrust Inc.
1000 Innovation Drive, Ottawa, Ontario, Canada K2K 3E7
E-mail: robert.zuccherato@entrust.com

Library of Congress Control Number: 2004102410

CR Subject Classification (1998): E.3, D.4.6, K.6.5, F.2.1-2, C.2.0, H.4.3

ISSN 0302-9743
ISBN 3-540-21370-8 Springer-Verlag Berlin Heidelberg New York

Springer-Verlag is a part of Springer Science+Business Media

springeronline.com

Printed in Germany

Typesetting: Camera-ready by author, data conversion by DA-TeX Gerd Blumenstein
Printed on acid-free paper SPIN: 10996386 06/3142 5 4 3 2 1 0

Preface

SAC 2003 was the tenth in a series of annual workshops on Selected Areas in Cryptography. This marked the third time that the workshop had been held at Carleton University in Ottawa with previous workshops being held there in 1995 and 1997. The intent of the SAC workshops is to provide a relaxed atmosphere in which researchers in cryptography can present and discuss new work on selected areas of current interest.

The themes for the SAC 2003 workshop were:

- design and analysis of symmetric key cryptosystems,
- primitives for symmetric key cryptography, including block and stream ciphers, hash functions, and MACs,
- efficient implementation of cryptographic systems in public and symmetric key cryptography,
- cryptographic solutions for Web services security,
- cryptography and security of trusted and distributed systems.

A total of 85 papers were submitted to SAC 2003, two of which were subsequently withdrawn. After a review process that had all papers reviewed by at least three referees, 25 papers were accepted for presentation at the workshop. We would like to thank all of the authors who submitted papers, whether or not those papers were accepted, for submitting their high-quality work to this workshop.

As well, we were fortunate to have the following two invited speakers at SAC 2003:

- Nicolas Courtois (Schlumberger Smart Cards)
  Algebraic attacks and design of block ciphers, stream ciphers, and multivariate public key schemes
- Virgil D. Gligor (University of Maryland)
  Cryptolight: Perspective and Status

SAC 2003 was memorable for all those involved, not only because of the quality of the technical program, but also because of the massive power blackout that occurred. On August 14, 2003 much of the eastern part of the United States, and most of the province of Ontario were plunged into darkness. The city of Ottawa was without power from about 4:00 pm on August 14 through most of the day on August 15. Despite the lack of power, the workshop carried on in an "unplugged" format with all remaining talks presented in a makeshift lecture hall using chalk and blackboards. The staff of the Tour and Conference Centre at Carleton University deserve special recognition for helping the chairs make alternate arrangements to deal with the blackout. We would also like to thank all SAC attendees and, in particular, the presenters who persevered and made SAC 2003 a success, despite the trying circumstances.

We appreciate the hard work of the SAC 2003 Program Committee. We are also very grateful to the many others who participated in the review process: Gildas Avoine, Florent Bersani, Alex Biryukov, Eric Brier, Jean-Sebastien Coron, Joan Daemen, Christophe De Canniere, Jean-François Dhem, Zhi (Judy) Fu, Virgil Gligor, Florian Hess, Don Johnson, Pascal Junod, Hans-Joachim Knobloch, Joe Lano, John Malone-Lee, Tom Messerges, Jean Monnerat, Svetla Nikova, Dan Page, Pascal Paillier, Matthew Parker, Holger Petersen, Michael Quisquater, Håvard Raddum, Christophe Tymen, Frederik Vercauteren, and Michael Wiener. We apologize for any unintended errors or omissions in this list.

We are also appreciative of the financial support provided by Carleton University, Cloakware Corporation, Entrust, Inc., Mitsubishi Electric, and Queen's University Kingston.

Special thanks are due to Sandy Dare for providing administrative assistance and to the local arrangements committee consisting of Mike Just, Tao Wan, and Dave Whyte for their help.

On behalf of all those involved in organizing the workshop, we thank all the workshop participants for making SAC 2003 a success!

January 2004 Mitsuru Matsui and Robert Zuccherato

Organization

Program Committee

Carlisle Adams	University of Ottawa, Canada
Steve Babbage	Vodafone, UK
Josh Benaloh	Microsoft, USA
Lily Chen	Motorola, USA
Henri Gilbert	France Telecom, France
Helena Handschuh	Gemplus, France
Lars Knudsen	Technical University of Denmark, Denmark
Mitsuru Matsui	Mitsubishi Electric, Japan (Co-chair)
Alfred Menezes	University of Waterloo, Canada
Markus Michels	Secorvo, Germany
Kaisa Nyberg	Nokia, Finland
Bart Preneel	Katholieke Universiteit Leuven, Belgium
Nigel Smart	University of Bristol, UK
Doug Stinson	University of Waterloo, Canada
Paul Van Oorschot	Carleton University, Canada
Serge Vaudenay	EPFL, Switzerland
Robert Zuccherato	Entrust, Canada (Co-chair)

Local Arrangements Committee

Mike Just, Tao Wan, Dave Whyte, Robert Zuccherato

Sponsoring Institutions

Carleton University
Cloakware Corporation
Entrust, Inc.
Mitsubishi Electric
Queen's University Kingston

Table of Contents

Cryptanalysis II

Cryptographic Primitives

Stream Ciphers

Efficient Implementation

Low Cost Security: Explicit Formulae for Genus-4 Hyperelliptic Curves

Jan Pelzl, Thomas Wollinger, and Christof Paar

Department of Electrical Engineering and Information Sciences
Communication Security Group (COSY)
Ruhr-Universität Bochum, Germany
{pelzl,wollinger,cpaar}@crypto.rub.de

Abstract. It is widely believed that genus four hyperelliptic curve cryptosystems (HECC) are not attractive for practical applications because of their complexity compared to systems based on lower genera, especially elliptic curves. Our contribution shows that for low cost security applications genus-4 hyperelliptic curves (HEC) can outperform genus-2 HEC and that we can achieve a performance similar to genus-3 HEC. Furthermore our implementation results show that a genus-4 HECC is an alternative cryptosystem to systems based on elliptic curves.
In the work at hand we present for the first time explicit formulae for genus-4 HEC, resulting in a 60% speed-up compared to the best published results. In addition we implemented genus-4 HECC on a Pentium4 and an ARM microprocessor. Our implementations on the ARM show that for genus four HECC are only a factor of 1.66 slower than genus-2 curves considering group order $\approx 2^{190}$. For the same group order ECC and genus-3 HECC are about a factor of 2 faster than genus-4 curves on the ARM. The two most surprising results are: 1) for low cost security application, namely considering an underlying group of order 2^{128}, HECC with genus 4 outperform genus-2 curves by a factor of 1.46 and has similar performance to genus-3 curves on the ARM and 2) when compared to genus-2 and genus-3, genus-4 HECC are better suited to embedded microprocessors than to general purpose processors.

Keywords: Hyperelliptic curves, genus four, explicit formulae, efficient implementation, low cost security, embedded application, comparison HECC vs. ECC

1 Introduction

It is widely recognized that data security will play a central role in the design of future IT systems. One of the major tools to provide information security is public-key cryptography. Additionally, one notices that more and more IT applications are realized as embedded systems. In fact, 98% of all microprocessors sold today are embedded in household appliances, vehicles, and machines on factory floors [9, 3], whereas only 2% are used in PCs and workstations. Embedded

M. Matsui and R. Zuccherato (Eds.): SAC 2003, LNCS 3006, pp. 1–16, 2004.

processors have a 100 – 1000 times lower computational power than conventional PCs. In addition to many other challenges, the integration of security and privacy in the existing and new embedded applications will be a major one.

Since the invention of public-key (PK) cryptography in 1976, three different variants of PK cryptosystems of practical relevance have been introduced, namely cryptosystems based on the difficulty of integer factorization (e.g. RSA [36]), solving the discrete logarithm problem in finite fields (e.g. Diffie-Hellman [6]), and the discrete logarithm problem (DLP) in the group of points of an elliptic curve (EC) over a finite field [29, 17]. Hyperelliptic curve cryptosystems (HECC) are a generalization of elliptic curve cryptosystems (ECC) that were suggested in 1988 for cryptographic applications [18].

Considering the implementation aspects of the three public-key variants, one notices that a major difference is the bit-length of the operands. It is widely accepted that for commercial applications one needs 1024-bit operands for RSA or Diffie-Hellman. In the case of ECC or HECC applications, a group order of size $\approx 2^{160}$ is believed to be sufficient for moderate long-term security. In this contribution we consider genus-4 HECC over $\mathbb{F}_q$ and therefore we will need at least $4 \cdot \log_2 q \approx 2^{160}$. In particular, for these curves, we will need a field $\mathbb{F}_q$ with $|\mathbb{F}_q| \approx 2^{40}$, i.e., 40-bit long operands. However, in many low cost and embedded applications lower security margins are adequate. In practice, if a group order of 2^{128} is sufficient, the operations can be performed with an operand length of 32-bit. Thus, the underlying field operations can be implemented very efficiently if working with 32-bit microprocessors (e.g. ARM). It is important to point out that the small field sizes and the resulting short operand size of HECC compared to other cryptosystems makes HECC specially promising for the use in embedded environments. We discuss the security of such curves in Section 4.2.

Our Contributions

The work at hand presents for the first time explicit formulae for genus-4 curves. Genus-4 HECC did not draw a lot of attention in the past because they seem to be far less efficient than genus-2 HECC, genus-3 HECC, and ECC. Our contribution is a major step in accelerating this kind of cryptosystem and contrary to common belief we were able to develop explicit formulae that perform the scalar multiplication 72% and 60% faster than previous work by Cantor [5] and Nagao [32], respectively.

Genus-4 HECC are well suited for the implementation of public-key cryptosystems in constrained environments because the underlying arithmetic is performed with relatively small operand bit-lengths. In this contribution, we present our implementation of this cryptosystem on an ARM and a Pentium microprocessor. We were able to perform a 160bit scalar multiplication in 172 msec on the ARM@80MHz and in 6.9 msec on the Pentium4@1.8GHz. In addition, our implementations show, that genus-4 HECC are only a factor of 1.66 and 2.08 slower than genus-2 and genus-3 curves considering group order of $\approx 2^{190}$, respectively. Compared to ECC, the genus-4 HECC are a factor of 2 slower for the same group order .

Genus-4 HEC are well suited, especially for cryptographic applications with short term security. Performing arithmetic with 32-bit operands only, genus-4 HECC allow for a security comparable to of 128-bit ECC. We implemented genus-4 HECC with underlying field arithmetic for 32-bit. In this case one is able to perform arithmetic with only one word. Contrary to the general case, the implementation of genus-4 curves in groups of order $\approx 2^{128}$ outperform genus-2 curves by a factor of about 1.5. Furthermore, our implementation shows that, HECC with genus three and four have similar performance considering the group order $\approx 2^{128}$.

The remainder of the paper is organized as follows. Section 2 summarizes contributions dealing with previous implementations and efficient formulae of genus-4 HECC. Section 3 gives a brief overview of the mathematical background related to HECC and Section 4 considers the security of the implemented HECCs. Sections 5 and 6 present our new explicit formulae for genus-4 curves and methodology used for our implementation. Finally, we end this contribution with a discussion of our results and some conclusions.

2 Previous Work

We will first summarize previous improvements on genus-4 HEC group operations and second introduce implementations published in earlier contributions.

Improvements to HECC Group Operations of Genus-4 HECC Cantor [5] presented algorithms to perform the group operations on HEC in 1987. In recent years, there has been extensive research being performed to speed up the group operations on genus two HECC [32, 16, 27, 30] [43, 23, 24, 25] and genus three [32, 22, 34].
Only Nagao [32] tried to improve Cantor's algorithm for higher genera.

Nagao evaluated the computational cost of the group operations by applying the stated improvements for genus $2 \leq g \leq 10$. The most efficient group addition for genus-4 curves needs 2I + 289M/S or 3I + 286M/S (depending on the cost of the field inversion compared to multiplications, one or the other is more efficient). I refers to field inversion, M to field multiplication, S to field squaring, and M/S to field multiplications or squarings, since squarings are assumed to be of the same complexity as multiplications in these publications. For the computation of a group doubling in genus-4 curves one has to perform 2I + 268M/S or 3I + 260M/S. Notice that the ideas proposed by [32] are used to improve polynomial arithmetic.

Genus-4 HECC Implementations Since HECC were proposed, there have been several software implementations on general purpose machines [21, 38] [42, 39, 27, 30, 22, 23] and publications dealing with hardware implementations of HECC [46, 4]. Only very recently work dealing with the implementation of HECC on embedded systems was published in [33, 34].

Table 1. Execution times of recent HEC implementations in software

reference	processor	genus	field	$t_{scalarmult.}$ in ms
[21]	Pentium@100MHz	4	$\mathbb{F}_{2^{31}}$	1100
[38]	Alpha@467MHz	4	$\mathbb{F}_{2^{41}}$	96.6
	Pentium-II@300MHz	4	$\mathbb{F}_{2^{41}}$	10900
[39]	Alpha21164A@600MHz	4	$\mathbb{F}_{2^{41}}$	43

The results of previous genus-4 HECC software implementations are summarized in Table 1. All implementations use Cantor's algorithm with polynomial arithmetic. We remark that the contribution at hand is the first genus-4 HECC implementation based on explicit formulae.

3 Mathematical Background

The mathematical background described in this section is limited to the material that is required in our contribution. The interested reader is referred to [19, 28, 20] for more details.

3.1 HECC and the Jacobian

Let $\mathbb{F}$ be a finite field, and let $\overline{\mathbb{F}}$ be the algebraic closure of $\mathbb{F}$. A hyperelliptic curve C of genus $g \geq 1$ over $\mathbb{F}$ is the set of solutions $(u, v) \in \mathbb{F} \times \mathbb{F}$ to the equation

$$C : v^2 + h(u)v = f(u)$$

The polynomial $h(u) \in \mathbb{F}[u]$ is of degree at most g and $f(u) \in \mathbb{F}[u]$ is a monic polynomial of degree $2g + 1$. For odd characteristic it suffices to let $h(u) = 0$ and to have $f(u)$ square free.

A divisor $D = \sum m_i P_i$, $m_i \in \mathbb{Z}$, is a finite formal sum of $\overline{\mathbb{F}}$-points. The set of divisors of degree zero will be denoted by $\mathbb{D}^0$. Every rational function on the curve gives rise to a divisor of degree zero and is called principal. The the set of all principal divisors is denoted by $\mathbb{P}$. We can define the Jacobian of C over $\mathbb{F}$, denoted by $\mathbb{J}_C(\mathbb{F})$ as the quotient group $\mathbb{D}^0/\mathbb{P}$.

In [5] it is shown that the divisors of the Jacobian can be represented as a pair of polynomials $a(u)$ and $b(u)$ with $\deg b(u) < \deg a(u) \leq g$, with $a(u)$ dividing $b(u)^2 + h(u)b(u) - f(u)$ and where the coefficients of $a(u)$ and $b(u)$ are elements of $\mathbb{F}$ [31]. In the remainder of this paper, a divisor D represented by polynomials will be denoted by $div(a, b)$.

3.2 Group Operations in the Jacobian

This section gives a brief description of the algorithms used for adding and doubling divisors on $\mathbb{J}_C(\mathbb{F})$. Algorithm 1 describes the group addition. Doubling a divisor is easier than general addition and therefore, Steps 1,2, and 3 of Algorithm 1 can be simplified as follows:

Algorithm 1 Group addition

Require: $D_1 = \text{div}(a_1, b_1)$, $D_2 = \text{div}(a_2, b_2)$
Ensure: $D = \text{div}(a_3, b_3) = D_1 + D_2$
1: $d = \gcd(a_1, a_2, b_1 + b_2 + h) = s_1 a_1 + s_2 a_2 + s_3(b_1 + b_2 + h)$
2: $a'_0 = a_1 a_2 / d^2$
3: $b'_0 = [s_1 a_1 b_2 + s_2 a_2 b_1 + s_3(b_1 b_2 + f)] d^{-1} (\text{mod} a'_0)$
4: $k = 0$
5: **while** $\deg a'_k > g$ **do**
6: $\quad k = k + 1$
7: $\quad a'_k = \frac{f - b'_{k-1} h - (b'_{k-1})^2}{a'_{k-1}}$
8: $\quad b'_k = (-h - b'_{k-1}) \bmod a'_k$
9: **end while**
10: Output $(a_3 = a'_k, b_3 = b'_k)$

1: $d = \gcd(a, 2b + h) = s_1 a + s_3(2b + h)$
2: $a'_0 = a^2 / d^2$
3: $b'_0 = [s_1 ab + s_3(b^2 + f)] d^{-1} (\text{mod} a'_0)$

3.3 Harley's Algorithm

The algorithms given in the previous section for the group operations in the Jacobian of HEC require the use of polynomial arithmetic for polynomials with coefficients in the definition field. An alternative approach for genus-2 curves was proposed by Harley in [15]. Harley computes the necessary coefficients from the steps of Cantor's algorithm directly in the definition field without the use of polynomial arithmetic, resulting in a faster execution time.

In [15], the authors found out that it is essential to know the weight of the input divisor to determine explicit formulae. For each case, implementations of different explicit formulae are required. However, for practical purposes it is sufficient to only consider the most frequent cases[1] which occur with probability of $1 - O(1/q)$, where q is the group order. General formulae for the most frequent case for genus-2 curves and arbitrary characteristic were presented in [23].

Algorithm 2 and 3 describe the most frequent case of group addition and doubling for genus-4 curves, respectively.

In Section 5 we develop for the first time explicit formulae of Cantor's Algorithm for genus-4 curves.

4 Security of the Implemented HECC

4.1 Security of HECC with High Genera

The DLP on $\mathbb{J}(\mathbb{F})$ can be stated as follows: given two divisors $D_1, D_2 \in \mathbb{J}(\mathbb{F})$, determine the smallest integer m such that $D_2 = mD_1$, if such an m exists.

[1] For addition the inputs are two co-prime polynomials and for doubling the input is a square free polynomial.

Algorithm 2 Most Frequent Case for Group Addition (g=4)

Require: $D_1 = \text{div}(a_1, b_1)$, $D_2 = \text{div}(a_2, b_2)$
Ensure: $D_3 = \text{div}(a_3, b_3) = D_1 + D_2$
1: $k = \frac{f - b_1 h - b_1^2}{a_1}$ (exact division)
2: $s \equiv \frac{b_2 - b_1}{a_1} \bmod a_2$
3: $z = s a_1$
4: $a = \frac{k - s(z + h + 2b_1)}{a_2}$ (exact division)
5: $a' = a$ made monic
6: $b' \equiv -(h + z + b_1) \bmod a'$
7: $a_3 = \frac{f - b'h - (b')^2}{a'}$ (exact division)
8: $b_3 \equiv -(b' + h) \bmod a_3$

Algorithm 3 Most Frequent Case for Group Doubling (g=4)

Require: $D_1 = \text{div}(a_1, b_1)$
Ensure: $D_2 = \text{div}(a_2, b_2) = 2D_1$
1: $k = \frac{b^2 - bh - f}{a}$ (exact division)
2: $s \equiv \frac{k}{h + 2b} \bmod a$
3: $a' = s^2 + \frac{k - s(h + 2b)}{a}$ (exact division)
4: $a'' = a'$ made monic
5: $b'' \equiv -(h + sa + b) \bmod a'$
6: $a_2 = \frac{f - b''h - (b'')^2}{a''}$ (exact division)
7: $b_2 \equiv -(b'' + h) \bmod a_2$

The Pollard rho method and its variants [35, 45, 13] solve the DLP with complexity $O(\sqrt{n})$ in generic groups of order n. In [11, 37] attacks against special cases of HECC were discovered with complexity smaller than $O(\sqrt{n})$. An algorithm to compute the DL in subexponential time for sufficiently large genera and its variants were published in [1, 10, 7, 14, 8]. The complexity of this algorithm is only better than the Pollard's rho method for $g \geq 3$. In [14] it is shown that index-calculus algorithms in the Jacobian of HEC have a higher complexity than the Pollard rho method for curves of genus greater than 4. Recent results by Thériault [44] show progress in attacks against HEC of genus 4. An asymptotic running time of $O(n^{14/9})$ compared to $O(n^2)$ for Pollard's rho can be achieved. However, an actual attack on curves of group order of $\approx 2^{128}$ is currently infeasible due to high storage usage. Furthermore, the values given in [44] are asymptotical, thus, large constant factors might influence the running times for small group orders.

4.2 Security of 128-bit HECC

In [26], Lenstra and Verheul argue, that for commercial security in the year 2003, 136-bit ECC should be considered. Furthermore, the authors state that ECC using 136-bit keys are as secure as 1068-bit keys for RSA or DSS. This notion of commercial security is based on the hypothesis that a 56-bit block cipher offered adequate security in 1982.

It is also worth to point out that the factorization of the 512-bit RSA challenge took only about 2% of the time required to break the ECC2K-108 challenge (or to break DES). This implies that ECC or HECC in groups of order 2^{128} offer far more security than a 512-bit RSA system. Nevertheless, RSA with a 512-bit key is still in use, for example in fielded smart card applications.

5 First Explicit Formulae for Genus-4 HECC

For the derivation of the explicit formulae, all polynomial calculations have to be mapped onto field operations.

The work at hand is the first approach using explicit formulae to optimize the group operations for genus-4 HEC. Table 7 presents the explicit formulae for a group addition and Table 8 those for a group doubling. The complexity of the formulae shown in the tables is based on the assumption that the coefficients h_i of $h(x) = h_4x^4 + h_3x^3 + h_2x^2 + h_1x + h_0$ are from $\{0, 1\}$. In addition, we can set f_8 to zero by substituting $x' = x + \frac{f_8}{9}$. Thus, all multiplications with the coefficients h_i for $i \in \{0, 1, 2, 3, 4\}$ and f_8 are neglected in the total operation count. A comparison of the computational complexity of our approach with the results of previously done work on genus-4 curves is illustrated in Table 2.

An extensive description on the methodology to reduce the complexity of the group operation can be found in [22, 23, 33].

A detailed analysis of the explicit formulae give rise to certain types of curves with good properties, i.e. optimum performance regarding the number of required field operations for the execution of the group operations. As a result of this analysis, curves of the form $y^2 + y = f(x)$ over extension fields of characteristic two turn out to be ideal. Unfortunately this kind of curve is supersingular and therefore not suited for use in cryptography [14, 12, 40]. Thus, we propose to use HEC of the form $y^2 + xy = f(x)$ over $\mathbb{F}_{2^n}$, which seem to be the best choice without any security limitations. With these curves, we can save 12 multiplications in the case of the group addition and 118 multiplications the for group doubling.

The following comparison is based on the assumption that a scalar multiplication with an n-bit scalar is realized by the sliding window method. Hence, the approximated cost of the scalar multiplication is $n \cdot$ doublings $+ 0.2 \cdot n \cdot$ additions for a 4-bit window size [2]. For arbitrary curves over fields of general characteristic, we achieve a 24% improvement[2] compared to the results presented in [32]. In the case of HEC over $\mathbb{F}_{2^n}$ with $h(x) = x$, we can reach an improvement up to 60% compared[2] to the best known formulae for genus-4 curves. When comparing our result to the original formulae presented by Cantor, the speed up is 72% and 47% for curves with $h(x) = x$ and general curves[2], respectively.

[2] We assumed, that the computation time for one inversion is approximately the same as for 8 multiplications. This value is fortified by several implementations targeting HECC on 32-bit processors, see Appendix A.

Table 2. Complexity comparison of the group operations on HEC of genus four

	field characteristic	curve properties	cost addition	cost doubling
Cantor [32]	general		$6I + 386M/S$	$6I + 359M/S$
Nagao [32]	odd	$h(x) = 0,\ f_i \in \mathbb{F}_2$	$2I + 289M/S$	$2I + 268M/S$
This work (Tables 7, 8)	general	$h_i \in \mathbb{F}_2,\ f_8 = 0$	$2I + 160M + 4S$	$2I + 193M + 16S$
	two	$h(x) = x,\ f_8 = 0$	$2I + 148M + 6S$	$2I + 75M + 14S$

6 HECC Implementation

We implemented the derived explicit formulae for genus-4 HECC from Section 5 on a Pentium4 and on an ARM microprocessor. This contribution is the first to implement explicit formulae for genus-4 HECC and is also the first to run this cryptosystem on an embedded processor as the ARM7TDMI.

6.1 Methodology

This subsection provides a short overview of the tools and the methodology used which finally lead to a successful implementation of the group operations.
The methodology is as follows:

1. Test the explicit formulae: NTL-based [41] implementation of Cantor's algorithm and of the new explicit formulae.
2. Speeding up the implementation: We developed our own library for the required field and group operations.
3. Testing the code on the Pentium.
4. Portation to the ARM: The code was loaded into the ARM7TDMI@80MHz (ARMulator).
5. Running and testing genus-4 HECC on the ARM7TDMI (ARMulator).
6. Detailed timing analysis for different field sizes and curves.

6.2 The ARM Processor

As primary target platform, we choose the popular embedded 32-bit ARM microprocessor which can be found in mobile communication devices and consumer electronics. ARM stands for *Advanced RISC Machine* and shows a typical RISC architecture with additional features like flag-depending instruction execution. ARM 7 is based on a von Neuman architecture. It is well suited for small hand held devices such as PDAs. As a reference and for testing we implemented all cryptosystems as well on a Pentium4.

7 Results

In this section we present our implementation results for the ARM and the Pentium. In the first part we discuss our results for standard commercial security application, whereas the second part concentrates on low cost security with genus-4 curves.

7.1 Pentium and ARM Timings

Tables 3 and 4, present the execution times for genus-4 HECC operations on the ARM processor and the Pentium, respectively. We provide timings for the group addition, group doubling and the scalar multiplication for different group orders. In addition we present the timings for genus-3 HECC, genus-2 HECC, and ECC using the same underlying library running on the same processor for comparison [34]. The formulae used for HECC implementation of genera two [23] and three [34] are to our knowledge the most efficient. In the case of ECC projective coordinates were used.

Contrary to common believe, the results show that genus-4 curves are worth to implement on 32-bit processors, though their performance for group orders larger than 2^{160} is slightly worse than that of HECC with genus $g \leq 3$. Considering a group order of approximately 2^{190}, genus-2 and genus-3 curves are a factor of 1.66 and a factor of 2.08, respectively, better than the introduced formulae for genus-4 HECC on the ARM7TDMI. Similarly, we obtain speed-ups of a factor of 1.72 and factor of 2.77 when using genus-2 and genus-3, respectively, com-

Table 3. Timings of group operations with ARMulator ARM7TDMI@80MHz (explicit formulae)

Genus	Field	Group order	Group addition in μs	Group doubling in μs	Scalar. mult. in ms
4	$\mathbb{F}_{2^{40}}$	2^{160}	1315	740	172.43
	$\mathbb{F}_{2^{41}}$	2^{164}	1304	734	174.80
	$\mathbb{F}_{2^{44}}$	2^{176}	1319	747	190.07
	$\mathbb{F}_{2^{46}}$	2^{184}	1323	752	199.49
	$\mathbb{F}_{2^{47}}$	2^{188}	1310	745	201.89
	$\mathbb{F}_{2^{63}}$	2^{252}	1372	797	286.51
3	$\mathbb{F}_{2^{63}}$	2^{189}	615	219	72.09
2	$\mathbb{F}_{2^{95}}$	2^{190}	511	504	121.49
1	$\mathbb{F}_{2^{191}}$	2^{191}	598	358	100

Table 4. Timings of group operations on the Pentium4@1.8GHz (explicit formulae)

Genus	Field	Group order	Group addition in μs	Group doubling in μs	Scalar. mult. in ms
4	$\mathbb{F}_{2^{40}}$	2^{160}	51.0	29.3	6.88
	$\mathbb{F}_{2^{41}}$	2^{164}	49.7	27.6	6.96
	$\mathbb{F}_{2^{44}}$	2^{176}	49.9	27.9	7.50
	$\mathbb{F}_{2^{46}}$	2^{184}	50.1	28.2	7.92
	$\mathbb{F}_{2^{47}}$	2^{188}	50.3	29.3	8.05
	$\mathbb{F}_{2^{63}}$	2^{252}	51.6	29.8	8.43
3	$\mathbb{F}_{2^{63}}$	2^{189}	23.4	8.6	2.91
2	$\mathbb{F}_{2^{95}}$	2^{190}	19.1	18.8	4.68
1	$\mathbb{F}_{2^{191}}$	2^{191}	15.4	8.7	2.78

pared to genus-4 curves on the Pentium4 for the same group order. Compared to ECC, genus-4 HECC performs a factor of 2.90 and a factor of 2.02 worse on the Pentium and ARM7TDMI, respectively.

Notice that the relative performance of genus-4 HECC is always better on the ARM microprocessor compared to the Pentium. Hence, we conclude that genus-4 HECC are well suited for the encryption in constraint environments and we encourage the research community to put more effort into the further development of this system.

7.2 Low Cost Security

In contrast to the facts mentioned in Section 7.1, there is a clear benefit of using genus-4 HECC over a 32-bit finite field. For hyperelliptic curve cryptosystems with a group order of $\approx 2^{128}$, genus-4 group operations only require 32-bit field arithmetic. Thus, the processor word is optimal utilized and the cryptosystem does not need additional multi-precision arithmetic.

Analyzing the results for a group order of around 2^{128} as presented in Table 5, a major advantage of genus-4 HEC is noticeable. The comparison of the timings yield to following facts (numbers in parenthesis are for the Pentium timings):

- Genus-4 HECC outperforms genus-2 HECC by a factor of 1.46 (1.24)
- HECC of genus 3 are slightly faster by a factor of 1.04 (1.08) than genus-4 HECC

As a result of this comparison, we suggest the use of genus-4 HECC for short term security applications. Despite the high number of required field operations compared to HEC with genus $g \leq 3$, group operations on genus-4 HEC are easier to implement. This fact relies on the relatively simple field arithmetic based on operands of length no longer than 32 bits.

Table 5. Timings on the ARM7TDMI@80MHz and Pentium4@1.8GHz for group order $\approx 2^{128}$ (explicit formulae)

ARMulator ARM7TDMI@80MHz					
Genus	Field	Group order	Group addition in μs	Group doubling in μs	Scalar. mult. in ms
4	$\mathbb{F}_{2^{32}}$	2^{128}	441	260	49.07
3	$\mathbb{F}_{2^{43}}$	2^{129}	603	199	47.13
2	$\mathbb{F}_{2^{63}}$	2^{126}	450	443	71.54
Pentium4@1,8GHz					
4	$\mathbb{F}_{2^{32}}$	2^{128}	17.3	11.6	2.14
3	$\mathbb{F}_{2^{43}}$	2^{129}	23.6	8.2	1.98
2	$\mathbb{F}_{2^{63}}$	2^{126}	16.8	15.9	2.66

8 Conclusions

The work at hand presents major improvements to hyperelliptic curve cryptosystems of genus 4. We were able to reduce the average complexity of a scalar multiplication by up to 60% compared to the currently best known formulae. The steps of the explicit formulae used to compute the group operations are presented for the first time for the case of genus-4 curves.

Additionally, we showed with the first implementation of genus-4 HECC on an embedded microprocessor that this cryptosystem is better suited for the use in embedded environments, than to general purpose processors. Contrary to common believe, our timing results show the practical relevance of this system.

Especially for applications based on asymmetric algorithms with group orders around 2^{128}, genus-4 HECC can be consider a viable choice. Not only the underlying field operations consist of simple 32-bit operations, but also we get better performance than genus-2 curves and similar speed than genus-3 curves.

References

[1] L. M. Adlemann, J. DeMarrais, and M.-D. Huang. A subexponential algorithm for discrete logarithms over the rational subgroup of the jacobians of large genus hyperelliptic curves over finite fields. In *The 1st Algorithmic Number Theory Symposium — ANTS I*, pages 28 – 40, Berlin, May 1994. Springer-Verlag. LNCS 877. 6

[2] I. F. Blake, G. Seroussi, and N. P. Smart. *Elliptic Curves in Cryptography.* London Mathematical Society Lecture Notes Series 265. Cambridge University Press, Reading, Massachusetts, 1999. 7

[3] G. Borriello and R. Want. Embedded computation meets the world wide web. *Communications of the ACM*, 43(5):59–66, May 2000. 1

[4] N. Boston, T. Clancy, Y. Liow, and J. Webster. Genus Two Hyperelliptic Curve Coprocessor. In *Workshop on Cryptographic Hardware and Embedded Systems — CHES 2002*, New York, 2002. Springer Verlag. LNCS 2523. 3

[5] D. G. Cantor. Computing in Jacobian of a Hyperelliptic Curve. In *Mathematics of Computation*, volume 48(177), pages 95 – 101, January 1987. 2, 3, 4

[6] W. Diffie and M. E. Hellman. New directions in cryptography. *IEEE Transactions on Information Theory*, IT-22:644–654, 1976. 2

[7] A. Enge. Computing discrete logarithms in high-genus hyperelliptic jacobians in provably subexponential time. Preprint; Available at `http://www.math.waterloo.ca/CondO_Dept/CORR/corr99.html`, 1999. 6

[8] A. Enge and P. Gaudry. A general framework for subexponential discrete logarithm algorithms. *Acta Arith.*, 102:83 – 103, 2002. 6

[9] D. Estrin, R. Govindan, and J. Heidemann. Embedding the Internet. *Communications of the ACM*, 43(5):39–41, May 2000. 1

[10] R. Flassenberg and S.Paulus. Sieving in function fields. Available at `ftp://ftp.informatik.tu-darmstadt.de/pub/TI/TR/TI-97-13.rafla.ps.gz`, 1997. To appear in Experimental Mathematics. 6

[11] G. Frey and H.-G. Rück. A remark concerning m-divisibility and the discrete logarithm in the divisor class group of curves. *Mathematics of Computation*, 62(206):865–874, April 1994. 6

[12] S. D. Galbraith. Supersingular Curves in Cryptography. In *Advances in Cryptology — ASIACRYPT 2001*, pages 495–517, 2001. LNCS 2248. 7

[13] R. Gallant, R. Lambert, and S. Vanstone. Improving the parallelized Pollard lambda search on anomalous binary curves. *Mathematics of Computation*, 69(232):1699–1705, 2000. 6

[14] P. Gaudry. An algorithm for solving the discrete log problem on hyperelliptic curves. In Bart Preneel, editor, *Advances in Cryptology — EUROCRYPT 2000*, pages 19–34, Berlin, Germany, 2000. Springer-Verlag. LNCS 1807. 6, 7

[15] P. Gaudry and R. Harley. Counting Points on Hyperelliptic Curves over Finite Fields. In W. Bosma, editor, *The 4th Algorithmic Number Theory Symposium — ANTS IV*, pages 297 – 312, Berlin, 2000. Springer Verlag. LNCS 1838. 5

[16] R. Harley. Fast Arithmetic on Genus Two Curves. Available at http://cristal.inria.fr/~harley/hyper/, 2000. 3

[17] N. Koblitz. Elliptic Curve Cryptosystems. *Mathematics of Computation*, 48:203–209, 1987. 2

[18] N. Koblitz. A Family of Jacobians Suitable for Discrete Log Cryptosystems. In Shafi Goldwasser, editor, *Advances in Cryptology — Crypto '88*, pages 94 – 99, Berlin, 1988. Springer-Verlag. LNCS 403. 2

[19] N. Koblitz. Hyperelliptic Cryptosystems. In Ernest F. Brickell, editor, *Journal of Cryptology*, pages 139 – 150, 1989. 4

[20] N. Koblitz. *Algebraic Aspects of Cryptography*. Algorithms and Computation in Mathematics. Springer-Verlag, 1998. 4

[21] U. Krieger. signature.c. Master's thesis, Universität Essen, Fachbereich 6 (Mathematik und Informatik), February 1997. (Diplomarbeit). 3, 4

[22] J. Kuroki, M. Gonda, K. Matsuo, Jinhui Chao, and Shigeo Tsujii. Fast Genus Three Hyperelliptic Curve Cryptosystems. In *The 2002 Symposium on Cryptography and Information Security, Japan - SCIS 2002*, Jan.29-Feb.1 2002. 3, 7

[23] T. Lange. Efficient Arithmetic on Genus 2 Hyperelliptic Curves over Finite Fields via Explicit Formulae. Cryptology ePrint Archive, Report 2002/121, 2002. http://eprint.iacr.org/. 3, 5, 7, 9

[24] T. Lange. Inversion-Free Arithmetic on Genus 2 Hyperelliptic Curves. Cryptology ePrint Archive, Report 2002/147, 2002. http://eprint.iacr.org/. 3

[25] T. Lange. Weighted Coordinates on Genus 2 Hyperelliptic Curves. Cryptology ePrint Archive, Report 2002/153, 2002. http://eprint.iacr.org/. 3

[26] A. Lenstra and E. Verheul. Selecting Cryptographic Key Sizes. In Hideki Imai and Yuliang Zheng, editors, *Third International Workshop on Practice and Theory in Public Key Cryptography — PKC 2000*, Berlin, 2000. Springer-Verlag. LNCS 1751. 6

[27] K. Matsuo, J. Chao, and S. Tsujii. Fast Genus Two Hyperelliptic Curve Cryptosystems. In *ISEC2001-31, IEICE*, 2001. 3

[28] A. J. Menezes, Y.-H. Wu, and R. Zuccherato. An elementary introduction to hyperelliptic curves. In N. Koblitz, editor, *Algebraic Aspects of Cryptography*, Berlin, Heidelberg, 1996. Springer Verlag. 4

[29] V. Miller. Uses of Elliptic Curves in Cryptography. In H. C. Williams, editor, *Advances in Cryptology — CRYPTO '85*, pages 417–426, Berlin, Germany, 1986. Springer-Verlag. LNCS 218. 2

[30] Y. Miyamoto, H. Doi, K. Matsuo, J. Chao, and S. Tsuji. A Fast Addition Algorithm of Genus Two Hyperelliptic Curves. In *SCIS, IEICE Japan*, pages 497 – 502, 2002. in Japanese. 3

[31] D. Mumford. Tata lectures on theta II. In *Prog. Math.*, volume 43. Birkhäuser, 1984. 4

[32] K. Nagao. Improving group law algorithms for Jacobians of hyperelliptic curves. In W. Bosma, editor, *ANTS IV*, pages 439 – 448, Berlin, 2000. Springer Verlag. LNCS 1838. 2, 3, 7, 8

[33] J. Pelzl. Hyperelliptic Cryptosystems on Embedded Microprocessors. Master's thesis, Fakultät für Elektrotechnik und Informationstechnik, Ruhr-Universität Bochum, September 2002. (Diplomarbeit). 3, 7

[34] J. Pelzl, T. Wollinger, J. Guajardo, and C. Paar. Hyperelliptic Curve Cryptosystems: Closing the Performance Gap to Elliptic Curves. In C. D. Walter, C. K. Koc, and C. Paar, editors, *Workshop on Cryptographic Hardware and Embedded Systems — CHES 2003*, pages 351–365, Berlin, 2003. Springer Verlag. LNCS 2779. 3, 9

[35] J. M. Pollard. Monte Carlo methods for index computation mod p. *Mathematics of Computation*, 32(143):918–924, July 1978. 6

[36] R. L. Rivest, A. Shamir, and L. Adleman. A Method for Obtaining Digital Signatures and Public-Key Cryptosystems. *Communications of the ACM*, 21(2):120–126, February 1978. 2

[37] H.-G. Rück. On the discrete logarithm in the divisor class group of curves. *Mathematics of Computation*, 68(226):805–806, 1999. 6

[38] Y. Sakai and K. Sakurai. Design of Hyperelliptic Cryptosystems in small Characteristic and a Software Implementation over $\mathbb{F}_{2^n}$. In *Advances in Cryptology — ASIACRYPT '98*, pages 80 – 94, Berlin, 1998. Springer Verlag. LNCS 1514. 3, 4

[39] Y. Sakai and K. Sakurai. On the Practical Performance of Hyperelliptic Curve Cryptosystems in Software Implementation. In *IEICE Transactions on Fundamentals of Electronics, Communications and Computer Sciences*, volume E83-A NO.4, pages 692 – 703, April 2000. . 3, 4

[40] J. Scholten and J. Zhu. Hyperelliptic curves in characteristic 2. *International Mathematics Research Notices*, 2002(17):905 – 917, 2002. 7

[41] V. Shoup. NTL: A libary for doing Number Theory (version 5.0c), 2001. http://www.shoup.net/ntl/index.html. 8

[42] N. P. Smart. On the Performance of Hyperelliptic Cryptosystems. In *Advances in Cryptology - EUROCRYPT '99*, pages 165 – 175, Berlin, 1999. Springer-Verlag. LNCS 1592. 3

[43] M. Takahashi. Improving Harley Algorithms for Jacobians of Genus 2 Hyperelliptic Curves. In *SCIS, IEICE Japan*, 2002. in Japanese. 3

[44] N. Thériault. Index calculus attack for hyperelliptic curves of small genus, 2003. To appear in: Advances in Cryptology — ASIACRYPT '03. 6

[45] D. H. Wiedemann. Solving Sparse Linear Equations Over Finite Fields. *IEEE Transactions on Information Theory*, IT-32(1):54–62, January 1986. 6

[46] T. Wollinger. Computer Architectures for Cryptosystems Based on Hyperelliptic Curves. Master's thesis, ECE Department, Worcester Polytechnic Institute, Worcester, Massachusetts, USA, May 2001. 3

A Timings for Field Operation

In this section we present the timings for field operations for selected field orders.

Table 6. Timings field operations for genus-4 HECC

ARMulator ARM7TDMI@80MHz				
Field	Group order	Field inversion in μs	Field multiplication in μs	inversion / multiplication
$\mathbb{F}_{2^{32}}$	2^{128}	26.8	2.6	10.16
$\mathbb{F}_{2^{40}}$	2^{160}	49.2	7.3	6.73
$\mathbb{F}_{2^{47}}$	2^{188}	77.5	7.3	10.5
Pentium4@1.8GHz				
Field	Group order	Field inversion in ns	Field multiplication in ns	inversion / multiplication
$\mathbb{F}_{2^{32}}$	2^{128}	1650	168	9.82
$\mathbb{F}_{2^{40}}$	2^{160}	2519	413	6.04
$\mathbb{F}_{2^{47}}$	2^{188}	3752	402	9.33

B Explicit Formulae Genus-4 HECC

Table 7. Explicit formulae for adding on a HEC of genus four

Input	Weight four reduced divisors $D_1 = (a_1, b_1)$ and $D_2 = (a_2, b_2)$ where: $a_1 = x^4 + ax^3 + bx^2 + cx + d$; $b_1 = ix^3 + jx^2 + kx + l$ $a_2 = x^4 + ex^3 + fx^2 + gx + h$; $b_2 = mx^3 + nx^2 + ox + p$ $h = h_4x^4 + h_3x^3 + h_2x^2 + h_1x + h_0$, where $h_i \in \{0, 1\}$; $f = x^9 + f_7x^7 + f_6x^6 + f_5x^5 + f_4x^4 + f_3x^3 + f_2x^2 + f_1x + f_0$
Output	A weight four reduced divisor $D_3 = (a_3, b_3) = D_1 + D_2$ where: $a_3 = x^4 + \tilde{a}x^3 + \tilde{b}x^2 + \tilde{c}x + \tilde{d}$; $b_3 = \tilde{i}x^3 + \tilde{j}x^2 + \tilde{k}x + \tilde{l}$

Step	Procedure (For simplicity, only the implemented case is given.)	Cost	
1	Almost inverse $inv = r/a_1 \bmod a_2 = inv_3x^3 + inv_2x^2 + inv_1x + inv_0$: $r_{23} = e + a$; $r_{22} = f + b$; $r_{21} = g + c$; $r_{20} = h + d$; $t_{20} = 1$; $r_{33} = r_{23} \cdot a + r_{22}$; $r_{32} = r_{23} \cdot b + r_{21}$; $r_{31} = r_{23} \cdot c + r_{20}$; $r_{30} = r_{23} \cdot d$; $t_{31} = 1$; $t_{30} = r_{23}$; $r_{42} = r_{33} \cdot r_{22} + r_{23} \cdot r_{32}$; $r_{41} = r_{33} \cdot r_{21} + r_{23} \cdot r_{31}$; $r_{40} = r_{33} \cdot r_{20} + r_{23} \cdot r_{30}$; $t_{41} = r_{23}$; $t_{40} = r_{33} + r_{23}^2$; $r_{52} = r_{42} \cdot r_{32} + r_{33} \cdot r_{41}$; $r_{51} = r_{42} \cdot r_{31} + r_{33} \cdot r_{40}$; $r_{50} = r_{42} \cdot r_{30}$; $t_{52} = r_{33} \cdot t_{41}$; $t_{51} = r_{42} + r_{33} \cdot t_{40}$; $t_{50} = r_{42} \cdot r_{23}$; $r_{61} = r_{52} \cdot r_{41} + r_{42} \cdot r_{51}$; $r_{60} = r_{52} \cdot r_{40} + r_{42} \cdot r_{50}$; $t_{62} = r_{42} \cdot t_{52}$; $t_{61} = r_{52} \cdot t_{41} + r_{42} \cdot t_{51}$; $t_{60} = r_{52} \cdot t_{40} + r_{42} \cdot t_{50}$; $r_{71} = r_{61} \cdot r_{51} + r_{52} \cdot r_{60}$; $r_{70} = r_{61} \cdot r_{50}$; $t_{73} = r_{52} \cdot t_{62}$; $t_{72} = r_{61} \cdot t_{52} + r_{52} \cdot t_{61}$; $t_{71} = r_{61} \cdot t_{51} + r_{52} \cdot t_{60}$; $t_{70} = r_{61} \cdot t_{50}$; $r_{80} = r_{71} \cdot r_{60} + r_{61} \cdot r_{70}$; $inv_3 = r_{61} \cdot t_{73}$; $inv_2 = r_{71} \cdot t_{62} + r_{61} \cdot t_{72}$; $inv_1 = r_{71} \cdot t_{61} + r_{61} \cdot t_{71}$; $inv_0 = r_{71} \cdot t_{60} + r_{61} \cdot t_{70}$;	$45M + 1S$	$46M$
2	$s' = rs \equiv (b_2 - b_1)inv \bmod a_2 = s'_3x^3 + s'_2x^2 + s'_1x + s'_0$ (Karatsuba): $t_a = m + i$; $t_b = n + j$; $t_c = o + k$; $t_d = p + l$; $t_e = inv_3$; $t_f = inv_2$; $t_g = inv_1$; $t_h = inv_0$; $t_0 = t_c \cdot t_g$; $t_1 = t_b \cdot t_f$; $t_2 = t_a \cdot t_e$; $t_3 = t_b \cdot t_g$; $t_4 = t_c \cdot t_f$; $t_{10} = t_d \cdot t_h$; $t_{11} = (t_c + t_d) \cdot (t_g + t_h) + t_0 + t_{10}$; $t_{12} = (t_b + t - d) \cdot (t_f + t_h) + t_{10} + t_1 + t_0$; $t_{13} = (t_a + t_d) \cdot (t_e + t_h) + t_{10} + t_2 + t_3 + t_4$; $t_{14} = (t_a + t_c) \cdot (t_e + t_g) + t_2 + t_0 + t_1$; $t_{15} = (t_a + t_b) \cdot (t_e + t_f) + t_2 + t_1$; $t_{16} = t_2$; $t_{17} = t_{15} + e \cdot t_{16}$; $t_{18} = e \cdot t_{17} + t_{16} \cdot f + t_{14}$; $s'_3 = e \cdot t_{18} + f \cdot t_{17} + g \cdot t_{16} + t_{13}$; $s'_2 = f \cdot t_{18} + g \cdot t_{17} + h \cdot t_{16} + t_{12}$; $s'_1 = g \cdot t_{18} + h \cdot t_{17} + t_{11}$; $s'_0 = h \cdot t_{18} + t_{10}$;	$23M$	$23M$
3	$s = x^3 + s_2x^2 + x_1x + s_0 = s'$ made monic: $t_1 = r_{80} \cdot s'_3$; $w_6 = t_1^{-1}$; $w_7 = r_{80} \cdot w_6$; $w_4 = r_{80} \cdot w_7$; $w_3 = s'^2_3 \cdot w_6$; $w_5 = w_4^2$; $s_0 = s'_0 \cdot w_7$; $s_1 = s'_1 \cdot w_7$; $s_2 = s'_2 \cdot w_7$;	$I + 7M + 2S$	$I + 7M + 2S$
4	$z = sa_1 = x^7 + z_6x^6 + z_5x^5 + z_4x^4 + z_3x^3 + z_2x^2 + z_1x + z_0$ (Karats.): $t_0 = c \cdot s_1$; $t_1 = b \cdot s_2$; $z_0 = s_0 \cdot d$; $z_1 = (c + d) \cdot (s_1 + s_0) + t_0 + z_0$; $z_2 = (b+d) \cdot (s_2+s_0) + z_0 + t_1 + t_0$; $z_3 = (a+d) \cdot (1+s_0) + z_0 + a + b \cdot s_1 + c \cdot s_2$; $z_4 = (a+c) \cdot (1+s_1) + a + t_0 + t_1 + s_0$; $z_5 = (a+b) \cdot (1+s_2) + a + t_1 + s_1$; $z_6 = a + s_2$; $z_7 = 1$;	$10M$	$10M$
5	$a' = [s(z + w_4(h + 2b_1)) - w_5((f - b_1h - b_1^2)/a_1)]/a_2$ $= x^6 + u'_5x^5 + u'_4x^4 + u'_3x^3 + u'_2x^2 + u_1x + u_0$: $t_1 = s_2 \cdot w_4$; $t_2 = s_1 \cdot w_4$; $diff_4 = s_2 \cdot z_6 + z_5 + s_1 + f$; $diff_3 = g + z_4 + s_0 + s_2 \cdot z_5 + s_1 \cdot z_6$; $diff_2 = h + z_3 + s_2 \cdot z_4 + s_1 \cdot z_5 + s_0 \cdot z_6$; $diff_1 = s_2 \cdot z_3 + s_1 \cdot z_4 + s_0 \cdot z_5 + z_2 + w_5$; $diff_0 = w_4 + s_2 \cdot z_2 + s_1 \cdot z_3 + s_0 \cdot z_4 + w_5 \cdot a + z_1$; $u'_5 = z_6 + s_2 + e$; $u'_4 = diff_4 + e \cdot u'_5$; $u'_3 = diff_3 + e \cdot u'_4 + f \cdot u'_5$; $u'_2 = diff_2 + e \cdot u'_3 + f \cdot u'_4 + g \cdot u'_5$; $u'_1 = diff_1 + e \cdot u'_2 + f \cdot u'_3 + g \cdot u'_4 + h \cdot u'_5$; $u'_0 = diff_0 + e \cdot u'_1 + f \cdot u'_2 + g \cdot u'_3 + h \cdot u'_4$;	$29M$	$34M$
6	$b' = -(w_3z + h + b_1) \bmod a' = v'_5x^5 + v'_4x^4 + v'_3x^3 + v'_2x^2 + v'_1x + v'_0$: $t_1 = u'_5 + z_6$; $v'_5 = w_3 \cdot (+u'_5 \cdot t_1 + u'_4 + z_5)$; $v'_4 = w_3 \cdot (+u'_4 \cdot t_1 + u'_3 + z_4)$; $v'_3 = w_3 \cdot (+u'_3 \cdot t_1 + u'_2 + z_3) + i$; $v'_2 = w_3 \cdot (+u'_2 \cdot t_1 + u'_1 + z_2) + j$; $v'_1 = w_3 \cdot (+u'_1 \cdot t_1 + u'_0 + z_1) + 1 + k$; $v'_0 = w_3 \cdot (+u'_0 \cdot t_1 + z_0) + l$;	$12M$	$12M$
7	$a'_3 = (f - b'h - b'^2)/a' = u_{34}x^4 + u_{33}x^3 + u_{32}x^2 + u_{31}x + u_{30}$: $diff_3 = 1$; $diff_2 = v'^2_4$; $diff_1 = f_7$; $diff_0 = f_6 + v'_5 + v'^2_3$; $u_{34} = v'^2_5$; $u_{33} = diff_3 + u_{34} \cdot u'_5$; $u_{32} = diff_2 + u_{34} \cdot u'_4 + u_{33} \cdot u'_5$; $u_{31} = diff_1 + u_{34} \cdot u'_3 + u_{33} \cdot u'_4 + u_{32} \cdot u'_5$; $u_{30} = diff_0 + u_{34} \cdot u'_2 + u_{33} \cdot u'_3 + u_{32} \cdot u'_4 + u_{31} \cdot u'_5$;	$10M + 3S$	$16M + 2S$
8	$a_3 = x^4 + \tilde{a}x^3 + \tilde{b}x^2 + \tilde{c}x + \tilde{d} = a'_3$ made monic: $t_0 = u_{34}^{-1}$; $\tilde{a} = u_{33} \cdot t_0$; $\tilde{b} = u_{32} \cdot t_0$; $\tilde{c} = u_{31} \cdot t_0$; $\tilde{d} = u_{30} \cdot t_0$;	$I + 4M$	$I + 4M$
9	$b_3 = -(b' + h) \bmod a_3 = \tilde{i}x^3 + \tilde{j}x^2 + \tilde{k}x + \tilde{l}$: $t_0 = v'_4 + v'_5 \cdot a_3$; $\tilde{i} = \tilde{a} \cdot t_0 + \tilde{b} \cdot v'_5 + v'_3$; $\tilde{j} = \tilde{b} \cdot t_0 + \tilde{c} \cdot v'_5 + v'_2$; $\tilde{k} = \tilde{c} \cdot t_0 + \tilde{d} \cdot v'_5 + v'_1 + 1$; $\tilde{l} = \tilde{d} \cdot t_0 + v'_0$;	$8M$	$8M$
Total	in fields of arbitrary characteristic in fields of characteristic 2 and $h(x) = x$	 $2I{+}148M{+}6S$	$2I{+}160M{+}4S$

Table 8. Explicit formulae for doubling on HEC of genus four

Input	A weight four reduced divisor $D_1 = (a_1, b_1)$ where: $a_1 = x^4 + ax^3 + bx^2 + cx + d$; $b_1 = ix^3 + jx^2 + kx + l$ $h = h_4x^4 + h_3x^3 + h_2x^2 + h_1x + h_0$, where $h_i \in \{0, 1\}$; $f = x^9 + f_7x^7 + f_6x^6 + f_5x^5 + f_4x^4 + f_3x^3 + f_2x^2 + f_1x + f_0$;		
Output	A weight four reduced divisor $D_2 = (a_2, b_2) = [2]D_1$ where: $a_2 = x^4 + \tilde{a}x^3 + \tilde{b}x^2 + \tilde{c}x + \tilde{d}$; $b_2 = \tilde{i}x^3 + \tilde{j}x^2 + \tilde{k}x + \tilde{l}$		
Step	Procedure (For simplicity, only the implemented case is given.)	Cost	
1	Almost inverse $inv = r/(h + 2b_1) \bmod a_1$ $= inv_3x^3 + inv_2x^2 + inv_1x + inv_0$: $inv_3 = 1$; $inv_2 = a$; $inv_1 = b$; $inv_0 = c$;	–	$45M$
2	$z = ((f - hb_1 - b_1^2)/a_1) \bmod a_1 = x^4 + z_3x^3 + z_2x^2 + z_1x + z_0$: $diff_2 = i^2 + c$; $diff_0 = j^2 + i$; $z'_4 = a$; $z'_3 = b + a^2 + f_7$; $z'_2 = diff_2 + a \cdot (z'_3 + b) + f_6$; $z'_1 = d + a \cdot (z'_2 + c) + b \cdot z'_3 + f_5$; $z'_0 = diff_0 + a \cdot (z'_1 + d) + b \cdot z'_2 + c \cdot z'_3 + f_4$; $z_3 = b + z'_3$; $z_2 = c + z'_2$; $z_1 = d + z'_1$; $z_0 = z'_0$;	$6M + 3S$	$16M + 2S$
3	$s' = zinv \bmod a_1 = s'_3x^3 + s'_2x^2 + s'_1x + s'_0$ (Karatsuba): $t_1 = z_1 \cdot inv_1$; $t_2 = z_2 \cdot inv_2$; $t_{10} = z_0 \cdot inv_0$; $t_{16} = z_3 \cdot inv_3$; $t_{15} = (z_3 + z_2) \cdot (inv_3 + inv_2) + t_{16} + t_2$; $t_{14} = (z_3 + z_1) \cdot (inv_3 + inv_1) + t_{16} + t_1 + t_2$; $t_{13} = (z_3 + z_0) \cdot (inv_3 + inv_0) + t_{10} + t_{16} + z_2 \cdot inv_1 + z_1 \cdot inv_2$; $t_{12} = (z_2 + z_0) \cdot (inv_2 + inv_0) + t_{10} + t_2 + t_1$; $t_{11} = (z_1 + z_0) \cdot (inv_1 + inv_0) + t_1 + t_{10}$; $t_3 = t_{15} + a \cdot t_{16}$; $t_4 = a \cdot t_3 + b \cdot t_{16} + t_{14}$; $s'_0 = d \cdot t_4 + t_{10}$; $s'_1 = c \cdot t_4 + d \cdot t_3 + t_{11}$; $s'_2 = b \cdot t_4 + c \cdot t_3 + d \cdot t_{16} + t_{12}$; $s'_3 = a \cdot t_4 + b \cdot t_3 + c \cdot t_{16} + t_{13}$;	$23M$	$23M$
4	$s = x^3 + s_2x^2 + x_1x + s_0 = s'$ made monic: $t_1 = d \cdot s'_3$; $w_6 = t_1^{-1}$; $w_7 = d \cdot w_6$; $w_4 = d \cdot w_7$; $w_3 = s_3'^2 \cdot w_6$; $w_5 = w_4^2$; $s_0 = s'_0 \cdot w_7$; $s_1 = s'_1 \cdot w_7$; $s_2 = s'_2 \cdot w_7$;	$I + 7M + 2S$	$I + 7M + 2S$
5	$G = sa_1 = x^7 + g_6x^6 + g_5x^5 + g_4x^4 + g_3x^3 + g_2x^2 + g_1x + g_0$ (Karat.): $t_0 = c \cdot s_1$; $t_1 = b \cdot s_2$; $g_0 = s_0 \cdot d$; $g_1 = (c + d) \cdot (s_1 + s_0) + t_0 + g_0$; $g_2 = (b+d) \cdot (s_2+s_0)+g_0+t_1+t_0$; $g_3 = (a+d) \cdot (1+s_0)+g_0+a+b \cdot s_1+c \cdot s_2$; $g_4 = (a+c) \cdot (1+s_1)+a+t_0+t_1+s_0$; $g_5 = (a+b) \cdot (1+s_2)+a+t_1+s_1$; $g_6 =$ $a + s_2$;	$10M$	$10M$
6	$a' = a_1^{-2}[(G + w_4b_1)^2 + w_4hG + w_5(hb_1 - f)]$ $= x^6 + u'_5x^5 + u'_4x^4 + u'_3x^3 + u'_2x^2 + u_1x + u_0$: $t_0 = a^2$; $t_1 = b^2$; $t_2 = c^2$; $t_3 = g_6^2$; $t_4 = g_5^2$; $u'_5 = 0$; $u'_4 = t_3 + t_0$; $u'_3 = 0$; $u'_2 = t_4 + t_1 + t_0 \cdot (t_3 + t_0)$; $u'_1 = w_5$; $u'_0 = g_4^2 + w_4 + t_2 + t_0 \cdot u'_2 + t_1 \cdot (t_0 + t_3)$;	$3M + 6S$	$52M + 10S$
7	$b' = -(w_3z + h + b_1) \bmod a' = v'_5x^5 + v'_4x^4 + v'_3x^3 + v'_2x^2 + v'_1x + v'_0$: $v'_5 = w_3 \cdot (u'_4 + g_5)$; $v'_4 = w_3 \cdot (u'_4 \cdot g_6 + g_4)$; $v'_3 = w_3 \cdot (u'_2 + g_3) + i$; $v'_2 = w_3 \cdot (u'_2 \cdot g_6 + u'_1 + g_2) + j$; $v'_1 = w_3 \cdot (u'_1 \cdot g_6 + u'_0 + g_1) + 1 + k$; $v'_0 = w_3 \cdot (u'_0 \cdot g_6 + g_0) + l$;	$10M$	$12M$
8	$a'_2 = (f - b'h - b'^2)/a' = u_{24}x^4 + u_{23}x^3 + u_{22}x^2 + u_{21}x + u_{20}$: $diff_3 = 1$; $diff_2 = v_4'^2$; $diff_1 = f_7$; $diff_0 = f_6 + v'_5 + v_3'^2$; $u_{24} = v_5'^2$; $u_{23} = diff_3$; $u_{22} = diff_2 + u_{24} \cdot u'_4$; $u_{21} = diff_1 + u_{23} \cdot u'_4$; $u_{20} = diff_0 + u_{24} \cdot u'_2 + u_{22} \cdot u'_4$;	$4M + 3SQ$	$16M + 2SQ$
9	$a_2 = x^4 + \tilde{a}x^3 + \tilde{b}x^2 + \tilde{c}x + \tilde{d} = a'_2$ made monic: $t_0 = u_{24}^{-1}$; $\tilde{a} = u_{23} \cdot t_0$; $\tilde{b} = u_{22} \cdot t_0$; $\tilde{c} = u_{21} \cdot t_0$; $\tilde{d} = u_{20} \cdot t_0$;	$I + 4M$	$I + 4M$
10	$b_2 = -(b' + h) \bmod a_2 = \tilde{i}x^3 + \tilde{j}x^2 + \tilde{k}x + \tilde{l}$: $t_0 = v'_4 + v'_5 \cdot a_2$; $\tilde{i} = \tilde{a} \cdot t_0 + \tilde{b} \cdot v'_5 + v'_3$; $\tilde{j} = \tilde{b} \cdot t_0 + \tilde{c} \cdot v'_5 + v'_2$; $\tilde{k} = \tilde{c} \cdot t_0 + \tilde{d} \cdot v'_5 + v'_1 + 1$; $\tilde{l} = \tilde{d} \cdot t_0 + v'_0$;	$8M$	$8M$
Total	in fields of arbitrary characteristic in fields of characteristic 2 with $h(x) = x$	 $2I+75M+14S$	$2I+193M+16S$

On the Selection of Pairing-Friendly Groups

Paulo S. L. M. Barreto[1], Ben Lynn[2], and Michael Scott[3]

[1] Universidade de São Paulo, Escola Politécnica
Av. Prof. Luciano Gualberto, tr. 3, 158
BR 05508-900, São Paulo(SP), Brazil
pbarreto@larc.usp.br

[2] Computer Science Department, Stanford University, USA
blynn@cs.stanford.edu

[3] School of Computer Applications
Dublin City University
Ballymun, Dublin 9, Ireland
mscott@indigo.ie

Abstract. We propose a simple algorithm to select group generators suitable for pairing-based cryptosystems. The selected parameters are shown to favor implementations of the Tate pairing that are at once conceptually simple and efficient, with an observed performance about 2 to 10 times better than previously reported implementations, depending on the embedding degree. Our algorithm has beneficial side effects: various non-pairing operations become faster, and bandwidth may be saved.

Keywords: pairing-based cryptosystems, group generators, elliptic curves, Tate pairing.

1 Introduction

Pairing-based cryptosystems are currently one of the most active areas of research in elliptic curve cryptography, as we see from the abundance of recent literature on the subject. This interest is not unfounded, as previously unsolved problems have been cracked by using pairings.

To date, most suitable pairings are based on the Tate pairing over certain elliptic curve groups, a notable exception being that of Boneh, Mironov and Shoup [6] based on the String RSA assumption. Unfortunately, the Tate pairing is an expensive operation and is often the bottleneck in such systems.

Efficient pairings for supersingular curves have been proposed [2, 9, 12]. However, there is a widespread feeling that supersingular curves should be avoided whenever possible, as they may be more susceptible to attacks than ordinary curves. Moreover, for technical reasons, one is often forced to use fields of small characteristic [16, section 5.2.2], which are more vulnerable to Coppersmith's discrete logarithm attack [7]. Protecting against this attack increases bandwidth requirements (larger fields), and while this may not be an issue in some situations, it is a central concern in many cases (e.g. short BLS signatures [5]).

M. Matsui and R. Zuccherato (Eds.): SAC 2003, LNCS 3006, pp. 17–25, 2004.

Thus we would like to find similar optimizations for ordinary curves over fields of large characteristics containing subgroups of manageable embedding degree [3, 8, 18].

We show how to select groups in nonsupersingular curves where many optimizations proposed for supersingular curves [2] have a counterpart, and obtain running times that are up to ten times better than previously reported results [13]. In particular, we show how to perform elimination of irrelevant factors and denominators during the computation of the Tate pairing, which is rendered conceptually simpler and substantially more efficient. Additionally, it turns out that operations of pairing-based schemes that do not rely on pairings, such as key generation, become more efficient with our choice of groups.

This paper is organized as follows. Section 2 recalls some concepts essential to the discussion of pairings. Section 3 describes our group selection algorithm. Section 4 explains how the selected groups lead to efficient implementation of the Tate pairing. We compare our results with previous work in Section 5, and present our conclusions in Section 6.

2 Preliminaries

A subgroup G of (the group of points of) an elliptic curve $E(\mathbb{F}_q)$ is said to have *embedding degree* k if its order r divides $q^k - 1$, but does not divide $q^i - 1$ for all $0 < i < k$. We assume $k > 1$. The group $E[r] \cong \mathbb{F}_r \times \mathbb{F}_r$ of r-torsion points lies in $E(\mathbb{F}_{q^k})$ [1].

In what follows, let $\mathbb{F}_q$ be a field of odd characteristic and $E(\mathbb{F}_q)$ an elliptic curve containing a subgroup of prime order r with embedding degree k, and assume that r and k are coprime.

2.1 The Twist of a Curve

Let $E(\mathbb{F}_q)$ given by the short Weierstraß equation $y^2 = x^3 + ax + b$, let d be a factor of k and let $v \in \mathbb{F}_{q^d}$ be some quadratic non-residue. The *twist* of E over $\mathbb{F}_{q^d}$ is the curve $E'(\mathbb{F}_{q^d}) : y^2 = x^3 + v^2 a\, x + v^3 b$. The orders of the groups of rational points of these curves satisfy the relation $\#E(\mathbb{F}_{q^d}) + \#E'(\mathbb{F}_{q^d}) = 2q^d + 2$ [4, section III.3].

In the above equation, if v is instead a quadratic residue, then it is easy to check that an isomorphism $E \to E'$ given by $(X, Y) \mapsto (vX, v\sqrt{v}Y)$ exists.

2.2 Divisors and the Tate Pairing

For our purposes, a *divisor* on E is a formal sum $D = \sum_{P \in E(\mathbb{F}_{q^k})} n_P(P)$ where $n_P \in \mathbb{Z}$.

The set of points $P \in E(\mathbb{F}_{q^k})$ such that $n_P \neq 0$ is called the support of D. The degree of D is the value $\deg(D) = \sum_P n_P$. The null divisor, denoted 0, has all $n_P = 0$. The sum of two divisors $D = \sum_P n_P(P)$ and $D' = \sum_P n'_P(P)$ is the divisor $D + D' = \sum_P (n_P + n'_P)(P)$.

Given a nonzero rational function $f : E(\mathbb{F}_{q^k}) \to \mathbb{F}_{q^k}$, the *divisor of* f is the divisor $(f) = \sum_P \mathrm{ord}_P(f)(P)$ where $\mathrm{ord}_P(f)$ is the multiplicity of f at P. It follows from this definition that $(fg) = (f) + (g)$ and $(f/g) = (f) - (g)$ for any two nonzero rational functions f and g defined on E; moreover, $(f) = 0$ if and only if f is a nonzero constant.

We say two divisors D and D' are equivalent, $D' \sim D$, if there exists a function g such that $D' = D + (g)$. For any function f and any divisor $D = \sum_P n_P(P)$ of degree zero, we define $f(D) = \prod_P f(P)^{n_P}$.

The *Tate pairing* is a bilinear mapping $e : E(\mathbb{F}_q)[r] \times E(\mathbb{F}_{q^k}) \to \mathbb{F}_{q^k}^*$. Specifically, let $P \in E(\mathbb{F}_q)$ be a point of order r, let f be a function whose divisor satisfies $(f) = r(P) - r(O)$, let $Q \in E(\mathbb{F}_{q^k})$, and let $D \sim (Q) - (O)$ be a divisor whose support is disjoint from the support of (f). We define the (reduced) Tate pairing as

$$e(P, Q) = f(D)^{(q^k-1)/r}.$$

One can show [11] that this mapping is indeed bilinear, and also nondegenerate for linearly independent P and Q if r divides the order of Q.

More generally, if D' is a divisor satisfying $D' \sim (P) - (O)$ then we can substitute any f' for f such that $(f') = rD'$, so long as the support of D' is disjoint to that of D.

Note that raising $f(D)$ to $(q^k - 1)/r$ ensures that the result is either 1 or an element of order r. This property is useful in efficiently preventing small subgroup attacks [15]. There is no need to multiply Q by a large cofactor to avoid these attacks, as checking the pairing value is sufficient.

2.3 The Frobenius Endomorphism

The *Frobenius endomorphism* is the mapping $\Phi : E(\mathbb{F}_{q^k}) \to E(\mathbb{F}_{q^k})$, $(X, Y) \mapsto (X^q, Y^q)$. Thus a point $P \in E(\mathbb{F}_{q^k})$ is defined over $\mathbb{F}_{q^i}$ if and only if $\Phi^i(P) = P$; in particular, $\Phi^k(P) = P$ for any $P \in E(\mathbb{F}_{q^k})$.

2.4 The Trace Map

The *trace map* is the mapping $\mathrm{tr} : E(\mathbb{F}_{q^k}) \to E(\mathbb{F}_q)$ defined as $\mathrm{tr}(P) = P + \Phi(P) + \Phi^2(P) + \cdots + \Phi^{k-1}(P)$. We have $\mathrm{tr}(\Phi(P)) = \Phi(\mathrm{tr}(P)) = \mathrm{tr}(P)$ for any $P \in E(\mathbb{F}_{q^k})$, (which shows that the range of the map is indeed $E(\mathbb{F}_q)$).

We describe the two eigenspaces of the trace map on $E[r]$. The eigenvalues are k and 0.

Lemma 1. *The k-eigenspace of the trace map is* $E(\mathbb{F}_q)[r]$.

Proof. Clearly, all points $R \in E(\mathbb{F}_q)[r]$ satisfy $\mathrm{tr}(R) = [k]R$, hence we only need to show that all points $R \in E[r]$ such that $\mathrm{tr}(R) = [k]R$ are defined over $\mathbb{F}_q$. Indeed, if $\mathrm{tr}(R) = [k]R$, then $\Phi(\mathrm{tr}(R)) = \Phi([k]R) = [k]\Phi(R)$, but since $\Phi(\mathrm{tr}(R)) = \mathrm{tr}(R)$, it follows that $[k]\Phi(R) = \mathrm{tr}(R) = [k]R$ and thus $[k](\Phi(R) - R) = O$. As k is coprime to the order of R, necessarily $\Phi(R) - R = O$, hence R must be defined over $\mathbb{F}_q$, that is, $R \in E(\mathbb{F}_q)[r]$. □

It is easy to verify that for any $R \in E(\mathbb{F}_{q^k})$ the point $Q = R - \Phi(R)$ satisfies $\mathrm{tr}(Q) = O$. This provides a way of generating points of trace zero. Since at least one finite point Q can be constructed in this fashion (provided $k > 1$), we see that the other eigenvalue of the trace map is indeed zero. We know that this space must be one-dimensional, since the other dimension has been accounted for by $E(\mathbb{F}_q)[r]$.

We now describe the eigenspaces of the Frobenius map on $E[r]$. The characteristic polynomial of the Frobenius endomorphism is the polynomial $\pi(u) = u^2 - tu + q$. The value t is called the trace of the Frobenius endomorphism, not to be confused with the trace map. The polynomial π factorizes as $\pi(u) = (u-1)(u-q) \pmod r$, so the eigenvalues are 1 and q.

Lemma 2. *The* 1*-eigenspace of* Φ *is* $E(\mathbb{F}_q)[r]$.

Proof. A point of $E(\mathbb{F}_{q^k})$ is fixed under Φ if and only if it lies in $E(\mathbb{F}_q)$. □

Lemma 3. *The* q*-eigenspace of* Φ *consists of all points* $R \in E[r]$ *satisfying* $\mathrm{tr}(R) = O$.

Proof. If a point R satisfies $\mathrm{tr}(R) = (1 + \Phi + \ldots + \Phi^{k-1})R = O$, then $\mathrm{tr}(\Phi(R)) = (\Phi + \ldots + \Phi^k)R = O$. In other words, the points of trace zero are mapped to points of trace zero under Φ and hence must constitute an eigenspace. As the 1-eigenspace has already been accounted for, the set of points of trace zero must be the q-eigenspace of Φ. □

3 Parameter Generation

Assume k is even and set $d = k/2$. We propose a method for selecting group generators that makes the pairing more efficient, and additionally improves the performance of operations in pairing-based schemes that do not use the pairing, such as key generation.

Let E be given by $y^2 = x^3 + ax + b$, and consider its twist over $\mathbb{F}_{q^d}$, namely, the curve $E'(\mathbb{F}_{q^d}) : y^2 = x^3 + v^2 a\, x + v^3 b$ for some quadratic non-residue $v \in \mathbb{F}_{q^d}$. In $\mathbb{F}_{q^k}$, v is a quadratic residue, which means the map $\Psi : (X, Y) \mapsto (v^{-1}X, (v\sqrt{v})^{-1}Y)$ is an isomorphism that maps the group of points of $E'(\mathbb{F}_{q^d})$ to a subgroup of points of $E(\mathbb{F}_{q^k})$.

Let $Q' = (X, Y) \in E'(\mathbb{F}_{q^d})$, and set $Q = \Psi(Q') = (v^{-1}X, (v\sqrt{v})^{-1}Y) \in E(\mathbb{F}_{q^k})$. By construction, the x-coordinate of Q is an element of $\mathbb{F}_{q^d}$, allowing the denominator elimination optimization that will be described in the next section. This suggests the following group selection algorithm.

Group Selection Algorithm:

1. Randomly generate a point $P \in E(\mathbb{F}_q)$ of order r.
2. Randomly generate a point $Q' \in E'(\mathbb{F}_{q^d})$.

We view the domain of the Tate pairing as $\langle P \rangle \times \langle Q \rangle$, where $Q = \Psi(Q')$. It may be desirable to explicitly check that $e(P, Q) \neq 1$, but as this occurs with overwhelming probability, in some situations it could be safe to skip this check. Note that only P is required to have order r.

Operations that do not use the pairing such as key generation and point transmission can be performed using only arithmetic on $\mathbb{F}_{q^d}$. Points of $E'(\mathbb{F}_{q^d})$ are mapped back to points on $E(\mathbb{F}_{q^k})$ only when needed for a pairing computation. This avoids many $\mathbb{F}_{q^k}$ operations and halves bandwidth requirements.

For instance, if $k = 2$, pairing-based protocols can be implemented using $E(\mathbb{F}_q)$ arithmetic, readily available in a highly optimized form in many code libraries, along with support for simple $\mathbb{F}_{q^2}$ operations for the pairing computation. For higher k, we suggest implementing $\mathbb{F}_{q^k}$ as $\mathbb{F}_q[x]/R_k(x)$, where $R_k(x)$ is the sparsest possible polynomial containing only terms of even degree. In this case, elements in $\mathbb{F}_{q^d}$ are polynomials lacking any term of odd degree.

3.1 Some Remarks on the Selected Groups

We mention a few observations on the groups selected by our algorithm.

Lemma 4. *Let* $Q = (X, Y) \in E(\mathbb{F}_{q^k})$ *be a* ▫*nite point. Then* $\Phi^d(Q) = -Q$ *if and only if* $X^{q^d-1} = 1$ *(i.e.* $X \in \mathbb{F}_{q^d}$*) and* $Y^{q^d-1} = -1$.

Proof. Since $-Q = (X, -Y)$ (for a suitable Weierstraß form), we conclude that $\Phi^d(X, Y) = (X^{q^d}, Y^{q^d}) = (X, -Y)$ if and only if $X^{q^d-1} = 1$ (i.e. $X \in \mathbb{F}_{q^d}$) and $Y^{q^d-1} = -1$. □

Thus $\Psi(E'(\mathbb{F}_{q^d}))$ is precisely the group of points in $E(\mathbb{F}_{q^k})$ satisfying $\Phi^d(Q) = -Q$, which is a subgroup of the trace zero points of $E(\mathbb{F}_{q^k})$.

Hence an alternative way to pick Q in our algorithm is to choose a random $R \in E(\mathbb{F}_{q^k})$ and set $Q \leftarrow R - \Phi^d(R)$. However this is slower than finding points of $E'(\mathbb{F}_{q^d})$, and we also do not obtain the bonus of speeding up non-pairing operations.

Lastly, we note that the above lemma can be used to show that r-torsion points of trace zero have a special form.

Corollary 1. *Let* $Q = (X, Y) \in E(\mathbb{F}_{q^k})[r]$ *be a* ▫*nite point with* $\mathrm{tr}(Q) = O$. *Then* $X \in \mathbb{F}_{q^d}$ *and* $Y^{q^d-1} = -1$.

Proof. As $\mathrm{tr}(Q) = O$, the point Q lies in the q-eigenspace of the Frobenius map Φ, that is, $\Phi(Q) = [q]Q$. We have $q^d \equiv -1 \pmod{r}$, because $q^{2d} \equiv 1 \pmod{r}$ and $2d = k$ is the smallest integer for which this holds. Thus $\Phi^d(Q) = -Q$. By Lemma 4 we have $X^{q^d-1} = 1$ and $Y^{q^d-1} = -1$. □

4 Tate Pairing Computation

We review Miller's algorithm [17] for computing the Tate pairing and describe how to optimize it for the subgroups constructed according to our algorithm.

Let $P \in E(\mathbb{F}_q)[r]$ and $Q \in E(\mathbb{F}_{q^k})$ be linearly independent points. Let f be the rational function with divisor $(f) = r(P) - r(O)$. We wish to compute the Tate pairing $e(P,Q) = f(D)^{(q^k-1)/r}$, where D satisfies $D \sim (Q) - (O)$, and the support of D does not contain P or O.

For this section, instead of requiring k to be even and setting $d = k/2$, we generalize so that d now represents any proper factor of k, that is, $d \mid k$ and $d < k$.

Lemma 5. *$q^d - 1$ is a factor of $(q^k - 1)/r$.*

Proof. We start with the factorization $q^k - 1 = (q^d - 1)\sum_{i=0}^{k/d-1} q^{id}$. Since the embedding degree is $k > 1$, we have $r \mid q^k - 1$ and $r \nmid q^d - 1$. Thus $r \mid \sum_{i=0}^{k/d-1} q^{id}$, and $q^d - 1$ survives as a factor of $(q^k - 1)/r$. □

Corollary 2 (Irrelevant factors). *One can multiply $f(D)$ by any nonzero $x \in \mathbb{F}_{q^d}$ without aecting the pairing value.*

Proof. To compute the pairing, $f(D)$ is raised to the exponent $(q^k - 1)/r$. By Lemma 5, this exponent contains a factor $q^d - 1$, thus by Fermat's Little Theorem for finite fields [14, lemma 2.3], $x^{(q^k-1)/r} = 1$. □

The next theorem generalizes a result originally established only for certain supersingular curves [2, Theorem 1]:

Theorem 1. *Let $P \in E(\mathbb{F}_q)[r]$ and $Q \in E(\mathbb{F}_{q^k})$ be linearly independent points. Then $e(P,Q) = f(Q)^{(q^k-1)/r}$.*

Proof. Suppose $R \notin \{O, -P, Q, Q - P\}$ is some point on the curve. Let f' be a function with divisor $(f') = r(P+R) - r(R) \sim (f)$, so that $e(P,Q) = f'((Q) - (O))^{(q^k-1)/r}$. Because f' does not have a zero or pole at O, we have $f'((Q) - (O)) = f'(Q)/f'(O)$, and since P has coordinates in $\mathbb{F}_q$, we know that $f'(O) \in \mathbb{F}_q^*$. Corollary 2 then ensures that $f'(O)$ is an irrelevant factor and can be omitted from the Tate pairing computation, i.e. $e(P,Q) = f'(Q)^{(q^k-1)/r}$.

Now $(f') = r((P + R) - (R)) = r((P) - (O) + (g)) = (f) + r(g)$ for some rational function g, since $(P + R) - (R) \sim (P) - (O)$. Thus $f' = fg^r$, and because Q is not a zero or pole of f or f' (so that $g(Q) \in \mathbb{F}_{q^k}^*$ is well defined) it follows that $f'(Q)^{(q^k-1)/r} = f(Q)^{(q^k-1)/r} g(Q)^{q^k-1} = f(Q)^{(q^k-1)/r}$. □

The case of linearly dependent P and Q is trivially handled, as then we have $e(P,Q) = 1$.

In what follows, which we quote directly from Barreto et al. [2, Theorem 2], for each pair $U, V \in E(\mathbb{F}_q)$ we define $g_{U,V} : E(\mathbb{F}_{q^k}) \to \mathbb{F}_{q^k}$ to be (the equation of) the line through points U and V (if $U = V$, then $g_{U,V}$ is the tangent to the curve at U, and if either one of U, V is the point at infinity O, then $g_{U,V}$ is the vertical line at the other point). The shorthand g_U stands for $g_{U,-U}$. In affine coordinates, $E : y^2 = x^3 + ax + b$, for $U = (x_U, y_U)$, $V = (x_V, y_V)$ and $Q = (x, y)$, we have:

$$
\begin{aligned}
g_{U,V}(Q) &= 1, \ Q \in \langle P \rangle. \\
g_{U,U}(Q) &= \lambda_1(x - x_U) + y_U - y, \ Q \notin \langle P \rangle. \\
g_{U,V}(Q) &= \lambda_2(x - x_U) + y_U - y, \ Q \notin \langle P \rangle, \ U \neq V. \\
g_U(Q) &= x - x_U, \ Q \notin \langle P \rangle.
\end{aligned}
$$

where

$$\lambda_1 = \frac{3x_U^2 + a}{2y_U}, \quad \lambda_2 = \frac{y_V - y_U}{x_V - x_U}.$$

Lemma 6 (Miller's formula). *Let P be a point on $E(\mathbb{F}_q)$ and f_c be a function with divisor $(f_c) = c(P) - ([c]P) - (c-1)(O)$, $c \in \mathbb{Z}$. For all $a, b \in \mathbb{Z}$, $f_{a+b}(Q) = f_a(Q) \cdot f_b(Q) \cdot g_{[a]P,[b]P}(Q)/g_{[a+b]P}(Q)$.*

Proof. See Barreto et al. [2, Theorem 2]. □

Notice that $(f_0) = (f_1) = 0$, so that by corollary 2 we can set $f_0(Q) = f_1(Q) = 1$. Furthermore, $f_{a+1}(Q) = f_a(Q) \cdot g_{aP,P}(Q)/g_{(a+1)P}(Q)$ and $f_{2a}(Q) = f_a(Q)^2 \cdot g_{[a]P,[a]P}(Q)/g_{[2a]P}(Q)$. Recall that $r > 0$ is the order of P. Let its binary representation be $r = (r_t, \ldots, r_1, r_0)$ where $r_i \in \{0, 1\}$ and $r_t \neq 0$. Miller's algorithm computes $f(Q) = f_r(Q)$, $Q \notin \{O, P\}$, by coupling the above formulas with the double-and-add method to calculate $[r]P$:

Miller's Algorithm:

```
set f ← 1 and V ← P
for i ← t − 1, t − 2, ..., 1, 0 do {
    set f ← f² · g_{V,V}(Q)/g_{[2]V}(Q) and V ← 2V
    if r_i = 1 then set f ← f · g_{V,P}(Q)/g_{V+P}(Q) and V ← V + P
}
return f
```

Miller's algorithm can be simplified further if k is even, as established by the following generalization of a previous result [2, Theorem 2]:

Theorem 2 (Denominator elimination). *Let $P \in E(\mathbb{F}_q)[r]$. Suppose $Q = (X, Y) \in E(\mathbb{F}_{q^k})$ and $X \in \mathbb{F}_{q^d}$. Then the $g_{[2]V}$ and g_{V+P} denominators in Miller's algorithm can be discarded without changing the value of $e(P, Q)$.*

Proof. The denominators in Miller's formula have the form $g_U(Q) \equiv x - u$, where $x \in \mathbb{F}_{q^d}$ is the abscissa of Q and $u \in \mathbb{F}_q$ is the abscissa of U. Hence $g_U(Q) \in \mathbb{F}_{q^d}$. By corollary 2, they can be discarded without changing the pairing value. □

Table 1. Complexity of computing the Tate pairing

algorithm	coordinates	$k = 2$, $\lvert q\rvert = 512$	$k = 6$, $\lvert q\rvert = 171$
[13]	projective	20737.6M	33078.3M
ours, w/o precomp.	projective	4153.2M	15633.0M
ours, with precomp.	projective	2997.6M	14055.4M
ours, with precomp.	affine	1899.6M	11110.2M

5 Results

To illustrate the effectiveness of our method for the computation of the Tate pairing, we compare our results with those of Izu and Takagi [13] for non-supersingular curves with $k = 2$ and $k = 6$.

The computation of $e(P, Q)$ requires all of the intermediate points computed during the scalar multiplication $[r]P$. If P is fixed, these can be precalculated and stored, with considerable savings. In this case affine coordinates are faster, and require less storage. Otherwise we follow Izu and Takagi [13] and use projective coordinates. Additional savings could be obtained with the method of Eisentraeger, Lauter and Montgomery [10], but we have not implemented it.

Table 1 summarizes the results, where M denotes the computing time of a multiplication in $\mathbb{F}_q$, and assuming that the time taken by one squaring is about $0.8M$.

6 Conclusions

We have shown how to select cryptographically significant groups where the Tate pairing can be efficiently implemented.

Specifically, we have argued that the Tate pairing $e(P, Q)$ is most efficiently calculated when $P \in E(\mathbb{F}_q)[r]$ and $Q \in E(\mathbb{F}_{q^k})$ satisfies $\Phi^{k/2}(Q) = -Q$. We have also provided an algorithm to choose such P and Q so that $e(P, Q)$ is nondegenerate.

An interesting line of further research is the extension of our methods to hyperelliptic curves, possibly with enhancements. This has already been done for the supersingular case [9].

Acknowledgements

We wish to thank Waldyr Benits, Steven Galbraith, and Florian Heß for valuable comments about this work.

References

[1] R. Balasubramanian and N. Koblitz. The improbability that an elliptic curve has subexponential discrete log problem under the Menezes-Okamoto-Vanstone algorithm. *Journal of Cryptology*, 11(2):141–145, 1998. 18

[2] P. S. L. M. Barreto, H. Y. Kim, B. Lynn, and M. Scott. Efficient algorithms for pairing-based cryptosystems. In *Advances in Cryptology – Crypto'2002*, volume 2442 of *Lecture Notes in Computer Science*, pages 377–87. Springer-Verlag, 2002. 17, 18, 22, 23

[3] P. S. L. M. Barreto, B. Lynn, and M. Scott. Constructing elliptic curves with prescribed embedding degrees. In *Security in Communication Networks – SCN'2002*, volume 2576 of *Lecture Notes in Computer Science*, pages 263–273. Springer-Verlag, 2002. 18

[4] I. Blake, G. Seroussi, and N. Smart. *Elliptic Curves in Cryptography*. Cambridge University Press, London, 1999. 18

[5] D. Boneh, B. Lynn, and H. Shacham. Short signatures from the Weil pairing. In *Advances in Cryptology – Asiacrypt'2001*, volume 2248 of *Lecture Notes in Computer Science*, pages 514–532. Springer-Verlag, 2002. 17

[6] D. Boneh, I. Mironov, and V. Shoup. A secure signature scheme from bilinear maps. In *Topics in Cryptology – CT-RSA'2003*, volume 2612 of *Lecture Notes in Computer Science*, pages 98–110, San Francisco, USA, 2003. Springer-Verlag. 17

[7] D. Coppersmith. Fast evaluation of logarithms in fields of characteristics two. In *IEEE Transactions on Information Theory*, volume 30, pages 587–594, 1984. 17

[8] R. Dupont, A. Enge, and F. Morain. Building curves with arbitrary small MOV degree over finite prime fields. Cryptology ePrint Archive, Report 2002/094, 2002. `http://eprint.iacr.org/2002/094`. 18

[9] I. Duursma and H.-S. Lee. Tate-pairing implementations for tripartite key agreement. Cryptology ePrint Archive, Report 2003/053, 2003. `http://eprint.iacr.org/2003/053`. 17, 24

[10] K. Eisentraeger, K. Lauter, and P. L. Montgomery. Fast elliptic curve arithmetic and improved Weil pairing evaluation. In *Topics in Cryptology – CT-RSA'2003*, volume 2612 of *Lecture Notes in Computer Science*, pages 343–354. Springer-Verlag, 2003. 24

[11] G. Frey and H.-G. Rück. A remark concerning m-divisibility and the discrete logarithm problem in the divisor class group of curves. In *Mathematics of Computation*, volume 62, pages 865–874, 1994. 19

[12] S. Galbraith, K. Harrison, and D. Soldera. Implementing the Tate pairing. In *Algorithm Number Theory Symposium – ANTS V*, volume 2369 of *Lecture Notes in Computer Science*, pages 324–337. Springer-Verlag, 2002. 17

[13] T. Izu and T. Takagi. Efficient computations of the Tate pairing for the large MOV degrees. In *5th International Conference on Information Security and Cryptology (ICISC 2002)*, volume 2587 of *Lecture Notes in Computer Science*, pages 283–297. Springer-Verlag, 2003. 18, 24

[14] R. Lidl and H. Niederreiter. *Finite Fields*. Number 20 in Encyclopedia of Mathematics and its Applications. Cambridge University Press, 2nd edition, 1997. 22

[15] C. H. Lim and P. J. Lee. A key recovery attack on discrete log-based schemes using a prime order subgroup. In *Advances in Cryptology – Crypto'97*, volume 1294 of *Lecture Notes in Computer Science*, pages 249–263. Srpinger-Verlag, 1997. 19

[16] A. J. Menezes. *Elliptic Curve Public Key Cryptosystems*. Kluwer Academic Publishers, 1993. 17

[17] V. Miller. Short programs for functions on curves. unpublished manuscript, 1986. 22

[18] A. Miyaji, M. Nakabayashi, and S. Takano. New explicit conditions of elliptic curve traces for FR-reduction. *IEICE Transactions on Fundamentals*, E84-A(5):1234–1243, 2001. 18

Counting Points for Hyperelliptic Curves of Type $y^2 = x^5 + ax$ over Finite Prime Fields

Eisaku Furukawa[1], Mitsuru Kawazoe[2], and Tetsuya Takahashi[2]

[1] Fujitsu Kansai-Chubu Net-Tech Limited
[2] Department of Mathematics and Information Sciences
College of Integrated Arts and Sciences
Osaka Prefecture University
1-1 Gakuen-cho Sakai Osaka 599-8531 Japan
{kawazoe,takahasi}@mi.cias.osakafu-u.ac.jp

Abstract. Counting rational points on Jacobian varieties of hyperelliptic curves over finite fields is very important for constructing hyperelliptic curve cryptosystems (HCC), but known algorithms for general curves over given large prime fields need very long running time. In this article, we propose an extremely fast point counting algorithm for hyperelliptic curves of type $y^2 = x^5 + ax$ over given large prime fields $\mathbb{F}_p$, e.g. 80-bit fields. For these curves, we also determine the necessary condition to be suitable for HCC, that is, to satisfy that the order of the Jacobian group is of the form $l \cdot c$ where l is a prime number greater than about 2^{160} and c is a very small integer. We show some examples of suitable curves for HCC obtained by using our algorithm. We also treat curves of type $y^2 = x^5 + a$ where a is not square in $\mathbb{F}_p$.

1 Introduction

Let C be a hyperelliptic curve of genus 2 over $\mathbb{F}_q$. Let J_C be the Jacobian variety of C and $J_C(\mathbb{F}_q)$ the group of $\mathbb{F}_q$-rational points of J_C. We call the group $J_C(\mathbb{F}_q)$ the Jacobian group of C. Since $J_C(\mathbb{F}_q)$ is a finite abelian group, we can construct a public-key-cryptosystem with it. This cryptosystem is called a "hyperelliptic curve cryptosystem (HCC)". The advantage of HCC to an elliptic curve cryptosystem (ECC) is that we can construct a cryptosystem at the same security level as an elliptic one by using a defining field in a half size. More precisely, we need a 160-bit field to construct a secure ECC, but for HCC we only need an 80-bit field. The order of the Jacobian group of a hyperelliptic curve defined over an 80-bit field is about 160-bit. It is said that $\sharp J_C(\mathbb{F}_q) = c \cdot l$ where l is a prime number greater than about 2^{160} and c is a very small integer is needed for a secure HCC. We call a hyperelliptic curve "suitable for HCC" if its Jacobian group has such a suitable order.

As in the case of ECC, computing the order of the Jacobian group $J_C(\mathbb{F}_q)$ is very important for constructing HCC. But it is very difficult for hyperelliptic curves defined over 80-bit fields and there are very few results on it: Gaudry-Harley's algorithm [9, 15] can compute the order for random hyperelliptic curves

M. Matsui and R. Zuccherato (Eds.): SAC 2003, LNCS 3006, pp. 26–41, 2004.

over 80-bit fields but their algorithm needs very long running time, e.g. 1 week or longer. For a hyperelliptic curve with complex multiplication, there are known efficient algorithms (we call them "CM-methods") to construct a curve with its Jacobian group having a 160-bit prime factor. But CM-methods also need rather long time and do not give an algorithm to compute the order of the Jacobian group over a given defining field. There is another way. For special curves, it is possible to obtain a fast point counting algorithm for given defining fields. Buhler-Koblitz [2] obtained such algorithm for special curves of type $y^2 + y = x^n$ over prime fields $\mathbb{F}_p$ where n is an odd prime such that $p \equiv 1 \pmod{n}$.

In this article, we propose an extremely fast algorithm to compute the order of the Jacobian group $J_C(\mathbb{F}_p)$ for hyperelliptic curves C defined by the equation $y^2 = x^5 + ax$ over large prime fields $\mathbb{F}_p$. Curves of this type are different from Buhler-Koblitz's curves [2]. Though the curves of this type have complex multiplication, by using our algorithm we can obtain suitable curves for HCC much faster than by using CM-methods. The expected running time of our algorithm is $O(\ln^4 p)$. The program based on our algorithm runs instantaneously on a system with Celeron 600MHz CPU and less than 1GB memory. It only takes less than 0.1 seconds even for 160-bit prime fields. Moreover we study on the reducibility of the Jacobian variety over extension fields and the order of the Jacobian group for the above curves. After these studies, we determine the necessary condition to be suitable for HCC. In Section 5, we describe our algorithm and give some examples of hyperelliptic curves suitable for HCC obtained by using it. In the last section of this article, we treat another hyperelliptic curves of type $y^2 = x^5 + a$, $a \in \mathbb{F}_p$. When a is square in $\mathbb{F}_p$, it is a kind of Buhler-Koblitz's curves [2]. Here we consider the case that a is not square. It is not appeared in Buhler-Koblitz's curves. We describe our point counting algorithm for this type and show the result of search for suitable curves for HCC. In fact, Jacobian groups with prime order are obtained in a very short time over 80-bit prime fields.

2 Basic Facts on Jacobian Varieties over Finite Fields

Here we recall basic facts on the order of Jacobian groups of hyperelliptic curves over finite fields. (cf. [9, 11])

2.1 General Theory

Let p be an odd prime number, $\mathbb{F}_q$ is a finite field of order $q = p^l$ and C a hyperelliptic curve of genus g defined over $\mathbb{F}_q$. Then the defining equation of C is given as $y^2 = f(x)$ where $f(x)$ is a polynomial in $\mathbb{F}_q[x]$ of degree $2g + 1$.

Let J_C be the Jacobian variety of a hyperelliptic curve C. We denote the group of $\mathbb{F}_q$-rational points on J_C by $J_C(\mathbb{F}_q)$. Let $\chi_q(t)$ be the characteristic polynomial of q-th power Frobenius endomorphism of C. Then, the order $\sharp J_C(\mathbb{F}_q)$ is given by

$$\sharp J_C(\mathbb{F}_q) = \chi_q(1).$$

The following "Hasse-Weil bound" is a famous inequality which bounds $\sharp J_C(\mathbb{F}_q)$:

$$\lceil(\sqrt{q}-1)^{2g}\rceil \leq \sharp J(\mathbb{F}_q) \leq \lfloor(\sqrt{q}+1)^{2g}\rfloor.$$

Due to Mumford [16], every point on $J_C(\mathbb{F}_q)$ can be represented uniquely by a pair $\langle u(x), v(x)\rangle$ where $u(x)$ and $v(x)$ are polynomials in $\mathbb{F}_q[x]$ with $\deg v(x) < \deg u(x) \leq 2$ such that $u(x)$ divides $f(x) - v(x)^2$. The identity element of the addition law is represented by $\langle 1, 0\rangle$. We refer this representation as "Mumford representation" in the following. By using Mumford representation of a point on $J_C(\mathbb{F}_q)$, we obtain an algorithm for adding two points on $J_C(\mathbb{F}_q)$ (cf. Cantor's algorithm [3], Harley's algorithm [9]).

2.2 Hasse-Witt Matrix and the Order of $J_C(\mathbb{F}_q)$

There is a well-known method to calculate $\sharp J_C(\mathbb{F}_q) \pmod{p}$ by using the Hasse-Witt matrix. The method is based on the following two theorems ([14, 22]).

Theorem 1. *Let $y^2 = f(x)$ with $\deg f = 2g+1$ be the equation of a genus g hyperelliptic curve. Denote by c_i the coecient of x^i in the polynomial $f(x)^{(p-1)/2}$. Then the Hasse-Witt matrix is given by $A = (c_{ip-j})_{1\leq i,j\leq g}$.*

For $A = (a_{ij})$, put $A^{(p^i)} = (a_{ij}^{p^i})$. Then we have the following theorem.

Theorem 2. *Let C be a curve of genus g de□ned over a □nite □eld $\mathbb{F}_q$ where $q = p^l$. Let A be the Hasse-Witt matrix of C, and let $A_\phi = AA^{(p)}A^{(p^2)}\ldots A^{(p^{l-1})}$. Let $\kappa(t)$ be the polynomial given by $\det(I_g - tA_\phi)$ where I_g is the $(g\times g)$ identity matrix and χ_q the characteristic polynomial of the q-th power Frobenius endomorphism. Then $\chi_q(t) \equiv (-1)^g t^g \kappa(t) \pmod{p}$.*

Due to the above two theorems, we can calculate $\sharp J_C(\mathbb{F}_q) \pmod{p}$ by the following formula:

$$\sharp J_C(\mathbb{F}_q) \equiv (-1)^g \kappa(1) \pmod{p}.$$

But this method is not practical in general when p is very large.

3 Basic Idea for Our Algorithm

We only consider the case of genus 2 in the following. Let $f(x)$ be a polynomial in $\mathbb{F}_q[x]$ of degree 5 with no multiple root, C a hyperelliptic curve over $\mathbb{F}_q$ of genus 2 defined by the equation $y^2 = f(x)$. Then, the characteristic polynomial $\chi_q(t)$ of the q-th power Frobenius endomorphism of C is of the form:

$$\chi_q(t) = t^4 - s_1t^3 + s_2t^2 - s_1qt + q^2, \quad s_i \in \mathbb{Z}, \quad |s_1| \leq 4\sqrt{q}, \quad |s_2| \leq 6q.$$

Hence the order of $J_C(\mathbb{F}_q)$ is given by the following formula:

$$\sharp J_C(\mathbb{F}_q) = q^2 + 1 - s_1(q+1) + s_2.$$

We also note on the well-known fact that s_i are given by

$$s_1 = 1 + q - M_1 \quad \text{and} \quad s_2 = (M_2 - 1 - q^2 + s_1^2)/2$$

where M_i is the number of $\mathbb{F}_{q^i}$-rational points on C (cf. [11]).

The following sharp bound is useful for calculating $\sharp J_C(\mathbb{F}_q)$.

Lemma 1 (cf. [17, 15]). $\lceil 2\sqrt{q}|s_1| - 2q \rceil \le s_2 \le \lfloor s_1^2/4 + 2q \rfloor$.

In the following we consider the case of $q = p$. When $q = p$, we obtain the following lemma as a collorary of Theorem 1 and 2.

Lemma 2. *Let $f(x)$, s_i, p be as above and c_i the coecient of x^i in $f(x)^{(p-1)/2}$. Then $s_1 \equiv c_{p-1} + c_{2p-2} \pmod p$ and $s_2 \equiv c_{p-1}c_{2p-2} - c_{p-2}c_{2p-1} \pmod p$.*

Remark 1. Since $|s_1| \le 4\sqrt{p}$, if $p > 64$ then s_1 is uniquely determined by c_{p-1}, c_{2p-2}. Moreover, by Lemma 1, if s_1 is determined, then there are only at most five possibilities for the value of s_2.

Even in the case $q = p$ and $g = 2$, it is difficult in general to calculate $s_i \pmod p$ by using Lemma 2 when p is very large. But for hyperelliptic curves of special type, it is possible to calculate them in a remarkably short time even when p is extremely large, e.g. 160-bit.

Here we consider hyperelliptic curves of type $y^2 = x^5 + ax$, $a \in \mathbb{F}_p$. We show the following theorem which is essential to construct our algorithm.

Theorem 3. *Let a be an element of $\mathbb{F}_p$, C a hyperelliptic curve de□ned by the equation $y^2 = x^5 + ax$ and $\chi_p(t)$ the characteristic polynomial of the p-th power Frobenius endomorphism of C. Then s_1, s_2 in $\chi_p(t)$ are given as follows.*

1. *if $p \equiv 1 \pmod 8$, then*

$$s_1 \equiv (-1)^{(p-1)/8} 2c(a^{3(p-1)/8} + a^{(p-1)/8}) \pmod p,$$
$$s_2 \equiv 4c^2 a^{(p-1)/2} \pmod p$$

   where c is an integer such that $p = c^2 + 2d^2$, $c \equiv 1 \pmod 4$ and $d \in \mathbb{Z}$.
2. *if $p \equiv 3 \pmod 8$, then $s_1 \equiv 0 \pmod p$ and $s_2 \equiv -4c^2 a^{(p-1)/2} \pmod p$ where c is an integer such that $p = c^2 + 2d^2$ and $d \in \mathbb{Z}$.*
3. *Otherwise, $s_1 \equiv 0 \pmod p$ and $s_2 \equiv 0 \pmod p$.*

Proof. Since $(x^5 + ax)^{\frac{p-1}{2}} = \sum_{r=0}^{(p-1)/2} \binom{\frac{p-1}{2}}{r} x^{4r+(p-1)/2} a^{(p-1)/2-r}$, the necessary condition for an entry c_{ip-j} of the Hasse-Witt matrix $A = \begin{pmatrix} c_{p-1} & c_{p-2} \\ c_{2p-1} & c_{2p-2} \end{pmatrix}$ of C being non-zero is that there must be an integer r, $0 \le r \le (p-1)/2$ such that $4r + (p-1)/2 = ip - j$. Then there are the following three possibilities: (i) $A = \begin{pmatrix} c_{p-1} & 0 \\ 0 & c_{2p-2} \end{pmatrix}$ if $p \equiv 1 \pmod 8$, (ii) $A = \begin{pmatrix} 0 & c_{p-2} \\ c_{2p-1} & 0 \end{pmatrix}$ if $p \equiv 3 \pmod 8$, (iii) $A = O$ if $p \not\equiv 1, 3 \pmod 8$.

Case (i). Put $f = (p-1)/8$. Then, since $4r+(p-1)/2 = p-1$ for c_{p-1}, we have $r = (p-1)/8 = f$ and $c_{p-1} = \binom{4f}{f}a^{3f}$. For c_{2p-2}, since $4r + (p-1)/2 = 2p-2$, we have $r = 3(p-1)/8 = 3f$ and $c_{2p-2} = \binom{4f}{3f}a^{f}$. From the result of Hudson-Williams [10, Theorem 11.2], we have $\binom{4f}{f} \equiv (-1)^f 2c \pmod{p}$ where $p = c^2+2d^2$ and $c \equiv 1 \pmod{4}$. Since $\binom{4f}{f} = \binom{4f}{3f}$, we have the case (1).

Case (ii). By the condition, it is obvious that $s_1 \equiv 0 \pmod{p}$. Put $f = (p-3)/8$. Then, since $4r + (p-1)/2 = p-2$ for c_{p-2}, we have $r = (p-3)/8 = f$ and $c_{p-2} = \binom{4f+1}{f}a^{3f+1}$. For c_{2p-1}, since $4r + (p-1)/2 = 2p-1$, we have $r = (3p-1)/8 = 3f+1$ and $c_{2p-1} = \binom{4f+1}{3f+1}a^{f}$. From the result of Berndt-Evans-Williams [1, Theorem 12.9.7], $\binom{4f+1}{f} \equiv -2c \pmod{p}$ where $p = c^2+2d^2$ and $c \equiv (-1)^f \pmod{4}$. Since $\binom{4f+1}{3f+1} = \binom{4f+1}{f}$, we have $s_2 \equiv -\binom{4f+1}{f}^2 a^{4f+1} \equiv -4c^2a^{(p-1)/2} \pmod{p}$. Thus we obtain the case (2).

Case (iii). This is obvious and we obtain the case (3). □

Remark 2. Note that the order of $J_C(\mathbb{F}_p)$ for a curve of type $y^2 = x^5 + ax$ is always even because $J_C(\mathbb{F}_p)$ has a point of order 2. By Lemma 1, if $p > 64$, then there are only at most three possibilities for the value of s_2.

By using Theorem 3 and Remark 2, we can calculate (at most three) possibilities of $\sharp J_C(\mathbb{F}_p)$ in a very short time. Then to determine $\sharp J_C(\mathbb{F}_p)$, we only have to multiply a random point on $J_C(\mathbb{F}_p)$ by each possible order. The following remark is also important.

Remark 3. If $p > 16$ for the case (2) and (3) in Theorem 3, we have $s_1 = 0$.

4 Study on the Structure of the Jacobian Group

Before describing our point counting algorithm, we study the structure of the Jacobian group for $y^2 = x^5 + ax$ more precisely. First, we study the reducibility of the Jacobian variety over extension fields of the defining field $\mathbb{F}_p$. Second, we determine the characteristic polynomial of the p-th power Frobenius endomorphism for many cases and give a necessary condition to be suitable for HCC explicitly.

4.1 Reducibility of the Jacobian Variety

We recall a few basic facts on the relation between the reducibility of the Jacobian variety and the characteristic polynomial of the Frobenius endomorphism. The following famous result was proved by Tate [18]:

Theorem 4. *Let A_1, A_2 be abelian varieties over $\mathbb{F}_q$ and $\chi_1(t)$, $\chi_2(t)$ characteristic polynomials of q-th power Frobenius endomorphisms of A_1, A_2, respectively. Then, A_1 is isogenous to A_2 over $\mathbb{F}_q$ if and only if $\chi_1(t) = \chi_2(t)$.*

The characteristic polynomial of the q-th power Frobenius endomorphism for a simple abelian variety of dimension two over $\mathbb{F}_q$ is determined as follows:

Theorem 5 ([21], cf. [17, 19]). *All possible characteristic polynomials $\chi_q(t)$ of q-th power Frobenius endomorphisms for simple abelian varieties of dimension two over $\mathbb{F}_q = \mathbb{F}_{p^r}$ are the followings:*

1. $\chi_q(t) = t^4 - s_1t^3 + s_2t^2 - qs_1t + q^2$ *is irreducible in* $\mathbb{Z}[t]$, *where* s_1, s_2 *satisfy some basic conditions,*
2. $\chi_q(t) = (t^2 - q)^2$, r *is odd,*
3. $\chi_q(t) = (t^2 + q)^2$, r *is even and* $p \equiv 1 \pmod 4$,
4. $\chi_q(t) = (t^2 \pm q^{1/2}t + q)^2$, r *is even and* $p \equiv 1 \pmod 3$.

For the reducibility of $\chi_{q^2}(t)$, the following lemma holds:

Lemma 3. *Let C be a hyperelliptic curve over $\mathbb{F}_q$ and $\chi_q(t) = t^4 - s_1t^3 + s_2t^2 - qs_1t + q^2$ the characteristic polynomial of q-th power Frobenius endomorphism of C, $\chi_{q^2}(t)$ the one of q^2-th power Frobenius endomorphism. Assume that $\chi_q(t)$ is irreducible in $\mathbb{Z}[t]$. Then $\chi_{q^2}(t)$ is reducible in $\mathbb{Z}[t]$ if and only if $s_1 = 0$.*

Proof. Let α, $\bar{\alpha}$, β, $\bar{\beta}$ be four roots of $\chi_q(t)$ where $\bar{\ }$ means complex conjugate. Then it is a well-known fact that $\chi_{q^2}(t) = (t - \alpha^2)(t - \bar{\alpha}^2)(t - \beta^2)(t - \bar{\beta}^2)$.

Assume that $s_1 = 0$. Put $\omega_1 = \alpha + \bar{\alpha}$ and $\omega_2 = \beta + \bar{\beta}$. Then from $s_1 = 0$ and $s_2 \in \mathbb{Z}$, we have $\omega_1 + \omega_2 = 0$ and $\omega_1\omega_2 + 2q \in \mathbb{Z}$. Put $m = \omega_1\omega_2 + 2q$. Then $\alpha^2 + \bar{\alpha}^2 = \omega_1^2 - 2q = -m$. We also have $\beta^2 + \bar{\beta}^2 = -m$. Hence we have $\chi_{q^2}(t) = (t^2 + mt + q^2)^2$.

Assume that $\chi_{q^2}(t)$ is not irreducible over $\mathbb{Z}$. First we consider the case $\chi_{q^2}(t)$ factors into a product of two polynomials of degree 2 over $\mathbb{Z}$. In this case, there are two possibilities: (a) $(t - \alpha^2)(t - \bar{\alpha}^2)$, $(t - \beta^2)(t - \bar{\beta}^2) \in \mathbb{Z}[t]$, (b) $(t - \alpha^2)(t - \beta^2)$, $(t - \bar{\alpha}^2)(t - \bar{\beta}^2) \in \mathbb{Z}[t]$. In case (a), $(\alpha + \bar{\alpha})^2 = \alpha^2 + \bar{\alpha}^2 + 2q \in \mathbb{Z}$. We also have $(\beta + \bar{\beta})^2 \in \mathbb{Z}$. Since $\chi_q(t)$ is irreducible over $\mathbb{Z}$, $\alpha + \bar{\alpha}$ and $\beta + \bar{\beta}$ are irrational numbers and we obtain that $s_1 = (\alpha + \bar{\alpha}) + (\beta + \bar{\beta})$ must be zero. In case (b), since $\alpha^2 + \beta^2$, $\bar{\alpha}^2 + \bar{\beta}^2$, $\alpha^2\beta^2$, $\bar{\alpha}^2\bar{\beta}^2$ are all in $\mathbb{Z}$, we have $\alpha^2 + \beta^2 = \bar{\alpha}^2 + \bar{\beta}^2$ and $\alpha^2\beta^2 = \bar{\alpha}^2\bar{\beta}^2$. Then $\alpha^2 = \bar{\alpha}^2$ or $\alpha^2 = \bar{\beta}^2$. Since $\chi_q(t)$ is irreducible, it cannot have a double root. So we have $\alpha = -\bar{\alpha}$ or $\alpha = -\bar{\beta}$. Moreover $\alpha = -\bar{\alpha}$ does not occur because if $\alpha = -\bar{\alpha}$ then $\chi_q(t)$ has a factor $(t - \alpha)(t - \bar{\alpha}) = t^2 + q$ over $\mathbb{Z}$. Hence we obtain $\alpha = -\bar{\beta}$. Then $\alpha + \bar{\beta} = 0$ and we have $s_1 = (\alpha + \bar{\beta}) + (\bar{\alpha} + \beta) = 0$. Finally, we consider the case that $\chi_{q^2}(t)$ has a factor of degree 1 over $\mathbb{Z}$. But if $t - \alpha^2 \in \mathbb{Z}[t]$ then we obtain $\alpha^2 = \bar{\alpha}^2$. As we showed in case (b), it does not occur. □

Now we consider the reducibility for the Jacobian variety of our curve $y^2 = x^5 + ax$.

Lemma 4. *Let p be an odd prime and C a hyperelliptic curve de□ned by $y^2 = x^5 + ax$, $a \in \mathbb{F}_p^\times$ and $\mathbb{F}_q = \mathbb{F}_{p^r}$, $r \geq 1$. If $a^{1/4} \in \mathbb{F}_q$, then J_C is isogenous to the product of the following two elliptic curves E_1 and E_2 over $\mathbb{F}_q$:*

$$E_1 : Y^2 = X(X^2 + 4a^{1/4}X - 2a^{1/2}),$$

$$E_2 : Y^2 = X(X^2 - 4a^{1/4}X - 2a^{1/2}).$$

Proof. Let α be an element of $\mathbb{F}_q$ such that $\alpha^4 = a$. We can construct maps $\varphi_i : C \to E_i$ explicitly as follows: $\varphi_i^*(X) = (x - (-1)^i\alpha)^2/x, \varphi_i^*(Y) = (x - (-1)^i\alpha)y/x^2$, $i = 1, 2$. Since pull-backs of regular 1-forms dX/Y on E_i's generate the space of regular 1-forms on C, $\varphi_1 \times \varphi_2$ induces an isogeny from J_C to $E_1 \times E_2$ (cf. [13, 12]). □

The Jacobian variety for curves of type $y^2 = x^5 + ax$ is reducible over $\mathbb{F}_{p^4}$ by the above lemma. From a cryptographic point of view, if the Jacobian variety splits over an extension field of degree two, HCC for these curves might lose its advantage to ECC. Hence in the following, it is important to see whether the Jacobian splits over an extension field $\mathbb{F}_{p^r}$ of lower degree, i.e. $r = 1, 2$.

Remark 4. If $\mathbb{F}_q$ includes a 4-th primitive root of unity, E_1 and E_2 in Lemma 4 are isomorphic to each other by the following transformation: $X \to -X$, $Y \to \zeta_4 Y$ where ζ_4 is a 4-th primitive root of unity in $\mathbb{F}_q$.

4.2 Determining the Characteristic Polynomial of the p-th Power Frobenius Endomorphism

Due to Theorem 3, we divide the situation into the following three cases: (1) $p \equiv 1 \pmod 8$, (2) $p \equiv 3 \pmod 8$, (3) $p \equiv 5, 7 \pmod 8$.

The Case of $p \equiv 1 \pmod 8$.

Lemma 5. *Let p be a prime number such that $p \equiv 1 \pmod 8$ and C a hyperelliptic curve over $\mathbb{F}_p$ defined by an equation $y^2 = x^5 + ax$. If $a^{(p-1)/2} = 1$, then 4 divides $\sharp J_C(\mathbb{F}_p)$. Moreover, if $a^{(p-1)/4} = 1$, then 16 divides $\sharp J_C(\mathbb{F}_p)$.*

Proof. First note that there is a primitive 8-th root of unity, ζ_8, in $\mathbb{F}_p$ because 8 divides $p-1$. If $a^{(p-1)/2} = 1$, then there exists an element $b \in \mathbb{F}_p$ such that $b^2 = a$. Then

$$x^5 + ax = x^5 + b^2x = x(x^2 + \zeta_8^2 b)(x^2 - \zeta_8^2 b).$$

It is easy to see that $\langle x, 0\rangle$ and $\langle x^2 + \zeta_8^2 b, 0\rangle$, which are points on $J_C(\mathbb{F}_p)$ in the Mumford representation, generate a subgroup of order 4 in $J_C(\mathbb{F}_p)$. Hence 4 divides $\sharp J_C(\mathbb{F}_p)$.

If $a^{(p-1)/4} = 1$, there is an element u in $\mathbb{F}_p$ such that $a = u^4$. Then

$$x^5 + ax = x^5 + u^4x = x(x + \zeta_8 u)(x - \zeta_8 u)(x + \zeta_8^3 u)(x - \zeta_8^3 u).$$

It is easy to see that $\langle x, 0\rangle$, $\langle x + \zeta_8 u, 0\rangle$, $\langle x - \zeta_8 u, 0\rangle$ and $\langle x + \zeta_8^3 u, 0\rangle$ generate a subgroup of order 16 in $J_C(\mathbb{F}_p)$. Hence 16 divides $\sharp J_C(\mathbb{F}_p)$. □

Theorem 6. *Let p be a prime number such that $p > 64$, $p \equiv 1 \pmod 8$ and C a hyperelliptic curve over $\mathbb{F}_p$ defined by an equation $y^2 = x^5 + ax$. If $\left(\frac{a}{p}\right) = 1$, then $\chi_p(t)$ are as follows:*

1. *if* $p \equiv 1 \pmod{16}$ *and* $a^{(p-1)/8} = 1$, *then* $\chi_p(t) = (t^2 - 2ct + p)^2$,
2. *if* $p \equiv 9 \pmod{16}$ *and* $a^{(p-1)/8} = 1$, *then* $\chi_p(t) = (t^2 + 2ct + p)^2$,
3. *if* $p \equiv 1 \pmod{16}$ *and* $a^{(p-1)/8} = -1$, *then* $\chi_p(t) = (t^2 + 2ct + p)^2$,
4. *if* $p \equiv 9 \pmod{16}$ *and* $a^{(p-1)/8} = -1$, *then* $\chi_p(t) = (t^2 - 2ct + p)^2$,
5. *otherwise,* $\chi_p(t) = t^4 + (4c^2 - 2p)t^2 + p^2$,

where $p = c^2 + 2d^2$, $c, d \in \mathbb{Z}$ *and* $c \equiv 1 \pmod 4$.

Proof. First of all, from Theorem 3, $s_1 \equiv (-1)^{(p-1)/8} 2c\left(a^{3(p-1)/8} + a^{(p-1)/8}\right) \pmod p$ and $s_2 \equiv 4c^2 \pmod p$ for all cases.

For the case (1), from Theorem 3 we have $s_1 \equiv 4c \pmod p$. By the definition of c, $c^2 < p$ and hence $0 < |4c| < 4\sqrt{p}$. Since $p > 64$ and Remark 1, we have that $s_1 = 4c$. Moreover since $\lceil 2\sqrt{p}|s_1| - 2p \rceil \le s_2 \le \lfloor s_1^2/4 + 2p \rfloor$ and $0 < 4c^2 < 4p$, s_2 is of the form $4c^2 + mp$, $-5 \le m \le 2$, $m \in \mathbb{Z}$. Then $\sharp J_C(\mathbb{F}_p) = 1 + p^2 - 4c(1+p) + 4c^2 + mp$ where m is an integer such that $-5 \le m \le 2$. Since $\sharp J_C(\mathbb{F}_p) \equiv 0 \pmod{16}$ from Lemma 5, $1 + p^2 - 4c(1+p) + 4c^2 + mp \equiv 0 \pmod{16}$. Since $p \equiv 1 \pmod{16}$ and $c \equiv 1 \pmod 4$, we have $mp \equiv 2 \pmod{16}$ and then $m = 2$. Hence we obtain $\chi_p(t) = t^4 - 4ct^3 + (4c^2 + 2p)t^2 - 4cpt + p^2 = (t^2 - 2ct + p)^2$.

For the cases (2), (3), (4), we can show in the same way.

For the case (5), $a^{(p-1)/8}$ is a primitive 4-th root of unity and $a^{3(p-1)/8} + a^{(p-1)/8} = 0$. So we have that $s_1 = 0$ by Theorem 3 and $p > 64$. Since $|s_2| \le 2p$ in this case by Lemma 1 and $0 < 4c^2 < 4p$ by the definition of c, s_2 is of the form $4c^2 + mp$, $-5 \le m \le 1$, $m \in \mathbb{Z}$. On the other hand, since $1 + p^2 \equiv 2 \pmod 4$ and $\sharp J_C(\mathbb{F}_p) \equiv 0 \pmod 4$ by Lemma 5, we have that $m = -2$. Hence we obtain $\chi_q(t) = t^4 + (4c^2 - 2p)t^2 + p^2$. □

Hence in particular if $p \equiv 1 \pmod 8$ and $\left(\frac{a}{p}\right) = 1$, then C with $a^{(p-1)/4} = 1$ is not suitable for HCC because $\sharp J_C(\mathbb{F}_p) = (p \pm 2c + 1)^2$ and $|c| < \sqrt{p}$. In addition, J_C in case (5) is isogenous to the product of two elliptic curves over $\mathbb{F}_{p^2}$ because $a^{1/4} \in \mathbb{F}_{p^2}$.

The Case of $p \equiv 3 \pmod 8$.

Lemma 6. *For a hyperelliptic curve* $C : y^2 = x^5 + ax$, $a \in \mathbb{F}_p$ *where* $p \equiv 3 \pmod 4$, *the followings hold:*

1. *if* $\left(\frac{a}{p}\right) = 1$, *then* $\sharp J_C(\mathbb{F}_p) \equiv 0 \pmod 4$,
2. *if* $\left(\frac{a}{p}\right) = -1$, *then* $\sharp J_C(\mathbb{F}_p) \equiv 0 \pmod 8$.

Proof. If $\left(\frac{a}{p}\right) = 1$, then there exists an element $b \in \mathbb{F}_p$ such that $a = b^2$. Since $\left(\frac{-1}{p}\right) = -1$ by $p \equiv 3 \pmod 4$, either $2b$ or $-2b$ is a square. If $2b = u^2$, then

$$x^5 + ax = x\{(x^2 + b)^2 - 2bx^2\} = x(x^2 + ux + b)(x^2 - ux + b)$$

over $\mathbb{F}_p$ and $\langle x, 0\rangle$ and $\langle x^2+ux+b, 0\rangle$ generate a subgroup of order 4 in $J_C(\mathbb{F}_p)$. If $-2b = u^2$,

$$x^5 + ax = x\{(x^2-b)^2 - (-2b)x^2\} = x(x^2+ux-b)(x^2-ux-b)$$

over $\mathbb{F}_p$ and $\langle x, 0\rangle$ and $\langle x^2+ux-b, 0\rangle$ generate a subgroup of order 4 in $J_C(\mathbb{F}_p)$.

If $\left(\frac{a}{p}\right) = -1$, then x^5+ax factors into a form $x(x+\beta)(x-\beta)(x^2+\gamma)$ over $\mathbb{F}_p$. It is easy to see that $\langle x, 0\rangle$, $\langle x+\beta, 0\rangle$ and $\langle x-\beta, 0\rangle$ generate a subgroup of order 8 in $J_C(\mathbb{F}_p)$. □

Theorem 7. *Let p be a prime number such that $p > 16$, $p \equiv 3 \pmod 8$ and C a hyperelliptic curve over $\mathbb{F}_p$ defined by the equation $y^2 = x^5 + ax$. If $\left(\frac{a}{p}\right) = 1$, then $\chi_p(t) = (t^2+2ct+p)(t^2-2ct+p)$ where $p = c^2 + 2d^2$, $c, d \in \mathbb{Z}$.*

Proof. The order of $J_C(\mathbb{F}_p)$ is given by $1+p^2+s_2$ because $s_1 = 0$. Moreover $s_2 \equiv -4c^2a^{(p-1)/2} \equiv -4c^2 \pmod p$. Since $|s_2| \le 2p$, $s_2 = -4c^2 + mp$ where $m \in \mathbb{Z}$ such that $-2p \le -4c^2 + mp \le 2p$. By the definition of c, $0 < c^2 < p$ and $-4p < -4c^2 < 0$. Hence we have $-1 \le m \le 5$.

On the other hand, since 4 divides $\sharp J_C(\mathbb{F}_p)$ by Lemma 6, we have $(1+p^2+mp-4c^2) \equiv 0 \pmod 4$. By $p \equiv 3 \pmod 8$ and $c^2 \equiv 1 \pmod 4$, we have the condition $1+p^2+mp-4c^2 \equiv 2+3m \equiv 0 \pmod 4$ and we obtain $m = 2$. Hence $\chi_p(t) = t^4 + (2p-4c^2)t^2 + p^2 = (t^2+2ct+p)(t^2-2ct+p)$. □

Theorem 8. *Let p be a prime number such that $p > 16$, $p \equiv 3 \pmod 8$ and C a hyperelliptic curve over $\mathbb{F}_p$ defined by the equation $y^2 = x^5 + ax$. If $\left(\frac{a}{p}\right) = -1$, then $\chi_p(t) = t^4 + (4c^2-2p)t^2 + p^2$ where $p = c^2 + 2d^2$, $c, d \in \mathbb{Z}$.*

Proof. In this case, $\sharp J_C(\mathbb{F}_p) = 1+p^2+mp+4c^2$ where $-2p \le mp+4c^2 \le 2p$ and $-5 \le m \le 1$. Since 8 divides $\sharp J_C(\mathbb{F}_p)$ by Lemma 6, $1+p^2+mp+4c^2 \equiv 6+3m \equiv 0 \pmod 8$ and we obtain $m = -2$. Hence $\chi_p(t) = t^4 + (4c^2-2p)t^2 + p^2$. □

Hence in this case, $\sharp J_C(\mathbb{F}_p)$ only depends on p and the value of the Legendre symbol for $\left(\frac{a}{p}\right)$. And in particular, C is not suitable for HCC if $\left(\frac{a}{p}\right) = 1$ because $\sharp J_C(\mathbb{F}_p) = (p+2c+1)(p-2c+1)$ and $|c| < \sqrt{p}$. In addition, J_C for the case of $\left(\frac{a}{p}\right) = -1$ is isogenous to the product of two elliptic curves over $\mathbb{F}_{p^2}$ because $a^{1/4} \in \mathbb{F}_{p^2}$.

The Case of $p \equiv 5, 7 \pmod 8$. This is the case that the Jacobian variety J_C is supersingular because $s_1 \equiv s_2 \equiv 0 \pmod p$ (cf. [21]).

Lemma 7. *Let p be a prime number such that $p > 16$ and $p \equiv 5 \pmod 8$. For a hyperelliptic curve $C : y^2 = x^5 + ax$, $a \in \mathbb{F}_p$, the followings hold:*

1. *if $a^{(p-1)/4} = 1$, then $\sharp J_C(\mathbb{F}_p) \equiv 0 \pmod 4$,*
2. *if $a^{(p-1)/4} = -1$, then $\sharp J_C(\mathbb{F}_p) \equiv 0 \pmod 8$.*

Proof. Note that $\mathbb{F}_p$ has a 4-th primitive root of unity, ζ_4, because $p - 1 \equiv 0 \pmod 4$. Since $\left(\frac{a}{p}\right) = 1$ in both cases, there exists an element $b \in \mathbb{F}_p$ such that $a = b^2$ and $x^5 + ax = x(x^2 + \zeta_4 b)(x^2 - \zeta_4 b)$. Hence $\langle x, 0\rangle$, $\langle x^2 + \zeta_4 b, 0\rangle$ generates a subgroup of order 4 in $J_C(\mathbb{F}_p)$.

If $a^{(p-1)/4} = -1$, $\left(\frac{b}{p}\right) = -1$ and then $x^2 - \zeta_4 b$ factors into the form $(x + \beta)(x - \beta)$ because $\left(\frac{\zeta_4}{p}\right) = -1$. Hence in case (2), $\langle x, 0\rangle$, $\langle x + \beta, 0\rangle$, $\langle x - \beta, 0\rangle$ generate a subgroup of order 8 in $J_C(\mathbb{F}_p)$. □

Using the above lemma and Lemma 6, we obtain the following theorem.

Theorem 9. *Let p be a prime number such that $p > 16$, $p \equiv 5, 7 \pmod 8$ and C a hyperelliptic curve over $\mathbb{F}_p$ de*□*ned by the equation $y^2 = x^5 + ax$. Then,*

1. *if $p \equiv 5 \pmod 8$ and $a^{(p-1)/4} = 1$, then $\chi_p(t) = (t^2 + p)^2$,*
2. *if $p \equiv 5 \pmod 8$ and $a^{(p-1)/4} = -1$, then $\chi_p(t) = (t^2 - p)^2$,*
3. *if $p \equiv 5 \pmod 8$ and $\left(\frac{a}{p}\right) = -1$, then $\chi_p(t) = t^4 + p^2$,*
4. *if $p \equiv 7 \pmod 8$, then $\chi_p(t) = (t^2 + p)^2$.*

Proof. The order of $J_C(\mathbb{F}_p)$ is given by $1 + p^2 + s_2$ because $s_1 = 0$. Moreover, $s_2 = 0$ or $\pm 2p$ by Lemma 1 and Remark 2. Note that $1 + p^2 \equiv 2 \pmod 8$.

In case (1), $a^{1/4} \in \mathbb{F}_p$. Then J_C is isogenous to the product of two elliptic curves over $\mathbb{F}_p$ by Lemma 4. Hence by the list of Theorem 5, $\chi_p(t)$ must be $(t^2 + p)^2$.

In case (2), $\sharp J_C(\mathbb{F}_p) \equiv 0 \pmod 8$ by Lemma 7. Then we obtain $s_2 = -2p$ and the result.

In case (3), we use the relation $s_2 = (M_2 - 1 - p^2 + s_1^2)/2$ where $M_2 = \sharp C(\mathbb{F}_{p^2})$. Since $s_1 = 0$, $s_2 = (M_2 - 1 - p^2)/2$ and M_2 is given by $1 + \sharp R + 2\sharp S$ where $R = \{x \in \mathbb{F}_{p^2} | x^5 + ax = 0\}$ and $S = \{x \in \mathbb{F}_{p^2} | x^5 + ax \text{ is a non-zero square }\}$. Since $\mathbb{F}_{p^2}$ has a primitive 8-th root of unity, ζ_8, we easily see that if $u \in S$ then $\zeta_8^2 u \in S$. Hence we have that 4 divides $\sharp S$. In the case of $p \equiv 5 \pmod 8$ and $\left(\frac{a}{p}\right) = -1$, $\sharp R = 1$ and we have $M_2 \equiv 2 \pmod 8$. Hence in this case, $s_2 \equiv 0 \pmod 4$ and we have that $s_2 = 0$.

In case (4), we divide the situation by the value of the Legendre symbol $\left(\frac{a}{p}\right)$. If $\left(\frac{a}{p}\right) = 1$ then $a^{1/4} \in \mathbb{F}_p$ because $\left(\frac{-1}{p}\right) = -1$. By this fact, if $\left(\frac{a}{p}\right) = 1$ then J_C is isogenous to the product of two elliptic curves over $\mathbb{F}_p$ and we obtain the result as in case (1). For the case of $\left(\frac{a}{p}\right) = -1$, we have $s_2 = 2p$ by Lemma 6. □

So in this case, C is not suitable for HCC if $p \equiv 5 \pmod 8$ with $\left(\frac{a}{p}\right) = 1$ or $p \equiv 7 \pmod 8$, because $\sharp J_C(\mathbb{F}_p) = (p \pm 1)^2$. If $p \equiv 5 \pmod 8$ and $\left(\frac{a}{p}\right) = -1$, $\chi_{p^2}(t)$ is split because $s_1 = 0$ but J_C is simple over $\mathbb{F}_{p^2}$ by Theorem 5.

4.3 Necessary Condition to be Suitable for HCC

From the results in 4.2, we have the following corollary.

Corollary 1. *Let p be a prime number and C a hyperelliptic curve de□ned by an equation $y^2 = x^5 + ax$ where $a \in \mathbb{F}_p$. Then C is not suitable for HCC if one of the followings holds: (1) $p \equiv 1 \pmod 8$, $a^{(p-1)/4} = 1$, (2) $p \equiv 3 \pmod 8$, $\left(\frac{a}{p}\right) = 1$, (3) $p \equiv 5 \pmod 8$, $\left(\frac{a}{p}\right) = 1$, (4) $p \equiv 7 \pmod 8$.*

In addition to the above cases, if $p \equiv 1 \pmod 8$ with $a^{(p-1)/4} = -1$ or $p \equiv 3 \pmod 8$ with $\left(\frac{a}{p}\right) = -1$, J_C is isogenous to the product of two elliptic curves over $\mathbb{F}_{p^2}$.

5 Point Counting Algorithm and Searching Suitable Curves

In this section we search suitable curves for HCC among hyperelliptic curves of type $y^2 = x^5 + ax$, $a \in \mathbb{F}_p$. From the result of the previous section, all the cases which can have suitable orders are the followings: (1) $p \equiv 1 \pmod 8$ with $\left(\frac{a}{p}\right) = -1$, (2) $p \equiv 1 \pmod 8$ with $a^{(p-1)/4} = -1$, (3) $p \equiv 3 \pmod 8$ with $\left(\frac{a}{p}\right) = -1$, (4) $p \equiv 5 \pmod 8$ with $\left(\frac{a}{p}\right) = -1$. But as we remarked in 4.2 and 4.3, J_C's are reducible over $\mathbb{F}_{p^2}$ in the case (2) and (3). Moreover J_C is supersingular in the case (4) as we remarked in 4.2. Hence we exclude these cases and only focus on the remaining case (1): $p \equiv 1 \pmod 8$ with $\left(\frac{a}{p}\right) = -1$.

On the other hand, the Jacobian group $J_C(\mathbb{F}_p)$ for our curve has a 2-torsion point (Remark 2), the best possible order of $J_C(\mathbb{F}_p)$ is $2l$ where l is prime. The case (1) in the above is the case that we can obtain the best possible order.

For the case (1) we cannot determine the characteristic polynomial of the p-th power Frobenius endomorphism by using the same method in 4.2. So we need a point counting algorithm for $J_C(\mathbb{F}_p)$. First we describe our algorithm and next we show the result of the search based on our algorithm.

5.1 Point Counting Algorithm for $p \equiv 1 \pmod 8$ and $\left(\frac{a}{p}\right) = -1$

We describe our algorithm based on Theorem 3. The algorithm is as follows:

Algorithm 1
`Input`: *$a \in \mathbb{F}_p$ where $p \equiv 1 \pmod 8$ and $p > 64$*
`Output`: *$\sharp J_C(\mathbb{F}_p)$ (C : a hyperelliptic curve of genus 2 de□ned by $y^2 = x^5 + ax$)*

1. *Calculate an integer c such that $p = c^2 + 2d^2$, $c \equiv 1 \pmod 4$, $d \in \mathbb{Z}$ by using Cornacchia's Algorithm.*

2. *Determine* s_1*:*
   $s \leftarrow (-1)^{(p-1)/8} 2c(a^{3(p-1)/8} + a^{(p-1)/8}) \pmod p \qquad (0 \le s \le p-1)$
   `If` $s < 4\sqrt{p}$, `then` $s_1 \leftarrow s$, `else` $s_1 \leftarrow s - p$.
3. *Determine the list* S *of candidates for* s_2*:*
   $t \leftarrow 4c^2 a^{(p-1)/2} \pmod p \qquad (0 \le t \le p-1)$
   `If` t: *even,* `then` $S \leftarrow \{t + 2mp \mid 2\sqrt{p}|s_1| - 2p \le t + 2mp \le s_1^2/4 + 2p\}$,
   `else` $S \leftarrow \{t + (2m+1)p \mid 2\sqrt{p}|s_1| - 2p \le t + (2m+1)p \le s_1^2/4 + 2p\}$.
4. *Determine the list* L *of candidates for* $\sharp J_C(\mathbb{F}_p)$*:*
   $L \leftarrow \{1 + p^2 - s_1(p+1) + s_2 \mid s_2 \in S\}$. ($\sharp L \le 3$ *by Remark* 2.)
5. `If` $\sharp L = 1$, `then` *return the unique element of* L,
   `else` *determine* $\sharp J_C(\mathbb{F}_p)$ *by multiplying a random point* D *on* $J_C(\mathbb{F}_p)$ *by each element of* L.

It is easy to show that the expected running time of the above algorithm is $O(\ln^4 p)$. (For an estimation for Cornacchia's algorithm and so on, see Cohen's book [5] for example.)

5.2 Searching Suitable Curves for HCC and Results

Here we show the result that we have searched hyperelliptic curves suitable for HCC among hyperelliptic curves of type $y^2 = x^5 + ax$, $a \in \mathbb{F}_p$.

Our search is based on the algorithm which we proposed in 5.1. All computation below were done by *Mathematica* 4.1 on Celeron 600MHz.

Example 1. The followings are examples of curves such that the orders of their Jacobian groups are in the form 2·(prime).

$$p = 1208925819614629175095961(81\text{-bit}), a = 3,$$
$$J_C(\mathbb{F}_p) = 2 \cdot 730750818666480869498570026461293846666412451841(160\text{-bit})$$

(The computation for counting points took 0.04s.)

$$p{=}2923003274661805836407369665432566039311865180529(162\text{-bit}), a{=}371293,$$
$$J_C(\mathbb{F}_p){=}2{\cdot}4271974071841820164790042159200669057836414062331724137933\backslash$$
$$6519382596868657626708008708198483809 7(321\text{-bit})$$

(The computation for counting points took 0.07s.)

In the above examples, J_C's are simple over $\mathbb{F}_{p^2}$. Since $\sharp J_C(\mathbb{F}_p)$ has a large prime factor, the characteristic polynomial of the p-th power Frobenius endomorphism must be irreducible. Moreover since $s_1 \ne 0$ over $\mathbb{F}_p$, the characteristic polynomial of p^2-th power Frobenius endomorphism cannot split by Lemma 3.

Furthermore, one can easily check that large prime factors of the above $\sharp J_C(\mathbb{F}_p)$ do not divide $p^r - 1$, $r = 1, 2, \ldots, 2^3\lfloor \log^2 p \rfloor$. Hence these curves are not weak against the Frey-Rück attack [7].

Example 2. The following table shows the result of search in many p's. We can find the following number of suitable curves for each search range.

search range (r, s) for p, $r < p < s$	num. of primes $p \equiv 1 \pmod 8$	num. of curves s.t. $\sharp J_C(\mathbb{F}_p) = 2\times(\text{prime})$	time (seconds)
$2^{80}, 2^{80} + 10^6$	4441	366	416.67
$2^{81}, 2^{81} + 10^6$	4309	352	409.72
$2^{161}, 2^{161} + 10^6$	2276	93	497.49
$2^{325}, 2^{325} + 10^6$	1100	30	731.52

Remark 5. From the result of Duursma, Gaudry and Morain [6], an automorphism of large order can be exploited to accelerate the Pollard's rho algorithm. If there is an automorphism of order m, we can get a speed up of $\sqrt{m}$. The order of any automorphism of $y^2 = x^5 + ax$ is at most 8. So the Pollard's rho algorithm for these curves can be improved only by a factor $\sqrt{8}$.

6 Point Counting Algorithm for another Curve: $y^2 = x^5 + a$

In this section, we consider another curve $y^2 = x^5 + a$, $a \in \mathbb{F}_p$. For the case a is square in $\mathbb{F}_p$, it is a kind of Buhler-Koblitz's curves [2]. Hence we consider the case a is non-square.

Theorem 10. *Let p be an odd prime number such that $p \equiv 1 \pmod 5$. C a hyperelliptic curve de□ned by the equation $y^2 = x^5 + a$ where $a \in \mathbb{F}_p$. Moreover let $J_5(\chi, \chi) = \sum_{s=0}^{p-1} \chi(s)\chi(1-s)$ be the Jacobi sum for a character χ of $\mathbb{F}_p$ which maps a □xed non-quintic element in $\mathbb{F}_p$ to $\zeta = e^{2\pi i/5}$ and c_1, c_2, c_3, c_4 be coecients of ζ^i in the expression $J_5(\chi, \chi) = c_1\zeta + c_2\zeta^2 + c_3\zeta^3 + c_4\zeta^4$. Then for the characteristic polynomial $t^4 - s_1t^3 + s_2t^2 - s_1pt + p^2$ of the p-th power Frobenius endomorphism of C, s_1, s_2 are given as follows:*

$$s_1 \equiv \frac{1}{2}\alpha^3 (-z + \beta)\, a^{3(p-1)/10} + \frac{1}{2}\alpha (-z - \beta)\, a^{(p-1)/10} \pmod p$$
$$s_2 \equiv \frac{1}{4}\alpha^4 \left(z^2 - \beta^2\right) a^{2(p-1)/5} \pmod p$$

where $\alpha = 2^{(p-1)/5} \pmod p$, $\beta = \frac{w(z^2-125w^2)}{4(zw+uv)}$ *and* z, u, v, w *are given by* $z = -(c_1 + c_2 + c_3 + c_4)$, $5u = c_1 + 2c_2 - 2c_3 - c_4$, $5v = 2c_1 - c_2 + c_3 - 2c_4$, $5w = c_1 - c_2 - c_3 + c_4$.

Proof. Since $(x^5 + a)^{(p-1)/2} = \sum_{r=0}^{(p-1)/2} \binom{\frac{p-1}{2}}{r} x^{5r} a^{(p-1)/2-r}$ and $p \equiv 1 \pmod 5$, the Hasse-Witt matrix of C is of the form $\begin{pmatrix} c_{p-1} & 0 \\ 0 & c_{2p-2} \end{pmatrix}$. Put $f = (p-1)/10$. Then $s_1 \equiv \binom{5f}{2f} a^{3f} + \binom{5f}{4f} a^f \pmod p$ and $s_2 \equiv \binom{5f}{2f}\binom{5f}{4f} a^{4f} \pmod p$. From the result of [10, Theorem 13.1], $\binom{5f}{2f} = \frac{1}{2}\alpha^3 \left(-z + \frac{w(z^2-125w^2)}{4(zw+uv)}\right)$ and $\binom{5f}{f} = \frac{1}{2}\alpha \left(-z - \frac{w(z^2-125w^2)}{4(zw+uv)}\right)$. Hence we obtain the result. □

Remark 6. If $p \not\equiv 1 \pmod 5$, then the Hasse-Witt matrix is of the form $\begin{pmatrix} 0 & c_{p-2} \\ 0 & 0 \end{pmatrix}$ or $\begin{pmatrix} 0 & 0 \\ c_{2p-1} & 0 \end{pmatrix}$. Hence $s_1 \equiv s_2 \equiv 0 \pmod p$ and J_C is supersingular [21].

From the above theorem, we obtain a point counting algorithm for curves of type $y^2 = x^5 + a$ over $\mathbb{F}_p$ when $p \equiv 1 \pmod 5$. The algorithm is as follows:

Algorithm 2
`Input`: *$a \in \mathbb{F}_p$ where $p \equiv 1 \pmod 5$ and $p > 64$.*
`Output`: *$\sharp J_C(\mathbb{F}_p)$ (C: a hyperelliptic curve of genus 2 de◻ned by $y^2 = x^5 + a$).*

1. *Calculate coecients c_1, c_2, c_3, c_4 in $J_5(\chi, \chi) = \sum_{i=1}^{4} c_i \zeta^i$ in Theorem 10 by using the LLL algorithm. (See [2] for details.)*
2. *Determine s_1 by Theorem 10 and the bound $|s_1| < 4\sqrt{p}$.*
3. *Determine the list of candidates for s_2 by Theorem 10 and Lemma 1.*
4. *Determine the list L of candidates for $\sharp J_C(\mathbb{F}_p)$ from results of Step 2 and 3. ($\sharp L \leq 5$ by Remark 1.)*
5. `If` *$\sharp L = 1$,* `then` *return the unique element of L,* `else` *determine $\sharp J_C(\mathbb{F}_p)$ by multiplying a random point D on $J_C(\mathbb{F}_p)$ by each element of L.*

We show the result that we have searched suitable curves for HCC among hyperelliptic curves of type $y^2 = x^5 + a$, $a \in \mathbb{F}_p$ where a is non-square. All computation below were done by *Mathematica* 4.1 on Celeron 600MHz.

Example 3. The followings are examples of curves whose Jacobian groups have prime orders.

$$p = 1208925819614629174708801(81\text{-bit}), a = 1331,$$
$$J_C(\mathbb{F}_p) = 1461501637326815988079848163961117521046955445901(160\text{-bit})$$
(The computation for counting points took 0.18s.)

$$p = 1208925819614629174709941(81\text{-bit}), a = 2,$$
$$J_C(\mathbb{F}_p) = 1461501637331762771847359428275278989652932675771(161\text{-bit})$$
(The computation for counting points took 24.58s.)

In these examples, J_C's are simple over $\mathbb{F}_{p^2}$ by Lemma 3 and not weak against the Frey-Rück attack.

Example 4. The following table shows the result of search in many p's. We can find the following number of suitable curves for each search range.

search range (r, s) for p, $r < p < s$	num. of primes $p \equiv 1 \pmod 5$	num. of curves s.t. $\sharp J_C(\mathbb{F}_p)$ =prime	time (seconds)
$2^{80}, 2^{80} + 10^4$	50	7	237.67
$2^{81}, 2^{81} + 10^4$	40	7	224.16
$2^{82}, 2^{82} + 10^4$	39	5	297.13
$2^{100}, 2^{100} + 10^4$	33	5	335.76

Remark 7. The order of any automorphism of $y^2 = x^5 + a$ is at most 10. So as same as we remarked in Remark 5, the Pollard's rho algorithm for these curves can be improved only by a factor $\sqrt{10}$.

References

[1] B. C. Berndt, R. J. Evans and K. S. Williams, Gauss and Jacobi Sums, Canadian Mathematical Society Series of Monographs and Advanced Texts **21**, A Wiley-Interscience Publication, 1998, 30

[2] J. Buhler and N. Koblitz, *Lattice Basis Reduction, Jacobi Sums and Hyperelliptic Cryptosystems*, Bull. Austral. Math. Soc. **58** (1998), pp. 147–154, 27, 38, 39

[3] D. G. Cantor, *Computing in the Jacobian of hyperelliptic curve*, Math. Comp. **48** (1987), pp. 95–101, 28

[4] Y. Choie, E. Jeong and E. Lee, *Supersingular Hyperelliptic Curves of Genus 2 over Finite Fields*, Cryptology ePrint Archive: Report 2002/032 (2002), http://eprint.iacr.org/2002/032/,

[5] H. Cohen, A Course in Computational Algebraic Number Theory, Graduate Texts in Mathematics **138**, Springer, 1996, 37

[6] I. Duursma, P. Gaudry and F. Morain, *Speeding up the Discrete Log Computation on Curves with Automorphisms*, Advances in Cryptology – ASIA CRYPT '99, Springer-Verlag LNCS 1716, 1999, pp. 103–121, 38

[7] G. Frey and H.-G. Rück, *A Remark Concerning m-divisibility and the Discrete Logarithm in the Divisor Class Group of Curves*, Math. Comp. **62**, No.206 (1994) pp. 865–874, 37

[8] S. G. Galbraith, *Supersingular Curves in Cryptography*, Advances in Cryptology – ASIACRYPT 2001, Springer-Verlag LNCS 2248, 2001, pp. 495–513,

[9] P. Gaudry and R. Harley, *Counting Points on Hyperelliptic Curves over Finite Fields*, ANTS-IV, Springer-Verlag LNCS 1838, 2000, pp. 297–312, 26, 27, 28

[10] R. H. Hudson and K. S. Williams, *Binomial Coefficients and Jacobi Sums*, Trans. Amer. Math. Soc. **281** (1984), pp. 431–505, 30, 38

[11] N. Koblitz, Algebraic Aspects of Cryptography, Algorithms and Computation in Mathematics Vol. 3, Springer-Verlag, 1998, 27, 29

[12] S. Lang, Abelian Varieties, Springer-Verlag, 1983, 32

[13] F. Leprévost and F. Morain, *Revêtements de courbes elliptiques à multiplication complexe par des courbes hyperelliptiques et sommes de caractères*, J. Number Theory **64** (1997), pp. 165–182, 32

[14] Ju. I. Manin, *The Hasse-Witt Matrix of an Algebraic Curve*, Amer. Math. Soc. Transl. Ser. **45** (1965), pp. 245–264, 28

[15] K. Matsuo, J. Chao and S. Tsujii, *An improved baby step giant step algorithm for point counting of hyperelliptic curves over finite fields*, ANTS-V, Springer-Verlag LNCS 2369, 2002, pp. 461–474, 26, 29

[16] D. Mumford, Tata Lectures on Theta II, Progress in Mathematics **43**, Birkhäuser, 1984, 28

[17] H-G. Rück, *Abelian surfaces and Jacobian varieties over finite fields*, Compositio Math. **76** (1990), pp. 351–366, 29, 31

[18] J. Tate, *Endomorphisms of abelian varieties over finite fields*, Invent. Math. **2** (1996), pp. 134–144, 30

[19] W. C. Waterhouse, *Abelian varieties over finite fields*, Ann. Sci. École Nor. Sup. (4) **2** (1969), pp. 521–560, 31

[20] S. Wolfram, The Mathematica Book, 4th ed., Wolfram Media/Cambridge University Press, 1999,
[21] C. Xing, *On supersingular abelian varieties of dimension two over finite fields*, Finite Fields and Their Appl. **2** (1996), pp. 407–421, 31, 34, 39
[22] N. Yui, *On the Jacobian Varieties of Hyperelliptic Curves over Fields of Characteristic* $p > 2$, J. Alg. **52** (1978), pp. 378–410. 28

Longer Keys May Facilitate Side Channel Attacks

Colin D. Walter

Comodo Research Lab
10 Hey Street, Bradford, BD7 1DQ, UK
Colin.Walter@comodogroup.com

Abstract. Increasing key length is a standard counter-measure to cryptanalysis. However, longer key length generally means greater side channel leakage. For embedded RSA crypto-systems the increase in leaked data outstrips the increase in secret data so that, in contrast to the improved mathematical strength, longer keys may, in fact, lead to lower security. This is investigated for two types of implementation attack. The first is a timing attack in which squares and multiplications are differentiated from the relative frequencies of conditional subtractions over several exponentiations. Once keys are large enough, longer length seems to decrease security. The second case is a power analysis attack on a single m-ary exponentiation using a single k-bit hardware multiplier. For this, despite certain counter-measures such as exponent blinding, uncertainty in determining the secret bits decreases so quickly that longer keys appear to be noticeably less secure.

Keywords: RSA Cryptosystem, Key Length, Side Channel Attacks, Timing Attack, Power Analysis, DPA.

1 Introduction

So-called *side channel attacks* on smartcards to discover secret keys contained therein follow a well-established tradition pursued by the military and secret services, and exemplified by the long-running Tempest project of the US [27]. That project concentrated on detecting and obscuring electro-magnetic radiation (EMR) and led to both heavily shielded monitors (for those based on electron beam technology) and TV detector vans. EMR can be, and is, used to break smartcards – but with a somewhat smaller aerial, one some 3mm long or less [5]. If correctly placed and set up with sufficiently sensitive equipment, these can detect useful variations in EMR non-invasively.

Side-channel leakage occurs through data dependent variation in the use of resources such as time and hardware. The former results from branching in the code or compiler optimisation [2, 9], and the latter manifests itself through current variation as well as EMR [10, 12, 13]. For the RSA crypto-system [17], conditional modular subtractions should be removed to make the time constant [18, 19, 21]. Bus activity is the major cause of power variation, with a strong relationship

M. Matsui and R. Zuccherato (Eds.): SAC 2003, LNCS 3006, pp. 42–57, 2004.

between it and the Hamming weight of the data on the bus. Instructions and memory locations pass along the bus and, in the context of the limited computational resources of a smartcard, potentially also large quantities of data. This is partly solved by encryption of the bus [1, 11].

For all the popular crypto-systems used in practice where the key length is variable, the greater the key length, the greater the *mathematical* strength of the system against attack is believed to be. Indeed, a brute force attack will take time exponential in the key length. However, longer key lengths require more computation for encryption and decryption or signature and verification. Hence there is more data which leaks through timing, current and EMR variation. In an embedded crypto-system to which an attacker has access, such as a smartcard, a valid question to ask is whether or not the increased data from side channel leakage actually makes longer keys *more* vulnerable to attack.

In the symmetric crypto-systems of DES, 3-DES and AES [25, 26], the block length is fixed and the number of rounds is proportional to the key length (comparing DES with 3-DES, and AES with different choices for its parameter Nk). Hence the data leakage is also proportional to the key length and the *implementation* strength of the cipher is unlikely to decrease as key length increases.

However, public key cryptography such as in RSA, DSA, ECC, Diffie-Hellman or El-Gamal [3, 4, 14, 17, 24], usually involves exponentiation in some form, where the block length and exponent are proportional to the key length. Assuming multiplication of double-length arguments takes four times the time for single-length arguments on the same hardware, total decryption/signing time is proportional to the cube of the key length. Consequently, *more* leaked data is available per key bit as key length grows. Indeed, if the multiplicative operations of the exponentiation are performed sequentially using one of the standard algorithms [7, 8] and no form of blinding, then there is more data per exponent bit for longer key lengths and one should expect the implementation strength to decrease.

Two attacks illustrate that such an outcome may be possible from increasing the key length. The first is a timing attack [21] whose success is apparently easier for very short and very long key lengths. By its very nature, the attack assumes essentially none of the currently expected standard counter-measures which would ensure no data-dependent time variations and would introduce random variation in the exponent. Each key bit is determined by data proportional to the square of the key length.

The second attack [20] requires more expensive monitoring equipment to perform and uses power analysis and/or EMR. It is applied to a single exponentiation and so avoids any difficulty arising from employing exponent blinding as a counter-measure. Key bits are determined independently with each using all available data, that is, with data proportional to the cube of the key length. Individual exponent bits are now identified correctly with an accuracy which increases sufficiently quickly to compensate for the increased number of key bits. Consequently the attack becomes easier with longer key lengths.

Having assessed the vulnerabilities, our conclusion is that indeed increased key length will normally lead to a weaker implementations unless appropriate counter-measures are taken. As this is counter-intuitive, it achieves the main aim of the paper, namely to provide the justification for cautioning readers strongly against the temptation to assume that counter-measures to cryptanalysis can be used successfully as counter-measures to side channel leakage.

2 Security Model

The contexts for the two attacks [20, 21] are slightly different, but, for convenience, in both cases we assume a similar, but realistic, scenario. For each, a smartcard is performing RSA with limited resources and must be re-usable after the attack. The attacker is therefore limited in what he is allowed to do: he can only monitor side channel leakage. He cannot choose any inputs, nor can he read inputs or outputs. In most well-designed crypto-systems, the I/O will be blinded and the attacker will be able to see at most the unblinded data which is not used directly in the observed computations. However, the attacker is allowed to know the algorithms involved, perhaps as a result of previous destructive studies of identical cards, insider information and public specifications. His goal is to determine the secret exponent D whether or not the Chinese Remainder Theorem has been used, and he may use knowledge of the public modulus M and public exponent E to confirm proposed values. It is assumed that the m-ary exponentiation algorithm is used, but similar arguments apply to other classical (i.e. non-randomised) algorithms, such as sliding windows.

The timing attack [21] assumes the use of a modular multiplication algorithm which includes a final, conditional subtraction of the modulus. We assume the consequent timing variations enable the attacker to record accurately almost all occurrences of these subtractions. He then observes a number of exponentiations for which the same, unblinded exponent is used. We demonstrate the attack using an implementation of Montgomery's method which is described in the next section.

Power use, and hence also EMR, varies with the amount of switching activity in a circuit. The average number of gates switched in a multiplier is close to linear in the sum of the Hamming weights of the inputs, and the same is true for the buses taking I/O to and from the multiplier. So, by employing a combination of power and EMR measurements from carefully positioned probes [5], it should be assumed that an attacker can obtain some data, however minimal, which is related to the sum of the Hamming weights of these inputs. His problem is to combine these in a manner which reveals the Hamming weights with sufficient accuracy to deduce the digits of the exponent. The differential power analysis (DPA) attack [20] shows how this might be done from observations of a *single* exponentiation. Hence it does not matter if the exponent has been masked by the addition of, say, a 32-bit random multiple of $\phi(M)$ [9].

3 Notation

As above, we assume an n-bit modulus M and private exponent D for the RSA crypto-system. Ciphertext C has to be converted to plaintext $C^D \bmod M$ using a single, small k-bit multiplier. Hence, except for the exponent, the n-bit numbers X involved in the exponentiation are represented using base $r = 2^k$ and (non-redundant) digits x_i ($0 \le i < s$, say) in the range $[0, r)$. Thus $X = \sum_{i=0}^{s-1} x_i r^i$ and, without loss of generality, $n = ks$.

The exponent D is represented with a different base m, typically 2 or 4, depending on the exponentiation algorithm. Exponentiation is usually performed using the binary "square-and-multiply" algorithm, processing the exponent bits in either order, or the generalisation of the most-to-least significant case, called m-ary exponentiation [7, 8], in which D is represented in radix m using, say, t digits, and some powers of $C^{(i)} = C^i \bmod M$ ($1 \le i < m$) which are pre-computed:

The m-ary (Modular) Exponentiation Algorithm

```
C(1) ← C ;
For i ← 2 to m-1 do
    C(i) ← C(i-1) × C mod M ;
P ← C(d_{t-1}) ;
For i ← t-2 downto 0 do
Begin
    P ← P^m mod M ;
    If d_i ≠ 0 then P ← P×C(d_i) mod M ;
End ;
```

Output: $P = C^D \bmod M$ for $D = \sum_{i=0}^{t-1} d_i m^i$

The modular products here are too large for the smartcard multiplier to perform in one operation. Typically a form of Montgomery's modular multiplication algorithm (MMM) is used [16]. This gives an output related to $(A \times B) \bmod M$ via a scaling factor $R = r^s$ which is determined by the number of digits in input A. The form of interest here includes a final conditional subtraction which reduces the output to less than M, but causes variation in the time taken.

Montgomery's Modular Multiplication Algorithm (MMM)

```
P := 0 ;
For i := 0 to s-1 do
Begin
    P  := P + a_i×B ;
    q_i := (-p_0 m_0^-1) mod r ;
    P  := (P + q_i×M) div r ;
End ;
If P >= M then P := P-M
```

Output: $P = ABr^{-s} \bmod M$ for $A = \sum_{i=0}^{s-1} a_i r^i < M$ and $B < M$.

Here ${m_0}^{-1}$ under the mod r is the unique residue modulo r with the property ${m_0}^{-1}\times m_0 \equiv 1 \bmod r$, i.e. the multiplicative inverse of m_0 mod r. Similarly, r^{-s} appearing under the mod M is the inverse of r^s modulo M. The digit products such as $a_i \times B$ are generated over s cycles by using the k-bit multiplier to compute each digit by digit product $a_i \times b_j$ for $0 \le j < s$ from least to most significant digit of B, propagating carries on the way so that a non-redundant representation can be used.

Using induction it is readily verified for $R = r^s$ that:

Theorem 1. [22] *The MMM loop has post-condition* $ABR^{-1} \le P < ABR^{-1} + M$.

With the advent of timing attacks [9], the conditional subtractions should be avoided. This is easy to achieve by having extra loop iterations [6, 19, 22]. Alternatively, a non-destructive subtraction can always be performed if space is available, and the correct answer selected using the sign of the result. However, EMR measurements might still reveal this choice.

4 The Timing Attack

Walter and Thompson [21] observed that the final, conditional subtraction takes place in Montgomery's algorithm with different frequencies for multiplications and squarings. Indeed, different exponent digits are also distinguished. It is assumed that the attacker can partition the traces of many exponentiations correctly into sub-traces corresponding to each execution of MMM and use their timing differences to determine each instance of this final subtraction. This gives him a matrix $Q = (q_{ij})$ in which q_{ij} is 1 or 0 according to whether or not there is an extra subtraction at the end of the ith modular multiplication of the jth exponentiation. We now estimate the distance between two rows of this matrix.

With the possible exception of the first one or two instances, it is reasonable to assume that the I/O for each MMM within an exponentiation is uniformly distributed over the interval $0..M-1$ since crypto-systems depend on multiplications performing what seem to be random mappings of multiplicands onto $0..M-1$. Suppose π_{mu} is the probability that the final subtraction takes place in MMM for two independent, uniformly distributed inputs. Let A, B and Z be independent, uniformly distributed, discrete random variables over the interval of integers $0..M-1$ which correspond to the MMM inputs and the variation in output within the bounds given in Theorem 1. Then $\pi_{mu} = pr(Z + ABR^{-1} \ge M)$ $= \frac{1}{M^3}\sum_{Z=0}^{M-1}\sum_{A=0}^{M-1}\sum_{B=0}^{M-1}(Z + ABR^{-1} \ge M) = \frac{1}{M^3}\sum_{A=0}^{M-1}\sum_{B=0}^{M-1} ABR^{-1}$. So $\pi_{mu} \approx \frac{1}{4}MR^{-1}$ because M is large.

On the other hand, suppose π_{sq} is the probability that the final subtraction takes place when MMM is used to square a uniformly distributed input. For A and Z as above, $\pi_{sq} = pr(Z + A^2R^{-1} \ge M) = \frac{1}{M^3}\sum_{Z=0}^{M-1}\sum_{A=0}^{M-1}(Z + A^2R^{-1} \ge M)$ $= \frac{1}{M^3}\sum_{A=0}^{M-1} A^2R^{-1}$, whence $\pi_{sq} \approx \frac{1}{3}MR^{-1}$.

The difference between π_{mu} and π_{sq} means that multiplications can be distinguished from squares if a sufficiently large sample of exponentiations is available. π_{mu} and π_{sq} are given approximately by averaging the entries in the rows of Q.

If the binary or "square-and-multiply" exponentiation method is used, then the pattern of squares and multiplies given by these row averages reveals the bits of the secret exponent D.

If the m-ary or sliding windows method is used for the exponentiation then it is also necessary to distinguish between multiplications corresponding to different exponent digits. This is done by using the fact that in the jth exponentiation, the same pre-computed multiplier $C_j^{(i)}$ is used whenever the exponent digit is i. Let π_{ij} be the probability that the MMM input $A = C_j^{(i)}$ induces the conditional subtraction when the argument B is uniformly distributed on $0..M{-}1$. For Z as before, $\pi_{ij} = pr(Z{+}C_j^{(i)}BR^{-1}{\geq}M) = \frac{1}{M^2}\sum_{Z=0}^{M-1}\sum_{B=0}^{M-1}(Z{+}C_j^{(i)}BR^{-1}{\geq}M)$ $= \frac{1}{M}\sum_{B=0}^{M-1}C_j^{(i)}BR^{-1} = \frac{1}{2}C_j^{(i)}R^{-1}$. The $C_j^{(i)}$ are uniformly distributed as j varies. So the average value of π_{ij} as j varies is, by definition, π_{mu}. Also, the average value of $\pi_{ij}{}^2$ as j varies is $\pi^{(2)} = \frac{1}{M}\sum_{C=0}^{M-1}\frac{1}{4}C^2R^{-2} \approx \frac{1}{12}M^2R^{-2}$.

The distance between two rows of Q is defined here as the average Hamming distance between corresponding entries. This is, in a sense, independent of the sample size N, i.e. the number of columns. Thus the expected distance between two rows which correspond to the *same* exponent digit i is $d_{ii} = \frac{2}{N}\sum_j \pi_{ij}(1{-}\pi_{ij})$. Its average value is therefore $\overline{d_{eq}} = \overline{d_{ii}} = 2(\pi_{mu}{-}\pi^{(2)}) \approx 2(\frac{1}{4}MR^{-1} - \frac{1}{12}M^2R^{-2}) = MR^{-1}(\frac{1}{2} - \frac{1}{6}MR^{-1})$, which is independent of N and, indeed, of i.

Now assume that the distributions of $C_j^{(i)}$ and $C_j^{(i')}$ are independent if $i \neq i'$. This is reasonable since the RSA crypto-system relies on the fact that application of a public exponent $E{=}3$ to any ciphertext C should randomly permute values modulo M. Then, if two rows of Q correspond to *distinct* digits i and i', their distance apart is approximately $d_{ii'} = N^{-1}(\sum_j \pi_{ij}(1{-}\pi_{i'j}) + \sum_j \pi_{i'j}(1{-}\pi_{ij}))$. The average value of this is $\overline{d_{neq}} = \overline{d_{ii'}} = 2(\pi_{mu}{-}\pi_{mu}{}^2) \approx MR^{-1}(\frac{1}{2}{-}\frac{1}{8}MR^{-1})$.

It is also possible to compare two squarings or a multiplication with a squaring. In an exponentiation, except perhaps for the first one or two squarings, the inputs to these would be independent. For a square and a multiplication involving exponent digit i, the expected distance between the rows of Q is $d_{sq,mu} = N^{-1}(\sum_j \pi_{ij}(1{-}\pi_{sq}) + \sum_j \pi_{sq}(1{-}\pi_{ij}))$. The average value of this is $\overline{d_{sq,mu}} = \pi_{mu}{+}\pi_{sq}{-}2\pi_{mu}\pi_{sq} = MR^{-1}(\frac{7}{12} - \frac{1}{6}MR^{-1})$. For two squares the expected distance between the (different) rows of Q is $d_{sq,sq} = 2N^{-1}\sum_j \pi_{sq}(1{-}\pi_{sq})$. The average value of this is $\overline{d_{sq,sq}} = 2\pi_{sq}(1{-}\pi_{sq}) = MR^{-1}(\frac{2}{3} - \frac{2}{9}MR^{-1})$.

Observe that $\overline{d_{eq}}$, $\overline{d_{neq}}$, $\overline{d_{sq,mu}}$ and $\overline{d_{sq,sq}}$ must all be distinct because $M < R$. As variance in these distances is proportional to $\frac{1}{N}$, the distance between two rows of Q will tend to one of these four distinct values as the sample size increases, making it easier to determine whether the rows represent, respectively, two multiplications corresponding to the same exponent digit, two multiplications corresponding to different exponent digits, a squaring and a multiplication, or two squarings.

It is easy to develop a suitable algorithm to traverse the rows of Q and classify all the multiplicative operations into subsets which represent either squarings or the same exponent digit. One such algorithm was given in [20]. The classification might, for example, minimise the sum of the differences between the expected and actual distances between all pairs of rows. The set in which a pre-multiplication lies determines the exponent digit associated with that set. There are a few consistency checks which might highlight any errors, such as enforcing exactly one pre-multiplication in each set of multiplications, and squarings having to appear only in multiples of $\log_2 m$ consecutive operations. This enables the secret exponent key D to be reconstructed with sufficiently few errors to enable its precise determination providing the sample size N is large enough.

5 Doubling the Key Length

Suppose the key length is increased. Does the timing attack become more or less successful when the ratio M/R, the base m and the sample size N are kept the same? We will assume that the detection rate for the conditional subtraction is unchanged because the detection method is unspecified. However, it seems likely that the subtractions will be easier to spot for longer keys since, although the same detectable operations are performed in both cases, there are more of them. The detection assumption means that, by counting only the subtractions in each row of Q, the same proportion of errors will be made in classifying an operation as a square or a multiply. Doubling n will then double the number of such errors. However, using *pairs* of rows rather than *single* rows for this classification improves the likelihood of classifying multiplications correctly.

First note that the distributions for the four types of distances between two rows are independent of n because the row length N is unchanged and the probability of a conditional subtraction is unchanged. Suppose the rows have already been roughly partitioned into one set for each non-zero exponent digit and one set for squares (m subsets in all). A row is classified, or its classification checked, by taking the distance between it and each of these sets. This distance is the average between the chosen row and each row of the group. Doubling n doubles the size of the group and so provides *twice* the number of distances from the row. So, as the other parameters are unchanged, the average distance from the row to the group will have *half* the variance when the key length is doubled. This will markedly reduce the probability of mis-classifying a row.

There are two main types of error to consider, namely those which are detectable through inconsistencies and those which are not. Inconsistencies arise when squares do not appear in sequences of m or multiplications are not separated by squares. For convenience, suppose that the inconsistent errors can be corrected with computationally feasible effort for both key lengths n and $2n$ because this is a minor part of the total cost. Hence it is assumed that a possible pattern of squares and multiplies has been obtained. For simplicity, we assume this is the correct pattern. Ambiguities also appear when a multiplication appears to be near to two or more different subsets of rows or near to none. The attacker then knows to check each of up to m possibilities for that multiplication. However, his main problem is the number of incorrect, but consistent decisions.

A mis-classified row has to be too far away from its correct subset *and* too close to one other set in order to be assigned to an incorrect exponent digit. For convenience, suppose that average distances from one row to the subset of rows representing a given exponent digit are normally distributed, and that appropriate scaling is performed so that the distances are $N(0,1)$. (Although the distances are bound within the interval $[0,1]$, the previous section shows their averages are not close to either end, and so increasing the sample size N will improve the match with a normal distribution.) Let Z be a random variable with such a distribution, and let δ be the (similarly scaled) distance at which the row is equally likely to be in the group as not in it. (A similar discussion is given in more detail in §7 for the other attack where these notions are made more precise.) Then the mis-classification occurs with probability $pr(Z{>}\delta)^2$. Since δ is inversely proportional to standard deviation it is dependent on the key length. Thus $\delta = \delta_n$ increases by a factor $\sqrt{2}$ when the key length is doubled.

Suppose p_n is the probability of correctly classifying one multiplication. Since keys with $2n$ bits require twice as many multiplications on average, we need $p_n < {p_{2n}}^2$ for the attack to become easier for the longer key. From the above, $p_n = 1{-}pr(Z{>}\delta_n)^2$ where Z is $N(0,1)$ and so the condition becomes $1{-}pr(Z{>}\delta)^2 < (1{-}pr(Z{>}\sqrt{2}\delta)^2)^2$. A quick glance at tables of the normal distribution shows that this is true providing $\delta > 0.616$. In other words, longer keys are easier to attack if distances between rows of Q are accurate enough. This just requires the sample size N to be large enough, or the experimental methods to be made accurate enough, or, indeed, n to be large enough. In conclusion, with all other aspects fixed there appears to be an optimal key length providing maximum security against this attack with shorter and longer keys being more unsafe.

However, with more leaked data per exponent bit as key length increases, it is not impossible that the attack may be developed further so that there is no longer an optimal secure key length and all increases in key length become unsafe. For example, some exponentiations are more helpful than others in discriminating between one exponent digit and any others because the associated multiplicands are unusually large or unusually small. These instances become apparent while performing the attack just described. Then a weighted Hamming distance which favours these cases should improve the correct detection of the corresponding exponent digit. Increasing key length provides more useful data for detecting such cases, further decreasing the strength of longer keys.

6 The Power Analysis Attack

The other attack considered here is one based on data-dependent power and/or EMR variation from the smartcard multiplier [20]. The long integer multiplication $A{\times}B$ requires every product of digits $a_u{\times}b_v$ to be computed. For each index u, the power or EMR traces from the multiplier are averaged as v ranges over its s values. In general, the digits of B are sufficiently random for this averaging process to provide a trace which is reasonably indicative of the Hamming weight of a_u. Concatenating these averaged traces for all a_u provides a single trace from which the vector of the Hamming weights of the digits of A is obtained with reasonable accuracy. Unless s is small, the Euclidean distance between the Hamming weight vectors for different, randomly chosen values of A has much smaller variance than its average. So this distance enables equal arguments A to be identified and unequal ones to be distinguished. By defining distance between power traces via the Hamming weight vectors in this way, the attacker can expect to distinguish between, or identify, the multipliers $C^{(i)}$ used in the modular multiplications of an exponentiation. This enables the exponent digits to be discovered and hence the secret key D to be determined.

In detail, each digit product $a_u \times b_v$ contributes $|a_u|+|b_v|+x$ to the trace-averaging process where $|d|$ is the Hamming weight of digit d and x is an instance of a random variable X which represents measurement errors and variation caused by the initial condition of the multiplier and other hardware. Without loss of generality, we assume $\mu_X=0$. Averaging over the s digits of B provides $\frac{1}{s}|B|+|a_u|+x_s$ as the uth co-ordinate of the vector for $A\times B$. Here the average for x_s is the same as for X (namely 0) but, with realistic independence assumptions, the variance is less by a factor s. As the s digits have k bits each and their Hamming weights are binomially distributed, this has a mean of $\frac{k}{2}+|a_u|$ and variance $\frac{k}{4s}+\frac{1}{s}\sigma_X^2$. Thus, overall, the coordinates have mean k and variance $\frac{k}{4}(1+\frac{1}{s})+\frac{1}{s}\sigma_X^2$. Now, comparing the vectors from two independent multipliers $C^{(i)}$ and $C^{(i')}$, the mean square difference in the uth co-ordinate is $\frac{k}{2}(1+\frac{1}{s})+\frac{2}{s}\sigma_X^2$, leading to a mean Euclidean distance between the vectors of $\sqrt{\frac{k}{2}(s+1)+2\sigma_X^2}$. However, if the multipliers are equal, i.e. $i = i'$, then the Euclidean distance between the two vectors contains no contribution from $C^{(i)}$ and $C^{(i')}$. So its mean is derived entirely from the variance $\frac{k}{4s}+\frac{1}{s}\sigma_X^2$ in each co-ordinate, namely $\sqrt{\frac{k}{2}+2\sigma_X^2}$. Hence there is a $\sqrt{s+1}$-fold difference in size between the distances between vectors for the same and for different multiplicands when the data is "clean". Other variation from measurement error and hardware initialisation is only significant for small s, which is not the case here.

These vectors are used to form a matrix $Q = (q_{ij})$ similar to that in the timing attack: q_{ij} is the weight derived from the jth digit of the ith multiplication. As before, the distances (now Euclidean) between rows are used to distinguish squares from multiplies, and identify rows corresponding to the same exponent digits. Squares have no arguments in common with other operations, so that they have distances from all other rows which behave in the same way as described above for distances between multiplications for different exponent digits; they are not close to any other rows in the way that rows are for multiplications associated with the same exponent digit. Thus, as before, the attacker can potentially determine the secret key D.

7 Increasing the Key Length

The formulae in the previous section make explicit some of the results of increasing the key length n, and hence also the number of digits s. First, the trace averaging process is improved for individual entries in Q by reducing their variance. Secondly, as a consequence, the larger number of columns in Q increases the Euclidean distance between rows corresponding to different exponent digits without changing the distance between rows corresponding to the same digit. This enables each row to be classified more accurately. Thirdly, as in the timing attack, the larger number of rows in Q reduces the variance in the average distance of the row from the sets of rows which represent the various exponent digits. This, too, enables rows to be classified more accurately. So, as well as the increased difference in average separation, doubling the key length halves the variance in the separation since the sets for each exponent digit contain twice as many rows on average. At a theoretical level, this more than squares the probability of mis-classifying a digit so that the total number of digit errors actually *decreases* when key length increases. The question, as before, is whether such improved accuracy in classification really does achieve this in practice.

Modelling the attack by randomly generating Hamming weights is potentially inaccurate for several reasons. For example, bus encryption should hide Hamming weight effectively. Secondly, the multiplier does not necessarily yield the Hamming weight of inputs with much accuracy. Lastly, the multiplier does not operate independently on different input digits: processing one digit of a long integer input sets the multiplier in a biased state which affects the amount of switching when the next digit is processed.

So it was decided to assume the attacker made observations of EMR from, and power use by, the multiplier which would enable him to estimate the number of gates being switched in the multiplier. A model was built of the typical gate layout in a 2^k-bit multiplier using full adders and half adders in a Wallace tree without Booth re-coding. Random long integers were generated, and their digits fed sequentially into the multiplier as in a long integer multiplication. Gate switching activity was counted for each clock cycle, and the averaging and concatenation processes of the previous section were used to generate a row of the matrix Q. In this way m-ary exponentiation was modelled and a large number of values obtained for Q. Key length was varied to obtain an insight into general behaviour and confirm the improved feasibility of the attack as n increases.

Figures from the simulation of 8-ary exponentiation with a standard 32-bit multiplier and various key lengths are given in Table 1. This is the largest multi-

Table 1. Gate Switch Statistics for 32-bit Multiplier with $m = 8$

Bit length n	32	64	128	256	512	1024	2048
Av btwn same	266	255	234	201	177	176	171
SD btwn same	191	161	137	129	106	110	100
Av min to diff	68.4	146	324	434	843	1453	2153
SD min to diff	53.4	87.9	78	102	140	131	118
%age errors	83	71	16	1.8	0.02	0.00	0.00
SDs btwn avs	–	–	0.84	2.02	5.41	10.6	18.2
p_c (lowr. bnd.)	–	–	0.439	0.711	0.9932	0.999...	0.999...

plier likely to be found in current smartcards. Standard m-ary exponentiation was used, not the sliding windows version, so that there were $m-1$ pre-computed powers for use in multiplications. These choices of k, m and algorithm make the correct association of exponent digits more difficult than is typically the case. So the setting here provides one of the most unfavourable scenarios for the attack, except for the absence of measurement noise. Moreover, the refinement of making comparisons between every pair of rows was neglected: just making comparisons of a row with each of the pre-computed multiplications was enough to establish the principle that longer key lengths may be less secure.

The column headings in Table 1 provide the key length: the number of bits n used in both the modulus M and the exponent D. Values are chosen to illustrate the effect of doubling key length. Although the smaller values are totally insecure, they allow a much clearer appreciation of the overall trends, especially in the last three rows of the table where values tend to their limits very quickly. The first line of data provides the average distance between vectors formed from multiplications which correspond to equal, exponent digits. These confirm the theory of the previous section: for equal digits, the average distance is essentially constant except for a slight decline arising from reduced noise as key length increases. The second line records the standard deviation in the figures of the first line. These also show a steady decrease as n increases. They are consistently about two thirds of the associated means over the given range.

The third and fourth lines provide the average distance, and its standard deviation, of a multiplication from the nearest pre-computed case which corresponds to a different exponent digit. If exponent digits are assigned to multiplications on the basis of the nearest pre-computation trace, these lines give a basis for estimating the number of errors that would be made. The percentage of such errors encountered in the simulations is given in the following line. For the very smallest cases, the nearest pre-computation vector is, on average, *nearer* than that corresponding to the same exponent digit. So a large number of errors are made. For the 128-bit or larger keys that are encountered in practice, the nearest pre-computation is usually the correct one. Due to its marginally different definition, the average tabulated in line 3 behaves slightly differently from the average between any pair of multiplications corresponding to different exponent digits. However, as with the formula in the previous section, this distance increases markedly with the key length, so that multiplications corresponding to different exponent digits are distinguished more easily. The standard deviations in line 4 varied noticeably between different samples generated by the multiplier simulation even for large samples (with the largest s.d. being around 50% greater than the smallest), but there seems to be a gradual trend upwards.

Both lines of standard deviations are included in order to calculate how many distances might be incorrectly classified as corresponding to equal or unequal digits. The average was taken of the two standard deviations in each column and the number of them which separate the two averages in the column was computed. This is tabulated in the second last line. The final line of the table contains an estimate from normal distribution tables for the probability p_c that the nearest trace of a pre-computation correctly determines the exponent digit associated with a multiplication, given that the operation is indeed a multiplication rather than a squaring. This assumes that the distances between traces sharing the same multiplicand are normally distributed with the tabulated expectation and variance and, similarly, that the minimum distance between one trace and a set of $m-2$ traces, all with different multiplicands, is normally distributed with the given expectation and variance.

Thus, let Z_c be a random variable with distribution $N(\mu_c, {\sigma_c}^2)$ which gives the distance to the correct trace, and let Z_d be a random variable with distribution $N(\mu_d, {\sigma_d}^2)$ which gives the distance to the nearest incorrect trace (one for a different digit). Then the probability of a correct decision is $p_c \approx Pr(Z_c < Z_d)$. Since, by the table, the means are so many standard deviations apart for typical values of n, a good approximation is given by

$$Pr(Z_c < Z_d) \quad \approx \quad Pr\left(Z_c < \tfrac{\sigma_c\mu_d+\sigma_d\mu_c}{\sigma_c+\sigma_d}\right) \times Pr\left(\tfrac{\sigma_c\mu_d+\sigma_d\mu_c}{\sigma_c+\sigma_d} < Z_d\right)$$

This yields $p_c \approx Pr(Z < \frac{\mu_d-\mu_c}{\sigma_d+\sigma_c})^2$ where Z is an $N(0,1)$ random variable. The last line of the table gives these values direct from tables of the normal distribution. This is approximately the probability of identifying the correct exponent digit given that the operation is a multiplication. It is consistent with the observed number of errors recorded in the table.

These probabilities goes up much faster than the square root as key length is doubled: $p_c^{(128)} = 0.4386$, $p_c^{(256)} = 0.7114$, $p_c^{(512)} = 0.9932$ and $p_c^{(1024)} = 1 - 2.5\times10^{-7}$ easily satisfy $p_c^{(128)} < \{p_c^{(256)}\}^2$, $p_c^{(256)} < \{p_c^{(512)}\}^2$ and $p_c^{(512)} < \{p_c^{(1024)}\}^2$. This means that it is easier to identify the exponent digits correctly for a pair of multiplications where the key has $2n$ bits than it is to identify the exponent digit correctly for a single multiplication where the key has only n bits. Thus fewer errors will be made for the $2n$-bit key. Indeed, the total number of predicted errors decreases rapidly towards zero over the range of the table. Thus, since squares are detected in a very similar way (they are not close to any of the pre-computed powers), at least in the simulation it becomes easier to deduce the full secret exponent as key length increases.

The analysis above has not taken into account comparisons between all possible pairs of product traces – distances between pairs of computation stage operations can be evaluated as well. As noted earlier, each row of Q can be compared with $O(n)$ other rows instead of just $O(1)$ rows. This decreases the variances involved and thereby improves the above decision process as n increases. Hence, as key length increases, a full scale attack will become even easier to process correctly than is indicated by the table.

8 A Particular Example

Consider the case from Table 1 which is closest to that in a typical current smartcard, namely a key length of 1024 bits. This will require about 1023 squares, which will occur in 341 triplets for $m = 2^3$, and about $7/8\times1023/3 \approx 298$ multiplications. By examining the exponent from left to right, of all the squares it is necessary to identify only the first of each triplet correctly. Hence there are approximately $341+298 = 639$ operations to identify as squares or multiplications, after which each multiplication must be associated with a digit value.

Let μ_{sq} and μ_{mu} be the average distances of a square and multiplication from the nearest of the $m-1$ pre-computation traces and let σ_{sq} and σ_{mu} be the corresponding standard deviations. A multiplication is assumed if, and only if, the distance is less than $\frac{\sigma_{mu}\mu_{sq}+\sigma_s\mu_{mu}}{\sigma_{mu}+\sigma_{sq}}$. The probability p_{sm} of this being the correct decision is then $Pr(Z < \frac{\mu_{sq}-\mu_{mu}}{\sigma_{sq}+\sigma_{mu}})$ for an $N(0,1)$ random variable Z. For larger m as here, $\mu_{mu} \approx \mu_c$ and $\mu_{sq} \approx \mu_d$ so that $p_{sm} \approx \sqrt{p_c}$. So all the squares and multiplications are identified correctly with probability at least ${p_{sq}}^{639} \approx {p_c}^{319.5}$. Correct determination of the exponent digits for the 298 or so multiplications is done with probability about ${p_c}^{298}$. Hence, without making any use of the considerable data given by comparing the $(1023+298)^2/2$ or so pairs of computation phase traces, deduction of the correct exponent will occur with probability at least about ${p_c}^{298+319.5} \approx (1-2.5\times10^{-7})^{617.5} \approx 0.9998$.

At least theoretically, this very high probability should give cause for concern. In practice, it is to be hoped that measurement noise will substantially reduce the ability to identify the correct multiplicand $C^{(i)}$. Even a modest reduction in the probabilities p_{mu} and p_{sq} would be helpful since both must be raised to a power linear in the number of bits in the key in order to obtain the probability that the key is identified correctly first time without further computing to try the next best alternatives. It is computationally feasible to correct only one or two errors.

9 Counter-Measures

Counter-measures for the timing attack are straightforward, and were covered in the introduction: the exponent can be randomly blinded [9] and the subtraction can either be performed every time or be omitted every time [6, 19, 22].

The power analysis attack is harder to perform, but also harder to defeat. Exponent blinding is not a defence. The attack does rely on re-use of the pre-computed powers. Hence performing m-ary exponentiation in the opposite order, namely from least to most significant digit, may be a solution. This can be done without significant extra computation time [15, 23]. For $m = 2$, the normal square-and-multiply algorithm can be modified to square-and-always-multiply, but this is more expensive time-wise.

Apart from hardware counter-measures such as a Faraday cage to shield the processor and capacitors to smooth out the power trace, a larger multiplier also helps. This reduces the number of digits s over which averages are taken and reduces the number s of concatenated traces. Thus it reverses the effect of increased key length on the traces. Moreover, with larger numbers of words sharing the same Hamming weight, it becomes less easy to use the Euclidean metric to separate the different multiplicands. Further, one might use two multipliers in parallel. Montgomery's modular multiplication algorithm naturally uses two.

Then the power used by one might successfully shield observation of the power used by the other. Thus safety can be bought, but perhaps only at a price.

10 Conclusion

Two attacks on smartcard implementations of RSA have been outlined, one a timing attack and the other a power analysis attack. In each case the effect of increasing the key length was studied for its impact on the number of bit errors made in deducing the secret key. For the timing attack, leaked data is proportional to the square of the key length and it appears that there is an optimal secure length with both shorter and longer keys being less safe. For the power analysis attack, leaked data is proportional to the cube of the key length and the analysis shows that longer keys are less safe.

There are a number of both algorithmic and hardware counter-measures which improve resistance against such side channel attacks and they should provide the extra safety that one has been traditionally led to expect from longer key lengths. However, the main conclusion is that counter-measures to cryptanalysis must not be assumed to be suitable as counter-measures to side channel leakage. In particular, increasing key length on its own appears to be quite unsuitable as a counter-measure in embedded RSA cryptosystems.

References

[1] R. M. Best, *Crypto Microprocessor that Executes Enciphered Programs*, U. S. Patent 4,465,901, 14 Aug. 1984. 43

[2] J.-F. Dhem, F. Koeune, P.-A. Leroux, P. Mestré, J.-J. Quisquater & J.-L. Willems, *A practical implementation of the Timing Attack*, Proc. CARDIS 1998, J.-J. Quisquater & B. Schneier (editors), Lecture Notes in Computer Science, **1820**, Springer-Verlag, 2000, pp. 175–190. 42

[3] W. Diffie & M. E. Hellman, *New Directions in Cryptography*, IEEE Trans. Info. Theory, **IT-22**, no. 6, 1976, pp. 644–654. 43

[4] T. El-Gamal, *A Public-Key Cryptosystem and a Signature Scheme Based on Discrete Logarithms*, IEEE Trans. Info. Theory, **IT-31**, no. 4, 1985, pp. 469–472. 43

[5] K. Gandolfi, C. Mourtel & F. Olivier, *Electromagnetic Analysis: Concrete Results*, Cryptographic Hardware and Embedded Systems – CHES 2001, Ç. Koç, D. Naccache & C. Paar (editors), Lecture Notes in Computer Science, **2162**, Springer-Verlag, 2001, pp. 251–261. 42, 44

[6] G. Hachez & J.-J. Quisquater, *Montgomery exponentiation with no final subtractions: improved results*, Cryptographic Hardware and Embedded Systems (Proc CHES 2000), C. Paar & Ç. Koç (editors), Lecture Notes in Computer Science, **1965**, Springer-Verlag, 2000, pp. 293–301. 46, 54

[7] D. E. Knuth, The Art of Computer Programming, vol. 2, *Seminumerical Algorithms*, 2nd Edition, Addison-Wesley, 1981, pp. 441–466. 43, 45

[8] Ç. K. Koç, *Analysis of Sliding Window Techniques for Exponentiation*, Computers and Mathematics with Applications, **30**, no. 10, 1995, pp. 17–24. 43, 45

[9] P. Kocher, *Timing attack on implementations of Diffie-Hellman, RSA, DSS, and other systems*, Proc. Crypto 96, N. Koblitz (editor), Lecture Notes in Computer Science, **1109**, Springer-Verlag, 1996, pp. 104–113. 42, 44, 46, 54
[10] P. Kocher, J. Jaffe & B. Jun, *Differential Power Analysis*, Advances in Cryptology – Crypto '99, M. Wiener (editor), Lecture Notes in Computer Science, **1666**, Springer-Verlag, 1999, pp. 388–397. 42
[11] M. G. Kuhn, *Cipher Instruction Search Attack on the Bus-Encryption Security Microcontroller DS5002FP*, IEEE Transactions on Computers, **47**, No. 10, October 1998, pp. 1153–1157. 43
[12] R. Mayer-Sommer, *Smartly Analyzing the Simplicity and the Power of Simple Power Analysis on Smartcards*, Cryptographic Hardware and Embedded Systems (Proc CHES 2000), C. Paar & Ç. Koç (editors), Lecture Notes in Computer Science, **1965**, Springer-Verlag, 2000, pp. 78–92. 42
[13] T. S. Messerges, E. A. Dabbish & R. H. Sloan, *Power Analysis Attacks of Modular Exponentiation in Smartcards*, Cryptographic Hardware and Embedded Systems (Proc CHES 99), C. Paar & Ç. Koç (editors), Lecture Notes in Computer Science, **1717**, Springer-Verlag, 1999, pp. 144–157. 42
[14] V. Miller, *Use of Elliptic Curves in Cryptography*, Proc. CRYPTO '85, H. C. Williams (editor), Lecture Notes in Computer Science, **218**, Springer-Verlag, 1986, pp. 417–426. 43
[15] Bodo Möller, *Parallelizable Elliptic Curve Point Multiplication Method with Resistance against Side Channel Attacks*, Information Security – ISC 2002, A. H. Chan & V. Gligor (editors), Lecture Notes in Computer Science, **2433**, Springer-Verlag, 2002, pp. 402–413. 54
[16] P. L. Montgomery, *Modular Multiplication without Trial Division*, Mathematics of Computation, **44**, no. 170, 1985, pp. 519–521. 45
[17] R. L. Rivest, A. Shamir & L. Adleman, *A Method for obtaining Digital Signatures and Public-Key Cryptosystems*, Comm. ACM, **21**, 1978, pp. 120–126. 42, 43
[18] W. Schindler, *A Timing Attack against RSA with Chinese Remainder Theorem*, Cryptographic Hardware and Embedded Systems (Proc CHES 2000), C. Paar & Ç. Koç (editors), Lecture Notes in Computer Science, **1965**, Springer-Verlag, 2000, pp. 109–124. 42
[19] C. D. Walter, *Montgomery Exponentiation Needs No Final Subtractions*, Electronics Letters, **35**, no. 21, October 1999, pp. 1831–1832. 42, 46, 54
[20] C. D. Walter, *Sliding Windows succumbs to Big Mac Attack*, Cryptographic Hardware and Embedded Systems – CHES 2001, Ç. Koç, D. Naccache & C. Paar (editors), Lecture Notes in Computer Science, **2162**, Springer-Verlag, 2001, pp. 286–299. 43, 44, 48, 49
[21] C. D. Walter & S. Thompson, *Distinguishing Exponent Digits by Observing Modular Subtractions*, Topics in Cryptology – CT-RSA 2001, D. Naccache (editor), Lecture Notes in Computer Science, **2020**, Springer-Verlag, 2001, pp. 192–207. 42, 43, 44, 46
[22] C. D. Walter, *Precise Bounds for Montgomery Modular Multiplication and Some Potentially Insecure RSA Moduli*, Topics in Cryptology – CT-RSA 2002, B. Preneel (editor), Lecture Notes in Computer Science, **2271**, Springer-Verlag, 2002, pp. 30–39. 46, 54
[23] C. D. Walter, *MIST: An Efficient, Randomized Exponentiation Algorithm for Resisting Power Analysis*, Topics in Cryptology – CT-RSA 2002, B. Preneel (editor), Lecture Notes in Computer Science, **2271**, Springer-Verlag, 2002, pp. 53–66. 54
[24] *Digital Signature Standard* (DSS), FIPS 186, http://csrc.nist.gov/publications/, US National Institute of Standards and Technology, May 1994. 43

[25] *Data Encryption Standard* (DES), FIPS 46-3, http://csrc.nist.gov/publications/, US National Institute of Standards and Technology, October 1999. 43

[26] *Advanced Encryption Standard* (AES), FIPS 197, http://csrc.nist.gov/publications/, US National Institute of Standards and Technology, November 2001. 43

[27] *Index of National Security Telecommunications Information Systems Security Issuances*, NSTISSC Secretariat, US National Security Agency, 9 January 1998. 42

On Randomizing Private Keys to Counteract DPA Attacks

Nevine Ebeid and M. Anwar Hasan

Department of Electrical and Computer Engineering
University of Waterloo, Waterloo, Ontario, Canada N2L 3G1
nebeid@uwaterloo.ca
ahasan@ece.uwaterloo.ca

Abstract. Differential power analysis (DPA) attacks can be of major concern when applied to cryptosystems that are embedded into small devices such as smart cards. To immunize elliptic curve cryptosystems (ECCs) against DPA attacks, recently several countermeasures have been proposed. A class of countermeasures is based on randomizing the paths taken by the scalar multiplication algorithm throughout its execution which also implies generating a random binary signed-digit (BSD) representation of the scalar. This scalar is an integer and is the secret key of the cryptosystem. In this paper, we investigate issues related to the BSD representation of an integer such as the average and the exact number of these representations, and integers with maximum number of BSD representations within a specific range. This knowledge helps a cryptographer to choose a key that provides better resistance against DPA attacks. Here, we also present an algorithm that generates a random BSD representation of an integer starting from the most significant signed bit. We also present another algorithm that generates all existing BSD representations of an integer to investigate the relation between increasing the number of bits in which an integer is represented and the increase in the number of its BSD representations.

Keywords: Differential power analysis, elliptic curve cryptosystems, binary signed-digit representation, scalar multiplication, smart cards.

1 Introduction

Smart cards and wireless devices are vulnerable to a special type of attacks, those are side-channel attacks. For these systems, a correct implementation of a strong protocol is not necessarily secure if this implementation does not take into account the leakage of secret key information through side channels. Examples of side channels are execution time [8], computational faults [1] and power consumption [9, 12, 13]. The mentioned systems are vulnerable since the task of monitoring the power consumption or the execution time of cryptographic protocols running on them is relatively easy.

Power Analysis attacks are those based on monitoring and analyzing the power consumption of devices while executing a cryptographic algorithm in order to obtain significant information about the secret key. Kocher et al. were the

M. Matsui and R. Zuccherato (Eds.): SAC 2003, LNCS 3006, pp. 58–72, 2004.

first to present attacks based on *simple* and *dierential* power analysis (referred to as SPA and DPA respectively). In SPA, a single power trace of a cryptographic execution is measured and analyzed to identify large features of a cryptographic algorithm and specific operations that are typical of the underlying cryptosystem. On the other hand, to mount a DPA attack, an attacker collects hundreds of power signal traces, and manipulates them with statistical techniques to extract the *dierential* signal. Therefore, DPA is in general more powerful than SPA.

Coron [3] has explained how power analysis attacks can be mounted on ECCs – which are more suitable for memory limited devices because of the small size of their keys – and suggested countermeasures against both types of attacks. Other authors have proposed DPA countermeasures for both general and specific types of elliptic curves [4, 5, 6, 10, 15, 16]. Specifically, the approach followed by the authors in [4, 16] was based each on randomizing the number and the sequence of execution of operations in the scalar multiplication algorithm. This randomization consists of inserting a random decision in the process of building the representation of the scalar k. The algorithms to which this randomization is applied were originally proposed to speed up the elliptic curve (EC) scalar multiplication. They are based on replacing the binary representation of the *scalar* k by another representation with a fewer number of nonzero symbols by allowing negative symbols to be inserted (e.g. *binary signed-digit* (BSD) representation of an integer). This yields a fewer number of executions of the point addition (or subtraction) in the EC scalar multiplication algorithm. This speedup was possible using the fact that the negative of a point on an elliptic curve is available at no extra computational cost. The algorithms proposed were computing what we referred to as the *canonical* BSD (also known as the *sparse* or NAF) representation of the integer k by scanning the bits of its binary representation starting from the least significant bit. A brief overview of the EC scalar multiplication and the possible power attacks on it is presented in Sect. 2.

When we consider the DPA countermeasures based on randomizing the BSD representation of the integer k some natural questions arise, those are: What is the average number of BSD representations for an integer k represented in n bits, where the BSD representations are to be of length l signed bits – which we will refer to as *sbits* – for both cases $l = n$ and $l = n+1$? For integers represented in n bits, which one has the maximum number of BSD representations since this may affect the choice of the secret scalar for cryptosystems that will adopt this countermeasure? In this paper, we are interested in answering those questions and the answers are presented in Sect. 3. Also, in the same section, we present an algorithm that calculates the exact number of those representations for any integer k in $\mathcal{O}(n)$.

In Sect. 4, we present an algorithm that generates a random BSD representation for an integer k by scanning its bits starting from the most significant bit in $\mathcal{O}(n)$ and another algorithm that generates all BSD representations for an integer k in $\mathcal{O}(3^{\lfloor \frac{n}{2} \rfloor})$ in the worst case. We also demonstrate the effect of increasing n on the number of BSD representations of k. Many of the proofs and examples have been omitted due to the space limitations. For a complete version of this article, we refer the reader to the corresponding CACR technical report published at `http://www.cacr.math.uwaterloo.ca/techreports/2003/corr2003-11.ps`

2 EC Scalar Multiplication and Power Analysis Attacks

In the context of ECCs, the EC scalar multiplication is the core cryptographic operation performed. This operation computes $Q = kP$, i.e. the addition of P to itself k times, where Q and P are two points on a predefined elliptic curve over a finite field and are public, and k is a secret integer. The EC scalar multiplication is conventionally performed using the *double-and-add* algorithms which are also referred to as the *binary algorithms* [7, Sect. 4.6.3]. The doubling of a point and the addition of two points on an elliptic curve are operations performed using basic finite field operation as explained in [11].

The side channel attacks on the EC scalar multiplication aim to discover the value of k. We assume that the attacker gets hold of the cryptographic token performing the EC scalar multiplication. Coron [3] has explained the possible SPA and DPA attacks that can be mounted on this token. He suggested a reasonable SPA countermeasure at the expense of the execution time of the algorithm. We will focus here on DPA countermeasures.

To mount a DPA attack, the attacker inputs to the token a large number of points and collects the corresponding power traces. As Coron [3] and Hasan [5] have explained, knowing the input point to the algorithm, the attacker starts by guessing the bits of the scalar k starting by the first bit involved in the computation, and accordingly computes the intermediate value for each point he inputs to the algorithm after the bit considered is processed. Based on the representation of the intermediate results, he chooses some partitioning function to partition the power traces he collects and processes them with statistical techniques, such as averaging, to conclude the real value of the bit considered. The attacker then repeats this procedure with every bit of the scalar.

Many of the countermeasures proposed to defeat DPA where based mainly on some form of randomization. They suggested either randomizing (or *blinding*) the point P or the scalar k. For example, one of the countermeasures proposed by Coron [3] suggested randomizing the value of k modulo the order of the point P, this is done as the first step in the scalar multiplication algorithm. Another type of countermeasures, that is of interest to us, is based on modifying the representation of the scalar k throughout the execution of the scalar multiplication algorithm. The representation of k in [4, 16] on which this approach is applied is the BSD representation. The underlying idea is as follows. The right-to-left EC scalar multiplication can be speed up by computing the NAF of k along with performing the corresponding doubling and addition (or subtraction) of points [14]. Random decisions can be inserted in the NAF generating algorithms so that they do not generate the NAF of k but any of the possible BSD representations of k (including the NAF). A different representation for the scalar k is chosen, and hence a different sequence of EC operations is followed, every time the algorithm is executed. We refer the reader to the paper by Oswald and Aigner [16] and the one by Ha and Moon [4] for the details since they are not relevant to the work presented here.

3 Number of Binary Signed Digit Representations

Considering the binary representation of k as one of its BSD representations, different BSD representations for k can be obtained by replacing 01 with $1\bar{1}$ and vice versa and by replacing $0\bar{1}$ with $\bar{1}1$ and vice versa [17, equations 8.4.4- and 8.4.5-]. The binary representation of k, must include at least one 0 that precedes a 1, so that starting from it we can obtain other BSD representations.

We consider in this case positive integers k, i.e. $0 \leq k < 2^n$. In general, the integers x, represented in $l = n$ sbits in BSD system, would be in the range $-2^l < x < 2^l$. There are 3^l different combinations for x. Also, in this system, for every positive integer corresponds a negative one obtained by exchanging the 1s with $\bar{1}$s and vice versa. Hence, the total number of non-negative combinations is $\frac{3^l+1}{2}$. This result can be confirmed using the lemmas below.

3.1 Useful Lemmas

In this subsection, we present a number of lemmas related to the number of BSD representations of an integer k. These lemmas will be used to derive the main results of this article.

Let $\lambda(k, n)$ be the number of BSD representations of k for $0 \leq k < 2^n$ that are $l = n$ sbits long. Then the following lemmas hold.

Lemma 1. (i) $\lambda(0, n) = 1$, (ii) $\lambda(1, n) = n$, (iii) $\lambda(2^i, n) = n - i$.

Lemma 2. *For* $2^{n-1} \leq k \leq 2^n - 1$, $\lambda(k, n) = \lambda(k - 2^{n-1}, n - 1)$.

Lemma 3. *For* k *even,* $\lambda(k, n) = \lambda(\frac{k}{2}, n - 1)$.

Lemma 4. *For* k *odd,*

$$\lambda(k, n) = \lambda(k - 1, n) + \lambda(k + 1, n) \ ,$$

or

$$\lambda(k, n) = \lambda\left(\left\lfloor \frac{k}{2} \right\rfloor, n - 1\right) + \lambda\left(\left\lfloor \frac{k}{2} \right\rfloor + 1, n - 1\right) \ .$$

3.2 Number of BSD Representations of Length $l = n + 1$

The algorithms that we are concerned with as DPA countermeasures are based on algorithms that generate the NAF representation of an integer. Since the NAF of an integer may be one sbit longer than its binary representation, we are interested in knowing the number of BSD representations of an integer k that are l sbits long, where in this case $l = n + 1$.

A part of these representations are the ones that are n sbits long and their number is $\lambda(k, n)$. For $l = n + 1$, those representations will have a 0 as the most significant sbit. If we were to change this 0 to a 1, i.e. add 2^n to the value of k, we should subtract $2^n - k$ in the remaining n sbits, that is the 2's complement of k. $2^n - k$ has $\lambda(2^n - k, n)$ BSD representations of length n. The negative of these representations is obtained by interchanging 1s and $\bar{1}$s. Thus, if we let $\delta(k, n)$ represent the number of BSD representations of k in $n + 1$ sbits for $1 \le k < 2^n$, we have

$$\delta(k, n) = \lambda(k, n) + \lambda(2^n - k, n) \ . \tag{1}$$

The same argument applies to the 2's complement of k

$$\delta(2^n - k, n) = \lambda(2^n - k, n) + \lambda(k, n) = \delta(k, n) \ . \tag{2}$$

For $k = 0$, $\delta(0, n) = \lambda(0, n) = 1$. From (2), we conclude that, for k in the defined range, the distribution of $\delta(k, n)$ is symmetric around $k = 2^{n-1}$.

Let $\varsigma(n)$ be the total number of BSD representations of length $n + 1$ for all integers $k \in [0, 2^n - 1]$, we can prove that

$$\varsigma(n) = 3^n \ . \tag{3}$$

Remark 1. *We conclude that, for any n-bit integer, the average number of its – $(n + 1)$ sbits long – BSD representations, i.e. of possible random forms it can take, is roughly* $\left(\frac{3}{2}\right)^n$.

It is clear from the definitions of $\lambda(k, n)$ and $\delta(k, n)$ that, for $0 \le k < 2^{n-1}$,

$$\lambda(k, n) = \delta(k, n - 1) \tag{4}$$

since in this range, the binary representation of k has a 0 as the leftmost bit. In other words, the algorithm that computes $\lambda(k, n)$ presented in the following section can be used to compute $\delta(k, n)$ as

$$\delta(k, n) = \lambda(k, n + 1) \ . \tag{5}$$

3.3 Algorithm to Compute the Number of BSD Representations for an Integer

Here we will present an algorithm that computes $\lambda(k, n)$ for any integer $k \in [0, 2^n - 1]$. This algorithm is based on the lemmas presented in Sect. 3.1.

Algorithm 1. Number of BSD representations of an integer k in $l = n$ sbits

---

INPUT: $k \in [0, 2^n - 1]$, n
OUTPUT: $C = \lambda(k, n)$
external $\lambda 2(k_e, k_o, w_e, w_o, n)$ /*computed by Algorithm 2 that follows*/
1. if $(k = 0)$ then
   $C \leftarrow 1$
2. else if $(k = 1)$ then
   $C \leftarrow n$

3. else if ($k \geq 2^{n-1}$) then
   $C \leftarrow \lambda(k - 2^{n-1}, n-1)$
4. else if (k is even) then
   $C \leftarrow \lambda(\frac{k}{2}, n-1)$
5. else
   5.1 if ($k \equiv 1 \pmod 4$) then
      $C \leftarrow \lambda2(\lfloor \frac{k}{2} \rfloor, \lfloor \frac{k}{2} \rfloor + 1, 1, 1, n-1)$
   5.2 else
      $C \leftarrow \lambda2(\lfloor \frac{k}{2} \rfloor + 1, \lfloor \frac{k}{2} \rfloor, 1, 1, n-1)$
6. return C

Algorithm 1 uses Lemma 1(i) and 1(ii) to return the value of $\lambda(k, n)$ directly if the value of k is either 0 or 1. Otherwise, it uses Lemmas 2 and 3 to trim k recursively from any leading 1's or trailing 0's since they don't add to the number of BSD representations of k. Then this algorithm calls Algorithm 2 to find the actual number of BSD representations of k which is then an odd integer in the range $[0, 2^{n'-1} - 1]$, for some $n' \leq n$. Hence, Lemma 4 is applicable to this k.

Algorithm 2. Auxiliary algorithm used by Algorithm 1 to compute $\lambda(k, n)$

INPUT: k_e, k_o, w_e, w_o, n
OUTPUT: $c = \lambda2(k_e, k_o, w_e, w_o, n)$
1. if ($k_o = 1$ AND $k_e = 2$) then
   $c \leftarrow n * w_o + (n-1) * w_e$
2. else
   2.1 if ($k_e \equiv 0 \pmod 4$) then
      2.1.1 if ($k_o \equiv 1 \pmod 4$) then
         $c \leftarrow \lambda2(\frac{k_e}{2}, \frac{k_e}{2} + 1, w_o + w_e, w_o, n-1)$
      2.1.2 else
         $c \leftarrow \lambda2(\frac{k_e}{2}, \frac{k_e}{2} - 1, w_o + w_e, w_o, n-1)$
   2.2 else
      2.2.1 if ($k_o \equiv 1 \pmod 4$) then
         $c \leftarrow \lambda2(\frac{k_e}{2} - 1, \frac{k_e}{2}, w_o, w_o + w_e, n-1)$
      2.2.2 else
         $c \leftarrow \lambda2(\frac{k_e}{2} + 1, \frac{k_e}{2}, w_o, w_o + w_e, n-1)$
3. return c

Using Lemma 4, $\lambda(k, n)$ for k odd constitutes of two other evaluations of the same function λ; one is for an even integer, k_e which is the closest even integer to $k/2$, and the other is for the preceding or the following odd integer, k_o. If we start using Lemmas 3 and 4 recursively to evaluate λ for k_e and k_o respectively, at each iteration there will be always two terms for the λ function multiplied by a certain weight each, w_e and w_o. In general, at the ith iteration

$$\lambda(k, n) = w_{e,n-i}\ \lambda(k_{e,n-i}, n-i) + w_{o,n-i}\ \lambda(k_{o,n-i}, n-i)\ .$$

At the beginning, $w_{e,n} = w_{o,n} = 1$. It can be shown that when $k_{e,n-i} \equiv 0 \pmod 4$, the weights are updated as follows

$$w_{e,n-i-1} = w_{o,n-i} + w_{e,n-i}\ , \qquad w_{o,n-i-1} = w_{o,n-i}\ ,$$

and when $k_{e,n-i} \equiv 2 \pmod 4$, they are updated as

$$w_{e,n-i-1} = w_{o,n-i} \ , \qquad w_{o,n-i-1} = w_{o,n-i} + w_{e,n-i} \ .$$

For the complexity of Algorithm 1 – including its usage of Algorithm 2 – it is clear that it runs in $O(n)$ time and occupies $O(n)$ bits in memory. This time complexity results from the fact that both algorithms deal with the integer k one bit at a time. For the space complexity of Algorithm 1, even in its recursive form, the new values that it generates for k and n can replace the old values in memory. The same argument is valid for Algorithm 2 regarding the new values of k_e, k_o, w_e, w_o and n.

3.4 Integer with Maximum Number of BSD Representations

From the view point of DPA countermeasure, while choosing a secret key k, it is desirable to know which integer $k \in [0, 2^n - 1]$, for a certain number of sbits $l = n$ or $l = n + 1$, has the maximum number of BSD representations. We note from (4) that this integer with the largest $\delta(k, n)$ is the same one with the largest $\lambda(k, n + 1)$. Also from the symmetry of $\delta(k, n)$ around 2^{n-1}, we note that there are two values of k for which $\delta(k, n)$ is the maximum value. We will denote them as $k_{max_1,n}$ and $k_{max_2,n}$.

From Lemma 3 and Lemma 4, $k_{max_1,n}$ and $k_{max_2,n}$ must be odd integers. There are two cases:

Case 1: $k_{max_1,n} \equiv 1 \pmod 4$
In this case, $\delta(k_{max_1,n} + 1, n) > \delta(k_{max_1,n} - 1, n)$, since $k_{max_1,n} - 1$ has two zeros as the least significant sbits while $k_{max_1,n} + 1$ has only one zero. Those rightmost zeros are trimmed by Algorithm 1.
Thus, from Lemma 4, we have

$$k_{max_1,n+1} = k_{max_1,n} + k_{max_1,n} + 1 = 2\ k_{max_1,n} + 1 \equiv 3 \pmod 4. \tag{6}$$

Case 2: $k_{max_1,n} \equiv 3 \pmod 4$
In this case, $\delta(k_{max_1,n} - 1, n) > \delta(k_{max_1,n} + 1, n)$. Thus, we have

$$k_{max_1,n+1} = k_{max_1,n} + k_{max_1,n} - 1 = 2\ k_{max_1,n} - 1 \equiv 1 \pmod 4. \tag{7}$$

With every increment of n, cases 1 and 2 alternate. Case 1 occurs when n is even and Case 2 occurs when n is odd.

We can use recursive substitution to find that, for n even,

$$k_{max_1,n} = \frac{1}{3}(2^n - 1) \tag{8}$$

and for n odd,

$$k_{max_1,n} = \frac{1}{3}(2^n + 1) \ . \tag{9}$$

Since $k_{max_1,n}$ and $k_{max_2,n}$ are equidistant from 2^{n-1}, we can obtain $k_{max_2,n}$ for n even as follows

$$k_{max_2,n} = 2^{n-1} + 2^{n-1} - k_{max_1,n} = 2^n - \frac{1}{3}(2^n - 1)$$
$$= \frac{1}{3}(2^{n+1} + 1) = k_{max_1,n+1} \tag{10}$$

where the last equality follows from (9).

Similarly, for n odd, we have

$$k_{max_2,n} = \frac{1}{3}(2^{n+1} - 1) = k_{max_1,n+1} \ . \tag{11}$$

Finally we should notice that, for n even, $k_{max_1,n}$ is of the form $(\langle 0\ 1\rangle^{\frac{n}{2}})_2$ and, for n odd, $k_{max_1,n}$ is of the form $(\langle 0\ 1\rangle^{\frac{n-1}{2}}1)_2$.

Knowing the integer with maximum number of BSD representations can help the cryptographer choose a secret key as follows. He can run Algorithm 1 with that integer as input to know the maximum number of representations. Then, he can pick an integer at random and run the same algorithm again to compare the number of BSD representations of that integer with the maximum one and accept that integer as the secret key if the number of its representations is within a predefined range of the maximum number. In general, from Lemma 4, odd integers have a number of BSD representations of order of twice that of their neighboring even integers. We have also observed that integers having a good random distribution of their bits are more probable to have larger number of BSD representations.

4 Left-to-Right BSD Randomization and Generation Algorithms

The algorithms mentioned in Sect. 2 that are used to generate a random BSD representation of k are modified versions of NAF generation algorithms. Those latter ones scan the bits of the integer k from right-to-left and hence, perform the EC scalar multiplication from right to left.

Sometimes, it is advantageous to perform the EC scalar multiplication from left to right, especially when a mixed coordinate (projective and affine) system is used for saving computational cost in scalar multiplication [2].

In this section, we will present an algorithm that generates a random – $(n+1)$ sbits long – BSD representation of k while scanning it from left to right. Also we will present another algorithm that generates *all* of these possible BSD representations of k.

4.1 Left-to-Right Randomization Algorithm

The underlying idea of the algorithm is that the binary representation of k is subdivided into groups of bits – of different lengths – such that each group is formed by a number of consecutive 0s ending with a single 1. For each of these groups a random BSD representation is chosen. Whenever the choice yields a $\bar{1}$ at the end of a group – which happens when any representation for that group other than the binary one is chosen – and a 1 at the beginning of the next group – which happens when the representation chosen for the next group is the one that has no 0s – another random decision is taken so as whether to leave those two sbits (i.e., $\bar{1}1$) as they are or to change them to $0\bar{1}$.

The choice of a random representation for a certain group is done by counting the number of 0s in it, say z, and choosing a random integer $t \in [0, z]$ which will be the number of 0s to be written to the output. If t is equal to z, the last sbit to be written to the output for this group is 1, and it is actually written. Otherwise, after writing the t 0s, a 1 and only $z - t - 1$ $\bar{1}$s are written, that is the last $\bar{1}$ is not written, but saved as the value of a variable labeled as *last*. We then do the same for the next group. If for the next group $t = 0$, we take a random decision whether to write $\bar{1}1$ to the output or $0\bar{1}$ at the boundary of the two groups. This leads to the following algorithm.

Algorithm 3. Left-to-Right Randomization of an integer's BSD representation

INPUT: $k = (k_{n-1} \ \dots \ k_0)_2$
OUTPUT: $k' = (k'_n \ \dots \ k'_0)_{\mathrm{BSD}}$, a random BSD representation of k

1. Set $k_n \leftarrow 0$; $i \leftarrow n + 1$; $last \leftarrow 1$
2. for j from n down to 0 do
   if $(k_j = 1)$ then
   2.1 $t \leftarrow_R [0, i - j - 1]$
   2.2 if $(t = 0$ AND $last \neq 1)$ then
      2.2.1 $c \leftarrow_R \{0, 1\}$
      2.2.2 if $(c = 0)$ then
         $k'_i \leftarrow \bar{1}$; $i \leftarrow i - 1$; $k'_i \leftarrow 1$
      2.2.3 else
         $k'_i \leftarrow 0$
   2.3 else
      2.3.1 if $(last \neq 1)$ then
         $k'_i \leftarrow \bar{1}$
      2.3.2 while $(t > 0)$ do
         $i \leftarrow i - 1$; $k'_i \leftarrow 0$; $t \leftarrow t - 1$
      2.3.3 $i \leftarrow i - 1$; $k'_i \leftarrow 1$
   2.4 if $(i = j)$ then
      $last \leftarrow 1$
   2.5 else
      2.5.1 while $(i > j + 1)$ do
         $i \leftarrow i - 1$; $k'_i \leftarrow \bar{1}$
      2.5.2 $i \leftarrow i - 1$; $last \leftarrow \bar{1}$
3. if $(last \neq 1)$ then
   $k'_i \leftarrow \bar{1}$
4. while $(i > 0)$ do
   $i \leftarrow i - 1$; $k'_i \leftarrow 0$

The algorithm runs in $O(n)$ time. The bits of k' can be used as they are generated in left-to-right scalar multiplication algorithms in EC cryptosystems or in left-to-right exponentiation algorithms in RSA or ElGamal cryptosystems. This means that there is no need to store k'.

4.2 Left-to-Right Generation Algorithm

The algorithm presented here is a modified version of Algorithm 3 that recursively and extensively substitutes every group of 0s ending with a 1 with one of its possible forms. It also takes into consideration the alternative substitutions at the group boundary when the representation of a group ends with a $\bar{1}$ and that of the next group starts with 1. This algorithm can be used as a straight-forward check that Algorithm 3 is capable of generating any possible – $(n+1)$ sbits long – BSD representation of an integer k in the range $[1, 2^n - 1]$, i.e. there is no BSD representation of k that cannot be generated by that algorithm. It was tested on small values of n.

Algorithm 4. Left-to-Right Generation of all BSD representations of k

---

INPUT: $k = (k_{n-1} \ \ldots \ k_0)_2$
OUTPUT: all possible strings $k' = (k'_n \ \ldots \ k'_0)_{\text{BSD}}$

1. Subdivide k from left to right into groups of consecutive 0s each ending with a single 1. Store the length of each group in a look-up table G. Let g be the index of the table.
2. Set $g \leftarrow 0$; $i \leftarrow n+1$;
   $last \leftarrow 1$; $j \leftarrow i - G[g]$; $k' \leftarrow \langle\rangle$
3. for $t = 0$ to $i - j - 1$ do
   ChooseForm$(k, g, t, i, j, last, k')$

Algorithm 5. ChooseForm$(k, g, t, i, j, last, k')$, a recursive procedure employed by Algorithm 4

INPUT: k, g, t, i, j, $last$, k'
OUTPUT: returns k', a string of sbits, as a possible BSD representation of k.

1. if $(t > 0)$ OR $(last = 1)$ then //this step is equivalent to step 2.3 in Algorithm 4
   1.1 if $(last \neq 1)$ then
       $k' \leftarrow k'|\bar{1}$ //concatenate k' with $\bar{1}$
   1.2 while $(t > 0)$ do
       $i \leftarrow i - 1$; $k' \leftarrow k'|0$; $t \leftarrow t - 1$
   1.3 $i \leftarrow i - 1$; $k' \leftarrow k'|1$
2. if $(i = j)$ then
   $last \leftarrow 1$
3. else
   3.1 while $(i > j + 1)$ do
       $i \leftarrow i - 1$; $k \leftarrow k'|\bar{1}$
   3.2 $i \leftarrow i - 1$; $last \leftarrow \bar{1}$
4. if $(j = 0)$ then
   4.1 if $(last \neq 1)$ then
       $k' \leftarrow k'|\bar{1}$

4.2 return k'
5. $g \leftarrow g+1;\ j \leftarrow j - G[g]$
6. if $(j = 0)$ AND (k is even) then
6.1 if $(i > 0)$ then
6.1.1 if $(last \neq 1)$ then
$k' \leftarrow k'|\bar{1}$
6.1.2 while $(i > 0)$ do
$i \leftarrow i-1;\ k' \leftarrow k'|0$
6.2 return k'
7. $t = 0$
8. if $(last \neq 1)$ then
ChooseForm$(k, g, t, i-1, j, last, k'|\bar{1}1)$
ChooseForm$(k, g, t, i, j, last, k'|0)$
9. else
ChooseForm$(k, g, t, i, j, last, k')$
10. for $t = 1$ to $i - j - 1$ do
ChooseForm$(k, g, t, i, j, last, k')$

To better explain how this algorithm works we present in Fig. 1 the tree explored by the algorithm for $k = 21$ and $n = 5$. This tree is explored by the algorithm in a *depth-first* fashion. That is, the recursive function *ChooseForm* is first called from Algorithm 4 at node a in the figure. Then this function calls itself at node b and then at node c where it returns with the first BSD representation for $k = 21$ which is $1\bar{1}1\bar{1}1\bar{1}$. With the flow control at node b the function calls itself at node d where the second BSD representation is generated and so forth.

The algorithm works as follows. The integer k is first subdivided into groups of bits where each group consists of consecutive 0s and a single 1 at the end as for Algorithm 3. We should mention that a 0 is prepended to the binary representation of k, so that the BSD representations, k' of k are $(n+1)$ sbits long. Starting from the leftmost group, a particular BSD representation for that

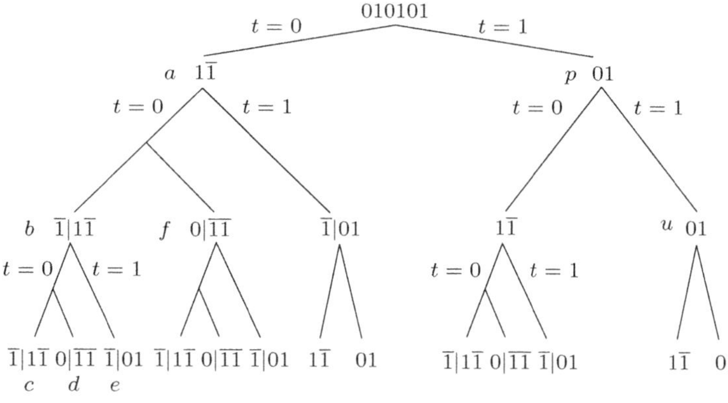

Fig. 1. The tree explored by Algorithm 4 for $k = 21$ and $n = 5$

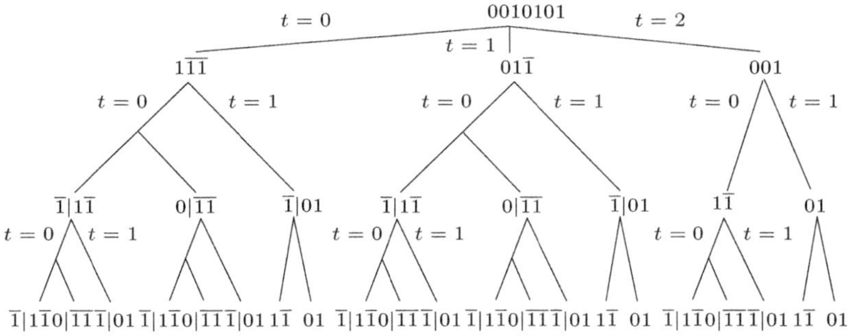

Fig. 2. The tree explored by Algorithm 4 for $k = 21$ and $n = 6$

group is chosen starting with the one that contains no 0s (i.e. t, the number of 0s to be written to the output for that group, is equal to 0). The representation is formed inside the function *ChooseForm* which takes t as one of its arguments. In turn, this function goes through the possible values of t for the following group and, for each one, calls itself to form the corresponding BSD representation of that group. When t is equal to 0, the two possible alternatives at the group boundary are considered as was explained in Sect. 4.1. For example, in Fig. 1, the last sbit in the group at node a may remain $\bar{1}$ or change to 0 depending on the random decision taken at the group boundary when $t = 0$ for the next group. This is why this last sbit is written at nodes b and f before the symbol '|' which designates the boundary between the groups.

The *worst-case* complexity analysis of Algorithm 4 is presented in the following. The worst case occurs for the integer with the maximum number of BSD representations in the range $[1, 2^n - 1]$. There are actually two integers with this property for any given n, which we referred to as $k_{max_1,n}$ and $k_{max_2,n}$ in Sect. 3.4. We mentioned that, for n even, $k_{max_1,n}$ is of the form $(\langle 0\ 1\rangle^{\frac{n}{2}})_2$. For example, $k_{max_1,6} = 21 = (010101)_2$ (see Fig. 2). We also mentioned that, for any n, $k_{max_2,n} = k_{max_1,n+1}$. For example, $k_{max_1,5} = 11 = (01011)_2$ and $k_{max_2,5} = 21 = (10101)_2$ (see Fig. 2). Therefore, our analysis is conducted on those integers k of the binary form $(\langle 0\ 1\rangle^{\frac{n}{2}})_2$ for n even and $(1\langle 0\ 1\rangle^{\frac{n-1}{2}})_2$ for n odd. In the following discussion, we will drop the subscript n from $k_{max_1,n}$ and $k_{max_2,n}$ for simplicity, since it will be obvious from the context.

For n even, we have the following.

$n = 2$: $k_{max_1} = k_{max_2} = 1 = (01)_2$, $\delta(1,2) = \lambda(1,3) = 3$.
The tree explored here is the same as the one having as root the node b in Fig. 1. The difference is that in this case t can take the values 0, 1 and 2 with only one representation for $t = 0$.

$n = 4$: $k_{max_1} = 5 = (0101)_2$, $\delta(5,4) = \lambda(5,5) = 8 = 3 \cdot 3 - 1$.
The tree explored for this integer is the same as the one having as root a in Fig. 1.

$n = 6$: $k_{max_1} = 21 = (010101)_2$, $\delta(21,6) = \lambda(21,7) = 21 = 3 \cdot 3 \cdot 3 - (3.1 + 3)$.
The tree explored for this integer is illustrated in Fig. 2.

Let $m = \frac{n}{2}$. By induction we can deduce the following

$$\begin{aligned}\lambda(k_{max_1}, n+1) &= 3^m - (m-1)3^{m-2} + \left(\sum_{i_1=1}^{m-3} i_1\right) 3^{m-4} \\ &- \left(\sum_{i_1=1}^{m-5}\sum_{i_2=1}^{i_1} i_2\right) 3^{m-6} + \left(\sum_{i_1=1}^{m-7}\sum_{i_2=1}^{i_1}\sum_{i_3=1}^{i_2} i_3\right) 3^{m-8} - \cdots .\end{aligned} \tag{12}$$

Also, for n odd, by induction we can deduce the following

$$\begin{aligned}\lambda(k_{max_2}, n+1) &= 2\cdot 3^m - \left[3^{m-1} + 2(m-1)3^{m-2}\right] \\ &+ \left[(m-2)3^{m-3} + 2\left(\sum_{i_1=1}^{m-3} i_1\right) 3^{m-4}\right] \\ &- \left[\left(\sum_{i_2=1}^{m-4} i_2\right) 3^{m-5} + 2\left(\sum_{i_1=1}^{m-5}\sum_{i_2=1}^{i_1} i_2\right) 3^{m-6}\right] \\ &+ \left[\left(\sum_{i_2=1}^{m-6}\sum_{i_3=1}^{i_2} i_3\right) 3^{m-7} + 2\left(\sum_{i_1=1}^{m-7}\sum_{i_2=1}^{i_1}\sum_{i_3=1}^{i_2} i_3\right) 3^{m-8}\right] \\ &- \cdots\end{aligned} \tag{13}$$

where $m = \frac{n-1}{2}$.

From this discussion, we state the following theorem.

Theorem 1. *For any n, the number of BSD representations generated by Algorithm 4 is, in the worst case, $\mathcal{O}(3^{\lfloor \frac{n}{2} \rfloor})$.*

4.3 Effect of Increasing n on the Number of BSD Representations of an Integer k

In an attempt to improve DPA countermeasure, one may increase the length of the binary representation of the integer k. Below we show how the number of BSD representations of k increases if we lengthen its binary representation by adding 0s at the most significant end.

If we compare Fig. 1 with Fig. 2, we see that for the same integer $k = 21$, increasing n from 5 to 6 had the effect of increasing the number of branches emerging from the root by one. The added branch has the same tree structure as the leftmost branch a in Fig. 1. This is because the number of BSD representations of the first group – recall how the integer is subdivided into groups – has increased by one. Since all representations of a group, except for the original binary representation, end with a $\bar{1}$, the added representation would generate two alternatives when $t = 0$ for the next group. If we increase n to 7, another subtree like the one having as root a will be added to the tree. The same subtree is repeated with every 0 prepended to the binary representation of k. It is easy to verify that this is true for any integer k.

As was mentioned before, the subtree having as root the node a is the tree explored for $k = 5$ and $n = 4$. In general, the subtree that is repeated is the one formed for the integer with the binary representation having the same groups as k except for the leftmost group. That is

$$\Delta(k) = \lambda(k, n+1) - \lambda(k, n) = \lambda(k - 2^{\lfloor \log_2 k \rfloor}, \lfloor \log_2 k \rfloor + 1) \tag{14}$$

where $\Delta(k)$ is the number of leaves in the repeated subtree.

We notice that $\Delta(k)$ does not depend on n and hence, based on (14), we have the following theorem.

Theorem 2. *The number of BSD representations of an integer increases linearly with the number of bits in which it is represented in its binary form.*

5 Conclusion

In this paper, we have presented a number of cryptographically important issues related to the binary-signed digit (BSD) representation of integers, such as the average number of BSD representations of an integer k in the range $[0, 2^n - 1]$, the integer in this range that has maximum number of BSD representations. Our results provide a mechanism for choosing integers (i.e. cryptographic keys) with larger space of BSD representations and hence, with better resistance to DPA attacks. We have presented an algorithm that calculates for any integer k represented in n bits the exact number of BSD representations with the same length in $\mathcal{O}(n)$. We have also presented an algorithm that generates a random BSD representation of an integer by scanning its bits starting from the most significant end which can be used where the EC scalar multiplication is to be performed from left to right to reduce computational cost using a mixed coordinate system. This algorithm runs in $\mathcal{O}(n)$. In addition, we presented an algorithm that can generate all BSD representations of an integer, which runs in $\mathcal{O}(3^{\lfloor \frac{n}{2} \rfloor})$ in the worst case, i.e. in the case of the integer with maximum number of BSD representations in the range $[0, 2^n - 1]$. We have also proved that the number of BSD representations of an integer increases linearly with the number of bits in which it is represented.

Acknowledgements

This work has been supported in part by NSERC (Natural Sciences and Engineering Research Council of Canada), OCIPEP (Office of Critical Infrastructure Protection and Emergency Preparedness) and RIM (Research in Motion) through an NSERC strategic project.

References

[1] Dan Boneh, Richard A. DeMillo, and Richard J. Lipton. On the importance of eliminating errors in cryptographic computations. *Journal of Cryptology*, 14:101–119, 2001. This is an expanded version of an earlier paper that appeared in *Proc. of EUROCRYPT '97*. 58

[2] Henri Cohen, Atsuko Miyaji, and Takatoshi Ono. Efficient elliptic curve exponentiation using mixed coordinates. In *Advances in Cryptology – ASIACRYPT '98*, volume 1514 of *LNCS*, pages 51–65. Springer-Verlag, 1998. 65

[3] Jean-Sébastien Coron. Resistance against differential power analysis for elliptic curve cryptosystems. In Ç. K. Koç and C. Paar, editors, *Cryptographic Hardware and Embedded Systems – CHES '99*, volume 1717 of *LNCS*, pages 292–302. Springer-Verlag, 1999. 59, 60

[4] JaeCheol Ha and SangJae Moon. Randomized signed-scalar multiplication of ECC to resist power attacks. In *Cryptographic Hardware and Embedded Systems – CHES '02*, volume 2523 of *LNCS*, pages 551–563. Springer-Verlag, 2002. 59, 60, 61

[5] M. A. Hasan. Power analysis attacks and algorithmic approaches to their countermeasures for Koblitz curve cryptosystems. *IEEE Transactions on Computers*, 50(10):1071–1083, October 2001. 59, 60

[6] M. Joye and J. J. Quisquater. Hessian elliptic curves and side-channel attacks. In *Cryptographic Hardware and Embedded Systems – CHES '01*, volume 2162 of *LNCS*, pages 402–410. Springer-Verlag, 2001. 59

[7] D. E. Knuth. *The Art of Computer Programming/Seminumerical Algorithms*, volume 2. Addison-Wesley, second edition, 1973. 60

[8] Paul Kocher. Timing attacks on implementations of Diffie-Hellman, RSA, DSS and other systems. In N. Koblitz, editor, *Advances in Cryptology – CRYPTO '96*, volume 1109 of *LNCS*, pages 104–113. Springer-Verlag, August 1996. 58

[9] Paul Kocher, Joshua Jaffe, and Benjamin Jun. Differential power analysis. In Michael Wiener, editor, *Advances in Cryptology – CRYPTO '99*, volume 1666 of *LNCS*. Springer-Verlag, 1999. 58

[10] P. Y. Liardet and N. P. Smart. Preventing SPA/DPA in ECC systems using the Jacobi form. In *Cryptographic Hardware and Embedded Systems – CHES '01*, volume 2162 of *LNCS*, pages 391–401. Springer-Verlag, 2001. 59

[11] Alfred J. Menezes. *Elliptic Curve Public Key Cryptosystems*. Kluwer Academic Publishers, 1993. 60

[12] T. Messerges, E. Dabbish, and R. Sloan. Investigations of power analysis attacks on smart cards. In *USENIX Workshop on Smart-card Technology*, pages 151–161, May 1999. 58

[13] T. Messerges, E. Dabbish, and R. Sloan. Power analysis attacks of modular exponentiation in smart cards. In Ç. K. Koç and C. Paar, editors, *Cryptographic Hardware and Embedded Systems – CHES '99*, volume 1717 of *LNCS*, pages 144–157. Springer-Verlag, August 1999. 58

[14] François Morain and Jorge Olivos. Speeding up the computations on an elliptic curve using addition-subtraction chains. *Informatique théorique et Applications/Theoritical Informatics and Applications*, 24(6):531–544, 1990. 60

[15] K. Okeya and K. Sakurai. Power analysis breaks elliptic curve cryptosystems even secure against the timing attack. In *Advances in Cryptology – INDOCRYPT '00*, volume 1977 of *LNCS*, pages 178–190. Springer-Verlag, 2000. 59

[16] Elisabeth Oswald and Manfred Aigner. Randomized addition-subtraction chains as a countermeasure aginst power attacks. In Ç. K. Koç, D. Naccache, and C. Paar, editors, *Cryptographic Hardware and Embedded Systems – CHES '01*, volume 2162 of *LNCS*, pages 39–50. Springer-Verlag, 2001. 59, 60, 61

[17] G. W. Reitwiesner. Binary arithmetic. *Advances in Computers*, 1:231–308, 1960. 61

Zero Common-Knowledge Authentication for Pervasive Networks

André Weimerskirch[1] and Dirk Westhoff[2]

[1] Communication Security Group, Ruhr-University Bochum, Germany
weika@crypto.rub.de

[2] NEC Europe Ltd. - Network Laboratories, Heidelberg, Germany
dirk.westhoff@ccrle.nec.de

Abstract. Ad-hoc networks and even more intrinsic pervasive networks face huge security lacks. In the most general case entities need to build up a well-defined security association without any pre-established secret or common security infrastructure. Under these circumstances it turns out that without unrealistic assumptions authentication of previously unknown parties is not achievable. However, for a wide spectrum of scenarios much weaker authentication forms are reasonable, e.g., for routing protocols and other protocols aiming to intensify cooperation. Like in real world when foreign subjects meet for the very first time, inferring the opposites identity is impossible. Nevertheless even from this zero common-knowledge status some minor level of trust establishment is possible for both scenarios, in real world and on a technical level. In this paper we will present a very light-weight still provably secure authentication protocol not aiming at inferring the involved entities' identities but re-recognizing foreign communication partners whenever necessary. We do not make any assumptions to the scenario, and we also have no requirements for the devices' abilities. For the technical realization we propose extremely efficient security primitives applicable for nearly all types of restricted devices. Our solution is more efficient than a public-key operation by some orders of magnitude.

Keywords: Authentication, Pervasive Networks, Ad-hoc Networks, Key-Chains, Public-Key, Symmetric Ciphers

1 Introduction

Wireless ad-hoc networks and pervasive networks face huge security lacks. In the most general case entities need to be able to establish well-defined security associations without any pre-established secret or common security infrastructure. Unlike in military or closed networks where there is a single logical and commonly agreed trust authority we cannot assume such a situation in the general case. For example, assume two entities that have a certificate issued by two different authorities. In an ad-hoc network with entities belonging to different administrative domains there might be no pre-defined association between these

M. Matsui and R. Zuccherato (Eds.): SAC 2003, LNCS 3006, pp. 73–87, 2004.

two authorities, or the nodes might not be able to reach the authorities. In both cases entities cannot easily establish a trust relationship.

In this paper we follow a fully infrastructure-less approach of establishing trust relationships in pervasive networks that are highly dynamic. We define that a network is of *pure* kind (or just pure) if there exist neither central services nor does a fixed infrastructure exist, and if there are no pre-established knowledge between two entities in a general manner. We do not assume that the network has a special topology, specifically it might be a wireless multi-hop network that is exposed to several attacks such as a man-in-the-middle attack. We define a *weak device* to be a simple device without any further assumptions. Such assumptions would be tamper resistance, or a unique identification number. We assume the most general case in meaning that there is no common trusted third party (TTP), and the ad-hoc network is indeed pure.

We define our security objective, which we call *zero common-knowledge authentication (ZCK)* as follows: A is able to authenticate B in a zero common-knowledge fashion if A is able to identify again the authority that runs B, i.e., B is able to convince A that both had some relationship in the past. We also say that A *recognizes* B, or that B *authenticates* to A. For example, if B was forwarding a data-packet for A, then later on A is able to recognize B to forward another packet, probably in exchange for another service. Now it is clear what we want to achieve: ZCK authentication in a pure pervasive network consisting of weak devices where there are no pre-established secrets, i.e., we do not use any assumptions like tamper resistant devices, devices that are able to perform expensive public-key operations, special access structures for deploying a distributed PKI, and so on. We believe that such an approach is more practical and realistic, yet still sufficient. Certainly, we are not able to determine a user's identity as it is necessary for financial transactions. However, in many cases like the financial one the problem of authentication does not differ to the problem in traditional networks and can be solved with schemes similar to the ones that are used in today's Internet. Clearly, this involves further assumptions or infrastructure. Our approach focuses on problems that are inherent to pure pervasive and ad-hoc networks. For example, our solution is suited to cooperation and motivation based schemes [7][3][9] as well as secure routing methods. These schemes require a large number of authentication steps for which ZCK authentication is strong enough. Our scheme also makes sense for all kinds of client-server and peer-to-peer relations, respectively.

A limited authentication based on re-recognition is reasonable. We cannot achieve as much as other authentication schemes, but we can keep our promises without any assumptions. Especially for pure ad-hoc and pervasive networks this is a realistic approach. Furthermore, in a pure network we believe that we cannot promise anything more than our objective. We formulate this as follows:

Claim. Under the assumption that there exists no public-key scheme that works without any pre-established knowledge[1] or without a common TTP, recognition is the best we can achieve in a pure network.

We cannot provide a formal proof but only intuitive arguments. If we were able to achieve more than ZCK authentication in a pure network, i.e., identify a user instead of recognizing him, then we had a public-key scheme that works without any pre-established knowledge or TTP. Today this seems to be impossible though.

Imagine two foreigners that meet in the real world. Usually, and obviously strongly related to the considered level and type of interaction these people do not doubtlessly identify each other, e.g., by showing their passports. Assuming there is nobody else available to ask about the opposite's reputation the best both can do is to establish step-by-step a trust relationship build on their bilateral, personal experiences. To do so, it is mandatory that these two people recognize again the next time they meet. In our model we do not assume geographical proximity though.

The main contribution of this paper is a new authentication scheme especially suited to pervasive networks. The scheme only requires one-way hash-functions and is suited to nearly any computationally weak device since it is more efficient than any public-key scheme by some order of magnitudes. Our scheme provides provably secure authentication against passive adversaries and secure message authentication against active adversaries, where the scheme is as sound as the underlying one-way hash function. We also present solutions for slightly different application scopes. The paper is organized as follows. Section 2 gives a description of our ZCK authentication scheme in a general framework. Section 3 introduces our new scheme. Section 4 compares the different instantiations of our general authentication scheme and rates them by comparing their complexity and by giving advise for which scope they are applicable. Finally, the last section concludes this work.

2 General ZCK Authentication Scheme

In this section we describe our scheme in a general kind. Consider the case where an entity A wants to be able to recognize an entity B after an initial contact. Obviously the communication channel they use is insecure. In this scenario, B might be a service provider and A the client. In the first step B provides A with some data that allows the later one to recognize B. Let S be a set of secrets, and $x \in S$ be a secret. B is able to prove that it knows x in such a way that A is not able to impersonate B. Furthermore B is able to use x in such a way that A can verify that a message origins of B, i.e., B is able to perform a message authentication by using the key x. Let $(m)_x$ be an authentication of a message m, then A can verify the origin by checking $((m)_x)_{f(x)} = m$,

[1] Note that we consider a unique global and tamper resistant ID for each device as pre-established knowledge.

where f is a mapping on S such that the knowledge of $f(x)$ enables a prover to check if a verifier knows x, i.e., $f(x)$ is a public key. A simple example is a private/public-key pair of a digital signature scheme. The protocol runs as follows. The entity B sends the public key $f(x)$ to A. Then A and B perform a challenge-response protocol as described in [8] such that A is able to verify that B knows the secret x. A simplified version of the protocol looks as follows:

$1:$ B `generates` $x \in S$ `at random`
$2:$ B `sends` $f(x)$ `to` A
`Repeat Steps 3 to 5 for each authentication process`
$3:$ A `sends random` r `to` B
$4:$ B `sends authenticated` $(r)_x$ `to` A
$5:$ A `checks if` $((r)_x)_{f(x)} = r$
~ `If 'yes',` A *accepts*, `otherwise she` *rejects*

Remarks:
- Step 1 only needs to be performed once for each authority and/or entity. An authority might hold several devices such that each device can hold the same secret x or that each device has its own secret x_i.
- Step 2 needs to be performed once for each communication pair A and B.
- Steps $3-5$ have to be performed for each authentication process.
- Step 4 usually consists of a message block r', $(r, r')_x$ with random r' to avoid chosen-text attacks. Since this is no threat to a ZCK scheme we omit it here.

We consider as main objective of this scheme the capability to ensure that entities are able to re-recognize another entity in order to receive a service they requested. Hence the public key $f(x)$ always has to be send together with the offered service, i.e., service and key have to be bound together to avoid that a malicious entity can inject his public key to a service that he did not offer at all. It follows that the authentication scheme we are envisioning here usually is connected to some offered service, i.e., to messages that are exchanged. Therefore we add the following steps to *authenticate messages* that replace Steps $3-5$:

`Repeat Steps 3 to 4 for each message to authenticate`
$3':$ B `sends` $(m)_x$ `to` A
$4':$ A `checks if` $((m)_x)_{f(x)} = m$
~ `If 'yes',` A *accepts*, `otherwise she` *rejects*

Note that message integrity and also freshness, i.e. that the data is recent and not replayed, comes with the message authentication. In contrast to PKI scenarios where there is a logical central certificate directory, A has to store B's public key (together with B's ID string) to be able to recognize B. After A deletes B's public key from her memory A is not able anymore to build a connection to a previous relationship with B. Note that in many applications a mutual authentication process is required. The above protocol can easily be extended for this case.

We now consider the traditional security objectives, namely authentication, confidentiality, integrity, and non-repudiation [8]. The above scheme ensures

ZCK authentication. It does not allow a key-exchange by itself, hence it cannot establish confidentiality. However, it is possible to establish integrity of messages by authenticating these messages as shown above. Obviously the scheme does not provide non-repudiation. However, for some type of scenario a weaker form of non-repudiation may also be appropriate. We define *ZCK non-repudiation* to be the service which prevents an entity to deny a commitment or action chain. In our case this means that an entity A is able to prove to a third party that a number of actions or commitments were taken by the same (probably unknown) entity B. Obviously a scheme that provides signatures satisfies the ZCK non-repudiation objective.

The presented protocol is as secure as the underlying security scheme, i.e., to break the protocol an adversary has to construct an authenticated message $(m)_x$ for given m and $f(x)$. Note that a man-in-the-middle attack is always possible, and consider what this means at an example. There is an entity B that offers a service, an entity A that seeks this service, and a malicious entity M. The entity B sends $f(x_B)$ to A. M interrupts this message, and sends $f(x_M)$ to A. Then M satisfies the needs of A by offering its services. All that A is interested in was that service. She does not care who provided the service, but she wants to receive the service in the same quality again. It becomes now clear that a man-in-the-middle attack is no threat to our protocol.

Two instantiations of the ZCK authentication scheme that immediately arise are based on traditional signature schemes as well as symmetric ciphers. Authentication is done by the proof of knowledge of the secret key in a challenge and response manner. The verifier sends a challenge r, and the prover signs the challenge or computes a message authentication code (MAC) of r. As we argued before, a man-in-the-middle attack is possible but irrelevant in the sense of our intention. In the case of digital signatures the scheme ensures ZCK authentication and ZCK non-repudiation, and also message authentication. In most cases public-key operations overstrain the capabilities of weak devices. Hence for our scope of weak devices, only very efficient public-key schemes such as NTRU [6] are appropriate, while RSA and even ECC might be too slow and too resource consuming.

In the case of a symmetric cipher a secret key s has to be shared a priori, i.e., the protocol requires a secret channel to exchange the shared secret. It is suited for applications where devices are geographically close, e.g., where devices can exchange the keys by infrared channel, or where there is only a single trust authority. If the key s is a t-bit string, and an authenticated message $(m)_s$ is a t-bit string, then the protocol requires storage of $t/8$ bytes and the exchange of $2t/8$ bytes which are split into two messages. For a security level similar to 1024-bit RSA we choose $t = 80$. A protocol run then requires the exchange of 20 bytes in two messages, where the key has a size of 10 bytes. Clearly, a secure channel for key-exchange could also be established by a secure key-exchange such as Diffie-Hellman. Such a key-exchange has to be performed for each communication pair. Since a key-exchange demands computationally powerful devices and the heavily changing topology of pervasive networks of mobile nodes induces many key-exchanges such a solution is not suited to weak devices.

3 Key-Chain Scheme

This section introduces our new protocol for ZCK authentication that only requires one-way hash functions but no expensive public-key operations. Doing so our scheme is extremely efficient and by orders of magnitudes faster than any public-key scheme. Again Bob wants to authenticate to Alice. Let x_B^G be a t-bit string which is Bob's global private key. Let each device have a network identifier ID[2], in our case ID_A and ID_B. Let f be a function that maps the identity ID to a bit-string, r_{ID} be t-bit random strings, and $\oplus$ be an operation on bit strings. Then x_0^B is Bob's private key for the communication with Alice which is derived from Bob's global key, Alice's identity and r_B such that $x_0^B = x_B^G \oplus f(ID_A) \oplus r_B$. Likewise $x_0^A = x_A^G \oplus f(ID_B) \oplus r_A$ is Alice's private key for the communication with Bob. The private key for the communication with an entity having the identifier ID can later again be derived by the stored associated string r_{ID} and the global private key. Note that these keys are only applicable to the communication pair Alice and Bob, and to no one else.

We define a hash chain, which is also known as Lamport's hash chain [8], as $h(x_i) = x_{i+1}$ with x_0 being the anchor and h being an unkeyed one-way hash function that has a security of t-bits, i.e., which maps bit-strings to t bits. Our scheme is based on such hash chains with x_0^A and x_0^B being the anchors. Let $x_{n_A}^A$ and $x_{n_B}^B$ be the final elements of the hash chains, respectively. We call these the public keys of Alice and Bob. We can use a key-value of the chain to generate an authenticated message by a MAC (keyed hash function). Let $(m)_x$ be the MAC of a message m by the key x. The core idea of our protocol is as follows: First exchange a value $f(x)$ which the receiver will tie together with some experience. Then prove knowledge of the pre-image of $f(x)$, i.e. x, in order to authenticate by establishing a relationship to $f(x)$ and the past experience. Since we want to be able to repeat the authentication step arbitrary many times we propose the use of a key-chain based on a one-way hash function. Our protocol works as follows:

---

[2] For the protocol this is an identifier to recognize another entity again. We do neither assume that the ID cannot be tampered with nor that IDs are unique. A just has to be able to map B to some name ID_B.

1 : A `sends her public key` $x^A_{n_A}$ `to` B`, who stores` $(x^A_{n_A}, r_B, n_B, 1)$
2 : B `sends his public key` $x^B_{n_B}$ `to` A`, who stores` $(x^B_{n_B}, r_A, n_A, 1)$
`Repeat Steps 3 to 9 for each authentication process`
3 : `Assume` A `stores` (x^B_i, r_A, j, u) `and` B `stores` (x^A_j, r_B, i, v)
4 : `(+)` A `sends authenticated messages` $(m)_{x^A_{j-u-1}}$ `to` B
5 : `(+)` B `sends authenticated messages` $(m)_{x^B_{i-v}}$ `to` A
6 : A `opens her key by sending` x^A_{j-1} `to` B.
7 : B `checks if` $h(x^A_{j-1}) = x^A_j$
8 : `For` $k = 1$ `to` $k' \leftarrow \max\{u, v\}$ `repeat Steps 8.1 to 8.5`
8.1 : B `opens his key by sending` x^B_{i-k} `to` A
8.2 : A `checks if` $h(x^B_{i-k}) = x^B_{i-k+1}$
8.3 : A `opens her key by sending` x^A_{j-k-1} `to` B
8.4 : B `checks if` $h(x^A_{j-k-1}) = x^A_{j-k}$
8.5 : `If any check fails, or the loop is interrupted,` A `and` B `stop execution. Then` A `stores` $(x^B_i, r_A, j, \max\{u, k+1\})$ `and` B `stores` $(x^A_j, r_B, i, \max\{v, k+1\})$.
9 : A `and` B `store the new values` $(x^B_{i-k'}, r_A, j-k'-1, 1)$ `and` $(x^A_{j-k'-1}, r_B, i-k', 1)$

Remarks:

- Steps $1-2$ ensure the exchange of public-keys which is done only once per pair A and B.
- Steps $3-9$ are done for each authentication process.
- For each authentication process we assume that A stores B's key x^B_i and that B stores A's key x^A_j (Step 3). Furthermore A and B store information to compute the subsequent keys, i.e., they store the random value r_A and r_B to compute the chain anchor from the global key x^G_A and x^G_B, respectively. Furthermore they store i and j to obtain the chain value from the anchor. In the initialization, i.e., after Steps 1-2, A and B store tuples $(x^B_{n_B}, r_A, n_A, 1)$ and $(x^A_{n_A}, r_B, n_B, 1)$. These are replaced later by updated tuples.
- Steps 4 and 5 provide messages authentication and are optional. The messages are guaranteed to be fresh.
- The messages sent in Steps $4-5$ can be read but are not authenticated at this moment. It has to be ensured that all messages are received, e.g., by the underlying routing protocol or by further steps in the authentication protocol. Messages can be checked after the keys were opened.
- Before Step 6 is performed it has to be ensured that A and B send the last messages in Steps 4-5 (if any). A might send a message to B expressing that she finished sending messages, and B sends after receiving such a message to A. To reduce the overhead of additional messages a flag-bit in the packet header might be used to indicate a final message. Note that this information has to be protected by a MAC as well to prevent forgery, e.g., it might be part of the final message $(m_f)_{x^A_{j-u-1}}$ and $(m_f)_{x^B_{i-v}}$, respectively.

- The loop in Step 8 avoids an attack, where a malicious entity starts an authentication process, interrupts it after he gained a key, and uses that key to the other benign entity. The idea is that A assumes after a faulty execution, that an attacker uses the gained key to obtain another key from B. Hence A does not accept a single key anymore but requires knowledge of the next two keys, and so on. B acts in the same way.
- After the public keys are exchanged, $u, v = 1$. Also after a successful protocol run, u and v are reset to 1. Hence in a normal protocol run the loop is only executed once, i.e., $k' = 1$.
- If A opens a key which B does not receive due to network faults, A can send the key again without endangering the security of the scheme until B gets the key, or until A halts the execution of the protocol due to a time-out error. The same holds for keys opened by B.
- A and B do not need to know $k' = \max\{u, v\}$ before the execution of the loop. The entities just continue running the loop until both signalize their satisfaction.
- The scheme uses mutual authentication to avoid that a key of Bob is stolen by a malicious entity that pretends to be Alice, and later on used by the malicious entity to impersonate Alice when authenticating to Bob. Note that all complexities for our scheme obtained below are for mutual authentication whereas the previous scheme instantiations only ensured mutual authentication at additional cost.
- A and B always have to be in the same role, i.e., for a pair A and B, the same entity always has to act as A. This limitation can be removed at the cost of a further message by requiring that A and B open at least two keys. The following steps which replace Step 9 implement such a case:

  $9'$: B `opens his key by sending` $x^B_{i-k'-1}$ `to` A
  $10'$: A `checks if` $h(x^B_{i-k'-1}) = x^B_{i-k'}$
  ~ `If the check fails, or the execution is interrupted,`
  ~ A `stores` $(x^B_i, r_A, j, \max\{u, k'+1\})$
  $11'$: A `and` B `store the new values` $(x^B_{i-k'-1}, r_A, j-k'-1, 1)$
  ~ `and` $(x^A_{j-k'-1}, r_B, i-k'-1, 1)$

- A man-in-the-middle attack at execution time is possible as it is for most other authentication schemes including the public-key scheme.
- The man-in-the-middle attack is not possible to forge authenticated messages since the messages are already exchanged at the time when the authentication starts.
- The scheme is not resistant to denial-of-service attacks (as is neither of the other schemes). A malicious entity can try to exhaust the keys of the key chain by starting an authentication process with A, gaining A's next key, using it against B to obtain B's key, using it again for A, and so on. An implementation can take care of this attack by forcing an exponentially increasing time interval between two authentication processes.

- The security of the scheme is as sound as the security of the underlying one-way hash-function and the underlying message authentication code. A formal proof of all above mentioned security properties can be found in the Appendix.
- The public key is only send once. Usually, the loop is only executed once, thus an authentication process requires three messages (Steps 6, 8.1, and 8.3), each of them a t-bit string
- To compute an arbitrary element of a hash chain, A only needs to know B's ID and the random seed r_A used for B.
- Assume that A and B use hash chains of length n. To compute x^A_{i-1} and x^B_{j-1} in Steps 4 and 5 from the global private key, this requires on average $n/2$ applications of the hash function h. Since A needs twice as many keys as B for an authentication, he might want to use chains that are twice as long.
- For each communication pair of A with any B, she needs to store a tuple (x^B_i, r_A, j, u), i.e., the public key. Assuming that we use short key-chains the indices j and u can be expressed in 2 bytes. Then A requires storage of $(2t + 32)/8$ bytes. Assuming that A stores data of p communication parters, she needs storage of $p(2t + 32)/8$ bytes.

Considering a hash function that maps strings to t bits, the probability to find a collision for any pair of strings (collision resistance) is $2^{-t/2}$ whereas the probability to find a collision to a given message (target collision resistance) is 2^{-t}. We believe that target collision resistance suffices our demands. It is widely believed that computing a collision to a given message in a one-way hash function with $t = 80$ is as hard as factoring an RSA modulus of 1024 bits. Hence to establish a security level similar to 1024-bit RSA we assume $t = 80$. Let the size of the average key-chain be $n = 100$ which should meet the demands of most short-lived pervasive networks. As we said before authentication in a pervasive network is usually connected to some service that is offered or requested, i.e., authentication is bound to messages that are exchanged. Altogether the scheme requires on average 50 applications of the hash function, and three message exchanges each of 10 bytes. It furthermore requires 24 bytes of storage on the prover's and verifier's side which are far less than an RSA public key and about the same size of a 160-bit ECC public key (assuming each entity uses the same curve parameters). Note that in our scheme the prover and the verifier have to store the other entity's public key. Since most relationships in a pervasive network are mutual we do not believe this to be a disadvantage but a feature. A hash function has very low running time. For example, the SHA-1 implementation in [1] obtains hashing speeds of 48.7 Mbit/s whereas an RSA verification (which is the most efficient signature verification scheme) runs in roughly 1 ms [5]. Thus an application of a hash function is faster than an RSA verification by almost a factor of 10^6, and the repeated application of a hash function nearly is for free for 50 or even more iterations. If a device has on average contacts to $p = 50$ communication parters, there is storage needed of 1200 bytes.

The number of hash function iterations can be reduced at the cost of storage, or by using shorter key-chains. To store the elements of a chain we can store each element of the chain, or only store the anchor and compute the elements on demand. A storage efficient mechanism was proposed in [4] which only requires $\log n$ storage and $\log n$ computation to access an element in a chain of n elements. For instance, if $n = 100$ we can reduce the number of average hash-function iterations to 7 at the cost of 7 more storage entries.

To safe memory and to avoid extensive computations short key-chains are used. We now show how to establish a new key-chain without breaking the trust relationship. Let x_i be the values of an old key-chain that is nearly used up, and x'_i be the values of a new key-chain. These key-chains use different anchors x_0 and x'_0 which are derived of the same global private key x^G and different random seeds, i.e., $x_0 = x^G \oplus f(ID) \oplus r$ and $x'_0 = x^G \oplus f(ID) \oplus r'$ with $r \neq r'$. We consider x_1^A, x_0^A, and $x'^A_{n_A}$ as the involved elements, where the first two keys are the last keys of the old chain and the last one is the first key of the new chain. Let r_A and r'_A be the random seeds of the old and new key-chain. The following protocol presents a way for Alice to introduce a new key-chain to Bob.

1 : `Assume` A `stores` (x_i^B, r_A, j) `and` B `stores` (x_1^A, r_B, i)
2 : A `sends` B `the new chain start value` $(x_{n_A}^A)_{x_0^A}$
3 : `Do Steps 6 to 8 as in the previous protocol`
4 : `Finally, if all checks were successfully,` A `stores`
$(x_{i-k'}^B, r'_A, n_A, 1)$ `and` B `stores` $(x'^A_n, r_B, i-k', 1)$.

Remarks:

- To avoid a man-in-the-middle attack as for the previous protocol we introduce Step 3.
- As before, keys always have to be checked for correctness, e.g., after Step 5.
- It is wise not to use the anchor x_0 in the protocol. It is better to keep some elements before initializing a new key-chain to avoid a complete loss of the trust relation due to network errors or malicious interceptions.

4 Comparison of the Schemes

In the previous sections we presented three instantiations of the ZCK authentication scheme. Table 1 gives an overview over all three instantiations. The first rows describe the complexity whereas the following rows describe features. Note that the values for the public-key scheme depend on the used scheme. Where applicable, a 'x' means that the scheme provides a feature, a '-' means that it does not, and a 'o' means that the scheme can provide the feature with modifications (at higher computational cost). The symmetric-key scheme is the most efficient one but it requires geographical proximity for a key exchange, or a single trust authority such as in military scenarios or such as for application in a private home. A secure key-exchange could be established by means of public-key schemes. At this point the symmetric-key scheme integrates in the public-key scheme.

Table 1. Overview of ZCK authentication schemes

	Key-Chain	Public-Key	Sym. Key
public-key size (bytes)	24	‡	10†
exchanged messages	3	2	2
exchanged bytes	30	‡	20
computational effort	0	2 PK Op.	0
ZCK authentication	x	x	x♯
message authentication §	x	x	x♯
ZCK non-repudiation	-	x	-
key-exchange	-	x	-
signature	-	x	-
mutual authentication	x	o	o

† size of the shared key
‡ depends on the used public-key scheme
♯ requires secure channel for key-exchange
§ includes message integrity and freshness

That one requires computationally demanding operations that are significantly more expensive than all other schemes but provides ZCK non-repudiation as well as a key-exchange. Our new scheme nearly has the same complexity as the symmetric scheme without its shortcomings. It is not capable of providing ZCK non-repudiation and a key-exchange, but comes with a mutual authentication for free. It is extremely efficient in providing ZCK authentication and message authentication in the view of computational as well as network resources.

Finally we want to give a remark about key distribution. A core benefit of a public-key infrastructure (PKI) compared to some infrastructure using symmetric keys is the key distribution. In a PKI each user has a public/private key pair that enables an entity to communicate with each other entity, whereas a symmetric key infrastructure (SKI) requires a shared key between any entity pair. Thus for n entities a PKI requires n key pairs whereas a SKI requires up to $n(n-1)/2$ shared keys if any entity wants to be able to communicate with any other entity. In our scheme, there are even $n(n-1)$ key-chains, i.e. keys, required if any pair of entities established a relationship. Thus one could conclude that our key-chain scheme has this disadvantage compared to a public-key scheme. However, in our scope of ZCK authentication the facts are different. Clearly there are no central directories of public-keys in a pure pervasive network as we are envisioning it. Furthermore, each user stores foreign entities' keys and binds them to some common past or experience. If an entity does a broadcast of its public key the receivers will not take notice of that key since they are not able to establish a relationship to that key. Each key has to be hand over bound to a service as we said before. Hence in our case, the complexity of a full distribution of all keys is always $n(n-1)$, both in the symmetric and asymmetric case.

5 Conclusions

In this work we presented a basic understanding of authentication for pervasive networks. Our approach is simplistic yet still realistic. It presents the most general case of authentication in pervasive networks which we call zero common-knowledge (ZCK) authentication. We presented three instantiations. The public-key scheme will not suffice our requirements for weak devices since it is not efficient enough. The symmetric-key scheme is most efficient but requires geographical proximity for a key exchange, or a single trust authority. Our new key-chain scheme is a general and still extremely efficient solution. It virtually needs no computation, 30 exchanged bytes in 3 messages, and 24 bytes to store a public key, and it provides mutual authentication for free. Therefore in many applications our new hash-chain based ZCK authentication scheme is very well suited to pervasive computing devices since it provides ZCK authentication and message authentication and requires nearly no computational power, and very low bandwidth and memory storage.

References

[1] A. Bosselaers. Even faster hashing on the Pentium. *Rump session of Eurocrypt'97*, 1997. 81

[2] M. Burrows, M. Abadi, R. Needham. A Logic of Authentication. *DEC SRC Research Report 39*, revised version, 1990. 85

[3] L. Buttyán and J.-P. Hubaux. Nuglets: a Virtual Currency to Stimulate Cooperation in Self-Organized Mobile Ad Hoc Networks. *Technical Report DSC/2001/001*, Swiss Federal Institute of Technology – Lausanne, Department of Communication Systems, 2001. 74

[4] D. Coppersmith and M. Jakobsson. Almost optimal hash sequence traversal. In *Proceedings of the Fourth Conference on Financial Cryptography (FC '02)*, Springer-Verlag, 2002. 82

[5] E. De Win, S. Mister, B. Preneel and M. Wiener. On the performance of signature based on elliptic curves. In *Proceedings of ANTS III*, LNCS 1423, Springer-Verlag, 1998. 81

[6] J. Hoffstein, J. Pipher, J. H. Silverman. NTRU: A Ring-Based Public Key Cryptosystem. In *Proceedings of ANTS III*, LNCS 1423, Springer-Verlag, 1998. 77

[7] B. Lamparter, K. Paul, D. Westhoff. Charging Support for Ad Hoc Stub Networks. In *Elsevier Journal of Computer Communication, Special Issue on 'Internet Pricing and Charging: Algorithms, Technology and Applications'*, Vol. 26, Issue 13, August 2003. 74

[8] A. Menezes, P. C. van Oorschot, and S. A. Vanstone. *Handbook of Applied Cryptography*, CRC Press, 1997. 76, 78

[9] S. Zhong, J. Chen, Y. R. Yang. Sprite: A Simple, Cheat-Proof, Credit-Based System for Mobile Ad-Hoc Networks, to appear in *Proceedings of INFOCOM 2003*, 2003. 74

A Security Proof of Key-Chain Scheme

In the following we give a security proof of our new key-chain authentication scheme. We will first analyze and evaluate the protocol as proposed by the BAN-logic [2]. Then we prove that our authentication scheme is secure against a passive eavesdropper, and that our scheme for message authentication is even secure against an active adversary.

A.1 Evaluation with BAN-Logic

We start the analysis of our protocol with means of the BAN-logic by presenting an *idealized version* of the authentication steps. Message authentication is based on the authentication steps and comes with it. For ease of description we omit the random seeds r_i without loss of generality.

A `stores` (x_i^B, j, u) `and` B `stores` (x_j^A, i, v)
$1:\ A \rightarrow B:\ x_{j-1}^A$
$2:$ `For` $k = 1$ `to` $k' \leftarrow \max\{u, v\}$ `do`
  $2.1:\ B \rightarrow A:\ x_{i-k}^B$
  $2.2:\ A \rightarrow B:\ x_{j-k-1}^A$
  $2.3:$ `If failure then`
   $2.3.1:\ A$ `stores` $(x_i^B, j, \max\{u, k+1\})$
   $2.3.2:\ B$ `stores` $(x_j^B, i, \max\{v, k+1\})$
  `End If`
`End For`
A `stores` $(x_{i-k'}^B, j-k'-1, 1)$ `and` B `stores` $(x_{j-k'-1}^A, i-k', 1)$

We first recall the basic constructs of the BAN-Logic:

- $A|\!\equiv X$: *A believes* X, or A would be entitled to believe X. In particular, the principal A may act as though X is true.
- $A|\!\sim X$: *A once said* X. The principal A at some time sent a message including a statement X. It is not known whether the message was sent long ago or during the current run of the protocol, but it is known that A believed X when he sent the message.
- $\#X$: The formula X is *fresh*, that is, X has not been sent in a message at any time before the current run of the protocol.

Now we can give some *assumptions* which are immediately derived from the stored values:

$$A|\!\equiv (x_i^B, j, u)\ B|\!\equiv (x_j^A, i, v)$$

It easily follows the *conclusions* :

$$A|\!\equiv (x_{i-k'}^B, j-k'-1, 1)\ B|\!\equiv (x_{j-k'-1}^A, i-k', 1) \tag{1}$$

The *objective* of our authentication scheme is to ensure that the last opened key is fresh, i.e., was not send before. Based on the security of a one-way hash function, only the right entity could have opened this key for authentication. We denote this formally as follows:

$$A \models B \mid\sim x^B_{i-k'} \quad A \models \#x^B_{i-k'} \tag{2}$$

$$B \models A \mid\sim x^A_{j-k'-1} \; B \models \#x^A_{j-k'-1} \tag{3}$$

The proof outline below shows the idea of the proof. For easier understanding, we suppress details. First we analyze the execution of a loop. If a key is received by A she can verify by applying the hash function and known key-chain values that B has once sent this key.

$$\forall k \leq k'.\ A \models B \mid\sim x^B_{i-k}\ \forall k \leq k'.\ B \models A \mid\sim x^A_{j-k-1} \tag{4}$$

By construction of the loop, all key values that are larger than u and v, respectively, have to be fresh in a general fashion, i.e., A and B believe that they are fresh. This is ensured by the failure condition in Step 2.3.

$$\forall k \geq v.\ A \models \#x^B_{i-k}\ \forall k \geq u.\ B \models \#x^A_{j-s-1} \tag{5}$$

Since $k' \geq u, v$, our objective (Equations (2) and (3)) easily follows from Equations (4) and (5) for the last iteration of the loop ($k = k'$). It is also clear that the conclusions (Equation (1)) immediately follow from the data seen by A and B. If there is a failure Step 2.3 ensures that the authentication process is not successful, and that Equation (5) still holds. The proof needs only slight adjustment to cover the case where A and B open at least two keys as described in Section 4.

Message authentication is done with the keys x^A_{j-u-1} or x^B_{i-v} respectively. Assuming that the message authentication code is secure, it immediately follows that all authenticated messages were sent by A or B, respectively, and that all messages are fresh.

A.2 Security Proofs

As we said before, our authentication scheme is secure against a passive adversary but not an active one. However, we can show that the message authentication property of our scheme is also secure against active adversaries. More precisely, we will prove that our schemes are as sound as the underlying one-way hash function.

Theorem 1. *Our authentication scheme is as sound as the one-wayness of the underlying hash function against passive adversaries.*

Proof: *Assume the scheme is based on a one-way hash function* h. *As we evaluated before by BAN-Logic an entity has to send a fresh key value to be authenticated. We allow an eavesdropper to listen to arbitrary many values* $x_{i+k}, k \geq 1$, *with* $x_{i+k+1} = h(x_{i+k})$. *The adversary has to present the key* x_i *to be successfully authenticated. Assume the adversary could authenticate successfully, then he could derive the key* x_i *of all the keys* x_{i+k} *with* $k \geq 1$. *Hence we could use the adversary to invert the hash function, which is a contradiction to its one-wayness.*

Finally we prove that our scheme provides provably secure message authentication. We assume that the authentication steps starts after all messages are sent, which can easily be provided by a flag in the authenticated message header. Note that at the point the final message $(m)_{x_i}$ is received it is not already authenticated but hold for authentication. However, this suffices as assumption since an adversary would have to forge the last message before the authentication steps start.

Theorem 2. *Our message authentication scheme is as sound, i.e. as secure against message forgery, as the underlying message authentication code against active adversaries.*

Proof: *Assume that the authentication step starts after all the messages are exchanged, and that the scheme is based on a one-way hash function* h. *We allow the adversary to listen to arbitrary many messages* $(m)_{x_{i+k}}$ *and* $x_{i+k}, k \geq 1$, *with* $x_{i+k+1} = h(x_{i+k})$. *Now assume an adversary can forge a message, i.e., he is capable of producing a valid* $(m)_{x_i}$. *As before the last opened key* x_i *has to be fresh, i.e., it was not sent before by* A *or* B. *But then we could use the adversary to produce a forged message authentication code without knowing the key. This is a contradiction to the security assumptions of the MAC.*

Multiple-Time Signature Schemes against Adaptive Chosen Message Attacks

Josef Pieprzyk[1], Huaxiong Wang[1], and Chaoping Xing[2]

[1] Centre for Advanced Computing – Algorithms and Cryptography
Department of Computing, Macquarie University, Australia
{josef,hwang}@ics.mq.edu.au

[2] Department of Mathematics, National University of Singapore, Singapore
Department of Mathematics, University of Science and Technology of China, China
matxcp@nus.edu.sg

Abstract. Multiple-time signatures are digital signature schemes where the signer is able to sign a predetermined number of messages. They are interesting cryptographic primitives because they allow to solve many important cryptographic problems, and at the same time offer substantial efficiency advantage over ordinary digital signature schemes like RSA. Multiple-time signature schemes have found numerous applications, in ordinary, on-line/off-line, forward-secure signatures, and multicast/stream authentication. We propose a multiple-time signature scheme with very efficient signing and verifying. Our construction is based on a combination of one-way functions and cover-free families, and it is secure against *the adaptive chosen-message attack*.

1 Introduction

One-time signature schemes proposed by Lamport [18] and Rabin [24] were among the earliest signatures based on the idea of committing to secret keys by one-way functions. For more than 25 years, various variants of Lamport and Rabin's schemes have been proposed and investigated by many researchers (see, for example, [3, 5, 6, 13, 20]). In general, digital signatures can be divided into two classes. The first class includes one-time signatures and their variants based on one-way functions. These schemes can be used to sign a predetermined number of messages, we will call them *multiple-time signature schemes* (e.g., one-time signature by Lamport and Rabin). The second class of schemes is based on public-key cryptography and they can be used to sign unlimited number of messages. Examples of this class of schemes include RSA and ElGamal signatures.

Despite the limit imposed on the number of messages signed, multiple-time signatures are very interesting cryptographic primitives as they typically offer more efficient generation and verification of signatures than the schemes based on public-key cryptography. Besides, multiple-time signatures can be constructed based on an arbitrary one-way function without requiring a trapdoor function. Multiple-time signatures have found many applications, for example, in the design of public-key signature schemes [21, 3, 10], on-line/off-line signatures [12],

M. Matsui and R. Zuccherato (Eds.): SAC 2003, LNCS 3006, pp. 88–100, 2004.

digital signatures with forward security properties [1], broadcast authentication protocol [23] and stream-oriented authentication [27], just to mention a few.

All the previous multiple-time signature schemes follow the general idea that the secret key is used as the input to a sequence of one-way functions which generate a sequence of intermediate results and finally the public key. One-wayness of the functions implies that it is infeasible to compute the secret key, or any intermediate result of the computation, from the public key. For example, the idea of the basic scheme of Lamport [18] is very simple: given a one-way function f, one selects two random strings x_0, x_1 as the secret key, and publishes $f(x_0), f(x_1)$ as the public key. Then, a single-bit message $b \in \{0, 1\}$ can be signed by revealing x_b. Bleichenbacher and Maurer in their series of papers [6, 7, 8], developed the general model of these schemes based on the use of "graphs of one-way functions". The security proof under this model has been investigated recently by Hevia and Micciancio [14].

Motivated by the applications of signatures to stream authentication and broadcast authentication, Perrig in [23] proposes a one-time signature called "BiBa", which has the advantages of fast verification and being short signature (perhaps, BiBa has the fastest verification of all previously known one-time signature schemes). The disadvantage of BiBa is, however, the signing time that is longer than in other previous schemes.

Reyzin and Reyzin in [25] proposed a new one-time (r-time) signature, called *HORS* (for Hash to Obtain Random Subset). HORS improves the BiBa scheme with respect to the time overhead necessary for verifying and signing, and reduces the key and signature sizes. This makes HORS the fastest one-time signature scheme available so far. We note that the security of BiBa can be proved in the random-oracle model while the security of HORS relies on the assumption of the existence of one-way functions and the *subset-resilience* .

Our Contribution In this paper, we propose a new multiple-time signature scheme. The scheme has the following advantages with respect to the security: (i) the security relies solely on one-wayness of the functions used to generate commitments (whereas BiBa is based on the assumption of random oracle and HORS is based on one-wayness and subset-resilience); (ii) the scheme achieves security against the r-adaptive chosen-message attack.

The new multiple-time signature is based on a one-way function and uses a combinatorial object, called the *cover-free family* . It is worth pointing out that the cover-free families introduced by Erdös *et al* [11], have also found numerous other application in cryptography and communication [17, 30].

The main advantage of our new scheme is that it achieves the highest level of security against the adaptive chosen-message attack. In comparison to the BiBa and HORS schemes, however, our scheme is slightly worse with respect to the time overhead needed for signing and verifying, and the length of signature. Moreover, the security of our scheme solely relies on the one-wayness of the function used to generate public keys. This assumption is substantially weaker than those required for the BiBa and HORS signatures (BiBa uses the random oracle assumption while the HORS security relies on subset resilience).

First, we give the generic construction from cover-free families and show that the efficiency of the scheme can be measured by the parameters of the underlying cover-free families. We then present three, very efficient, constructions. These constructions apply polynomials, error-correcting codes, and algebraic curves over finite fields. We further extend the scheme to increase the number of messages to sign, using the concepts of *one-way hash chains* .

The paper is organised as follows. In Section 2, we review the generic scheme proposed by Reyzin and Reyzin [25] that was used to construct their HORS and our schemes. In Section 3, we propose the new multiple-time signature scheme, the scheme is generic in the sense that is combines any one-way function with a cover-free family with appropriate parameters. In Section 4, we demonstrate efficiency of ne new proposed scheme by giving three constructions from polynomials over finite fields, error-correct codes and algebraic curves over finite fields. In Section 5 we extend our scheme and show how to increase the number of messages to sign, using the hash chains. We conclude the paper in Section 6.

2 Reyzin-Reyzin Scheme

The HORS scheme proposed by Reyzin and Reyzin [25] is an extension of their simpler scheme in the same paper, which we will call the RR scheme. We start with the description of the RR signature.

The RR scheme Let b, t, k be integers such that $\binom{t}{k} \geq 2^b$. Let T denote the set $\{1, 2, \ldots, t\}$ and $\mathcal{T}_k$ be the family of k-subsets of T. Let S be a one-to-one mapping from $\{0, 1, \ldots, 2^b - 1\}$ to $\mathcal{T}_k$ such that $S(m)$ is the m-th k-element subset of $\mathcal{T}_k$. Let f be a one-way function operating on ℓ-bit strings, for a security parameter ℓ. The scheme works as follows.

Key generation: The secret key is $SK = (s_1, \ldots, s_t)$, where s_i are random ℓ-bit strings. The public key is $PK = (v_1, \ldots, v_t)$, where $v_1 = f(s_1), \ldots, v_t = f(s_t)$.

Signing: To sign a b-bit message m, the message is first interpreted as an integer between 0 and $2^b - 1$, and next the mapping S is used to compute $S(m) = \{i_1, \ldots, i_k\} \in \mathcal{T}_k$. The value $s_{i_1}, \ldots, s_{i_k}$ is the signature of m.

Verifying: To verify a signature $(s'_1, s'_2, \ldots, s'_k)$ on a message m, again the message is interpreted as an integer between 0 and $2^b - 1$, and then the sequence $\{i_1, \ldots, i_k\}$ is recalculated as the m-th k-element subset of $\mathcal{T}_k$. Finally, it is checked if $f(s'_1) = v_{i_1}, \ldots, f(s'_t) = v_{i_t}$ holds.

Note that the Bos and Chaum's scheme [2] is a special case of the above RR scheme in which $k = t/2$. We also note that for $k = t/2$, Stinson [29] (page 217) gave an algorithm that reduces the size of signature to half of the original size of Bos-Chaum scheme.

The security of this scheme relies on one-wayness of f. Indeed, in order to forge a signature for a new message (or apply the adaptive chosen-message attack), the adversary is forced to invert at least one of the $t - k$ values in the public key for which the corresponding part of the secret key has not been revealed.

We look at the efficiency of the scheme. The key generation requires t evaluations of one-way function. The secret key size is $t\ell$ bits, and the public key size is $f_\ell t$ bits, where f_ℓ is the length of the one-way function output on the input length ℓ. The signature is $k\ell$ bit long. The signing algorithm takes as long as the running time of the algorithm for S: the time required to find the m-th k-element subset of a t-element set. In [25], Reyzin and Reyzin gives two algorithms for implementation of the mapping S:

Algorithm 1 is based on the following equation:

$$\binom{t}{k} = \binom{t-1}{k-1} + \binom{t-1}{k},$$

and has the computation cost of $O(tk\log^2 t)$, provided $O(k^2 log^2 t)$ bits extra storage available.

Algorithm 2 is based on the following a slightly more complicated equation:

$$\binom{t}{k} = \sum_{i=0}^{k} \binom{\lceil t/2 \rceil}{i} \binom{\lfloor t/2 \rfloor}{k-i},$$

and has the computation cost of $O(k^2 \log t \log k)$, provided $O(k^2 log^2 t)$ bits extra storage available.

The verifying algorithm of the RR scheme takes the same amount of time as signing, plus k evaluations of the one-way function.

Obviously, the most expensive part of the RR scheme is the computation of the function S. Note that for the function S, it is *impossible* to find any two distinct m_1 and m_2 such that $S(m_2) \subseteq S(m_1)$. To improve efficiency of the RR scheme, Reyzin and Reyzin proposed HORS in which the function S in the RR scheme is replaced by another function H with a weaker property that it is *infeasible* to find two messages, m_1 and m_2 such that $H(m_2) \subseteq H(m_1)$, the function H with such a property is called a *subset-resilient* function. In HORS, a **conjectured** subset-resilient function is constructed from certain cryptographic hash functions.

One drawback with the RR scheme is that each public key/private key can be used to sign a single message. Of course, to sign r messages, one can simply apply the scheme r times independently. This means that the cost of the scheme will be linear in the number of messages r. The question is: can we have a more efficient solution for signing r messages, where $r > 1$? Allowing to sign multiple messages introduces a new attack on the scheme: *the adaptive chosen-messages attack* , where the adversary can choose the message for signature after seeing a collection of messages and their signatures. Unlike the

RR scheme, HORS can be used for signing multiple messages, but its security is based on a much stronger assumption, i.e., *subset-resilient* function. In this work, we propose a new multiple-time signature scheme that provides security against the adaptive chosen-message attack, thus our scheme can be viewed as a generalisation of Bos-Chaum scheme with improved efficiency and of HORS with enhanced security.

3 The Scheme

As we have seen, both the Bos-Chaum scheme and the RR scheme can be used to sign a single message. We intend to generalise their scheme so it can be used for multiple signatures. We observe that the the basic requirement of S is such that for any distinct messages m_1, m_2, we have $S(m_1) \not\subseteq S(m_2)$ in the family of subsets $\mathcal{T}$. If the function S has, however, the property that for any $r+1$ messages $m_1, m_2, \ldots, m_{r+1}$, $S(m_{r+1}) \not\subseteq \cup_{i=1}^{r} S(m_i)$, then the scheme can be used to sign up to r messages. The required property of S can be captured by a well known combinatorial object, called the *cover-free family* introduced by Erdös *et al* [11].

Definition 1. *A set system* $(X, \mathcal{B})$ *with* $X = \{x_1, \ldots, x_t\}$ *and* $\mathcal{B} = \{B_i \subseteq X \mid i = 1, \ldots, n\}$ *is called an* (n, t, r)-cover-free family *(or* (n, t, r)*-CFF for short) if for any subset* $\Delta \subseteq \{1, \ldots, n\}$ *with* $|\Delta| = r$ *and any* $i \notin \Delta$*,*

$$\left| B_i \setminus \bigcup_{j \in \Delta} B_j \right| \geq 1.$$

Our new scheme HORS++ is based on a one-way function and a CFF with appropriate parameters.

HORS++ Scheme Let $(X, \mathcal{B})$ be an (n, t, r)-CFF and let b be an integer such that $2^b \leq n$, where b is the length of the message m to be signed. If the message length is greater than b, then a collision-resistant hash function is used to produce a b-bit digest of m. The signature is generated for the digest.

Assume S is a one-to-one mapping from $\{0,1\}^b$ to $\mathcal{B}$ (Since $n \geq 2^b$ such a mapping S exists). The scheme works as follows.

Key generation: For the given security parameter 1^ℓ, generate t random ℓ-bit numbers s_i and let the secret key be $SK = (s_1, \ldots, s_t)$. Compute the public key as follows: $PK = (v_1, \ldots, v_t)$, where $v_1 = f(s_1), \ldots, v_t = f(s_t)$ and f is a one-way function.

Signing: To sign a message $m \in \{0,1\}^b$, compute $S(m) = \{i_1, \ldots, i_k\} \in \mathcal{B}$. Reveal $(s_{i_1}, s_{i_2}, \ldots, s_{i_k})$ as a signature.

Verifying: To verify a signature $(s'_1, s'_2, \ldots, s'_k)$ on a message m, recompute $S(m) = \{i_1, \ldots, i_k\} \in \mathcal{B}$. Verify that $f(s'_1) = v_{i_1}, \ldots, f(s'_t) = v_{i_t}$.

Security Suppose that the adversary has seen r valid signatures for the message $m_1, \ldots, m_r$ chosen adaptively. In order to forge a signature on a new message, the adversary would have to invert the one-way function f on the value associated to the points of $S(m_{r+1}) \setminus \cup_{i=1}^r S(m_i)$ in the public key. Since $(X, \mathcal{B})$ is an (n,t,r)-CFF, it yields that $|S(m_{r+1}) \setminus \cup_{i=1}^r S(m_i)| \geq 1$. That means that the adversary has to invert the one-way function on at least one value, and so the security of the signature is reduced to the one-wayness of f. Furthermore, it is fairly easy to see that the property of the r-cover freeness guarantees that the scheme is secure against the r-adaptive chosen-message attack.

Efficiency To measure the efficiency of the scheme, we consider two aspects of performance: (i) the time needed for key generation, signing, and verifying; (ii) the length of secret key, public key, and signature. The key generation requires t evaluations of one-way function, the signing takes as long as the running time of the algorithm for S and the verifying algorithm takes the same time as signing, plus at most t evaluations of the one-way function. The size of public and secret key is determined by t and the size of signature is determined by the size of blocks $|B_i|$ in $\mathcal{B}$.

Thus, the performance of the scheme is virtually determined by the parameters of the underlying cover-free family. Without considering the complexity of algorithm S, it is expected that the underlying (n,t,r)-cover-free family has the desired property that for given n and r, the parameter t is as small as possible. Constructions and bounds for (n,t,r)-CFF were studied by numerous authors (see, for example, [11, 17, 30]). It is shown in [30] that for (n,t,r)-CFF with $t \geq 2$, $t \geq c\frac{r^2}{\log r}\log n$ for some constant $c \approx 1/8$. On the other hand, Erdös *et al* [11] showed that for any $n > 0$, there exists an (n,t,r)-CFF with $t = O(r^2 \log n)$ and $|B_i| = O(r \log n)$. Therefore, we obtain the following theorem.

Theorem 1. *Given a one-way function f with the ℓ-bit input and f_ℓ-bit output. There exists a r-time signature scheme secure against the adaptive chosen-message attack with the secret key size $O(r^2 f_\ell \ell)$-bits, public key size $O(r^2 f_\ell^2)$-bits, and with the size of signature $O(r f_\ell \ell)$.*

Proof. Taking $n = 2^{f_\ell}$ and applying the results of cover-free family, the construction will result in a scheme with the desired properties in Theorem 1.

However, Theorem 1 is only of theoretical interest, because it doesn't take into account the time cost of the implementation for the function S, so it is only an existence result. As in the RR scheme, implementation of the function S is the most time consuming part of the system. To make the proposed scheme practical, we have to specify the function S and provide an algorithm for its evaluation.

4 Constructions

In this section we give several constructions of S for HORS++. Observe that in the RR scheme, the parameters t, k of the function S are chosen in order to minimise the expression $\binom{t}{k} - 2^b$ so the size of secret key/public key (corresponding to t) and the size of signature (corresponding to k) is minimal (note that there are some trade-offs between t and k). In other words, the family $\mathcal{T}_k$ of k-subsets of T is minimal such that there is a one-to-one mapping from $\{0, 1, \ldots, 2^b - 1\}$ to $\mathcal{T}_k$. The minimal size of $\mathcal{T}_k$ seems, however, to increase the difficulty (cost) of the implementation of S. To efficiently implement S, we allow the size of the range of S, i.e., the size of the blocks in the cover-free family, to be slightly larger than the minimal value and then we can expect to have an easy implementation for the one-to-one mapping S. We will elaborate this idea in this section, giving several explicit constructions for S.

4.1 Construction of S Based on Polynomials

Consider polynomials of degree less that d over $GF(2^c)$, where $b = dc$. For each such polynomial g, we associate a set

$$B_g = \{(x, g(x)\} \subseteq GF(2^c) \times GF(2^c).$$

Let $X = GF(2^c) \times GF(2^c)$ and

$$\mathcal{B} = \{B_g \mid g \text{ is a polynomial of degree at most } d - 1\}.$$

It is easy to see that $|B_g| = 2^c$ and $|\mathcal{B}| = 2^{dc} = 2^b$. Now if $g_1 \neq g_2$, then $|B_{g_1} \cap B_{g_2}| \leq d - 1$ since $g(x) = g_1(x) - g_2(x)$ is a polynomial of degree $d - 1$ with at most $d-1$ different solution for the equation $g(x) = 0$. We can show that $(X, \mathcal{B})$ is a $(2^b, 2^c, r)$-CFF provided $2^c \geq r(d-1)+1$. Indeed, for any $g, g_1, \ldots, g_r$ of polynomial of degree less than d over $GF(2^c)$, we have

$$\begin{aligned} |B_g \setminus (B_{g_1} \cup \cdots \cup B_{g_r})| &\geq |B_g| - (|B_g \cap B_{g_1}| + \cdots + |B_g \cap B_{g_r}|) \\ &\geq 2^c - r(d-1) \\ &\geq 1. \end{aligned}$$

It should be noted that the above cover-free family construction is not new, it was first given by Erdös in [11] and further extended by many other authors. Our main point is to give the explicit construction of S in an efficient way.

To fulfil the task for signing messages of arbitrary length, we propose using a cryptographic hash function H, for example SHA-1 or RIPEMD and assume that the output of the hash function is of b bits. To sign a message m, we first hash m using H and construct the one-to-one mapping S as follows.

- Split $H(m)$ into d substrings of length c-bit each, where $b = cd$.
- Interpret each c-bit substring as an element in $GF(2^c)$, denote these d elements as $a_0, a_1, \ldots, a_{d-1}$ and construct a polynomial $g_m(x) = a_0 + a_1x + \cdots, a_{d-1}x^{d-1}$.
- We define the mapping S from $\{0, 1\}^b$ to $\mathcal{B}$ as follows,

$$S(H(m)) = \{(\alpha, g_m(\alpha)) \mid \alpha \in GF(2^c)\}.$$

The implementation of S only involves in the direct evaluation of polynomials over the finite field $GF(2^c)$. So both the sign and verification are very fast. The sizes of key and signature are slightly worse than the RR scheme.

4.2 Error-Correcting Code Construction

A more general explicit construction for the mapping S from the above polynomial construction is through error-correcting codes. In fact, the polynomial construction can be seen a special case of the construction from Reed-Solomon codes.

Let Y be an alphabet of q elements. An (N, M, D, q) *code* is a set $\mathcal{C}$ of M vectors in Y^N such that the Hamming distance between any two distinct vectors in $\mathcal{C}$ is at least D.

Consider an (N, M, D, q) code $\mathcal{C}$. We write each codeword as $c_i = (c_{i1}, \dots, c_{iN})$ with $c_{ij} \in Y$, where $1 \leq i \leq M, 1 \leq j \leq N$. Set $X = \{1, \dots, N\} \times Y$ and $\mathcal{B} = \{B_i : 1 \leq i \leq M\}$, where for each $1 \leq i \leq M$ we define $B_i = \{(j, c_{ij}) : 1 \leq j \leq N\}$. It is easy to check that $|X| = Nq$, $|\mathcal{B}| = M$ and $|B_i| = N$. For each pair of i, k, we have $|B_i \cap B_k| = |\{(j, c_{ij}) : 1 \leq j \leq N\} \cap \{(j, c_{kj}) : 1 \leq j \leq N\}| = |\{j : c_{ij} = c_{kj}\}| \leq N - D$.

Using an identical argument to the one applied in the polynomial construction, it is easy to see that $(X, \mathcal{B})$ is (M, Nq, r)-CFF if the condition $r < \frac{N}{N-D}$ holds. We thus obtain that if there is an (N, M, D, q) code, then there exists an (M, Nq, r)-CFF provided $r < \frac{N}{N-D}$.

Note that the above coding construction is explicit. That is, given a code word $c_i \in \mathcal{C}$, it is straightforward to find its corresponding block B_i. Now to explicitly construct the mapping S, we only need to find the one-to-one mapping from $\{H(m) \mid m \text{ in the message space}\}$ to $\mathcal{B}$, which is the same as the encoding algorithm in the error-correcting code, and so can be very efficient. In the following we show how to construct S using a linear error-correcting codes.

Let $\mathcal{C}$ be an (N, q^d, D, q) linear error-correcting code with a d by N generating matrix A. Each code word can be indexed by the elements in $GF(q)^d$, using the encoding algorithm: $(y_1, y_2, \dots, y_N) = (x_1, x_2, \dots, x_d)A, \forall (x_1, x_2, \dots, x_d) \in \mathcal{C}$. For the implementation consideration we may further assume, without loss of generality, that $q = 2^c$ and the hash output of the messages to be signed is of cd bits. The one-to-one mapping S is then constructed as follows.

- Split $H(m)$ into d substrings of length c-bit each, where $b = cd$.
- Interpret each c-bit substrings as an element in $GF(2^c)$, and denote $H(m)$ as a d-vector $(x_1, x_2, \dots, x_d) \in (GF(2^c))^d$.
- Define the one-to-one mapping $S : \{0,1\}^b \to \mathcal{B}$ as follows,

$$\begin{aligned} S(H(m)) &= \{(j, y_j) : 1 \leq j \leq N\} \\ &= \{(1, y_1), (2, y_2), \dots, (N, y_N)\}, \end{aligned}$$

  where $(y_1, y_2, \dots, y_N) = (x_1, x_2, \dots, x_d)A = H(m)A$.

Again, the algorithm for the S implementation is quite efficient as it only involves in the matrix multiplication over a finite field. A further interesting question is to find the good codes satisfying the required conditions that should result in a good performance for the proposed scheme.

4.3 Algebraic Curve Construction

If we apply the code construction of CFFs in Section 4.2 to algebraic geometry codes, we immediately obtain the following result (the reader may refer to [22] for the background on algebraic codes and curves).

Corollary 1. *Let $\mathcal{X}/GF(q)$ be an algebraic curve of genus g with $N+1$ rational points. Then for any integer d with $g \le d < N$, there exists a $(q^{d-g+1}, Nq, \lfloor (N-1)/d \rfloor)$-CFF.*

To study the asymptotic behaviour of CFFs in Corollary 1, we need some notation from algebraic geometry (see [22]). Define

$$A(q) := \limsup_{g(\mathcal{X})\to\infty} \frac{N(\mathcal{X})}{g(\mathcal{X})},$$

where $N(\mathcal{X})$ stands for the number of the rational points of the curve $\mathcal{X}$ defined over $GF(q)$, and $g(\mathcal{X})$ for the genus of $\mathcal{X}$. By [22] (Example 5.4.1), we know that $A(q) = \sqrt{q} - 1$ if q is a square prime power.

Combining Corollary 1 with the definition of $A(q)$, we obtain the following asymptotic result.

Corollary 2. *For a* □*xed r and a square prime power q with $r < \sqrt{q} - 1$, there exists a sequence of CFFs with parameters*

$$(q^{d_i-g+1}, N_i q, r)$$

such that

$$\lim_{i\to\infty} \frac{\log q^{d_i-g+1}}{N_i q} = \frac{\log q}{q} \times (\frac{1}{r} - \frac{1}{\sqrt{q}-1}). \tag{1}$$

Remark Corollary 2 shows that for any fixed r there are infinite families of (n,t,r)-CFF in which $t = O(\log n)$. In fact, the constructions are explicit in the sense that the mapping S can be constructed explicitly as long as the curves have explicit equations.

For the rest of this section, we are going to improve the asymptotic result in Corollary 2.

Let $\mathcal{X}$ be an algebraic curve of genus g with at least $n+g+1$ rational points. By using an identical argument in the proof of [28] (Proposition I.6.10), we can show that there exist $n+1$ rational points $P_\infty, P_1, \ldots, P_n$ such that

$$\mathcal{L}(rdP_\infty - \sum_{i=1}^{n} P_i) = \{0\},$$

if $rd - n \le g - 1$, where $\mathcal{L}(D)$ stands for the Rieman-Roch space for a divisor D, i.e.,

$$\mathcal{L}(D) := \{\text{functions } f : \mathrm{div}(F) + D \ge 0\}.$$

For each $f \in \mathcal{L}(dP_\infty)$, we denote $B_f = \{(P_i, f(P_i)) \mid i = 1, 2, \ldots, n\}$. For any $r+1$ distinct $f_1, f_2, \ldots, f_r, f \in \mathcal{L}(dP_\infty)$, we have $\prod_{i=1}^r (f - f_i) \in \mathcal{L}(dP_\infty)$ as $f \neq f_i$ for any $i = 1, \ldots, r$. On the other hand, Since $\prod_{i=1}^r (f - f_i) \neq 0$, we have $\prod_{i=1}^r (f - f_i) \notin \mathcal{L}(rdP_\infty - \sum_{i=1}^n P_i)$. Therefore, there exists a P_j such that $\prod_{i=1}^r (g - g_i)(P_j) \neq 0$, i.e., $f(P_j) \neq f_i(P_j)$, $\quad \forall i = 1, 2, \ldots, n$, We then conclude $(P_j, f(P_j)) \in B_f$ and $(P_j, f(P_j)) \notin \cup_{i=1}^r B_{f_i}$. That is,

$$|B_f \setminus \cup_{i=1}^r B_{f_i}| \geq 1.$$

This shows that there exists a $(|\mathcal{L}(dP_\infty)|, nq, r)$-CFF or, equivalently, a (q^{d-g+1}, nq, r)-CFF. Moreover, if we let $r = \lfloor g - 1 + n/d \rfloor$ then we obtain a

$$(q^{d-g+1}, nq, \lfloor g - 1 + n/d \rfloor) - \text{CFF}.$$

Thus, we have proved the following corollary.

Corollary 3. *If q is a square prime power, then for a* ﬁ*xed r we obtain a sequence of CFFs with parameters*

$$(q^{d_i-g+1}, N_i q, r)$$

such that

$$\lim_{i\to\infty} \frac{\log q^{d_i-g+1}}{N_i q} = \frac{\log q}{q} \times \left(\frac{1}{r} - (1 - \frac{1}{r})\frac{1}{\sqrt{q} - 2}\right). \qquad (2)$$

Obviously, bound (1) improves bound (2) for $r < \sqrt{q} - 1$.

Remarks

(i) Corollary 2 and 3 shows that the existence bounds of CFFs in [11, 30] can be asymptotically met by the explicit constructions.
(ii) Most previous explicit constructions for CFFs typically apply the tricks from coding constructions of Section 4.2. Thus, Corollary 3 can be also used to improve previous results on cover-free families, for example, the explicit construction from algebraic geometry codes in [17].

5 Extensions

Consider the following question: suppose that r is the maximal value that HORS++ scheme can be used to sign up to r messages, i.e., r is maximal for which the set system $(X, \mathcal{B})$ is a (n, t, r)-cover-free family (for the fixed n and t). What will happen if we want the scheme to sign $r+1$ or more than $r+1$ messages? In this section we will suggest a solution to extend the scheme to increase the number of messages to sign.

One-way hash chains , or simply *one-way chains* , are build on using a one-way function repeatly to a random input, they are a frequently used cryptographic primitive in the design of secure protocols [19, 26, 15]. By a one-way chain we mean a sequence of values $< s_0, s_1, \ldots, s_d >$, where s_d is a value chosen uniformly at random from $\{0,1\}^\ell$, and $s_i = f((s_{i+1})$, where $f : \{0,1\}^* \to \{0,1\}^\ell$ is a hash function or a publicly computable one-way function.

We can employ one-way hash chains to our basic scheme to increase the number of the messages to be signed.

1. Create a sequence of secret keys and their public keys:
$$\begin{array}{cccc} s_{1,d}, & s_{1,d-1}, & \cdots & s_{1,1},\ s_{1,0} \to v_1 \\ s_{2,d}, & s_{2,d-1}, & \cdots & s_{2,1},\ s_{2,0} \to v_2 \\ \vdots & & \vdots & \vdots \\ s_{t,d}, & s_{t,d-1}, & \cdots & s_{t,1},\ s_{t,0} \to v_t \end{array}$$
such that $s_{i,j-1} = f(s_{i,j})$ for $i = 1, \ldots, t$ and $j = 1, \ldots, d$ while $v_i = f(s_{i,0})$ and f is a one-way function. The secret key is $(s_{1,d}, \ldots, s_{t,d})$ and the public key is $(v_1, \ldots, v_t)$.
2. To sign a sequence of messages using HORS++, the signer first uses the first level of secret keys (i.e., $(s_{1,0}, \ldots, s_{t,0})$) to sign the r message and go backwards to the second level of secret keys (i.e., $(s_{1,1}, \ldots, s_{t,1})$ for the next r messages, and so on.
3. Verification of the signatures is exactly the same as HORS++

Using this approach, the scheme can be used to sign up to $(d+1)r$ messages. The properties of one-way chains leave room to improve the time overhead of the signature verification. Note that given an existing authenticated element of a one-way hash chain, it is possible to verify elements later in the sequence of use within the chain, without evaluating all the sequence of the hash function. For example, if $d_{i,j}$ has been used to sign among the $(j+1)$th r messages and its value is revealed, then $d_{i,j+3}$ can be used to sign the message from the $(j+4)$th r messages, by simply computing $f(f(f(s_{i,j+3})))$ and verifying that the resulting value equals $s_{i,j}$, rather than computing $f^{j+4}(s_{i,j+3})$ and verifying its equality with v_i. Recently, Jakobsson [16] and Coppersmith and Jakobsson [9] propose a computation-efficient mechanism for one-way chains, it requires only $O(\log d)$ computation to verify the elements for a one-way chain of d elements, rather than the $O(d)$ computation of the trivial approach. An interesting research problem to ask is whether their techniequs can be incorporated into our scheme to improve the time overhead.

Also, it is worth pointing out that the above extended scheme is not secure against the adaptive chosen-message attacks, but only against the random chosen-message attacks.

6 Conclusion

In this paper, we proposed a multiple-time signature scheme with security against adaptive-chosen-message attacks. Our construction is based on a one-way function and a cover-free family in which the security solely relies on the one-wayness of the one-way function, whereas the efficiency can be measured by the underlying cover-free family. We show several constructions of cover-free families can be used to construct this new multiple-time signature scheme in an effective way.

Acknowledgements

We wish to thank Leonid Reyzin for his insightful comments and suggestions on an earlier draft of the paper. The work is in part supported by Australian Research Council Discovery grants DP0345366 and DP0344444.

References

[1] M. Abdalla and L. Reyzin. A new forward-secure digital signature scheme, *Advances in Cryptology – Asiacrypt'00*, LNCS, **1976**(2000), 116-129. 89

[2] J. N. E. Bos and D. Chaum. Provably unforgeable signature, *Advances in Cryptology – Crypto'92*, LNCS, **740**(1993), 1-14. 90

[3] M. Bellare and S. Micali. How to sign given any trapdoor function. *Journal of Cryptology,* **39**(1992), 214-233. 88

[4] M. Bellare and S. Miner. A forward-secure digital signature scheme, *Advances in Cryptology – Crypto'99*, LNCS, **1666**(1999), 431-448.

[5] M. Ballare and S. G. Neven. Transitive signatures based on factoring and RSA, *Advances in Cryptology – Asiacrypt'02*, LNCS, **2501**(2002), 397-314. 88

[6] D. Bleichenbacher and U. Maurer. Directed acyclic graphs, one-way functions and digital signatures, *Advances in Cryptology – Crypto'94*, LNCS, **839**(1994), 75-82. 88, 89

[7] D. Bleichenbacher and U. Maurer. On the efficiency of one-time digital signatures, *Advances in Cryptology – Asiacrypt'96*, LNCS, **1163**(1996, 145-158. 89

[8] D. Bleichenbacher and U. Maurer. Optimal tree-based one-time digital signature schemes, *STACS'96*, LNCS, **1046**(1996), 363-374. 89

[9] D. Coppersmith and M. Jakobsson. Almost optimal hash sequence traversal, *Financial Cryptography (FC'02)*, LNCS, 2002, to appear. 98

[10] C. Dwork and M. Naor. An efficient existentially unforgeable signature scheme and its applications, *Advances in Cryptology – Crypto'94*, LNCS, **839**(1994), 234-246. 88

[11] P. Erdös, P. Frankl, and Z. Furedi, Families of finite sets in which no set is covered by the union of r others, *Israel Journal of Mathematics*, **51**(1985), 79-89. 89, 92, 93, 94, 97

[12] S. Even, O. Goldreich and S. Micali. On-line/off-line digital signatures, *Journal of Cryptology,* **9**(1996), 35-67. 88

[13] S. Goldwasser, S. Micali and R. Rivest. A digital signature scheme secure against adaptive chosen-message attacks, *SIAM Journal on Computing*, **17**(1988), 281-308. 88

[14] A. Hevia and D. Micciancio. The provable security of graph-based one-time signatures and extensions to algebraic signature schemes. *Advances in Cryptology – Asiacrypt'02*, LNCS, **2501**(2002), 379-396. 89

[15] Y.-C Hu, A. Perrig and D. B. Johnson. Packet Leashes: A defense against wormhole attacks in wireless Ad Hoc Networks, *Proceedings of the 22nd Annual Joint Conference of the IEEE Computer and Communications Societies (INFOCOM 2003)*, 2003, to appear. 97

[16] M. Jakobsson. Fractal hash sequence representation and traversal, *Proceedings of the IEEE International Symposium on Information Theory (ISIT02)*, 2002, 437-444. 98

[17] R. Kumar, S. Rajagopalan and A. Sahai, Coding constructions for blacklist in problems without computational assumptions, *Advances in Cryptology – CRYPTO '99*, LNCS, **1666**(1999), 609-623. 89, 93, 97
[18] L. Lamport. Constructing digital signatures from a one way function, *Technical Report CSL-98*, SRI International, 1979. 88, 89
[19] L. Lamport. Password authentication with insecure communication, *Communication of the ACM*, **24**(11), 1981, 770-772. 97
[20] R. C. Merkle. A digital signature based on a conventional function, *Advances in Cryptology – Crypto'87*, LNCS, **293**(1987), 369-378. 88
[21] R. C. Merkle. A certified digital signature. *Advances in Cryptology – Crypto'87*, LNCS, **435**(1990), 218-238. 88
[22] H. Niederreiter and C. P. Xing, *Rational Points on Curves over Finite Fields: Theory and Applications,* Cambridge University Press, LMS 285, 2001. 96
[23] A. Perrig. The BiBa one-time signature and broadcast authentication. *Eighth ACM Conference on Computer and Communication Security*, ACM, 2001, 28-37. 89
[24] M. O. Rabin. Digitalized signatures, *Foundations of Secure Communication*, Academic Press, 1978, 155-168. 88
[25] L. Reyzin and N Reyzin. Better than BiBa: Short one -time signatures with fast signing and verifying. *Information Security and Privacy (ACISP02)*, LNCS 2384, 144-153. 89, 90, 91
[26] R. Rivest and A. Shamir. PayWord and MicroMint: two simple micro payment schemes, *Tech. Rep.,* MIT Lab. for Computer Science, 1996. 97
[27] P. Rohatgi. A compact and fast hybrid signature scheme for multicast packet authentication, *6th ACM conference on Computer and Communication Security*, 1999, 93-100. 89
[28] H. Stichtenoth. *Algebraic function fields and codes*, Berlin: Springer 1993. 96
[29] D. R. Stinson. Cryptography: theory and practice, CRC Press, 1995. 90
[30] D. R. Stinson, R. Wei and L. Zhu. Some new bounds for cover-free families, *Journal of Combinatorial Theory, A*, **90**(2000), 224-234. 89, 93, 97

Broadcast Enforced Threshold Schemes with Disenrollment

Mingyan Li and Radha Poovendran*

Network Security Laboratory
Department of Electrical Engineering, University of Washington
{myli,radha}@ee.washington.edu

Abstract. Blakley, Blakley, Chan and Massey conjectured a lower bound on the entropy of broadcast messages in threshold schemes with disenrollment. In an effort to examine the conjecture, we identify their original scheme definition has a limitation: a coalition of participants can reconstruct all shared secrets without broadcast from the dealer, and hence render the dealer no control over disenrollment. We introduce a constraint that delays this lack of control of the dealer over disenrollment. We also establish the lower bounds on the entropy of broadcast messages in such a model. We demonstrate the need for new models by presenting a construction under an open problem.

Keywords: secret sharing, threshold schemes with disenrollment, entropy

1 Introduction

A (t, n) threshold scheme is a technique to split a secret among a group of n participants in such a way that any subset of t or more participants can reconstruct the shared secret by pooling the information they have, while any subset of participants of cardinality less than t is unable to recover the secret [2, 15]. The information held by a participant is called a *share*, which is distributed securely by a trusted third party, called *dealer*, to the participant on initialization. Threshold schemes find important applications in cryptography and security, such as secure distributed storage of a master key, secure file sharing, and threshold signature [16].

Threshold schemes were first introduced by Shamir [15] and Blakley [2] and were generalized to secret sharing schemes, which allow reconstruction of a shared secret among a more general combination of subsets of participants. An excellent survey on secret sharing can be found in [16], and a bibliography is provided online in [17].

There are scenarios in which the share of a participant is stolen or is disclosed deliberately by the malicious participant. Then, for security reasons, the share

* This research is funded in part by NSF grant ANI-0093187 and ARO grant DAAD 190210242.

M. Matsui and R. Zuccherato (Eds.): SAC 2003, LNCS 3006, pp. 101–116, 2004.

has to be assumed to have become public knowledge, and the effective threshold among the group is reduced by 1, because any $t-1$ shares from the group plus the disclosed share suffice to reconstruct the secret. It is preferable that the same level of security, i.e., the same threshold size t, be preserved even if shares are disclosed. This may not present a problem if secure channel is available all the time, since the dealer can choose a new shared secret, construct a $(t, n-1)$ threshold scheme, and deliver new shares securely to the remaining participants. However, an expensive secure channel is normally set up only to distribute initial shares and is no longer available after initialization. An alternative is to use public broadcast by the dealer. The problem of *maintaining the threshold via only broadcast* in case of share disclosure or loss was considered by Blakley, Blakley, Chan and Massey in [3], and the solutions were called *threshold schemes with disenrollment capability*. Blakley *et al.* formally defined *threshold schemes with L-fold disenrollment capability* as the schemes that have the capability of disenrolling L participants successively, one at a time, without reducing the threshold. In the model of a threshold scheme with disenrollment capability [3], it is assumed that no secure channel is available after initialization between the dealer and each participant or between participants, and a new secret is chosen to be shared among the group after each disenrollment. The scheme is different from a proactive secret sharing scheme [9], in which a long-term secret is protected against gradual break in by refreshing the share of each participant periodically using public key cryptosystems.

Share size and broadcast size are used to characterize a threshold scheme with disenrollment. While small share size may lead to low storage requirement, it reduces the search space of an adversary. Broadcast size indicates communication cost, and a broadcast message of smaller size is less likely to be corrupted during transmission when compared with a longer message. In [3], Blakley *et al.* established a lower bound on the size of shares in a threshold scheme with L-fold disenrollment capability and conjectured a lower bound on the size of public broadcast. Barwick *et al.* confirmed a revised version of the lower bound on the broadcast size in [1].

Our Contribution: We show that the model of a threshold scheme with disenrollment capability originally defined in [3] and also used in [1] can lead to *the disenrollment not under the control of the dealer*. We illustrate this point by studying a scheme in which a coalition of $t+i$ participants can recover the shared secret $K_0, ..., K_i$ before the ith disenrollment, without requiring any broadcast from the dealer. In order to resolve the problem, we propose a broadcast enforced model of threshold schemes with disenrollment by adding one condition to the original scheme definition to ensure public broadcast from the dealer is necessary in the reconstruction of the current shared secret. Although Barwick *et al.* [1] stated that they do not constrain $t+i$ participants from constructing the shared secret K_i in advance, they also noted that if it is a potential problem, then a stronger model is necessary. Our broadcast enforced model can be viewed as the first step in seek of such a stronger model, and our model prevents the collusion of *any number* of participants from recovering new shared secrets without a broadcast message from the dealer. We establish lower bounds on broadcast messages in the new model. We also note that inherent limitation of the original disenrollment model by showing that even with our condition, the dealer can only delay the lack of control under user collusion. We discuss this problem in Section 5 and present examples showing the need for new directions.

Other related work on threshold schemes with disenrollment includes [4, 6, 8, 12, 13, 18]. In [12], disenrollment of untrustworthy participants was discussed for general secret sharing schemes, but no analytical study on the bounds of share size or broadcast size was provided. Blundo *et al.* [4] addressed a more general problem of enabling participants of different sets to reconstruct different secrets at different times via insecure public channel, and established lower bounds on share size. However, they did not investigate the lower bound on the broadcast size for a threshold scheme with disenrollment. Charnes *et al.* [6] presented a computationally secure threshold scheme with disenrollment using the hardness of discrete logarithm. In [8], secure channels between participants were employed to refresh valid participants with new shares in order to recover new secrets. A scheme was proposed to realize disenrollment without changing shares in [18], but was later shown to be flawed in [13].

This paper is organized as follows. In Section 2, we review the definition of threshold schemes with disenrollment capability [3] and previous results on the lower bounds of share size [3] and broadcast size [1]. In Section 3, we show by one example that the original definition of threshold scheme with disenrollment potentially can render the dealer no control over disenrollment process. To fix the problem, we propose to add one broadcast enforcement term to the definition. In Section 4, we derive lower bounds on the size of broadcast messages in the model with the new property added. We finally conclude the paper with our contributions and one open problem in Section 5.

2 Preliminaries

In this section, we review the definitions of a threshold scheme and a threshold scheme with disenrollment in an information-theoretic approach, and summarize the results of previous study on the bounds of share size and broadcast size. For clarity of presentation, we list the notations used in this paper in Table 1.

2.1 Threshold Schemes

A (t, n) threshold scheme is a protocol to divide a secret into n shares so that the knowledge of at least t shares allow full reconstruction of the secret [2, 15]. Let K be the shared secret that is a random variable that takes values from space $\mathcal{K}$, and S be a share that is a random variable that takes values from space $\mathcal{S}$. Let S_j be the share held by participant j, for $j \in N = \{1, .., n\}$.

Definition 1. *A (t, n) threshold scheme is a sharing of a secret K among n participants so that*

Table 1. Notation

$H(\cdot)$	Shannon Entropy [7]
$I(\cdot)$	Mutual Information [7]
t	threshold
n	total number of participants
L	maximum allowable number of disenrollments
N	set of all the indices of n participants, i.e., $N = \{1, ..., n\}$
i	index for update stages
j	index for participants
S_j	share held by participant j
K_i	secret to be shared at stage i
P_i	broadcast message at stage i
d_i	index of the disenrolled participant at stage i
D_i	set of indices of all disenrolled participants up to stage i, i.e., $D_i = \{d_1, ..., d_i\}$
v_l	index of valid participants with a dummy counting index l
$S_j^{(i)}$	subshare of participant j corresponding to the shared secret K_i
R	random string used to hide a shared secret or a share
$X_{a:b}$	set $\{X_a, X_{a+1}, ...X_b\}$ for $a < b$

1. *The secret* K *is recoverable from at least* t *shares. That is, for any set of* k *(*$t \leq k \leq n$*) indices* $\{l_1, l_2, ..., l_k\} \subset \{1, ..., n\}$,

$$H(K|S_{l_1:l_k}) = 0 \qquad \textit{for} \qquad t \leq k \leq n \tag{1}$$

2. *The secret* K *remains uncertain with the knowledge of* $(t-1)$ *or less shares. That is,*

$$H(K|S_{l_1:l_k}) > 0 \qquad \textit{for} \qquad k < t. \tag{2}$$

A (t, n) threshold scheme is called *perfect* in an information theoretic sense if $(t-1)$ or fewer shares reveal absolutely no information on the secret K. That is,

$$H(K|S_{l_1:l_k}) = H(K) \quad \text{for} \quad k < t. \tag{3}$$

It has been shown in [14] that a necessary condition to have a perfect threshold scheme is

$$H(S_j) \geq H(K) \qquad \text{for} \qquad j = 1, ..., n. \tag{4}$$

A perfect threshold scheme is called *ideal* if share size achieves the lower bound in (4), i.e., $H(S_j) = H(K)$ for all j.

2.2 Threshold Schemes with Disenrollment

A threshold scheme with L-fold disenrollment capability deals with the problem of maintaining a threshold via insecure broadcast channel when disenrolling an untrustworthy participant at each of L successive updates [3]. Let $i = 1, ..., L$

be the indices of update stages. At the ith update, let K_i denote the shared secret, P_i denote the broadcast message, $d_i \in N \backslash D_{i-1}$ be the index of the disenrolled participant at the ith update, and $v_l \in N \backslash D_i$ for $l = 1, ..., n-i$ be an index of one of the remaining valid participants.

Definition 2. *A (t,n) threshold scheme with L-fold disenrollment capability with $n - L \geq t$ is a collection of shares S_j for $j = 1, ..., n$; shared secrets K_i for $i = 0, ..., L$; and public broadcast messages P_i for $i = 1, ..., L$, that satis□es the following conditions:*

1. *Initially (i.e., at stage $i = 0$), the scheme is a (t,n) threshold scheme that shares the secret K_0 among n participants.*
2. *At stage i for $i = 1, ..., L$, one additional share S_{d_i} is disenrolled, any set of k $(t \leq k \leq n-i)$ valid shares $S_{v_1}, ..., S_{v_k}$ plus the broadcast messages $P_1, ..., P_i$ can reconstruct the new secret K_i, i.e.,*

$$H(K_i|S_{v_1:v_k}, P_{1:i}) = 0 \quad \textit{for} \quad t \leq k \leq n-i. \tag{5}$$

3. *At stage i for $i = 1, ..., L$, given broadcast information $P_1, ..., P_i$ and all disenrolled shares $S_{d_1}, ..., S_{d_i}$, the shared secret K_i is not solvable if the number of valid shares is less than t. That is,*

$$H(K_i|S_{v_1:v_k}, S_{d_1:d_i}, P_{1:i}) > 0 \quad \textit{for} \quad k < t. \tag{6}$$

A (t,n) threshold scheme with L-fold disenrollment capability is called *perfect* if

$$H(K_i|S_{v_1:v_k}, S_{d_1:d_i}, P_{1:i}) = H(K_i) \quad \text{for} \quad k < t. \tag{7}$$

From Definition 2, it follows that a threshold scheme with disenrollment capability at stage i is equivalent to a $(t, n-i)$ threshold scheme sharing K_i among $n-i$ valid participants. In order to be able to collectively reconstruct K_i, each participant must have a component in his share corresponding to K_i. Note that S_j is a collection of components to reconstruct $K_0, ..., K_L$. Let $S_j^{(i)}$ denote the component in S_j corresponding to K_i, and we call $S_j^{(i)}$ a *subshare* of participant j. The subshare satisfies

$$H(K_i|S_{v_1:v_k}^{(i)}, P_{1:i}) = 0 \quad \text{for} \quad t \leq k \leq n-i. \tag{8}$$

The necessary condition (4) can be extended to subshares as

$$H(S_j^{(i)}) \geq H(K_i) \quad \text{for} \quad j = 1, .., n \quad i = 0, ..., L \tag{9}$$

The share by participant j, S_j, is the union of all its subshares over L disenrollment stages, i.e., $S_j = \{S_j^{(0)}, S_j^{(1)}, ..., S_j^{(L)}\}$. Since the shared secrets K_i's at different stage $i = 0, ..., L$ are independent, the subshares of one participant that are used to recover different secrets are independent in a share size efficient scheme.

2.3 Previous Results on Bounds of Share Size and Broadcast Size

For a threshold scheme with disenrollment capability defined in Definition 2, Blakley *et al.* [3] established a lower bound on the entropy of each share, as stated in Theorem 1.

Theorem 1. *Let $S_{1:n}, P_{1:L}, K_{0:L}$ form a (t,n) perfect threshold scheme with L-fold disenrollment capability and $H(K_i) = m$ for $i = 0, 1, ..., L$. Then,*

$$H(S_j) \geq (L+1)m \qquad \textit{for} \quad j = 1, 2, ..., n. \tag{10}$$

The proof of Theorem 1 provided by Blakley *et al.* is built on their Lemma 5 in [3]. We find that the original proof of the Lemma 5 on page 543 of [3] fails in the last line. A correct proof of their Lemma 5 is presented in Appendix.

A perfect threshold scheme with disenrollment in which each share achieves its lower bound is called *share minimal* [1], i.e.,

$$H(S_j) = (L+1)m, \quad \text{for} \quad j = 1, ..., n \tag{11}$$

where $H(K_i) = m$ for $i = 0, ..., L$.

Blakley *et al.* [3] also proposed a conjecture on the lower bound of the entropy of broadcast. A modified version of the conjecture was proven by Barwick *et al.* in [1]. Theorem 2 summarizes the result of Barwick *et al.* on the entropy of broadcast.

Theorem 2. *Let $S_{1:n}, P_{1:L}, K_{0:L}$ form a (t,n) share minimal perfect threshold scheme with L-fold disenrollment capability satisfying properties (5), (7), and (11), then*

$$\sum_{l=1}^{i} H(P_l) \geq \sum_{l=1}^{i} \min(i, n-i-t+1)m \quad \textit{for} \quad i = 1, ..., L. \tag{12}$$

2.4 Useful Lemmas

In this section, we present some lemmas that will be useful in proving our theorems. Proofs are provided in our technical report [11] but omitted here due to space limit.

Lemma 1. *Let X, Y, Z and W be random variables. Given $H(X|Y,W) = 0$, $H(X|Z,W) = H(X), H(X) = H(Y)$, then $I(Y;Z) = 0$.*

Lemma 2. *Let X, Y and Z be random variables. Given $H(X|Y,Z) = 0, H(X|Z) = H(Y|Z)$, then $H(Y|X,Z) = 0$.*

3 Broadcast Enforced Threshold Scheme with Disenrollment

In this section, we will show Definition 2 in Section 2.2 is not adequate when centralized control from the dealer is required, by examining a scheme that satisfies Definition 2 (originally appeared in [3] as Definition 2) but leaves the dealer no control over disenrollment process.

Let us consider the following scheme.

- Participant j holds the share $S_j = \{S_j^{(0)}, S_j^{(1)}, ..., S_j^{(L)}\}$ after initialization, where subshare $S_j^{(i)}$ corresponds to a share of a $(t+i, n)$ ideal perfect threshold scheme sharing the secret K_i.
- At stage i, the dealer broadcasts $P_i = S_{d_i}$

If $t+i$ participants collaborate by exchanging their shares, then they can decipher $K_0, ..., K_i$ in advance and the disenrollment of an invalidated participant involving the update of K_{i-1} to K_i at stage i is not under the control of the dealer. Therefore, for the dealer to have control at each disenrollment, we should seek a model in which broadcast P_i is necessary in reconstructing the secret K_i, and each disenrollment is not possible without a broadcast message from the dealer.

The scheme presented above satisfies Definition 2 but *requires no broadcast from the dealer if* $t+i$ *participants collude* . In order for the dealer have control over each disenrollment, we suggest adding the following broadcast enforcement term:

$$I(K_i; S_{1:n}, P_{1:i-1}) = 0 \quad \text{for} \quad i = 1, ..., L. \tag{13}$$

Condition (13) states that the mutual information of K_i and all shares S_j for $j = 1...n$ and all previous broadcast message $P_1, ..., P_{i-1}$ is zero. By jointly considering (5) and (13), we note that (13) expresses the importance of broadcast message P_i at stage i: without the message, no information on the new shared secret K_i can be obtained even if all shares S_j and all previous broadcast messages $P_1, ..., P_{i-1}$ are known. Futhermore, by enforcing a broadcast message from the dealer, it allows the dealer the freedom to choose a secret to be shared when disenrolling untrustworthy participants; while in the scheme presented, all the shared secrets are predetermined before distributing shares to participants.

In [1], Barwick *et al.* used the same model defined in (5) and (7) when deriving a lower bound on the entropy of broadcast. However, one of their lemmas, Lemma 2, implies the necessity of broadcast in recovering the shared secret. From now on, we use capitalized **LEMMA** to refer to the lemmas cited from [1] and [3], and **Lemma** or Lemma for our lemmas.

LEMMA 2 in [1] In a $(1, n)$ threshold scheme with L-fold disenrollment capability, let $l_1, ..., l_L$ be distinct elements of $N = \{1, ..., n\}$,

$$H(K_i | S_{l_1:l_i}, K_{0:i-1}) = H(K_i) \qquad \text{for} \qquad i = 1, ..., L. \tag{14}$$

They claim that (14) holds regardless of $S_{l_1:l_i}$ being valid or not. We will show in the following lemma for (14) to hold when at least one of $S_{l_1:l_i}$ is valid, an additional condition that suggests the importance of broadcast message needs to be satisfied.

Lemma 3. *For (14) to hold for the case in which at least one of the shares* $\{S_{l_1}, ..., S_{l_i}\}$ *is valid at stage* i*, a necessary and sucient condition is*

$$I(K_i; P_{1:i}|S_{l_1:l_i}, K_{0:i-1}) = H(K_i). \tag{15}$$

Proof. Necessity:

Since at least one of the shares $S_{l_1:l_i}$ is valid, for a $(1, n)$ threshold scheme, we have $H(K_i|S_{l_1:l_i}, P_{1:i}) = 0$ from (5), and therefore $H(K_i|S_{l_1:l_i}, P_{1:i}, K_{0:i-1}) = 0$.

$$\begin{aligned} H(K_i) &= H(K_i|S_{l_1:l_i}, K_{0:i-1}) \\ &= H(K_i|S_{l_1:l_i}, K_{0:i-1}) - H(K_i|S_{l_1:l_i}, P_{1:i}, K_{0:i-1}) \\ &= I(K_i; P_{1:i}|S_{l_1:l_i}, K_{0:i-1}) \end{aligned} \tag{16}$$

Sufficiency:

$$\begin{aligned} H(K_i) &= I(K_i; P_{1:i}|S_{l_1:l_i}, K_{0:i-1}) \\ &= H(K_i|S_{l_1:l_i}, K_{0:i-1}) - H(K_i|S_{l_1:l_i}, P_{1:i}, K_{0:i-1}) \\ &\leq H(K_i|S_{l_1:l_i}, K_{0:i-1}) \end{aligned}$$

Since $H(K_i) \geq H(K_i|S_{l_1:l_i}, K_{0:i-1})$, we have $H(K_i) = H(K_i|S_{l_1:l_i}, K_{0:i-1})$.

Condition (15) emphasizes the importance of broadcast messages, i.e., even with the knowledge of enough valid shares and all previous shared secrets, *broadcast messages up to now are needed in deciphering the current shared secret* . In fact, the proposed term (13) is a sufficient condition for **LEMMA 2** as shown in the following lemma.

Lemma 4. *Condition (13) is a sucient condition for (14), where* $l_i \in N$ *for* $i = 1, ..., L$.

Proof.

$$\begin{aligned} H(K_i|S_{l_1:l_i}, K_{0:i-1}) &\geq H(K_i|S_{1:n}, K_{0:i-1}, P_{0:i-1}) \\ &= H(K_i|S_{1:n}, P_{0:i-1}) + I(K_i; K_{0:i-1}|S_{1:n}, P_{0:i-1}) \\ &= H(K_i|S_{1:n}, P_{0:i-1}) + H(K_{0:i-1}|S_{1:n}, P_{0:i-1}) \\ &\quad -H(K_{0:i-1}|S_{1:n}, P_{0:i-1}, K_i) \\ &\overset{(a)}{=} H(K_i|S_{1:n}, P_{0:i-1}) \\ &= H(K_i) - I(K_i; S_{1:n}, P_{0:i-1}) \\ &\overset{(b)}{=} H(K_i) \end{aligned}$$

Equation (a) holds because of (5), and Equation (b) holds due to the broadcast enforcement term (13). Since $H(K_i|S_{l_1:l_i}, K_{0:i-1}) \leq H(K_i)$, it follows that (14) holds.

We will address how the broadcast enforcement term (13) affects the previously derived lower bounds on the broadcast size. Adding (13) to the definition only puts additional constraints on requiring broadcast at each disenrollment, and hence it will not affect the lower bounds on the share size.

4 Lower Bounds on Broadcast Entropy

In this section, we will establish lower bounds on the entropy of broadcast in a perfect threshold scheme with disenrollment satisfying (5), (7) and (13). We consider two cases, (i) no constraints on the share size; (ii) the size of each share achieves its lower bound (11), i.e., share minimal perfect threshold schemes with disenrollment.

Theorem 3. *Let $S_{1:n}, P_{1:L}, K_{0:L}$ form a perfect (t, n) threshold scheme with L-fold disenrollment capability satisfying properties (5), (7) and (13), and $H(K_i) = m$ for $i = 0, 1, ..., L$, then*

$$H(P_i) \geq H(K_i) = m \qquad i = 1, ..., L. \tag{17}$$

Proof.

$$\begin{aligned} H(P_i) &\overset{(a)}{\geq} H(P_i|S_{1:n}, P_{1:i-1}) \\ &\overset{(b)}{\geq} H(P_i|S_{1:n}, P_{1:i-1}) - H(P_i|S_{1:n}, P_{1:i-1}, K_i) \\ &\overset{(c)}{=} I(P_i; K_i|S_{1:n}, P_{1:i-1}) \\ &\overset{(d)}{=} H(K_i|S_{1:n}, P_{1:i-1}) - H(K_i|S_{1:n}, P_{1:i-1}, P_i) \\ &\overset{(e)}{=} H(K_i|S_{1:n}, P_{1:i-1}) \\ &\overset{(f)}{=} H(K_i) - I(K_i; S_{1:n}, P_{1:i-1}) \\ &\overset{(g)}{=} H(K_i) = m. \end{aligned}$$

Inequality (a) comes from the fact that conditioning reduces entropy. Inequality (b) holds due to non-negativity of entropy. Equations (c), (d) and (f) follow from the definition of mutual information. The second term of (d) is zero due to (5), so Equation (e) follows. Equation (g) holds from property (13).

Theorem 3 is the main result of our previous paper [10]. It shows that the entropy of a broadcast message is at least that of the shared secret for all updates. The same result is mentioned in [1] for the original threshold scheme with disenrollment model, but without rigorous proof.

Now we consider share minimal perfect threshold schemes with L-fold disenrollment, i.e., the case in which $H(S_j) = (L+1)m$ for $j = 1, .., n$. It will be proven for this case,

$$H(P_i) \geq \min(i+1, n-i-t+1)m \qquad i = 1, ..., L. \tag{18}$$

if all previous broadcast P_l's sastify lower bounds $\min(l+1, n-l-t+1)m$ for $l = 1, .., i-1$.

In order to establish the bound (18), we first prove some lemmas as follows.

Lemma 5. *In a $(1,n)$ share minimal perfect threshold scheme with L-fold disenrollment, any $i+1$ subshares $S_{l_1}^{(i)}, ..., S_{l_{i+1}}^{(i)}$ are independent.*

Proof. A $(1,n)$ perfect threshold scheme with disenrollment satisfies the following two equations in terms of subshares.

$$H(K_i | S_{v_1}^{(i)}, P_{1:i}) = 0 \tag{19}$$

$$H(K_i | S_{d_1:d_i}^{(i)}, P_{1:i}) = H(K_i) = m \tag{20}$$

where (19) is from (8) and (20) is obtained from (7).

Substituting $X = K_i$, $Y = S_{v_1}^{(i)}$, $Z = S_{d_1:d_i}^{(i)}$ and $W = P_{1:i}$ into Lemma 1, we have from (19), (20) and $H(S_j^{(i)}) = H(K_i)$ that

$$I(S_{v_1}^{(i)}; S_{d_1}^{(i)}, ..., S_{d_i}^{(i)}) = 0. \tag{21}$$

We now prove the independence between subshares by contradiction.

Assume there is one set of $i+1$ subshares $\{S_{l_1}^{(i)}, ..., S_{l_{i+1}}^{(i)}\}$ that are not independent. That is, in $\{S_{l_1}^{(i)}, ..., S_{l_{i+1}}^{(i)}\}$, there is at least one subshare that is not independent of the rest i subshares. Without loss of generality, we assume that $S_{l_1}^{(i)}$ is dependent on $S_{l_2}^{(i)}, ..., S_{l_{i+1}}^{(i)}$

$$I(S_{l_1}^{(i)}; S_{l_2}^{(i)}, ..., S_{l_{i+1}}^{(i)}) > 0 \tag{22}$$

However, if $\{l_2, ..., l_{i+1}\} = \{d_1, .., d_i\}$, these subshares fail to form a valid $(1,n)$ threshold scheme with L-fold disenrollment since (22) contradicts with (21).

In order to be able to disenroll any i participants while maintaining the threshold at stage i, any $i+1$ subshares $S_{l_1}^{(i)}, ..., S_{l_{i+1}}^{(i)}$ have to be independent.

Lemma 6. *In a $(1,n)$ share minimal perfect threshold scheme with L-fold disenrollment,*

$$H(P_i) \geq \min(i+1, n-i)m, \tag{23}$$

if all previous broadcast messages meet their lower bound on entropy, i.e., $H(P_w) = \min(w+1, n-w)$ for $w = 0, ..., i-1$. When $H(P_i)$ achieves its minimum at $(i+1, n-i)m$, then $I(P_i; S_j^{(l)}) = 0$ for $l = i+1, ..., L$ and $j = 1, ..., n$, i.e., P_i is independent of subshares used to reconstruct future shared secrets.

Proof. We will first show $H(S^{(i)}_{v_1:v_u}|K_i, P_{1:i}) = 0$, where $u = \min(i+1, n-i)$. Let S_{v_l} denote one valid share in the set $\{S_{v_1}, ..., S_{v_k}\}$.

$$\begin{aligned} H(S^{(i)}_{v_l}|P_{1:i}) &\geq I(S^{(i)}_{v_l}; K_i|P_{1:i}) \\ &= H(K_i|S^{(i)}_{v_l}) - H(K_i|S^{(i)}_{v_l}, P_{1:i}) \\ &= H(K_i) = m \end{aligned}$$

Since $H(S^{(i)}_{v_l}|P_{1:i}) \leq H(S^{(i)}_{v_l}) = m$, we have $H(S_{v_l}|P_{1:i}) = m$. From (20), we obtain $H(K_i|P_{1:i}) = H(K_i) = m$. By letting $X = K_i$, $Y = S^{(i)}_{v_l}$ and $Z = P_{1:i}$ and applying Lemma 2, we obtain $H(S^{(i)}_{v_l}|K_i, P_{1:i}) = 0$.

$$0 \leq H(S^{(i)}_{v_1:v_u}|K_i, P_{1:i}) \leq \sum_{l=1}^{u} H(S^{(i)}_{v_l}|K_i, P_{1:i}) = 0 \tag{24}$$

Therefore, $H(S^{(i)}_{v_1:v_u}|K_i, P_{1:i}) = 0$.

Then we will prove the lower bound of $H(P_i)$ by induction.

At stage $k = 1$, there are $n-1$ valid participants, $u = \min(k+1, n-k) = \min(2, n-1)$

$$\begin{aligned} H(P_1) &\geq I(P_i; S^{(1)}_{v_1:v_u}|K_1) \\ &= H(S^{(1)}_{v_1:v_u}|K_1) - H(S^{(1)}_{v_1:v_u}|K_1, P_1) \\ &\overset{(a)}{=} H(S^{(1)}_{v_1:v_u}, K_1) - H(K_1) \\ &= H(S^{(1)}_{v_1:v_u}) + H(K_1|S^{(1)}_{v_1:v_u}) - H(K_1) \\ &\overset{(b)}{=} H(S^{(1)}_{v_1:v_u}) + H(K_1) - H(K_1) \\ &\overset{(c)}{=} \sum_{l=1}^{u} H(S^{(1)}_{v_l}) \\ &= um = \min(2, n-1)m \end{aligned}$$

Equation (a) holds because $H(S^{(1)}_{v_1:v_u}|K_1, P_1) = 0$. Without P_1, $H(K_1|S^{(1)}_{v_1:v_u}) = H(K_1)$ and hence (b) holds. Equation (c) holds due to the independence of $S^{(i)}_{v_l}$'s for $l = 1, ..., i+1$ shown in Lemma 5.

Now we show if $H(P_1) = \min(2, n-1)m$, then $I(P_1; S^{(l)}_j) = 0$ for $l = 2, ..., L$ and $j = 1, ..., n$.

$$\begin{aligned} H(P_1) &\geq I(P_1; S^{(l)}_j, K_1, S^{(1)}_{v_1:v_u}) \\ &\geq I(P_1; S^{(l)}_j) + I(P_i; S^{(1)}_{v_1:v_u}|K_1, S^{(l)}_j) \\ &= I(P_1; S^{(l)}_j) + H(S^{(1)}_{v_1:v_u}|K_1, S^{(l)}_j) - H(S^{(1)}_{v_1:v_u}|K_1, P_1, S^{(l)}_j) \\ &= I(P_1; S^{(l)}_j) + H(S^{(1)}_{v_1:v_u}|S^{(l)}_j) + H(K_1|S^{(l)}_j) - H(K_1) \\ &\overset{(d)}{=} I(P_1; S^{(l)}_j) + H(S^{(1)}_{v_1:v_u}) \\ &= I(P_1; S^{(l)}_j) + \min(2, n-1)m \end{aligned}$$

Equation (d) holds because of independence of subshares of one participant and condition (13). From $H(P_1) \geq I(P_1; S_j^{(l)}) + \min(2, n-1)m$, a necessary condition for $H(P_1)$ to achieve its lower bound is $I(P_1; S_j^{(l)}) = 0$ for $l = 2, ..., L$.

Assume Lemma 6 is true for stage $k = i - 1$, i.e., $H(P_{i-1}) \geq \min(i, n - i + 1)m$ if all previous broadcast messages reach their lower bound on entropy, i.e., $H(P_w) = \min(w + 1, n - w)$ for $w = 0, ..., i - 2$, and $I(P_{i-1}; S_j^{(l)}) = 0$ for $l = i, ..., L$.

When $k = i$, $u = \min(k + 1, n - i) = \min(i + 1, n - i)$

$$
\begin{aligned}
H(P_i) &\geq I(P_i; S_{v_1:v_u}^{(i)} | K_i, P_{1:i-1}) \\
&= H(S_{v_1:v_u}^{(i)} | K_i, P_{1:i-1}) - H(S_{v_1:v_u}^{(i)} | K_i, P_{1:i}) \\
&= H(S_{v_1:v_u}^{(i)}, K_i | P_{1:i-1}) - H(K_i | P_{1:i-1}) \\
&= H(S_{v_1:v_u}^{(i)} | P_{1:i-1}) + H(K_i | S_{v_1:v_u}^{(i)}, P_{1:i-1}) - H(K_i | P_{1:i-1}) \\
&= H(S_{v_1:v_u}^{(i)} | P_{1:i-1}) + H(K_i) - H(K_i) \\
&= H(S_{v_1:v_u}^{(i)} | P_{1:i-1}) \\
&= H(S_{v_1:v_u}^{(i)}) \\
&= um = \min(i + 1, n - i)m
\end{aligned}
$$

The proof of $I(P_i; S_j^{(l)}) = 0$ for $l = i + 1, ..., L$ when $H(P_i)$ achieves its minimum at $(i + 1, n - i)m$ is similar to the base case ($k = 1$) and thus is omitted.

Now we can establish the lower bound of $H(P_i)$ for a share minimal perfect threshold scheme with disenrollment.

Theorem 4. *Let $S_{1:n}, P_{1:L}, K_{0:L}$ form a share minimal perfect (t, n) threshold scheme with L-fold disenrollment capability satisfying properties (5), (7), (11) and (13), then*

$$
H(P_i) \geq \min(i + 1, n - i - t + 1)m \qquad i = 1, ..., L. \tag{25}
$$

if all previous broadcast messages P_l's for $l = 1, .., i - 1$ achieve their lower bounds as $\min(l + 1, n - l - t + 1)m$.

Proof. As shown in [1], if $\{S_{1:n}, P_{1:L}, K_{0:L}\}$ form a (t, n) share minimal perfect threshold scheme with L-fold disenrollment capability, then

$$
\{S_{l_1:l_{n-t+1}} | S_{v_1:v_{t-1}}, P_{1:L} | S_{v_1:v_{t-1}}, K_{0:L} | S_{v_1:v_{t-1}}\}
$$

form a $(1, n-t+1)$ share minimal perfect threshold scheme with L-fold disenrollment capability, where $|$ denote conditioned on and $\{l_1, ..., l_{n-t+1}\} = N \backslash \{v_1, ..., v_{t-1}\}$. For the $(1, n - t + 1)$ threshold scheme with disenrollment, we have $H(P_i | S_{v_1:v_k}) \geq \min(i+1, n-t+1-i)m$ from Lemma 6, if all previous broadcast messages meet their lower bound on their entropy.

Since $H(P_i) \geq H(P_i|S_{v_1:v_k})$, then

$$H(P_i) \geq \min(i+1, n-t+1-i)m.$$

Therefore, Theorem 4 holds.

Comparing Theorem 2 and Theorem 4, we notice that when adding (13) into the definition to ensure the dealer to have control over disenrollment, the lower bound on broadcast size is different from (12) as expected.

5 Conclusions and an Open Problem

During the process of examining the conjecture on the lower bound of broadcast entropy [3], we found that the original model of threshold schemes with disenrollment [3] is inadequate to ensure the dealer of the control over each disenrollment. We presented a broadcast enforced model which ensures that the public broadcast from the dealer is required for disenrollment, by adding an additional term to the original definition. We showed that in related previous work to establish a lower bound on broadcast size [1], though the original model is used, the validity of **LEMMA 2** does require the broadcast from the dealer. In the new model, the coalition of any number of participants is unable to reconstruct the shared secret K_i before the ith disenrollment stage. We also derived lower bounds on the entropy of broadcast messages in such a model, which are refined from the bound obtained in [1].

There is an open problem with threshold scheme with disenrollment. Consider the following schemes.

Scheme 1

- Participant j has share $S_j = \{S_j^{(0)}, S_j^{(1)}, ..., S_j^{(L)}\}$, where $S_j^{(i)}$ is a share of a $(t+i, n)$ ideal perfect threshold scheme sharing $K_i + R_i$ with R_i being a string of length m chosen by the dealer.
- At update i, the dealer broadcasts $P_i = \{R_i, S_{d_1}^{(i)}, ..., S_{d_i}^{(i)}\}$.

This scheme satisfies (5), (7) and (13) and achieves the lower bound (25) in Theorem 4 if $L < \lfloor \frac{n-t}{2} \rfloor$. But if $t+L$ participants collude in advance, then they can construct $K_0+R_0, ..., K_L+R_L$. Under this construction, dealer looses the ability to disenroll a participant of its choice. The best the dealer can do is to delay broadcast and hence the reconstruction of the shared secrets! Therefore, there are schemes that satisfy all the properties including the broadcast requirement and still not allow the dealer to have control over the disenrollment process. At first it might appear as the problem with the setup of the original model in [3].

We now present a model attributed to Brickell and Stinson in [3] and show that it is possible to construct schemes that allow the dealer to have full control over the disenrollment with (5), (7) and (13).

Scheme 2 Brickell-Stinson's Scheme [3]

- The share held by participant j is $S_j = \{S_j^{(0)}, R_j^{(1)}, ..., R_j^{(L)}\}$ where $R_j^{(i)}$ denotes encryption/decryption key of m bits for participant j at disenrollment stage i.
- At stage i, the dealer updates only valid participants with new shares, so $P_i = \{S_{v1}^{(i)} + R_{v1}^{(i)}, ..., S_{v_{n-i}}^{(i)} + R_{v_{n-i}}^{(i)}\}$.

This scheme prevents a coalition of any number of participants from obtaining any shared secrets as long as the dealer does not update those colluded participants with new shares.

From the above observation, we note that the predistribution of multiple shares can lead to unwanted key exposure. Finding alternate models that allow more control to the dealer remains an open problem.

Acknowledgements

The authors wish to thank InTae Kang for insightful discussion and useful comments that significantly improve the presentation of this paper. They also wish to thank anonymous reviewers for their helpful suggestion.

References

[1] S. G .Barwick, W. A. Jackson, K. M. Martin, and P .R. Wild, Size of broadcast in threshold schemes with disenrollment, *ACISP 2002, Lecture Notes in Computer Science 2384*, pp. 71-88, 2002. 102, 103, 106, 107, 109, 112, 113

[2] G. R. Blakley, Safeguarding cryptographic keys, *Proceedings AFIPS 1979 National Computer Conference*, pp. 313-317, 1979. 101, 103

[3] B. Blakley, G. R. Blakley, A. H. Chan, and J. Massey, Threshold schemes with disenrollment, *Advances in Cryptology – CRYPTO'92, E. F. Brickell, ed., Lecture Notes in Computer Science* vol. 740, pp. 540-548, 1993. 102, 103, 104, 106, 107, 113, 114, 115

[4] C. Blundo, A. Cresti, A. De Santis, U. Vaccaro, Fully dynamic secret sharing schemes, *Advances in Cryptology – CRYPTO '93, D. R. Stinson, ed., Lecture Notes in Computer Science*, vol. 773, pp. 110-125, 1994. 103

[5] C. Blundo, A note on dynamic threshold schemes, *Information Processing Letters*, vol. 55, pp. 189-193, August 1995.

[6] C. Charnes, J. Pieprzyk, and R. Safavi-Naini, Conditionally secure secret sharing schemes with disenrollment capability, *Proceedings of the 2nd ACM Conference on Computer and communications security*, pp. 89-95, 1994. 103

[7] T. M. Cover and J. A. Thomas, *Elements of Information Theory*, John Wiley & Sons Inc, 1991. 104

[8] Y. Desmedt and S. Jajodia, Redistributing secret shares to new access structures and its application, *Technical Report ISSE TR-97-01*, George Mason University, July 1997 103

[9] A. Herzberg, S. Jarecki, H. Krawczyk, M. Yung, Proactive secret sharing or: How to cope with perpetual leakage, *Advances in Cryptology – CRYPTO'95, Lecture Notes in Computer Science* vol. 963, Springer Verlag, pp. 339–352, 1995. 102

[10] M. Li and R. Poovendran, A note on threshold schemes with disenrollment, *Proceedings of 37th annual Conference on Information Sciences and Systems (CISS)*, John Hopkins University, March 2003. 109

[11] M. Li and R. Poovendran, Broadcast Enforced Threshold Schemes with Disenrollment, *UWEETR-2003-0014*, University of Washington, 2003 106

[12] K. M. Martin, Untrustworthy participants in perfect secret sharing schemes, *Cryptography and Coding III*, M. J. Ganley, ed., Oxford University Press, pp. 255-264, 1993. 103

[13] K. M. Martin, J. Nakahara Jr, Weakness of protocols for updating the parameters of an established threshold scheme, *IEE Proceedings Computers and Digital Techniques*, Vol. 148, No. 1, pp. 45-48, 2001. 103

[14] E. D. Karnin, J. W. Greene and M. E. Hellman, On secret sharing systems, *IEEE Transactions on Information Theory*, vol. 29, pp. 35-41, 1983. 104

[15] A. Shamir, How to share a secret, *Communications of the ACM*, vol. 22, pp. 612-613, 1979 101, 103

[16] D. R. Stinson, An explication of shared secret sharing schemes, *Design, Codes and Cryptography*, vol. 2, pp. 357-390, 1992 101

[17] D. R. Stinson, R. Wei, Bibliography on secret sharing schemes, [Online], Available: `http://cacr.math.uwaterloo.ca/ dstinson/ssbib.html.` 101

[18] U. Tamura, M. Tada, and E. Okamoto, Update of access structure in Shamire's (k, n) threshold scheme, *Proceedings of the 1999 symposium on cryptography and information security*, pp. 26-29, January 1999. 103

Appendix

In the appendix, we present a correct proof to **LEMMA 5** in [3].

LEMMA 5 in [3] Let $S_{1:n}, P_{1:L}, K_{0:L}$ be a perfect (t, n) threshold scheme with L-fold disenrollment capability,

$$I(K_i; S_{v_1:v_k}, S_{d_1:d_i}, P_{1:i}, K_{0:i}) = 0 \quad \text{for} \quad k \leq t-1. \tag{26}$$

In the original proof of **LEMMA 5** in [3], they made use of (5), which holds for only $k \geq t$.

Proof. Let us consider $k = t-1$ first. At stage $w = 0, ..., i-1$, $t-1$ valid shares plus S_{d_i} which was also valid at stage w suffice to recover K_w, i.e.,

$$H(K_w | S_{v_1:v_{t-1}}, S_{d_1:d_i}, P_{1:i}) = 0 \quad \text{for} \quad w = 0, ..., i-1, \tag{27}$$

which is a necessary condition for (7).

$$\begin{aligned}
&I(K_i; S_{v_1:v_{t-1}}, S_{d_1:d_i}, P_{1:i}, K_{0:i-1}) \\
&= I(K_i; S_{v_1:v_{t-1}}, S_{d_1:d_i}, P_{1:i}) + \sum_{w=0}^{i-1} I(K_i; K_w | S_{v_1:v_{t-1}}, S_{d_1:d_i}, P_{1:i}, K_{0:w-1}) \\
&= H(K_i) - H(K_i | S_{v_1:v_{t-1}}, S_{d_1:d_i}, P_{1:i})
\end{aligned}$$

$$+\sum_{w=0}^{i-1}[H(K_w|S_{v_1:v_{t-1}}, S_{d_1:d_i}, P_{1:i}, K_{0:w-1})$$
$$-H(K_w|S_{v_1:v_{t-1}}, S_{d_1:d_i}, P_{1:i}, K_{0:w-1}, K_i)] \stackrel{(a)}{=} 0.$$

Equation (a) holds because of (7) and (27). For $k < t-1$,

$$0 \le I(K_i; S_{v_1:v_k}, S_{d_1:d_i}, P_{1:i}, K_{0:i-1}) \le I(K_i; S_{v_1:v_{t-1}}, S_{d_1:d_i}, P_{1:i}, K_{0:i-1}) = 0$$

Therefore, **LEMMA 5** holds for $k \le t-1$.

A New Meet-in-the-Middle Attack on the IDEA Block Cipher

Hüseyin Demirci[1], Ali Aydın Selçuk[2], and Erkan Türe[3]

[1] Tübitak UEKAE, 41470 Gebze, Kocaeli, Turkey
huseyind@uekae.tubitak.gov.tr
[2] Department of Computer Engineering
Bilkent University, 06800, Ankara, Turkey
selcuk@cs.bilkent.edu.tr
[3] Marmara University, Faculty of Engineering
Göztepe Campus, 81040 Kuyubaşı, İstanbul, Turkey
ture@eng.marmara.edu.tr

Abstract. In this paper we introduce a novel meet-in-the-middle attack on the IDEA block cipher. The attack consists of a precomputation and an elimination phase. The attack reduces the number of required plaintexts significantly for 4 and 4.5 rounds, and, to the best of our knowledge, it is the first attack on the 5-round IDEA.

1 Introduction

Events that happen with probability one (or zero) have been widely used in cryptanalysis. The cryptanalysis of Enigma is a historical example whereas the impossible differential attacks [1, 2] on the block ciphers Skipjack, IDEA, Khufu, and Khafre are more recent examples. In this paper, we present a new attack on the reduced-round versions of IDEA which generalizes the idea of "an event with probability one" to "a set of candidate events with probability one". The attack utilizes a set of events among which one is sure to happen. Key candidates are checked against this criterion, and those which do not realize any of the events are eliminated as wrong candidates.

The attack presented in this paper is a chosen-plaintext, meet-in-the-middle attack consisting of two phases: First there is a precomputation phase where a "sieving set" whose elements are the possible outcomes of a specific event is generated. Then there is the key elimination phase where the candidate keys which do not produce any of the events in the sieving set are eliminated. This attack can be considered as a combination of the Chaum-Evertse's meet in the middle approach [5] and the multi-set approach by Gilbert and Minier [9] to form collisions in the inner rounds of the cipher.

This paper proceeds as follows: In Section 2, we briefly describe the IDEA block cipher. In Section 3, we prove certain properties of IDEA essential to our attack. In Section 4, we develop the attack, beginning with three rounds and gradually advancing it to five rounds. In Section 5, we analyze the complexity of the attack. Finally in Section 6, we conclude the paper with possible directions for future research.

M. Matsui and R. Zuccherato (Eds.): SAC 2003, LNCS 3006, pp. 117–129, 2004.

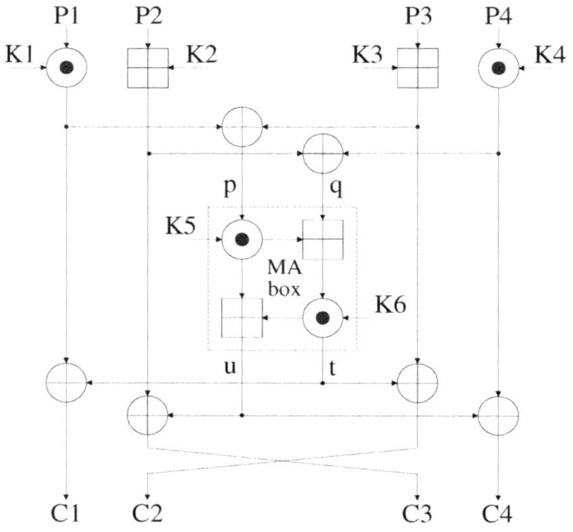

Fig. 1. One round of IDEA

1.1 Notation

Throughout this paper we will be using the following notation: We use the symbol $\oplus$ for the bitwise exclusive-or (XOR) and for the modular addition, for both 8- and 16-bit variables; carry($x \quad y$) denotes the overflow carry bit from the modular addition of x and y. We denote the plaintext by (P_1, P_2, P_3, P_4) and the ciphertext by (C_1, C_2, C_3, C_4) where the separated parts show the 16-bit subblocks. The round numbers are denoted by superscripts. As an example, $C_1^{(2)}$ denotes the first subblock of the ciphertext after 2 rounds. In the i-th round we use six round-key subblocks where $K_1^{(i)}, K_2^{(i)}, K_3^{(i)}, K_4^{(i)}$ are the round key subblocks used in the transformation part and $K_5^{(i)}, K_6^{(i)}$ are the round key subblocks used in the MA-box. The first input of the MA-box $(P_1 \odot K_1) \oplus (P_3 \quad K_3)$ is denoted by p and the second input $(P_2 \quad K_2) \oplus (P_4 \odot K_4)$ is denoted by q. The output words of the MA-box are denoted by t and u, respectively.

The least significant and the most significant bits of a variable x are denoted by lsb(x) and msb(x), respectively. The least significant eight bits of x are denoted by $\text{lsb}_8(x)$ and the most significant eight bits by $\text{msb}_8(x)$. The notation $(x|y)$ denotes the concatenation of x and y. Finally, $K_j^{(i)}[m \dots n]$ means that the round key subblock $K_j^{(i)}$ is being considered which uses the bits from m to n of the master key.

2 IDEA Block Cipher

The IDEA block cipher is a modified version of the PES block cipher [12, 13]. The main design concept is to mix operations from different algebraic groups. There are three different "incompatible" group operations on 16-bit subblocks: XOR, modular addition, and the "IDEA multiplication", which is a modified multiplication modulo $2^{16}+1$ where 0 is interpreted as 2^{16} to make the multiplication invertible. If the result of the multiplication is 2^{16}, it is converted to 0.

IDEA admits a 128-bit key, has a 64-bit block size and consists of 8.5 rounds. The data is processed in 16-bit words. The round function consists of two parts: First there is a transformation part where each plaintext subblock is operated with a round key subblock, i.e.,

$$T : (P_1, P_2, P_3, P_4) \rightarrow (P_1 \odot K_1, P_2 \quad K_2, P_3 \quad K_3, P_4 \odot K_4).$$

In the second part, there is a multiplication-addition structure which is called the MA-box. MA-box uses two 16-bit inputs $p = (P_1 \odot K_1) \oplus (P_3 \quad K_3)$ and $q = (P_2 \quad K_2) \oplus (P_4 \odot K_4)$ to produce two 16-bit output words t and u. The output words are calculated as $t = ((p \odot K_5) \quad q) \odot K_6$ and $u = (p \odot K_5) \quad t$. Then the outputs of the MA-box are XORed with the outputs of the transformation part, and the two middle subblocks are exchanged. After one round, the ciphertext is of the form (C_1, C_2, C_3, C_4), where

$$\begin{aligned} C_1 &= (P_1 \odot K_1) \oplus t, \\ C_2 &= (P_3 \quad K_3) \oplus t, \\ C_3 &= (P_2 \quad K_2) \oplus u, \\ C_4 &= (P_4 \odot K_4) \oplus u. \end{aligned}$$

The encryption algorithm consists of eight full rounds and an extra transformation part. The key schedule processes the 128-bit master key into an array of 16-bit round subkeys by cyclic shifts; 16 bits are taken from this array each time a new round key subblock is required in the algorithm.

Decryption is done using the same algorithm, but with different round key subblocks. In the transformation part the multiplicative and additive inverses of the round key subblocks are used, whereas the same key subblocks are used in the MA-Box since it is an involution.

Following its proposal, various cryptanalytic attacks have been applied on reduced-round versions of IDEA. These include differential [14, 6], linear [11], differential-linear and truncated-differential [4], impossible differential [2], and square [15, 8] attack techniques. There are also related key attacks [15], and some classes of weak keys have been observed [7, 10, 3].

Currently the most effective attack on IDEA is due to Biham, Biryukov, and Shamir [2]. They used the impossible differential technique to sieve the key space for 3.5, 4, and 4.5 rounds. The 4.5-round attack requires the encryption of 2^{64} plaintexts which is the whole space.

Table 1 gives a comparison of the performance of the attacks described in this paper and of the attacks developed earlier.

Table 1. Plaintext, memory, and time complexity of chosen plaintext attacks on reduced-round versions of IDEA

Paper	Rounds	Type	No. of C. Plaintexts	Memory Memory	Total Complexity
[14]	2	differential	2^{10}	2^{32}	2^{42}
[8]	2	square-like	23	small	2^{64}
[14]	2.5	differential	2^{10}	2^{96}	2^{106}
[6]	2.5	differential	2^{10}		2^{32}
[15]	2.5	square	3.2^{16}	small	$3.2^{63} + 2^{48}$
[8]	2.5	square-like	55	small	2^{81}
[4]	3	differential-linear	2^{29}	2^{16}	2^{44}
[8]	3	square-like	71	small	2^{71}
This paper	3	collision	2^{33}	2^{58}	2^{64}
[4]	3.5	truncated-differential	2^{56}	2^{32}	2^{67}
[2]	3.5	impossible-differential	$2^{38.5}$	2^{48}	2^{53}
[8]	3.5	square-like	2^{34}	small	2^{82}
[8]	3.5	square-like	103	small	2^{103}
This paper	3.5	collision	2^{24}	2^{58}	2^{73}
[2]	4	impossible-differential	2^{37}	2^{48}	2^{70}
[8]	4	square-like	2^{34}	small	2^{114}
This paper	4	collision	2^{24}	2^{58}	2^{89}
[2]	4.5	impossible-differential	2^{64}	2^{32}	2^{112}
This paper	4.5	collision	2^{24}	2^{58}	2^{121}
This paper	5	collision	2^{24}	2^{58}	2^{126}

3 Some Properties of IDEA

In this section, we present some observations on the IDEA block cipher. Theorem 1 states the main result of this section which plays a key role in our attack:

Theorem 1. *Let* $\mathcal{P} = \{(P_1, P_2, P_3, P_4)\}$ *be a set of 256 plaintexts such that*

- P_1, P_3, $\mathrm{lsb}_8(P_2)$ *are fixed,*
- $\mathrm{msb}_8(P_2)$ *takes all possible values over* $0, 1, \ldots, 255$,
- P_4 *varies according to* P_2 *such that* $(P_2 \quad K_2^{(1)}) \oplus (P_4 \odot K_4^{(1)})$ *is fixed.*

For $p^{(2)}$ *denoting the first input of the MA-box in the second round, the following properties will hold in the encryption of the set* $\mathcal{P}$:

- $\mathrm{lsb}_8(p^{(2)})$ *is fixed,*
- $\mathrm{msb}_8(p^{(2)})$ *takes all possible values over* $0, 1, \ldots, 255$.

Moreover, the $p^{(2)}$ *values, when ordered according to their plaintexts'* $\mathrm{msb}_8(P_2)$*, beginning with* $\mathrm{msb}_8(P_2) = 0$*, will be of the form*

$$(y_0|z), (y_1|z), \ldots, (y_{255}|z)$$

for some fixed, 8-bit z*, and* $y_i = (((i \quad a) \oplus b) \quad c) \oplus d$*, for* $0 \leq i \leq 255$ *and fixed, 8-bit* a*,* b*,* c*,* d*.*

Proof. Consider the input of the second round $(P_1^{(2)}, P_2^{(2)}, P_3^{(2)}, P_4^{(2)})$. We have

$$p^{(2)} = (P_1^{(2)} \odot K_1^{(2)}) \oplus (P_3^{(2)} \quad K_3^{(2)}),$$

where

$$P_1^{(2)} = (P_1 \odot K_1^{(1)}) \oplus t^{(1)},$$
$$P_3^{(2)} = (P_2 \quad K_2^{(1)}) \oplus u^{(1)}.$$

Therefore,

$$p^{(2)} = (((P_1 \odot K_1^{(1)}) \oplus t^{(1)}) \odot K_1^{(2)}) \oplus (((P_2 \quad K_2^{(1)}) \oplus u^{(1)}) \quad K_3^{(2)})$$

where the only variable term is $\text{msb}_8(P_2)$. If we order the $p^{(2)}$ values of the 256 plaintexts in $\mathcal{P}$ according to their plaintexts' $\text{msb}_8(P_2)$, beginning with $\text{msb}_8(P_2) = 0$, the resulting sequence will be $(y_0|z), (y_1|z), \ldots, (y_{255}|z)$, where

$$z = \text{lsb}_8(((P_1 \odot K_1^{(1)}) \oplus t^{(1)}) \odot K_1^{(2)}) \oplus \text{lsb}_8(((P_2 \quad K_2^{(1)}) \oplus u^{(1)}) \quad K_3^{(2)})$$

which is a constant over the set $\mathcal{P}$, and

$$y_i = (((i \quad a) \oplus b) \quad c) \oplus d$$

where the only variable term is i and

$$a = \text{msb}_8(K_2^{(1)}) + \text{carry}(\text{lsb}_8(P_2) \quad \text{lsb}_8(K_2^{(1)}))$$
$$b = \text{msb}_8(u^{(1)})$$
$$c = \text{msb}_8(K_3^{(2)}) + \text{carry}(((\text{lsb}_8(P_2) \quad \text{lsb}_8(K_2^{(1)})) \oplus \text{lsb}_8(u^{(1)})) \quad \text{lsb}_8(K_3^{(2)}))$$
$$d = \text{msb}_8(((P_1 \odot K_1^{(1)}) \oplus t^{(1)}) \odot K_1^{(2)})$$

are constants over $\mathcal{P}$. □

Theorem 2. *In the encryption of the plaintext set* $\mathcal{P}$ *defined in Theorem 1,* $\text{lsb}(K_5^{(2)} \odot p^{(2)})$ *equals either* $\text{lsb}(C_2^{(2)} \oplus C_3^{(2)})$ *or* $\text{lsb}(C_2^{(2)} \oplus C_3^{(2)}) \oplus 1$ *for all the 256 plaintexts in* $\mathcal{P}$.

Proof. Note that

$$C_2^{(2)} = (((P_2 \quad K_2^{(1)}) \oplus u^{(1)}) \quad K_3^{(2)}) \oplus t^{(2)},$$
$$C_3^{(2)} = (((P_3 \quad K_3^{(1)}) \oplus t^{(1)}) \quad K_2^{(2)}) \oplus u^{(2)}.$$

Since the least significant bits of P_2, P_3, $t^{(1)}$, $u^{(1)}$ are all fixed, we have either $\text{lsb}(C_2^{(2)} \oplus C_3^{(2)}) = \text{lsb}(t^{(2)} \oplus u^{(2)})$ or $\text{lsb}(C_2^{(2)} \oplus C_3^{(2)}) = \text{lsb}(t^{(2)} \oplus u^{(2)}) \oplus 1$ for all plaintexts in $\mathcal{P}$. By Lemma 1 of [8], which we also state below, $\text{lsb}(K_5^{(2)} \odot p^{(2)}) = \text{lsb}(t^{(2)} \oplus u^{(2)})$ and the result follows. □

Now observe that in the middle subblocks C_2 and C_3, only addition and XOR operations are used between the ciphertext, the round key, and the MA-box output subblocks. Since the only difference between addition and XOR is the carry bit, some information can leak from these variables. It seems that the variable $\text{lsb}(C_2 \oplus C_3)$ is a candidate for being the Achilles' heel for the IDEA encryption algorithm.

Recall the following lemma from [8]:

Lemma 1. $\text{lsb}(t \oplus u) = \text{lsb}(p \odot K_5)$.

Proof. Since $u = t \quad (p \odot K_5)$ and the least significant bit XOR is the same as addition, we have $\text{lsb}(t \oplus u) = \text{lsb}(p \odot K_5)$. □

This property is useful for us because one bit of information related to the MA-box outputs can be obtained using only one input and one round key subblocks. This simple observation will play an important role in the attack.

Corollary 1. $\text{lsb}(C_2^{(i)} \oplus C_3^{(i)} \oplus (K_5^{(i)} \odot (C_1^{(i)} \oplus C_2^{(i)}))) = \text{lsb}(C_2^{(i-1)} \oplus C_3^{(i-1)} \oplus K_2^{(i)} \oplus K_3^{(i)})$.

Proof. By Lemma 1 we have $\text{lsb}(t_i \oplus u_i) = \text{lsb}(K_5^{(i)} \odot (C_1^{(i)} \oplus C_2^{(i)}))$. Consider the middle blocks $C_2^{(i)} = (C_3^{(i-1)} \quad K_3^{(i)}) \oplus t_i$ and $C_3^{(i)} = (C_2^{(i-1)} \quad K_2^{(i)}) \oplus u_i$. Since the least significant bit addition is equivalent to XOR, we have the result. □

By this corollary, we are able to relate the variables $\text{lsb}(C_2^{(i-1)} \oplus C_3^{(i-1)})$ and $\text{lsb}(C_2^{(i)} \oplus C_3^{(i)})$ of two successive rounds. We can generalize this idea. For two successive rounds, we have the following result:

Corollary 2. $\text{lsb}(C_2^{(i)} \oplus C_3^{(i)} \oplus (K_5^{(i)} \odot (C_1^{(i)} \oplus C_2^{(i)})) \oplus (K_5^{(i-1)} \odot (C_1^{(i-1)} \oplus C_2^{(i-1)}))) = \text{lsb}(C_2^{(i-2)} \oplus C_3^{(i-2)} \oplus K_2^{(i)} \oplus K_3^{(i)} \oplus K_2^{(i-1)} \oplus K_3^{(i-1)})$.

Proof. Consider the middle blocks in the i-th round,

$$C_2^{(i)} = (((C_2^{(i-2)} \quad K_2^{(i-1)}) \oplus u_{i-1}) \quad K_3^{(i)}) \oplus t_i,$$
$$C_3^{(i)} = (((C_3^{(i-2)} \quad K_3^{(i-1)}) \oplus t_{i-1}) \quad K_2^{(i)}) \oplus u_i.$$

By Lemma 1, we have $\text{lsb}(t_{i-1} \oplus u_{i-1}) = K_5^{(i-1)} \odot (C_1^{(i-1)} \oplus C_2^{(i-1)})$ and $\text{lsb}(t_i \oplus u_i) = K_5^{(i)} \odot (C_1^{(i)} \oplus C_2^{(i)})$. Then the result follows. □

We will use Corollary 2 to get information about the second round variables using the output of the fourth round.

4 Attack on IDEA

In this section we describe our attack on IDEA using the results of the previous section. We first give a general outline, then describe the attack in detail.

4.1 The General Outline of the Attack

The first phase of the attack is a precomputation where all possible orderings of $\mathrm{lsb}(C_2^{(2)} \oplus C_3^{(2)})$ are calculated for some particular sequence of plaintexts. Second there is a partial decryption phase. In this phase, different key candidates are tried to partially decrypt some particularly selected plaintext-ciphertext set. When the right key is tried, it is certain that there will be a match between the precomputed set and the set obtained by the partial decryption. Otherwise, it is extremely unlikely that such a match will occur by chance, and this criterion can be used safely to sieve out the wrong key candidates.

The construction of the precomputed set and the set used for the partial decryption is based on the results of the previous section. For a given set of 256 plaintexts as in the hypothesis of Theorem 1, we know, from Theorem 2, that in the second round, the variable $\mathrm{lsb}(C_2^{(2)} \oplus C_3^{(2)})$ can be guessed from the variable $\mathrm{lsb}(K_5^{(2)} \odot p^{(2)})$. Also from Theorem 1, we know that, when ordered according to $\mathrm{msb}_8(P_2)$, the sequence of the 256 $p^{(2)}$s must have the form

$$(y_0|z), (y_1|z), \ldots, (y_{255}|z).$$

In the precomputation phase of the attack, we compute and store all possible 256-bit sequences of the form

$$\mathrm{lsb}(k \odot (y_0|z)), \mathrm{lsb}(k \odot (y_1|z)), \ldots, \mathrm{lsb}(k \odot (y_{255}|z)),$$

for y_i, z as in Theorem 1 and for all possible k values.

On the other hand, we use Corollary 1 or Corollary 2 to make a partial decryption from the end of the cipher to get the bit sequence $\mathrm{lsb}(C_2^{(2)} \oplus C_3^{(2)})$, trying all possible values exhaustively for the key subblocks involved in this partial decryption. If the bit sequence obtained from such a decryption exists in the precomputed set, the key subblocks used for that decryption are a possible candidate. Otherwise, that key can be eliminated. This procedure is repeated until a single[1] candidate key remains.

4.2 Attack on 3-Round IDEA

To attack on 3 rounds of IDEA, we proceed through the following steps:

1. Prepare the *sieving set* , a set of 256-bit strings, as follows:

$$S = \{f(a, b, c, d, z, K_5^{(2)}) : \ 0 \le a, b, c, d, z < 2^8, \ \ \le K_5^{(2)} < 2^{16}\}$$

   where f is a function, mapping a given $(a, b, c, d, z, K_5^{(2)})$ to a 256-bit string, defined bitwise by

$$f(a, b, c, d, z, K_5^{(2)})[i] = \mathrm{lsb}(K_5^{(2)} \odot (y_i|z))$$

   for $y_i = (((i \quad a) \oplus b) \quad c) \oplus d$, $0 \le i \le 255$.

[1] Actually, two candidates will remain: The right key and a "conjugate".

2. Take a set of 2^{24} plaintexts $\mathcal{P} = \{(P_1, P_2, P_3, P_4)\}$ such that P_1, P_3 and the least significant 8 bits of P_2 are fixed, and P_4 and the most significant 8 bits of P_2 take each of the possible 2^{24} values once. Encrypt this set with 3 rounds of IDEA.
3. For each value of $K_2^{(1)}$ and $K_4^{(1)}$, take 256 plaintexts from the set $\mathcal{P}$ such that the most significant 8 bits of P_2 change from 0 to 255 and $(P_2 \quad K_2^{(1)}) \oplus (P_4 \odot K_4^{(1)})$ are constant. For each candidate value for $K_5^{(3)}$, calculate

$$\mathrm{lsb}(C_2^{(3)} \oplus C_3^{(3)} \oplus (K_5^{(3)} \odot (C_1^{(3)} \oplus C_2^{(3)}))) \tag{1}$$

over the selected 256 plaintexts.
At this point, if the key value $K_5^{(3)}$ in (1) is correct, the computed $\mathrm{lsb}(C_2^{(3)} \oplus C_3^{(3)} \oplus (K_5^{(3)} \odot (C_1^{(3)} \oplus C_2^{(3)})))$s are all equal either to $\mathrm{lsb}(C_2^{(2)} \oplus C_3^{(2)})$ or to $\mathrm{lsb}(C_2^{(2)} \oplus C_3^{(2)}) \oplus 1$, by Corollary 1.
4. Sort the 256 bits obtained in Step 3 according to the plaintexts' $\mathrm{msb}_8(P_2)$, for $0 \leq \mathrm{msb}_8(P_2) \leq 255$.
Recall that, by Theorem 2, $\mathrm{lsb}(C_2^{(2)} \oplus C_3^{(2)})$ equals either $\mathrm{lsb}(K_5^{(2)} \odot p^{(2)})$ or $\mathrm{lsb}(K_5^{(2)} \odot p^{(2)}) \oplus 1$, and that the $p^{(2)}$ values, when sorted according to $\mathrm{msb}_8(P_2)$, follow the pattern given in Theorem 1. Therefore, the sorted 256-bit sequence that corresponds to the right choice of $(K_2^{(1)}, K_4^{(1)}, K_5^{(3)})$ must be present in the sieving set S.
Check whether the sorted 256-bit sequence is present in S. If not, eliminate the corresponding key combination $(K_2^{(1)}, K_4^{(1)}, K_5^{(3)})$.[2]
5. If more than two key combinations survive, return to Step 2 and change the plaintext set $\mathcal{P}$. Continue until only two combinations remain.

The attack finds the right combination of $K_2^{(1)}$, $K_4^{(1)}$, and $K_5^{(3)}$ explicitly. The correct value of $K_5^{(2)}$ is found implicitly from the element of the sieving set S that matches the remaining 256-bit string.

4.3 Attacking the Decryption Operation

A chosen-ciphertext version of this attack is also possible which can be applied on the inverse cipher (i.e., the decryption operation) to obtain additional subblocks of the key. When the number of rounds is not an integer (i.e., 2.5, 3.5, etc.) the attack on the inverse cipher would proceed exactly like the one on the normal cipher, using the decryption subkeys instead of the encryption ones. When the

[2] As mentioned above, when the correct key values are tried, we will have $\mathrm{lsb}(C_2^{(3)} \oplus C_3^{(3)} \oplus (K_5^{(3)} \odot (C_1^{(3)} \oplus C_2^{(3)})))$ equal to either $\mathrm{lsb}(K_5^{(2)} \odot p^{(2)})$ or $\mathrm{lsb}(K_5^{(2)} \odot p^{(2)}) \oplus 1$. For the former, the 256-bit sequence obviously has to be in S. If the latter is the case, note that $\mathrm{lsb}(K_5^{(2)} \odot p^{(2)}) \oplus 1 = \mathrm{lsb}(k' \odot p^{(2)})$, for all $p^{(2)}$, where $k' = 2^{16} + 1 - K_5^{(2)}$. Hence, the sequence again has to be present in S. (This also implies a conjugate key triple $(K_2^{(1)}, K_4^{(1)}, K_5^{(3)\prime})$ that exists along with the right triple $(K_2^{(1)}, K_4^{(1)}, K_5^{(3)})$ which cannot be eliminated by sieving in S.)

number of rounds is an integer, a slight modification would be needed to deal with the effect of the MA-box half-round at the end. We suggest the following method on the 3-round IDEA, which makes use of the fact that the MA-box operation is an involution. The idea here is to obtain a set of 2^{24} chosen ciphertexts for the output of the first 2.5 rounds of the cipher that conforms to the plaintext specification of Theorem 1. Once such a set is obtained, the attack can be applied to the first 2.5 rounds of the cipher from the reverse direction.

We first generate a set C' of 2^{24} 64-bit blocks in the form of the set $\mathcal{P}$ in Step 2 of the original attack. Then we try the possible values for $K_5^{(3)}$ and $K_6^{(3)}$ and encrypt C' with an MA-box half-round using the guessed $K_5^{(3)}$ and $K_6^{(3)}$ values. Then we decrypt this set with the 3-round IDEA. If the values tried for $K_5^{(3)}$ and $K_6^{(3)}$ are correct, this combined operation of the half-round encryption and the 3-round decryption will be equivalent to a 2.5-round IDEA decryption, and the original attack can be applied in the reverse direction, using C' instead of $\mathcal{P}$. If wrong values are tried for $K_5^{(3)}$ and $K_6^{(3)}$, no meaningful results will be obtained.

Note that in the original attack, $K_5^{(3)}$ was among the key subblocks discovered. Moreover, seven bits of $K_6^{(3)}$, namely $K_6^{(3)}[67\ldots73]$, are also known since they are in common with the already discovered key subblock of $K_5^{(2)}$. Hence, it suffices to guess only the remaining nine bits of $K_6^{(3)}$. This makes it possible to launch the attack with a set of $2^9 \times 2^{24} = 2^{33}$ ciphertexts.

This decryption attack ends up discovering the key subblocks of $K_5^{(3)}[51\ldots66]$, $K_6^{(3)}[67\ldots82]$, $K_2^{(3)}[106\ldots121]$, $K_4^{(3)}[10\ldots25]$, which, together with the 3-round encryption attack, provides 73 bits of the master key.

4.4 Attack on 3.5-Round IDEA

In the attack on the 3.5-round IDEA, Steps 1 and 2 are identical to that of the 3-round attack, except that the plaintexts are encrypted with 3.5 rounds instead of 3. Then the attack proceeds as follows:

3. As in the 3-round attack, for every value of $K_2^{(1)}$ and $K_4^{(1)}$, take the 256 plaintext blocks from $\mathcal{P}$ that keep $(P_2 \quad K_2^{(1)}) \oplus (P_4 \odot K_4^{(1)})$ constant. For every value of the round key subblocks $K_1^{(4)}$ and $K_2^{(4)}$, do a partial decryption of the ciphertexts to obtain the $C_1^{(3)}$ and $C_2^{(3)}$ values. Then calculate, for each candidate $K_5^{(3)}$,

$$\mathrm{lsb}(C_2^{(3.5)} \oplus C_3^{(3.5)} \oplus (K_5^{(3)} \odot (C_1^{(3)} \oplus C_2^{(3)}))). \qquad (2)$$

Note that $\mathrm{lsb}(C_2^{(3.5)} \oplus C_3^{(3.5)})$ is either $\mathrm{lsb}(C_2^{(3)} \oplus C_3^{(3)})$ or $\mathrm{lsb}(C_2^{(3)} \oplus C_3^{(3)}) \oplus 1$, and the bit computed in (2) equals either $\mathrm{lsb}(C_2^{(2)} \oplus C_3^{(2)})$ or $\mathrm{lsb}(C_2^{(2)} \oplus C_3^{(2)}) \oplus 1$ for all the ciphertexts. If the choices for $K_2^{(1)}$, $K_4^{(1)}$, $K_1^{(4)}$, $K_2^{(4)}$, and $K_5^{(3)}$ are correct, the derived 256-bit sequence must exist in the set S. Steps 4 and 5 are executed as in the 3-round attack and the key elimination is carried out. The remaining key bits are found with an exhaustive search.

4.5 Attack on 4 and 5 Rounds of IDEA

The attack on the 4-round IDEA follows the same logic. The only difference is in the partial decryption part in Step 3. In this part, we first make a partial decryption to find out $C_1^{(3)}$ and $C_2^{(3)}$ using the round key subblocks $K_1^{(4)}$, $K_2^{(4)}$, $K_5^{(4)}$, and $K_6^{(4)}$. Then we calculate the 256 values of

$$\mathrm{lsb}(C_2^{(4)} \oplus C_3^{(4)} \oplus (K_5^{(4)} \odot (C_1^{(4)} \oplus C_2^{(4)}))) \oplus (K_5^{(3)} \odot (C_1^{(3)} \oplus C_2^{(3)}))). \quad (3)$$

By Corollary 2, we have $\mathrm{lsb}(C_2^{(4)} \oplus C_3^{(4)} \oplus (K_5^{(4)} \odot (C_1^{(4)} \oplus C_2^{(4)}))) \oplus (K_5^{(3)} \odot (C_1^{(3)} \oplus C_2^{(3)})))$ equal either to $\mathrm{lsb}(C_2^{(2)} \oplus C_3^{(2)})$ or to $\mathrm{lsb}(C_2^{(2)} \oplus C_3^{(2)}) \oplus 1$ for all the 256 ciphertexts. From these bits, the 256-bit sequence is produced by sorting the bits according to their plaintexts' $\mathrm{msb}_8(P_2)$; and the key elimination is carried out as in the aforementioned attacks.

To attack on 4.5 and 5 rounds of IDEA, in Step 3 we first make a decryption to reach the outputs of round 4, and then continue the same steps as in the 4-round attack. For 4.5 rounds of IDEA, we search for the round key subblocks $K_1^{(5)}$, $K_2^{(5)}$, $K_3^{(5)}$, and $K_4^{(5)}$, whereas for 5 rounds we search for $K_5^{(5)}$ and $K_6^{(5)}$ in addition to these subblocks to reach the end of round 4.

5 Complexity of The Attack

To assess the elimination power of the attack, we need to calculate the probability of a wrong key avoiding elimination by chance. Given a random sequence of 256 bits, what is the probability that this sequence exists in a set of 2^{56} elements whose elements are again random bit sequences of 256 bits? The probability that two random 256-bit sequences are equal is $1/2^{256}$. The probability that a 256-bit sequence does not exist in a set of 2^{56} elements is $(1-1/2^{256})^{(2^{56})} \approx e^{-2^{-200}} \approx 1$. The probability that all wrong keys will be eliminated by sieving in the set S at the first trial, with n_k denoting the number of key bits tried in the attack, is approximately

$$\left(\left(1 - \frac{1}{2^{256}}\right)^{(2^{56})}\right)^{(2^{n_k})} \approx e^{-2^{-200+n_k}}$$

which is ≈ 1 when $n_k \leq 128$, which will always be the case for the 128-bit key size of IDEA.

Steps 1 and 2 are the same in every attack. In Step 1, we first make 2^{64} precomputations to form the sieving set. We also need 2^{64} bits of memory to store these computations—equivalent to the storage of 2^{58} IDEA blocks. In Step 2 we make 2^{24} encryptions.

In Step 3, for the 3-round version of the attack, we try all possibilities for the round key subblocks,

$$K_2^{(1)}[17\ldots32], K_4^{(1)}[49\ldots64], K_5^{(3)}[51\ldots66].$$

which altogether make up 34 distinct bits of the master key. For each different combination of these key bits, we compute $\text{lsb}(C_2^{(3)} \oplus C_3^{(3)} \oplus (K_5^{(3)} \odot (C_1^{(3)} \oplus C_2^{(3)})))$ over 256 ciphertexts, which makes $2^{34} \times 2^8 = 2^{42}$ computations in total. Moreover, each of the 2^{34} 256-bit strings computed must be compared against the sieving set for a possible match. This can be done efficiently by using a hash table for storing and searching the sieving set. Once the correct key value is found, the key subblock $K_5^{(2)}[58 \ldots 73]$ can be deduced from the matching string, providing another distinct 7 bits of the master key.

After the 3-round encryption attack is completed, the attack can be repeated on the decryption operation as described in Section 4.3, providing the subkey blocks $K_5^{(3)}[51 \ldots 66]$, $K_6^{(3)}[67 \ldots 82]$, $K_2^{(3)}[106 \ldots 121]$, $K_4^{(3)}[10 \ldots 25]$. The two attacks together provide 73 bits of the master key with a complexity of about 2^{41} partial encryptions and the remaining 55 key bits can be found by exhaustive search. However, there is also the complexity of computing the sieving set S that needs to be considered. This precomputation phase takes 2^{64} encryptions, dominating the complexity of the 3-round attack.

Consider the attack on 3.5-round IDEA. In Step 3, we use the round key subblocks

$$K_2^{(1)}[17 \ldots 32], K_4^{(1)}[49 \ldots 64], K_5^{(3)}[51 \ldots 66], K_1^{(4)}[83 \ldots 98], K_2^{(4)}[99 \ldots 114]$$

to find the sequences. Therefore, there are $2^{66} \times 2^8 = 2^{74}$ partial decryptions and 2^{66} comparisons. Seven additional master key bits will come from $K_5^{(2)}[58 \ldots 73]$, and the remaining 55 bits will have to be searched exhaustively. In this case, the computational complexity of the attack is dominated by the partial decryption phase. If we consider the complexity of a partial decryption to be half of the complexity of an encryption, the computational complexity of the attack is about 2^{73} encryptions.

Consider the attack on the 4-round IDEA. We use the round key subblocks $K_2^{(1)}$, $K_4^{(1)}$, $K_5^{(3)}$, $K_1^{(4)}$, $K_2^{(4)}$, $K_5^{(4)}$, and $K_6^{(4)}$ for obtaining the bit sequences. Although we are searching seven subblocks, because of the simple cyclic structure of the key schedule, these subblocks provide only 82 distinct bits of the master key. Therefore in the inner-most loop we are doing $2^{82} \times 2^8 = 2^{90}$ partial decryptions and 2^{82} comparisons against the set S. The main work is about 2^{89} encryptions.

For the 4.5 round IDEA, we additionally search for the round key subblocks

$$K_1^{(5)}[76 \ldots 91], K_2^{(5)}[92 \ldots 107], K_3^{(5)}[108 \ldots 123], K_4^{(5)}[124 \ldots 11]$$

in Step 3 of the attack. Most of these key bits are among those previously mentioned. There are 114 bits to be searched in total. The computational complexity is about $2^{114} \times 2^8 = 2^{122}$ partial decryptions. The data complexity is 2^{24} chosen plaintext blocks, which is a significant reduction from the 2^{64} chosen plaintexts of the best previously known attack [2]. But this reduction is at the expense of computational complexity, which is higher by a factor of 2^9.

Finally, for 5 rounds of IDEA, we also search the key subblocks $K_5^{(5)}[12\ldots27]$ and $K_6^{(5)}[28\ldots43]$. This brings 5 extra bits to search. The total complexity is about $(2^{119} \times 2^8) = 2^{127}$ partial decryptions. The data complexity is again 2^{24}.

Note that the decryption attack described in Section 4.3 on the 3-round IDEA can also be utilized to obtain additional key bits in higher-round attacks. However, the gain from those decryption attacks would be marginal. This is due to the fact that the encryption attacks on the IDEA versions with more than 3 rounds provide more than half of the 128 key bits with a complexity of between 2^{73}–2^{126} encryptions, making the complexity of searching the remaining key bits in those attacks relatively insignificant.

6 Conclusion

We introduced a new meet-in-the-middle attack against the reduced-round versions of the IDEA block cipher. The 4- and 4.5-round versions of the attack provide a significant reduction in the attack's data complexity over all previously known IDEA attacks. As for the 5-round version, this is the first attack developed against 5 rounds of IDEA faster than exhaustive search, to the best of our knowledge.

It may be possible to generalize the logic of this attack to other ciphers: Choose a group of plaintexts that will guarantee the occurrence of a certain kind of event in the upper part of the cipher. Then, from the lower end of the cipher, search the key bits that would give a partial decryption providing a match with the events expected to happen in the upper part. The key combinations which do not give any such match will be discarded as wrong candidates. The elimination will continue until a single or just a few candidates remain. It is an interesting question how such events can be found and the sieving sets can be constructed for other block ciphers.

Acknowledgements

We would like to thank an anonymous referee for his many insightful comments on the paper, in particular for his suggestion of using the decryption operation for obtaining additional key bits.

References

[1] E. Biham, A. Biryukov, A. Shamir, *Cryptanalysis of Skipjack Reduced to 31 Rounds Using Impossible Differentials*, LNCS 1592, Proceedings of EUROCRYPT' 99, pp. 12-23, Springer-Verlag, 1999. 117

[2] E. Biham, A. Biryukov, A. Shamir, *Miss in the Middle Attacks on IDEA and Khufu*, LNCS 1636, Proceedings of Fast Software Encryption - 6th International Workshop, FSE' 99, pp. 124-138, Springer-Verlag, 1999. 117, 119, 120, 127

[3] A. Biryukov, J. Nakahara Jr., B. Preneel, J. Vandewalle, *New Weak-Key Classes of IDEA*, LNCS 2513, ICICS'2002, pp. 315-326, Springer-Verlag, 2002. 119

[4] J. Borst, L. R. Knudsen, V. Rijmen, *Two Attacks on Reduced IDEA (extended abstract)*, LNCS 1223, Advances in Cryptology - Proceedings of EUROCRYPT'97, pp. 1-13, Springer-Verlag, 1997. 119, 120

[5] D. Chaum, J. H. Evertse, *Cryptanalysis of DES with a Reduced Number of Rounds: Sequences of Linear Factors in Block Ciphers,* LNCS 218, CRYPTO'85, pp. 192-211, Springer-Verlag, 1986. 117

[6] J. Daemen, R. Govaerts, J. Vandewalle, *Cryptanalysis of 2.5 round of IDEA (extended abstract),* Technical Report ESAC-COSIC Technical Report 93/1, Department Of Electrical Engineering, Katholieke Universiteit Leuven, March 1993. 119, 120

[7] J. Daemen, R. Govaerts, J. Vandewalle, *Weak Keys of IDEA,* LNCS 773, CRYPTO'93, pp. 224-231, Springer-Verlag, 1994. 119

[8] H. Demirci, *Square-like Attacks on Reduced Rounds of IDEA,* LNCS 2595, SAC'2002, pp. 147-159, Springer-Verlag, 2003. 119, 120, 121, 122

[9] H. Gilbert, M. Minier, *A Collision Attack on 7 Rounds of Rijndael,* AES Candidate Conference 2000, pp. 230-241. 117

[10] P. Hawkes, *Differential-Linear Weak Key Classes of IDEA,* LNCS 1403, EUROCRYPT'98, pp. 112-126, Springer-Verlag, 1998. 119

[11] P. Hawkes, L. O'Connor, *On Applying Linear Cryptanalysis to IDEA,* LNCS 1163, ASIACRYPT'96, pp. 105-115, Springer-Verlag, 1996. 119

[12] X. Lai, J. L. Massey, *A Proposal for a New Block Encryption Standard,* LNCS 473, Advances in Cryptology - Proceedings of EUROCRYPT'90, pp. 389-404, Springer-Verlag, 1991. 118

[13] X. Lai, J. L. Massey and S. Murphy, *Markov Ciphers and Differential Cryptanalysis,* LNCS 547, Advances in Cryptology - Proceedings of EUROCRYPT'91, pp. 17-38,Springer-Verlag, 1991. 118

[14] W. Meier, *On the Security of the IDEA Block Cipher,* LNCS 765, Advances in Cryptology - Proceedings of EUROCRYPT'93, pp. 371-385, Springer-Verlag, 1994. 119, 120

[15] J. Nakahara Jr., P. S. L. M. Barreto, B. Preneel, J. Vandewalle, H. Y. Kim, *SQUARE Attacks Against Reduced-Round PES and IDEA Block Ciphers,* IACR Cryptology ePrint Archive, Report 2001/068, 2001. 119, 120

A Implementing the Attack

It is desirable to verify the correctness of the attack and our estimates for its success probability with an experimental implementation, possibly on a reduced version of IDEA. A major handicap for such an implementation with the 64-bit IDEA is the size of the sieving set, which would take 2^{64} encryptions for creation and 2^{64} bits of memory for storage.

Implementing the attack on a reduced version of IDEA, possibly with an 8-, 16-, or 32-bit block size, can be a more feasible alternative. However, with these block sizes, it turns out that the attack looses almost all of its elimination power: For w denoting the bit length of an IDEA word, i.e., one quarter of a block, the search string in the attack is $2^{w/2}$ bits long, having a domain size of $2^{2^{w/2}}$. On the other hand, the sieving set consists of $2^{3.5w}$ such strings, covering virtually every possibility if we take $w = 2$, 4, or 8, and hence rendering the key elimination phase of the attack useless.

At the time of this writing, no practical ways are known for an experimental testing of the attack, and the authors would gratefully welcome every suggestion on this issue.

Cryptanalysis of the Alleged SecurID Hash Function*

Alex Biryukov**, Joseph Lano***, and Bart Preneel

Katholieke Universiteit Leuven, Dept. Elect. Eng.-ESAT/SCD-COSIC
Kasteelpark Arenberg 10, B-3001 Leuven-Heverlee, Belgium
{alex.biryukov,joseph.lano,bart.preneel}@esat.kuleuven.ac.be

Abstract. The SecurID hash function is used for authenticating users to a corporate computer infrastructure. We analyse an alleged implementation of this hash function. The block cipher at the heart of the function can be broken in few milliseconds on a PC with 70 adaptively chosen plaintexts. The 64-bit secret key of 10% of the cards can be discovered given two months of token outputs and 2^{48} analysis steps. A larger fraction of cards can be covered given more observation time.

Keywords: Alleged SecurID Hash Function, Differential Cryptanalysis, Internal Collision, Vanishing Differential.

1 Introduction

The SecurID authentication infrastructure was developed by SDTI (now RSA Security). A SecurID token is a hand-held hardware device issued to authorized users of a company. Every minute (or every 30 seconds), the device generates a new pseudo-random token code. By combining this code with his PIN, the user can gain access to the computer infrastructure of his company. Software-based tokens also exist, which can be used on a PC, a mobile phone or a PDA.

More than 12 million employees in more than 8000 companies worldwide use SecurID tokens. Institutions that use SecurID include the White House, the U.S. Senate, NSA, CIA, The U.S. Department of Defense, and a majority of the Fortune 100 companies.

The core of the authenticator is the proprietary SecurID hash function, developed by John Brainard in 1985. This function takes as an input the 64-bit secret key, unique to one single authenticator, and the current time (expressed in seconds since 1986). It generates an output by computing a pseudo-random function on these two input values.

SDTI/RSA has never made this function public. However, according to V. McLellan [5], the author of the SecurID FAQ, SDTI/RSA has always stated

* The work described in this paper has been supported by the Concerted Research Action (GOA) Mefisto.

** F.W.O. researcher, sponsored by the Fund for Scientific Research – Flanders

*** Research financed by a Ph.D. grant of the Institute for the Promotion of Innovation through Science and Technology in Flanders (IWT-Vlaanderen)

M. Matsui and R. Zuccherato (Eds.): SAC 2003, LNCS 3006, pp. 130–144, 2004.

that the secrecy of the SecurID hash function is not critical to its security. The hash function has undergone cryptanalysis by academics and customers under a non-disclosure agreement, and has been added to the NIST "evaluated products"-list, which implies that it is approved for U.S. government use and recommended as cryptographically sound to industry.

The source code for an alleged SecurID token emulator was posted on the Internet in December 2000 [10]. This code was obtained by reverse engineering, and the correctness of this code was confirmed in some reactions on this post. From now on, this implementation will be called the "Alleged SecurID Hash Function" (ASHF). Although the source code of the ASHF has been available for more than two years, no article discussing this function has appeared in the cryptographic literature, except for a brief note [6]. This may be explained by a huge number of subrounds (256) and by the fact that the function looses information and thus standard techniques for analysis of block-ciphers may not be applicable.

In this paper, we will analyse the ASHF and show that the block-cipher at the core of this hash function is very weak. In particular this function is non-bijective and allows for an easy construction of *vanishing* differentials (*i.e.* collisions) which leak information on the secret key. The most powerful attacks that we show are differential [1] adaptive chosen plaintext attacks which result in a complete secret key recovery in just a few milliseconds on a PC (See Table 1 for a summary of attacks).

For the real token, vanishing differentials do occur for 10% of all keys given only two months of token output and for 35% of all keys given a year of token output. We describe an algorithm that recovers the secret key given one single vanishing differential. The complexity of this algorithm is 2^{48} SecurID encryp-

Table 1. The attacks presented in this paper

Function attacked	Type of Attack	Data Compl. (#texts**)	Time Compl.**	Result	Sect.
Block-cipher (256 subrounds)	Adaptively chosen plaintext	70	2^{10}	full key recovery	3.3
Full ASHF	Adaptively chosen plaintext	2^{17}	2^{17}	few key bits	4.1
Full ASHF	Chosen + Adaptively chosen plaintext	$2^{24}+2^{13}$	2^{24}	full key recovery	4.1
Full ASHF+ time duplication	Known plaintext⋆	$2^{16}-2^{18}$	2^{48}	full key recovery, for $10-35\%$ of the keys	4.2
Full ASHF+ time duplication	Known plaintext* + Network monitoring	2^{18}	2^{18}	Possible network intrusion	4.2

⋆ A full output of the 60-second token for 2-12 months.

* A full output of the 60-second token for one year.

** Data complexity is measured in full hash outputs which would correspond to two consecutive outputs of the token.

⋆⋆ Time complexity is measured in equivalent SecurID encryptions.

tions. These attacks motivate a replacement of ASHF by a more conventional hash function, for example one based on the AES.

In Sect. 2, we give a detailed description of the ASHF. In Sect. 3, we show attacks on the block cipher-like structure, the heart of the ASHF. In Sect. 4, we show how to use these weaknesses for the cryptanalysis of the full ASHF construction. Sect. 5 presents the conclusions.

2 Description of the Alleged SecurID Hash Function

The alleged SecurID hash function (ASHF) outputs a 6 to 8-digit word every minute (or 30 seconds). All complexity estimates further in this paper, if not specified otherwise, will correspond to 60-second token described in [10] though we expect that our results apply to 30-second tokens with twice shorter observation period. The design of ASHF is shown in Fig. 1. The secret information contained in ASHF is a 64-bit secret key. This key is stored securely and remains

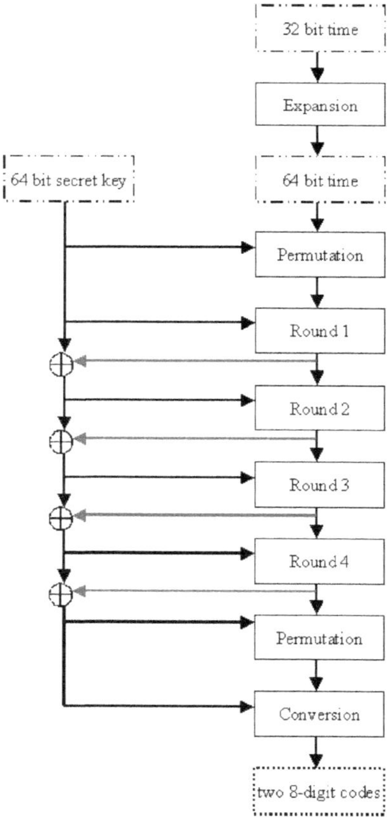

Fig. 1. Overview of the ASHF hash function

the same during the lifetime of the authenticator. Every 30 or 60 seconds, the time is read from the clock. This time is then manipulated by the expansion function (which is not key-dependent), to yield a 64-bit time.

This 64-bit time is the input to the key-dependent transformation, which consists of an initial permutation, four rounds of a block cipher-like function, a final permutation and a conversion to decimal. After every round the key is changed by XORing the key with the output of that round, hence providing a simple key scheduling algorithm. The different building blocks of the hash function will now be discussed in more detail.

In the following, we will denote a 64-bit word by b, consisting of bytes B_0, $B_1, \ldots B_7$, of nibbles $\mathrm{B}_0\mathrm{B}_1 \ldots \mathrm{B}_{15}$ and of bits $b_0 b_1 \ldots b_{63}$. B_0 is the Most Significant Byte (MSB) of the word, b_0 is the most significant bit (msb).

2.1 The Expansion Function

We consider the case where the token code changes every 60 seconds. The time is read from the clock into a 32-bit number, and converted first into the number of minutes since January 1, 1986, 0.00 GMT. Then this number is shifted to the left one position and the two least significant bits are set to zero. We now have a 32-bit number $B_0B_1B_2B_3$. This is converted into the 64-bit number by repeating the three least significant bytes several times. The final time t is then of the form $B_1B_2B_3B_3B_1B_2B_3B_3$. As the two least significant bits of B_3 are always zero, this also applies to some bits of t. The time t will only repeat after 2^{23} minutes (about 16 years), which is clearly longer than the lifetime of the token.

One can notice that the time only changes every two minutes, due to the fact that the last two bits are set to zero during the conversion. In order to get a different one-time password every minute, the ASHF will at the end take the 8 (or 6) least significant digits at even minutes, and the 8 (or 6) next digits at odd minutes. This may have been done to economize on computing power, but on the other hand this also means that the hash function outputs more information. From an information-theoretic point of view, the ASHF gives 53 bits (40 bits) of information if the attacker can obtain two consecutive 8 digit (6 digit) outputs. This is quite high considering the 64-bit secret key.

2.2 The Key-Dependent Initial and Final Permutation

The key-dependent bit permutation is applied before the core rounds of the hash function and after them. It takes a 64-bit value u and a key k as input and outputs a permutation of u, called $y = P(u, k)$.

This is how the permutation works: The key is split into 16 nibbles $\mathrm{K}_0\mathrm{K}_1 \ldots \mathrm{K}_{15}$, and the 64 bits of u are put into an array. A pointer p jumps to bit u_{K_0}. The four bits strictly before p will become the output bits $y_{60}y_{61}y_{62}y_{63}$.

The bits that have already been picked are removed from the array, and the pointer is increased (modulo the size of the array) by the next key nibble K_1. Again the four bits strictly before p become the output bits $y_{56}y_{57}y_{58}y_{59}$. This process is repeated until the 16 nibbles of the key are used up and the whole output word y is determined.

An interesting observation is that the 2^{64} keys only lead to $2^{60.58}$ possible permutations. This can be easily seen: when the array is reduced to 12 values, the key nibble can only lead to 12 different outputs, and likewise for an array of length 8 or 4.[1]

This permutation is not strong: given one input-output pair (u, y), one gets a lot of information on the key. An algorithm has been written that searches all remaining keys given one pair (u, y). On average, 2^{12} keys remain, which is a significant reduction. Given two input-output pairs, the average number of remaining keys is 17.

In Sect. 3 and 4, we will express the complexity of attacks in the number of SecurID encryptions. In terms of processing time, one permutation is equivalent to 5% of a SecurID encryption.

2.3 The Key-Dependent Round

One round takes as input the 64-bit key k and a 64-bit value b^0. It outputs a 64-bit value b^{64}, and the key k is transformed to $k = k \oplus b^{64}$. This ensures that every round (and also the final permutation) gets a different key. The round consists of 64 subrounds, in each of these one bit of the key is used. The superscript ^{i} denotes the word after the i-th round. Subround i ($i = 1 \ldots 64$) transforms b^{i-1} into b^i and works as follows (see Fig. 2):

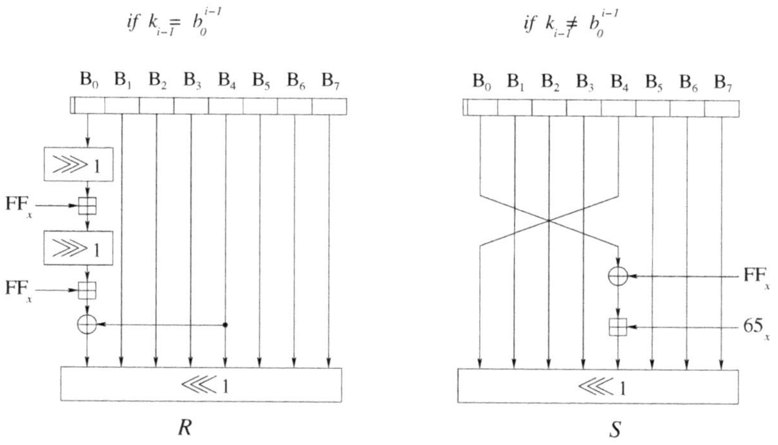

Fig. 2. Sub-round i defined by the operations R and S

[1] The description of the permutation given here is more transparent than the actual implementation. This equivalent representation and the observation on the number of permutations has also been found independently by Contini [3].

1. Check if the key bit k_{i-1} equals b_0^{i-1}.
   - if the answer is yes:

$$\begin{cases} B_0^i = ((((B_0^{i-1} \quad 1) - 1) \quad 1) - 1) \oplus B_4^{i-1} \\ B_j^i = B_j^{i-1} \text{ for } j = 1, 2, 3, 4, 5, 6, 7 \end{cases} \tag{1}$$

   where $\quad i$ denotes a cyclic shift to the right by i positions and $\oplus$ denotes an exclusive or. This function will be called R.
   - if the answer is no:

$$\begin{cases} B_0^i = B_4^{i-1} \\ B_4^i = 100 - B_0^{i-1} \mod 256 \\ B_j^i = B_j^{i-1} \text{ for } j = 1, 2, 3, 5, 6, 7 \end{cases} \tag{2}$$

   This function will be called S.
2. Cyclically shift all bits one position to the left:

$$b^i = b^i \quad 1\,. \tag{3}$$

After these 64 iterations, the output b^{64} of the round is found, and the key is changed according to $k = k \oplus b^{64}$.

In terms of processing time, one round is equivalent to 0.21 SecurID encryptions.

2.4 The Key-Dependent Conversion to Decimal

After the initial permutation, the 4 rounds and the final permutation, the 16 nibbles of the data are converted into 16 decimal symbols. These will be used to form the two next 8 (or 6)-digit codes.

This is done in a very straightforward way: the nibbles $0_x, 1_x, \ldots 9_x$ are simply transformed into the digits $0, 1, \ldots 9$. A_x, C_x and E_x are transformed into $0, 2, 4, 6$ or 8, depending on the key; and B_x, D_x and F_x are transformed into $1, 3, 5, 7$ or 9, also depending on the key.

3 Cryptanalysis of the Key-Dependent Rounds

The four key-dependent rounds are the major factor for mixing the secret key and the current time. The ASHF could have used any block cipher here (for example DES), but a dedicated design has been used instead. The designers had the advantage that the rounds do not have to be reversible, as the cipher is only used to encrypt. In this section we will show some weaknesses of this dedicated design.

3.1 Avalanche of 1-Bit Differences

It is instructive to look at how a differential propagates through the rounds. As has been explained in Sect. 2.3, in every subround one bit of the key is mixed in by first performing one R or S-operation and then shifting the word one position to the left.

A standard differential trail, for an input difference in b_{63}, is shown in Table 2 in Appendix A. As long as the difference does not enter B_0 or B_4, there is no avalanche at all: the difference is just shifted one position to the left after each subround. But once the difference enters into B_0 and B_4, avalanche occurs quite rapidly. This is due to two factors: S and R are nonlinear (though very close to linear) and mainly due to a choice between the two operations S or R, conditional on the most significant bit b_0 of the text.

Another complication is that, unlike in regular block ciphers, the round output is XORed into the subkey of the following round. This leads to difference propagation into the subkeys which makes the mixing even more complex. Because of the many subrounds (256), it seems that avalanche will be more than sufficient to resist differential cryptanalysis.

3.2 Differential Characteristics

We now search for interesting differential characteristics. Two texts are encrypted and the differential trail is inspected. A difference in the lsb of B_7 will be denoted by 1_x, in the second bit of B_7 by 2_x, etc... Three scenarios can occur in a subround:

- If the difference is not in B_0 or B_4, it will undergo a linear operation: the difference will always propagate by shifting one position to the left: 1_x will become 2_x, 2_x will become 4_x, etc.
- If the difference is in B_0 and/or B_4, and the difference in the msb of B_0 equals the difference in the key, both texts will undergo the same operation (R or S). These operations are not completely linear, but a difference can only go to a few specific differences. A table has been built that shows for every differential the differentials it can propagate to together with the probability.
- If the difference is in B_0 and/or B_4, and the difference in the msb of B_0 does not equal the difference in the key, one text will undergo the R operation and the other text will undergo the S operation. This results in a uniform distribution for the output differences: each difference has probability 2^{-16}.

Our approach has been to use an input differential in the least significant bits of B_3 and B_7. This differential will then propagate "for free" for about 24 subrounds. Then it will enter B_0 and B_4. We will pay a price in the second scenario (provided the msb of the differential in B_0 is not 1) for a few subrounds, after which we want the differential to leave B_0 and B_4 and jump to B_7 or B_3. Then it can again propagate for free for 24 rounds, and so on.

That way we want to have a difference in only 1 bit after 64 subrounds. This is the only difference which will propagate into the key, and so we can hope to push the differentials through more rounds.

The best differential for one round that we have found has an input difference of 2_x in B_3 and 5_x in B_7, and gives an output difference of 1_x in B_6 with probability 2^{-15}.

It is possible that better differentials exist. One could try to push the characteristic through more rounds, but because of the difference in the keys other paths will have to be searched. For now, it is unclear whether a path through the four rounds can be found with probability larger than 2^{-64}, but it may well be feasible. In any case, this approach is far less efficient than the approach we will discuss in the following section.

3.3 Vanishing Differentials

Because of the specific application in which the ASHF is used, the rounds do not have to be bijections. A consequence of this non-bijective nature is that it is possible to choose an input differential to a round, such that the output differential is zero, *i.e.*, an internal collision. An input differential that causes an internal collision will be called a vanishing differential[2].

This can be derived as follows. Suppose that we have two words at the input of the i-th subround, b^{i-1} and b'^{i-1}. A first condition is that:

$$b_0^{i-1} \neq b'^{i-1}_0 . \tag{4}$$

Then one word, assume b^{i-1}, will undergo the R operation, and the other word b'^{i-1} will undergo the S operation. We impose a second condition, namely:

$$B_j^{i-1} = B'^{i-1}_j \text{ for } j = 1, 2, 3, 5, 6, 7. \tag{5}$$

We now want to find an input differential in B_0 and B_4 that vanishes. This is easily achieved by simply setting b^i equal to b'^i after S or R:

$$\begin{cases} B_0^i = B'^i_0 \Rightarrow B'^{i-1}_4 = ((((B_0^{i-1} \quad 1) - 1) \quad 1) - 1) \oplus B_4^{i-1} \\ B_4^i = B'^i_4 \Rightarrow B'^{i-1}_0 = 100 - B_4^{i-1} , \end{cases} \tag{6}$$

As both R and S are bijections, there will be 2^{16} such tuples $(B_0^{i-1}, B_4^{i-1}, B'^{i-1}_0, B'^{i-1}_4)$. The extra condition that the msb of B_0^{i-1} and B'^{i-1}_0 have to be different will filter out half of these, still leaving 2^{15} such pairs.

This observation leads to a very easy attack on the full block cipher. We choose two plaintexts b^0 and b'^0 that satisfy the above conditions. We encrypt these with the block cipher (the 4 rounds), and look at the difference between the outputs. Two scenarios are possible:

---

2 Notice that the ASHF scheme can be viewed both as a block cipher with partially non-bijective round function or as a MAC where current time is authenticated with the secret key. The fact that internal collisions in MACs may lead to forgery or key-recovery attacks was noted and exploited against popular MACs in [7, 8, 4].

- b^0 undergoes the R operation and b'^0 undergoes the S operation in the first subround: this means that b^1 will be equal to b'^1. As the difference is equal to zero, this will of course propagate to the end and we will observe this at the output. This also implies that $k_0 = b_0^0$, because that is the condition for b^0 to undergo the R operation.
- b^0 undergoes the S operation and b'^0 undergoes the R operation in the first subround: this means that b^1 will be different from b'^1. This difference will propagate further (with very high probability), and we will observe a nonzero output difference. This also implies that $k_0 = b'^0_0$, because that is the condition for b'^0 to undergo the R operation.

To summarize, this gives us a very easy way to find the first bit of the secret key with two chosen plaintexts: choose b^0 and b'^0 according to (4), (5) and (6) and encrypt these. If outputs will be equal, then $k_0 = b_0^0$. If not, then $k_0 = b'^0_0$!

This approach can be easily extended to find the second, third, ... bit of the secret key by working iteratively. Suppose we have determined the first $i-1$ bits of the key. Then we can easily find a pair (b^0, b'^0), that will be transformed by the already known key bits of the first $i-1$ subrounds into a pair (b^{i-1}, b'^{i-1}) that satisfies (4), (5) and (6). The search for an adequate pair is performed offline, and once we have found a good pair offline it will always be suitable for testing on the real cipher. The procedure we do is to encrypt a random text with the key bits we have deduced so far, then we choose the corresponding second text there for a vanishing differential, and for this text we then try to find a preimage. Correct preimages can be found with high probabilities (75% for the 1st bit, 1.3% for 64th bit), hence few text pairs need to be tried before an adequate pair is found. Now we can deduce k_i in the same way we deduced k_0 above.

This algorithm has been implemented in C on a Pentium. Finding the whole secret key requires at most 128 adaptively chosen plaintexts. This number will in practice mostly be reduced, because we can often reuse texts from previous subrounds in the new rounds. Simulation shows that on average only 70 adaptively chosen plaintexts are needed. The complexity of this attack can be calculated to be 2^{10} SecurID encryptions. Finding the 64-bit secret key for the whole block cipher, with the search for the appropriate plaintexts included, requires only a few milliseconds. Of course, it is possible to perform a trade-off by only searching the first i key bits. The remaining $64 - i$ key bits can then be found by doing a reduced exhaustive search.

4 Extending the Attack with Vanishing Differentials to the Whole ASHF

So far, we have shown how to break the four key-dependent rounds of the ASHF. In this paragraph, we will first try to extend the attack of Sect. 3.3 to the full ASHF, which consists of a weak initial key-dependent permutation, the four key-dependent rounds, a weak final key-dependent permutation and the key-dependent conversion to decimal. Then we will mount the attack when taking the symmetrical time format into account.

4.1 The Attack on the Full ASHF

The attack with vanishing differentials of Sect. 3.3 is not defeated by the final permutation. Even a perfect key-dependent permutation would not help. The only thing an attacker needs to know is whether the outputs are equal, and this is not changed by the permutation. The lossy conversion to decimal also doesn't defeat the attack. There still are 53 bits (40 bits) of information, so the probability that two equal outputs are caused by chance (and thus are not caused by a vanishing differential) remains negligibly small.

However, the initial key-dependent permutation causes a problem. It prevents the attacker from choosing the inputs to the block cipher rounds. A new approach is needed to extract information from the occurrence of vanishing differentials.

The attack starts by searching a vanishing differential by randomly choosing 2 inputs that differ in 1 bit, say in bit i. Approximately 2^{17} pairs need to be tested before such a pair can be found. Information on the initial permutation (and thus on the secret key) can then be learned by flipping a bit j in the pair and checking whether a vanishing differential is still observed. If this is so, this is an indication that bit j is further away from B_0 and B_4 than bit i.

An algorithm has been implemented that searches for a vanishing pair with one bit difference in all bits i, and then flips a bit for all bits j. This requires 2^{24} chosen and 2^{13} adaptively chosen plaintexts. A $64 \cdot 64$ matrix is obtained that carries a lot of information on the initial permutation. Every element of the matrix establishes an order relationship, every row i shows which bits j can be flipped for an input differential in bit i, and every column shows how often flipping bit i will preserve the vanishing differential. This information can be used to extract the secret key. The first nibble of the key determines which bits go to positions $b_{60}, \ldots b_{63}$. By inspecting the matrix, one can see that this should be the four successive bits between bit 60 and bit 11 that have the lowest row weight and the highest column weight.

Once we have determined the first nibble, we can work recursively to determine the following nibbles of the secret key. The matrix will not always give a unique solution, so then it will be necessary to try all likely scenarios. Simulation indicates that the uncertainty seems to be lower than the work required to find the vanishing differentials.

The data complexity of this attack may be further reduced by using fewer vanishing differentials, but thereby introducing more uncertainty.

4.2 The Attack on the Full ASHF with the Time Format

The attack is further complicated by the symmetrical time format. A one-bit difference in the 32-bit time is expanded into a 2-bit difference (if the one-bit difference is in the second or third byte of the 32-bit time) or into a 4-bit difference (if the one-bit difference is in least significant byte of the 32-bit time).

A 4-bit difference caused by a one-bit difference in the 32-bit time will yield a vanishing differential with negligible probability, because the initial permutation will seldom put the differences in an ordered way that permits a vanishing

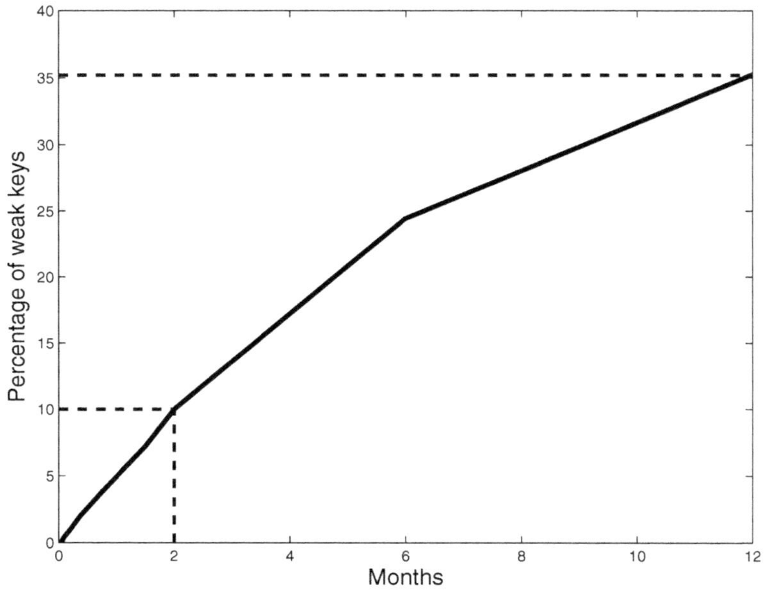

Fig. 3. Percentage of keys that have at least one VD

differential to occur. A 2-bit difference, however, will lead to a vanishing differential with high probability: taking a random key, an attacker observes two equal outputs for one given 2-bit difference with probability 2^{-19}. This can be used to distinguish the SecurID stream from a random stream, as two equal outputs would normally only be detected with probability 2^{-53} ($2^{-26.5}$ if only one 8-digit tokencode is observed).

In the following, we assume that an attacker can observe the output of the 60-second token during some time period. This attack could simulate a "curious user" who wants to know the secret key of his own card, or a malicious internal user who has access to the SecurID cards before they are deployed. The attacker could put his token(s) in front of a PC camera equipped with OCR software, automating the process of reading the numbers from the card. The attacker then would try to detect vanishing differentials in the sampled data. Figure 3 shows the percentage of the tokens for which at least one vanishing differential is detected, as a function of the observation time.

Two interesting points are the following: after two months, about 10% of the keys have one or more vanishing differentials; after one year, 35% of keys have at least one vanishing differential. Below, we show two ways in which an attacker can use the information obtained by the observation of the token output.

Full Key Recovery. In this attack, we recover the key from the observation of a single vanishing differential. In the following, it is assumed that we are given one pair of 64-bit time inputs (t, t') that leads to a vanishing differential, and that there is a 2-bit difference between the two inputs (the attack can also be mounted with other differences). We know that the known pair (t, t') will be permuted into an unknown pair (b, b'), and that the difference will vanish after an unknown number of subrounds N. The outputs of the hash, o and o', are also known and are of course equal.

The idea of the attack is to first guess the subround N in which the vanishing differential occurs, for increasing $N = 1, 2, \ldots$ For each value of N, a filtering algorithm is used that searches the set of keys that make such a vanishing differential possible. We then search this set to find the correct key. We will now describe the filtering algorithm for the case $N = 1$. For other values of N the algorithm will be similar.

When guessing $N = 1$, we assume the vanishing differential to happen in the first subround. This means that the only bits that play a role in the vanishing differential are the key bit k_0, and the bytes B_0, B_4, B'_0 and B'_4 of the two words after the permutation. Out of the 2^{33} possible values, we are only interested in those combinations that have a 2-bit difference between the texts and lead to a vanishing differential. We construct a list of these values during a precomputation phase, which has to be performed only once for all attacks. In the precomputation phase, we let a guess of the word b, called b_v, take on all values in bytes B_{v0} and B_{v4} (the other values are set to a fixed value), and let k_0 be 0 or 1. We perform one subround for all these values and store the outputs. For each value of k_0, we then search for equal outputs for which the inputs b_v, b'_v have 2-bit difference. We then have found a valid combination, which we store as a triplet (k_0, b_v, b'_v). Note that in b_v and b'_v only two bytes are of importance, we refer to such words as "partially filled". Only 30 such valid triplets are found.

The list of scenarios found in the precomputation phase will be used as the start for a number of guessing and filtering steps. In the first step, for each scenario (k_0, b_v, b'_v), we try all possible values of $k_1, \ldots k_{27}$. Having guessed the first 28 key bits, we know the permutation of the last 28 bits. We call these partially guessed values $b_p = P(t, k)$ and $b'_p = P(t', k)$. Under this scenario, we now have two partial guesses for both b and b', namely b_v, b_p and b'_v, b'_p. One can see that b_v and b_p overlap in the nibble B_9. If $\mathrm{B}_{v9} = \mathrm{B}_{p9}$ and $\mathrm{B'}_{v9} = \mathrm{B'}_{p9}$, the scenario $(k_0 \ldots k_{27}, b_v, b'_v)$ is possible and will go to the next iteration. If there's a contradiction, the scenario is impossible and can be filtered out.

In the second step, a scenario that survived the first step is taken as input and the key bits $k_{28} \ldots k_{31}$ are guessed. Filtering is done based on the overlap between the two guesses for nibble B_8. In the third step we guess key bits $k_{32} \ldots k_{59}$ and filter for the overlap in nibble B_1. Finally, in the fourth step the key bits $k_{60} \ldots k_{63}$ are guessed and the filtering is based on the overlap in nibble B_0. Every output of this fourth step is a key values that leads to a vanishing differential in the first subround for the given inputs t and t'. Each key that survives the filtering algorithm will then be checked to see if it is the correct key.

We perform this algorithm for $N = 1, 2, \ldots$. Note that for higher N, the overlap will be higher (because more bits play a role in the vanishing differential) and thus the filtering will be stronger. Simulation on 10000 samples indicated that more than 50% of the vanishing differentials (observed in two-month periods) occur before the 12th subround. So in order to get a success probability of 50%, it suffices to run the attack for N up to 12.

The time complexity of the precomputation step increases with N. One can see that for a vanishing differential in subround N, $2 \cdot N + 14$ bits of the text and N bits of the key are of importance. It can be calculated that the total time complexity to precompute the tables for N up to 12 will be 2^{44} SecurID encryptions. The size of the precomputed table is increasing by a factor of about 8 with increasing N. About 500 GB of hard disk is required to store these tables.

The time complexity of the attack itself is dependent on the strength of the filtering. This may vary from input to input, but simulations indicate the following averages for $N = 1$: the 30 scenarios go to 2^{27} possibilities after the first step. These are reduced to 2^{25} after the second step, go to 2^{45} after the third step and reduce to 2^{41} after the fourth step. The most expensive step in this algorithm is the third step: 28 bits of the key are guessed in 2^{25} scenarios. At every iteration, two partial permutations (28 bits in each) have to be done. This means that the total complexity in terms of SecurID encryptions of this step is:

$$2^{25} \cdot 2^{28} \cdot \frac{28}{64} \cdot 2 \cdot 0.05 \approx 2^{48.5} , \tag{7}$$

where the factor 0.05 is the relative complexity of the permutation.

The time complexity of the third (and forth) step can be further improved by using the fact that there are only $2^{60.58}$ possible permutations, as described in Sect. 2.2. By searching for the permutations instead of the key, we reduce the complexity of the attack by a factor $\frac{12}{16} \cdot \frac{8}{16}$ to 2^{47}. The memory requirements, apart from the storage of the precomputed tables, are negligible.

For $N > 1$, we expect the complexity of the attack to be lower due to the stronger filtering. Our estimate for the total complexity of the attack is equivalent to 2^{48} SecurID encryptions. We expect that further refinements are possible that reduce the complexity to 2^{45}. For a more thorough treatment of the attack and of its complexity analysis, see [2].

Network Intrusion. An attacker can also use the one year output without trying to recover the secret key of the token. In this attack scenario it is assumed that the attacker can monitor the traffic on the network in the following year. When an attacker monitors a token at the (even) time t, he will compare this with the value of the token 2^{19} minutes (about 1 year) earlier. If both values are equal, this implies that a vanishing differential is occurring. This vanishing differential will also hold at the next (odd) time $t + 1$. The attacker can thus predict at time t the value of the token at time $t + 1$ by looking it up in his database, and can use this value to log into the system.

Simulation shows that 4% of the keys [3] will have such vanishing differentials within a year, and that these keys will have 6 occurrences of vanishing differentials on average. Higher percentages of such weak keys are possible if we assume the attacker is monitoring several years.

The total probability of success of an attacker depends on the number of cards from which he could collect the output during one year, and on the number of logins of the users in the next year. It is clear that the attack will not be very practical, since the success probability for a single user with 1000 login attempts per year will be $2^{-19} \cdot 1000 \cdot 6 \cdot 0.04/2 \approx 2^{-12}$. This is however, much higher than what would be expected from the password length (*i.e.*, $2^{-26.5}$ and 2^{-20} for 8- and 6-digit tokens respectively). Note that this attack does not produce failed login attempts and requires only passive monitoring.

5 Conclusion

In this paper, we have performed a cryptanalysis of the Alleged SecurID Hash Function (ASHF). It has been shown that the core of this hash, the four key-dependent block cipher rounds, is very weak and can be broken in a few milliseconds with an adaptively chosen plaintext attack, using vanishing differentials.

The full ASHF is also vulnerable: by observing the output during two months, we have a 10% chance to find at least one vanishing differential. We can use this vanishing differential to recover the secret key of the token with expected time complexity 2^{48}. We can also use the observed output to significantly increase our chances of network intrusion.

The ASHF does not deliver the security that one would expect from a present-day cryptographic algorithm. See Table 1 for an overview of the attacks presented in this paper. We thus would recommend to replace the ASHF-based tokens by tokens implementing another algorithm that has undergone extensive open review and which has 128-bit internal secret. The AES seems to be a good candidate for such a replacement and indeed, from February 2003 RSA has started phasing in AES-based tokens [9].

References

[1] E. Biham, A. Shamir, *Differential Cryptanalysis of DES-like Cryptosystems,* Journal of Cryptology, volume 4, number 1, pp. 3–72, 1991. 131

[2] A. Biryukov, J. Lano, B. Preneel, *Cryptanalysis of the Alleged SecurID Hash Function (extended version)*, http://eprint.iacr.org/2003/162/, 2003. 142

[3] S. Contini, *The Effect of a Single Vanishing Differential on ASHF,* sci.crypt post, Sept. 6, 2003. 134

[4] Internet Security, Applications, Authentication and Cryptography, University of California, Berkeley, *GSM Cloning* http://www.isaac.cs.berkeley.edu/isaac/gsm-faq.html. 137

[3] Decreased key fraction is due to the restriction of the input difference to a specific one year difference.

[5] V. McLellan, *Re: SecurID Token Emulator*, post to BugTraq, http://cert.uni-stuttgart.de/archive/bugtraq/2001/01/msg00090.html 130
[6] Mudge, Kingpin, *Initial Cryptanalysis of the RSA SecurID Algorithm*, www.atstake.com/ research/reports/acrobat/initial_securid_analysis.pdf 131
[7] B. Preneel, P. van Oorschot, *MDx-MAC and Building Fast MACs From Hash Functions*, CRYPTO'95, LNCS 963, D. Coppersmith, Ed., Springer-Verlag, pp. 1–14, 1995. 137
[8] B. Preneel, P. van Oorschot, *On the Security of Two MAC Algorithms,* Eurocrypt 96, LNCS 1070, U. Maurer, Ed., Springer-Verlag, pp. 19–32, 1996. 137
[9] RSA security website, http://www.rsasecurity.com/company/news/releases/pr.asp?doc_id=1543 143
[10] I.C. Wiener, *Sample SecurID Token Emulator with Token Secret Import*, post to BugTraq, http://archives.neohapsis.com/archives/bugtraq/2000-12/0428.html 131, 132

A Differential Trail

Table 2. Unrestricted differential trail for the first 50 subrounds (avalanche demonstration)

Subround	B_0	B_1	B_2	B_3	B_4	B_5	B_6	B_7
0	00	00	00	00	00	00	00	01
1	00	00	00	00	00	00	00	02
2	00	00	00	00	00	00	00	04
3	00	00	00	00	00	00	00	08
...								
24	00	00	00	00	01	00	00	00
25	02	00	00	00	02	00	00	00
26	1a	00	00	00	04	00	00	01
27	08	00	00	00	1c	00	00	02
28	38	00	00	00	70	00	00	04
29	f4	00	00	00	e0	00	00	08
30	68	00	00	01	40	00	00	11
31	4c	00	00	02	80	00	00	22
32	22	00	00	05	00	00	00	45
33	00	00	00	0a	cc	00	00	8a
34	98	00	00	15	98	00	01	15
35	2c	00	00	2b	88	00	02	2a
36	10	00	00	56	28	00	04	55
37	50	00	00	ac	e0	00	08	aa
38	c0	00	01	58	a0	00	11	55
39	c2	00	02	b1	10	00	22	ab
40	0e	00	05	63	ec	00	45	56
41	e4	00	0a	c7	d8	00	8a	ac
42	c2	00	15	8f	3e	01	15	59
43	72	00	2b	1e	50	02	2a	b2
44	a0	00	56	3c	64	04	55	64
45	9c	00	ac	78	9c	08	aa	c9
46	14	01	58	f0	b8	11	55	92
47	4a	02	b1	e1	70	22	ab	25
48	e0	05	63	c2	94	45	56	4a
49	b6	0a	c7	84	0a	8a	ac	94
50	3e	15	8f	08	0b	15	59	29
...								

Authenticated On-Line Encryption

Pierre-Alain Fouque, Antoine Joux, Gwenaëlle Martinet, and Frédéric Valette

DCSSI Crypto Lab
51, Boulevard de Latour Maubourg
75700 Paris 07 SP, FRANCE
Pierre-Alain.Fouque@ens.fr, Antoine.Joux@m4x.org
Gwenaelle.Martinet@worldonline.fr, Fred.Valette@wanadoo.fr

Abstract. In this paper, we investigate the authenticated encryption paradigm, and its security against blockwise adaptive adversaries, mounting chosen ciphertext attacks on on-the-fly cryptographic devices. We remark that most of the existing solutions are insecure in this context, since they provide a decryption oracle for any ciphertext. We then propose a generic construction called Decrypt-Then-Mask, and prove its security in the blockwise adversarial model. The advantage of this proposal is to apply minimal changes to the encryption protocol. In fact, in our solution, only the decryption protocol is modified, while the encryption part is left unchanged. Finally, we propose an instantiation of this scheme, using the encrypted CBC-MAC algorithm, a secure pseudorandom number generator and the Delayed variant of the CBC encryption scheme.

Keywords: Symmetric encryption, authenticated encryption, chosen ciphertext attacks, blockwise adversaries, provable security.

1 Introduction

An authenticated encryption scheme is a secret key scheme providing both privacy and integrity. In [7], Bellare and Namprempre have studied how to combine encryption scheme and message authentication code (MAC) to construct a secure composition against chosen ciphertext attacks. They have proved that the generically secure way is to first encrypt the data with a symmetric encryption scheme and then compute a MAC of the ciphertext. They called this method the "Encrypt-Then-MAC" paradigm. From the receiver point of view, the "Verify-Then-Decrypt" method is performed by first checking the MAC and if (and only if) the tag is correct, by decrypting.

Some other constructions for authenticated encryption have recently been proposed, [18, 21]. All these constructions ensure both integrity and confidentiality in a single pass and are thus more efficient than the Encrypt-Then-MAC composition. Furthermore, the decryption method is now slightly different: integrity is checked at the end of the decryption process. A lot of papers have also studied how to ensure integrity and confidentiality in a single pass (as in [8, 1]). The main result of these papers is that providing integrity with an encryption

M. Matsui and R. Zuccherato (Eds.): SAC 2003, LNCS 3006, pp. 145–159, 2004.

scheme with redundancy and/or encoding is not generically secure. Some requirements are needed on the encoding scheme for the composition to be generically secure. For example, Vaudenay has shown in [23] that using a public redundancy is not a secure way to provide security against chosen ciphertext attacks. Indeed, some reaction attacks are possible: this shows that encoding schemes are usually not sufficient to provide authenticity. Another reaction attack has recently been proposed in [6] against the SSH binary Packet Protocol, proving that this scheme may be insecure in some contexts. However, lot of schemes are now well known to be secure in the strong sense, as the generic Encrypt-then-MAC composition, or single pass schemes as IACBC [18], OCB [21]... Thus constructing authenticated encryption schemes does not seem to be an open problem anymore.

However, in some practical applications the sender and the receiver of an authenticated ciphertext use a cryptographic device to perform the encryption, the checking and the decryption operations. In many cases, this cryptographic module uses a smart card with a limited storage. Due to memory restrictions, the card cannot store the whole ciphertext C to first check the tag τ and then decrypt C if τ was valid, as assumed in the standard model (or store the whole plaintext after decryption, check its integrity and output it only if valid).

To overcome this problem, interactions between the card and the rest of the world are usually performed on-the-fly. However, in [17], a new security flaw of on-line implementations was pointed out. The basic idea is to notice that with such implementations, messages are no longer atomic objects, as assumed in the usual security proofs. This idea leads to a new class of attacks called *blockwise adaptive*. Adversaries using such attacks see the kth ciphertext block before having supplied the $(k+1)$th plaintext block. Note that some techniques used in [6] to attack the SSH protocol are linked with this kind of attackers. In [17], only blockwise adaptive chosen plaintext attacks were considered. In this paper, we focus on *blockwise adaptive chosen ciphertext attacks* and look at the precautions that have to be taken, not only during the encryption phase, but also during the decryption phase, both executed on-the-fly.

Recently another work has been published, formalizing the remotely keyed authenticated encryption [11]. It solves the problem of authenticated encryption on a high bandwidth and insecure channel using a limited bandwidth and memory but highly secure cryptographic device. The work of [11] also proposes a generic way to solve this problem, but the solution they give transforms both the encryption and the decryption parts. In their solution, and in the previous work of [9], the main idea is to use a session key to encrypt the data. The cryptographic device just encrypts this session key and authenticates a hash of the ciphertext. However, in well-established standards such as SSH or SSL, designers cannot accept to change the protocol only for low memory devices. Consequently, our aim is to provide a solution that only modifies the decryption protocol.

Our Results. In this paper we study how authenticated encryption can be securely implemented when dealing with blockwise adaptive adversaries using chosen ciphertext attacks. We show how to securely implement on-line decryption.

In particular, an adversary should not be able to feed a decryption oracle with an invalid ciphertext and obtain the corresponding plaintext. We first describe the usual on-the-fly implementations of the Encrypt-Then-MAC composition and of authenticated encryption in one pass. We show how such implementations lead to totally insecure schemes when considering blockwise adversaries. Trivial attacks are possible: they provide to the adversary a decryption oracle without any check of the integrity. Since the basic encryption schemes are generally not secure against chosen ciphertext attacks, this leads to major security flaws.

After having formally described the blockwise adaptive security model, both for confidentiality and integrity, we propose, as an alternative to existing solutions, a new generic construction and we prove its security. This solution requires an encryption scheme only secure against blockwise adversaries mounting chosen plaintext attacks, together with a new decryption protocol. The main idea is to blind the plaintext blocks obtained after decryption by XORing them with a pseudorandom sequence of bits. Then, when the integrity of the ciphertext is checked, the seed used to generate the pseudorandom sequence is returned. Thus the cryptographic device does not need neither memory to store the plaintext nor multiple sending of the ciphertext. Finally, section 6 of this paper presents a practical instantiation of this generic composition.

2 Blockwise Attacks against Naive Implementations

In smart cards or with online protocols, authenticated encryption schemes use on-the-fly interactions. In such a setting, the decryption process is not easy to implement, since both privacy and integrity should be provided. Most of the existing solutions are insecure since these interactive processes greatly facilitate chosen ciphertext attacks. Indeed, they do not prevent attackers from getting decryptions of invalid messages. The following paragraphs describe why classical constructions are insecure.

In practice, two naive methods are widely used. Both implement the Encrypt-Then-MAC composition or single pass authenticated encryptions. Let (C, τ) be an authenticated ciphertext. For the first decryption process, the ciphertext C is sent block by block to the smart card, which gradually returns for each block the corresponding plaintext block. In the same time, the crypto device updates the MAC computation. At the end, the tag τ is sent to the card which checks its validity. With this method, the user learns the plaintext even if the ciphertext was invalid, since integrity is checked after the plaintext has been returned. For example, with the OCB authenticated encryption scheme (see [21] for further details on this scheme), the authenticated ciphertext $C = C_1 \| \dots \| C_m \| \tau$ is sent block by block to the card: it decrypts each block C_i into M_i, sends it to the receiver and updates the `Checksum` for the MAC computation. When the card receives the tag τ it just checks its validity by comparing it with the value it has computed. The result of this comparison does not matter since the adversary has received the plaintext. As a consequence, the card provides a decryption oracle for the underlying encryption scheme. Since most of the existing encryption modes are not secure against chosen ciphertext attacks, such a technique often leads to insecure schemes.

The second naive technique works as follows: an authenticated ciphertext (C, τ) is sent to the smart card, block by block, or buffer by buffer. The card just checks its validity: if τ is valid, in a second pass, the ciphertext C is sent again to the card. The transmission is made on-the-fly, *i.e.*, for each ciphertext block sent, the card outputs the corresponding plaintext block. The main drawback of this protocol is that no verification can be made to check whether the same ciphertext has been sent twice. This leads to a major security flaw: in a first pass, an adversary can send any valid ciphertext, in the sense of integrity, and in the second pass, another one, possibly invalid, which will be nonetheless decrypted.

Such security flaws call for a formal definition of security for authenticated encryption schemes secure against blockwise adaptive adversaries, and for schemes ensuring this security level.

3 Preliminaries

Recently in [17], some results appeared concerning the insecurity of some encryption schemes in a new adversarial model. This notion is meaningful when implementing digital signed streams as in [15], or when considering on-line encryption schemes which do not require the whole plaintext before beginning the encryption. In this section we formally describe these adversaries and the associated security model for both privacy and integrity against chosen plaintext and ciphertext attacks.

3.1 Privacy

Privacy in the Standard Model. In the standard model, privacy of an encryption scheme is viewed as ciphertext indistinguishability (IND), defined in [3]. This notion is modeled through a "left-or-right"(LOR) game: the adversary is allowed to feed the *left-or-right encryption oracle* $\mathcal{E}_K(\mathcal{LR}(\cdot,\cdot,b))$ with queries of the form (M_0^i, M_1^i) where M_0^i and M_1^i are two equal length messages. First, the oracle chooses a random bit b, and, for all queries (M_0^i, M_1^i), always encrypts the message M_b^i and returns a ciphertext C_b^i. The adversary's goal is to guess the bit b with non-negligible advantage in polynomial time. If an encryption scheme $\mathcal{SE}$ withstands an adversary performing a *chosen plaintext attack* (CPA), then we say that $\mathcal{SE}$ is IND-CPA secure. If the adversary has access, in addition, to a decryption oracle, taking as input a ciphertext C and outputting the corresponding plaintext M, the adversary is said to mount a *chosen ciphertext attack* (CCA). For a complete description of these notions the reader can refer to [3].

Privacy in the Blockwise Adversarial Model. In this setting, adversaries are adaptive during their queries to the different encryption oracles. The *blockwise left or right* encryption oracle $\mathcal{E}_K^{bl}(\mathcal{LR}(\cdot,\cdot,b))$ can be requested in an online manner. The adversaries send queries block by block, i.e. they submit

$(m_0^i[k], m_1^i[k])$. The oracle encrypts message block $m_b^i[k]$ according to the bit b chosen at the beginning of the game, and immediately outputs the ciphertext block $c_b^i[k]$, without waiting for the next plaintext block. The adversary can now adapt each plaintext block according to the previous ciphertext blocks. In the case of chosen ciphertext attacks, the adversary has also access to a blockwise decryption oracle, taking as input a ciphertext block $c[k]$ and returning the corresponding plaintext block $m[k]$. This better models implementations for which interactions are made on-the-fly between a user and his crypto device. Such adversaries are called *blockwise adaptive* . Note that when dealing with smart cards, more than one block can be stored and interactions could contain larger buffers. However adversaries can still adapt their queries between each buffer, and thus one can assume that single blocks are sent (here, the word block is redefined to cover a complete buffer). This leads to the notions of Blockwise Chosen Plaintext Attacks (BCPA) or Blockwise Chosen Ciphertext Attacks (BCCA).

A recent work of Fouque, Martinet and Poupard [14] has formalized this notion in a stronger way: in their work they have considered *concurrent blockwise adaptive adversaries* . In this setting, the adversaries may run a polynomial number (in the security parameter) of encryption and/or decryption sessions in parallel. Such a notion is clearly stronger than the one we need here. A scheme proved secure in their model is thus clearly also secure in the weaker model considered here. The formal definition and description of the experiments we consider are given in appendix A.1.

3.2 Integrity of Ciphertexts

The notion of *integrity of ciphertexts* (INT-CTXT) has been first introduced in [19] and independently in [7]. It formalizes the idea that it should be computationally infeasible for a polynomial-time adversary performing a chosen message attack (CMA), to produce an authenticated ciphertext, for a message, not previously queried to the oracle (weak unforgeability) or even already queried (strong unforgeability). The chosen message attack is modeled by giving access to an oracle, that takes as input a message M and returns an authenticated ciphertext (C, τ), and to a verification oracle, taking as input an authenticated ciphertext (C, τ) and returning a bit b depending on the validity of the tag. The strongest security notion used for integrity is the strong unforgeability. Of course this distinction with the weak unforgeability does not have sense in the case of deterministic MAC schemes. However, for probabilistic ones, this security notion is the stronger one we can expect for a MAC scheme.

In the case of integrity, the blockwise adversarial model modifies the encryption oracle: it is requested with on-line queries and it outputs the authenticated ciphertext blocks on-the-fly. During the game, the verification oracle does not output anything and just waits until the end of the query. If it is valid, it returns $b = 1$ and otherwise, it returns $b = 0$. The queries are made on-the-fly but this does not make any change in the formalism of the experiment, as no intermediate results are provided to the adversary. Thus, integrity in the blockwise adversarial model is only slightly different from the standard model, since the encryption oracle is blockwise oriented. A description of the adversary experiment is given in appendix A.2. In the following we say that a scheme is B-INT-CTXT secure if any "reasonable" adversary cannot win this game with significant probability.

4 Authenticated Encryption in the Blockwise Setting

To construct an authenticated encryption scheme, the classical method is to use an encryption scheme along with a Message Authentication Code (MAC). In [7], Bellare and Namprempre have shown that if an authenticated encryption scheme is both IND-CPA secure and INT-CTXT secure, then it is also IND-CCA secure. They have also studied how to combine encryption and MAC schemes so that the construction is generically secure: the right way to securely combine them is to first encrypt the plaintext and then MACing the ciphertext: if the underlying encryption scheme is only IND-CPA secure and if the MAC scheme is strongly unforgeable, then the Encrypt-Then-MAC composition is IND-CCA secure.

If one considers now blockwise adaptive adversaries, one can see that the Encrypt-Then-MAC composition is no longer secure against chosen ciphertext attacks. Indeed, as we have seen above, such adversaries allow to break the naive implementations of the Encrypt-Then-MAC. Thus, not only the encryption part of the composition has to be studied against blockwise adversaries, but also the decryption part, which may lead to insecure schemes.

To secure these compositions, the first idea is to move the requirements on the underlying schemes to the blockwise setting. However, this is not sufficient since the MAC verification and the decryption process are no longer linked. Thus even if the scheme is IND-BCPA and B-INT-CTXT secure, the composition could be insecure against chosen ciphertext attacks. For example, we consider the composition of the CBC encryption scheme with delay, denoted by DCBC (fully described and proved secure in [14]), along with the EMAC authentication algorithm, strongly unforgeable ([20, 5]). This scheme, DCBC-Then-EMAC, provides IND-BCPA and B-INT-CTXT security. However, the already known chosen ciphertext attack on the CBC can be performed in the blockwise setting (see [16] for a detailed description of it) even if the DCBC is combined with the secure EMAC authentication scheme. This proves that the composed scheme is not IND-BCCA secure. This remark allows us to give the following proposition:

Proposition 1. *There exists a symmetric encryption encryption scheme providing both IND-BCPA and B-INT-CTXT security but which is not IND-BCCA secure. That is, we have:*

$$\textbf{IND-BCPA} + \textbf{B-INT-CTXT} \not\Rightarrow \textbf{IND-BCCA}$$

This shows that when dealing with blockwise adaptive adversaries some other and stronger requirements have to be made on the underlying schemes. The classical Encrypt-Then-MAC composition and all the known authenticated encryption schemes cannot be used as it to ensure both confidentiality and integrity. The protocol itself has to be modified to take into account blockwise adaptive adversaries.

5 The Decrypt-Then-Mask Secure Generic Composition

In this section we describe a practical solution to the Verify-Then-Decrypt paradigm. The composition simply modifies the decryption protocol and thus is backward compatible with existing schemes. The encryption phase is supposed to be secure in the blockwise model against chosen plaintext attacks. We also assume that the cryptographic device is memory limited (cannot store the whole plaintext), but stores the long term secret key. Moreover the receiver of an authenticated ciphertext is assumed to have access to a Pseudorandom Number Generator (PRNG), also implemented in the crypto device in charge of the decryption. In this context, we propose a new decryption process, generically secure against blockwise adaptive adversaries, mounting chosen ciphertext attacks.

5.1 Description

The main idea behind this construction is that the crypto device should not give any information on the plaintext before having checked the ciphertext integrity. However, because of its restricted storage capability, it cannot store the plaintext M, verify the MAC and output M only when valid. Instead, the crypto device will use a Pseudorandom Number Generator (PRNG) to mask the plaintext blocks so that they can be returned on-the-fly.

A PRNG consists in two parts: a seed generation algorithm (initialization) taking as input a security parameter and outputting an initial state s_0 ; and a generation algorithm, taking as input the current state s_{i-1}, and outputting the random string r_i along with the next state s_i. Note that in the model presented in [10], the initialization algorithm also produces a key which selects one particular PRNG out of a whole family. However, we suppose here the PRNG is without key and that the only secret resides in the initial state. In the following we denote by $\mathcal{CC}$ the cryptographic device and by $\mathcal{R}$ the user of this device. We assume the existence of an authenticated encryption scheme $\mathcal{SE}$, taking as input a key K along with a plaintext M, and returning an authenticated ciphertext. Without loss of generality, it is denoted by (C, τ), where C is the ciphertext and τ the MAC on it, although privacy and authenticity could be provided in a single pass (with IACBC, OCB, ...).

The user $\mathcal{R}$ will use $\mathcal{CC}$ to decrypt an authenticated ciphertext (C, τ). The main idea is to blind the plaintext blocks obtained after decryption of C by XORing them with a pseudorandom sequence of bits. Then, if the tag τ is valid, the seed used to generate the pseudorandom sequence is returned. Thus the cryptographic device does not need neither memory to store the plaintext nor multiple sending of the ciphertext. Formally, the decryption protocol between $\mathcal{CC}$ and $\mathcal{R}$, described in figure 1, works as follow:

Stage 0 $\mathcal{R}$ is given the ciphertext $C = c_1\|\ldots\|c_n$ along with a tag τ. He wants to first check its integrity and, if valid, to decrypt it.

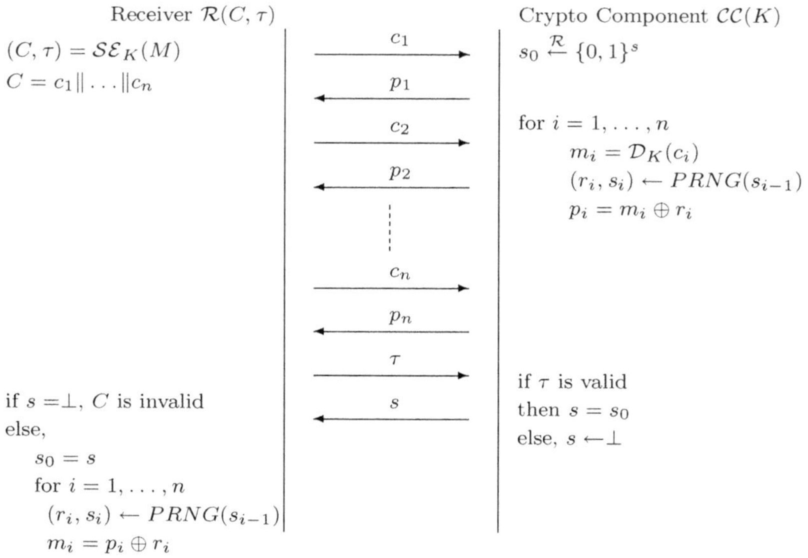

Fig. 1. The Decrypt-Then-Mask protocol

Stage 1 $\mathcal{CC}$ runs the seed generation algorithm to get a random seed $s_0 \in \{0,1\}^s$ for the PRNG (where s is a security parameter) and generates $(r_1, s_1) = \text{PRNG}(s_0)$. $\mathcal{R}$ sends to his crypto device $\mathcal{CC}$ the first ciphertext block c_1. $\mathcal{CC}$ initializes the tag computation, decrypts c_1 to obtain $m_1 = \mathcal{D}_K(c_1)$, computes $p_1 = m_1 \oplus r_1$ and returns p_1 to $\mathcal{R}$.

Stage 2 $\mathcal{R}$ sends the ciphertext on-the-fly. For each ciphertext block c_i he receives, $\mathcal{CC}$ updates the tag computation, decrypts c_i using the secret key, and masks it as $p_i = m_i \oplus r_i$ where $(r_i, s_i) = \text{PRNG}(s_{i-1})$. $\mathcal{CC}$ finally outputs p_i. This process continues until the last ciphertext block c_n is sent and $\mathcal{CC}$ returns p_n.

Stage 3 $\mathcal{R}$ finally sends the tag τ to $\mathcal{CC}$ which checks its validity. If valid, $\mathcal{CC}$ returns to $\mathcal{R}$ the seed s_0 used as initial state for the PRNG. Otherwise it outputs the predefined symbol $\perp$.

Stage 4 If (C, τ) was valid, $\mathcal{R}$ can decrypt the ciphertext $P = p_1 \| \dots \| p_n$ using s_0: for $i = 1, \dots, n$, $(r_i, s_i) = \text{PRNG}(s_{i-1})$ and $m_i = p_i \oplus r_i$. Then $M = m_1 \| \dots \| m_n$ is the plaintext corresponding to C. Otherwise, if $\mathcal{R}$ receives $\perp$, he cannot recover the plaintext.

Even if the last stage requires a cryptographic operation (One Time Pad with a pseudorandom sequence of bits), it can be safely performed outside the crypto device, since no permanent secret is involved. Note that if the tag was valid, the user $\mathcal{R}$ recovers the message M by generating all the r_i values from the seed s_0. Otherwise, no information on the plaintext is given to the adversary, according to the security of the PRNG. Indeed, as the receiver has no information on the seed and since the one time pad blinds the message, any plaintext could have been encrypted in P if the PRNG outputs are indistinguishable from random strings. Thus the security assumption on the PRNG is to be indistinguishable from truly random against Known Key Attacks[1], as defined in [10]: the adversary knows the key used to generate the r_i values but the seed s_0 and the states s_i are all hidden.

Note that the main point here is to use the initialization algorithm for each decryption and then generate a new initial state each time a decryption is requested. Indeed, the final state of the generator should not be used as initial state in the next use of the PRNG, as often done in practice.

In the sequel, we prove the IND-BCCA security of this Decrypt-Then-Mask decryption process when using an authenticated encryption scheme IND-BCPA and B-INT-CTXT secure, along with a IND-KKA secure PRNG.

Remark 1. Hereafter, we assume that the decryption process is regularly clocked, *i.e.*, if k blocks of ciphertext have been sent, $k - l$ plaintext blocks have been returned, where l is a public parameter of the scheme. For example, the CBC encryption scheme is such that $l = 1$ since the first block corresponds to the IV. Note that this property is needed during the proof. Otherwise, insecure schemes can be built, with delayed decryption outputs depending on the plaintext block. For sake of simplicity, we assume in the sequel that $l = 0$, meaning that plaintexts and ciphertexts, excluding the tag, are of the same length. However, the proof holds for any value of l.

5.2 Security Proof

In this part we prove that when using the Decrypt-Then-Mask protocol proposed above, with a IND-BCPA and B-INT-CTXT secure scheme, then the scheme is also IND-BCCA secure.

Theorem 1 (With the Decrypt-Then-Mask protocol, IND-BCPA and B-INT-CTXT ⇒ IND-BCCA). *Let $\mathcal{SE}$ an authenticated encryption scheme using the decryption protocol described in the* ◘*gure 1. If $\mathcal{SE}$ is B-INT-CTXT secure and IND-BCPA secure, and if the PRNG used in the decryption protocol is IND-KKA secure, then $\mathcal{SE}$ is IND-BCCA secure. Moreover, we have:*

$$\begin{aligned}\mathbf{Adv}_{\mathcal{SE}}^{\mathrm{IND-BCCA}}(k,t,q_e,q_d,\mu_e,\mu_d) \leq\ & \mathbf{Adv}_{\mathcal{SE}}^{\mathrm{B-INT-CTXT}}(k,t,q_e,q_d,\mu_e,\mu_d)\\ &+ \mathbf{Adv}_{PRNG}^{\mathrm{IND-KKA}}(k,t,q_d,\mu_d)\\ &+ \mathbf{Adv}_{\mathcal{SE}}^{\mathrm{IND-BCPA}}(k,t,q_e,\mu_e)\end{aligned}$$

Proof. We consider the adversary's IND-BCCA game defined in section 3.1. We recall that the adversary has access to a "left-or-right" blockwise oracle $\mathcal{LR}_{\mathcal{B}}(\cdot,\cdot,b)$ taking as input two plaintexts and encrypting one of them depending on a random bit b. The adversary has also access to a decryption oracle $\mathcal{D}^*(\cdot,\cdot)$ taking as input a ciphertext C and a candidate tag τ for it, block by block,

[1] Here the PRNG we use is supposed to be without any key. Thus one can assume the key is known and then use this security model.

and responding the queries as described in the protocol: first, it generates a seed s_0 for its PRNG. Then interactions with the adversary $\mathcal{A}$ begin. $\mathcal{A}$ sends to the decryption oracle the ciphertext C, on-the-fly. Each ciphertext block c_i is first decrypted into m_i using the decryption algorithm $\mathcal{D}_k$. Then the PRNG generates a random block r_i and the oracle outputs $p_i = m_i \oplus r_i$. At the end of the interactions, the decryption oracle receives the tag τ for the ciphertext. If it is valid, it outputs the seed s_0 for the PRNG. Otherwise, it sends a predefined symbol $\perp$, meaning that the ciphertext is invalid.

The adversary's goal is to guess with non negligible advantage the bit b used by the encryption oracle. The adversary $\mathcal{A}$ we consider runs in time t, submits at most q_e test messages of at most μ_e blocks, and q_d decryption queries, of at most μ_d blocks.

We start from the initial game G_0 and we will transform this game to obtain games G_1, G_2, and G_3. For $i = 0, 1, 2, 3$, we denote by S_i the event that $\mathcal{A}$ guesses the bit b in game G_i.

Game G_0. This is the original game, where encryption and decryption oracles are as described above. S_0 is defined to be the event that $\mathcal{A}$ correctly guesses the value of the hidden bit b, in the game G_0. Following the definition of security given in annex A.1, the relation holds:

$$\mathbf{Adv}_{\mathcal{SE},\mathcal{A}}^{\mathrm{IND-BCCA}}(k) = |\Pr(S_0) - 1/2|$$

Game G_1. This game is the same as G_0 except that the decryption algorithm never outputs the seed of the PRNG. Let E_1 be the event that some valid ciphertexts are rejected in game G_1. Note that in the security model, $\mathcal{A}$ is not allowed to feed the decryption oracle with outputs of the $\mathcal{LR}_{\mathcal{B}}$ oracle. Thus the decryption queries are necessarily forgeries: at least one ciphertext block or the tag have been modified in a query copied from an answer of the encryption oracle. Since $\mathcal{SE}$ is B-INT-CTXT secure, $\mathcal{A}$ cannot forge a valid ciphertext, except with probability at most $\mathbf{Adv}_{\mathcal{SE},\mathcal{A}}^{\mathrm{B-INT-CTXT}}(k)$, depending on the scheme. Then it follows that:

$$\Pr(E_1) \leq \mathbf{Adv}_{\mathcal{SE},\mathcal{A}}^{\mathrm{B-INT-CTXT}}(k)$$

Using lemma 1 of [22] and after some probability manipulations, we get:

$$|\Pr(S_1) - \Pr(S_0)| \leq \mathbf{Adv}_{\mathcal{SE},\mathcal{A}}^{\mathrm{B-INT-CTXT}}(k)$$

Game G_2. This game is the same as G_1, except that the outputs r_i of the PRNG are replaced by purely random blocks R_i. As before, for all decryption blocks queries c_i, the value $p_i = m_i \oplus R_i$ is returned.

The crucial point here is that the adversary knows the random values returned by the decryption box. Indeed, assume that $\mathcal{A}$ wants to have the encryption of message M. Then he queries the left-or-right oracle for the pair of equal messages (M, M) so that the ciphertext (C, τ) he receives necessarily encrypts M. Since the adversary cannot request the decryption oracle directly with

(C, τ), either one block of C or the tag τ has to be modified to be sent. Thus, one can suppose that $\mathcal{A}$ feeds $\mathcal{D}^*(\cdot,\cdot)$ with the legitimate query (C, τ'), where $\tau' \neq \tau$. As a consequence, according to the encryption scheme, the adversary gets, in the best case, the values $p_i = m_i \oplus r_i$. Since he already knows m_i, he can deduce r_i. Therefore, we assume that $\mathcal{A}$ always knows the random values generated by the decryption box.

In this game, $\mathcal{A}$ can detect the modification in two different ways:

- if $\mathcal{A}$ obtains the seed s_0, then he can detect the oracle's misbehavior. Indeed, he runs the PRNG to obtain the values r_i that would have been generated, and detects that the oracle is cheating, since $r_i \neq R_i$ except with negligible probability. However, since we specified in game G_1 that the oracle never outputs s_0, this event cannot occur.
- if $\mathcal{A}$ can distinguish the PRNG outputs from random bits sequences, he can also detect the oracle's misbehavior. However, the PRNG is supposed to be indistinguishable from random, and thus this bad event occurs with probability at most $\mathbf{Adv}_{PRNG,\mathcal{A}}^{\text{IND-KKA}}(k)$.

Finally, since the adversary never obtains the seed for the PRNG, the adversary's advantage between the two games G_1 and G_2 depends only on the security of the PRNG. Thus, we have:

$$|\Pr(S_2) - \Pr(S_1)| \leq \mathbf{Adv}_{PRNG,\mathcal{A}}^{\text{IND-KKA}}(k)$$

where $\mathbf{Adv}_{PRNG}^{\text{IND-KKA}}(k, t, q_d, \mu_d) = \max_{\mathcal{A}}\{\mathbf{Adv}_{PRNG,\mathcal{A}}^{IND-KKA}(k)\}$ is defined to be the maximum adversary's advantage in distinguishing the output of the PRNG from a truly random string, with at most q_d queries of length at most μ_d, and in time t, when the secret key is known and all the states are hidden. A precise definition is given in the full version paper [13].

Game G_3. We start from G_2 and we modify the decryption oracle's behavior as follows: instead of decrypting the ciphertext block c_i into m_i, and then masking it with a random block R_i, the decryption oracle generates a random block P_i and outputs it directly. Here the adversary gains no information from the decryption oracle since he receives random values independent of the previous computations and oracle calls. Furthermore since the one time pad is unconditionally secure in the information theoretic sense, and since the outputs of the PRNG are indistinguishable from random strings, no information leaks about the plaintext in the previous game. Thus the adversary gains no advantage between these two games and we have:

$$\Pr(S_3) = \Pr(S_2)$$

Moreover the decryption oracle clearly gives no information to the adversary. So the game of the adversary is the same as for a chosen plaintext attack in the blockwise sense. Thus, his advantage of guessing the bit b in this game implies:

$$|\Pr(S_3) - 1/2| \leq \mathbf{Adv}_{\mathcal{SE},\mathcal{A}}^{\text{IND-BCPA}}(k)$$

Finally, adding all advantages involved in the different games gives the theorem.

6 Practical Instantiation

In this section, we propose a practical implementation of the Decrypt-Then-Mask composition with the Delayed CBC, proposed in [17] and proved secure in [14], along with the FIPS 186 Pseudorandom Number Generator (see [12, 10]).

The Delayed-CBC encryption scheme, denoted by DCBC, has been proposed as a countermeasure against the blockwise adaptive attack on the classical CBC, in [17]. In the DCBC encryption mode, the encryption process is on-line : when it receives the kth input block, it computes the kth output block and returns the $(k-1)$th one. Finally, when it receives the `stop` command, the encryption process returns the last block. The security proof for the DCBC has been recently made in [14]. In that paper, the authors prove the DCBC secure against blockwise chosen plaintext attacks, in the sense of the concurrent left-or-right security. As mentioned in section 3.1, this notion is stronger than the one we need here.

The generic composition Decrypt-Then-Mask uses a symmetric authenticated encryption scheme secure in the sense of indistinguishability and integrity. As shown above, the Delayed CBC can be used to ensure BCPA security. Combined in the Encrypt-Then-MAC composition with the encrypted MAC, called EMAC [20], it also provides integrity. Thus, the composition DCBC-Then-EMAC is a secure instantiation of the scheme in the Decrypt-Then-Mask setting.

However, to implement the Decrypt-Then-Mask protocol, a Pseudorandom Number Generator should be used. Such generators have been proposed in the literature with different security proofs, depending on the model we consider. The requirements we have here on the generator are very strong. Indeed, since the receiver of the ciphertext should also have an implementation of it, we should assume that the key is known to the adversary and that the only secret is the initial state chosen by the crypto device. Such security notion has been defined in [10]. In that paper the authors studied the security of two popular Pseudorandom Number Generators, the ANSI X9.17 and the FIPS 186. In our setting, the ANSI X9.19 is not appropriate since it is totally insecure when the key is known to the adversary. However, the FIPS 186 generator is proved secure against Known Key Attacks, when the states of the generator are hidden, and when the inputs are not under control of the adversary. This is exactly our setting and thus we propose to use it in our scheme. The full version of this paper [13] recalls this security framework and the theorem of [10] for the security of the FIPS 186 generator. One of the constructions provided by the FIPS 186 specifications [12] is based on the core SHA-1 function with the underlying assumption that it can be considered as a random function. This assumption is not new and has already been used in some papers as in [4] and [2]. This seems realistic in practice since no attack that could suggest such a weakness has been found for this function.

References

[1] J. H. An and M. Bellare. Does encryption with redundancy provide authenticity. In B. Pfitzmann, editor, *Advances in Cryptology – Eurocrypt'01*, volume 2045 of *LNCS*, pages 512 – 528. Springer-Verlag, 2001. 145

[2] M. Bellare, R. Canetti, and H. Krawczyk. Pseudorandom Functions Revisited: The Cascade Construction and its Concrete Security. In *Proceedings of the 37th Symposium on Foundations of Computer Science*. IEEE, 1996. 156

[3] M. Bellare, A. Desai, E. Jokipii, and P. Rogaway. A Concrete Security Treatment of Symmetric Encryption: Analysis of the DES Modes of operation. In *Proceedings of the 38th Symposium of Foundations of Computer Science*, pages 394 – 403. IEEE Computer Security Press, 1997. 148

[4] M. Bellare, R. Guérin, and P. Rogaway. XOR-MACs: New Methods for Message Authentication using Finite Pseudorandom Functions. In D. Coppersmith, editor, *Advances in Cryptology – Crypto'95*, volume 963 of *LNCS*, pages 15 – 28. Springer-Verlag, 1995. 156

[5] M. Bellare, J. Kilian, and P. Rogaway. The Security of the Cipher Block Chaining Message Authentication Code. In Y. Desmedt, editor, *Advances in Cryptology – Crypto'94*, volume 839 of *LNCS*, pages 341 – 358. Springer-Verlag, 1994. 150

[6] M. Bellare, T. Kohno, and C. Namprempre. Authenticated Encryption in SSH: Provably Fixing the SSH Binary Packet Protocol. In *Ninth ACM Conference on Computer and Communications Security*, pages 1 – 11. ACM Press, 2002. 146

[7] M. Bellare and C. Namprempre. Authenticated Encryption: Relations among notions and analysis of the generic composition paradigm. In T. Okamoto, editor, *Advances in Cryptology – Asiacrypt'00*, volume 1976 of *LNCS*, pages 531 – 545. Springer-Verlag, 2000. 145, 149, 150

[8] M. Bellare and P. Rogaway. Encode then encipher encryption: How to exploit nounces or redundancy in plaintexts for efficient cryptography. In T. Okamoto, editor, *Advances in Cryptology – Asiacrypt'00*, volume 1976 of *LNCS*, pages 317 – 330. Springer-Verlag, 2000. 145

[9] M. Blaze, J. Feigenbaum, and M. Naor. A Formal Treatment of Remotely Keyed Encryption. In K. Nyberg, editor, *Advances in Cryptology – Eurocrypt'98*, volume 1403 of *LNCS*, pages 251 – 265. Springer-Verlag, 1998. 146

[10] A. Desai, A. Hevia, and Y. L. Yin. A Practice-Oriented Treatment of Pseudorandom Number Generators. In L. Knudsen, editor, *Advances in Cryptology – Eurocrypt 2002*, volume 2332 of *LNCS*, pages 368 – 383. Springer-Verlag, 2002. 151, 153, 156

[11] Y. Dodis and J. H. An. Cancelment and its Applications to Authenticated Encryption. In E. Biham, editor, *Advances in Cryptology – Eurocrypt'03*, LNCS. Springer-Verlag, 2003. 146

[12] FIPS PUB 186-2. Digital Signature Standard. Technical report, National Institute of Standards and Technologies, 2001. 156

[13] P.-A. Fouque, A. Joux, G. Martinet, and F. Valette. Authenticated On-line Encryption, 2003. Full version of this paper. Available at `http://www.di.ens.fr/~fouque`. 155, 156

[14] P.-A. Fouque, G. Martinet, and G. Poupard. Practical Symmetric On-line Encryption. In T. Johansson, editor, *Proceedings of the Fast Software Encryption Workshop 2003*, LNCS. Springer-Verlag, 2003. 149, 150, 156

[15] R. Gennaro and P. Rohatgi. How to Sign Digital Streams. In B. Kaliski, editor, *Advances in Cryptology – Crypto'97*, volume 1294 of *LNCS*, pages 180 – 197. Springer-Verlag, 1997. 148

[16] S. Goldwasser and M. Bellare. Lecture Notes on Cryptography, 2001. Available at `http://www-cse.ucsd.edu/users/mihir`. 150

[17] A. Joux, G. Martinet, and F. Valette. Blockwise-Adaptive Attackers. Revisiting the (in)security of some provably secure Encryption Modes: CBC, GEM, IACBC.

In M. Yung, editor, *Advances in Cryptology – Crypto'02*, volume 2442 of *LNCS*, pages 17 – 30. Springer-Verlag, 2002. 146, 148, 156

[18] C. Jutla. Encryption Modes with Almost Free Message Integrity. In B. Pfitzmann, editor, *Advances in Cryptology – Eurocrypt'01*, volume 2045 of *LNCS*, pages 529 – 544. Springer-Verlag, 2001. 145, 146

[19] J. Katz and M. Yung. Unforgeable Encryption and Chosen Ciphertext Secure Modes of Operation. In B. Schneier, editor, *Proceedings of the Fast Software Encryption Workshop 2000*, volume 1978 of *LNCS*, pages 284 – 299. Springer-Verlag, 2000. 149

[20] E. Petrank and C. Rackoff. CBC-MAC for Real-Time Data Sources. *Journal of Cryptology*, 13(3):315 – 338, 2000. 150, 156

[21] P. Rogaway, M. Bellare, J. Black, and T. Krovetz. OCB: A Block-Cipher Mode of Operation for Efficient Authenticated Encryption. In *Proceedings of the 8th Conference on Computer and Communications Security*, pages 196 – 205. ACM Press, 2001. 145, 146, 147

[22] V. Shoup. OAEP reconsidered (Extended Abstract). In J. Kilian, editor, *Advances in Cryptology – Crypto'01*, volume 2139 of *LNCS*, pages 239 – 259. Springer-Verlag, 2001. 154

[23] S. Vaudenay. CBC Padding: Security Flaws Induced by CBC Padding - Applications to SSL, IPSEC, WTLS,... In L. Knudsen, editor, *Advances in Cryptology – Eurocrypt 2002*, volume 2332 of *LNCS*, pages 534 – 545. Springer-Verlag, 2002. 146

A Formal Definitions

A.1 Privacy

Here are described the experiments we consider:

$\mathsf{Expt}^{\mathrm{IND-BCPA}}_{\mathcal{SE},\mathcal{A}}(k)$	$\mathsf{Expt}^{\mathrm{IND-BCCA}}_{\mathcal{SE},\mathcal{A}}(k)$
Pick a random bit $b \in \{0,1\}$	Pick a random bit $b \in \{0,1\}$
$K \overset{\mathcal{R}}{\leftarrow} \mathcal{K}(k)$	$K \overset{\mathcal{R}}{\leftarrow} \mathcal{K}(k)$
$d \leftarrow \mathcal{A}^{\mathcal{E}^{bl}_K(\mathcal{LR}(\cdot,\cdot,b))}$	$d \leftarrow \mathcal{A}^{\mathcal{E}^{bl}_K(\mathcal{LR}(\cdot,\cdot,b)),\mathcal{D}^{bl}_K(\cdot)}$
if $d = b$, return 1, else return 0	if $d = b$, return 1, else return 0

where $\mathcal{E}^{bl}_K(\mathcal{LR}(\cdot,\cdot,b))$ is an encryption oracle taking as input two blocks of messages and returning the encryption of one of them depending on the bit b, and where $\mathcal{D}^{bl}_K(\cdot)$ is a decryption oracle taking as input a ciphertext block and returning the corresponding plaintext. We denote by IND-BCPA (respectively by IND-BCCA) the security in the blockwise model against chosen plaintext attacks (respectively chosen ciphertext attacks). The adversary's advantage in winning the IND-BCPA and the IND-BCCA games are defined as:

$$\mathbf{Adv}^{\mathrm{IND-BCPA}}_{\mathcal{SE},\mathcal{A}}(k) = \left|\Pr[\mathsf{Expt}^{\mathrm{IND-BCPA}}_{\mathcal{SE},\mathcal{A}}(k) = 1] - 1/2\right|$$

$$\mathbf{Adv}^{\mathrm{IND-BCCA}}_{\mathcal{SE},\mathcal{A}}(k) = \left|\Pr[\mathsf{Expt}^{\mathrm{IND-BCCA}}_{\mathcal{SE},\mathcal{A}}(k) = 1] - 1/2\right|$$

Therefore, we define the security bound of the scheme in the IND-BCPA and in the IND-BCCA senses by:

$$\mathbf{Adv}_{\mathcal{SE}}^{\mathrm{IND-BCPA}}(k,t,q_e,\mu_e) = \max_{\mathcal{A}}\{\mathbf{Adv}_{\mathcal{SE},\mathcal{A}}^{\mathrm{IND-BCPA}}(k)\}$$
$$\mathbf{Adv}_{\mathcal{SE}}^{\mathrm{IND-BCCA}}(k,t,q_e,q_d,\mu_e,\mu_d) = \max_{\mathcal{A}}\{\mathbf{Adv}_{\mathcal{SE},\mathcal{A}}^{\mathrm{IND-BCCA}}(k)\}$$

where the maximum is over all legitimate $\mathcal{A}$ having time-complexity t, asking to the oracle at most q_e encryption queries totaling μ_e blocks, and possibly q_d decryption queries totaling μ_d blocks. The time complexity is defined to be the worst case total execution time of the experiment plus the size of the code of the adversary. We consider that the time complexity is polynomially bounded in the security parameter k. A secret-key encryption scheme is said to be IND-BCPA (respectively IND-BCCA) secure, if for all polynomial time, probabilistic adversaries, the advantage in the respective games is negligible as a function of the security parameter k.

A.2 Integrity

The experiment we consider is as follows:

$\mathsf{Expt}_{\mathcal{SE},\mathcal{A}}^{\mathrm{B-INT-CTXT}}(k)$

$K \overset{\mathcal{R}}{\leftarrow} \mathcal{K}(k)$

If $\mathcal{A}^{\mathcal{E}_K^{bl}(\cdot),\mathcal{D}_K^*(\cdot,\cdot)}(k)$ makes a query (C,τ) to the oracle $\mathcal{D}_K^*(\cdot,\cdot)$ such that

- $\mathcal{D}_K^*(C,\tau)$ returns 1, and
- (C,τ) was never an output of $\mathcal{E}_K(\cdot)$

then return 1, else return 0.

where $\mathcal{E}_K^{bl}(\cdot)$ is a blockwise authenticated encryption oracle taking as input a plaintext M on-the-fly and returning a pair (C,τ) of ciphertext and tag, and where $\mathcal{D}_K^*(\cdot,\cdot)$ is a decryption oracle taking as input a ciphertext C along with a candidate tag τ for it, and returning a bit b such that $b=1$ if valid and $b=0$ otherwise. Note that the adversary $\mathcal{A}$ is not allowed to feed the decryption oracle $\mathcal{D}_K^*(\cdot,\cdot)$ with outputs of the encryption oracle. Otherwise, he could trivially win the game. So, if (C,τ) is an output of the encryption oracle, then the adversary should modify at least one block of C or the tag τ before calling the decryption oracle.

The adversary's advantage in winning the B-INT-CTXT game is defined as:

$$\mathbf{Adv}_{\mathcal{SE},\mathcal{A}}^{\mathrm{B-INT-CTXT}}(k) = \Pr[\mathsf{Expt}_{\mathcal{SE},\mathcal{A}}^{\mathrm{B-INT-CTXT}}(k) = 1]$$

Therefore, we define the security bound of the scheme in the B-INT-CTXT sense by:

$$\mathbf{Adv}_{\mathcal{SE}}^{\mathrm{B-INT-CTXT}}(k,t,q_e,q_d,\mu_e,\mu_d) = \max_{\mathcal{A}}\{\mathbf{Adv}_{\mathcal{SE},\mathcal{A}}^{\mathrm{B-INT-CTXT}}(k)\}$$

where the maximum is over all legitimate $\mathcal{A}$ having time-complexity t, asking to the oracle at most q_e encryption queries totaling at most μ_e blocks, and at most q_d decryption queries totaling at most μ_d blocks.

Five Practical Attacks for "Optimistic Mixing for Exit-Polls"

Douglas Wikström

Swedish Institute of Computer Science (SICS)
Box 1263, S-164 29 Kista, Sweden
douglas@sics.se

Abstract. Golle, Zhong, Boneh, Jakobsson, and Juels [9] recently presented an efficient mix-net, which they claim to be both robust and secure. We present five practical attacks for their mix-net, and break both its privacy and robustness.

The first attack breaks the privacy of any given sender *without corrupting any mix-server*. The second attack requires that the first mix-server is corrupted. Both attacks are adaptations of the "relation attack" introduced by Pfitzmann [24, 23].

The third attack is similar to the attack of Desmedt and Kurusawa [4] and breaks the privacy of *all* senders. It requires that all senders are honest and that the last mix-server is corrupted.

The fourth attack may be viewed as a novel combination of the ideas of Lim and Lee [16] and Pfitzmann [24, 23]. It breaks the privacy of any given sender, and requires that the first and last mix-servers are corrupted. This attack breaks also Jakobsson [14], including the fixed version of Mitomo and Kurosawa [18].

The fifth attack breaks the robustness in a novel way. It requires corruption of some senders and the first mix-server. This attack breaks also Jakobsson and Juels [15].

1 Introduction

The notion of a mix-net was invented by Chaum [3] and further developed by a number of people. Properly constructed a mix-net enables a set of senders to send messages anonymously.

Informally the requirements on a mix-net are: correctness, privacy, robustness, availability, and efficiency. Correctness implies that the result is correct given that all mix-servers are honest. Privacy implies that if a fixed minimum number of mix-servers are honest privacy of the sender of a message is ensured. Robustness implies that if a fixed number of mix-servers are honest, then any attempt to cheat is detected and defeated.

A mix-net consists of a number of mix-servers that collectively execute a protocol. The idea is that each mix-server receives a list of encrypted messages, transforms them, using partial decryption or random re-encryption, reorders them, and then outputs the randomly transformed and reordered list of cleartext messages. The secret permutation is shared among the mix-servers.

M. Matsui and R. Zuccherato (Eds.): SAC 2003, LNCS 3006, pp. 160–175, 2004.

1.1 Previous Work and Applications of Mix-Nets

The mixing paradigm has been used to accomplish privacy in many different scenarios. Chaum's original "anonymous channel" [3, 21] enables a sender to securely send mail anonymously. When constructing election schemes [3, 6, 22, 25, 20] the mix-net is used to ensure that the vote of a given voter can not be revealed. Also in the construction of electronic cash systems [13] mix-nets have been used to ensure privacy.

Abe gives an efficient construction of a general mix-net [1] and argues about its properties. Jakobsson has written a number of more general papers on the topic of mixing [12, 14] also focusing on efficiency.

There has been a breakthrough in the construction of zero-knowledge proofs of a correct shuffle recently. Furukawa and Sako [7], and Neff [19] respectively have both found efficient ways to design such proofs.

A new approach to practical mixing is given by Golle et al. [9]. They combine a robustness test based partly on work by Jakobsson and Juels, with the notion of "double enveloping". The latter notion is introduced independently by Wikström [29], except that he uses different keys for the two layers, and a proof of knowledge of the inner most cleartext.

Desmedt and Kurosawa [4] describe an attack on a protocol by Jakobsson [12]. Similarly Mitomo and Kurosawa [18] exhibit a weakness in another protocol by Jakobsson [14]. Pfitzmann has given some general attacks on mix-nets [24, 23], and Michels and Horster give additional attacks in [17].

This paper is based on two technical reports [30, 31]. Apparently Abe [2] has independently found attacks similar to those of the first of our technical reports, i.e. the first two attacks in this paper.

2 Review of "Optimistic Mixing for Exit-Polls"

We present a short review of the relevant parts of the protocol of Golle et al. [9]. The description given here is as close as possible to the original, but we avoid details irrelevant to our attacks and change some notation to simplify the exposition of the attacks. For details we refer the reader to [9].

2.1 Participants and Setup

The protocol assumes the existence of a bulletin board on which each participant has a dedicated area on which only she can write. No participant can erase anything on the bulletin board, but all participants can read everything.

The participants of the protocol are N *senders*, and a relatively small number of *mix-servers* , $M_1, \ldots, M_k$. Each sender encrypts its message, and writes it on the bulletin board. The mix-servers then execute the mix-net protocol.

The protocol employs an El Gamal [5] cryptosystem in a subgroup G_Q of prime order Q of the multiplicative group modulo a prime P, i.e. $\mathbb{Z}_P^*$. A private key x is generated by choosing $x \in \mathbb{Z}_Q$ uniformly and independently at random. The corresponding public key is (g, y), where g is a generator of G_Q, and $y = g^x$. Encryption of a message $m \in G_Q$ using the public key (g, y) is given by $E_{(g,y)}(m, r) = (g^r, y^r m)$, where r is chosen uniformly at random from $\mathbb{Z}_Q$, and decryption of a cryptotext on the form $(u, v) = (g^r, y^r m)$ using the private key x is given by $D_x(u, v) = u^{-x} v = m$. The El Gamal system also has the re-encryptability[1] property, i.e. given (u, v) and the public key (g, y), anybody can "update" the randomness used in the encryption of m, by forming $(g^{r'} u, y^{r'} v) = (g^{r+r'}, y^{r+r'} m) = E_{(g,y)}(m, r + r')$.

In the setup stage each mix-server M_j is somehow given a random $x_j \in \mathbb{Z}_Q$, and $y_l = g^{x_l}$ for $l \neq j$. The value x_j is also shared with the other mix-servers using a threshold verifiable secret sharing (VSS) scheme[2]. Thus, if any mix-server M_j is deemed to be cheating the other mix-servers can verifiably reconstruct its private key x_j. The mix-servers can also compute $y = \prod_{j=1}^{k} y_j$, which gives a joint public key (g, y), with secret corresponding private key $x = \sum_{j=1}^{k} x_j$.

A practical advantage of the mix-net is that it can be used to execute several mix-sessions using the same set of keys, i.e. the El Gamal keys are not changed between mix-sessions. To be able to do this the proofs of knowledge below are bound to a mix-session identifier id that is unique to the current mix-session.

2.2 Sending a Message to the Mix-Net

A typical honest sender, Alice, computes the following to send a message m to the mix-net:

$$(u, v) = E_{(g,y)}(m), \qquad w = h(u, v), \text{ and}$$
$$\alpha = [E_{(g,y)}(u), E_{(g,y)}(v), E_{(g,y)}(w)] = [(\mu_1, \mu_2), (\nu_1, \nu_2), (\omega_1, \omega_2)] \ ,$$

where $h : \{0,1\}^* \to G_Q$ is a hash function modeled by a random oracle. Then Alice computes a zero-knowledge proof of knowledge $\pi_{\mathrm{id}}(u, v, w)$, in the random oracle model of u, v and w, which depends on the current mix-session identifier id. Finally Alice writes $(\alpha, \pi_{\mathrm{id}}(u, v, w))$ on the bulletin board.

2.3 Execution of the Mix-Net

First the mix-servers remove any duplicate inputs to the mix-net, and discard input tuples that contain components not in the subgroup G_Q. Then the mix-servers discard all input tuples where the proof of knowledge is not valid for the current mix-session. Let $L_0 = \{[(a_{0,i}, b_{0,i}), (c_{0,i}, d_{0,i}), (e_{0,i}, f_{0,i})]\}_{i=1}^{N}$ be the resulting list of triples of El Gamal pairs. The mixing then proceeds in the following stages.

---

[1] Related terms are "homomorphic property", or "malleability property".

[2] Golle et al. [9] discuss different variants for sharing keys, but we choose to present a simple variant, since it has no impact on our attacks.

First Stage: Re-randomization and Mixing. This step proceeds as in all re-randomization mix-nets based on El Gamal. One by one, the mix-servers $M_1, \ldots, M_k$ randomize all the inputs and their order. (Note that the components of triples are not separated from each other during the re-randomization.) In addition, each mix-net must give a proof that the product of the plaintexts of all its inputs equals the product of the plaintexts of all its outputs. The protocol proceeds as follows.

1. Each mix-server M_j reads from the bulletin board the list L_{j-1} output by the previous mix-server.
2. The mix-server then chooses $r_{ji}, s_{ji}, t_{ji} \in \mathbb{Z}_Q$, for $i = 1, \ldots, N$, randomly and computes the re-randomized list:

   $$\{[(g^{r_{ji}} a_{j-1,i}, y^{r_{ji}} b_{j-1,i}), (g^{s_{ji}} c_{j-1,i}, y^{s_{ji}} d_{j-1,i}), (g^{t_{ji}} e_{j-1,i}, y^{t_{ji}} f_{j-1,i})]\}_{i=1}^{N} \ .$$

   The above list of triples is then randomly permuted, and the resulting list: $L_j = \{[(a_{j,i}, b_{j,i}), (c_{j,i}, d_{j,i}), (e_{j,i}, f_{j,i})]\}_{i=1}^{N}$ is written on the bulletin board.
3. Define $a_j = \prod_{i=1}^{N} a_{j,i}$, and define b_j, c_j, d_j, e_j, and f_j correspondingly. The mix-server proves in zero-knowledge that $\log_g a_j/a_{j-1} = \log_y b_j/b_{j-1}$, $\log_g c_j/c_{j-1} = \log_y d_j/d_{j-1}$, and $\log_g e_j/e_{j-1} = \log_y f_j/f_{j-1}$. This implies that $D_x(a_j, b_j) = D_x(a_{j-1}, b_{j-1})$, and similarly for the pairs (c_j, d_j) and (e_j, f_j), i.e. the component-wise product of the inner triples remains unchanged by the mix-server.

Remark 1. Since $\log_y b_j/b_{j-1} = \log_g a_j/a_{j-1} = \sum_{i=1}^{N} r_{ji}$, and M_j knows the latter sum, the proof in Step 3) can be implemented by a standard zero-knowledge proof of knowledge in the random oracle model, and similarly for the pairs (c_j, d_j), and (e_j, f_j). Such proofs are similar to Schnorr signatures [26].

Second Stage: Decryption of the Inputs.

1. A quorum of mix-servers jointly decrypt each triple of ciphertexts in L_k to produce a list L on the form $L = \{(u_i, v_i, w_i)\}_{i=1}^{N}$. Since the method used to do this is irrelevant to our attacks, we do not present it here.
2. All triples for which $w_i = h(u_i, v_i)$ are called *valid*.
3. Invalid triples are investigated according to the procedure described below. If the investigation proves that all invalid triples are *benign* (only senders cheated), we proceed to Step 4. Otherwise, the decryption is aborted, and we continue with the back-up mixing.
4. A quorum of mix-servers jointly decrypt the ciphertexts (u_i, v_i) for all valid triples. This successfully concludes the mixing. The final output is defined as the set of plaintexts corresponding to valid triples.

Special Step: Investigation of Invalid Triples. The mix-servers must reveal the path of each invalid triple through the various permutations. For each invalid triple, starting from the last server, each server reveals which of its inputs corresponds to this triple, and how it re-randomized this triple. One of two things may happen:

- **Benign case (only senders cheated):** if the mix-servers successfully produce all such paths, the invalid triples are known to have been submitted by users. The decryption resumes after the invalid triples have been discarded.
- **Serious case (one or more servers cheated):** if one or more servers fail to recreate the paths of invalid triples, these mix-servers are accused of cheating and replaced, and the mix-net terminates producing no output. In this case, the inputs are handed over to the back-up mixing procedure below.

Back-Up Mixing. The *outer-layer* encryption of the inputs posted to the mix-net is decrypted by a quorum of mix-servers. The resulting list of *inner-layer* ciphertexts becomes the input to a standard re-encryption mix-net based on El Gamal (using, for example Neff's scheme described in [19]). Then the output of the standard mix-net is given as output by the mix-net.

Remark 2. It is impossible to find two lists $\{(u_i, v_i)\}_{i=1}^N \neq \{(u'_i, v'_i)\}_{i=1}^N$ such that $\prod_{i=1}^N h(u_i, v_i) = \prod_{i=1}^N h(u'_i, v'_i)$, if the product is interpreted in a group where the discrete logarithm problem is hard. This is stated as a theorem by Wagner[3] [28], and appears as a lemma in Golle et al. [9].

During the re-encryption and mixing stage each mix-server proves in zero-knowledge that it leaves the component-wise product $(\prod u_i, \prod v_i, \prod w_i)$, of the inner triples (u_i, v_i, w_i) unchanged, but individual triples may still be corrupted. Then invalid triples are traced back. This leaves only valid inner triples in the output and the proofs of knowledge of each server are used to conclude that the component-wise product of these valid inner triples was left unchanged by the mix-net. Golle et al. [9] then refer to the lemma and conclude that the set of valid triples in the output is identical to the set of valid triples hidden in the double encrypted input to the mix-net.

Unfortunately, this intuitively appealing construction is flawed as we explain in Section 3.5. Furthermore, our third attack in Section 3.3 shows that it is possible to cheat without changing the set of inner triples.

3 The Attacks

The goal of the adversary Eve is to break the privacy of our typical honest sender Alice and cheat without detection. Each of our attacks illustrates a separate weakness of the protocol. The first two attacks are adaptations of the "relation attack", introduced by Pfitzmann [24, 23], to the setting with double enveloping. The idea of the "relation attack" is that to break the privacy of Alice, Eve computes a cryptotext of a message related to Alice's message. Then the mix-net is run as usual. The output of the mix-net contains two messages related in

[3] Wagner credits Wei Dai with this observation.

a way chosen by Eve. Some relations enable Eve to determine the message sent by Alice. The third attack is similar to the attack of Desmedt and Kurosawa [4] in that it exploits intermediate results of the protocol and fools a "product test". The fourth attack may be viewed as a novel combination of the ideas of Lim and Lee [16] and Pfitzmann [24, 23]. The fifth attack is novel.

3.1 First Attack: Honest Mix-Servers

We show that the adversary Eve can break the privacy of the typical sender Alice. All that is required is that Eve can send two messages to the mix-net, which is a natural assumption in most scenarios. In the following we use the notation for the cryptotext of Alice introduced in Section 2.2. Eve does the following:

1. Eve chooses δ and γ randomly in $\mathbb{Z}_Q$, and computes:

$$w_\delta = h(\mu_1^\delta, \mu_2^\delta),\ \ \alpha_\delta = (E_{(g,y)}(\mu_1^\delta), E_{(g,y)}(\mu_2^\delta), E_{(g,y)}(w_\delta))\ \ , \text{ and}$$
$$w_\gamma = h(\mu_1^\gamma, \mu_2^\gamma),\ \ \alpha_\gamma = (E_{(g,y)}(\mu_1^\gamma), E_{(g,y)}(\mu_2^\gamma), E_{(g,y)}(w_\gamma))\ \ .$$

   Then Eve computes corresponding proofs of knowledge $\pi_{\mathrm{id}}(\mu_1^\delta, \mu_2^\delta, w_\delta)$ and $\pi_{\mathrm{id}}(\mu_1^\gamma, \mu_2^\gamma, w_\gamma)$. This gives Eve two perfectly valid pairs $(\alpha_\delta, \pi_{\mathrm{id}}(\mu_1^\delta, \mu_2^\delta, w_\delta))$, $(\alpha_\gamma, \pi_{\mathrm{id}}(\mu_1^\gamma, \mu_2^\gamma, w_\gamma))$, that she sends to the bulletin board (possibly by corrupting two senders).
2. Eve waits until the mix-net has successfully completed its execution. During the execution of the mix-net the mix-servers first jointly decrypt the "outer layer" of the double encrypted messages. After benign tuples have been removed the result is a list of valid triples

$$((u_1, v_1, w_1), \ldots, (u_N, v_N, w_N))\ \ . \tag{1}$$

   The final output of the mix-net is the result of decrypting each inner El Gamal pair (u_i, v_i) and results in a list of cleartext messages $(m_1, \ldots, m_N)$.
3. Eve computes the list $(m_1', \ldots, m_N') = (m_1^{\delta/\gamma}, \ldots, m_N^{\delta/\gamma})$, and then finds a pair (i, j) such that $m_i = m_j'$. From this she concludes that with very high probability $m_j = u^\gamma$. Then she computes $z = m_j^{1/\gamma}$, and finds a triple (u_l, v_l, w_l) in the list (1) such that $z = u_l$. Finally she concludes that with very high probability m_l was the message sent by Alice to the mix-net.

Remark 3. At additional computational cost it suffices for Eve to send 2 messages to break the privacy of K senders. Suppose Eve wants to break the privacy also of Bob who sent m' encrypted as $(u', v') = E_{(g,y)}(m')$, $w' = h(u', v')$, and $\alpha' = [E_{(g,y)}(u'), E_{(g,y)}(v'), E_{(g,y)}(w')] = [(\mu_1', \mu_2'), (\nu_1', \nu_2'), (\omega_1', \omega_2')]$. Then Eve performs the attack above with the change that she starts with a single pair $(\mu_1^\zeta {\mu'}_1, \mu_2^\zeta {\mu'}_2)$ for some randomly chosen ζ instead of the two distinct pairs (μ_1, μ_2), and (μ_1', μ_2') that would have given two "unrelated" attacks. The original third step of the attack first gives Eve $z = u^\zeta u'$. To finish the attack she finds a pair (l, l') such that $u_l^\zeta u_{l'} = z$, and concludes that with high probability Alice sent m_l and Bob sent $m_{l'}$. The approach is generalized to higher dimensions in the natural way to break the privacy of several senders (K must clearly be reasonably sized).

Why the Attack Is Possible. The attack exploits two different flaws of the protocol. The first is that the sender of a message, e.g. Alice, proves only knowledge of the inner El Gamal pair (u, v) and the hash value $w = h(u, v)$, and not knowledge of the message m. The second flaw is that identical El Gamal keys are used for both the inner and outer El Gamal system.

Anybody can compute a single encrypted message $(\mu_1^\delta, \mu_2^\delta) = (g^{r\delta}, y^{r\delta}u^\delta) = E_{(g,y)}(u^\delta, r\delta)$ of a power u^δ of the first component u of the *inner* El Gamal pair (u, v) of the triple α sent by Alice. Anybody can also compute a proof of knowledge of $(\mu_1^\delta, \mu_2^\delta)$ and $w_\delta = h(\mu_1^\delta, \mu_2^\delta)$ (and similarly for $(\mu_1^\gamma, \mu_2^\gamma)$ and ω_γ).

The first flaw allows Eve to input triples of El Gamal pairs with such proofs of knowledge to the mix-net. The second flaw allows Eve to use the mix-net to decrypt $(\mu_1^\delta, \mu_2^\delta)$, and thus get her hands on u^δ (and similarly for u^γ). Eve can then identify (u, v) as the inner El Gamal pair of Alice and break her privacy.

3.2 Second Attack: Different Keys and Corrupt Mix-Server

Suppose we change the protocol slightly by requiring that the mix-servers generate separate keys for the outer and inner El Gamal systems, to avoid the first attack of Section 3.1. We assume that there are two different key pairs $((g, y_{\mathrm{in}}), x_{\mathrm{in}})$ and $((g, y_{\mathrm{out}}), x_{\mathrm{out}})$, for the inner and outer El Gamal layers respectively. We also assume that these keys have been shared similarly as the original key pair $((g, y), x)$. This is the type of double enveloping proposed by Wikström [29]. For the second attack to succeed we need some additional assumptions.

Unclear Details and Additional Assumptions. We start by quoting Section 5, under "Setup." point 4 of Golle et al. [9], which presents the proof of knowledge $\pi_{\mathrm{id}}(u, v, w)$ of the sender Alice:

> 4. This proof of knowledge should be bound to a unique mix-session identifier to achieve security over multiple invocations of the mix. Any user who fails to give the proof is disqualified, and the corresponding input is discarded.

If different keys are used for each mix-session, then the above makes no sense, since the proof of knowledge of u, v and w already depends on the public key of the outer El Gamal system. There is clearly practical value in not changing keys between mix-sessions. We assume that the keys are not changed between mix-sessions even if a mix-server is found to be cheating. If a mix-server is found to be cheating, its shared keys are instead reconstructed by the remaining mix-servers using the VSS-scheme, and in later mix-sessions the actions of the cheating mix-server are performed in the open (the details of this does not matter to our attack). Under these assumptions we can give an attack on the protocol.

The original paper of Golle et al. [9] does not explicitly say if the discovery of the corrupted mix-server results in a new execution of the key generation protocol. Apparently the intention of the authors is to let the remaining mix-servers generate a new set of keys if any cheating is discovered [10].

The attack is interesting even though this interpretation is not the one intended by the authors, since it shows the importance of explicitly defining all details of protocols and highlights some issues with running several concurrent mix-sessions using the same set of keys.

The Attack. Apart from the above assumptions, the attack only requires that the first mix-server in the mix-chain is corrupted. The attack is employed during two mix-sessions using the same keys and the corrupted mix-server is identified as a cheater in the first mix-session. In the following we describe the actions of Eve during the first and second mix-sessions, respectively.

THE FIRST MIX-SESSION. We assume that Alice and some other arbitrary sender Bob have sent inputs to the mix-net (and use the notation of Remark 3 for the input of Bob). Eve corrupts M_1. It then replaces α and α' with: $[E_{y_{\text{out}}}(u), E_{y_{\text{out}}}(v), E_{y_{\text{out}}}(w')]$, and $[E_{y_{\text{out}}}(u'), E_{y_{\text{out}}}(v'), E_{y_{\text{out}}}(w)]$ respectively, in its input list, i.e. the third components of the two triples are shifted. Then Eve forces M_1 to simulate a completely honest mix-server on the resulting altered list $L'_0 = \{[(a'_{0,i}, b'_{0,i}), (c'_{0,i}, d'_{0,i}), (e'_{0,i}, f'_{0,i})]\}_{i=1}^{N}$. Note that $\prod_{i=1}^{N} a'_{0,i} = a_0$, and similarly for b_0, c_0, d_0, e_0, and f_0. Thus the simulated honest mix-server outputs perfectly valid zero-knowledge proofs that the product of the inner triples are unchanged.

At the end of the mixing the mix-servers verify the tuples and discover the invalid tuples (u, v, w') and (u', v', w). These tuples are traced back all the way to the first mix-server, which is revealed as a cheater. In this process Eve is able to link Alice to (u, v) (and Bob to (u', v')). Finally the honest mix-servers finish the protocol by using the general constructions based on the work by Neff [19] as in Golle et al. [9].

THE SECOND MIX-SESSION. To allow the mix-net to execute a second mix-session using the same set of keys, the cheater's key is reconstructed and revealed by a quorum of the mix-servers.

To determine the contents of the El Gamal pair (u, v), Eve waits for the second mix-session using the same set of keys. Then she uses a "relation attack" [24, 23, 12] in the second mix-session to decrypt (u, v), i.e. Eve does the following:

1. Eve chooses δ and γ randomly in $\mathbb{Z}_Q$, and computes:
   $w_\delta = h(u^\delta, v^\delta)$, $\alpha_\delta = (E_{y_{\text{out}}}(u^\delta), E_{y_{\text{out}}}(v^\delta), E_{y_{\text{out}}}(w_\delta))$, and
   $w_\gamma = h(u^\gamma, v^\gamma)$, $\alpha_\gamma = (E_{y_{\text{out}}}(u^\gamma), E_{y_{\text{out}}}(v^\gamma), E_{y_{\text{out}}}(w_\gamma))$.
   Then Eve computes corresponding proofs of knowledge $\pi_{\text{id}}(u^\delta, v^\delta, w_\delta)$ and $\pi_{\text{id}}(u^\gamma, v^\gamma, w_\gamma)$. This gives Eve two perfectly valid pairs $(\alpha_\delta, \pi_{\text{id}}(u^\delta, v^\delta, w_\delta))$, $(\alpha_\gamma, \pi_{\text{id}}(u^\gamma, v^\gamma, w_\gamma))$, which she sends to the bulletin board (possibly by corrupting two senders).
2. Eve waits until the mix-net has successfully completed its execution. The final output of the mix-net is a list of cleartext messages $(m_1, \ldots, m_N)$.

3. Note that $m_i = m^\delta$ and $m_j = m^\gamma$ for some i and j. Eve computes $\delta\gamma^{-1}$ mod Q, computes the list $(m'_1, \ldots, m'_N) = (m_1^{\delta/\gamma}, \ldots, m_N^{\delta/\gamma})$, and finally finds a pair (i, j) such that $m_i = m'_j$. Then she concludes that with high probability $m_j^{1/\gamma}$ is the message sent by Alice to the mix-net in the first mix-session.

Remark 4. The attack is easily generalized to break the privacy of several senders by using a circular shift of the third components during the first mix-session. It is also easy to see that Remark 3 can be applied to reduce the number of messages sent by Eve during the second mix-session.

Why the Attack Is Possible. The attack exploits that the sender of a message only proves knowledge of the inner triple (u, v, w). At the cost of detected cheating Eve finds a (u, v) corresponding to Alice, and then uses the second mix-session as a decryption oracle to get her hands on m.

A Note on Concurrent Mix-Sessions. Ignoring the other attacks, a simple countermeasure to the second attack above, is to stipulate that if a cheating mix-server is identified new keys must be generated for the next mix-session.

A disadvantage of this countermeasure is that the mix-net can not be allowed to execute several concurrent mix-sessions using the same keys. If one mix-session is still receiving messages while another mix-session discovers a cheating mix-server the second attack of Section 3.2 can still be applied. The problem is not solved by running the back-up mix-net of Neff [19] on all mix-sessions using the same keys at this point.

This problem of concurrency may seem academic, since in most election scenarios it is not very cumbersome to have different keys for each mix-session, but in future applications of mix-nets it may be useful to run several concurrent mix-sessions using the same keys.

3.3 Third Attack: Honest Senders and One Corrupt Mix-Servers

In this section we assume that all senders and all mix-servers, except the last mix-server M_k, are honest. The last mix-server M_k is corrupted by the adversary Eve and performs the attack. The attack breaks both robustness and privacy.

To simplify our notation we write $L_0 = \{\alpha_i\}_{i=1}^N$ for the input list, where we define $\alpha_i = [(a_{0,i}, b_{0,i}), (c_{0,i}, d_{0,i}), (e_{0,i}, f_{0,i})]$ to be the tuple sent by sender S_i. Instead of following the protocol, M_k proceeds as follows in the first stage.

1. It computes the 6-tuple: $(a', b', \ldots, f') = (a_{k-1}/a_0, b_{k-1}/b_0, \ldots, f_{k-1}/f_0)$, and the tuple $\alpha'_1 = [(a' a_{0,1}, b' b_{0,1}), (c' c_{0,1}, d' d_{0,1}), (e' e_{0,1}, f' f_{0,1})]$.
2. Then it forms the list $L'_{k-1} = \{\alpha'_1, \alpha_2, \ldots, \alpha_N\}$, i.e. a copy of L_0 with the first tuple α_1 replaced by α'_1.
3. When M_k is supposed to re-randomize and permute the output L_{k-1} of M_{k-1} it instead simulates the actions of an honest mix-server on the corrupted input L'_{k-1}. The output list written to the bulletin board by the simulated mix-server is denoted L_k.

4. Eve waits until the inner layer has been decrypted and uses her knowledge of the permutation that relates L_k to L_0 to break the privacy of all senders.

We show that the attack goes undetected, i.e. the mix-servers decrypt the inner layer. This implies that the attack succeeds.

Firstly, consider the proof of knowledge that M_k produces during the re-encryption and mixing stage. Define $a'_{k-1} = (a'a_{0,1})\prod_{i=2}^{N} a_{0,i}$, and similarly for for b'_{k-1}, c'_{k-1}, d'_{k-1}, e'_{k-1}, and f'_{k-1}. In Step 3 above, the simulated honest mix-server outputs proofs of knowledge of the logarithms: $\log_g a_k/a'_{k-1} = \log_y b_k/b'_{k-1}$, $\log_g c_k/c'_{k-1} = \log_y d_k/d'_{k-1}$, and $\log_g e_k/e'_{k-1} = \log_y f_k/f'_{k-1}$. By construction we have that $a'_{k-1} = (a'a_{0,1})\prod_{i=2}^{N} a_{0,i} = a'\prod_{i=1}^{N} a_{0,i} = \frac{a_{k-1}}{a_0}a_0 = a_{k-1}$, and similarly for b_{k-1}, c_{k-1}, d_{k-1}, e_{k-1}, and f_{k-1}. This implies that the proof of knowledge produced by M_k is deemed valid by the other mix-servers.

Secondly, consider the investigation of invalid inner triples. Tracing back invalid triples is difficult to M_k, since it does not know the re-encryption exponents and the permutation relating L_{k-1} and L_k. We show that there are no invalid inner triples. Suppose we define the sums $r = \sum_{j=1}^{k-1}\sum_{i=1}^{N} r_{ji}$, $s = \sum_{j=1}^{k-1}\sum_{i=1}^{N} s_{ji}$, and $t = \sum_{j=1}^{k-1}\sum_{i=1}^{N} t_{ji}$, i.e. we form the sum of all re-encryption exponents used by all mix-servers except the last, for the first second and third El Gamal pairs respectively. Since all mix-servers except M_k are honest, we have $(a', b', c', d', e', f') = (g^r, y^r, g^s, y^s, g^t, y^t)$, which implies that α'_1 is a valid re-encryption of α_1. Thus M_k does not corrupt any inner triple by simulating an honest mix-server on the input L'_{k-1}. Since all senders are honest and the set of inner triples hidden in L_0 and L'_{k-1} are identical, there are no invalid inner triples. Thus cheating is not detected and robustness is broken.

We conclude that the mix-servers decrypt the inner triples, i.e. the privacy of *all* senders is broken.

Why the Attack Is Possible. The third attack above exploits that the last mix-server M_k is not forced to take the output L_{k-1} of the next to last mix-server as input. This allows M_k to use a slightly modified version of L_0 instead, which breaks the privacy of all senders.

3.4 Fourth Attack: Two Corrupt Mix-Servers

In this section we assume that the first and last mix-servers, M_1 and M_k, are corrupted. We give a novel attack that breaks the privacy of any given sender Alice. Let $L_0 = \{\alpha_i\}_{i=1}^{N}$, where $\alpha_i = [(a_{0,i}, b_{0,i}), (c_{0,i}, d_{0,i}), (e_{0,i}, f_{0,i})]$. Without loss we let α_1 and α_2 be the tuples sent by Alice and Bob respectively. Let $\xi \in \mathbb{Z}_P^* \backslash G_Q$. Eve corrupts M_1 and M_k, and they proceed as follows.

1. M_1 computes the elements $\alpha'_1 = [(\xi a_{0,1}, b_{0,1}), (c_{0,1}, d_{0,1}), (e_{0,1}, f_{0,1})]$ and $\alpha'_2 = [(\xi^{-1} a_{0,2}, b_{0,2}), (c_{0,2}, d_{0,2}), (e_{0,2}, f_{0,2})]$, and forms the modified list $L'_0 = \{\alpha'_1, \alpha'_2, \alpha_3, \ldots, \alpha_N\}$. Then M_1 simulates an honest mix-server on input L'_0.

2. M_k simulates an honest mix-server on input L_{k-1}, but it does not write the output L_k of this simulation on the bulletin board. Let $L_k = \{\beta_i\}_{i=1}^N$, where $\beta_i = [(a_{k,i}, b_{k,i}), (c_{k,i}, d_{k,i}), (e_{k,i}, f_{k,i})]$. M_k finds $l, l' \in \{1, \ldots, N\}$ such that $a_{k,l}^Q = \xi^Q$ and $a_{k,l'}^Q = \xi^{-Q}$.
   Then it computes the tuples $\beta'_l = [(\xi^{-1}a_{k,l}, b_{k,l}), (c_{k,l}, d_{k,l}), (e_{k,l}, f_{k,l})]$ and $\beta'_{l'} = [(\xi a_{k,l'}, b_{k,l'}), (c_{k,l'}, d_{k,l'}), (e_{k,l'}, f_{k,l'})]$, and writes L'_k, where $L'_k = \{\beta_1, \ldots, \beta_{l-1}, \beta'_l, \beta_{l+1}, \ldots, \beta_{l'-1}, \beta'_{l'}, \beta_{l'+1}, \ldots, \beta_N\}$, on the bulletin board.
3. The mix-net outputs $(m_1, \ldots, m_N)$ and Eve concludes that Alice sent m_l.

Since all mix-servers except M_1 and M_k are honest there exists $l, l' \in \{1, \ldots, N\}$ and $r, r' \in \mathbb{Z}_Q$ such that $a_{k,l} = g^r \xi a_{0,1}$ and $a_{k,l'} = g^{r'} \xi^{-1} a_{0,2}$. This implies that $a_{k,l}^Q = \xi^Q (g^r a_{0,1})^Q = \xi^Q$ and $a_{k,l'}^{-Q} = \xi^{-Q}$, since $\beta^Q = 1$ for any $\beta \in G_Q$. We have $\xi^Q \neq 1 \neq \xi^{-Q}$, since the order of ξ does not divide Q. On the other hand we have $a_{k,i}^Q = 1$ for $i \neq l, l'$, since $a_{k,i} \in G_Q$ for $i \neq l, l'$. Thus Eve successfully identifies Alice's cryptotext if the cheating of M_1 and M_k is not detected.

Clearly, the values of b_1, c_1, d_1, e_1, and f_1 are not changed by replacing L_0 with L'_0 in Step 1. Neither is a_1, since $(\xi a_{0,1})(\xi^{-1} a_{0,2}) \prod_{i=3}^N a_{0,i} = \prod_{i=1}^N a_{0,i} = a_1$. Similarly, b_k, c_k, d_k, e_k, and f_k are not changed by replacing L_k with L'_k in Step 2. Neither is a_k, since $(\xi^{-1} a_{k,l})(\xi a_{k,l'}) \prod_{i \neq l,l'}^N a_{k,i} = \prod_{i=1}^N a_{k,i}$. Similarly as in the second attack of Section 3.3, we conclude that the proofs of knowledge produced by M_1 and M_k are deemed valid by the other mix-servers. If we assume that Alice and Bob are honest, their inner triples are never traced back and cheating is not detected.

If $\xi = \xi^{-1}$ Eve can only conclude that Alice sent a message from the set $\{m_l, m_{l'}\}$. This breaks the privacy of Alice, but Eve can also identify Alice's message uniquely by choosing Bob to be a corrupted sender.

Remark 5. Our attack may be viewed as a novel combination of the ideas in Lim and Lee [16] and Pfitzmann [24, 23] in that we use elements in $\mathbb{Z}_P^* \backslash G_Q$ to execute a "relation attack". However, Lim and Lee [16] focus on *extracting the secret key* , and their attack requires that $P - 1$ contains a relatively large smooth factor. Their proposed countermeasure is to choose P such that $(P-1)/2$ consists of large prime factors. This implies that the protocol leaks at most one bit. Our attack on the other hand use elements of $\mathbb{Z}_P^* \backslash G_Q$ more subtly, and is applicable[4] and practical *for any* choice of P. In particular the type of P proposed by Lim and Lee.

Why the Attack Is Possible. The attack exploits that a mix-server M_j does not verify that all elements in its input L_{j-1} are in G_Q. M_1 uses this to "tag" elements in L_0, which lets them be identified by the last mix-server M_k.

[4] More generally, if the implementation of arithmetic for G_Q is induced from a larger group $G \supset G_Q$ such that $|G|$ is known and the protocol fails to verify that inputs are in G_Q and not only in G, then our attack is applicable.

3.5 Fifth Attack: One Corrupt Mix-Server

In Proposition 3 of Golle et al. [9] the authors claim that their protocol satisfies the following strong definition of public verifiability if there is a group G_Q in which the discrete logarithm problem is hard.

Definition 1. *(Public Veri□ability (cf. [9])) A mix net is* public verifable *if there exists a polynomially bounded veri□er that takes as input the transcript of the mixing posted on the bulletin board, outputs "valid" if the set of valid outputs is a permuted decryption of all valid inputs, and otherwise outputs "invalid" with overwhelming probability. Note that to prove public veri□ability, we consider an adversary that can control all mix-servers and all users.*

Unfortunately, Proposition 3 of [9] is false. This is seen as follows.

Suppose that there are 4 senders, and that the adversary corrupts two of the senders and the first mix-server M_1. Let $(u_i, v_i, w_i) = (g^{r_i}, y^{r_i}m_i, H(u_i, v_i))$, and set $\alpha_i = ((a_{0,i}, b_{0,i}), (c_{0,i}, d_{0,i}), (e_{0,i}, f_{0,i})) = (E_y(u_i), E_y(v_i), E_y(w_i))$ for $i = 1, 2, 3, 4$. Then define $\alpha'_3 = ((a_{0,3}, b_{0,3}), (c_{0,3}, ad_{0,3}), (e_{0,3}, f_{0,3}))$ and $\alpha'_4 = ((a_{0,4}, b_{0,4}), (c_{0,4}, a^{-1}d_{0,4}), (e_{0,4}, f_{0,4}))$, for some $1 \neq a \in G_Q$. Suppose that α_1 and α_2 are sent to the mix-net by honest senders, and α'_3 and α'_4 are sent to the mix-net by the corrupted senders, with corresponding proofs of knowledge.

M_1 replaces α'_3, and α'_4 with α_3 and α_4. This does not change the value of the component-wise product $d_1 = v_1v_2v'_3v'_4$ since $v'_3v'_4 = v_3v_4$, and the cheating is not detected, since α_3 and α_4 corresponds to valid inner triples, and thus not traced back. On the other hand the tuples α'_3 and α'_4 correspond to invalid inner triples (u_3, v_3, aw_3) and $(u_4, v_4, a^{-1}w_4)$. We conclude that the sets of valid inner triples in the input and output respectively differ, public verifiability is broken, and Proposition 3 of [9] is false.

Some may argue that this is not important since the adversary may only choose to correct invalid messages which she has previously prepared for this particular purpose. However, note that the adversary may *choose* whether to correct α'_3 and α'_4. If she chooses not to correct invalid triples they are simply traced back and considered benign.

The following application shows the importance of this subtlety. We use the mix-net construction to run two independent elections (using different keys). First all votes for both elections are collected, and after some time both elections are closed. Then the mix-net is executed for the first election. Finally the mix-net is executed for the second election. In this scenario the adversary can insert specially prepared invalid triples (i.e. votes) in the second election, and then decide whether to correct these triples *based on the outcome* of the first election. This should clearly not be allowed, but may be acceptable in certain non-voting scenarios.

Why the Attack Is Possible. The attack exploits the fact that the first mix-server can choose whether to correct specially prepared invalid inner triples or not without detection.

4 Further Applications and Future Work

The attacks of sections 3.1, 3.2, and 3.3 all exploit the particular structure of the protocol of Golle et al. [9]. We have found no other protocol vulnerable to these attacks. In particular the protocol by Jakobsson [14] with similar structure is not vulnerable to the attack of Section 3.2.

The attack of Section 3.4 can be applied to break the privacy of Jakobsson [14], including the fixed protocol[5] Mitomo and Kurosawa [18], and the attack of Section 3.5 breaks the robustness of Jakobsson and Juels [15]. These attacks are sketched in Appendices A and B.

An interesting open question is what other protocols are vulnerable to attacks based on malicious use of elements in $\mathbb{Z}_P^* \backslash G_Q$.

5 Conclusion

We have presented several practical attacks for the mix-net recently proposed by Golle, Zhong, Boneh, Jakobsson, and Juels [9], claimed secure by the authors. In particular we break privacy of any sender *without* corrupting any mix-server. Two of our attacks are easily adapted to break Jakobsson [14], including the Mitomo and Kurosawa [18] variant, and Jakobsson and Juels [15].

The attacks for mix-nets, presented here and in other papers [23, 23, 17, 4, 18], suggest that we should be careful with unproven claims of security for mix-nets.

Acknowledgements

I am grateful to Johan Håstad for his advise and support, and for providing a missing piece of the 4:th attack. My results would have been far fetched without the discussions I had with Gunnar Sjödin, Torsten Ekedahl, and Björn Grönvall. I also had discussions with Markus Jakobsson, Philippe Golle, Ari Juels, and Sheng Zhong. An anonymous referee pointed me to the work of Lim and Lee.

References

[1] M. Abe, *Universally Verifiable mix-net with Verification Work Independent of the Number of Mix-centers*, Eurocrypt '98, pp. 437-447, LNCS 1403, 1998. 161

[2] M. Abe, *Personal Communication*, april 2003, a paper will appear at ACISP '03. 161

[3] D. Chaum, *Untraceable Electronic Mail, Return Addresses and Digital Pseudonyms*, Communications of the ACM - CACM '81, Vol. 24, No. 2, pp. 84-88, 1981. 160, 161

[4] Y. Desmedt, K. Kurosawa, *How to break a practical MIX and design a new one*, Eurocrypt 2000, pp. 557-572, LNCS 1807, 2000. 160, 161, 165, 172

[5] T. El Gamal, *A Public Key Cryptosystem and a Signiture Scheme Based on Discrete Logarithms*, IEEE Transactions on Information Theory, Vol. 31, No. 4, pp. 469-472, 1985. 161

[5] We note that their proposal is given without security claims.

[6] A. Fujioka, T. Okamoto and K. Ohta, *A practical secret voting scheme for large scale elections*, Auscrypt '92, LNCS 718, pp. 244-251, 1992. 161

[7] J. Furukawa, K. Sako, *An efficient scheme for proving a shuffle*, Crypto 2001, LNCS 2139, pp. 368-387, 2001. 161

[8] S. Goldwasser, S. Micali, *Probabilistic Encryption*, Journal of Computer and System Sciences (JCSS), Vol. 28, No. 2, pp. 270-299, 1984.

[9] Golle, Zhong, Boneh, Jakobsson, Juels, *Optimistic Mixing for Exit-Polls*, Asiacrypt 2002, LNCS, 2002. 160, 161, 162, 164, 166, 167, 171, 172

[10] Golle, Zhong, Boneh, Jakobsson, Juels, *Private Communication*, 16 October 2002. 167

[11] M. Hirt, K. Sako, *Efficient Reciept-Free Voting Based on Homomorphic Encryption*, Eurocrypt 2000, LNCS 1807, pp. 539-556, 2000.

[12] M. Jakobsson, *A Practical Mix*, Eurocrypt '98, LNCS 1403, pp. 448-461, 1998. 161, 167

[13] M. Jakobsson, D. M'Raihi, *Mix-based Electronic Payments*, 5:th Workshop on Selected Areas in Cryptography - SAC'98, LNCS 1556, pp. 157-173, 1998. 161

[14] M. Jakobsson, *Flash Mixing*, 18:th ACM Symposium on Principles of Distributed Computing - PODC '98, pp. 83-89, 1998. 160, 161, 172, 174

[15] M. Jakobsson, A. Juels, *An optimally robust hybrid mix network*, 20:th ACM Symposium on Principles of Distributed Computing - PODC '01, pp. 284-292, 2001. 160, 172, 174

[16] C. H. Lim, P. J. Lee, *A Key Recovery Attack on Discrete Log-based Schemes Using a Prime Order Subgroup*, Crypto '97, LNCS 1294, pp. 249-263, 1997. 160, 165, 170

[17] M. Michels, P. Horster, *Some remarks on a reciept-free and universally verifiable Mix-type voting scheme*, Asiacrypt '96, pp. 125-132, LNCS 1163, 1996. 161, 172

[18] M. Mitomo, K. Kurosawa, *Attack for Flash MIX*, Asiacrypt 2000, pp. 192-204, LNCS 1976, 2000. 160, 161, 172, 174

[19] A. Neff, *A verifiable secret shuffle and its application to E-Voting*, 8:th ACM Conference on Computer and Communications Security - CCS 2001, pp. 116-125, 2001. 161, 164, 167, 168

[20] V. Niemi, A. Renvall, *How to prevent buying of votes in computer elections*, Asiacrypt'94, LNCS 917, pp. 164-170, 1994. 161

[21] W. Ogata, K. Kurosawa, K. Sako, K. Takatani, *Fault Tolerant Anonymous Channel*, Information and Communications Security - ICICS '97, pp. 440-444, LNCS 1334, 1997. 161

[22] C. Park, K. Itoh, K. Kurosawa, *Efficient Anonymous Channel and All/Nothing Election Scheme*, Eurocrypt '93, LNCS 765, pp. 248-259, 1994. 161

[23] B. Pfitzmann, *Breaking an Efficient Anonymous Channel*, Eurocrypt '94, LNCS 950, pp. 332-340, 1995. 160, 161, 164, 165, 167, 170, 172

[24] B. Pfitzmann, A. Pfitzmann, *How to break the direct RSA-implementation of mixes*, Eurocrypt '89, LNCS 434, pp. 373-381, 1990. 160, 161, 164, 165, 167, 170

[25] K. Sako, J. Killian, *Reciept-free Mix-Type Voting Scheme*, Eurocrypt '95, LNCS 921, pp. 393-403, 1995. 161

[26] C. Schnorr, *Efficient signature generation by smart cards*, Journal of Cryptology, No. 4, pp. 161-174, 1991. 163

[27] Y. Tsiounis, M. Yung, *On the Security of El Gamal based Encryption*, International workshop on Public Key Cryptography, LNCS 1431, pp. 117–134, 1998.

[28] D. Wagner, *A Generalized Birthday Problem*, Crypto 2002, LNCS 2442, pp. 288-304, 2002. 164

[29] D. Wikström, *An Efficient Mix-Net*, Swedish Institute of Computer Science (SICS) Technical Report T2002:21, ISSN 1100-3154, SICS-T-2002/21-SE, 2002, `http://www.sics.se`, (An implementation was demonstrated during the Conference of the Swedish Research Institute for Information Technology (SITI), feb 7, 2002). 161, 166

[30] D. Wikström, *How to Break, Fix, and Optimize "Optimistic Mix for Exit-Polls"*, Swedish Institute of Computer Science (SICS) Technical Report T2002:24, ISSN 1100-3154, ISRN SICS-T-2002/24-SE, 6 december 2002, `http://www.sics.se`. 161

[31] D. Wikström, *Four Practical Attacks for "Optimistic Mixing for Exit-Polls"*, Swedish Institute of Computer Science (SICS) Technical Report T2003:04, ISSN 1100-3154, ISRN SICS-T-2003/04-SE, 25 february 2003, `http://www.sics.se`. 161

A Attack for "Flash Mix"

Jakobsson [14] presents an efficient mix-net. We assume familiarity with his protocol, and sketch how it is broken using the attack of Section 3.3.

The adversary corrupts M_1 and M_k. During the "second re-encryption", M_1 "tags" two arbitrary El Gamal pairs in its input by multiplying their first components with ξ and ξ^{-1} respectively. Then the honest mix-servers perform their re-encryption and mixing. When the last mix-server M_k is about to re-encrypt and mix the output of the previous mix-server M_{k-1}, it identifies the "tagged" El Gamal pairs, removes the "tags" by multiplying the first components by ξ^{-1} and ξ respectively, and then finally re-encrypts and mix the resulting list honestly. After the verification of the "first re-encryption", this breaks the privacy of some randomly chosen sender, if the cheating goes undetected.

Cheating is detected if one of two things happen; the adversary by chance chooses a "dummy element" that is later traced back through the mix-chain, or if M_1 or M_k fails to play its part in the computation of the "relative permutations" correctly. The first event is very unlikely since by construction there are very few "dummy elements". Since the "tags" are removed by M_k, and both M_1 and M_k follow the protocol except for the use of the tags, it follows that the cheating is not detected. It is easy to see that the changes introduced by Mitomo and Kurosawa [18] do not counter the above attack.

B Attack for "An Optimally Robust Hybrid Mix Network"

Jakobsson and Juels [15] presents a hybrid mix-net. We assume familiarity with their protocol and sketch how it is broken using the attack of Section 3.5.

Suppose that there are four senders, and that the i:th sender forms a cryptotext $(c_0^{(i)}, \mu_0^{(i)}, y_0^{(i)})$ of a message m_i. The adversary corrupts the last two senders and modifies their cryptotexts as follows before they hand them to the mix-net. It replaces $y_0^{(3)}$ by $\overline{y}_0^{(3)} = a y_0^{(3)}$ by and $y_0^{(4)}$ by $\overline{y}_0^{(4)} = a^{-1} y_0^{(4)}$ for some $a \neq 1$.

The adversary corrupts M_1. M_1 then replaces $\overline{y}_0^{(3)}$ by $y_0^{(3)}$ and $\overline{y}_0^{(4)}$ by $y_0^{(4)}$ and simulates an honest M_1 on the modified input. Similarly as in the original attack this does not change the component-wise product $P_0 = y_0^{(1)} y_0^{(2)} \overline{y}_0^{(3)} \overline{y}_0^{(4)} = y_0^{(1)} y_0^{(2)} y_0^{(3)} y_0^{(4)}$. The VerifyComplaint procedure is never invoked, since all cryptotexts are valid. Thus the cheating is not detected.

We conclude that the set of cleartext messages corresponding to the set of valid cryptotexts in the input differs from the set of cleartext messages in the output of the mix-net. This breaks the robustness, i.e. Definition 4(b).

Security Analysis of SHA-256 and Sisters*

Henri Gilbert[1] and Helena Handschuh[2]

[1] France Télécom R&D, FTRD/DTL/SSR
38-40 Rue du Général Leclerc, F-92131 Issy-Les Moulineaux
henri.gilbert@francetelecom.com
[2] GEMPLUS, Security Technologies Department
34 Rue Guynemer, F-92447 Issy-les-Moulineaux
helena.handschuh@gemplus.com

Abstract. This paper studies the security of SHA-256, SHA-384 and SHA-512 against collision attacks and provides some insight into the security properties of the basic building blocks of the structure. It is concluded that neither Chabaud and Joux's attack, nor Dobbertin-style attacks apply. Differential and linear attacks also don't apply on the underlying structure. However we show that slightly simplified versions of the hash functions are surprisingly weak : whenever symmetric constants and initialization values are used throughout the computations, and modular additions are replaced by exclusive or operations, symmetric messages hash to symmetric digests. Therefore the complexity of collision search on these modified hash functions potentially becomes as low as one wishes.

1 Introduction

A cryptographic hash function can be informally defined as an easy to compute but hard to invert function which maps a message of arbitrary length into a fixed length (m-bit) hash value, and satisfies the property that finding a collision, i.e. two messages with the same hash value, is computationally infeasible. Most collision resistant hash function candidates proposed so far are based upon the iterated use of a so-called compression function, which maps a fixed-length ($m+n$-bit) input value into a shorter fixed-length m-bit output value.

The most popular hash functions today are based on MD4 [20]. Following den Boer and Bosselaers [3], Vaudenay [23] and Dobbertin's work [7], it is no longer recommended to use MD4 for secure hashing, as collisions can now be computed in about 2^{20} compression function calls. In 1991, MD5 was introduced as a strengthened version of MD4. Although no collision has been found so far for MD5, pseudo-collisions were found on its compression function, so that MD5 is no longer considered as a very conservative hash function either [8, 9]. Other variants include RIPEMD, RIPEMD-128 and RIPEMD-160 [11, 19]. Attacks on

* This work is based on the result of an evaluation requested by the Japanese CRYPTREC project: http://www.ipa.go.jp/security/enc/CRYPTREC/index-e.html

M. Matsui and R. Zuccherato (Eds.): SAC 2003, LNCS 3006, pp. 175–193, 2004.

reduced versions of RIPEMD were published in [6, 10]. We call these functions the MD family of hash functions.

SHA, which also belongs to the MD family of hash functions, was introduced by the American National Institute for Standards and Technology and published as a FIPS standard in 1993. This early version is known as SHA-0. In 1994 a minor change to SHA-0 was made, and published as SHA-1 [14, 15]. The best attack known on SHA-0 is by Chabaud and Joux [4]. They show that in about 2^{61} evaluations of the compression function it is possible to find two messages hashing to the same value whereas a brute-force attack exploiting the birthday paradox would require about 2^{80} evaluations. The best known cryptanalysis reported on SHA-1 addresses the existence of slid pairs [22]. Finally a new generation of SHA functions with much larger message digest sizes, namely 256, 384 and 512 bits, called SHA-256, SHA-384 and SHA-512, was introduced in 2000 and adopted as a FIPS standard in 2002 [15]. As far as we know, the main motivation for introducing these new standard hash functions was to provide hash functions with security levels against collision search attacks consistent with the security levels expected from the three standard key sizes for the newly selected Advanced Encryption Standard (128, 192 and 256 bits) [16].

In this paper we study the security of these new functions against known attacks and report a very surprising property on a simplified version of these functions. For practical reasons, whenever our results apply to all three variants of SHA, we will denote these by SHA-2. For all other cases, the original name of the function will be used.

The rest of this paper is organised as follows. Section 2 briefly describes SHA-256, SHA-384, and SHA-512. Section 3 contains preliminary remarks on their main design features and a comparison with the corresponding features of SHA-1. Section 4 investigates the applicability of the currently known attacks of cryptographic hash functions to SHA-2. Section 5 shows that close variants of SHA-2 with modified constant values are not collision resistant, and sect. 6 concludes the paper.

2 Outline of SHA-256 and SHA-384/512

SHA-256, SHA-384, and SHA-512 belong to the MD family of hash functions. Since SHA-384 and SHA-512 are almost identical, we will describe both functions as a single algorithm SHA-384/512, and indicate their differences at the end of this Section. SHA-256 (resp. SHA-384/512) results from the iteration of a 256 + 512-bit to 256-bit (resp. 512 + 1024-bit to 512-bit) compression function. The hash computations are the following.

Padding: First the message is right-padded with a binary '1', followed by a sufficient number of zeros followed by a 64-bit suffix (resp. a 128-bit suffix) containing the binary length of the original message, so that the length of the resulting

$$
\begin{aligned}
T_1 &= h + \Sigma_1(e) + Ch(e,f,g) + K_t + W_t;\\
T_2 &= \Sigma_0(a) + Maj(a,b,c);\\
h &= g;\\
g &= f;\\
f &= e;\\
e &= d + T_1;\\
d &= c;\\
c &= b;\\
b &= a;\\
a &= T_1 + T_2;
\end{aligned}
$$

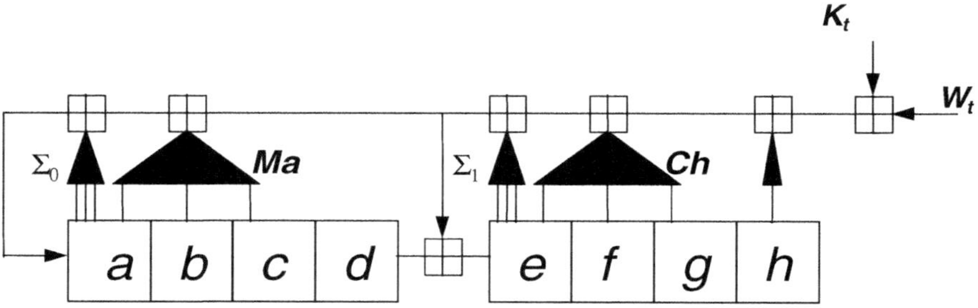

Fig. 1. State register update at each round of the compression function. The functions Ch, Maj, Σ_0 and Σ_1 do not depend on the round number, whereas K_t and W_t represent a constant and a message word the value of which depends on the round number t [15]

padded message becomes a multiple of 512 (resp. 1024) bits. The padded message is then cut into 512-bit blocks (resp. 1024-bit blocks). This form of padding is non-ambiguous and is an example of a valid padding for the Merkle-Damgård construction [5].

State Register Update: After the padding phase, the 8 state registers a, b, c, d, e, f, g, h are initialized to pre-determined 32-bit constants (resp. 64-bit constants) H_0 to H_7 (see [15] for a complete description) for the first message block, and to the current intermediate hash value for the following blocks. Next, 64 rounds (resp. 80 rounds) of the compression function are applied following the pseudo-code given below. Finally, the output value of the registers is added to the previous intermediate hash value according to the Davies-Meyer construction using addition (denoted '+') modulo 2^{32} (resp. 2^{64}) to give the new intermediate hash value.

In the case of SHA-256, the functions Ch, Maj, Σ_0 and Σ_1 operate on 32-bit input words, and produce the 32-bit words given by

$Ch(X,Y,Z) = (X \wedge Y) \oplus (\neg X \wedge Z);$

$Maj(X,Y,Z) = (X \wedge Y) \oplus (X \wedge Z) \oplus (Y \wedge Z);$

$\Sigma_0(X) = ROTR^{2}(X) \oplus ROTR^{13}(X) \oplus ROTR^{22}(X);$

$\Sigma_1(X) = ROTR^{6}(X) \oplus ROTR^{11}(X) \oplus ROTR^{25}(X).$

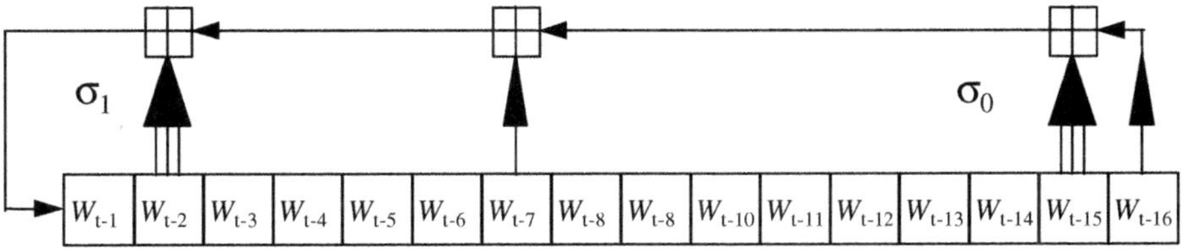

Fig. 2. Message schedule recurrence

In the case of SHA-384/512, the functions Ch, Maj, Σ_0 and Σ_1 operate on 64-bit input words, and produce the 64-bit words given by
$Ch(X,Y,Z) = (X \wedge Y) \oplus (\neg X \wedge Z)$;
$Maj(X,Y,Z) = (X \wedge Y) \oplus (X \wedge Z) \oplus (Y \wedge Z)$;
$\Sigma_0(X) = \mathit{ROTR}^{\,28}(\mathrm{X}) \oplus \mathit{ROTR}^{\,34}(\mathrm{X}) \oplus \mathit{ROTR}^{\,39}(\mathrm{X})$;
$\Sigma_1(X) = \mathit{ROTR}^{\,14}(\mathrm{X}) \oplus \mathrm{ROTR}^{18}(\mathrm{X}) \oplus \mathit{ROTR}^{\,41}(\mathrm{X})$.

Message Schedule: The 'message schedule' takes the original 512-bit message block (resp. the original 1024-bit message block) as input and expands these 16 32-bit words (resp. these 16 64-bit words) W_0 to W_{15} into 64 words W_0 to W_{63} (resp. into 80 words W_0 to W_{79}), one for every round of the compression function. This is done according to the following recurrence formula:

$$W_t = \sigma_1(W_{t-2}) + W_{t-7} + \sigma_0(W_{t-15}) + W_{t-16}$$

where σ_0 and σ_1 represent linear functions (see also Fig. 2). In the case of SHA-256, the functions σ_0 and σ_1 operate on 32-bit input words, and produce the 32-bit words given by $\sigma_0(\mathrm{X}) = \mathit{ROTR}^{\,7}(\mathrm{X}) \oplus \mathit{ROTR}^{\,18}(\mathrm{X}) \oplus \mathit{SHR}^{\,3}(\mathrm{X})$ and $\sigma_1(\mathrm{X}) = \mathit{ROTR}^{\,17}(\mathrm{X}) \oplus \mathit{ROTR}^{\,19}(\mathrm{X}) \oplus \mathit{SHR}^{\,10}(\mathrm{X})$. In the case of SHA-384/512, the functions σ_0 and σ_1 operate on 64-bit input words, and produce the 64-bit words given by $\sigma_0(\mathrm{X}) = \mathit{ROTR}^{\,1}(\mathrm{X}) \oplus \mathit{ROTR}^{\,8}(\mathrm{X}) \oplus \mathit{SHR}^{\,7}(\mathrm{X})$ and $\sigma_1(\mathrm{X}) = \mathit{ROTR}^{\,19}(\mathrm{X}) \oplus \mathrm{ROTR}^{61}(\mathrm{X}) \oplus \mathit{SHR}^{\,6}(\mathrm{X})$.

When all consecutive 512-bit message blocks (resp. all consecutive 1024-bit message blocks) have been hashed, the last intermediate hash value is the final overall hash value. The SHA-384 hash computations are exactly the same as those of SHA-512, up to the two following differences : the constants H_0 to H_7 used in SHA-384 are not the same as those used in SHA-512, and the SHA-384 output is obtained by truncating the final overall hash value to its 6 leftmost words.

3 Preliminary Remarks

3.1 Comparison with SHA-1

State Register Update Function: The overall structure of the 8-word state register (a, b, c, d, e, f, g, h) update performed at each round of the compression function of SHA-2 is close to the one of the 5-word state register (a, b, c, d, e) update performed at each round of SHA-1. However, one round of SHA-2 is more complex than one round of SHA-1: the Σ_0 and Σ_1 GF(2)-linear functions achieve a faster mixing than the circular rotations $ROTL^5$ and $ROTL^{30}$, the non-linear functions *Majority* and *Choice* are applied in each round whereas only one of the ternary functions *Choice*, *Majority* and *Xor* is applied in each SHA-1 round, and finally two register variables of SHA-2 are substantially modified at each round compared to only one for SHA-1. The SHA-2 round function is the same for all rounds except for the use of distinct constants K_t at each round, whereas SHA-1 involves four different types of round functions used in a subset of 20 consecutive rounds each. This lesser uniformity might represent a security advantage for SHA-1. But on the other hand equal constants K_t are used within each type of round function of SHA-1; unlike SHA-2, this makes SHA-1 vulnerable to Saarinen's sliding attack [22]. One can also notice that the number of rounds to state register length ratio, which represents the number of "full rotations" of the state register during each compression function computation, is much lower for SHA-2 than for SHA-1: its value is $64/8 = 8$ in the case of SHA-256 and $80/8 = 10$ in the case of SHA-384/512 instead of $80/5 = 16$ for SHA-1. The exact performance to security balance argumentation behind the substantial reduction of this ratio is unclear to us. This may look at first glance as a serious decrease of the security margin offered by SHA-2. On the other hand one can probably consider that this is at least partly compensated by the higher complexity of the round function (recall that two variables are updated in each round).

Message Schedule: Both the SHA-1 and the SHA-2 message schedules produce a recurring sequence of depth 16 initialized with the 16-word message block $M = M_0, M_1, \ldots, M_{15}$. However, unlike for SHA-1, the SHA-2 message schedule computations are not GF(2)-linear, because of the involvement of the '+' addition instead of '$\oplus$'. This makes the properties of the message schedule recurrence more difficult to analyze, because the set of possible difference patterns is no longer a linear code. The SHA-1 property following which (unlike in SHA-0) the recurrence relation mixes the various bit positions is strengthened thanks to the involvement of the bit rotations in σ_0 and σ_1 (which play a similar role as the $ROTL^1$ rotation of the SHA-1 recurrence) and also because of the diffusion effect introduced by the '+' addition.

3.2 Majority and Choice Functions

In this section we recall the elementary properties of the majority and choice functions as well as the modular addition operation [12]. Both the Choice and Majority functions operate on individual bits and are balanced on their respective input domains, as shown in their difference distribution table 1. The notation of table 1 is as follows: for every 3-bit input difference, a '0' denotes that the output difference is always zero, a '1' denotes that it is always one, and a '0/1' denotes that it is zero in half of the cases and one the rest of the time.

Table 1. Difference distribution table for a 3-bit input difference

X	Y	Z	*Choice*	*Majority*
0	0	0	0	0
0	0	1	0/1	0/1
0	1	0	0/1	0/1
0	1	1	1	0/1
1	0	0	0/1	0/1
1	0	1	0/1	0/1
1	1	0	0/1	0/1
1	1	1	0/1	1

For the subsequent sections, it is useful to note that both functions achieve a zero output difference (i.e. an internal collision) with average probability $\frac{1}{2}$ if exactly one of the three input differences is equal to 1.

Concerning the modular addition operation, one can easily see that if A and B differ in only the i-th bit, then with probability $\frac{1}{2}$ if a third word C is added to A and B, $(A+C)$ and $(B+C)$ also differ in only the i-th bit. The only special case here is when the difference is located in the most significant bit; in this case the carry bit does not propagate any difference, thus $(A+C)$ and $(B+C)$ differ also only in the most significant bit (with probability one) due to the modular reduction. This is already described in [12]. Thus on average, a one-bit difference before a modular addition does **not** propagate after the addition operation with probability $\frac{1}{2}$.

3.3 Sigma Functions

In this section we state some elementary properties of the functions Σ_0 and Σ_1 used in the state register update function and of the functions σ_0 and σ_1 used in the message schedule computations:

- **The GF(2)-linear mappings Σ_0 and Σ_1 are one to one.** In the case of SHA-256, this results from the fact that if 32-bit words are represented by polynomials over $GF(2)[X]/(X^{32}+1)$, then $\Sigma_0^{\{256\}}$ and $\Sigma_1^{\{256\}}$ are represented by multiplications by the polynomials $X^2+X^{13}+X^{22}$ and $X^6+X^{11}+X^{25}$, and these two polynomials are co-prime with $X^{32}+1=(X+1)^{32}$. Similarly, in the case of SHA-384/512, this results from the fact that the polynomials $X^{28}+X^{34}+X^{39}$ and $X^{14}+X^{18}+X^{41}$ are co-prime with the polynomial $X^{64}+1=(X+1)^{64}$.
- **The GF(2)-linear mappings σ_0 and σ_1 are one to one** (in order to check this property for SHA-256 and SHA-384/512, we computed the two 32×32 binary matrices (resp. the two 64×64 binary matrices) representing σ_0 and σ_1 and checked that the kernel of these matrices is restricted to the null vector.

These two observations tend to increase our confidence in the strength of SHA-2 versus SHA-1 as they provide for a much faster diffusion effect and, more importantly, no internal collisions can be achieved through either one of the Σ and σ functions.

4 Security of SHA-2 against Known Hash Function Attack Techniques

In this section we investigate the applicability of the currently known attacks of cryptographic hash functions to SHA-2.

4.1 Applicability of Chabaud and Joux's Attack Techniques

Chabaud and Joux's attack of SHA-0 is entirely differential in nature. It takes advantage of the absence of any mixing of the various bit positions in the SHA-0 message schedule expansion function and of its linearity to construct relatively low weight[1] differences on the W message schedule output which are likely to produce collisions during the SHA-0 compression.

This attack can be summarized as follows. First one considers the injection in one of the words W_t of a one-bit difference, and one identifies the corresponding corrective patterns, i.e. sets of differences in the subsequent words W_{t+i} that cancel with high probability the resulting differences in the state registers after a few rounds. Then we search for low weight sequences of 1-bit perturbative patterns satisfying the linear recurrence of the message schedule (and some extra technical conditions). Due to the structure of the SHA-0 message schedule, the difference pattern resulting from the superposition of these perturbative patterns and of the corresponding corrective pattern satisfies the linear recurrence. Therefore, numerous pairs of messages leading to one of these difference patterns are easy to construct and one of these pairs is likely to lead to a SHA-0 collision.

Following this attack, we investigate whether differential collisions may be obtained on SHA-2 faster than by exhaustive search. Using the differential properties of the non-linear functions shown in Sect. 3.2, we approximate each addition by an exclusive or operation with probability $\frac{1}{2}$, and the majority and choice functions by zero with probability $\frac{1}{2}$. We proceed in three steps:

- define a low weight perturbation and related corrective patterns;
- compute the probability that the corrective patterns produce a differential collision;
- produce heuristic evidence that these patterns may **not** be generated according to the SHA-2 message schedule.

Obviously, in order to obtain a minimum weight difference, the best strategy is to inject a one bit difference in a given message word W_i, and for each

[1] The difference weights encountered in this attack are higher by an order of magnitude than the extremely low difference weights encountered in Dobbertin's attacks.

Table 2. Hamming weight of a propagating difference for SHA-2

W	a	b	c	d	e	f	g	h
1	1	0	0	0	1	0	0	0
6	0	1	0	0	3	1	0	0
9	0	0	1	0	0	3	1	0
0	0	0	0	1	0	0	3	1
1	0	0	0	0	1	0	0	3
6	0	0	0	0	0	1	0	0
0	0	0	0	0	0	0	1	0
0	0	0	0	0	0	0	0	1
1	0	0	0	0	0	0	0	0

consecutive round, to disable the propagation into the register A by appropriate corrective patterns of the next message words. Allowing for more than a single bit difference is not realistic as each Σ function automatically multiplies the Hamming weight of the difference by three in each step, and trying to match these bit locations using several initial difference bits implies a fatal decrease of the probability to obtain such differential collisions. Therefore we believe that no other strategy can provide a sufficiently low weight perturbation pattern, hence an acceptable overall collision probability. The pattern has been obtained in a straightforward manner by setting the following equalities: let W_i be the word containing the perturbative **one-bit difference**. Then we define the next eight word **differences** by: $W_{i+1} = \Sigma_1(W_i) \oplus \Sigma_0(W_i)$; $W_{i+2} = \Sigma_1(\Sigma_0(W_i))$; $W_{i+3} = 0$; $W_{i+4} = W_i$; $W_{i+5} = \Sigma_1(W_i) \oplus \Sigma_0(W_i)$; $W_{i+6} = 0$; $W_{i+7} = 0$; $W_{i+8} = W_i$.
This leads to the propagation of minimum weight differences in the 8 registers as shown in table 2. Explicit examples of such a difference propagation is given in Appendix A.

Fact 1. *Using corrective patterns with weight one, six and nine in the message words as shown in the W column of the above table gives rise to a dierential collision pattern over 9 rounds.*

The next step is to evaluate the probability of the differential pattern. As we already mentioned, we approximate the addition operation by an exclusive or, and the non-linear functions by zero. Two relevant additions occur in every round per one bit difference in a message word. These are: the addition of T_1 and the register d to form the new register value e; the addition of T_1 and T_2 to form the new register value a. The probability of a carry bit appearing in one of these additions is bound by $\frac{1}{2}$ for each addition, thus we upper bound the overall probability for two additions per difference bit by $\frac{1}{4}$. There are a total of $1+6+9+1+6+1 = 24$ difference bits over the 9-round pattern. Hence the probability over all additions is upper bounded by $(2^{-24})^2 = 2^{-48}$.

As for the non-linear choice and majority functions, the average probability to obtain a zero difference is $\frac{1}{2}$ per difference bit. A total of 18 such difference bits occur in the non-linear functions over the 9 rounds; thus the overall associated probability is upper bounded by 2^{-18}.

Fact 2. *The overall probability associated to the 9-round dierential collision pattern is upper bounded by* 2^{-66}.

In the third and last step, we provide evidence that these patterns may **not** be concatenated (as is the case for SHA-0) in order to form message words that follow the correct message schedule.

For SHA-256 suppose there is a block of 9 consecutive message words with differences defined as above (i.e. following the differential collision pattern). This block may not be followed or preceded by more than 15 zero difference message words. Clearly if 16 consecutive words in the message schedule are identical, then the whole message schedule is identical over the 64 words. If we apply the pattern twice, we can separate both patterns by a block of zero difference words of length at most 15. Therefore at most 15+9+15+9+15=63 difference message words may be defined. This shows that at least 3 different patterns must be combined to follow the correct message schedule.

If two of these patterns are applied, the probability to obtain a differential collision becomes lower than 2^{-132} whereas the complexity of a birthday attack on SHA-256 only represents 2^{128} computations on average.

Conclusion. *The original attack by Chabaud and Joux on SHA-0 does not extend to SHA-256.*

For SHA-384/512 suppose there is a block of 9 consecutive message words with differences defined as above (i.e. following the differential collision pattern). This block may not be followed by more than 7 pairs of identical message schedule output words. Let us show why.

Recall that the simplified message schedule (i.e. where every addition has been replaced by an exclusive or) is defined by:

$$W_t = \sigma_1(W_{t-2}) \oplus W_{t-7} \oplus \sigma_0(W_{t-15}) \oplus W_{t-16}$$

Then assuming that W_i to W_{i+8} represent a differential collision pattern and that W_{i+9} to W_{i+15} are equal to zero, the difference in the 16-th message word is defined by:

$$\begin{aligned} W_{i+16} &= \sigma_1(W_{i+14}) \oplus W_{i+9} \oplus \sigma_0(W_{i+1}) \oplus W_i \\ &= \sigma_0(W_{i+1}) \oplus W_i \\ &= \sigma_0(\Sigma_1(W_i) \oplus \Sigma_0(W_i)) \oplus W_i \\ &\neq 0 \text{ for a 1-bit difference in } W_i. \end{aligned}$$

Hence no more than 7 consecutive identical words may separate two consecutive differential collision patterns, with the original message block difference having at least one non-zero word.

Combining up to four different patterns, we can define at most 15 + 9 + 7 + 9 + 7 + 9 + 7 + 9 + 7 = 79 difference message words satisfying the message schedule recurrence. This shows that at least 5 different patterns have to be combined to follow the correct message schedule.

If four of these patterns are applied, the probability to obtain a differential collision becomes lower than 2^{-264} whereas the complexity of a birthday attack on SHA-512 only represents 2^{256} computations on average.

Conclusion. *The original attack by Chabaud and Joux on SHA-0 does not extend to SHA-384/512.*

4.2 Applicability of Dobbertin's Attack Techniques

The hash function attack techniques introduced by H. Dobbertin in [7, 8, 9, 10] exploit the extremely simple structure of the message schedule of hash functions such as MD4 and MD5. In these functions, the 16-words of the message block are just repeated in permuted order a small number r of times (namely 3 times for MD4 and 4 times for MD5). Dobbertin's attacks use pairs (M, M^*) of almost equal messages, up to a difference of Hamming weight 1 in only one of their 16 words. The attack strategy consists in controlling the diffusion of the resulting low weight (e.g. r-bit) message schedule output differences pattern through the hash function computations, in order for the resulting state registers differences after the $r-1$ first (16-step) rounds to be cancelled by the last message schedule difference encountered in the last (16-steps) round. Depending on the round considered, the control method consists either in differential techniques or in more sophisticated equation solving techniques.

Due to the more complex and conservative expansion method used in the message schedules of the SHA family of hash function, and in particular in the message schedule of SHA-2, Dobbertin's attacks do not seem applicable to these functions. More explicitly, the recurrence relation of the SHA-2 function (in particular the term $\sigma_0(W_{t-2})$ in this recurrence) ensures a fast and strong diffusion of any low weight difference in the message block M, and prevents any (M, M^*) pair of message blocks from resulting in a very low weight difference (e.g. 3, 4 or 5) at the message schedule expansion output.

4.3 Differential Attacks

Link between Differential Properties and Collision Resistance. In this section we investigate differential properties of the compression function. The idea behind this is that if it were possible to find any pseudo-collisions of the special form $compress(H, M) = compress(H', M)$ on the compression function of SHA-2, then the Merkle-Damgård security argument [5] could not be applied. In other words, the existence of such pseudo-collisions on the compression function of SHA-2 would represent an undesirable property.

In order to search for pseudo-collisions of this special form, it is convenient to view the compression functions of SHA-256 and SHA-384/512 as a block cipher[2] encrypting a 256-bit (or 512-bit) input $H = (a, b, c, d, e, f, g, h)$ under key $[W_0, \ldots, W_{63}]$ (or key $[W_0, \ldots, W_{79}]$) followed by the addition of the output with the input H according to the Davies-Meyer construction. If it were possible to predict the differential behavior of this block cipher, it might help find high probability differential characteristics such that the output difference compensates the input difference in the final Davies-Meyer addition, and thus to find pseudo-collisions of the form $compress(H, M) = compress(H', M)$. A similar approach has already been taken for DES-based hash functions in [18] and for SHA-1 in [12] in order to investigate the security of the underlying block cipher. No high probability differentials (and thus no partial collisions) could be found for SHA-1. However it should be mentioned that slid pairs (which result in related-key attacks for block ciphers) have since been discovered on MD-type hash functions used as block ciphers, including SHACAL-1 and MD5 [22].
Next we study the differential behavior of the block ciphers underlying SHA-2.

Search for Low Weight Differential Characteristics over a Few Rounds As in Section 3.1, we approximate each addition by an exclusive or operation with probability $\frac{1}{2}$, and the majority and choice functions by zero with probability $\frac{1}{2}$, using the differential properties of the non-linear functions shown in Sect. 3.2.

The most efficient differential characteristic over a few consecutive rounds we have identified relates to 4 rounds, and has a probability of 2^{-8}. See Appendix B for details.

While this characteristic does not concatenate over the whole 64 rounds, we can conclude that the best overall differential probability for SHA-256 appears to be lower than $2^{-8*16} = 2^{-128}$ which results in a work factor much higher than the complexity of a collision search for a 256-bit hash function. Thus a standard differential attack on the compression function is very unlikely to succeed.

While this characteristic does not concatenate over the whole 80 rounds, for SHA-512 we can conclude that the best overall differential probability appears to be lower than $2^{-8*20} = 2^{-160}$. As opposed to the case of SHA-256, this does not result in a work factor which is higher than the complexity of a collision search on a 512-bit or even a 384-bit hash function. However, it remains to be seen whether a global differential characteristic may be constructed from this property. Having in mind that we need 80-round characteristics with input and output differences that compensate each other in the final Davies-Meyer addition, there is no obvious way to extend this result to the hash function itself.

Search for Iterative Differential Characteristics We have also investigated iterative differential differential characteristics of non-negligible probability on

[2] In the case of SHA-256, this block cipher is the SHACAL-2 algorithm [13] recently selected by the European NESSIE project

a reduced number of rounds. For that purpose we have approximated the actual differential transitions associated with each round of the SHA-2 register update function by a linear function L of $\{0,1\}^{256}$ (resp. $\{0,1\}^{512}$). In order to identify candidate iterative differential characteristics over a restricted number r of rounds, we computed, for the 32 first values of r, a basis of the vector space of difference vectors $\delta = (\delta a,\ \delta b,\ \delta c,\ \delta d,\ \delta e,\ \delta f,\ \delta g,\ \delta h)$ which stay invariant under L^r. See Appendix B for details. It was observed that for the first values of r, all the 32-bit or 64-bit words of the vectors of the identified spaces of iterative differences are "periodic", of period 32, 16 or 8 (resp of period 64, 32 or 16) and thus the weight of all candidate iterative differential characteristics we identified using this method is a multiple of 8. Therefore, we believe that this approach does not provide high probability iterative differentials for SHA-2.

Consequently, we find the differential behavior of the compression functions of SHA-2 to be sound and believe it is highly unlikely that even pseudo-collisions will be found through this approach.

5 Weakness in SHA-2 Variants Using Symmetric Constants and Exor

In this Section we show that if some relatively slight variations are made in the SHA-2 specification, the resulting modified hash function is no longer collision-resistant. The considered variations consist in replacing all constants encountered in the algorithm by highly symmetric values and all additions modulo 2^n by the exclusive or operation. In order to simplify the discussion, we only describe the case of SHA-256, but the transposition to SHA-384/512 is straightforward.

Let us denote by Ω the set $\{0,1\}^{32}$, and by Ω' the set of all symmetric 32-bit words consisting of two equal 16-bit halves:

$$\Omega' = \{C \in \{0,1\}^{32} \mid \exists c \in \{0,1\}^{16}, C = c\|c\}.$$

Let us denote by SHA'-256 the SHA-256 variant obtained by replacing:

- the words $H_0^{(0)}$ to $H_7^{(0)}$ of the initial hash value $H^{(0)}$ by any 8 constant 32-bit words belonging to Ω';
- the constants K_0 to K_{63} involved in the hash computation by any 64 32-bit words belonging to Ω';
- the operation '+'(mod 2^{32} addition) in the hash computation by '$\oplus$';
- the shift operation $SHR^3(x)$ in the function $\sigma_0^{\{256\}}$ by the circular shift operation $ROTR^3(x)$ and the shift operation $SHR^{10}(x)$ of the function $\sigma_1^{\{256\}}$ by the circular shift operation $ROTR^{10}(x)$.

Now it is easy to see that if $x, y \in \Omega'$ then $x \oplus y \in \Omega'$ and that if $x, y, z \in \Omega'$, then $Ch(x,y,z) \in \Omega'$ and $Maj(x,y,z) \in \Omega'$, so that if the $H^{(i-1)}$ and $M^{(i)}$ inputs to the compression function sha'-256 of SHA'-256 both consist of Ω' words, then the resulting $H^{(i)}$ output also consists of Ω' words. Consequently:

- the complexity of a collision search on the restriction of the sha'-256 compression function to input values belonging to Ω' is only 2^{64} instead of 2^{128} (since for such values a collision on the left half of each output word implies a collision on the whole output word);
- the complexity of a collision search on the SHA'-256 hash function is also only 2^{64} instead of 2^{128}: to construct such a collision, one can for instance first search two 512-bit initial message blocks M_1 and $M_1' \in \Omega'^{16}$ such that $sha'-256(H_0, M_1) = sha'-256(H_0, M_1')$. The complexity for this sha'-256 collision search is 2^{64}. Now given any binary suffix message of any length $M_2 \in \{0,1\}*$, the $M = M_1 \| M_2$ and $M' = M_1' \| M_2$ messages provide a collision for the SHA-256 hash function.

The above attack can easily be generalized to the SHA"-256; SHA"'-256, etc. variants of SHA-256 in which all constants are selected in the subsets $\Omega'' = \{C \in \{0,1\}^{32} \mid \exists c \in \{0,1\}^8, C = c\|c\|c\|c\}$, $\Omega''' = \{C \in \{0,1\}^{32} \mid \exists c \in \{0,1\}^4, C = c\|c\|c\|c\|c\|c\|c\|c\}$, etc., of Ω instead of Ω'. This results in collision attacks of complexity only $2^{256/4} = 2^{64}$ for SHA'-256, $2^{256/8} = 2^{32}$ for SHA"-256 and so on.

We have checked these results experimentally by implementing the case of SHA"'-256. In other words, for SHA-256, we applied the described modifications to the compression function such that all constants were replaced by 32-bit values showing 8 identical nibbles. Next we generated a large hash table and searched for collisions on the compression function for 2^{20} input messages of length one block (512 bits) showing 8 identical nibbles in each one of the 16 32-bit input words. On average, the number of collisions we expect to obtain is $\frac{2^{20} \times 2^{20}}{2 \times 2^{32}}$ which is about 2^7. These numbers were confirmed by our experiments.

As an illustration, in table 3 we provide two messages showing the required symmetry, a set of initial vectors showing the required symmetry, and the resulting collision we obtained on the compression function of SHA"'-256. (For this example, the 64 32-bit constants K_t were obtained by repeating 8 times their respective first nibble.)

Similarly, it is easy to define variants SHA'-512/384, SHA"-512/384, etc., of SHA-512 in which constants are replaced by more symmetric values, and to show that the collision search complexities for these variants are only $2^{512/4} = 2^{128}$, $2^{512/8} = 2^{64}$, 2^{32}, etc.

Thus with some very simple modifications, one obtains variants of the hash functions SHA-256 and SHA-384/512 which are surprisingly weak. We note that similar modifications on SHA-1 and on SHA-0 would have the same effect (and would not need any change in the message schedule). However, this does by no means imply that the original hash functions are insecure, not even remotely, but it casts some doubts on these designs.

6 Conclusion

We have investigated the security of SHA-2. We have shown that neither Dobbertin's nor Chabaud and Joux's attacks on MD-type hash functions seem to

Table 3. Example of two symmetric message blocks compressing to the same symmetric value

	Chaining variables
Initialisation vectors	0xaaaaaaaa 0xbbbbbbbb 0xcccccccc 0xdddddddd
	0xeeeeeeee 0xffffffff 0x00000000 0x11111111
Message 1	0x99999999 0xbbbbbbbb 0xffffffff 0x44444444
	0x99999999 0x00000000 0x00000000 0x00000000
	0x00000000 0x00000000 0x00000000 0x00000000
	0x00000000 0x00000000 0x00000000 0x00000000
Output 1	0x00000000 0xbbbbbbbb 0x77777777 0xeeeeeeee
	0x99999999 0x99999999 0x11111111 0x88888888
Message 2	0xeeeeeeee 0x00000000 0xffffffff 0x33333333
	0xffffffff 0x00000000 0x00000000 0x00000000
	0x00000000 0x00000000 0x00000000 0x00000000
	0x00000000 0x00000000 0x00000000 0x00000000
Output 2	0x00000000 0xbbbbbbbb 0x77777777 0xeeeeeeee
	0x99999999 0x99999999 0x11111111 0x88888888

apply to SHA-2. Most features of the basic components of SHA-2 seem to provide a better security level than for preceding hash functions, even though the relative number of rounds is somewhat lower than for SHA-1 for instance, and though the selection criteria and security arguments for some design choices are difficult to reconstruct from the specification, in the absence of any public design report. Finally, we have shown that a simplified version of SHA-2 where the round constants are symmetric and where addition is replaced by exclusive or, is insecure.

Acknowledgements

This work is based on the result of an evaluation requested by the Japanese CRYPTREC project: http://www.ipa.go.jp/security/enc/CRYPTREC/...
.../index-e.html. We would like to thank the members of the CRYPTREC project for having authorized this publication. We also thank the anonymous reviewers for their suggestions and comments.

References

[1] E. Biham, O. Dunkelmann, N. Keller, *Rectangle Attacks on 49-Round SHACAL-1*, in FSE 2003, Pre-proceedings of the conference, pages 39-48, 2003.

[2] J. Black, P. Rogaway, T. Shrimpton, *Black-Box Analysis of the Block-Cipher-Based Hash-Function Constructions from PGV*, in Advances in Cryptology - Crypto'02, pages 320-335, LNCS 2442, Springer-Verlag, 2002.

[3] B. den Boer and A. Bosselaers, *An attack on the last two rounds of MD4*, in Advances in Cryptology - Crypto'91, pages 194-203, LNCS 576, Springer-Verlag, 1992. 175
[4] F. Chabaud and A. Joux, *Differential Collisions in SHA-0*, in Advances in Cryptology - CRYPTO'98, LNCS 1462, pages 56-71, Springer-Verlag, 1998. 176
[5] I. B. Damgård, *A design principle for hash functions*, in Advances in Cryptology - Crypto'89, LNCS 435, pages 416-427, Springer Verlag, 1990. 177, 184
[6] C. Debaert, H. Gilbert, *The RIPEMD^L and RIPEMD^R Improved Variants of MD4 are not Collision Free,* in Fast Software Encryption - FSE'2001, LNCS 2355, Springer Verlag, 2001. 176
[7] H. Dobbertin, *Cryptanalysis of MD4*, in Journal of Cryptology vol.11 n.4, Springer-Verlag, 1998. 175, 184
[8] H. Dobbertin, *Cryptanalysis of MD5 Compress*, Presented at the rump session of Eurocrypt '96, May 14, 1996. 175, 184
[9] H. Dobbertin, *The status of MD5 after a recent attack*, CryptoBytes, vol. 2, n. 2, 1996. 175, 184
[10] H. Dobbertin, *RIPEMD with two round compress function is not collision-free*, in Journal of Cryptology vol.10 n.1, Springer-Verlag, 1997. 176, 184
[11] H. Dobbertin, A. Bosselaers and B. Preneel, *RIPEMD-160: a strengthened version of RIPEMD*, April 1996. http.esat.kuleuven.ac.be/pub/COSIC/bossselae/ripemd. 175
[12] H. Handschuh, L. Knudsen, M. Robshaw, *Analysis of SHA-1 in encryption mode,* in Topics in Cryptology - CT-RSA 2001, LNCS 2020, pages 70-83, Springer-Verlag, 2001. 179, 180, 185
[13] H. Handschuh, D. Naccache, *SHACAL: A Family of Block Ciphers* Submission to the NESSIE project, 2002. Available from `http://www.crytponessie.org` 185
[14] National Institute of Standards and Technology (NIST) *FIPS Publication 180-1: secure Hash Standard*, April 1994. 176
[15] National Institute of Standards and Technology (NIST), FIPS 180-2, 2002. `http://csrc.nist.gov/encryption/tkhash.html`. 176, 177
[16] National Institute of Standards and Technology (NIST) *FIPS Publication 197: Advanced Encryption Standard (AES)*, 2001. 176
[17] P. C. van Oorschot, M. J. Wiener, *Parallel Collision Search with Cryptanalytic Applications*, in Journal of Cryptology vol.12 n.1, Springer-Verlag, 1999.
[18] B. Preneel, R. Govaerts, J. Vandewalle, *Differential cryptanalysis of hash functions based on block ciphers*, Proc. 1st ACM Conference on Computer and Communications Security, pages 183-188, 1993. 185
[19] *RIPE Integrity Primitives for Secure Information Systems - Final Report of RACE Integrity Primitives Evaluation (RIPE-RACE 1040)*, LNCS 1007, Springer-Verlag, 1995. 175
[20] R. L. Rivest, *The MD4 message digest algorithm*, in Advances in Cryptology - Crypto'90, pages 303-311, Springer-Verlag, 1991. 175
[21] R. L. Rivest, *RFC1321: The MD5 message digest algorithm*, M. I. T. Laboratory for Computer Science and RSA Data Security, Inc., April 1992.
[22] M.-J. O. Saarinen, *Cryptanalysis of Block Ciphers Based on SHA-1 and MD5*, in FSE'2003, Pre-proceedings of the conference, pages 39-48, 2003. 176, 179, 185
[23] S. Vaudenay, *On the need for multipermutations: Cryptanalysis of MD4 and SAFER*, in Fast Software Encryption - FSE'95, LNCS 1008, pages 286-297, Springer-Verlag, 1995. 175

A Example of 9-Round Differential Collision Patterns

SHA-384/512 Case

The following values are an example of the consecutive contents of the differences in the SHA-384/512 registers a, b, c, d, e, f, g, h when a "perturbative pattern" of Hamming weight one followed by the corresponding "corrective pattern" is applied to nine consecutive message words W.

The values of the 9 consecutive differences in words W[0] to W[8] are the following :

W[i]: 0x20 0x 0	W[i+1]: 0x50000000 0x880208
W[i+2]: 0x8a31001 0x4200000	W[i+3]: 0x 0 0x 0
W[i+4]: 0x20 0x 0	W[i+5]: 0x50000000 0x880208
W[i+6]: 0x 0 0x 0	W[i+7]: 0x 0 0x 0
W[i+8]: 0x20 0x 0	W[i+9]: 0x 0 0x 0

The corresponding values of the 10 consecutive differences in registers a, b, c, d, e, f, g, h (represented by 2 32-bit half registers separated by a .) are the following:

Round i : 0x 0 0x 0 . 0x 0 0x 0 . 0x 0 0x 0 . 0x 0 0x 0 . 0x 0 0x 0 . 0x 0 0x 0 . 0x 0 0x 0 . 0x 0 0x 0

Round i+1 : 0x20 0x 0 . 0x 0 0x 0 . 0x 0 0x 0 . 0x 0 0x 0 . 0x20 0x 0 . 0x 0 0x 0 . 0x 0 0x 0 . 0x 0 0x 0

Round i+2 : 0x 0 0x 0 . 0x20 0x 0 . 0x 0 0x 0 . 0x 0 0x 0 . 0x40000000 0x208 . 0x20 0x 0 . 0x 0 0x 0 . 0x 0 0x 0

Round i+3 : 0x 0 0x 0 . 0x 0 0x 0 . 0x20 0x 0 . 0x 0 0x 0 . 0x 0 0x 0 . 0x40000000 0x208 . 0x20 0x 0 . 0x 0 0x 0

Round i+4 : 0x 0 0x 0 . 0x 0 0x 0 . 0x 0 0x 0 . 0x20 0x 0 . 0x 0 0x 0 . 0x 0 0x 0 . 0x40000000 0x208 . 0x20 0x 0

Round i+5 : 0x 0 0x 0 . 0x 0 0x 0 . 0x 0 0x 0 . 0x 0 0x 0 . 0x20 0x 0 . 0x 0 0x 0 . 0x 0 0x 0 . 0x40000000 0x208

Round i+6 : 0x 0 0x 0 . 0x 0 0x 0 . 0x 0 0x 0 . 0x 0 0x 0 . 0x 0 0x 0 . 0x20 0x 0 . 0x 0 0x 0 . 0x 0 0x 0

Round i+7 : 0x 0 0x 0 . 0x 0 0x 0 . 0x 0 0x 0 . 0x 0 0x 0 . 0x 0 0x 0 . 0x 0 0x 0 . 0x20 0x 0 . 0x 0 0x 0

Round i+8 : 0x 0 0x 0 . 0x 0 0x 0 . 0x 0 0x 0 . 0x 0 0x 0 . 0x 0 0x 0 . 0x 0 0x 0 . 0x 0 0x 0 . 0x20 0x 0

Round i+9 : 0x 0 0x 0 . 0x 0 0x 0 . 0x 0 0x 0 . 0x 0 0x 0 . 0x 0 0x 0 . 0x 0 0x 0 . 0x 0 0x 0 . 0x 0 0x 0

SHA-256 Case

The following values are an example of the consecutive contents of the differences in the SHA-256 registers a, b, c, d, e, f, g, h when a " perturbative pattern " (1-bit difference on the least significant bit) followed by a " corrective pattern " is applied to nine consecutive message words W.

Round i : 0x 0 0x 0 0x 0 0x 0 0x 0 0x 0 0x 0 0x 0
Round i+1 : 0x 1 0x 0 0x 0 0x 0 0x 1 0x 0 0x 0 0x 0
Round i+2 : 0x 0 0x 1 0x 0 0x 0 0x40080400 0x 1 0x 0 0x 0
Round i+3 : 0x 0 0x 0 0x 1 0x 0 0x 0 0x40080400 0x 1 0x 0
Round i+4 : 0x 0 0x 0 0x 0 0x 1 0x 0 0x 0 0x40080400 0x 1
Round i+5 : 0x 0 0x 0 0x 0 0x 0 0x 1 0x 0 0x 0 0x40080400
Round i+6 : 0x 0 0x 0 0x 0 0x 0 0x 0 0x 1 0x 0 0x 0
Round i+7 : 0x 0 0x 0 0x 0 0x 0 0x 0 0x 0 0x 1 0x 0
Round i+8 : 0x 0 0x 0 0x 0 0x 0 0x 0 0x 0 0x 0 0x 1
Round i+9 : 0x 0 0x 0 0x 0 0x 0 0x 0 0x 0 0x 0 0x 0

B Investigation of Differential Characteristics for SHA-2

Search for Low Weight Differential Characteristics over a Few Rounds:

The following table shows the evolution of the lowest weight differential characteristic over 4 rounds we found. Only the weight of the difference in each register is shown, as a circular rotation of the corresponding indexes of the initial difference bits achieves the same overall propagation pattern. We stress that in this setting, all the message words are identical: Only the input registers differ in a few bits.

probability	a	b	c	d	e	f	g	h
	0	0	0	0	1	0	0	3
1/16	0	0	0	0	0	1	0	0
1/2	0	0	0	0	0	0	1	0
1/2	0	0	0	0	0	0	0	1
1/4	1	0	0	0	1	0	0	0

- The first difference bit in register E affects both the *Choice* and the non-linear Σ_1 function. With probability $\frac{1}{2}$, the output of the Σ_1 function is equal to zero, and with probability 2^{-3} the 3 input difference bits in register H added to the 3 difference bits generated by the Σ_1 function do not generate any difference carry bits. Thus after the first round, with probability 2^{-4} only one difference bit propagates in register F.
- In rounds 2 and 3, with probability $\frac{1}{2}$, this difference bit does not cause any difference in the output of the *Choice* function. Thus we now have a one-bit difference in register H.
- In the last round of the characteristic, this one-bit difference is added respectively into register A and E, thus with probability $\frac{1}{4}$,the output difference is a 2-bit difference after 4 rounds.

Putting everything together, this low weight differential characteristic has a probability of 2^{-8}.

Search for Iterative Differential Characteristics

In order to investigate iterative differential characteristics for SHA-2 we approximated the actual differential transitions associated with each round of the SHA-2 register update function by a linear function of $\{0,1\}^{256}$ in the case of SHA-256 (resp. $\{0,1\}^{512}$ in the case of SHA-384/512) , by making the simplifying assumption that the output difference ($\delta a'$, $\delta b'$, $\delta c'$, $\delta d'$, $\delta e'$, $\delta f'$, $\delta g'$, $\delta h'$) associated with an input difference (δa, δb, δc, δd, δe, δf, δg, δh) is equal to the output difference one would obtain if SHA-2 the functions *Choice* and *Majority* were ignored and if '+' was replaced by '$\oplus$'. Let us denote by L the 256×256 (resp. 512×512) binary matrix over GF(2) representing the above linear mapping. Let us denote by A and E the matrices associated with Σ_0 and Σ_1 respectively and by I and O the identity and the null 32×32 (resp. 64×64) matrices. L can be described as the following 8x8 block matrix:

$$L = \begin{pmatrix} A & O & O & O & E & O & O & I \\ I & O & O & O & O & O & O & O \\ O & I & O & O & O & O & O & O \\ O & O & I & O & O & O & O & O \\ O & O & O & I & E & O & O & I \\ O & O & O & O & I & O & O & O \\ O & O & O & O & O & I & O & O \\ O & O & O & O & O & O & I & O \end{pmatrix}$$

We are then using the matrix L to search candidate iterative differential characteristics over a restricted number of rounds r. For that purpose, we computed for each value r in $\{1,16\}$ a basis of the kernel K_r of $L^r - I$,where I represents the 256×256 (resp. 512×512) identity matrix, using standard Gaussian reduction. Elements of K_r represent those input differences $\delta = (\delta a, \delta b, \delta c, \delta d, \delta e, \delta f, \delta g, \delta h)$ which stay invariant under r rounds, up to the approximation of the differential transition at each round by the linear function L. In other words, elements of K_r represent iterative characteristics for r rounds, provided the probabilities obtained when taking into account the approximations made in L are not too low.

In the case of SHA-256, we obtained for K_1 to K_{16} vector spaces of respective dimensions given by the following table.

$r =$	1	2	3	4	5	6	7	8	9	10	11	12	13	14	15	16
$dim(K_r) =$)	1	2	1	4	1	2	4	8	1	2	1	4	1	8	1	16

To develop on particular example more in detail, K_4 has dimension 4. If we denote by a^n the concatenation of n binary words equal to a (so that for instance $(0111)^2 = 01110111$, etc.), a basis $\{e_{40}, e_{41}, e_{42}, e_{43}\}$ of K_4 is given by:

$$e_{40} = ((10)^{16}, 0^{32}, (01)^{16}, 0^{32}, 0^{32}, (10)^{16}, 0^{32}, (01)^{16})$$

$$e_{41} = ((01)^{16}, 0^{32}, (10)^{16}, 0^{32}, 0^{32}, (01)^{16}, 0^{32}, (10)^{16})$$

$$e_{42} = (0^{32}, (01)^{16}, 0^{32}, (10)^{16}, (01)^{16}, 0^{32}, (10)^{16}, 0^{32})$$

$$e_{43} = (0^{32}, (10)^{16}, 0^{32}, (01)^{16}, (10)^{16}, 0^{32}, (01)^{16}, 0^{32})$$

In the case of SHA-384/512, we obtained for K_1 to K_{16} vector spaces which dimensions given by the following table.

$r =$	1	2	3	4	5	6	7	8	9	10	11	12	13	14	15	16
$dim(K_r =)$	2	4	2	8	2	4	8	16	2	4	2	8	2	16	2	32

As could be seen in the enumeration of the K_r base vectors for the first values of r, K_r elements are highly symmetric, i.e. they consist of differences $\delta = (\delta a, \cdots, \delta h)$ such that the 32-bit or 64-bit patterns δa to δh be periodic, of period 32 or 16 or 8 for SHA-256 (resp. 64, 32, 16 or 8 for SHA-512). Thus, any non zero element of the first sets K_r contains at least some non zero periodic words and thus cannot have an extremely low weight. Therefore we think that the approach described above does not provide high probability iterative differentials for SHA-2.

A Chosen IV Attack Against *Turing*

Antoine Joux and Frédéric Muller

DCSSI Crypto Lab, 18 rue du Docteur Zamenhof
F-92131 Issy-les-Moulineaux Cedex, France
{Antoine.Joux,Frederic.Muller}@m4x.org

Abstract. In this paper, we show that the key scheduling algorithm of the recently proposed stream cipher Turing suffers from important flaws. These weaknesses allow an attacker that chooses the initialization vector (IV) to recover some partial information about the secret key. In particular, when using Turing with a 256-bit secret key and a 128-bit IV, we present an attack that requires the ability to choose 2^{37} IV and then recovers the key with complexity 2^{72}, requiring 2^{36} bytes of memory.

1 Introduction

A stream cipher is a secret key cryptosystem that takes a short random string and transforms it into a long pseudo-random sequence. Usually this sequence is XORed bitwise with the plaintext in order to produce the ciphertext. This purpose can also be reached by iterating a block cipher, however it is widely believed that a dedicated design may offer a better encryption speed. In general, a stream cipher produces a pseudo random sequence $PRNG(K, IV)$ from a secret key K and an initialization vector IV. Then, the ciphertext C is computed from the plaintext P by:

$$C = PRNG(K, IV) \oplus P$$

The main idea behind the use of initialization vectors is to generate different pseudo-random sequences without necessarily changing the secret key, since it is totally insecure to use twice the same sequence. Similar problems may arise when using block ciphers, since they are purely deterministic objects. This is the reason why several modes of operations like CBC or OFB require an initialization vector. Actually, block ciphers are not well suited for that purpose and a more suitable primitive called "Tweakable Block Cipher" was recently proposed [12]. It includes an additional input called the "tweak" which basically plays a role similar to an initialization vector. In both situations, it is extremely difficult to control the mechanism producing the randomization source, since it will usually be provided by a non-cryptographic layer. For instance, it may be implemented using counters or using an unspecified random source. Given this lack of knowledge, any cipher should generally resist attacks where an attacker is able to choose the initialization vector.

Recent developments in the cryptanalysis of stream ciphers have shown the importance of these considerations. In particular, it appears the key scheduling

M. Matsui and R. Zuccherato (Eds.): SAC 2003, LNCS 3006, pp. 194–207, 2004.

algorithm should be analyzed carefully in order to secure real-life systems. The chosen IV attack against RC4 proposed in [7] is a good illustration of this point. Although RC4 still appears as a robust cipher, the key scheduling algorithm leaks partial information concerning the secret key, when observing the first bytes of keystream. Besides, initialization vectors were implemented in the Wireless Equivalent Privacy (WEP) - a standard for wireless network encryption - in a way that allows key reconstruction from chosen IV's. Further analysis has shown that this chosen IV attack was practical (see [18]) and that known IV's were in fact enough to recover the secret key of most wireless LAN's given a reasonable amount of network traffic.

In the context of stream ciphers, most applications require frequent changes of initialization vector. The first reason is that long sequences of keystream imply permanent synchronization, which can become painful especially with high speed connections (for instance, mobile phone communications). The second reason is to handle multiple simultaneous sessions encrypted with the same secret key (for instance with wireless LAN's: WEP or Bluetooth). These practical problems are usually solved by encrypting only short sequences (2745 bits in the case of Bluetooth) and changing the IV value between each sequence. As a consequence, attacks based on known or chosen IV's are made more realistic, while classical attacks are still possible over multiple sequences (see the recent attacks against Bluetooth [8]).

All these elements motivate an analysis of the key scheduling algorithm of new stream ciphers. Here, we focus on Turing, a stream cipher recently proposed by Rose and Hawkes [16]. According to them, Turing is designed in order to achieve a good efficiency in software applications and they claim performances 5 times faster than AES on optimized versions. The keystream generation is based on classical components:

- A large Linear Feedback Shift Register (LFSR) with elements in $GF(2^{32})$. Such registers offer good statistical properties and a large period, while making correlation and fast-correlation attacks difficult. Good examples of similar designs are SNOW [4], S32 [14] and SOBER-t32 [10].
- A Nonlinear Filter that takes 5 words in the LFSR and transforms them in a key-dependent, highly non-linear manner. The resulting keystream is 160 bits long and is masked using 5 words of the LFSR. This technique is usually called "Linear Masking" and has been extensively studied in [3].
- A Key Scheduling Algorithm using a key of length up to 256 bits and an initialization vector of varying length. This routine fills out a keyed S-box used in the Nonlinear Filter and also sets up the initial LFSR state.

In Section 2 we will briefly describe Turing. One should refer to [16] to obtain a more precise description. In Section 3 we show some weaknesses in the key scheduling algorithm of Turing, using chosen initialization vectors. Furthermore, we show how these weaknesses allow a key recovery attack. In Section 4, we show some extensions of our observations to other kind of attacks.

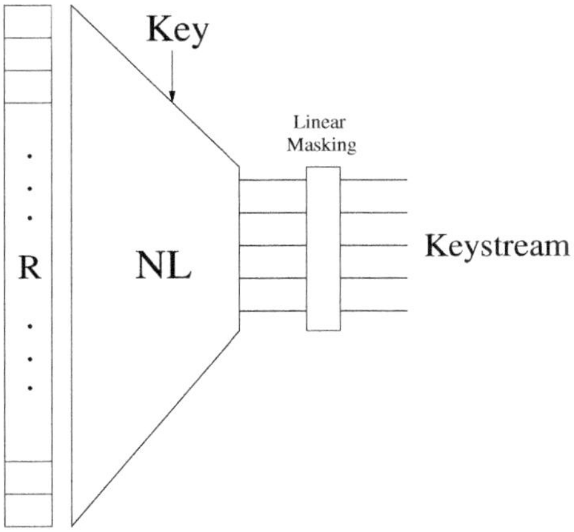

Fig. 1. General Structure of Turing

2 Description of *Turing*

The Turing keystream generation function is based on a classical structure : a linear feedback register R combined with a nonlinear filter NL . The particularity of this cipher lies in the key dependence of NL and on the linear masking. An overview of this structure is given in Figure 1.

Turing combines additions in GF(2^{32}) with additions modulo 2^{32}. To avoid any confusion, $\oplus$ will denote additions in GF(2^{32}), i.e. bitwise XOR, while $+$ will denote addition modulo 2^{32}.

Our description of the cipher mostly focuses on particular points that are relevant to our attacks. We dedicate a substantial space to describe several aspects of Turing that are only briefly described in the initial paper. They can be found by directly looking at the reference implementation code [2].

2.1 The LFSR

Turing uses a Linear Feedback Shift Register R operating on elements in GF(2^{32}). This choice allows good software performances on 32 bits processors. R has 17 cells, so the total number of internal state bits is 544. A register offering the same security with elements in GF(2) would require a very dense feedback polynomial, which would increase the cost of each advance. In the case of Turing, the following feedback polynomial was chosen :

$$x^{17} \oplus x^{15} \oplus x^4 \oplus \alpha$$

where α is a fixed element in GF(2^{32}). Thus, denoting by R_i the content of cell number i, the update function can be expressed as

$$z = R_{15} \oplus R_4 \oplus \alpha R_0$$

This new value z is introduced at position 16 and all cells are shifted by one position (R_0 is discarded).

Such registers are expected to offer good resistance against a wide class of attacks against stream ciphers based on LFSR, the correlation attacks [17] and fast correlation attacks [13]. The importance of choosing adequate feedback polynomials in this type of registers was recently shown by the new attacks against SNOW (see [3], [5] and [11]). However, the designers of Turing have apparently been very careful in the choice of polynomial to prevent similar attacks. Besides, the Nonlinear Filter being key-dependent, it seems very unlikely that a bias could be found independently of the secret key.

2.2 The Nonlinear Filter

The Nonlinear Filter (NL) of Turing is very similar to the construction of a block cipher round function. It combines two applications of a linear transformation on GF(2^{32}) and a layer of key-dependent 32-to-32 S-box applied to each word in-between the two linear layers. The input of NL consists in 5 cells of the LFSR : R_0, R_1, R_6, R_{13} and R_{16}.

The linear operation is the so-called Pseudo-Hadamard transform (PHT) (see [16] for more details). The keyed S-box is described more precisely in Section 2.4. Besides, a circular rotation is also applied to 3 of the 5 words before computing S in order to differentiate the trails followed by each input of NL.

2.3 Linear Masking

Linear Masking consists in adding to each output word of the Nonlinear Filter some word of the LFSR to hide any kind of undesirable statistical properties. Variants of this idea of a masking scheme have been used in SNOW [5] and SCREAM [9].

Here the linear masking is very simple. For each application of the Nonlinear filter, the LFSR is clocked twice :

- After the first clocking, the content of cells number 0, 1, 6, 13 and 16 is used as input of NL.
- After the second clocking, the same cells are used to mask the outputs of NL using a simple addition over GF(2^{32}).

This requires the LFSR to be clocked twice in order to produce $5 \times 32 = 160$ bits of keystream.

2.4 The Key Scheduling Algorithm

The Key Scheduling Algorithm of Turing receives a secret key K and an initialization vector IV. The number of words of K and IV are respectively denoted by n_K and n_I. Both should be multiples of 32 bits. Besides, n_K should not exceed 8 and $n_I + n_K$ should not exceed 12. Words of K are denoted by $\{K_i,$

$i = 0, \ldots, n_K - 1\}$. Each word K_i is further divided into four bytes which we denote by $\{K_{i,j},\ j = 0, \ldots, 3\}$. Similar notations are used for IV.

This initialization vector is only used to build the initial state of the LFSR while the secret key is used both in the keyed S-box S and to build the initial state of the LFSR. The Key Scheduling Algorithm of Turing basically consists in three steps.

The Key Transform To prevent related key attacks, the actual secret key K is turned into a secret value of the same length using a reversible transformation G applied to each word of K. The result is used to initialize the LFSR and to build the keyed S-box S. So the knowledge of this result is actually equivalent to the knowledge of K. That is why in the following sections, notation K will be used to represent this resulting value instead of the true secret key.

The Keyed S-box The keyed S-box S - also used in the nonlinear filter - is used to compute the initial state of the LFSR. It operates on a word w represented as four bytes $w = (w_0, w_1, w_2, w_3)$.

For each byte w_i, a 32-bit value $s_i(w_i)$ is computed using a 8-to-32 function depending on byte number i of each word K_j, denoted as $K_{j,i}$, for $0 \leq j < n_K$. For instance, $s_0(w_0)$ is computed using only the least significant byte of w and the least significant byte of each word of K. The four values $s_0(w_0), \ldots, s_3(w_3)$ are finally added bitwise :

$$S(w) = s_0(w_0) \oplus s_1(w_1) \oplus s_2(w_2) \oplus s_3(w_3)$$

Each s_i uses a chained construction similar to the CBC mode of operation on block ciphers and a 32 bits long accumulator. The general structure of s_i is summarized in Fig. 2 where key bytes are represented by $k0, \ldots, k7$. Two fixed S-boxes, Sb and Qb, are used during this computation. More details on these constants are given in [16] and [2]. Depending on which s_i is considered, the output byte of the CBC chain is appended at different positions in the final word and different key bytes are used.

The Initial State of the LFSR The LFSR is initially filled out as follows :

- The words of IV are processed using the transformation G previously applied to the key words and then copied at positions 0 to $n_I - 1$ in the LFSR. The transformation is fixed, so the value of these cells in the LFSR is initially known.
- The words of K are appended at positions n_I to $n_I + n_K - 1$.
- The binary value 0x010203$n_K n_I$ is appended at position $n_I + n_K$.
- The remaining cells R_i for $n_I + n_K < i < 17$ are computed by the formula

$$R_i = S(R_{i-1} + R_{i-n_K-n_I-1})$$

Finally, a 17-word Pseudo-Hadamard transform is applied :

$$T = \textstyle\sum_{i=0}^{i=16} R_i \qquad R_{16} := T \qquad R_i := R_i + T$$

for $i < 16$. Once this is done, keystream generation starts.

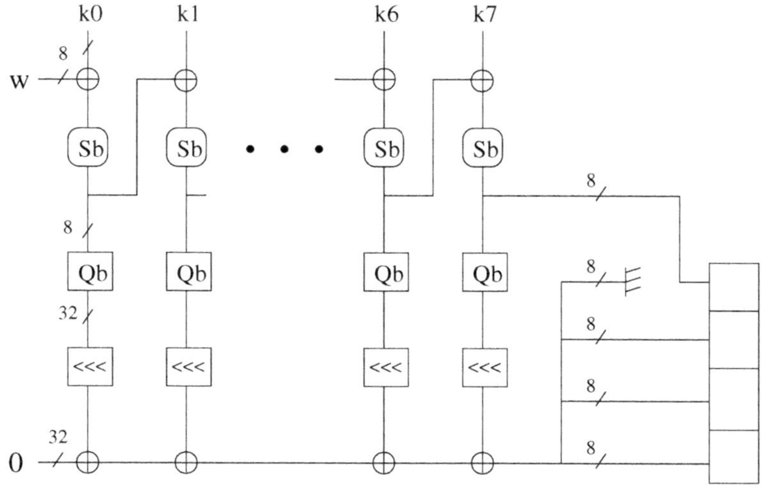

Fig. 2. Structure of s_i

3 A Chosen IV Attack

We observed that the influence of the initialization vector on the internal LFSR state is very limited. In spite of the Pseudo-Hadamard transform, it is possible that different IV's yield very similar initial states. In this case, the first words of keystream generated may even be equal.

To illustrate this, we will focus on the case where the secret key is 256 bits long (that is $n_K = 8$) and the initialization vector is 128 bits long (that is $n_I = 4$). The initial content of the LFSR - before the application of the PHT - is represented in Table 1.

In the following sections, we will fix the value of the secret key, IV_1 and IV_2. Then, we will study what is the influence on the initial state of successively randomizing IV_3 and IV_0.

Table 1. Initial State of the LFSR

$R_0 = G(IV_0)$	$R_9 = K_5$
$R_1 = G(IV_1)$	$R_{10} = K_6$
$R_2 = G(IV_2)$	$R_{11} = K_7$
$R_3 = G(IV_3)$	$R_{12} =$ 0x01020384
$R_4 = K_0$	$R_{13} = S(R_{12} + R_0)$
$R_5 = K_1$	$R_{14} = S(R_{13} + R_1)$
$R_6 = K_2$	$R_{15} = S(R_{14} + R_2)$
$R_7 = K_3$	$R_{16} = S(R_{15} + R_3)$
$R_8 = K_4$	

3.1 Randomizing IV_3

In the previous table, one sees that only R_3 and R_{16} actually depend on IV_3. Furthermore when the secret key and the first three words of the IV are fixed, it may happen for two distinct values of IV_3, say x and x', to observe the same value of $R_{16} + R_3$, before the PHT. Thus :

$$S(R_{15} + G(x)) + G(x) = S(R_{15} + G(x')) + G(x') \quad (1)$$

This is a birthday paradox situation. Thus, such an event should happen if about 2^{16} different values of IV_3 are tested.

In fact, this can be immediately detected. As a matter of fact, if (1) holds, the value of T computed by the PHT will be equal in both cases, and thus, only cell number 3 of the LFSR will differ after the PHT. Then, the first 5 words of keystream are computed as

$$(C_1, \ldots, C_5) = NL(X_1, X_2, X_7, X_{14}, X_{17}) \oplus (X_2, X_3, X_8, X_{15}, X_{18})$$

where C_i denotes the i-th keystream word and X_i the cell number i of the LFSR, after the PHT. There are only 17 cells in the LFSR, however we denote by X_{17} and X_{18} the following terms in the LFSR sequence :

$$X_{17} = X_{15} \oplus X_4 \oplus \alpha X_0$$
$$X_{18} = X_{16} \oplus X_5 \oplus \alpha X_1$$

Since no input of NL depends on IV_3, the value of C_1,C_2,C_3 and C_5 will be equal with both IV's. It is very unlikely that such keystream collisions on 128 bits will occur if (1) is not verified. Therefore, relation (1) can be efficiently detected by looking at the first words of keystream.

3.2 Randomizing IV_0

The keyed S-box S is not a permutation because of its particular structure based on 4 smaller functions. In fact, it should rather be seen as a pseudo-random function when the key is unknown. Therefore, we can expect to find collisions after 2^{16} queries to this S-box for an unknown secret key. Some experiments made on randomly chosen secret keys have confirmed this property.

It follows that different values - say y_1 and y_2 - for IV_0 may exist such that

$$S(G(y_1) + \texttt{0x01020384}) = S(G(y_2) + \texttt{0x01020384}) \quad (2)$$

The essential property is that values of IV_0 verifying (2) will induce the same value of R_{15}. Thus, they will verify (1) with the same IV_3's. The influence of these IV words on the first keystream words can be summarized by :

Indeed, the difference in the initial state brought by IV_0 vanishes when computing R_{13} because of (2). Then, when applying the PHT, the same value of T is computed for both IV_0's, since x_1 and x_1' verify (1). Therefore, collisions on S can be detected by looking at the keystream produced with different chosen initialization vectors.

IV_0	IV_3	First Keystream Words				
y_1	x_1	C_1	C_2	C_3	C_4	C_5
y_1	x'_1	C_1	$C_2 \oplus \Delta$	C_3	C_4	C_5
y_2	x_1	C'_1	C'_2	C'_3	C'_4	C'_5
y_2	x'_1	C'_1	$C_2 \oplus \Delta'$	C'_3	C'_4	C'_5

3.3 Efficient Detection of Collisions

In this section, we assume the attacker has access to the key schedule routine with a fixed unknown secret key and can choose the initialization vector. We also assume the attacker can observe the first words of keystream produced after this key schedule. We will show how such an attacker can efficiently recover collisions on S with chosen input values.

- Fix the secret key K
- Fix IV_1 and IV_2
- While (no relation (2) found)
  - Choose a value of IV_0
  - While (no relation (1) found)
    - Pick a random value of IV_3
    - Do a key scheduling with current value of IV words
    - Look for collisions on the first words of keystream
  - Store IV_0 with its two corresponding IV_3's
  - Do a key scheduling with current IV_0 and all previously stored pairs of IV_3
  - Look for collisions on the first words of keystream
- Output the two corresponding IV_0's (they verify (2))

Collisions described in the previous sections are observed after about 2^{16} queries. Thus, the total number of key scheduling necessary to observe once relation (2) is roughly

$$\sum_{i=1}^{i=2^{16}} (2(i-1) + 2^{16}) \simeq 2^{32}$$

We have implemented this basic technique with several different secret keys and managed to detect collisions on S quite efficiently.

An improved technique consists in fixing several values (say 2^{16}) of IV_3 before any key scheduling request. Then test, say M, different values of IV_0 with all these fixed IV_3's. Then, it is possible to detect which pairs of IV_0 among the M values considered yield collisions with the same pairs of IV_3's. These pairs verify relation (2). This technique allows to recover $M^2\ 2^{-32}$ S-box collisions after $M\ 2^{16}$ key scheduling requests although the chances of false alarm slightly increase. This technique is less expensive when more than one collision is needed.

3.4 A Key Recovery Attack

It turns out that these collisions on the keyed S-box reveal direct information about the secret key. More precisely, remember that collisions on S are obtained with chosen inputs. Moreover, outputs of S depend only on part of the key bits, when the corresponding inputs agree on a certain number of bytes. Accordingly, let us consider only collisions where inputs disagree on 3 bytes at most (for instance input values having the same most significant byte). This means only 2^{24} of all possible IV_0's may be tested. By choosing appropriate values for IV_0, the collisions will yield relations of the form :

$$S(w) = S(w')$$

where

$$S(w) = s_0(w_0) \oplus s_1(w_1) \oplus s_2(w_2) \oplus s_3(w_3)$$
$$S(w') = s_0(w'_0) \oplus s_1(w'_1) \oplus s_2(w'_2) \oplus s_3(w'_3)$$

and, since $w_0 = w'_0$,

$$s_1(w_1) \oplus s_2(w_2) \oplus s_3(w_3) = s_1(w'_1) \oplus s_2(w'_2) \oplus s_3(w'_3) \tag{3}$$

Thus, we get a relation involving only three of the four 8-to-32 key-dependent functions that constitute S. This brings some significant information about the 64 key bytes used in each of these functions. A straightforward approach would be to use relation (3) to decrease the complexity of an exhaustive search on the 256 bits of secret key. The number of triplets of outputs of s_1, s_2 and s_3 is :

$$(2^8)^3 = 2^{24}$$

Therefore the expected value for the number of existing relations is about

$$2^{24} \times 2^{24} \times 2^{-32} = 2^{16}$$

Hence, many relations similar to (3) should exist. They involve only 192 key bits, so a small number of them is sufficient to reduce the cost of key exhaustive search to 2^{192}. Furthermore, it may happen that collisions involving only 2 bytes exist. In that case, the cost of a brute-force attack may even be reduced to 2^{128}. However, this event occurs with small probability, so keys yielding these collisions may be considered as weak keys.

3.5 Solving the Underlying Linear System

However, we believe relations similar to (3) may be used in a more efficient manner to recover the secret key. Let us call $X_i = s_1(i)$, $Y_i = s_2(i)$ and $Z_i = s_3(i)$ for $0 \leq i \leq 255$. (3) is a linear relation between 6 of these $3 \times 256 = 768$ unknown values in GF(2^{32}), of the form :

$$X_i \oplus X'_i \oplus Y_j \oplus Y'_j \oplus Z_k \oplus Z'_k = 0 \tag{4}$$

for some i, i', j, j', k, k' between 0 and 255.

More generally, when many similar relations are available - at least 768 hopefully independent relations - one can expect to solve the underlying linear system. Unfortunately, it turns out it never has full rank. Indeed, all coefficients in relation (4) are either 0 or 1. Therefore this system can also be viewed as a linear system in GF(2) and, from each solution in GF(2^{32}), it is possible to build 32 solutions in GF(2). This implies a decrepancy of at least 32 in the rank of the system since at least one solution exists in GF(2^{32}), corresponding to the real outputs of the keyed S-box.

Furthermore, since all X_i's appear twice in each relation, adding a fixed word C to these 256 unknowns provides an extra non trivial solution. Similar considerations also hold for Y_i and Z_i, which implies an additional discrepancy of 3. So the kernel of the system has dimension at least $32 + 3 = 35$. An open question is to know whether this dimension is actually always 35. Using different secret keys, we built the corresponding system by observing all collisions on S. Then, we computed its rank using the software MAGMA [1]. We always obtained a rank equal to 733, which corresponds to the expected value

$$768 - 3 - 32 = 768 - 35 = 733$$

Besides, it appears from our experiments that, using about $1000 \simeq 2^{10}$ relations is enough to always obtain a system of maximal rank 733. In particular, testing 2^{21} values for IV_0 should be sufficient to obtain enough collision and thus a system of maximal rank :

$$2^{21} \times 2^{21} \times 2^{-32} = 2^{10}$$

Thus $2^{21} \times 2^{16} = 2^{37}$ chosen initialization vectors are needed.

Building a basis of the kernel of the underlying linear application can be done very quickly. We used the software MAGMA and, given the size of the system, it takes only a few seconds to complete this task. However, since the system has not full rank, linear algebra does not provide immediately a unique solution, but we can easily obtain a basis of the kernel and span its 2^{35} elements.

Using additional constraints resulting from the structure of the underlying keyed S-box, an efficient key recovery attack directly follows. Assume these 2^{35} solutions are sorted and stored in a table. An exhaustive search on the 64 key bits involved in s_3 will provide a candidate for $(Z_0, \ldots, Z_{255})$. Wrong guesses can be filtered out using the table, since the vector of least significant bits of all Z_i's must appear somewhere in this table, as part of a GF(2) solution. A similar technique can be used to find key bytes involved in s_1 and s_2 and the final 64 key bits can be guessed separately.

Therefore we obtain the 256 secret key bits, using a table containing 2^{35} words of 768 bits, with 2^{37} chosen IV's and $256 \times 2^{64} = 2^{72}$ steps of computation. A basic improvement is not to consider all solutions of the previous system in GF(2). Indeed, the output byte corresponding to the CBC chain (see Figure 2) in any function s_i is a permutation of the inputs (since this operation is reversible). Therefore, instead of verifying the least significant bit, we can use an other bit position corresponding to the output of this permutation and store only balanced vectors of 256 bits. Thus the size of the table required is reduced to the number of solutions balanced on these 256 bits, that is about 2^{31}, since

$$\binom{256}{128} \times 2^{-256} \times 2^{35} \simeq 2^{31}$$

Each entry of the table is a 256 bits vector. Thus, this attack requires 2^{36} bytes of memory.

4 Extensions of this Attack

The attack we have proposed is a little restrictive since it works only with 256 bits long secret key and 128 bits long IV's. In this section, we demonstrate that although this attack does not work in every case, some residual weaknesses of the key scheduling algorithm cannot be prevented.

4.1 Other Key and IV Lengths

The attack proposed in the previous section relies on the lack of diffusion brought by the PHT. This weakness exist for any key and IV length. However, the possibility to observe collisions on the first keystream words vary greatly depending on the choice of these parameters. We have demonstrated our attack when $n_K = 8$ and $n_I = 4$. When key length is less than 8 words but key and IV still sum up to 12 words, the attack proposed in Section 3 still works by keeping the additional IV words constant. The resulting attack has time complexity

$$2^8 \times 2^{8n_K}$$

Memory complexity is still about 2^{31} and the number of chosen IV's needed is still about 2^{37}.

To demonstrate residual weaknesses for other key lengths, we briefly give a sketch of a possible attack using 128 bits long secret key and IV in Appendix A. It seems very likely that similar residual weaknesses hold for most key length and IV length, although they seem to be more efficient when large keys and IV's are used. For shorter lengths (less than 64 bits), they might become even more difficult to exploit, however the security of the system does not reach the initial security goal.

4.2 Distinguishing Attacks

It is also worth noticing that collisions in the PHT can also be used to distinguish Turing from a truly Random Generator with a much smaller complexity than the key recovery attack. For instance, when considering the case of 256 bits long secret key and 128 bits long IV's, randomizing only IV_3 will yield keystream collisions very quickly - after about 2^{16} queries.

If, in practice, the IV's where implemented using a counter, it seems likely that only IV_3 would differ between two consecutive sessions. In that case, one could distinguish Turing from random by detecting these collisions. Moreover, a condition on S is obtained this way (literally, relation (1) with an unknown value of R_{15}). This relation does not appear to be very useful, however it may allow to reduce the complexity of brute-force attacks by a small constant.

Recently, Rose and Hawkes [15] proposed a distinction between "weak" and "powerful" distinguishing attacks, by arguing that many proposed distinguishers against stream ciphers (see [6] and [15]) were not related to the practical security of the cipher. We believe however that in this particular case, early distinguishers against Turing (with less than 2^{16} chosen IV's) already leak partial information about the secret key and should not be tolerated. Therefore, although one can argue that the key recovery attack we propose is not practical, since the use of 2^{37} different IV's with the same secret key can be avoided, we think the weaknesses of the key scheduling algorithm we identified should still be fixed somehow.

5 Conclusion

In this paper, we identified several weaknesses in the key scheduling algorithm of the new stream cipher Turing. We believe these attacks will significantly lower the security of this cryptosystem when the same secret key can be used with many different initialization vectors. Our best attack works on 256 bits long secret key and 128 bits long IV's. In this case, it recovers the key using 2^{37} chosen IV, 2^{72} of computation time and 2^{36} bytes of memory.

Altough our attacks concern only the key scheduling, we think Turing should be modified to remove this vulnerability resulting from chosen IV attacks. The classical and probably simplest way to achieve that is to clock the LFSR several times before starting the keystream generation (16 clocking should be sufficient to remove undesirable properties on the LFSR initial state resulting from the IV). This might slightly decrease the speed of the cipher when IV needs to be frequently changed but it appears like a sound countermeasure.

An open problem would be, given the particular structure of Turing S-boxes, to improve the resolution of the linear system of equations we obtain in Section 3.5.

References

[1] The Magma Home Page. `http://www.maths.usyd.edu.au:8000/u/magma/`. 203
[2] Turing reference source code. Available at `http://people.qualcomm.com/ggr/QC/turing.tqz`. 196, 198
[3] D. Coppersmith, S. Halevi, and C. Jutla. Cryptanalysis of Stream Ciphers with Linear Masking. In M. Yung, editor, *Advances in Cryptology – Crypto'02*, volume 2442 of *Lectures Notes in Computer Science*, pages 515–532. Springer, 2002. 195, 197

[4] P. Ekdahl and T. Johansson. SNOW - a New Stream Cipher. In *First Open NESSIE Workshop, KU-Leuven*, 2000. Submission to NESSIE. Available at `http://www.it.lth.se/cryptology/snow/`. 195

[5] P. Ekdahl and T. Johansson. A New Version of the Stream Cipher SNOW. In *Selected Areas in Cryptography – 2002*, Lectures Notes in Computer Science. Springer, 2002. 197

[6] P. Ekdahl and T. Johansson. Distinguishing Attacks on SOBER-t16 and t32. In J. Daemen and V. Rijmen, editors, *Fast Software Encryption – 2002*, volume 2365 of *Lectures Notes in Computer Science*, pages 210–224. Springer, 2002. 205

[7] S. Fluhrer, I. Mantin, and A. Shamir. Weaknesses in the Key Scheduling Algorithm of RC4. In S. Vaudenay and A.M. Youssef, editors, *Selected Areas in Cryptography – 2001*, volume 2259 of *Lectures Notes in Computer Science*, pages 1–24. Springer, 2001. 195

[8] J.Dj. Golic, V. Bagini, and G. Morgari. Linear Cryptanalysis of Bluetooth Stream Cipher. In L. Knudsen, editor, *Fast Software Encryption – 2002*, volume 2332 of *Lectures Notes in Computer Science*, pages 238–255. Springer, 2002. 195

[9] S. Halevi, D. Coppersmith, and C. Jutla. Scream : a Software-efficient Stream Cipher. In L. Knudsen, editor, *Fast Software Encryption – 2002*, volume 2332 of *Lectures Notes in Computer Science*, pages 195–209. Springer, 2002. 197

[10] P. Hawkes and G. Rose. Primitive Specification and Supporting Documentation for SOBER-t32. In *First Open NESSIE Workshop*, 2000. Submission to NESSIE. 195

[11] P. Hawkes and G. Rose. Guess-and-Determine Attacks on SNOW. In *Selected Areas in Cryptography – 2002*, Lectures Notes in Computer Science. Springer, 2002. 197

[12] M. Liskov, R. Rivest, and D. Wagner. Tweakable Block Ciphers. In M. Yung, editor, *Advances in Cryptology – Crypto'02*, volume 2442 of *Lectures Notes in Computer Science*, pages 31–46. Springer, 2002. 194

[13] W. Meier and O. Stafflebach. Fast Correlations Attacks on Certain Stream Ciphers. In *Journal of Cryptology*, pages 159–176. Springer-Verlag, 1989. 197

[14] G. Rose. S32: A Fast Stream Cipher based on Linear Feedback over $GF(2^{32})$. Unpublished report, QUALCOMM, Australia, Available at `http://people.qualcomm.com/ggr/QC/`. 195

[15] G. Rose and P. Hawkes. On the Applicability of Distinguishing Attacks Against Stream Ciphers, 2002. Available at `http://eprint.iacr.org/2002/142.pdf`. 205

[16] G. Rose and P. Hawkes. Turing : a Fast Stream Cipher. In T. Johansson, editor, *Fast Software Encryption – 2003*, Lectures Notes in Computer Science. Springer, 2003. To appear. 195, 197, 198

[17] T. Siegenthaler. Correlation-immunity of Nonlinear Combining Functions for Cryptographic Applications. In *IEEE Transactions on Information Theory*, volume 30, pages 776–780, 1984. 197

[18] A. Stubblefield, J. Ioannidis, and A.D. Rubin. Using the Fluhrer, Mantin and Shamir Attack to Break WEP, 2001. 195

A Possible Attacks on 128 bits Long Secret Key

We now briefly describe what happens during the key scheduling when considering 128 bits long key and IV's. In this case, using previous notations, the initial LFSR state - before the PHT - is given by :

$$\begin{aligned} R_0 &= G(IV_0) \\ R_1 &= G(IV_1) \\ R_2 &= G(IV_2) \\ R_3 &= G(IV_3) \\ R_4 &= K_0 \\ R_5 &= K_1 \\ R_6 &= K_2 \\ R_7 &= K_3 \\ R_8 &= \texttt{0x01020344} \end{aligned} \qquad \begin{aligned} R_9 &= S(R_8 + R_0) \\ R_{10} &= S(R_9 + R_1) \\ R_{11} &= S(R_{10} + R_2) \\ R_{12} &= S(R_{11} + R_3) \\ R_{13} &= S(R_{12} + R_4) \\ R_{14} &= S(R_{13} + R_5) \\ R_{15} &= S(R_{14} + R_6) \\ R_{16} &= S(R_{15} + R_7) \end{aligned}$$

The influence of the initialization vector on the initial state is more complex than previously and the first application of NL seems to resist any collision. However, when looking at the second application of NL, we have

$$(C_1, \ldots, C_5) = NL(X_3, X_4, X_9, X_{16}, X_{19}) \oplus (X_4, X_5, X_{10}, X_{17}, X_{20})$$

using the same notations as in Section 3. More precisely,

$$\begin{aligned} X_{17} &= X_{15} \oplus X_4 \oplus \alpha X_0 \\ X_{19} &= X_{15} \oplus X_6 \oplus X_4 \oplus \alpha(X_0 \oplus X_2) \end{aligned}$$

Assume we use two IV's that differ on IV_0 and IV_1, verify $IV_2 = IV_0$, and have the same value of IV_3. If simultaneously, collisions on R_9, R_{15} and the word T computed by the PHT occur, then inputs of the second application of NL will be equal. It is a birthday paradox situation and should be observed after $(2^{16})^3 = 2^{48}$ experiences. Only two masking words are guaranteed to be equal in that case, which is not enough to detect efficiently this event. However, false alarms can be discarded by repeating the same experience with an other value of IV_3. Furthermore, collisions on the keyed S-box are again detected, so an attack similar to the one of Section 3 will work.

To summarize, a key recovery attack can also be mounted in this case, although the data complexity will be higher than in the previous case. In practice, the number of chosen IV's needed will be more than 2^{48}.

Related-Key Differential Cryptanalysis of 192-bit Key AES Variants*

Goce Jakimoski and Yvo Desmedt

Computer Science Department, Florida State University
Tallahassee, Florida FL 32306-4530, USA
{jakimosk,desmedt}@cs.fsu.edu

Abstract. A related-key differential cryptanalysis is applied to the 192-bit key variant of AES. Although any 4-round differential trail has at least 25 active bytes, one can construct 5-round related-key differential trail that has only 15 active bytes and break six rounds with 2^{106} plaintext/ciphertext pairs and complexity 2^{112}. The attack can be improved using truncated differentials. In this case, the number of required plaintext/ciphertext pairs is 2^{81} and the complexity is about 2^{86}. Using impossible related-key differentials we can break seven rounds with 2^{111} plaintext/ciphertext pairs and computational complexity 2^{116}. The attack on eight rounds requires 2^{88} plaintext/ciphertext pairs and its complexity is about 2^{183} encryptions. In the case of differential cryptanalysis, if the iterated cipher is Markov cipher and the round keys are independent, then the sequence of differences at each round output forms a Markov chain and the cipher becomes resistant to differential cryptanalysis after sufficiently many rounds, but this is not true in the case of related-key differentials. It can be shown that if in addition the Markov cipher has $\mathcal{K} - f$ round function and the hypothesis of stochastic equivalence for related keys holds, then the iterated cipher is resistant to related-key differential attacks after sufficiently many rounds.

Keywords: Differential cryptanalysis, related keys, Markov ciphers, Advanced Encryption Standard

1 Introduction

On October 2, 2000, after a long and complex evaluation process, NIST announced that it has selected Rijndael [9] to propose for the Advanced Encryption Standard. A draft standard was published for public review and comment, and in 2001, FIPS-197 was approved as a Federal Information Processing Standard for the AES [1]. The AES algorithm is a symmetric block cipher that can process data blocks of 128 bits. It may be used with three different key lengths (128, 192, and 256 bits), and these different "flavors" are referred to as "AES-128", "AES-192", and "AES-256". It is expected that the algorithm "will be used by the U.S.

* A part of this research was funded by NSF CCR-0109425.

M. Matsui and R. Zuccherato (Eds.): SAC 2003, LNCS 3006, pp. 208–221, 2004.

Government, and on a voluntary basis, by the private sector" [8]. Therefore, it is very important to constantly reevaluate the security of AES.

Differential cryptanalysis [2] is a chosen-plaintext attack that can be applied to a large class of encryption algorithms. It analyzes the effect of the difference of a pair of plaintexts on the difference of succeeding round outputs in an iterated cipher. Because of its generality, differential cryptanalysis is extensively exploited tool for cryptanalysis of encryption algorithms [3] and for defining new attacks [15, 14]. Resistance to differential cryptanalysis became one of the basic criteria in the evaluation of the security of block encryption algorithms. Rijndael [9] is designed according to the wide trail strategy [10], and one of the goals of this strategy is resistance to differential cryptanalysis.

Related-key attacks [4, 13] allow the cryptanalyst to obtain p/c pairs by using different, but related keys. The relation between the keys can be chosen by the attacker. Ferguson et al [11] noticed that "compared to the cipher itself, the Rijndael key schedule appears to be more of an ad hoc design. It has much slower diffusion structure than the cipher, and contains relatively few non-linear elements." They exploited the slow diffusion of the Rijndael key schedule to mount a related-key attack on 9 rounds of 256-bit key Rijndael. The time complexity of the attack is 2^{224} and it requires 2^{85} plaintext/ciphertext pairs obtained under 256 related keys.

In this paper, we apply combinations of related-key and differential attacks to AES-192. The attacks exploit the effect of the difference of a pair of plaintexts on the difference of succeeding round outputs when the plaintexts are encrypted using distinct keys. The chosen relation between the keys is the key difference, which can be possibly obtained by fault insertion [17]. The complexity of the attack depends on the ability of the attacker to predict the propagation of the key difference during the key schedule. If we view the expanded key as a sequence of words, then the key schedule of AES-192 applies non-linear transformations to every sixth word, whereas the key schedules of AES-128 and AES-256 apply non-linear transformations to every fourth word. Therefore, we believe that AES-192 is more susceptible to related-key differential cryptanalysis than the other AES variants. We were able to break eight rounds of AES-192 using 2^{88} plaintext/ciphertext pairs. The time complexity of the attack is about 2^{183} encryptions and it suggests that the problem of designing block ciphers being resistant to related-key differential cryptanalysis is worth investigating.

The techniques used by related-key differential cryptanalysis are similar to the techniques used by differential cryptanalysis (e.g. finding highly probable differential trail). Markov cipher is a concept that was introduced to analyze the resistance of iterated ciphers to differential cryptanalysis. Namely, in [16], the authors showed that the sequence of differences at each round output forms a Markov chain if the iterated cipher is Markov and its round keys are independent. Assuming that the hypothesis of stochastic equivalence holds, then the cipher is secure against differential cryptanalysis after sufficiently many rounds. Revisiting the concept of Markov ciphers can give us some insight about the properties of a cipher that make it resistant to related-key differential cryptanalysis.

Hence, in this paper, we also address the question of sufficient conditions such that the sequence of differences forms a Markov chain in the case of related-keys.

Here is the outline of the paper. In Section 2, we give a definition of related-key differentials and describe a general related-key differential attack. In Section 3, we examine the resistance of the AES to related-key differential cryptanalysis. Some results about the properties that make iterated ciphers resistant to related-key differential cryptanalysis are derived in Section 4. The paper ends with the concluding remarks.

2 Related-Key Differential Attack

Differential cryptanalysis exploits the propagation of the differences when a pair of distinct plaintexts is submitted for encryption under the same key. Related-key differential cryptanalysis exploits the properties of the difference propagation when the plaintexts x_1 and x_2, which can be equal, are submitted for encryption under distinct keys k_1 and k_2 correspondingly.

Formally, an r-round related-key differential is a triple (α, β, δ), where α is the difference of the inputs at the input of the block encryption algorithm, β is the difference of the outputs of the r-th round and δ is the difference of the keys. The probability of r-round related-key differential is the probability that the difference of the outputs of the r-th round will be β, when the input difference is α, the key difference is δ, and the plaintext x_1 and the key k_1 are selected uniformly at random.

A possible related-key differential attack works as follows:

- Find highly probable $R-1$-round related-key differential, where R is the number of rounds of the block cipher.
- Select randomly x_1 and submit it for encryption under key k_1 to obtain ciphertext y_1. Compute $x_2 = x_1 + \alpha$ and submit it for encryption under key $k_2 = k_1 + \delta$ to obtain the ciphertext y_2.
- Find all possible last round key pairs (k_1^R, k_2^R) such that the difference between $d_{k_1^R}(y_1)$ and $d_{k_2^R}(y_2)$ is β, where $d_k(y)$ is the output of the first round of the decryption algorithm for input y and round key k. Add one to each counter that corresponds to one of the previously computed key pairs.
- Repeat previous two steps until one or more last round key pairs are counted significantly more than the others. Check these keys if they are the right keys.

Let K be the number of possible last round key pairs (k_1^R, k_2^R) and let l be the average number of suggested key pairs in the third step. Furthermore, let $p_{max} >> 2^{-m}$, where m is the block length and p_{max} is the probability of the related-key differential found in step 1 and let $N = c/p_{max}$ be the number of repetitions of steps two and three. Then the wrong key pairs will be counted lN/K times on average and the right key pair will be counted about c times on average. If $l \times c < K \times p_{max}$, then the wrong key pairs will be counted less then once on average. The order of the number of required plaintext/ciphertext pairs is $1/p_{max}$.

The related-key differential attack does not have to follow the pattern described above. In general, we will refer to any attack that exploits a related-key differentials as related-key differential attack.

3 Related-Key Differential Attacks on AES-192

In this section, we describe some attacks on reduced 192-bit key variants of AES. Description of the algorithm can be found in [1]. We will use the following notation: $x_i^I, x_i^S, x_i^P, x_i^M$ and x_i^O denote the input of the round i, the output after SubBytes, the output after ShiftRows, the output after MixColumns and the output after AddRoundKey transformation, correspondingly; k_i denotes the round i key and we will use $a_{i,j}, i, j \in \{0, 1, 2, 3\}$ to denote the byte j of the 32-bit word (column) i of a. For example, $x_{3,0,2}^P$ denotes the third byte of the first column of the output after the ShiftRows transformation in the round 3 (the initial key addition of the algorithm is considered as round 0). The encryption round can be transformed into equivalent one that uses key addition before the MixColumns. The round keys used in the equivalent encryption round will be denoted by z_i. Finally, we assume that the last round of the analyzed variants is a FinalRound.

3.1 Basic Attack

Differential cryptanalysis attacks are based on difference propagations over all but few rounds that have large enough prop ratio. For Rijndael, it is proven that any 4-round differential trail has at least 25 active bytes, that is there are no 4-round differential trails with predicted prop ratio above 2^{-150} [9, 10]. The idea of the attack described here is to use the round key differences in order to cancel the differences that exist before the key addition and reduce the number of active bytes.

The propagation of the key difference $(0000)(0000)(0\Delta00)(0\Delta00)(0000)(0000)$ is depicted in Table 1. If we submit two plaintexts x and x' for encryption under the keys k and $k' = k \oplus \Delta k$ correspondingly, such that $\Delta x = (0000)(0000)(0\Delta00)(0\Delta00)$, then a possible propagation of the difference is the one shown in Table 2.

Table 1. Propagation of the key difference

j	Δk_j
0	$(0000)(0000)(0\Delta00)(0\Delta00)$
1	$(0000)(0000)(0000)(0000)$
2	$(0\Delta00)(0000)(0000)(0000)$
3	$(0000)(0000)(0\Delta00)(0\Delta00)$
4	$(0\Delta00)(0\Delta00)(\Delta_1000)(\Delta_1000)$
5	$(\Delta_1\Delta00)(\Delta_1000)(\Delta_1\Delta00)(\Delta_1000)$
6	$(\Delta_100\Delta_2)(000\Delta_2)(\Delta_1\Delta0\Delta_2)(0\Delta0\Delta_2)$

Table 2. Possible propagation of the plaintext difference

j	Δx_j^I
0	$(0000)(0000)(0\Delta 00)(0\Delta 00)$
1	$(0000)(0000)(0000)(0000)$
2	$(0000)(0000)(0000)(0000)$
3	$(0\Delta 00)(0000)(0000)(0000)$
4	$(0000)(0000)(0\Delta 00)('03' \cdot \Delta' \| 0\Delta'\Delta')$
	$\Delta x_4^S = (0000)(0000)(0\Delta 00)(\Delta'' 0\Delta\Delta)$
5	$(\Delta 0 \| '03' \cdot \Delta \| '02' \cdot \Delta)('02' \cdot \Delta \| 0 \| '03' \cdot \Delta \| 0)$
	$(\Delta_1 000)('02' \cdot \Delta'' \oplus \Delta_1 \| \Delta''\Delta'' \| '03' \cdot \Delta'')$

The difference Δ' is selected to satisfy the relation $'02' \cdot \Delta' = \Delta$. In addition, the differences Δ, Δ' and Δ'' should be selected so that the probabilities $P_S(\Delta \to \Delta), P_S(\Delta \to \Delta'), P_S(\Delta' \to \Delta)$ and $P_S('03' \cdot \Delta' \to \Delta'')$ are greater than zero, where $P_S(a \to b)$ is the probability that the output difference of the S-box will be b when the input difference is a. When the previous conditions are satisfied, the 5-round related-key differential trail from Table 2 has 15 active bytes and its probability is $2^{-7\times 15} = 2^{-105}$ in the worst case. If we use 2^{106} plaintext/ciphertext pairs in a related-key differential attack on the six round variant, then the right key will be counted at least twice on average. The time complexity of the attack is about 2^{112} encryptions.

3.2 Improving the Basic Attack: Truncated Differentials

Let us consider the same plaintext and key differences as in the previous subsection. The probability that $\Delta x_{5,2}^I = \Delta_1 000$ is the same as the probability $P_S(\Delta \to \Delta')$ and it is 2^{-7} instead of 2^{-32}, which is the probability when the difference $\Delta x_{5,2}^I$ is uniformly distributed. This highly probable truncated differential [14] is exploited in the attack on six round version of AES. The attack is described below.

We assign counter to every 10-tuple

$$(\Delta_1, \Delta_2, k_{6,0,0}, k_{6,0,1}, k_{6,0,2}, k_{6,0,3}, k_{6,1,1}, k_{6,2,0}, k_{6,3,6}, z_{5,2,0})$$

that is possible for a given Δ. The attack is as follows:

- Select randomly a plaintext pair (x, x') such that the plaintext difference is $(0000)(0000)(0\Delta 00)(0\Delta 00)$ and the ciphertext difference is $\Delta y = (****)(0*0\Delta_2)(*\Delta 0\Delta_2)(0\Delta 0*)$, where '*' means any value, $y = E_k(x), y' = E_{k\oplus\delta}(x')$ and $\delta = (0000)(0000)(0\Delta 00)(0\Delta 00)(0000)(0000)$.
- For every possible 10-tuple, check whether $\Delta x_{5,2}^I = \Delta_1 000$. The value of $\Delta x_{5,2,0}^I$ can be determined from the ciphertext pair using the key differences and the five bytes of the key $k_{6,0,2}, k_{6,1,1}, k_{6,2,0}, k_{6,3,3}$ and $z_{5,2,0}$. Further, the difference $\Delta x_{6,i,j}^P$ is zero for all i and j such that $k_{6,i,j}$ is unknown. Hence, one can compute the differences Δx_5^O, and therefore,the value Δx_5^S can also

be computed due to the linearity of the MixColumns transformation. Now, it is easy to check whether the particular difference before the SubBytes transformation of the round 5 is zero. If $\Delta x^I_{5,2} = \Delta_1 000$, then add one to the counter that corresponds to the particular 10-tuple.

- Repeat the previous two steps until one or more of the 10-tuples are counted significantly more than the others. Take this values as possible values of the specified bytes of the key.

If we repeat the first two steps 2^8 times, then the right 10-tuple will be counted twice on average, while the wrong 10-tuples will be counted 2^{-24} times assuming that when we use wrong key values the probability distribution of $\Delta x^I_{5,2}$ is uniform. Further, the probability that the output difference Δy will be $(* * **)(0 * 0\Delta_2)(*\Delta 0\Delta_2)(0\Delta 0*)$, when the plaintext difference is $\Delta x = (0000)(0000)(0\Delta 00)\ (0\Delta 00)$, is $2^{-9\times 8} = 2^{-72}$. Therefore, the number of plaintext pairs required for the attack is about $2^{72} \times 2^8 = 2^{80}$. There are at most 2^{14} possible values of (Δ_1, Δ_2) for a given Δ. Hence, the complexity of the attack is about $2^8 \times 2^{14} \times 2^{8\times 8} = 2^{86}$ encryptions. The previously described attack is used to determine eight bytes of the key. It is not difficult to find the rest of the key using similar methods.

3.3 Impossible Related-Key Differentials Attack

Impossible differential attack against Rijndael reduced to five rounds was proposed by Biham and Keller [6]. Later, this attack was extended to six rounds [7]. In this section, we describe related-key impossible differentials attacks on 192-bit key variant reduced to seven and eight rounds.

The attack exploits a similar weakness in the key schedule as the previous attacks. Namely, if the key difference is $(0000)(0000)(\Delta 000)(\Delta 000)(0000)(0000)$, then this difference is propagated during the key generation as depicted in Table 3. We can see that the round 1 key difference is zero and the round 2 keys differ in only one byte. If we submit two plaintexts x and x' for encryption, such that $\Delta x = (0000)(0000)(\Delta 000)(\Delta 000)$, then Δx^I_1 is zero, and so is $\Delta x^O_1 = \Delta x^I_2$. Because of the round 2 key difference, the inputs of the third

Table 3. Propagation of the key difference

j	Δk_j
0	$(0000)(0000)(\Delta 000)(\Delta 000)$
1	$(0000)(0000)(0000)(0000)$
2	$(\Delta 000)(0000)(0000)(0000)$
3	$(0000)(0000)(\Delta 000)(\Delta 000)$
4	$(\Delta 000)(\Delta 000)(000\Delta_1)(000\Delta_1)$
5	$(\Delta 00\Delta_1)(000\Delta_1)(\Delta 00\Delta_1)(000\Delta_1)$
6	$(00\Delta_2\Delta_1)(00\Delta_2 0)(\Delta 0\Delta_2\Delta_1)(\Delta 0\Delta_2 0)$
7	$(00\Delta_2\Delta_1)(00\Delta_2 0)(0\Delta_3\Delta_2\Delta_1)(0\Delta_3 0\Delta_1)$

round will differ in only one byte $x^I_{3,0,0}$. Due to the MixColumn transformation and the round 3 key difference, the inputs of the round 4 will differ in six bytes $x^I_{4,0,1}, x^I_{4,0,2}, x^I_{4,0,3}, x^I_{4,1,1}, x^I_{4,1,2}$, and $x^I_{4,1,3}$. Hence, $\Delta x^M_{5,3} \neq 0000$ and $\Delta x^O_{5,3} \neq 000\Delta_1$.

The aforementioned fact can be used to find values of seven bytes of the last round key. Given Δ, for every possible 10-tuple

$$(\Delta_1, \Delta_2, k_{7,0,0}, k_{7,1,0}, k_{7,1,1}, k_{7,1,2}, k_{7,1,3}, k_{7,2,2}, k_{7,3,1}, z_{6,0,3})$$

do the following:

- Compute Δ_3 using $k_{7,1,2}$ and Δ_2.
- For a plaintext pair (x, x') such that $\Delta x = (0000)(0000)(\Delta 000)(\Delta 000)$ and the ciphertext difference is $\Delta y = (*0\Delta_2\Delta_1)(****)(0\Delta_3 * \Delta_1)(0*0\Delta_1)$, where $y = E_k(x), y' = E_{k\oplus\delta}(x')$ and $\delta = (0000)(0000)(\Delta 000)(\Delta 000)(0000)\ (0000)$, check whether $\Delta x^O_{5,3} = 000\Delta_1$. The value of $\Delta x^O_{5,3,3}$ can be determined from the ciphertext pair using the key differences and the five bytes of the key $k_{7,0,0}, k_{7,1,3}, k_{7,2,2}, k_{7,3,1}$ and $z_{6,0,3}$. Further, the difference $\Delta x^P_{7,i,j}$ is zero for all i and j such that $k_{7,i,j}$ is unknown. Hence, one can compute the differences Δx^O_6 and therefore Δx^S_6 due to the linearity of the MixColumns transformation. Once the value of Δx^S_6 is determined, it is not difficult to check whether $\Delta x^O_{5,3} = 000\Delta_1$. If $\Delta x^O_{5,3} = 000\Delta_1$, then mark the current 10-tuple as wrong.
- Repeat the previous step until the 10-tuple is marked as wrong or the maximum of 2^{38} tried plaintext pairs is reached.

The probability that the ciphertext difference will be $\Delta y = (*0\Delta_2\Delta_1)(****)(0\Delta_3 * \Delta_1)(0 * 0\Delta_1)$, when the plaintext x is randomly selected, is $2^{-9\times 8} = 2^{-72}$. Hence, the number of plaintext pairs required to obtain 2^{38} plaintext pairs with the desired property is about 2^{110}. Given Δ, the number of possible values of (Δ_1, Δ_2) is less than 2^{14}. Thus, the complexity of finding the possible 10-tuples is of order $2^{38} \times 2^{14} \times 2^{8\times 8} = 2^{116}$ encryptions. The probability that particular wrong 10-tuple will be marked as wrong using only one pair of plaintexts is 2^{-32}. The number of wrong 10-tuples that are not marked as wrong after applying the procedure 2^{38} times is on average $2^{14} \times 2^{64} \times (1 - 2^{-32})^{2^{38}} \approx 2^{78} \times e^{-2^6} \approx 2^{-14}$ i.e. most of the time there will be no wrong keys that are not marked as wrong. The previous procedure is used to find eight bytes of the key. The rest of the key can be determined using similar techniques with complexity which is negligible compared to the complexity of the overall attack.

The attack can be extended to eight rounds. We will use the same plaintext and key differences, but we will use the fact that $\Delta x^M_{5,1} \neq 0000$ and $\Delta x^O_{5,1} \neq 000\Delta_1$, which can be proved to be true by similar arguments as in the previous case.

Given Δ, for every possible 3-tuple

$$(k_8, z_{7,2,0}, z_{7,3,3})$$

do the following:

- Compute: $k_{7,0}, k_{7,1}, k_{6,3}, k_{5,2}, k_{5,3}, k_{4,1}$ and $z_{8,0,3}$ using k_8; Δ_1 using $k_{4,1}$ and Δ; Δ_2 using $k_{5,3}$ and Δ_1; Δ_3 using $k_{7,1}$ and Δ_2; and finally, $z_{5,2,3}$ using $z_{7,3,3}$ and $z_{8,0,3}$.
- For a plaintext pair (x, x') such that $\Delta x = (0000)(0000)(\Delta 000)(\Delta 000)$ and the difference $\Delta_7^{a,P}$ is $(****)(****)(*000)(000*)$, check whether $\Delta x_{5,1}^O = 000\Delta_1$. The difference $\Delta_7^{a,P}$ is the difference after the ShiftRows transformation of the round 7 computed using the assumed value k_8 from the ciphertext pair obtained when x is submitted for encryption under k and x' is submitted for encryption under $k \oplus \delta$. The value of $\Delta x_{5,1,3}^O$ can be determined from the ciphertext pair using the key differences, $k_8, k_{7,0}, k_{7,1}, z_{7,2,0}, z_{7,3,3}$ and $z_{5,2,3}$.Further, the difference $\Delta x_{7,i,j}^P$ is zero for all i and j such that $z_{7,i,j}$ can not be computed. Hence, one can compute the differences Δx_6^O, and therefore Δx_6^S also due to the linearity of the MixColumns transformation. Now, it is easy to check whether the particular difference before the SubBytes transformation of the round 6 is zero. If $\Delta x_{5,1}^O = 000\Delta_1$, then mark the current 3-tuple as wrong.
- Repeat the previous step until the 3-tuple is marked as wrong or the maximum of 2^{39} tried plaintext pairs is reached.

The probability that the difference $\Delta_7^{a,P}$ will be$(****)(****)(*000)(000*)$, when the plaintext x is randomly selected, is $2^{-6\times 8} = 2^{-48}$. The number of plaintext pairs required to obtain 2^{39} plaintext pairs with the desired property is about 2^{87}. There are $2^{128} \times 2^{2\times 8} = 2^{144}$ values of $(k_8, z_{7,2,0}, z_{7,3,3})$. Thus, the complexity of finding the "right" 3-tuples is of order $2^{39} \times 2^{144} = 2^{183}$ encryptions. The probability that particular wrong 3-tuple will be marked as wrong using only one pair of plaintexts is 2^{-32}. The number of wrong 3-tuples that are not marked as wrong after applying the procedure 2^{39} times is on average $2^{144} \times (1 - 2^{-32})^{2^{39}} \approx 2^{-40}$ i.e. the probability that only the right key will not be marked as wrong is very large. Once the right 3-tuple is determined, it is easy to determine the rest of the key using exhaustive search. One naive way to select the set of 2^{39} plaintext pairs with desired property from the set of 2^{87} available plaintext pairs is to check whether each pair leads to the required difference $\Delta x_7^{a,P}$ for the particular key k_8. In that case, the complexity will be $2^{87+144} = 2^{231}$. The differences $\Delta x_{7,2}^{a,P}$ and $\Delta x_{7,3}^{a,P}$ depend only on eight bytes of the key k_8 and the key differences Δ_1, Δ_2 and Δ_3. Hence, a better way to select the set is to assume first the values of these eight bytes and then compute the set for every possible value of Δ_1, Δ_2 and Δ_3. Then, we can assume the rest of the key, compute the real values of Δ_1, Δ_2 and Δ_3, and select the set that corresponds to the real values of the key differences. Selection can be made by selecting those pairs such that $\Delta x_{7,3}^{a,P} = (000*)$, and then selecting the pairs that satisfy $\Delta x_{7,2}^{a,P} = (*000)$ from the previously selected pairs. The complexity in this case is about $2^{4\times 8} \times 2^{3\times 7} \times 2^{87} = 2^{140}$. Table 4[1] compares the complexities of impossible related-key differential attacks to the complexities of the partial

[1] RK-CP stands for related-key chosen plaintext, and CP stands for chosen plaintext.

Table 4. Comparison of the impossible related-key differential attacks to partial sums attacks on AES-192

# of rounds	p/c pairs	Time	Attack
7	2^{111} RK-CP	2^{116}	impossible related-key differential
8	2^{88} RK-CP	2^{183}	impossible related-key differential
7	19×2^{32} CP	2^{155}	partial sums
7	$2^{128} - 2^{119}$ CP	2^{120}	partial sums
8	$2^{128} - 2^{119}$ CP	2^{188}	partial sums

sums attacks proposed in [11], which is the best attack on the 192-bit key variant known to the authors of this paper.

4 Markov Cipher Property Is Not Enough

The concept of Markov ciphers was introduced in order to analyze the security of iterated block ciphers against differential cryptanalysis. We give the following definition taken from [16]:

Definition 1. *An iterated cipher with round function $y = f(x, k)$ is* a Markov cipher *if there is a group operation for dening dierences such that, for all choices of α, $\alpha \neq e$ and β, $\beta \neq e$*

$$P_o(\Delta y = \beta | \Delta x = \alpha, x = \gamma)$$

is independent of γ when the subkey k is uniformly random, where $P_o(\Delta y = \beta | \Delta x = \alpha, x = \gamma)$ is the probability when the same round key is used to encrypt γ and $\gamma + \alpha$, and e is the identity element.

One can easily notice that *if an iterated cipher is Markov cipher, then the previous property holds even when $\alpha = e$ or $\beta = e$.* The differences in the previous definition are computed when the ciphertexts are obtained using the same key. It is shown that, if an iterated cipher is Markov and its round keys are independent, then the sequence of differences at each round output forms a Markov chain. Furthermore, if the Markov chain of differences has a steady state probability distribution, then this steady state distribution must be the uniform distribution. If we additionally assume that the hypothesis of stochastic equivalence holds for the Markov cipher, then, for almost all subkeys, this cipher is secure against a differential cryptanalysis attack after sufficiently many rounds (see [16] for more details).

The differences in the previous discussion are computed when the ciphertexts are obtained using the same key. In general, we can consider differences in the case when the ciphertexts are obtained using different keys. When the round keys are independent, it is obvious that we can construct highly probable related-key differentials by encrypting the same plaintext using keys that differ in one round key (the key of one of the last rounds). This is demonstrated by the following example.

Magenta [12] is 128-bit block encryption algorithm submitted for AES by Deutsche Telekom AG. It supports 128-bit, 192-bit and 256-bit key sizes. We will consider the 128-bit key variant, which consist of of six Feistel rounds. The key is divided into two 64-bit halves K_1 and K_2. The first part K_1 is used in rounds 1,2,5 and 6, and the second part K_2 is used in the remaining rounds 3 and 4. The algorithm is given by

$$E_K(M) = F_{K_1}(F_{K_1}(F_{K_2}(F_{K_2}(F_{K_1}(F_{K_1}(M)))))),$$

where

$$F_y(x) = ((x_8, \ldots, x_{15}), (x_0, \ldots, x_7) \oplus E^{(3)}(x_8, \ldots, x_{15}, y_0, \ldots, y_7)).$$

Let Δy and ΔE be two differences such that $P(\Delta E^{(3)} = \Delta E | \Delta y, \Delta x = 0)$ is significantly greater[2] than 2^{-64}. If we submit the same plaintext for encryption under the keys (K_1, K_2) and $(K_1, K_2 \oplus \Delta y)$, then the difference between the left halves at the input of the fourth round will be ΔE with probability significantly higher than 2^{-64}. We must note that, although the attack that exploits such related-key differential is more efficient than exhaustive search, the complexity of the attack is large compared to the attack proposed in [5]. It is obvious that we must take the subkey differences into account if we want to analyze the resistance of iterated ciphers to related-key differential cryptanalysis.

Definition 2. *We say that* the round function $y = f(x, k)$ is $\mathcal{K} - f$ *if for every* α , β *and* δ *one can* □*nd* α_1 *such that*

$$P(\Delta y = \beta | \Delta x = \alpha, \Delta k = \delta, x = \gamma) = P_o(\Delta y = \beta | \Delta x = \alpha_1, x = \gamma)$$

for any γ *and uniform distribution of the subkey* k.

Often, the round function is composed of key addition using bitwise XOR and bijective transformation (e.g. AES). In this case, the difference α_1 can be simply computed[3] as $\alpha_1 = \alpha \oplus \delta$. The definition of $\mathcal{K} - f$ round functions enforces relation between the probability distributions of the round output differences in the cases of zero and nonzero key differences. This is formally stated by the following theorem.

Theorem 1. *If the round function is* $\mathcal{K} - f$ *and the input* x *is independent of the input dierence* Δx *and round key dierence* Δk*, then for every* α , β *and* δ *one can* □*nd* α_1 *such that*

$$P(\Delta y = \beta | \Delta x = \alpha, \Delta k = \delta) = P_o(\Delta y = \beta | \Delta x = \alpha_1).$$

---

[2] Authors mention 2^{-40} as an upper bound for transition probabilities of $E^{(3)}$.

[3] This is the reason why we use a somewhat strange notation $\mathcal{K} - f$.

Proof.

$$\begin{aligned}
&P(\Delta y = \beta | \Delta x = \alpha, \Delta k = \delta) = \\
&= \sum_{\gamma} P(\Delta y = \beta | \Delta k = \delta, \Delta x = \alpha, x = \gamma) \times P(x = \gamma) = \\
&= \sum_{\gamma} P_o(\Delta y = \beta | \Delta x = \alpha_1, x = \gamma) \times P(x = \gamma) = \\
&= P_o(\Delta y = \beta | \Delta x = \alpha_1). \square
\end{aligned}$$

The Markov cipher property (round output difference to depend only on the the round input difference and not on the particular round inputs) is crucial in proving that the sequence of the round output differences forms a homogenous Markov chain. Therefore, it is convenient to define a similar property in the case of related-key differentials.

Definition 3. *An iterated cipher with round function* $y = f(x, k)$ *possesses* a Markov cipher property for related keys *if there is a group operation for de□n-ing dierences such that, for all choices of* α *and* β

$$P(\Delta y = \beta | \Delta x = \alpha, x = \gamma) = P(\Delta y = \beta | \Delta x = \alpha)$$

for any probability distribution of the round key dierences and uniformly distributed round key k.

The $\mathcal{K} - f$ property of the round function enables us to analyze the propagation of the related-key differences by observing the propagation of the differences when we use the same key for encryption of the pair of plaintexts. Therefore, it is not surprising that Markov ciphers with $\mathcal{K} - f$ round function possess a Markov cipher property for related keys.

Theorem 2. *If an iterated cipher is a Markov cipher with* $\mathcal{K} - f$ *round function, the round key is uniformly distributed, and the round key dierence is independent of the input and the input dierence, then the cipher possesses a Markov cipher property for related keys.*

Proof.

$$\begin{aligned}
&P(\Delta y = \beta | \Delta x = \alpha, x = \gamma) = \\
&= \sum_{\delta} P(\Delta y = \beta, \Delta k = \delta | \Delta x = \alpha, x = \gamma) = \\
&= \sum_{\delta} P(\Delta y = \beta | \Delta x = \alpha, \Delta k = \delta, x = \gamma) \times P(\Delta k = \delta | \Delta x = \alpha, x = \gamma) = \\
&= \sum_{\delta} P(\Delta k = \delta) \times P_o(\Delta y = \beta | \Delta x = \alpha_1, x = \gamma) \\
&= \sum_{\delta} P(\Delta k = \delta) \times P_o(\Delta y = \beta | \Delta x = \alpha_1)
\end{aligned}$$

$$= \sum_{\delta} P(\Delta k = \delta) \times P(\Delta y = \beta | \Delta x = \alpha, \Delta k = \delta)$$

$$= \sum_{\delta} P(\Delta k = \delta, \Delta y = \beta | \Delta x = \alpha)$$

$$= P(\Delta y = \beta | \Delta x = \alpha). \square$$

The previous results provide intuition for proving the following theorem.

Theorem 3. *If* (i) *an* r*-round iterated cipher is a Markov cipher with* $\mathcal{K} - f$ *round function,* (ii) *the round keys* k_i *are independent and uniformly random and* (iii) *the round key dierences are independent random variables, then the sequence of dierences* $\Delta x = \Delta y(0), \Delta y(1), \ldots \Delta y(r)$ *is a Markov chain. If additionally* (iv) *the probability distributions* $p(\Delta k_i)$ *are identical, then the Markov chain is homogeneous.*

Proof.

$$P(\Delta y(i) = \beta_i | \Delta y(i-1) = \beta_{i-1}, \ldots, \Delta x = \alpha) =$$

$$= \sum_{\gamma} P(\Delta y(i) = \beta_i, y(i-1) = \gamma | \Delta y(i-1) = \beta_{i-1}, \ldots, \Delta x = \alpha) =$$

$$= \sum_{\gamma} P(\Delta y(i) = \beta_i | y(i-1) = \gamma, \Delta y(i-1) = \beta_{i-1}, \ldots, \Delta x = \alpha) \times$$
$$P(y(i-1) = \gamma | \Delta y(i-1) = \beta_{i-1}, \ldots, \Delta x = \alpha) =$$

$$= \sum_{\gamma} P(\Delta y(i) = \beta_i | y(i-1) = \gamma, \Delta y(i-1) = \beta_{i-1}) \times$$
$$P(y(i-1) = \gamma | \Delta y(i-1) = \beta_{i-1}, \ldots, \Delta x = \alpha) =$$

$$= \sum_{\gamma} P(\Delta y(i) = \beta_i | \Delta y(i-1) = \beta_{i-1}) \times$$
$$P(y(i-1) = \gamma | \Delta y(i-1) = \beta_{i-1}, \ldots, \Delta x = \alpha) =$$
$$= P(\Delta y(i) = \beta_i | \Delta y(i-1) = \beta_{i-1})$$

If the probability distributions $P(\Delta k_i)$ are identical, then

$$P(\Delta y(i) = \beta | \Delta y(i-1) = \alpha) =$$

$$= \sum_{\delta} P(\Delta y(i) = \beta, \Delta k_i = \delta | \Delta y(i-1) = \alpha) =$$

$$= \sum_{\delta} P(\Delta y(i) = \beta | \Delta k_i = \delta, \Delta y(i-1) = \alpha) \times P(\Delta k_i = \delta) =$$

$$= \sum_{\delta} P_o(\Delta y = \beta | \Delta x = \alpha_1) \times P(\Delta k_i = \delta) =$$

$$= \sum_{\delta} P_o(\Delta y = \beta | \Delta x = \alpha_1) \times P(\Delta k_{i-1} = \delta) =$$

$$= P(\Delta y(i-1) = \beta | \Delta y(i-2) = \alpha). \square$$

Now, suppose that the round keys and round key differences are independent and uniformly distributed. If the round input difference is uniformly distributed, then the round output difference is also uniformly distributed. Hence, if the Markov chain formed by the round output differences has steady-state probability distribution, then this steady-state distribution must be the uniform distribution. Usually, the round keys are derived using some key generation algorithm, and, given the key and the key difference, the round keys and the round key differences are uniquely determined. If we assume that the probability of the related-key differentials when the round keys and round key differences are fixed, and the probability of the related-key differentials when the round keys and round key differences are independent and uniformly distributed are approximately equal, then the previously discussed Markov ciphers are secure against related-key differential attack after sufficiently many rounds. We will refer to this assumption as *hypothesis of stochastic equivalence for related keys* .

The previous discussion suggests that one way of dealing with related-key differential cryptanalysis is to use key scheduling algorithms whose output is "close" to random. We already mentioned that the success of a related-key attack depends on the attacker's ability to find highly probable (or impossible) related-key differential trails. Unpredictable key differences make the task of constructing such related-key differential trails very difficult.

5 Conclusion

We applied the related-key differential cryptanalysis to the 192-bit key variant of AES. The related-key differential attack on six rounds requires 2^{106} plaintext/ciphertext pairs and its complexity is 2^{112}. Using truncated differentials, we can improve the attack on six rounds. In this case, the number of required plaintext/ciphertext pairs is 2^{81} and the complexity is about 2^{86}. Impossible related-key differential cryptanalysis gave best results. The complexity of the attack on seven rounds is 2^{116} and requires 2^{111} plaintext/ciphertext pairs, and the complexity of the attack on eight rounds is about 2^{183} encryptions and requires 2^{88} plaintext/ciphertext pairs.

We also examined the additional constraints that should be satisfied so that the sequence of round output differences forms a Markov chain in the case of related keys. If the Markov cipher has $\mathcal{K} - f$ round function and the round key differences are independent variables with identical probability distribution, then the sequence forms a homogenous Markov chain. Assuming that the hypothesis of stochastic equivalence for related keys holds and steady-state probability distribution exists, then the steady-state probability distribution is the uniform distribution and the cipher is secure against related-key differential cryptanalysis after sufficiently many rounds.

References

[1] Advanced Encryption Standard (AES), FIPS Publication 197, November 26, 2001, available at http://csrc.nist.gov/encryption/aes. 208, 211
[2] E.Biham and A.Shamir, *"Differential cryptanalysis of DES-like cryptosystems,"* Journal of Cryptology, 4(1):3-72, 1991. 209
[3] E. Biham and A. Shamir, *"Differential Cryptanalysis of Snefru, Khafre, REDOC II, LOKI, and Lucifer,"* Advances in Cryptology, CRYPTO '91 Proceedings, Springer- Verlag, 1992, pp. 156-171. 209
[4] E. Biham, *"New Types of Cryptanalytic Attacks Using Related Keys,"* Journal of Cryptology, v. 7, n. 4, 1994, pp. 229-246. 209
[5] E. Biham, A. Biryukov, N. Ferguson, L. Knudsen, B. Schneier, A. Shamir, *"Cryptanalysis of MAGENTA"*, http:// csrc.nist.gov/ encryption/ aes/ round1/ conf2/ aes2conf.htm 217
[6] E.Biham and N.Keller, *"Cryptanalysis of Reduced Variants of Rijndael,"* http:// csrc.nist.gov/ encryption/ aes/ round2/ conf3/ aes3papers.html 213
[7] J. Cheon, M. Kim, K. Kim, J. Lee, and S. Kang, *"Improved Impossible Differential Cryptanalysis of Rijndael and Crypton,"* Information Security and Cryptology - ICISC 2001 4th International Conference Seoul, Korea, December 6-7, 2001, Proceedings, LNCS 2288,p. 39 ff. 213
[8] http:// csrc.nist.gov/ CryptoToolkit/ aes/ round2/ r2report.pdf 209
[9] J.Daemen and V.Rijmen, *"AES Proposal: Rijndael,"* http:// csrc.nist.gov/ encryption/ aes. 208, 209, 211
[10] J.Daemen, *"Cipher and hash function design strategies based on linear and differential cryptanalysis,"* Doctoral Dissertation, March 1995, K. U.Leuven. 209, 211
[11] N. Ferguson, J. Kelsey, B. Schneier, M. Stay, D. Wagner, D. Whiting, *"Improved Cryptanalysis of Rijndael"*, 7th International Workshop, FSE 2000, New York, NY, USA, April 2000, Proceedings, LNCS 1978, p. 213 ff. 209, 216
[12] M. J.Jacobson,Jr and K.Huber, *"The MAGENTA Block Cipher Algorithm,"* AES candidate, http:// csrc.nist.gov/ encryption/ aes. 217
[13] J.Kelsey, B.Schneier and D.Wagner, *"Key-schedule cryptanalysis of IDEA, GDES, GOST, SAFER, and Triple-DES,"* Advances in Cryptology, Proceedings Crypto'96, LNCS 1109, pp.237-252. 209
[14] L. R. Knudsen, *"Truncated and Higher Order Differentials,"* Fast Software Encryption, 2nd International Workshop Proceedings, Springer-Verlag, 1995, pp. 196-211. 209, 212
[15] X. Lai, *"Higher Order Derivations and Differential Cryptanalysis,"* Communications and Cryptography: Two Sides of One Tapestry, Kluwer Academic Publishers, 1994, pp. 227-233. 209
[16] X. Lai, J. Massey, and S. Murphy, *"Markov Ciphers and Differential Cryptanalysis,"* Advances in Cryptology, CRYPTO '91 Proceedings, Springer-Verlag, 1991, pp. 17-38. 209, 216
[17] Jean-Jacques Quisquater and David Samyde, *"Eddy current for Magnetic Analysis with Active Sensor"*, Proceedings of Esmart 2002 3rd edition, Nice, France, September 2002. 209

A Distinguishing Attack of SNOW 2.0 with Linear Masking Method

Dai Watanabe[1], Alex Biryukov[2], and Christophe De Cannière[2]

[1] Systems Development Laboratory, Hitachi, Ltd.,
292 Yoshida-cho, Totsuka-ku, Yokohama, 244-0817, Japan
daidai@sdl.hitachi.co.jp

[2] Katholieke Universiteit Leuven, Dept. Electrical Engineering-ESAT,
Kasteelpark Arenberg 10, B-3001 Heverlee, Belgium
{Alex.Biryukov,Christophe.DeCanniere}@esat.kuleuven.ac.be

Abstract. SNOW 2.0 was developed by Johansson and Ekdahl in 2002, as a modified version of SNOW 1.0. In this paper we present the application of linear (masking) attack to SNOW 2.0 stream cipher. Our attack requires 2^{225} output words (2^{230} bits) and 2^{225} steps of analysis to distinguish the output of SNOW 2.0 from a truly random bit sequence.

Keywords: Stream cipher, SNOW, Linear cryptanalysis

1 Introduction

A keystream generator (KSG) is a cryptographic primitive used for data encryption and random number generation. Many KSGs have been proposed so far. Most of them adopted bit-wise operations and used linear feedback shift registers (LFSRs). These KSGs are hardware oriented designs so that the cost (required gate size for the implementations) is quite small compared to most of block ciphers these days. In addition, the security evaluation for this class of KSGs is a well-studied problem. The output of the LFSRs has good statistical properties, e.g., long period, unbiased bit frequency, and so on. Only the weakness of the output of the LFSRs is the linear property derived from the update function and a lot of works relevant to the weakness have been presented [Ru86].

On the other hand, progress in the chip manufacturing technology relaxes the limitation of the gate count. In addition, the increase of cryptographic applications in software motivates recent KSG designs, for example SEAL [RC94] [RC98], Panama [DC98], SOBER [Ro98], MUGI [WFYP02], SNOW [EJ00] [EJ02b], Scream [CHJ02a], etc. The size of their internal state increases, and they adopt block-wise (e.g. 8-bit or 32-bit) operations for running fast on today's 8-bit- or 32-bit-processors. Some of them still adopt LFSRs as a primitive of their algorithms because of the well studied properties of the LFSRs.

SNOW family is a typical example of this class of KSGs. SNOW 1.0 is an LFSR-based stream cipher proposed by Johansson and Ekdahl [EJ00] and the

M. Matsui and R. Zuccherato (Eds.): SAC 2003, LNCS 3006, pp. 222–233, 2004.

key length is 128 or 256 bits. The significant property is the feedback polynomial defined over GF(2^{32}) and it enables SNOW 1.0 to run fast especially on 32-bit processors. SNOW was submitted to NESSIE (New European Schemes for Signatures, Integrity, and Encryption) project in 2000.

NESSIE project requires that a stream cipher provides *full security*, i.e., no security flaw can be found with calculation complexity less than exhaustive key search. We follow the style because the key length is often identified by the security of a cipher in real use, if no security bound is clearly defined.

SNOW 1.0 is designed to be secure as a 256-bit key cipher, but two different attacks have been presented. One is Guess-and-Determine attack by Hawkes and Rose [HR02]. This is a key recovery attack and the complexity of the attack is $O(2^{224})$. Another attack is a distinguishing attack by Coppersmith *et al.* [CHJ02b]. The complexity of this attack is about 2^{100}. The basic idea of this attack, developed by Golić [Go96], applies the technique of linear cryptanalysis on block ciphers [Ma94] for distinguishing the outputs of a KSG from a truly random bit sequence. This attack has been applied to RC4 [Go97], SOBER-t16 and t32 [EJ02a] so far. The attack of Coppersmith is the variant and is especially efficient for the cipher that consists of LFSRs with memory.

SNOW 2.0 is an improved version of SNOW 1.0 aimed to be secure against these attacks and remain to be efficient both in software and hardware implementations. However, no security evaluation against these attacks have been presented in the past proposal papers. In this paper we develop the distinguishing attack on SNOW 2.0 by linear masking method. This attack uses 2^{230} bits of the stream and 2^{225} steps of analysis, which is faster than exhaustive search for the 256-bit key. This result shows that though SNOW 2.0 has improved security against linear masking compared to SNOW 1.0 it is still vulnerable to this attack.

The rest of this paper is organized as follows. Firstly we briefly describe the algorithm of SNOW 1.0 in Sect. 2. Then we introduce linear masking method and show its application to SNOW 1.0 in Sect. 3. We describe the algorithm of SNOW 2.0 in Sect. 4 and show how to apply linear masking method to SNOW 2.0 in Sect. 5. At last we summarize the result in Sect. 6.

2 The Algorithm of SNOW 1.0

In this section, we present a brief description of the algorithm of SNOW 1.0. We ignore the key setup process because our attack is independent of this process.

SNOW 1.0 is a stream cipher which has a 128- or a 256-bit secret key and a 128-bit initial vector as inputs. It is based on LFSR over GF(2^{32}) and the feedback polynomial is given by

$$p(x) = x^{16} + x^{13} + x^7 + \alpha^{-1}, \tag{1}$$

where α is a root of the polynomial $y^{32} + y^{29} + y^{20} + y^{15} + y^{10} + y + 1 \in \mathrm{GF}(2)[y]$.

The state of LFSR is denoted by $(s_{t+16}, s_{t+15}, \ldots, s_{t+1})$. Each 32-bit word s_{t+i} is an element of GF(2^{32}).

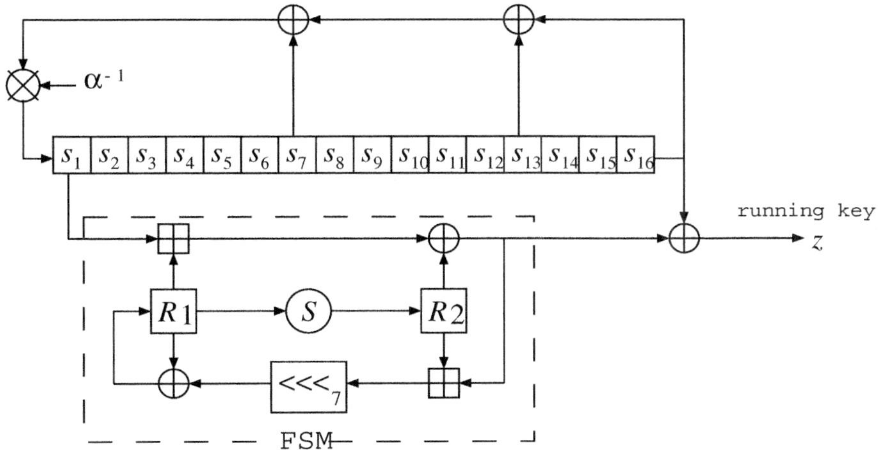

Fig. 1. The structure of SNOW 1.0

The Finite State Machine (FSM) is an additional internal state consisting of two 32-bit registers $R1$ and $R2$. The subscript t is used to specify the time, e.g. $R1_t$, $R2_t$. The output of the FSM F_t is given by

$$F_t = (s_{t+1} \quad R1_t) \oplus R2_t, \quad t \geq 0,$$

where is the addition modulo 2^{32} and $\oplus$ is the XORing operation. The keystream z_t is given by

$$z_t = F_t \oplus s_{t+16}, \quad t \geq 1.$$

Two registers $R1$ and $R2$ are updated as follows:

$$R1_{t+1} = (F_t \quad R2_t) \qquad 7) \oplus R1_t,$$
$$R2_{t+1} = S(R1_t).$$

The 32-bit non-linear transformation S consists of four identical 8-to-8 bit S-boxes and a permutation of the resulting bits. See [EJ00] for more detail.

3 Linear Masking Method

Distinguishing attack is a generic approach which allows to distinguish the output of the target KSG from a truly random sequence of the same length. The distinguishing method (or algorithm) is called a *distinguisher* . In this section, we explain the basic idea of linear masking method, which is a distinguishing attack proposed by Coppersmith *et al.* and show the application to SNOW 1.0.

3.1 General Description

Linear masking method [CHJ02b] is a general attack against a large class of KSGs. The basic idea of the attack is the same as linear cryptanalysis against block ciphers proposed by Matsui [Ma94].

The first step of linear cryptanalysis is to select several bit of inputs, outputs, and a fixed secret key. The sum of the selected bits is called a linear approximation. Then the attacker calculates the bias of selected bits through amount of known plaintexts. The target encryption function can be distinguished from a random permutation with this distinguisher if the bias is sufficiently large. Furthermore, the attacker can conjects the sum of key bits from the bias by maximum likelihood method. The main interest in the study of linear cryptanalysis is how to find the best approximation, which is the linear approximation with largest bias. Matsui shows how to construct the linear approximation in general by the iterative structure of block ciphers. His construction firstly searches for the best approximation of the round function of the target block cipher, and combines them to remove the terms of intermediate bits.

Linear masking method pays attention to the bias of the linear approximation consisting of only output bits and distinguishes the output of the target KSG from a truly random bit sequence. This attack is applicable if the internal state of the target KSG can be divided into the linear (or low-diffusion) part and non-linear part. The basic procedure of linear masking method is as follows:

Step 1. Divide the algorithm of a keystream generator into two parts; the linear part and the non-linear part. Let us denote the linear relation of the linear part by

$$\varphi(s,t) = \bigoplus_j c_j s_{t+j} = 0, \quad c_j \in \mathrm{GF}(2), \tag{2}$$

where $\{s_{t+j}\}_j$ is the internal state of the linear part.

Step 2. Find the best approximation of the non-linear part:

$$\bigoplus_i \Gamma_i s_{t+i} = \bigoplus_k \Gamma'_k z_{t+k}, \tag{3}$$

where $\{z_{t+k}\}_k$ is the output blocks. 32-bit values $\{\Gamma_i\}_i$ and $\{\Gamma'_k\}_k$ are called masks and $\Gamma_i s_{t+i}$ is the inner product of Γ_i and s_{t+i} over GF(2). Denote the probability that this equation holds by p, and define the bias ϵ_p by $p = 1/2 + \epsilon_p$. Let us denote the left hand of the equation by $f(s,t)$ and the right hand by $g(z,t)$ respectively. If the equation holds with the bias ϵ, about ϵ^2 rounds outputs is needed to distinguish the outputs from a truly random bit sequence.

Step 3. Construct the linear approximation consisting of only outputs by combining above two equations 2 and 3, and calculate the bias via *piling up lemma* [Ma94]:

$$0 = \bigoplus_i \Gamma_i \varphi(s, t+i) = \bigoplus_j c_j f(s, t+j) = \bigoplus_j c_j g(z, t+j). \tag{4}$$

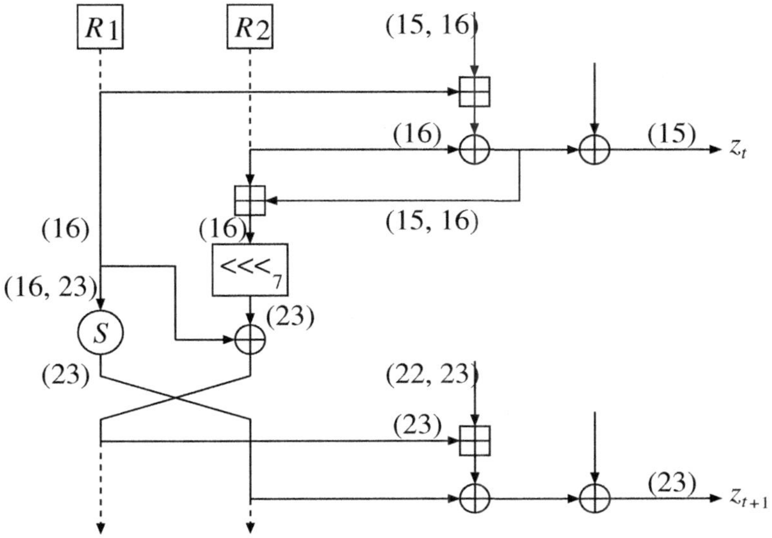

Fig. 2. The linear approximation of SNOW 1.0

3.2 Application to SNOW 1.0

The expression over GF(2) of the feedback polynomial yields a linear relation. But it has many coefficients so that linear masking method is not efficient. In [CHJ02b] Coppersmith *et al.* pointed out that the feedback polynomial has only one coefficient α which does not belong to GF(2). They used Frobenius map to eliminate α and constructed a linear relation over GF(2) with 6 terms. I.e., the polynomial

$$p(x)^{2^{32}} + p(x) = x^{16\times 2^{32}} + x^{13\times 2^{32}} + x^{7\times 2^{32}} + x^{16} + x^{13} + x^{7} \quad (5)$$

gives the linear relation. On the other hand, the linear approximation of non-linear part is given by the following 2-rounds approximation of FSM (See Fig. 2):

$$(s_{t+1})_{15,16} \oplus (s_{t+16})_{15} \oplus (s_{t+15})_{23} \oplus (s_{t+17})_{22,23} = (F_t)_{15} \oplus (F_{t+1})_{23}. \quad (6)$$

They declared that the bias of the approximation is at least $2^{-9.3}$. Hence, the linear approximation derived from Eq. 5, 6 is $2^5 \cdot 2^{-9.3\times 6} = 2^{-50.8}$ and $2^{101.6}$ rounds outputs is needed to distinguish the output of SNOW 1.0 from a truly random bit sequence.

4 The Algorithm of SNOW 2.0

In this section, we present a brief description of the algorithm of SNOW 2.0 except for the key setup process.

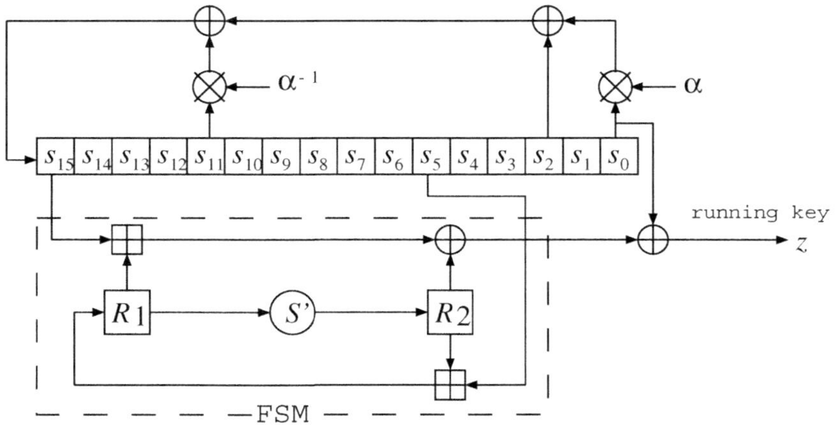

Fig. 3. The structure of SNOW 2.0

SNOW 2.0 is a stream cipher which has a 128- or a 256-bit secret key and a 128-bit initial vector. It is based on LFSR over GF(2^{32}) and the feedback polynomial is given by

$$\pi(x) = \alpha x^{16} + x^{14} + \alpha^{-1}x^5 + 1, \tag{7}$$

where α is a root of the polynomial $y^4 + \beta^{23}y^3 + \beta^{245}y^2 + \beta^{48}y + \beta^{239} \in \mathrm{GF}(2^8)[y]$, and β is a root of $z^8 + z^7 + z^5 + z^3 + 1 \in \mathrm{GF}(2)[z]$.

The state of LFSR is denoted by $(s_{t+15}, s_{t+14}, \ldots, s_t)$. Each s_{t+i} is an element of GF(2^{32}). Note that the sequence is opposite to that of SNOW 1.0 and the index starts at zero.

The Finite State Machine (FSM) has two 32-bit registers, $R1$ and $R2$. The output of the FSM F_t is given by

$$F_t = (s_{t+15} \quad R1_t) \oplus R2_t, \quad t \geq 0,$$

and the keystream z_t is given by

$$z_t = F_t \oplus s_t, \quad t \geq 1.$$

Two registers $R1$ and $R2$ are updated as follows:

$$R1_{t+1} = s_{t+5} \quad R2_t,$$
$$R2_{t+2} = S'(R1_t).$$

S' is the one column of AES, i.e. the combination of S-box layer (substitution byte) and the linear diffusion layer (mix column). The S-box and the matrix for the linear diffusion are denoted by S_R and M respectively.

5 The Attack on SNOW 2.0

5.1 The Basic Idea

The difficulty in applying linear masking method to SNOW family is caused by the multiplications over $GF(2^{32})$ in the LFSRs. Considering that the feedback polynomial is defined over GF(2) make it easy to apply linear masking method, however the number of terms of the polynomial becomes large. Hence the bias of whole linear approximation becomes small even though the bias of Eq. 3 is large so that the attack is no longer effective.

In the case of SNOW 1.0, Coppersmith *et. al.* noticed that only one coefficient of the feedback polynomial is not equal to 1 and use Frobenius map to remove this coefficient to construct another linear relation without the multiplication with the element of $GF(2^{32})$. On the other hand, the feedback polynomial of SNOW 2.0 has two different coefficients which belong to $GF(2^{32})$. This improvement of the feedback polynomial makes it difficult to apply the technique to SNOW 2.0 which is used against SNOW 1.0.

In the following, we examine to apply the feedback polynomial itself as the linear equation φ to combine the plural approximations of FSM. Assume that the linear approximation of FSM is given by

$$\bigoplus_i \Gamma_i s_{t+i} \oplus \bigoplus_j \Gamma'_j z_{t+j} = 0. \tag{8}$$

On the other hand, the internal state of LFSR s at time t satisfies the following linear relation for any mask Γ:

$$\Gamma(s_{t+16} \oplus \alpha^{-1} \cdot s_{t+11} \oplus s_{t+2} \oplus \alpha \cdot s_t) = 0. \tag{9}$$

Multiplying the element of the finite field is a linear transformation over GF(2), so that this equation can be re-written as follows:

$$\Gamma s_{t+16} \oplus (\Gamma \cdot \alpha^{-1}) s_{t+11} \oplus \Gamma s_{t+2} \oplus (\Gamma \cdot \alpha) s_t = 0, \tag{10}$$

where the multiplications $\Gamma \cdot \alpha$ and $\Gamma \cdot \alpha^{-1}$ are the composition of two linear transformation over GF(2).

Hence if Eq. 8 holds for the mask sets $\{\Gamma_i\}_i$, $\{\Gamma_i \cdot \alpha\}_i$, and $\{\Gamma_i \cdot \alpha^{-1}\}_i$ with a large bias, the attacker can construct the linear approximation consisting of only output bits with large bias from these linear approximations of FSM and the linear relation Eq. 10.

5.2 The Linear Approximation of FSM

Figure 4 shows the 2-rounds approximation of FSM:

$$\Gamma_0 s_t \oplus \Gamma_1 s_{t+1} \oplus \Gamma_5 s_{t+5} \oplus \Gamma_{15} s_{t+15} \oplus \Gamma_{16} s_{t+16} = \Gamma_0 z_t \oplus \Gamma_1 z_{t+1}. \tag{11}$$

In this subsection, we calculate the bias of Eq. 11.

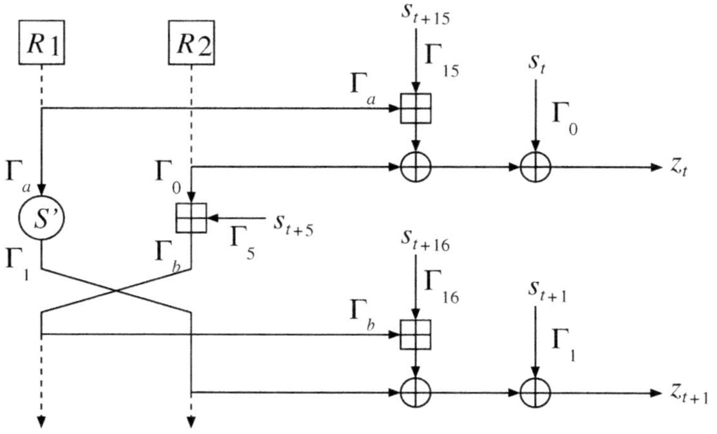

Fig. 4. The linear approximation of FSM

There are two non-linear operations in the linear approximation of FSM (11): one is the 32-bit permutation S' and the other is the additions modulo 2^{32} used three times. To simplify the search for the mask sets, we assume that the values of the masks do not change at three addition operands, i.e. we assume that the approximation $\Gamma x \oplus \Gamma y = \Gamma(x \quad y)$ has a large bias. In fact, this assumption holds in many cases.

Under the assumption, all masks Γ_i in the linear approximation (11) must have the same value. In the following, we ignore the subscripts and denote these masks as Γ. The linear approximation consisting of only outputs can be constructed from two equations Eq. 10 and 11:

$$\begin{aligned} 0 &= \Gamma(s_{t+16} \oplus \alpha^{-1} \cdot s_{t+11} \oplus s_{t+2} \oplus \alpha \cdot s_t) \\ &\oplus \Gamma(s_{t+17} \oplus \alpha^{-1} \cdot s_{t+12} \oplus s_{t+3} \oplus \alpha \cdot s_{t+1}) \\ &\oplus \Gamma(s_{t+21} \oplus \alpha^{-1} \cdot s_{t+16} \oplus s_{t+7} \oplus \alpha \cdot s_{t+5}) \\ &\oplus \Gamma(s_{t+31} \oplus \alpha^{-1} \cdot s_{t+26} \oplus s_{t+17} \oplus \alpha \cdot s_{t+15}) \\ &\oplus \Gamma(s_{t+32} \oplus \alpha^{-1} \cdot s_{t+27} \oplus s_{t+18} \oplus \alpha \cdot s_{t+16}) \\ &= \Gamma(z_{t+2} \oplus z_{t+3} \oplus z_{t+16} \oplus z_{t+17}) \\ &\oplus (\Gamma\alpha^{-1})(z_{t+11} \oplus z_{t+12}) \oplus (\Gamma\alpha)(z_t \oplus z_{t+1}). \end{aligned} \tag{12}$$

The search for the linear approximation of FSM is reduced to search the following two approximations:

$$\Gamma S'(x) \oplus \Gamma x = 0, \tag{13}$$

$$\Gamma x \oplus \Gamma y = \Gamma(x \quad y). \tag{14}$$

Let us denote the biases of Eq. 13 and 14 as $\epsilon_{S'}(\Gamma)$ and $\epsilon_{+}(\Gamma)$, and the bias of Eq. 11 as ϵ_{FSM} respectively. Then the bias of FSM corresponding to the mask

Γ is calculated with piling up lemma:

$$\epsilon(\Gamma) = 2 \cdot \epsilon_{S'}(\Gamma) \cdot 2^{3-1} \cdot \epsilon_{+}(\Gamma)^3. \tag{15}$$

Now we describe how to search the 3-tuples of mask values $(\Gamma, \Gamma \cdot \alpha, \Gamma \cdot \alpha^{-1})$ which satisfies Eq. 13 and 14 with large bias. The procedure of the search for mask values is as follows:

Step 1. Make a list of mask values Γ which satisfies Eq. 13 by using the linear profile of 8-bit permutation S_R and the matrix M, where linear profile means the table of the biases of S_R corresponding to all input and output masks.
Step 2. For each mask value Γ acquired in Step 1, check if Eq. 13 holds for $\Gamma \cdot \alpha$ and $\Gamma \cdot \alpha^{-1}$ with large biases. We discard the candidate if one of biases associated with the 3-tuple of masks is smaller than 2^{-20}.
Step 3. Calculate the biases of Eq. 14 for the 3-tuples of masks acquired in Step 2.

Executing this procedure for all 32-bit mask values is impractical even after the restriction of the mask values. Especially evaluating the biases of Eq. 14 for all masks in detail by experiment requires much computational power. As a matter of fact, we examined 2^{12} random inputs for x and y in Step 3, but the error was too large to rely on the result.

Hence we restrict the domain of mask values of Eq. 14 in addition. Generally the bias of Eq. 14 tends to depend on the hamming weight of the mask value Γ, and tends to become large when the hamming weight is small.

Let the byte representation of the mask be denoted by $\Gamma = (\gamma_3, \gamma_2, \gamma_1, \gamma_0)$. We fixed the hamming weight of each γ_i no more than two. The following lemma 1 and piling up lemma helps calculating the bias of 14.

Lemma 1 Let us denote the probability of the incidence of carry at n-th bit from the least significant bit (LSB) as p_n.

1. If the hamming weight of Γ is one (i.e. $\Gamma = 0\cdots010\cdots0$) and the n-th bit from the LSB is 1, then the bias $\epsilon_{+}(\Gamma)$ is equal to $p_n - 1/2$:

$$\epsilon_{+}(\Gamma) = p_n - 1/2 = 2^{-n} - 2^{-n-1}.$$

2. If the mask value is $\Gamma = 0\cdots0110\cdots0$, $\epsilon_{+}(\Gamma) = 1/4$.
3. If the mask value is $\Gamma = 0\cdots01010\cdots0$, $\epsilon_{+}(\Gamma) = 1/8$.
4. If the mask value is $\Gamma = 0\cdots011110\cdots0$, $\epsilon_{+}(\Gamma) = 1/8$.

5.3 The Result

Table 1 shows the best 3-tuples of approximation of FSM in our search.

The bias ϵ of the whole linear approximation Eq. 12 is estimated as follows:

$$\epsilon = 2^{4-1} \cdot \epsilon_{\mathrm{FSM}}(\Gamma)^2 \cdot \epsilon_{\mathrm{FSM}}(\Gamma \cdot \alpha) \cdot \epsilon_{\mathrm{FSM}}(\Gamma \cdot \alpha^{-1}) = 2^{-112.25}.$$

As a result, about 2^{225} outputs (2^{230} bits) are required to distinguish the output of SNOW 2.0 from a truly random bit sequence.

Table 1. 3-tuple of masks of FSM and their biases

	Mask value	$\epsilon_{S'}(\cdot)$	$\epsilon_{+}(\cdot)$	$\epsilon_{\mathrm{FSM}}(\cdot)$
Γ	0x0303600c	$2^{-15.61}$	$2^{-5.00}$	$2^{-27.61}$
$\Gamma \cdot \alpha$	0x0c030360	$2^{-15.61}$	$2^{-5.00}$	$2^{-27.61}$
$\Gamma \cdot \alpha^{-1}$	0x03600c63	$2^{-17.42}$	$2^{-6.00}$	$2^{-32.42}$

5.4 The Discussion

Our evaluation confirmed that SNOW 2.0 is well improved. Especially inducing an MDS matrix in the 32-bit non-linear permutation S' reinforces the resistance property against linear masking attack. In fact, the original attack against SNOW 1.0 approximates the only one S-box to construct the best approximation of FSM. Contrary, four S-boxes become active in all approximation we found. This property is also important to the bias of Eq. 14 because the hamming weight of masks increases in general. As a result, the bias of the best approximation of FSM becomes quite small, from about 2^{-8} to 2^{-30}.

On the other hand, the main reason this attack is applicable is caused by multiplying the primitive elements when we consider them as just a linear transformation over GF(2). This weakens the security of SNOW 2.0 against linear masking method. The choice of α or α^{-1} as the multiplier is effective in software implementation, but it weakens its security against linear masking attack. In fact, the mask Γ is transformed by multiplying α and α^{-1} as follows:

$$(\gamma_3, \gamma_2, \gamma_1, \gamma_0)\alpha = (\gamma', \gamma_3, \gamma_2, \gamma_1), \tag{16}$$
$$(\gamma_3, \gamma_2, \gamma_1, \gamma_0)\alpha^{-1} = (\gamma_2, \gamma_1, \gamma_0, \gamma''). \tag{17}$$

Exactly one byte value is changed in each transformation.

Furthermore the bias associated with the mask $\Gamma = (0, 0, 0, \gamma'')$ is independent of the higher bits so that the bias associated with γ'' tends to be large even though the value is changeable and this bias is easy to calculate. Therefore if the bias $\epsilon_{+}(\Gamma)$ is large, the other two biases $\epsilon_{+}(\Gamma \cdot \alpha)$, $\epsilon_{+}(\Gamma \cdot \alpha^{-1})$ tend to be large, too.

6 Conclusion

In this paper we present the application of the linear (masking) attack proposed in [CHJ02b] to SNOW 2.0. The modified version seems to develop resistance to the original attack, though the most primitive technique is still applicable.

Our attack requires 2^{225} rounds outputs (2^{230} bits) and 2^{225} steps of analysis to distinguish the output of SNOW 2.0 from a truly random bit sequence. This concludes that SNOW 2.0 generates sufficiently random sequences as a 128-bit key stream cipher, but is slightly weak as a 256-bit key stream cipher. The fast correlation decoding technique could be applicable to extract a key by using this bias. We leave this problem for further research.

Acknowledgement

We would like to thank Patrik Ekdahl. He pointed out that our experimental result in Table 1 was incorrect, and helped us to correct the values of the mask set and the corresponding biases.

References

[CHJ02a] D. Coppersmith, S. Halevi, and C. Jutla, "Scream: a software-efficient stream cipher," *Fast Software Encryption, FSE 2002*, LNCS 2365, pp. 195–209, 2002. 222

[CHJ02b] D. Coppersmith, S. Halevi, and C. Jutla, "Cryptanalysis of stream ciphers with linear masking," *Advances in Cryptology, CRYPTO 2002*, Springer-Verlag, LNCS 2442, pp. 515–532, 2002. 223, 225, 226, 231

[DC98] J. Daemen, C. Clapp, "Fast Hashing and Stream Encryption with PANAMA," *Fast Software Encryption, FSE'98*, Springer-Verlag, LNCS 1372, pp. 60–74, 1998. 222

[DR99] J. Daemen, V. Rijmen, "AES Proposal: Rijndael," AES algorithm submission, September 3, 1999, available at http://www.nist.gov/aes/.

[EJ00] P. Ekdahl and T. Johansson, "SNOW – a new stream cipher, " *NESSIE project submission*, 2000, available at http://www.cryptonessie.org. 222, 224

[EJ02a] P. Ekdahl and T. Johansson, "Distinguishing attacks on SOBER-t16 and t32, " *Fast Software Encryption, FSE 2002*, Springer-Verlag, LNCS 2365, pp. 210–224, 2002. 223

[EJ02b] P. Ekdahl and T. Johansson, "A new version of the stream cipher SNOW, " *Selected Areas in Cryptology, SAC 2002*, Springer-Verlag, LNCS 2595, pp. 47–61, 2002. 222

[Go96] J. Golić, "Linear models for keystream generator," *IEEE Trans. Computers*, vol. C-45, pp. 41–49, 1996. 223

[Go97] J. Golić, "Linear statistical weakness of alleged RC4 keystream generator," *Advances in Cryptology, Eurocrypt'97*, Springer-Verlag, LNCS 1233, pp. 226–238. 223

[HR02] P. Hawkes and G. Rose, "Guess-and-Determine Attacks on SNOW," *Selected Area of Cryptology, SAC 2002*, Springer-Verlag, LNCS 2595, pp. 37–46, 2002. 223

[Ma94] M. Matsui, "Linear cryptanalysis method for DES cipher," *Advances in Cryptology, Proceedings Eurocrypt'93*, Springer-Verlag, LNCS 765, pp. 159–169, 1994. 223, 225

[RC94] P. Rogaway, D. Coppersmith, "A Software-Optimized Encryption Algorithm," *Fast Software Encryption, FSE'94*, Springer-Verlag, LNCS 809, pp. 56–63, 1994. 222

[RC98] P. Rogaway, D. Coppersmith, "A Software-Optimized Encryption Algorithm," *Journal of Cryptography*, Vol. 11, No. 4, pp. 273–287, 1998. 222

[Ro98] G. Rose, "A Stream Cipher based on Linear Feedback over $GF(2^8)$," "Proc. Australian Conference on Information Security and Privacy," Springer-Verlag, 1998. 222

[Ru86] R. Rueppel, *Analysis and Design of Stream Ciphers*, Springer-Verlag, 1986. 222

[WFYP02] D. Watanabe, S. Furuya, H. Yoshida, and B. Preneel, "A new keystream generator MUGI," *Fast Software Encryption, FSE 2002*, Springer-Verlag, LNCS 2365, pp. 179–194, 2002. 222

On the Use of GF-Inversion as a Cryptographic Primitive

Kazumaro Aoki[1] and Serge Vaudenay[2]*

[1] NTT Laboratories
maro@isl.ntt.co.jp
[2] Swiss Federal Institute of Technology (EPFL)
Serge.Vaudenay@epfl.ch

Abstract. Inversion in Galois Fields is a famous primitive permutation for designing cryptographic algorithms e.g. for Rijndael because it has suitable differential and linear properties. Inputs and outputs are usually transformed by addition (e.g. XOR) to key bits. We call this construction the APA (Add-Permute-Add) scheme. In this paper we study its pseudorandomness in terms of k-wise independence.
We show that the pairwise independence of the APA construction is related to the impossible differentials properties. We notice that inversion has many impossible differentials, so $x \mapsto \frac{1}{x+a} + b$ is not pairwise independent.
In 1998, Vaudenay proposed the random harmonic permutation $h : x \mapsto \frac{a}{x-b} + c$. Although it is not perfectly 3-wise independent (despite what was originally claimed), we demonstrate in this paper that it is *almost* 3-wise independent. In particular we show that any distinguisher limited to three queries between this permutation and a perfect one has an advantage limited to $\frac{3}{q}$ where q is the field order. This holds even if the distinguisher has access to h^{-1}.
Finally, we investigate 4-wise independence and we suggest the cross-ratio as a new tool for cryptanalysis of designs involving inversion.

Inversion in Galois fields is quite a popular primitive permutation for making block ciphers. This comes from nice properties with respect to differential and linear cryptanalysis (see Nyberg [10]). It has been used e.g. in Rijndael [5]. Inversion is also known to have bad algebraic properties which can lead to interpolation attacks (see Jakobsen-Knudsen [7]) or quadratic equations (see Murphy-Robshaw [9] and Courtois-Pieprzyk [4]). In this paper we study randomness in terms of k-wise independence of constructions with inversion.

Since Carter and Wegman introduced the notion of universal hash function, a wide spectrum of extensions, including ε-almost k-wise independent functions, and constructions have been proposed. In cryptography, pairwise independent hash functions ($k = 2$) can be used in order to construct secure message authentication codes. (See Wegman-Carter [19].)

* This work started while this author was visiting NTT Labs.

M. Matsui and R. Zuccherato (Eds.): SAC 2003, LNCS 3006, pp. 234–247, 2004.

The k-wise independent *permutations* are also well suited properties of encryption functions. The perfect $k = 1$ case corresponds to the perfect secrecy in a Shannon sense [14]. This is however limited to one-time usage. More generally, perfect k-wise independence is linked to randomness when limited to k-time usage. The result is even quantitative in non perfect cases: for an ε-almost k-wise independent permutation, the best distinguisher between the permutation and an ideal one which is limited to k oracle calls has an advantage of $\frac{\varepsilon}{2}$. (When adopting an appropriate metrics, see Vaudenay [17, 18].) Furthermore, almost pairwise independence ($k = 2$) has application to block ciphers since there is an upper bound of the best differential and linear characteristics in terms of pairwise independence. (See Vaudenay [16, 18].) The 3-wise independent permutations recently found an application for strengthening short encryption keys (See Russel-Wang [13].)

Constructing k-wise independent functions over any finite field $\mathbf{K}$ is quite easy. Actually, a random polynomial of degree at most $k - 1$ is perfectly k-wise independent. However constructing k-wise independent *permutations* is not so easy but for the $k = 1$ and $k = 2$ cases. For $k = 1$, one notices that $h(x) = x + a$ with $a \in_U \mathbf{K}$ is perfectly 1-wise independent. For $k = 2$, the $h(x) = ax + b$ function with $(a, b) \in_U \mathbf{K}^* \times \mathbf{K}$ is perfectly 2-wise independent. In Rees [11] a nice perfect 3-wise independent permutation construction was proposed in $P_2(\mathbf{K})$ using $\mathrm{PGL}_2(\mathbf{K})$. This means that we can define the permutation family for a projective plane over $\mathbf{K}$ which is a set of cardinality $\#\mathbf{K} + 1$. This can never be equal to 2^{4n} since $15 = 2^4 - 1$ divides $2^{4n} - 1$ and is not a prime power. So this cannot help us in order to construct a 3-wise independent permutation over, for instance, a set of byte strings. In this paper we study the following construction over any finite field $\mathbf{K}$.

$$h(x) = a.\mathrm{inv}(x - b) + c$$

for $(a, b, c) \in_U \mathbf{K}^* \times \mathbf{K} \times \mathbf{K}$ where $\mathrm{inv}(t)$ is defined as being $1/t$ if $t \neq 0$ and 0 otherwise. We call it the *random harmonic permutation* construction. This construction was suggested in [16]. This paper claimed perfect 3-wise independence without proof. We show that this is not the case, but we still have almost independence. This provides a simple construction for almost 3-wise independent permutation over any finite field $\mathbf{K}$.

We also outline that the cross-ratio

$$R(t, u, v, w) = \left(\frac{t - u}{t - w}\right) / \left(\frac{v - u}{v - w}\right)$$

(for pairwise different t, u, v, w) is quite interesting from a cryptanalytic viewpoint since it is invariant under translation, multiplication, and inversion. We can distinguish the random harmonic permutation from an ideal one with only four queries t, u, v, w, so it is not 4-wise independent. We discuss about potential applications related to Rijndael.

We also study the pairwise independence of $h(x) = \mathrm{inv}(x - a) + b$ which is a kind of Even-Mansour [6] extension of the inversion. We show that for any permutation S, the pairwise independence of $h(x) = S(x + a) + b$ is related to impossible differentials for S. More precisely, we define a new measurement IDP (as for *Impossible Dierential Probability*) by

$$\mathrm{IDP}^S = \max_{\delta \neq 0} \frac{1}{q} \#\{\Delta; \mathrm{DP}^S(\delta, \Delta) = 0\}$$

where q is the output range size and DP is the regular differential probability, i.e.

$$\mathrm{DP}^S(\delta, \Delta) = \frac{1}{q} \#\{x; S(x + \delta) = S(x) + \Delta\}.$$

We demonstrate that the best advantage for distinguishing h from a random permutation with two queries is close to IDP^S. We also show that this quantity is quite bad for the inversion since we have IDP $\approx \frac{1}{2}$ in this case. This is however not a specific weakness of the inversion in characteristic 2: it is indeed linked to the choice of the XOR as the addition.

1 Previous Work and Definitions

There is a wide menagerie of universal functions. We recall here a few definitions. First of all, here are definitions related to perfect functions.

Definition 1 (Carter-Wegman [3], Wegman-Carter [19]). *Let A and B be two* □*nite sets. Let $\mathcal{F}(A, B)$ denote the set of all functions from A to B. Let H be a subset of $\mathcal{F}(A, B)$.*

1. *H is universal $_2$ if*

$$\forall x, y \in A \quad (x \neq y) \quad \Pr_{h \in_U H}[h(x) = h(y)] \leq \frac{1}{\#B}.$$

2. *H is strongly universal $_k$, or (perfect) k-wise independent function, if*

$$\forall x_1, \ldots, x_k \in A, \ \forall y_1, \ldots, y_k \in B, \quad (x_i \neq x_j \text{ for } i \neq j),$$
$$\Pr_{h \in_U H}[h(x_1) = y_1, \ldots, h(x_k) = y_k] = \frac{1}{\#B^k}.$$

3. *for $A = B$ when all functions of H are permutations, we say that H is a (perfect) k-wise independent permutation if*

$$\forall x_1, \ldots, x_k \in A, \ \forall y_1, \ldots, y_k \in B, \quad (x_i \neq x_j, y_i \neq y_j \text{ for } i \neq j),$$
$$\Pr_{h \in_U H}[h(x_1) = y_1, \ldots, h(x_k) = y_k] = \prod_{i=0}^{k-1} \frac{1}{\#B - i}.$$

Here are definitions related to imperfect functions.

Definition 2 (Stinson [15]). *Let A and B be two* □*nite sets. Let $\mathcal{F}(A, B)$ denote the set of all functions from A to B. Let H be a subset of $\mathcal{F}(A, B)$.*

1. *H is ε-almost universal* $_2$ *if*

$$\forall x, y \in A \quad (x \neq y) \quad \Pr_{h \in_U H}[h(x) = h(y)] \leq \varepsilon.$$

2. *H is ε-almost strongly universal* $_2$ *if*

$$\forall x_1 \in A,\ \forall y_1 \in B, \quad \Pr_{h \in_U H}[h(x_1) = y_1] = \frac{1}{\#B}$$

$$\forall x_1, x_2 \in A,\ \forall y_1, y_2 \in B, \quad (x_1 \neq x_2), \quad \Pr_{h \in_U H}[h(x_1) = y_1, h(x_2) = y_2] \leq \frac{\varepsilon}{\#B}.$$

Almost k-wise independence is well known to be harder to define since it depends on the metric choice.

In order to measure k-wise independence for cryptography, we take the following general definition.

Definition 3 (Vaudenay [16, 18]). *Let A and B be two finite sets. Let $\mathcal{F}(A,B)$ denote the set of all functions from A to B. Let $\mathcal{S}(A)$ denote the set of all permutations over A. Let H be a subset of $\mathcal{F}(A,B)$. Let $\mathcal{M}_k(A,B)$ be the set of all functions from $A^k \times B^k$ to the field* **R** *of real numbers. Let d be a distance over $\mathcal{M}_k(A,B)$. Let $k > 0$ be an integer. We define $[H]^k \in \mathcal{M}_k(A,B)$ by*

$$[H]^k(x_1, \ldots, x_k, y_1, \ldots, y_k) = \Pr_{h \in_U H}[h(x_1) = y_1, \ldots, h(x_k) = y_k].$$

1. *We say that H is an ε-d-almost k-wise independent function if $d([H]^k, [H^*]^k) \leq \varepsilon$ where $H^* = \mathcal{F}(A,B)$.*
2. *For $A = B$ and when H is a subset of $\mathcal{S}(A)$, we say that H is an ε-d-almost k-wise independent permutation if $d([H]^k, [H^*]^k) \leq \varepsilon$ where $H^* = \mathcal{S}(A)$.*

Several distances are quite significant in cryptography, including metrics induced by the $|||.|||_\infty$, $||.||_a$ and $||.||_s$ norms as defined in [16, 17, 18]:

$$|||f|||_\infty = \max_{(x_1,\ldots,x_k) \in A^k} \sum_{(y_1,\ldots,y_k) \in B^k} |f(x_1, \ldots, x_k, y_1, \ldots, y_k)|$$

$$||f||_a = \max_{x_1 \in A} \sum_{y_1 \in B} \ldots \max_{x_k \in A} \sum_{y_k \in B} |f(x_1, \ldots, x_k, y_1, \ldots, y_k)|$$

for $f \in \mathcal{M}_k(A,B)$. Obviously, $|||f|||_\infty \leq ||f||_a$. The $||.||_s$ norm is defined by

$$||f||_s = \max_{b_1 \in \{0,1\}} \max_{z_1^0 \in A} \sum_{z_1^1 \in A} \cdots \max_{b_k \in \{0,1\}} \max_{z_k^0 \in A} \sum_{z_k^1 \in A} |f(z_1^{b_1}, \ldots, z_k^{b_k}, z_1^{1-b_1}, \ldots, z_k^{1-b_k})|$$

for $f \in \mathcal{M}_k(A,A)$. Obviously, $|||f|||_\infty \leq ||f||_a \leq ||f||_s$. Here are some important properties which motivate these choices for cryptography.

Theorem 1 (Vaudenay [16, 17, 18]). *Let A and B be two finite sets. Let $\mathcal{F}(A,B)$ denote the set of all functions from A to B. Let $\mathcal{S}(A)$ denote the set of all permutations over A. Let H and H′ be subsets of $\mathcal{F}(A,B)$.*

1. *The best distinguisher between* H *and* H' *limited to* k *queries has an advantage of* $\frac{1}{2}||[H]^k - [H']^k||_a$. *It is* $\frac{1}{2}|||[H]^k - [H']^k|||_\infty$ *when we restrict to non adaptive attacks.*
2. *For* $A = B$ *and* H *and* H' *subsets of* $\mathcal{S}(A)$, *the best distinguisher between* $h \in_U H$ *and* $h \in_U H'$ *limited to* k *queries with access to both* h *and* h^{-1} *has an advantage of* $\frac{1}{2}||[H]^k - [H']^k||_s$.
3. *When* $A = B = \{0,1\}^n$ *and* H *is an* ε-$|||.|||_\infty$*-almost pairwise independent permutation, dierential and linear probabilities are bounded as follows.*

$$\forall b \ \ \forall a \neq 0 \quad \mathop{E}_{h \in_U H}(\mathrm{DP}^h(a,b)) \leq \frac{1}{2^n - 1} + \varepsilon$$

$$\forall a \ \ \forall b \neq 0 \quad \mathop{E}_{h \in_U H}(\mathrm{LP}^h(a,b)) \leq \frac{1}{2^n - 1} + 4\varepsilon$$

where

$$\mathrm{DP}^h(a,b) = \Pr_{X \in_U A}[h(X \oplus a) = h(X) \oplus b]$$

$$\mathrm{LP}^h(a,b) = \left(2 \Pr_{X \in_U A}[a \cdot X = b \cdot h(X)] - 1\right)^2 .$$

Therefore k-wise independence has nice interpretations in terms of randomness when limited to k uses. k-wise independence for $k \geq 2$ leads to upper bounds for the best differential and linear probabilities.

Given a finite field $\mathbf{K} = \mathrm{GF}(q)$, we let inv be the permutation defined by $\mathrm{inv}(x) = \frac{1}{x}$ for $x \neq 0$ and $\mathrm{inv}(0) = 0$. Note that $\mathrm{inv}(x) = x^{q-2}$ for all $x \in \mathbf{K}$ when $q > 2$. This permutation is widely used in cryptography, e.g. in the design of the substitution boxes of Rijndael [1, 5]. It is known to have nice differential properties. In particular Nyberg [10] proved that

$$\begin{array}{l}\mathrm{DP}^{\mathrm{inv}}(a,b) \leq \frac{4}{q} \text{ for all } a \neq 0 \text{ and all } b \\ \mathrm{LP}^{\mathrm{inv}}(a,b) \leq \frac{4}{q} \text{ for all } b \neq 0 \text{ and all } a.\end{array}$$

2 The Random Harmonic Permutation Construction

2.1 Our Result

Theorem 2. *Let* $\mathbf{K}$ *be a* ◻*nite* ◻*eld of cardinality* q. *For any* $a, b, c \in \mathbf{K}$ *such that* $a \neq 0$ *we de*◻*ne* $h_{a,b,c}(x) = a.\mathrm{inv}(x - b) + c$. *Let* H *be the set of all* $h_{a,b,c}$.

1. H *is a perfect 2-wise independent permutation.*
2. H *is not a perfect 3-wise independent permutation for* $q > 3$.
3. H *is a* $\frac{6}{q}$-$||.||_s$*-almost 3-wise independent permutation.*
4. H *is not a* $(2 - \frac{13}{q})$-$|||.|||_\infty$*-almost 4-wise independent permutation for* $q > 4$.

The proof is achieved over the following subsections.

As a corollary H is also a $\frac{6}{q}$-$||.||_a$-almost 3-wise independent permutation and a $\frac{6}{q}$-$|||.|||_\infty$-almost 3-wise independent permutation as well.

This result means that any distinguisher limited to two queries has no chance at all for distinguishing H from a random permutation. Its advantage is limited to $\frac{3}{q}$ when limited to three queries (even adaptive, even with access to the inverse of H). Its advantage can be pretty close to 1 when four queries are allowed.

2.2 On the Perfect 3-wise Independence

One can wonder whether H is perfect 3-wise independent.

The $q = 2$ and $q = 3$ cases are particular. For $q = 2$ or $q = 3$ we have $\mathrm{inv}(x) = x$ for all $x \in \mathbf{K}$. Hence

$$a.\mathrm{inv}(x-b)+c = a.(x-b)+c = ax + (-ab+c).$$

Therefore H has the same distribution as $H' = \{h_{a,b}; (a,b) \in \mathbf{K}^* \times \mathbf{K}\}$ defined by $h_{a,b}(x) = ax+b$. We further notice that all permutations are indeed affine in these fields. Therefore H is perfectly 3-wise independent for $q = 2$ or $q = 3$.

Next, we check that H is never perfectly 3-wise independent for $q > 3$. Actually if we take any x_1, x_2, x_3 pairwise different elements of $\mathbf{K}$ we can consider $(h(x_1), h(x_2), h(x_3))$ for $h \in H$. This triplet must take values among all $q(q-1)(q-2)$ triplets with pairwise different coordinates in a uniform way. But we have $q^2(q-1)$ elements h in H. Therefore this cannot be uniformly distributed unless $q-2$ divides q which leads to $q = 3$ or $q = 4$. The $q = 4$ is also special since $\mathrm{inv}(x) = x^2$ which is GF(2)-linear for all $x \in \mathbf{K}$. Hence

$$a.\mathrm{inv}(x-b)+c = a.(x-b)^2+c = ax^2 + (ab^2+c).$$

We thus notice that H defines the same distribution than the set of all $h_{a,b}$ defined by $h_{a,b}(x) = ax^2+b$ for $(a,b) \in \mathbf{K}^* \times \mathbf{K}$. This cannot be perfectly 3-wise independent since two (x_i, y_i) points offer no freedom for any third one. This proves Theorem 2 item 2.

We can manually compute $\varepsilon = |||[H]^3 - [H^*]^3|||_\infty$ for small q. We found

q	2	3	4	5	7	8	9	11	13	16	17	19	23	25	27	29	31	32
ε	0	0	1	$\frac{4}{15}$	$\frac{26}{35}$	$\frac{1}{2}$	$\frac{10}{21}$	$\frac{14}{33}$	$\frac{62}{143}$	$\frac{5}{14}$	$\frac{26}{85}$	$\frac{98}{323}$	$\frac{38}{161}$	$\frac{134}{575}$	$\frac{46}{225}$	$\frac{50}{261}$	$\frac{170}{899}$	$\frac{7}{40}$

We can notice that these numbers get closer to $\frac{6}{q}$ which seems to mean that our bound is tight.

2.3 Pairwise Independence

We notice that for any permutation S the set of all $a.S(x)+c$ for $(a,c) \in \mathbf{K}^* \times \mathbf{K}$ is perfectly pairwise independent. Hence H is a disjoint union of perfectly pairwise independent permutations. Therefore H is a perfect pairwise independent permutation. This proves Theorem 2 item 1.

2.4 Four-wise Independence

We construct a distinguisher which uses four input-output pairs (x_i, y_i) for $i = 1, 2, 3, 4$ by using the cross-ratio: let

$$R(t,u,v,w) = \frac{\frac{t-u}{t-w}}{\frac{v-u}{v-w}}$$

when t, u, v, w are pairwise different. We notice that R is invariant under translation, scalar multiplication, and inversion:

1. $R(t+\alpha, u+\alpha, v+\alpha, w+\alpha) = R(t,u,v,w)$ for any α,
2. $R(t.\beta, u.\beta, v.\beta, w.\beta) = R(t,u,v,w)$ for any $\beta \neq 0$,
3. $R(\text{inv}(t), \text{inv}(u), \text{inv}(v), \text{inv}(w)) = R(t,u,v,w)$ when t, u, v, w are nonzero.

Hence R is almost invariant under any h in H. The distinguisher works as follows: if $R(x_1, x_2, x_3, x_4) = R(y_1, y_2, y_3, y_4)$, yield 1, otherwise yield 0. The probability that the distinguisher yields 1 for $h \in H$ is at least than $1 - \frac{4}{q}$ since none of the inv input is zero with this probability. When y_1 takes all values but y_2, y_3, y_4, then $R(y_1, y_2, y_3, y_4)$ takes all but three values. So the probability that the distinguisher yields 1 for a random permutation is at most $\frac{1}{q-3}$. The advantage of the distinguisher is thus greater than $1 - \frac{4}{q} - \frac{1}{q-3}$. This is greater than $1 - \frac{13}{2q}$ for $q \geq 5$. The best non-adaptive distinguisher has thus an advantage greater than $1 - \frac{13}{2q}$. For the $|||.|||_\infty$-almost 4-wise independence we just need to multiply by 2 due to Theorem 1 item 1. This proves Theorem 2 item 4.

For $q = 4$ we notice that 4-wise independence is just like 3-wise independence for permutations: once three different input-output pairs are known, the fourth one is known as well. Thus H is 1-almost 4-wise independent for $q = 4$. For $q < 4$ the notion of 4-wise independence does not make sense.

Note that we can see Rijndael [1, 5] as parallel applications and mixtures of $h_{a,b,c}$ functions as was shown by Murphy and Robshaw [9].[1] The distinguisher above shows that if we reduce this scheme to a single branch then it is totally insecure when having only four known plaintexts.

2.5 Three-wise Independence

Let us now prove Theorem 2 item 3. Let $x = (x_1, x_2, x_3)$, $y = (y_1, y_2, y_3)$. Let $p(x, y)$ be as follows.

$$p(x,y) = \Pr_{(a,b,c) \in_U \mathbf{K}^* \times \mathbf{K} \times \mathbf{K}} [h_{a,b,c}(x_1) = y_1, h_{a,b,c}(x_2) = y_2, h_{a,b,c}(x_3) = y_3]$$

Similarly we let $p^*(x, y)$ be as follows.

$$p^*(x,y) = \Pr_{h \in_U \mathcal{S}(\mathbf{K})} [h(x_1) = y_1, h(x_2) = y_2, h(x_3) = y_3]$$

[1] This is also equivalent to the simple SHARK [12] that was studied by using interpolation attacks by Jakobsen and Knudsen [7].

We define $d(x,y) = p(x,y) - p^*(x,y)$. We want to compute

$$D^3_{|||.|||_\infty} = \max_x \sum_y |d(x,y)|$$

$$D^3_{||.||_a} = \max_{x_1} \sum_{y_1} \max_{x_2} \sum_{y_2} \max_{x_3} \sum_{y_3} |d(x,y)|$$

$$D^3_{||.||_s} = \max_{b_1,z_1^0} \sum_{z_1^1} \max_{b_2,z_2^0} \sum_{z_2^1} \max_{b_3,z_3^0} \sum_{z_3^1} |d(x,y)|$$

with $x_i = z_i^{b_i}$ and $y_i = z_i^{1-b_i}$. According to the definition of 3-wise independent permutation (see Def. 3), we should prove that $D^3_{.} \leq \frac{6}{q}$ for the three norms.

First, we notice that both $p(x,y)$ and $p^*(x,y)$ are zero when $x_i = x_j$ is not equivalent to $y_i = y_j$ since $h_{a,b,c}$ and h are permutations. Therefore the sums can be restricted to all y for which the equivalence holds. Second, we notice that terms in $D^3_{.}$ for which $x_i = x_j$ for some $i < j$ are already in the maximum defined for the pairwise independence. Since H is a perfect pairwise independent permutation these terms are all zero. We can thus focus on x terms for which we have $x_1 \neq x_2, x_2 \neq x_3, x_3 \neq x_1$. This means that we have

$$D^3_{|||.|||_\infty} = \max_{\substack{x \\ x_1 \neq x_2, x_2 \neq x_3, x_3 \neq x_1}} \sum_{\substack{y \\ y_1 \neq y_2, y_2 \neq y_3, y_3 \neq y_1}} |d(x,y)|$$

$$D^3_{||.||_a} = \max_{x_1} \sum_{y_1} \max_{\substack{x_2 \\ x_2 \neq x_1}} \sum_{\substack{y_2 \\ y_2 \neq y_1}} \max_{\substack{x_3 \\ x_3 \neq x_1, x_3 \neq x_2}} \sum_{\substack{y_3 \\ y_3 \neq y_1, y_3 \neq y_2}} |d(x,y)|.$$

We also consider

$$D = q(q-1) \max_{\substack{x_1,x_2,x_3,y_1,y_2 \\ x_1 \neq x_2, x_2 \neq x_3, x_3 \neq x_1, y_2 \neq y_1}} \sum_{\substack{y_3 \\ y_3 \neq y_1, y_3 \neq y_2}} |d(x,y)|.$$

Obviously we have $D^3_{|||.|||_\infty} \leq D^3_{||.||_a} \leq D$ so it is sufficient to prove that $D \leq \frac{6}{q}$. For the $||.||_s$ norm we also have $D^3_{||.||_s} \leq \max(D, D')$ with D' defined by

$$D' = q(q-1) \max_{\substack{x_1,x_2,y_1,y_2,y_3 \\ y_1 \neq y_2, y_2 \neq y_3, y_3 \neq y_1, x_2 \neq x_1}} \sum_{\substack{x_3 \\ x_3 \neq x_1, x_3 \neq x_2}} |d(x,y)|.$$

So it is sufficient to prove that $D \leq \frac{6}{q}$ and $D' \leq \frac{6}{q}$. Since the treatment for D' is similar to that for D, we focus on the $D \leq \frac{6}{q}$ inequality.

By the definition of $p(x,y)$, we are interested in the number of solutions $(a,b,c) \in \mathbf{K}^* \times \mathbf{K} \times \mathbf{K}$ of

$$\begin{cases} a.\mathrm{inv}(x_1 - b) + c = y_1 \\ a.\mathrm{inv}(x_2 - b) + c = y_2 \\ a.\mathrm{inv}(x_3 - b) + c = y_3 \end{cases} \tag{1}$$

By linear combination of those equations, we obtain.

$$\mathrm{inv}(x_1 - b)(y_3 - y_2) + \mathrm{inv}(x_2 - b)(y_1 - y_3) + \mathrm{inv}(x_3 - b)(y_2 - y_1) = 0 \qquad (2)$$

as a necessary condition. Then we realize that once a fixed b satisfies this equation, then, thanks to the hypothesis on x that $x_1 \neq x_2, x_2 \neq x_3, x_3 \neq x_1$, at least two out of the three equations of (1) are independent linear equations in a and c which leads to a unique solution (a, b, c). Therefore (1) and Eq. (2) have the same number of solutions. It is thus sufficient to count the number of solutions of Eq. (2).

Let $x = (x_1, x_2, x_3)$ be fixed and such that $x_1 \neq x_2, x_2 \neq x_3, x_3 \neq x_1$. Let y_1, y_2 be fixed and such that $y_1 \neq y_2$. We let $n_i(x, y_1, y_2)$ be the number of y_3 such that $y_2 \neq y_3, y_3 \neq y_1$ and such that the number of solutions b for (2) is exactly i. We also define

$$d_i = \frac{i}{q^2(q-1)} - \frac{1}{q(q-1)(q-2)}.$$

We notice that for $q > 3$ then d_0 and d_1 are the only negative terms. We have

$$D = q(q-1) \max_{x,y_1,y_2} \sum_{i=0}^{q} n_i(x, y_1, y_2)|d_i|.$$

Obviously, for any x_1, x_2, x_3, y_1, y_2 with x_1, x_2, x_3 pairwise different and $y_1 \neq y_2$, we have

$$\sum_{\substack{y_3 \\ y_3 \neq y_1, y_3 \neq y_2}} p(x, y) = \Pr_{(a,b,c) \in_U \mathbf{K}^* \times \mathbf{K} \times \mathbf{K}} [h_{a,b,c}(x_1) = y_1, h_{a,b,c}(x_2) = y_2]$$

and

$$\sum_{\substack{y_3 \\ y_3 \neq y_1, y_3 \neq y_2}} p^*(x, y) = \Pr_{h \in_U \mathcal{S}(\mathbf{K})} [h(x_1) = y_1, h(x_2) = y_2]$$

and both are equal since H is perfectly pairwise independent. Hence the sum for D without absolute values is zero thus

$$n_0(x, y_1, y_2)|d_0| + n_1(x, y_1, y_2)|d_1| = \sum_{i=2}^{q} n_i(x, y_1, y_2)|d_i|$$

thus

$$D = 2q(q-1) \max_{x,y_1,y_2} (n_0(x, y_1, y_2)|d_0| + n_1(x, y_1, y_2)|d_1|).$$

Let $n_{\leq 1}$ be $n_0 + n_1$. We now have

$$D = 2q(q-1) \max_{x,y_1,y_2} (n_0(x, y_1, y_2)(|d_0| - |d_1|) + n_{\leq 1}(x, y_1, y_2)|d_1|)$$

which expands into

$$D = 2 \max_{x,y_1,y_2} \left(\frac{n_0(x, y_1, y_2)}{q} + \frac{2n_{\leq 1}(x, y_1, y_2)}{q(q-2)} \right)$$

Since we have $n_{\leq 1}(x, y_1, y_2) \leq q - 2$, we have

$$D \leq \frac{4}{q} + \frac{2}{q} \max_{\substack{x_1,x_2,x_3,y_1,y_2 \\ x_1 \neq x_2, x_2 \neq x_3, x_3 \neq x_1, y_2 \neq y_1}} n_0(x, y_1, y_2).$$

Therefore we only have to show that we have no more than one y_3 for which we have no solution for b in Eq. (2).

Under the assumption that $b \notin \{x_1, x_2, x_3\}$ Eq. (2) is equivalent to

$$\begin{aligned} 0 &= b\,(y_1(x_3 - x_2) + y_2(x_1 - x_3) + y_3(x_2 - x_1)) \\ &\quad - ((x_3 - x_2)x_1y_1 + (x_1 - x_3)x_2y_2 + (x_2 - x_1)x_3y_3) \end{aligned}$$

When we have no solution at all we must have

$$y_1(x_3 - x_2) + y_2(x_1 - x_3) + y_3(x_2 - x_1) = 0. \quad (3)$$

For any choice of x, y_1, y_2 (with $x_1 \neq x_2$) there is at most one y_3 which verifies this condition. Similarly for any choice of x_1, x_2, y (with $y_1 \neq y_2$) there is at most one x_3 which verifies this condition. This concludes the proof. □

3 The APA Construction

In this section we investigate $h_{a,b}(x) = \mathrm{inv}(x + a) + b$. This kind of primitive is used in several block ciphers, e.g. Rijndael since inv is one substitution-box application and a and b are key additions. Interestingly, we can also consider $h_{a,b}$ as the Even-Mansour [6] extension of inv, like for DESX [8]. We first study the problem with fixed permutations in a more general context that we call the Add-Permute-Add (APA) construction.

Note that one may also like to investigate $x \mapsto a.\mathrm{inv}(x)+c$ or $x \mapsto a.\mathrm{inv}(x+b)$. We notice that the latter family is the inverse of the former one. We also notice that the former family is equivalent to $y \mapsto a.y + c$ which is a perfect pairwise independent permutation.

3.1 Pairwise Independence of the APA Construction

The following lemma provides an interesting link between pairwise independence and the number of impossible differentials.

Lemma 1. *Let G be a finite group of order $q \geq 2$. Let S be a (fixed) permutation over G. For $(a, b) \in G \times G$, we consider the permutation $h_{a,b}$ defined by $h_{a,b}(x) = a + S(x + b)$. We let H denote the set of all $h_{a,b}$.*

Given a nonzero input dierence δ in G, we let $\mathrm{IDP}^S(\delta)$ be the fraction of the number of nonzero Δ values in G such that the $S(x+\delta) = S(x)+\Delta$ equation has no solution, i.e.

$$\mathrm{IDP}^S(\delta) = \frac{\#\{\Delta \in G; \mathrm{DP}^S(\delta, \Delta) = 0\}}{\#G}$$

We further let IDP^S *be the maximum of* $\mathrm{IDP}^S(\delta)$ *for all nonzero* δ.

The best advantage Adv of a non-adaptive distinguisher between H *and a random permutation limited to two queries is such that*

$$\frac{q-2}{2q(q-1)} \leq \mathrm{Adv} - \mathrm{IDP}^S \leq \frac{1}{q}.$$

Note that $\mathrm{IDP}^S(\delta)$ denotes the number of impossible differentials (δ, Δ) in the sense of Biham et al. [2] with a fixed δ. Hence we have a nice link between pairwise independence and impossible differentials.

Due to the link between differential probabilities and pairwise independence (see Theorem 1), we notice the consequence that we have

$$\max_{a\neq 0,b} \mathop{E}_{h\in_U H}(\mathrm{DP}^h(a,b)) \leq \frac{1}{q-1} + \frac{2}{q} + 2.\mathrm{IDP}^S$$

where $E_{h\in_U H}(\mathrm{DP}^h(a,b))$ denotes the expected value of $\mathrm{DP}^h(a,b)$ for a random h uniformly distributed in H. Therefore we also have a nice link between differential probabilities and impossible differentials for the APA construction.

Proof. As in previous sections, and with similar notations, we observe that

$$D^2_{|||\cdot|||_\infty} = \max_{\substack{x_1,x_2\\x_1\neq x_2}} \sum_{\substack{y_1,y_2\\y_1\neq y_2}} |d(x,y)|.$$

We let

$$d_i = \frac{i}{q^2} - \frac{1}{q(q-1)}$$

and $n_i(x)$ be the number of y for which $d(x,y) = d_i$. We have

$$D^2_{|||\cdot|||_\infty} = \max_{\substack{x_1,x_2\\x_1\neq x_2}} \sum_{i=0}^{q(q-1)} n_i(x)|d_i|.$$

The sum without absolute values is zero and d_0 and d_1 are the only negative terms we obtain

$$D^2_{|||\cdot|||_\infty} = 2 \max_{\substack{x_1,x_2\\x_1\neq x_2}} (n_0(x)(|d_0| - |d_1|) + n_{\leq 1}(x)|d_1|)$$

where $n_{\leq 1}(x) = n_0(x) + n_1(x)$. Since $\sum_{i\geq 2} n_i(x) = q(q-1) - n_{\leq 1}(x)$ and $d_i \geq d_2$ for $i \geq 2$, we have

$$(q(q-1) - n_{\leq 1}(x))d_2 \leq \sum_{i=2}^{q(q-1)} n_i(x)d_i = n_0(x)|d_0| + n_1(x)|d_1| \leq n_{\leq 1}(x)|d_0|$$

thus

$$n_{\leq 1}(x) \geq q(q-1)\frac{d_2/|d_0|}{1 + d_2/|d_0|} = \frac{1}{2}q(q-2).$$

Furthermore $n_{\leq 1} \leq q(q-1)$, thus we obtain

$$\frac{q-2}{q(q-1)} \leq D^2_{|||.|||_\infty} - \frac{2}{q^2} \max_{\substack{x_1,x_2 \\ x_1 \neq x_2}} n_0(x) \leq \frac{2}{q}.$$

Now we notice that $n_0(x)$ counts the number of unreached (y_1, y_2) pairs by $h_{a,b}$. Since a perfectly randomizes the outputs $(h_{a,b}(x_1), h_{a,b}(x_2))$ up to a fixed difference, $n_0(x)$ is equal to q times the number of unreached differences. Since b perfectly randomizes the inputs $(x_1 + b, x_2 + b)$ of S, $n_0(x)$ is simply equal to $q^2.\mathrm{IDP}^S(x_2 - x_1)$. Hence we obtain the claimed inequalities. □

The lemma bounds the best advantage of a distinguisher (regardless of the complexity). We describe here a distinguisher whose advantage is very close to the best one.

1. Pick a random x_1, x_2 ($x_1 \neq x_2$) such that $\mathrm{IDP}^S(x_2 - x_1)$ is maximal.
2. Send x_1, x_2 to the oracle, get y_1, y_2 respectively.
3. If $y_2 - y_1$ is in the set of all $S(x + x_2) - S(x + x_1)$ when $x \in G$, then output 1, otherwise, output 0.

Obviously the advantage is IDP^S.

3.2 Application to inv

With notations of the previous lemma, we notice that $\mathrm{IDP}^{\mathrm{inv}}$ is pretty bad. Actually, $\mathrm{inv}(x + \delta) = \mathrm{inv}(x) + \Delta$ has no solution if, and only if the following conditions are satisfied

1. $\Delta \neq \mathrm{inv}(\delta)$.
2. The $x^2 + \delta x + \frac{\delta}{\Delta}$ polynomial has no root.

These conditions hold for half of all possible Δs hence $\mathrm{IDP}^{\mathrm{inv}} = \frac{1}{2}$ for q even and $\mathrm{IDP}^{\mathrm{inv}} = \frac{1}{2}(1 - q^{-1})$ for q odd. This suggests that $h_{a,b}$ has a pretty bad pairwise independence. With two samples $x_1 \mapsto y_1$ and $x_2 \mapsto y_2$, we can actually distinguish $h_{a,b}$ from a random permutation with high advantage by checking whether the above conditions hold for $\delta = x_1 - x_2$ and $\Delta = y_1 - y_2$. (This is the distinguisher of the previous section.) Since $\mathrm{IDP}^{\mathrm{inv}}$ is close to $\frac{1}{2}$, the advantage is close to $\frac{1}{2}$.

3.3 On the Choice of XOR as a Group Operation

The bad performance if inv in the previous construction is actually not exceptional when the group operation is equivalent to the XOR. Indeed, given a fixed $\delta \neq 0$ we know that $\mathrm{DP}^S(\delta, \Delta)$ is always an even multiple of q^{-1} (since x is a solution of $S(x + \delta) = S(x) + \Delta$ implies that $x + \delta$ is also a solution). It sums to 1 over all of the q choices of Δ, so at least half of them are zero. This means that $\mathrm{IDP}^S \geq \frac{1}{2}$ for all S. So inv does not perform so bad in the characteristic 2 case: it is just the maximum we can get from the the APA construction with the XOR addition and a fixed permutation.

4 Conclusion

We investigated properties of the random harmonic permutation construction. We demonstrated that it is perfect pairwise independent, and almost 3-wise independent. It implies that any distinguisher between those permutations and perfect ones which is limited to three queries has an advantage bounded by $\frac{3}{q}$ where q is the field order.

We also have shown that it is not 4-wise independent and can actually be easily distinguished from random permutations by using the cross-ratio. This suggests the cross-ratio as a new tool for cryptanalysis.

We investigated the pairwise independence of the APA construction. We have shown it relates to the impossible differentials. In particular, this construction used together with the inversion is not a good one since we can easily distinguish it with two oracle accesses, despite the good properties of inversion with respect to differential and linear cryptanalysis.

References

[1] Advanced Encryption Standard (AES). *Federal Information Processing Standards* Publication #197. U. S. Department of Commerce, National Institute of Standards and Technology, 2001. 238, 240

[2] E. Biham, A. Biryukov, A. Shamir. Cryptanalysis of Skipjack Reduced to 31 Rounds using Impossible Differentials. In *Advances in Cryptology EUROCRYPT'99*, Prague, Czech Republic, Lectures Notes in Computer Science 1592, pp. 12–23, Springer-Verlag, 1999. 244

[3] J.L. Carter, M.N. Wegman. Universal Classes of Hash Functions. *Journal of Computer and System Sciences*, vol. 18, pp. 143–154, 1979. 236

[4] N.T. Courtois, J. Pieprzyk. Cryptanalysis of Block Ciphers with Overdefined Systems of Equations. 234

[5] J. Daemen, V. Rijmen. *The Design of Rijndael*, Information Security and Cryptography, Springer-Verlag, 2002. 234, 238, 240

[6] S. Even, Y. Mansour. A Construction of a Cipher from a Single Pseudorandom Permutation. In *Advances in Cryptology ASIACRYPT'91*, Fujiyoshida, Japan, Lectures Notes in Computer Science 739, pp. 210–224, Springer-Verlag, 1993. Also in *Journal of Cryptology*, vol. 10, pp. 151–161, 1997. 235, 243

[7] T. Jakobsen, L.R. Knudsen. The Interpolation Attack on Block Ciphers. In *Fast Software Encryption'97*, Haifa, Israel, Lectures Notes in Computer Science 1267, pp. 28–40, Springer-Verlag, 1997. 234, 240

[8] J. Kilian, P. Rogaway. How to Protect DES Against Exhaustive Key Search. *Journal of Cryptology*, vol. 14, pp. 17–35, 2001. 243

[9] S. Murphy, M.J.B. Robshaw. Essential Algebraic Structure within the AES. In *Advances in Cryptology CRYPTO'02*, Santa Barbara, California, U.S.A., Lectures Notes in Computer Science 2442, pp. 1–16, Springer-Verlag, 2002. 234, 240

[10] K. Nyberg. Differentially Uniform Mappings for Cryptography. In *Advances in Cryptology EUROCRYPT'93*, Lofthus, Norway, Lectures Notes in Computer Science 765, pp. 55–64, Springer-Verlag, 1994. 234, 238

[11] E.G. Rees. *Notes on Geometry*, Springer-Verlag, 1983. 235

[12] V. Rijmen, J. Daemen, B. Preneel, A. Bosselaers, E. De Win. The Cipher SHARK. In *Fast Software Encryption'96*, Cambridge, United Kingdom, Lectures Notes in Computer Science 1039, pp. 99–112, Springer-Verlag, 1996. 240

[13] A. Russel, H. Wang. How to Fool an Unbounded Adversary with a Short Key. In *Advances in Cryptology EUROCRYPT'02*, Amsterdam, Netherland, Lectures Notes in Computer Science 2332, pp. 133–148, Springer-Verlag, 2002. 235

[14] C. E. Shannon. Communication Theory of Secrecy Systems. *Bell system technical journal*, vol. 28, pp. 656–715, 1949. 235

[15] D. R. Stinson. Universal Hashing and Authentication Codes. In *Advances in Cryptology CRYPTO'91*, Santa Barbara, California, U.S.A., Lectures Notes in Computer Science 576, pp. 74–85, Springer-Verlag, 1992. 236

[16] S. Vaudenay. Provable Security for Block Ciphers by Decorrelation. In *STACS 98*, Paris, France, Lectures Notes in Computer Science 1373, pp. 249–275, Springer-Verlag, 1998. 235, 237

[17] S. Vaudenay. Adaptive-Attack Norm for Decorrelation and Super-Pseudorandomness. In *Selected Areas in Cryptography'99*, Kingston, Ontario, Canada, Lectures Notes in Computer Science 1758, pp. 49–61, Springer-Verlag, 2000. 235, 237

[18] S. Vaudenay. Decorrelation: a Theory for Block Cipher Security. To appear in the Journal of Cryptology. 235, 237

[19] M. N. Wegman, J. L. Carter. New Hash Functions and their Use in Authentication and Set Equality. *Journal of Computer and System Sciences*, vol. 22, pp. 265–279, 1981. 234, 236

Cryptographic Applications of T-Functions

Alexander Klimov and Adi Shamir

Computer Science department, The Weizmann Institute of Science
Rehovot 76100, Israel
{ask,shamir}@wisdom.weizmann.ac.il

Abstract. A *T-function* is a mapping in which the i-th bit of the output can depend only on bits $0, 1, \ldots, i$ of the input. All the bitwise machine operations and most of the numeric machine operations in modern processors are T-functions, and their compositions are also T-functions. In this paper we show that T-functions can be used to construct exceptionally efficient cryptographic building blocks which can be used as nonlinear maximal length state transition functions in stream ciphers, as large S-boxes in block ciphers, and as non-algebraic multipermutations in hash functions.

1 Introduction

A function $f(x)$ from an n-bit input to an n-bit output is called a *T-function* (which is short for a *triangular function*) if it does not propagate information from left to right, that is, bit number i of the output (denoted by $[f(x)]_i$, where the LSB is defined as bit number 0 and the MSB is defined as bit number $n-1$) can depend only on bits $j = 0, \ldots, i$ of the input. This definition can be naturally extended to functions that map several n-bit inputs to several n-bit outputs. The special class of T-functions $f(x)$ for which the i-th bit of the output can depend only on bits $j = 0, \ldots, i-1$ of the input are called *parameters* and denoted by α, β, γ, et cetera. We can thus consider each T-function f as a parameterized collection of bit slice mappings from $[x]_i$ to $[f(x)]_i$, in which the parameters describe the dependence of the output bit on the previous input bits. The simplest example of such a representation is the addition of two variables x and y: The i-th bit of the output is the XOR of $[x]_i$, $[y]_i$, and a parameter which describes the carry from the addition of all the previous bit slices. Note that the mappings $x \to 2x \bmod 2^n$ and $x \to x^2 \bmod 2^n$ are T-functions which are also parameters.[1] If $f_0(x), \ldots, f_k(x)$ are parameters then $g(x) = \Psi(f_0(x), \ldots, f_k(x))$ is also a parameter for an arbitrary T-function Ψ.

Simple examples of T-functions are the following machine operations, which are available on almost any contemporary microprocessor with n-bit words: addition ($a + b \bmod 2^n$), subtraction ($a - b \bmod 2^n$), negation ($-a \bmod 2^n$), multiplication ($a \cdot b \bmod 2^n$), bit-wise complementation ($\overline{a}$), xor ($a \oplus b$), and ($a \wedge b$), or

[1] It can be shown that a T-function $f(x)$ is a parameter if and only if $\forall x : 0 \leq x < 2^n$ $f(x) = f(x + 2^n) \pmod{2^{n+1}}$ and it is easy to check that $2x = 2(x + 2^n) \pmod{2^{n+1}}$ and $x^2 = (x + 2^n)^2 \pmod{2^{n+1}}$ (except for $n = 0$).

M. Matsui and R. Zuccherato (Eds.): SAC 2003, LNCS 3006, pp. 248–261, 2004.

$(a \vee b)$. We call these eight machine instructions *primitive operations* . Any univariate or multivariate composition of primitive operations is a T-function, and in particular all the polynomials modulo 2^n are T-functions. Note that left shift could be added to the list since it is equivalent to multiplication by two modulo 2^n, but right shift and circular shift cannot be added to the list since they are not T-functions. The main purpose of this paper is to study the properties of cryptographic building blocks defined by T-functions, and in particular the properties of mappings defined as a composition of a small number of primitive operations which mix boolean and arithmetic operations over 32 or 64 bit words, and contain nonlinear subexpressions such as squaring. Such mappings have very efficient software implementations, and they are more likely to resist cryptanalysis, even though each one of them has to be tested carefully over a long period of time before it can be used as a secure building block in an actual cryptographic design.

2 Invertible T-Functions

The round function of a block cipher has to be invertible, since we have to undo its effect in order to decrypt the ciphertext. Even when we do not wish to apply the inverse operation, it is often desirable to use invertible building blocks (e.g., to avoid collisions in hash functions or to increase the expected cycle length in stream ciphers). In [3] it was shown that it is easy to test the invertibility of mappings which are based on arbitrary compositions of primitive operations. For example, the following three T-functions

$$x \to x + 2x^2$$
$$x \to x + (x^2 \vee 1)$$
$$x \to x \oplus (x^2 \vee 1)$$

require only three primitive operations over n-bit words, and they are invertible for any n. To prove this result, it is necessary and sufficient to prove that for all i the bit slice mappings $[x]_i \to [f(x)]_i$ are invertible, where all the bits of x are fixed except $[x]_i$. This condition can be easily checked by noting that x^2 is a parameter except in its the least significant bit, and the LSB problem can be fixed by either shifting it or "OR"ing it with 1. A simple generalization of this technique can show that multivariate mappings such as

$$x \to x \oplus 2(x \vee y),$$
$$y \to (y + 3x^3) \oplus x$$

are also invertible for any word size n.

3 Invertible T-Functions with a Single Cycle

The problem considered in this section is how to characterize those T-functions which are permutations with a single cycle of length 2^n for any word size n.

The cycle structure of an invertible T-function is particularly important when the function is used as a state transition function in a stream cipher, since in this application we iterate the function a large number of times and do not want the sequence of generated states to be trapped in a short cycle. The fact that we can easily test whether a linear feedback shift register (LFSR) has maximal length is one of the main reasons they are so popular in stream cipher designs, in spite of the cryptographic weaknesses implied by the linearity of the transition function. If a similar theory can be developed for compositions of primitive operations, we can use more complicated (nonlinear, and even non-algebraic) transition functions which are very efficient in software and which are guaranteed to have a maximal cycle length.

One added benefit is that in LFSRs, the existence of one fixed point (the all zero state) is unavoidable, and thus we have to make sure that we do not accidentally derive such an initial state from the random key (e.g., by forcing some of the bits to 1). This is cumbersome, and in some well known stream ciphers (e.g., A5/2) such a protective mechanism even leads to devastating attacks. With appropriately chosen T-functions, we can guarantee that all the states are on a single cycle of length 2^n, and thus there are no bad states which should be avoided during the initialization of the stream cipher.

Not every invertible T-function has a single cycle. Consider, for example, the RC6 mapping $x \to x + 2x^2 \pmod{2^n}$. It is easy to show that it has a very bad cycle structure since any one of the $2^{n/2}$ x values whose bottom half is zero is a fixed point of the mapping. The mapping $x \to x + (x^2 \vee 1)$ is better, but it does not have a single cycle. In [3], we used ad-hoc techniques to show that the mapping $x \to x + (x^2 \vee 5)$ (which also requires only three primitive operations on n-bit words) has a single cycle which contains all the 2^n possible values. In this section we develop a general technique for proving such results for other T-functions.

The cycle structure of T-functions was recently studied by Anashin [1], who used p-adic analysis and infinite power series to prove[2] (in theorem 2.7) that a T-function is invertible if and only if it can be represented in the form $c+x+2v(x)$, and that an invertible T-function defines a single cycle if and only if it can be represented in the form $1+x+2(v(x+1)-v(x))$, where c is some constant and $v(x)$ is some T-function. The sufficiency can be used to construct new single cycle permutations by using a $v(x)$ which is defined by a small number of primitive functions,[3] but the necessity is less useful since in many cases (e.g. the mapping $x+(x^2 \vee 5)$) we know from Anashin's theorem that $v(x)$ exists but it is not clear how to define it in order to show by his method that the mapping has a single cycle.

---

[2] He uses a completely different terminology of compatible, ergodic and measure preserving functions, so we translate his result to our terminology.

[3] Note, however, that the construction requires two evaluations of $v(x)$ and five additional operations, so even if $v(x) = x^2$, which requires a single operation, the constructed function requires seven primitive operations which is rather inefficient.

In the univariate case, there are only four possible bit slice mappings from one bit to one bit: 0, 1, x, $x \oplus 1$. Since only the last two are invertible and the choice between them can be a parameter depending on the previous bits, a T-function $f(x)$ is invertible if and only if it can be represented in the following form: $[f(x)]_i = [x]_i \oplus \alpha$, where α is a parameter. It is easy to show that the only possible lengths of cycles of a T-function are powers of two, so the sequence $\{x_{i+1} = f(x_i) \bmod 2^n\}$ has period 2^n if and only if $x_i \neq x_{i+2^{n-1}} \pmod{2^n}$. Since for any T-function $x_i = x_{i+2^{n-1}} \pmod{2^{n-1}}$, we can conclude that $f(x)$ defines a single cycle if and only if $[x_i]_{n-1} \neq [x_{i+2^{n-1}}]_{n-1}$, and thus $\bigoplus_{j=0}^{2^{n-1}} \alpha(x_{i+j}) = 1$. The function $\alpha(x)$ is a parameter, that is $\alpha(x + 2^{n-1}) = \alpha(x) \pmod{2^n}$. Moreover, $\{x_i \bmod 2^{n-1}\}$ has period 2^{n-1}, so $\{\alpha(x_{i+j})\}_{j=0}^{2^{n-1}}$ as a set is the same as $\{\alpha(j)\}_{j=0}^{2^{n-1}}$. This proves the following simple characterization:

Theorem 1. *The T-function $f(x)$ de□nes a single cycle modulo 2^n if and only if $[f(x)]_{n-1} = [x]_{n-1} \oplus \alpha([x]_{0,\ldots,n-2})$ and $\bigoplus_{x=0}^{2^{n-1}-1} \alpha(x) = 1$.*

Once again, this theorem completely characterizes those T-functions whose iteration defines a single cycle, but it is difficult to use it even in the simplest example of the mapping $x \to x + C \pmod{2^n}$, which is known to have a single cycle if and only if C is odd.

Since the general theorem is not very helpful in practice, let us consider an interesting special case of it. Suppose that $r(x)$ is a parameter, that is $r(x) = r(x + 2^{n-1}) \pmod{2^n}$. So, $r(x) = r(x + 2^{n-1}) + 2^n b(x) \pmod{2^{n+1}}$. Consider

$$B[r, n] = 2^{-n} \sum_{i=0}^{2^{n-1}-1} (r(i + 2^{n-1}) - r(i)) \pmod 2 = \bigoplus_{i=0}^{2^{n-1}-1} b(i). \qquad (1)$$

Let us introduce the notion of *even* and *odd* parameters according to the 0/1 value of B. Note that in the general case B is a function of n, and thus the parameter can be neither even nor odd if

$$\forall N\ \exists n_o > N, n_e > N: \qquad B[r, n_o] = 1,\ B[r, n_e] = 0.$$

Let us give several examples of even parameters. The simplest is an arbitrary constant $r(x) = C$: $r(x) = r(x + 2^{n-1})$ and so, $b = 0$ and $B = 0$. Let $r(x) = 2x$ then $r(x + 2^{n-1}) = r(x) + 2^n \pmod{2^{n+1}}$, so $b(x) = 1$ and B is even as long as 2^{n-1} is even, that is $n \geq 2$. If $r(x) = x^2$ then $r(x+2^{n-1}) = r(x)+2^n x+2^{2(n-1)}$, so $b(x) = [x]_0$ and B is even for $n \geq 3$.

The following function is an example of an odd parameter: $[r(x)]_i = [x]_0 \wedge [x]_1 \wedge \cdots \wedge [x]_{i-1}$. Bit number i of $r(x)$ depends only on bits up to $i-1$ of x, so it is a T-function and a parameter. Clearly $b(i) \neq 0$ if and only if $i = 1 \ldots 1$, so $B[r, n] = 1$ for $n \geq 1$.

Note that if a and b are even parameters then $a + b$, $a - b$, $a \oplus b$ are also even parameters. Suppose that we know the value of $B[r]$ and let us calculate $B[r \vee C]$, where C is a constant. If $[C]_i = 0$ then $[r(x) \vee C]_i = [r(x)]_i$, so $B[r, i] =$

$B[r \vee C, i]$. If $[C]_i = 1$ then $[r(x) \vee C]_i = 1$, so $b(x) = 0$ and $B[r \vee C, i] = 0$. Combining both cases we could say that if $r(x)$ is an even parameter then $r(x) \vee C$ is also an even parameter for an arbitrary constant C.

Theorem 2. *Let N_0 be such that $x \to x + r(x) \bmod 2^{N_0}$ de□nes a single cycle and for $n > N_0$ the function $r(x)$ is an even parameter. Then the mapping $x \to x + r(x) \bmod 2^n$ de□nes a single cycle for all n.*

Proof. Let us prove the theorem by induction. For $n \leq N_0$ the mapping defines a single cycle. Suppose that it is true for n (and $n-1$). Consider the sequence $\{x_i\}_{i=0}^{2^{n+1}-1}$, where $x_0 = 0$ and $x_i = x_{i-1} + r(x_{i-1}) \bmod 2^{n+1}$. In particular,

$$x_{2^n} = x_{2^n-1} + r(x_{2^n-1}) = \ldots = x_0 + \sum_{i=0}^{2^n-1} r(x_i) = \sum_{i=0}^{2^n-1} r(x_i) \pmod{2^{n+1}}. \quad (2)$$

From the inductive hypothesis it follows that all the x_i $(i = 0, \ldots, 2^n - 1)$ are different modulo 2^n, so as a set $\{x_i \bmod 2^n\}_{i=0}^{2^n-1} = \{i\}_{i=0}^{2^n-1}$. Using also the fact that $r(x) = r(x + 2^n) \pmod{2^{n+1}}$, we can rewrite the sum as follows:

$$\sum_{i=0}^{2^n-1} r(x_i) = \sum_{i=0}^{2^n-1} r(x_i \bmod 2^n) = \sum_{i=0}^{2^n-1} r(i)$$
$$= \sum_{i=0}^{2^{n-1}-1} r(i) + \sum_{i=0}^{2^{n-1}-1} r(i + 2^{n-1}) \pmod{2^{n+1}}.$$

Let us denote the first sum as S and the second as S'. From the fact that $x_0 \neq x_{2^{n-1}} \pmod{2^n}$, but $x_0 = x_{2^{n-1}} \pmod{2^{n-1}}$ it follows that $x_{2^{n-1}} = 2^{n-1} \pmod{2^n}$. Using also (2) (with n replaced by $n-1$), we can write

$$S = \sum_{i=0}^{2^{n-1}-1} r(i) = \sum_{i=0}^{2^{n-1}-1} r(x_i) = x_{2^{n-1}} = 2^{n-1} \pmod{2^n}.$$

So, there is a constant A, such that $S = A2^n + 2^{n-1} \pmod{2^{n+1}}$. From the fact that $r(x)$ is an even parameter it follows that $S' = S \pmod{2^{n+1}}$, so, $x_{2^n} = S + S' = 2(A2^n + 2^{n-1}) = 2^n \pmod{2^{n+1}}$. This means that $x_0 \neq x_{2^n} \pmod{2^{n+1}}$, and thus the mapping $x \to x + r(x) \bmod 2^{n+1}$ defines a single cycle for $n+1$.

The mapping $x \to x + C$, where C is an odd constant defines a single cycle. So, the condition "$x \to x + r(x) \bmod 2^{N_0}$ defines a single cycle" always holds if $r(x) \bmod 2^{N_0}$ is an odd constant. This is always true for $r(x) = r'(x) \vee C$, where $C = \underbrace{1\ldots1}_{N_0}{}_2$, although other constants are also possible.

We already know that for $n \geq 3$, x^2 is an even parameter. So, $x \to x + (x^2 \vee 111_2)$ defines a single cycle modulo 2^n for arbitrary n. It turns out that $\forall x, [x^2]_1 = 0$, so $x^2 \vee 101_2 \pmod{2^3}$ is also a constant. So, $x \to x + (x^2 \vee C)$

defines a single cycle if and only if $C = \star \cdots \star 1 \star 1_2$, where $\star$ denotes 0 or 1. (It is easy to check by direct calculation modulo 2^3 that it is also a necessary condition.) This shows that our theorem 2 is a generalization of the theorem which was proven in [3].

A further generalization of this result, which considers the cyclic use of several constants C, is

Theorem 3. *Consider the sequence* $\{(x_i, k_i)\}$ *de*□*ned by iterating*

$$x_{i+1} = x_i + (x_i^2 \vee C_{k_i}) \bmod 2^n,$$
$$k_{i+1} = k_i + 1 \bmod m,$$

where for any $k = 0, \ldots, m-1$ C_k *is some constant. Then the sequence of pairs* (x_i, k_i) *has a maximal period (* $m2^n$*) if and only if* m *is odd, and for all* k, $[C_k]_0 = 1$ *and* $\bigoplus_{k=0}^{m-1} [C_k]_2 = 1$.

The proof of this result is quite complicated, and is omitted due to space limitations.

4 Latin Squares

Let X be a finite set of values. A function $f : X \times X \to X$ is called a *latin square* of *order* $K = |X|$ if both $f(x, \cdot)$ and $f(\cdot, x)$ are invertible. Latin squares have a rich mathematical structure, and they were shown to be useful building blocks in a variety of cryptographic applications (especially in block ciphers and hash functions, see e.g. [6]). In order to check that a function $f(\cdot, \cdot)$ which is a composition of primitive operations is a latin square it is necessary and sufficient to check, using machinery developed in [3], that $f(x, C)$ and $f(C, x)$ are invertible for every value of C.

Let us prove, for example, that $(x \oplus y)(A(x \wedge y) + B)$ is a latin square, where A is any even number and B is any odd number (i.e., $[A]_0 = 0$ and $[B]_0 = 1$): $[(x \oplus C)(A(x \wedge C) + B)]_0 = ([x]_0 \oplus [C]_0)([A]_0 [x]_0 [C]_0 \oplus [B]_0) = [x]_0 \oplus [C]_0$, and $[(x \oplus C)(A(x \wedge C) + B)]_i = [x \oplus C]_i [(A(x \wedge C) + B)]_0 \oplus [x \oplus C]_0 [A(x \wedge C) + B]_i \oplus \alpha_1 = [x \oplus C]_i \oplus [x \oplus C]_0 ([A]_i [x]_0 [C]_0 \oplus [A]_0 [x]_i [C]_i \oplus [B]_i \oplus \alpha_2) \oplus \alpha_1 = [x]_i \oplus \alpha_3$.

A pair of latin squares (f, g) is called *orthogonal* [4] if

$$\forall (x, y) \neq (x', y'),\ (f(x, y), g(x, y)) \neq (f(x', y'), g(x', y')). \quad (3)$$

Such mappings are also known as multipermutations, and were used in several cryptographic constructions. They are known to exist for all orders except two and six. There is an easy construction of orthogonal latin squares of odd order K: $(f, g) = (x + y, 2x + y) \bmod K$. We will concentrate on $K = 2^n$. Let $\mathbb{F}$ be a finite

[4] As Euler used Greek and Latin letters to denote values of f and g respectively, they got also known as *Graeco-Latin* squares.

field with 2^n elements. If $\alpha, \beta \in \mathbb{F}$, $\alpha, \beta \neq 0$ and $\alpha \neq \beta$ then $(f, g) = (\alpha x + y, \beta x + y)$ are orthogonal. Actually, this is an abuse of the notation, since $f(x, y) = \phi^{-1}(\alpha\phi(x) + \phi(y))$, where $\phi : \{0 \ldots 2^n - 1\} \to \mathbb{F}$ is a one-to-one mapping between integers and the field elements. Unfortunately, most processors do not have built-in operations which deal with finite fields, and thus the mapping is quite slow when implemented in software. In addition, the resulting transformation is linear, and thus it is a very weak cryptographic building block.

In [5] it was shown that there are no orthogonal latin squares formed by a pair of polynomials modulo 2^n. Let us prove that this is true not only for polynomials modulo 2^n but also for the wider class of all the possible T-functions. Consider the latin square of order 2^n formed by a T-function $f(x, y)$. Given arbitrary $x_0, y_0 < 2^{n-1}$ let $x'_0 = x_0 + 2^{n-1}$ and $y'_0 = y_0 + 2^{n-1}$. Since f is a T-function and $(x_0, y_0) = (x'_0, y'_0) \pmod{2^{n-1}}$ it follows that $f(x_0, y_0) = f(x_0, y'_0) = f(x'_0, y'_0) \pmod{2^{n-1}}$. The function $f(x_0, y)$ is invertible modulo 2^n, so $f(x_0, y'_0) = f(x_0, y_0) + 2^{n-1} \pmod{2^n}$. For the same reason $f(x'_0, y'_0) = f(x_0, y'_0) + 2^{n-1} \pmod{2^n}$, so $f(x_0, y_0) = f(x'_0, y'_0) \pmod{2^n}$. Suppose that a pair (f, g), where f and g are T-functions is a pair of orthogonal latin squares. Similar to the above $g(x_0, y_0) = g(x'_0, y'_0) \pmod{2^n}$, so $(f(x_0, y_0), g(x_0, y_0)) = (f(x'_0, y'_0), g(x'_0, y'_0)) \pmod{2^n}$ which contradicts (3).

In spite of this negative result, we can construct a pair of orthogonal latin squares using T-functions, if we consider the top and bottom half of each variable as a separate entity. This is a natural operation in many processors, which allows us to consider each machine word either as one word of length $2n$ or as two consecutive words of length n. Every $0 \leq x < 2^{2n}$ could be represented as $x = x_u 2^n + x_v$, where $0 \leq x_u, x_v < 2^n$. There exist T-functions $f_u(x_u, x_v, y_v, y_v)$, $f_v(x_u, x_v, y_v, y_v)$, $g_u(x_u, x_v, y_v, y_v)$ and $g_v(x_u, x_v, y_v, y_v)$, such that $(f, g) = (f_u 2^n + f_v, g_u 2^n + g_v)$ is a pair of orthogonal latin squares of order 2^{2n}. Let us construct them.

Table 1. A pair of orthogonal latin squares of order four

0,0	1,1	2,2	3,3
1,2	0,3	3,0	2,1
2,3	3,2	0,1	1,0
3,1	2,0	1,3	0,2

Table 1 shows a pair of orthogonal latin squares of order four ($n = 1$). Columns correspond to x and rows to y, for example, $f(0, 1) = 1$ and $g(0, 1) = 2$ or more explicitly for arguments $(x_u = 0, x_v = 0, y_u = 0, y_v = 1)$ $f_u = 0$, $f_v = 1$, $g_u = 1$ and $g_v = 0$. Each of x_u, x_v, y_v and y_v consists of only a single bit, so f_u, f_v, g_u and g_v are clearly T-functions. Suppose we have a pair (f, g) of orthogonal latin squares of order 2^{2n}, where f_u, f_v, g_u and g_v are T-functions. To construct a pair (f', g') of orthogonal latin squares of order $2^{2(n+1)}$ we do the following. Let $[f'_u]_i \equiv [f_u]_i$, $[f'_v]_i \equiv [f_v]_i$, $[g'_u]_i \equiv [g_u]_i$ and $[g'_v]_i \equiv [g_v]_i$ for

$i = 0, \ldots, n-1$. This way bit number i of f' depends on the same bits of the arguments as f, which is a T-function and so, f' is also a T-function. The same holds for f_v, g_u and g_v. For every fixed $(x_u, x_v, y_u, y_v) \pmod{2^n}$ let us define (f', g') in such a way that $[f', g']_n$ forms a pair of orthogonal latin squares. Let us prove that f' and g' are latin squares. Suppose that there exists a row y_0 such that $\exists x_0, x_1 : f'(x_0, y_0) = f'(x_1, y_0)$. There are two possibilities: either $x_0 \neq x_1 \pmod{2^n}$, so, $f'(x_0, y_0) = f(x_0, y_0) \neq f(x_1, y_0) = f'(x_1, y_0) \pmod{2^n}$ or $x_0 = x_1 \pmod{2^n}$, but in this case $[f'(x_0, y_0)]_n \neq [f'(x_1, y_0)]_n$, because for any fixed n the least significant bits of arguments $[f']_n$ forms a latin square. The same proof applies to the columns of f', to g' and to the orthogonality of f' and g'.

Let us show some examples of orthogonal latin squares. First we need to encode table 1:[5]

$$
\begin{aligned}
f_u^\star &= \texttt{0011001111001100} = x_v \oplus y_v, \\
f_v^\star &= \texttt{0101101001011010} = x_u \oplus y_u, \\
g_u^\star &= \texttt{0011110011000011} = x_v \oplus y_u \oplus y_v, \\
g_v^\star &= \texttt{0101010110101010} = x_u \oplus y_v.
\end{aligned}
$$

The next question is how to define (f, g) in such a way that $[(f, g)]_n$ forms a pair of orthogonal latin squares for every fixed $(x_u, x_v, y_u, y_v) \bmod 2^n$. The simplest way is to use for $[f, g]_n$ the same functions $(f^\star, g^\star)$, that is $f = (x_v \oplus y_v, x_u \oplus y_u)$, $g = (x_v \oplus y_u \oplus y_v, x_u \oplus y_v)$. Note that if (f, g) is a pair of orthogonal latin squares and ϕ is an invertible mapping then $(\phi(f), g)$ is also a pair of orthogonal latin squares. The mapping $\phi(x) = x \oplus C$ is invertible, thus the bit trace $[f]_n = (f_u^\star \oplus \alpha, f_v^\star \oplus \beta)$, where α and β are parameters, is also admissible. So, for example, $f = (x_v \oplus y_v - (x_u^2 \vee 1), 7x_u + y_u)$ and $g = (x_v - (y_u \oplus y_v) + (x_u^2 \vee 1), x_u \oplus y_v)$ are nonlinear and non-algebraic orthogonal latin squares.

We are not limited to latin squares of size $2^{2n} \times 2^{2n}$, since using similar construction we can build a pair of orthogonal latin squares of size $2^{mn} \times 2^{mn}$ for any m. For example, if $m = 4$ and we represent the inputs as $x = 2^{3n}x_s + 2^{2n}x_t + 2^n x_u + x_v$ and $y = 2^{3n}y_s + 2^{2n}y_t + 2^n y_u + y_v$, then

$$
\begin{aligned}
f &= (x_s \oplus y_s + 2x_v y_u, \quad x_t + y_t, \quad x_u \oplus y_u + 2x_s x_v, \quad x_v + y_v + 2x_s y_t), \\
g &= (x_s + y_t \oplus 2x_u y_v, \quad x_t \oplus y_u, \quad x_u + y_v \oplus y_s, \quad x_v \oplus y_s \oplus (x_s^2 \vee 1))
\end{aligned}
$$

is an example of a nonlinear pair of orthogonal latin squares of size $2^{4n} \times 2^{4n}$.

5 The Minimality of Mappings

The mapping $x \to x + (x^2 \vee C)$, where $C = \star \cdots \star 1 \star 1_2$ is a nonlinear invertible function with a single cycle which requires only three primitive operations. The

---

[5] It is not a coincident that the functions are linear. The pair in table 1 was constructed by $(f, g) = (\alpha x + y, \beta x + y)$, where $\mathbb{F}$ is $GF_2[t]/(t^2 + t + 1)$, $\alpha = 1$, $\beta = t$. Addition in the field is just bitwise-xor — this completely explains $f^\star$, and multiplication by t is one bit left shift and xor with 11_2 in case of "carry".

natural question is whether there are any other mappings with these properties which are compositions of one, two, or three primitive operations. In the full version of the paper we describe the search technique we used to show that there are no nonlinear mappings with one or two primitive operations which have this property. In fact, the term "*number of operations* " has two possible interpretations: we can count the number of internal nodes in the parse tree of an expression, or we can count the number of instructions in a straight-line program which evaluates this expression. In the first case the only other nonlinear mapping with three operations which has a single cycle is $x \to x - (x^2 \vee C)$, where $C = \star \cdots \star 1 \star 1_2$ (note that if $x' = x + (x^2 \vee C)$ then $-x' = -x - ((-x)^2 \vee C)$ and thus each one of the sequences is the negation (mod 2^n) of the other sequence). This is true for any word size n and for any choice of n-bit constants in the mapping, and thus it is impossible to prove such a result by exhaustively searching the infinite space of all the possible mappings. In the second model there are exactly two additional families of single cycle mappings: $x \to x \pm (x \vee C)^2$, where C is any odd constant, which can be calculated with three machine operations: $r_1 = x \vee C$, $r_2 = r_1 \times r_1$, $r_3 = x \pm r_2$. However, since the squaring is not technically considered as a primitive operation, the parse tree of the expression is based on $x \pm (x \vee C)(x \vee C)$ and thus according to the previous model it has four operations. The latter model depends on the instruction set of the target CPU. For example, the `SPARC` instruction set has a command to evaluate $r_1 = x \vee C$, but in the `x86` instruction set the result in most operations is stored in place of the first operand, and thus to evaluate $r_1 = x \vee C$ we need to execute *two* operations: $r_1 = x$ and $r_1 = r_1 \vee C$. Because of this architecture dependency we use the former model in the rest of the section.

By using similar techniques, we can find the smallest number of primitive operations required to define a nonlinear latin square $f(x, y)$, where *nonlinear* means that there is a multiplication operation in which both sides depend on x and a multiplication operation in which both sides depend on y. One example is $C_0 + ((x + y) * (C_1 \vee (x + y)))$, where C_0 is odd and $C_1 = 1 \cdots 11_2$, which is actually equivalent to the linear mapping $C_0 + C_1(x + y)$. To avoid such cases we add another constraint: for any subexpression g (except C) there should be (x, y) and (x', y') such that $g(x, y) \neq g(x', y')$. Experiment shows that there are no expressions with fewer than five primitive operations satisfying these constrains and there are 188 such expressions with five primitive operations. All of them have the form $\beta * \gamma$ with four possible β and 47 possible γ.

6 Combinations of Permutations

Let $f(x)$ and $g(x)$ be arbitrary permutations over n-bit words. Their sum can never be a permutation, and their XOR is extremely unlikely to be a permutation. The problem of constructing "random looking" $f(x)$ and $g(x)$ such that $f(x)$, $g(x)$, and $f(x) \oplus g(x)$ are all permutations seems to be difficult, but we can easily construct such T-functions by analyzing their bit-slice mappings. In fact, we can choose $g(x)$ as the identity, and thus generate nonlinear and non-algebraic mappings for which both $f(x)$ and $f(x) \oplus x$ are permutations. We can easily generalize the technique and generate k permutations with the property that the XOR of any pair of them is also a permutation, or generate a single permutation $f(x)$ with the property that various polynomials in f (such as $f(f(f(x))) \oplus f(x) \oplus x$) are also permutations. Due to space limitations, we can only describe the basic idea of the construction, which is to split x into multiple variables $x_0, \ldots, x_{m-1}$, and to define $f_0, \ldots, f_{m-1}$ so that its bit-slice has the following form $[f_j]_i = \bigoplus_{k=0}^{m-1} [C_{j,k}]_i [x_k]_i \oplus \alpha_{j,i}$, where $(C_{i,j})$ is a constant matrix, such that both C and $C \oplus I$ (or both C and $C^3 \oplus C \oplus I$) are invertible.

7 Fast Iteration and Inversion of T-Functions

Consider the sequence $\{x_i\}$, where $x_{i+1} = f(x_i) \bmod 2^n$. The problem considered in this section is how to efficiently calculate x_k given x_0 and k without going through all the intermediate values. This problem has at least two cryptographic applications. If $f(x)$ is used as the state transition function in a stream cipher, the solution allows us to jump into an arbitrary position of the stream without calculating all the intermediate states. If $f(x)$ is used as the round function of a block cipher, then in order to decrypt the ciphertext we have to run $f(x)$ backwards (i.e., calculate x_{-1} in the above sequence) more efficiently than in the bit-by-bit manner considered so far. The length of each cycle of a T-function is 2^k for some $k \leq n$, and thus $x_{2^n} = x_0$ which implies that $f^{-1}(x) = x_{2^n-1}$.

Suppose that $f(x)$ is a polynomial $\hat{p}(x)$ of degree d, then the iterated expression $x_m = \hat{p}^{(m)}(x_0)$ is also some polynomial, but unfortunately its degree is d^m. Let k and l be constants such that $kl \geq n$. Any x could be represented in the following form: $x = 2^k y + r$, where $r = x \bmod 2^k$. For any fixed r there exists a polynomial p, such that $\hat{p}^{(m)}(x) = \hat{p}^{(m)}(2^k y + r) = p(2^k y)$. Although the degree of p could be as high as the degree of $p^{(m)}$, modulo 2^n all its coefficients except the first l are equal to zero: $a_i(2^k y)^i = a_i y^i 2^{ki} = 0 \pmod{2^n}$ for $i \geq l$.[6] There are 2^k possible values of r, so if we prepare a lookup table with the coefficients of p for each possible value of r then we could calculate x_k using $l-1$ multiplications and $l-1$ additions modulo 2^n.[7] Consider, for example, the RC6 function $p(x) = x + 2x^2$, and let $n = 64$, $k = 16$ and $l = 4$. The straightforward calculation of its inverse takes on average[8] $\approx \frac{n}{2} = 32$ calculations of

---

[6] Note that in order to calculate p modulo 2^n we do not need all the bits of the coefficients a_i, but only $a_i \bmod 2^{k(l-i)}$. So, in order to store the coefficients we need only $k(l + (l-1) + \cdots + 1) = \frac{kl(l+1)}{2}$ bits of memory.

[7] An interesting consequence of this is that most T-functions over n-bit words are not representable as a polynomial modulo 2^n, since in order to encode a general T-function we need $2^n + 2^{n-1} + \cdots + 2^1 = 2^{n+1} - 1$ bits of memory which is greater than the size of the table. This is in contrast to the fact that over a finite filed such as $\mathbb{Z}_p$ any function can be represented as a (very high degree) polynomial.

[8] Note that if we calculate $[f(x)]_i$ and find that $[x]_i = 0$ than we do not need to recalculate $f(x)$ in order to find $[f(x)]_{i+1}$.

$p(x)$, that is about 32 multiplications and 32 additions. Our method requires only three multiplications and three additions which is only three times slower than the forward calculation. The drawback is that our method needs a fixed precomputed table of $2^{k-1}kl(l+1) \approx 2^{23}$ bits ≈ 1 megabyte of memory, whereas the slow method does not need precomputations and memory. However, a one megabyte table is not a problem in many PC-based cryptographic applications.

To construct the lookup table we use the following property: $p^{(a+b)}(x) = p^{(a)}(p^{(b)}(x))$, so in order to calculate $p^{(2^n)}(x)$ we need n "symbolic" evaluations of polynomial of polynomial. Care must be taken to use $p[r]$ for the right r in each step, that is in the general case $r = x \bmod 2^k$ is not equal to $r' = p^{(b)}(x) \bmod 2^k$, so we need to calculate the whole table for $p^{(2^k)}(x)$ before constructing the table for $p^{(2^{k+1})}(x)$.

Unlike the RC6 function $x + 2x^2$, the function $f(x) = x + (x^2 \vee 5)$ is not a polynomial, but if $k = 3$ it is a polynomial for every possible value of r. For example, if $r = x \bmod 2^3 = 1$ then $x^2 \bmod 2^3 = 1$, whereas $x^2 \vee 5 \bmod 2^3 = 5$, so $f(x)$ can be represented by the polynomial $x + x^2 + 4$ for each such input x.

8 Cryptanalysis of $x \to x + (x^2 \vee C) \pmod{2^n}$

Our goal in this paper is to develop new efficient building blocks for larger cryptographic schemes, and in many cases the security of the building block depends on how it is used. In particular, we would like to use the $x \to x + (x^2 \vee 5) \pmod{2^n}$ mapping as a substitute for LFSRs or linear congruential `rand()` functions rather than as a stand-alone stream cipher. However, we did try to analyze the security of the exceptionally simple stream cipher which just iterates this function and sends the m most significant bits[9] of each n-bit state to the output, and discovered that it is surprisingly strong against all the attacks we could think of — the running time of all our attacks is exponential in n. The purpose of this section is to summarize our findings, but due to space limitations we outline only some of the attacks.

Any PRNG with an n-bit state could be attacked as follows. Precompute the outputs of the generator for random 2^t states, where the length of each output should be sufficient to identify uniquely the state. Sort them in order to be able to retrieve the state given the output sequence. Given 2^d actual outputs try to locate any one of them in the table. If the parameters are such that $t + d \approx n$ we have a significant probability of success. One possible choice of parameters is $t = d = \frac{n}{2}$.[10] In this case we use $O(2^{\frac{n}{2}})$ of memory and time, and thus the effective security of any PRNG is no more than $\frac{n}{2}$ bits.

---

[9] Note that the i-th least significant bit in any iterated single cycle T-function repeats every 2^i steps and depends only on the first i state bits, and thus the most significant bits are much stronger than the least significant bits in this application. In addition, we assume that $m \ll n$.

[10] Usually the processing time is cheaper than memory, and access to secondary memory takes a significant amount of time, so in practice it is better to have $t > d$. We do

Let us show how to attack our generator with the same complexity $O(2^{\frac{n}{2}})$ but without the preprocessing and additional memory, besides those which are used for the output sequence itself. Consider $x_i = \underbrace{\star\ldots\star}_{\frac{n}{2}}\underbrace{0\ldots0}_{\frac{n}{2}}$, that is $x_i = 2^{\frac{n}{2}}y$ for some y. In this case $x_i^2 = 0 \pmod{2^n}$, so $x_{i+1} = x_i + 5 \bmod 2^n$, and thus with high probability the most significant bits of x_{i+1} are the same as those of x_i. On the other hand if x_i does not end with $\frac{n}{2}$ zeros then the probability that the m most significant bits of x_i and x_{i+1} are the same is approximately 2^{-m}. Also note that if $x_i = 2^{\frac{n}{2}}y$ then $x_{i+2^{\frac{n}{2}}} = 2^{\frac{n}{2}}y'$. So, checking a few pairs of the outputs with a $2^{\frac{n}{2}}$ shift between the pairs we could identify the point at which the least significant halves of $x_{i+l2^{\frac{n}{2}}}$ are zeros. It is also guaranteed that one of any $2^{\frac{n}{2}}$ consecutive x_i's has this property.

We now describe an improved attack in which the data, time and memory complexities are of order $2^{\frac{n}{3}}$. Let $x = 2^{\frac{2n}{3}}x_u + 2^{\frac{n}{3}}x_v + x_w$ and suppose that $x_w = 0$. In this case $(2^{\frac{2n}{3}}x_u + 2^{\frac{n}{3}}x_v + x_w) \to (2^{\frac{2n}{3}}x_u + 2^{\frac{n}{3}}x_v + x_w) + ((2^{\frac{2n}{3}}x_u + 2^{\frac{n}{3}}x_v + x_w)^2 \vee 5) = 2^{\frac{2n}{3}}(x_u + x_v^2) + 2^{\frac{n}{3}}x_v + 5 \pmod{2^n}$, and so the difference between the most significant bits of consecutive outputs is approximately x_v^2. If x_v is known (and $x_w = 0$) we can easily calculate the value of x_v after $2^{\frac{n}{3}}k$ steps for several k. If we make a lookup table of these values for all possible x_v we can find x_v after inspecting a few pairs of the outputs with a $2^{\frac{n}{3}}$ shift between them.

To reduce the amount of data needed to attack the generator, we can use a different approach. In section 7 it was shown how to represent x_i as a polynomial of degree $l-1$ in $x_0 - r$ if $r = x_0 \bmod 2^k$ was guessed correctly. Given $\{x_i = a_{i,l-1}y_0^{l-1} + \cdots + a_{i,0}\}_{i=0}^{p-1}$ it is possible, as we will see below, to find $\{\beta_i \in \{-1,0,+1\}\}_{i=0}^{p-1}$ such that

$$\forall j, \sum_{i=0}^{p-1} \beta_i a_{i,j} = 0 \pmod{2^{k(l-j)}}. \tag{4}$$

If the sum is zero as a polynomial then $S = \sum \beta_i x_i = 0$ as long as the k least significant bits of x_0 are guessed correctly. On the other hand if the guess is incorrect then S is likely to be random. Provided that we could distinguish these cases we could find the k least significant bits of x_0 after about $\frac{2^k}{2}$ tests. Using the same technique while incrementing k we could find the rest of the state x_0. The only two remaining questions are:

- How to notice that $\sum \beta_i x_i = 0$ given only the m most significant bits of x_i?
- How to find those β_i?

---

not store all the preprocessed sequences but only those that have some distinguishable feature (like starting with l zeros), thus reducing memory and postprocessing time by factor of 2^l.

Let us denote by u_i the m most significant bits of x_i, that is $x_i = 2^{n-m}u_i + v_i$, where $v_i < 2^{n-m}$. This way

$$S = \sum_{i=0}^{p-1} \beta_i x_i = 2^{n-m} \sum_{i=0}^{p-1} \beta_i u_i + \sum_{i=0}^{p-1} \beta_i v_i = 2^{n-m} A \ + B \pmod{2^n}.$$

If the guess is correct, then $S = 0 \pmod{2^n}$, and thus $B = S = 0 \pmod{2^{n-m}}$. Let us denote $B' = \frac{B}{2^{n-m}}$. In the general case $B' = q2^m - A$, where $q \in \mathbb{Z}$ and $A \in [1, 2^m]$. If $p < 2^m$ then $B' < 2^m$ so an attacker could calculate $B' = -A \bmod 2^m$ and it should behave approximately as the sum of p uniformly distributed in $[0,1]$ random variables which is approximately normal with mean $\frac{p}{2}$. On the other hand if the guess is wrong A should be uniformly distributed in $[1, 2^m]$. An attacker can easily tell apart the cases by inspecting the expectation (average) of A for several different tuples $\{\beta_i\}$. If $p > 2^m$ the test of the expectation is not sufficient because B' is not guaranteed to be less than 2^m and thus q is not always 1. But if $p < 2^{2m}$ then $\mathrm{Var}(B') \approx \frac{p}{12}$ so the standard deviation is smaller than 2^{m-1} and thus with high probability $q = 1 + \lfloor \frac{p}{2^{m+1}} \rfloor$, so $A = q2^m - B'$ is normal and $\mathrm{Var}(A) \approx \frac{p}{12}$. On the other hand if the guess is incorrect $\mathrm{Var}A \approx \frac{2^{2m}}{12}$, so an attacker again could tell if his guess is correct.

The second question is more difficult. The probability that a random polynomial conform to (4) is 2^{-t}, where $t = \frac{kl(l+1)}{2}$. There are 3^p ways to assign $\{-1, 0, +1\}$ to $\{\beta_i\}_{i=0}^{p-1}$, so as long as $p > \tau t$, where $\tau = \frac{\log 3}{\log 2} \approx 0.63$ such tuple exists with high probability. For example if $k = 16$ and $l = 4$ then t$= 160$ and $p > 101$. Unfortunately, exhaustive search would take $O(t)$ time which is not practical even for a precomputation step. There are several *practical* approaches to the problem.

We could relax the problem of finding $\beta_i \in \{-1, 0, +1\}$ conforming to (4) to finding β_i which are small integers. The new problem could be solved by LLL reduction of the following (row) lattice:

$$\begin{pmatrix}
1\,0\,0 \cdots 0 & a_{0,0}\psi & a_{0,0}\psi & \cdots & a_{0,l-1}\psi \\
0\,1\,0 \cdots 0 & a_{1,0}\psi & a_{1,0}\psi & \cdots & a_{1,l-1}\psi \\
0\,0\,1 \cdots 0 & a_{2,0}\psi & a_{2,0}\psi & \cdots & a_{2,l-1}\psi \\
\vdots \quad \ddots \ \vdots & \vdots & \vdots & \vdots & \vdots \\
0\,0\,0 \cdots 1 & a_{p-1,0}\psi & a_{p-1,0}\psi & \cdots & a_{p-1,l-1}\psi \\
0\,0\,0 \cdots 0 & 2^{kl}\psi & 0 & \cdots & 0 \\
0\,0\,0 \cdots 0 & 0 & 2^{k(l-1)}\psi & \cdots & 0 \\
\vdots\,\vdots\,\vdots\ \vdots\ \vdots & \vdots & \vdots & \ddots & \vdots \\
0\,0\,0 \cdots 0 & 0 & 0 & \cdots & 2^{k}\psi
\end{pmatrix},$$

where ψ is a sufficiently large constant. If $p > \tau t$ we know that the squared length of the smallest vector in the lattice is smaller than p. On the other hand LLL algorithm with $\frac{1}{4} < \delta \leq 1$ is guaranteed to return a non-zero basis vector which is no more than $\left(\frac{1}{\delta - \frac{1}{4}}\right)^{p+l-1}$ times longer then the shortest vector in the lattice. This theoretical guarantee is not acceptable but in practice LLL behaves much better. For example, if[11] $p = 160$, the LLL algorithm returns after a few seconds on a standard PC a vector such that $\sum_i |\beta_i| = 108$ and $\max_i |\beta_i| = 9$.

In order to solve efficiently the exact problem we could use a variation [2] of Wagner's algorithm [7]. Given approximately 2^ω (for our purposes $\omega^2 = t$) members $\{x_i\}$ of a group $G' = G^\omega$ ($|G| = 2^\omega$) and the target value $z \in G'$ it finds $\{\beta_i\}$ from $\{-1, 0, +1\}$ such that $\sum_i \beta_i x_i = z$ using $O(2^\omega)$ time and memory. By using this approach we are not limited to zero on the right hand side of (4), so we could find $\{\beta_i\}$ such that $\sum_i \beta_i x_i(y) = 2^m y$ and thus reveal the m most significant bits of y or, equivalently, of x_0 instead of repeating with larger k's. For example, if $n = 64$, $k = 16$, $l = \frac{n}{k} = 4$, $t = \frac{kl(l+1)}{2} = 160$, $\omega = 13$, then preprocessing and checking each of 2^k consecutive positions needs roughly $O(2^{16})$ data, memory and time. Note that this attack works only if the constant C is smaller than 2^k, so if, for example, size of C is $\frac{n}{3}$ the attack is still exponential and requires $O(2^{\frac{n}{3}})$ time.

References

[1] V. Anashin, "Uniformly Distributed Sequences of p-adic integers, II", To appear in Diskretnaya Mathematika (Russian), English translation in Diskrete Mathematics (Plenum Publ.). Available from `http://www.arxiv.org/ps/math.NT/0209407`. 250

[2] A. Joux, "Cryptanalysis of the EMD Mode of Operation", EUROCRYPT 2003. 261

[3] A. Klimov and A. Shamir, "*A New Class of Invertible Mappings*", CHES 2002. 249, 250, 253

[4] R. Rivest, M. Robshaw, R. Sidney, and Y. L. Yin, "*The RC6 block cipher*". Available from `http://www.rsa.com/rsalabs/rc6/`.

[5] R. Rivest, "Permutation Polynomials Modulo 2^ω", 1999. 254

[6] S. Vaudenay, "On the need for multipermutations: Cryptanalysis of MD4 and SAFER", FSE 1995. 253

[7] D. Wagner, "A Generalized Birthday Problem", CRYPTO 2002. 261

[11] In fact $\{\beta_i = 0\}_{i=54}^{p-1}$, so the same vector is returned if $p = 54$.

On the Success of the Embedding Attack on the Alternating Step Generator

Jovan Dj. Golić

System on Chip, Telecom Italia Lab
Telecom Italia
Via Guglielmo Reiss Romoli 274, I-00148 Turin, Italy
jovan.golic@tilab.com

Abstract. The edit distance correlation attack on the well-known alternating step generator for stream cipher applications was proposed by Golić and Menicocci. The attack can be successful only if the probability of the zero edit distance, the so-called embedding probability, conditioned on a given segment of the output sequence, decreases with the segment length, and if the decrease is exponential, then the required segment length is linear in the total length of the two linear feedback shift registers involved. The exponential decrease for the maximal value of the embedding probability as a function of the given output segment was estimated experimentally by Golić and Menicocci. In this paper, by using the connection with the interleaving and decimation operations, the embedding probability is theoretically analyzed. Tight exponentially small upper bounds on the maximal embedding probability are thus derived. Sharp exponentially small lower and upper bounds on the minimal embedding probability are also determined.

Index Terms: Correlation attack, decimation, edit distance, embedding probability, interleaving, sequences.

1 Introduction

It is well known that stream ciphers based on irregularly clocked linear feedback shift registers (LFSR's) are suitable for hardware implementations and can achieve a reasonably high security against secret key reconstruction attacks in the known plaintext scenario. Correlation attacks are a general class of divide-and-conquer attacks that aim at reconstructing the initial states of a subset of the LFSR's and use appropriate correlation measures between the known output sequence and the output sequences of the targeted LFSR's when regularly clocked. Such attacks based on the appropriately defined edit distances and edit probabilities are introduced in [1] and [2], respectively, and further analyzed in [3]. They are applicable to LFSR's that are clocked at least once per each output bit produced. In the case of a single irregularly clocked LFSR, the edit distances measure the possibility and the edit probabilities measure the probability of obtaining the output sequence from the assumed LFSR sequence, where

M. Matsui and R. Zuccherato (Eds.): SAC 2003, LNCS 3006, pp. 262-274, 2004.

the sequence controlling the clocking is not known. Therefore, such attacks can be called the embedding and probabilistic correlation attacks, respectively, and the embedding attack is first introduced in [9].

The stop-and-go (stop/go) clocking is particularly interesting for high speed applications. At any time, a stop/go shift register is clocked once if the clock-control input bit is equal to 1 (or 0) and is not clocked at all otherwise. The well-known alternating step generator (ASG) proposed in [6] consists of two stop/go clocked binary LFSR's, LFSR_X and LFSR_Y, and a clock-control regularly clocked binary LFSR, LFSR_C. At each time, the clock-control bit defines which of the two LFSR's is clocked, and the output sequence is obtained as the bitwise sum of the two stop/go clocked LFSR sequences. Some standard cryptographic properties of the ASG, such as a long period, a high linear complexity, and approximately uniform relative frequency of short output patterns on a period are established in [6], under the assumption that the clock-control sequence is a de Bruijn sequence and that the feedback polynomials of LFSR_X and LFSR_Y are primitive. It is expected that similar results also hold if the the clock-control sequence is produced by another LFSR, LFSR_C, with a primitive feedback polynomial whose period is coprime to the periods of LFSR_X and LFSR_Y.

It is shown in [6] that the initial state of LFSR_C can be recovered by a specific divide-and-conquer attack based on the fact that if and only if the guess about the initial state of LFSR_C is correct, then the first (binary) derivative of the ASG output sequence can be deinterleaved into the first derivatives of the regularly clocked LFSR_X and LFSR_Y sequences, which are then easily tested for low linear complexity.

An edit distance correlation attack targeting LFSR_X and LFSR_Y simultaneously is proposed in [4]. The specific edit distance incorporating the stop/go clocking is defined between one output string and two input strings. The output string is a given segment of the ASG output sequence and the input strings are the segments of the output sequences of LFSR_X and LFSR_Y whose initial states are guessed. An efficient algorithm for computing the edit distance is derived in [4]. Note that the attack has a divide-and-conquer effect since the unknown initial state of LFSR_C is not guessed.

If the initial states of LFSR_X and LFSR_Y are guessed correctly, then the edit distance is equal to zero. The zero edit distance means that the given segment of the ASG output sequence can be obtained from the assumed segments of the output sequences of LFSR_X and LFSR_Y by the stop/go clocking as in the ASG. In other words, it means that the ASG-embedding is possible. If the guess is incorrect, then the probability of obtaining the zero edit distance from random input strings, i.e., the ASG-embedding probability has to decrease with the output segment length in order for the attack to be successful, and if this decrease is exponential, then the required output segment length is linear in the total length of LFSR_X and LFSR_Y. This is because the expected number of false candidates for the initial states of LFSR_X and LFSR_Y can be approximated as the product of the ASG-embedding probability and the total number of incorrect guesses.

The experimental results from [4] indicate that the decrease of the ASG-embedding probability is exponential and that the output segment length of about four total lengths of LFSR_X and LFSR_Y is sufficient for success. Theoretical derivation and analysis of the maximal, average, and minimal values of the ASG-embedding probability, as a function of the given output segment, is qualified in [4] as a nontrivial combinatorial problem. Its solution is practically important for proving that the zero-edit-distance correlation attack on the ASG is successful if the output segment length is sufficiently large.

A partial step in this direction is made in [7] where an exponentially small upper bound on the average ASG-embedding probability is established by using the connection with the interleaving operation. Of course, this does not imply an exponentially small upper bound on the maximal ASG-embedding probability, which is needed to solve the problem completely. The main objective of this paper is to provide a more effective solution to the problem by deriving exponentially small upper bounds on the maximal ASG-embedding probability. This is achieved by a mathematically more involved approach using the connection with the interleaving and decimation operations.

Although it is out of the scope of this paper, it is interesting to mention that a correlation attack on an individual LFSR, either LFSR_X or LFSR_Y, which is based on a specific edit probability is later developed in [5]. For a similar approach, more explicitly using the connection with the interleaving and decimation operations, see [8]. Note that for individual LFSR's, the edit distance attack cannot be successful, due to a result from [3] regarding the embedding attack on irregularly clocked shift registers. By experimental analysis of the underlying statistical hypothesis testing problem, it is shown in [5] that the output segment length equal to about forty lengths of the targeted LFSR is sufficient for success. Theoretical analysis of this problem is very difficult and is related to the theoretically still open capacity problem for a communication channel with deletion errors.

This paper is organized as follows. In Section 2, the mathematical definitions of the ASG-embedding probability and the related interleaving and decimation probabilities are introduced. Some basic relations among these probabilities are established in Section 3. By analyzing the decimation probability, various exponentially small upper bounds on the maximal ASG-embedding probability are derived in Section 4. By analyzing the interleaving probability, exponentially small lower and upper bounds on the minimal ASG-embedding probability are determined in Section 5. Conclusions are presented in Section 6.

2 Preliminaries

For a binary sequence $A = a_0, a_1, \cdots$ or $A = a_1, a_2, \cdots$, let $A_k = a_k, a_{k+1}, \cdots$ and let $A_k^n = a_k, a_{k+1}, \cdots, a_n$ denote a segment of length $n - k + 1$. Formally, A_k^n is empty if $k > n$ and, for simplicity, let $A^n = A_1^n$. Further, the first (binary) derivative of A is denoted by $\dot{A} = \dot{a}_0, \dot{a}_1, \cdots$, where $\dot{a}_i = a_i \oplus a_{i+1}$ and $\oplus$ stands for the binary (modulo 2) addition. The (binary) complement of A is denoted by

$\overline{A} = \overline{a}_0, \overline{a}_1, \cdots$, where $\overline{a}_i = a_i \oplus 1$. As usual, $A^m B^n$ denotes the concatenation of A^m and B^n, whereas a^n denotes a constant sequence $a, a, \cdots, a$.

Let X, Y, and C be the output sequences of LFSR$_X$, LFSR$_Y$, and LFSR$_C$ in the ASG, respectively. Assuming the step-then-add mode of operation, the ASG output sequence $Z = z_1, z_2, \cdots$ is generated as follows. Initially, the first bits of X and Y, that is, x_0 and y_0 are produced. For each $t \geq 1$, depending on whether c_{t-1} equals 1 or 0, the next bit of X or Y is produced, respectively, and the output bit z_t is obtained as the binary sum of the last produced bits of X and Y. The ASG output sequence produced from X_0^n, Y_0^n, and C_0^{n-1} is denoted as $Z^n = Z_1^n = \text{ASG}(X_0^n, Y_0^n, C_0^{n-1})$, where $n \geq 1$.

Let $W^n = \text{INT}(U^n, V^n, C^n)$ denote the sequence obtained by interleaving U^n and V^n according to C^n, w_i being taken from U^n if $c_i = 1$ and from V^n if $c_i = 0$. The ASG and interleaving operations are connected by

$$\dot{Z}_1^{n-1} = \begin{cases} \text{INT}(\dot{X}_1^{n-1}, \dot{Y}_0^{n-2}, C_1^{n-1}) \text{ if } c_0 = 1 \\ \text{INT}(\dot{X}_0^{n-2}, \dot{Y}_1^{n-1}, C_1^{n-1}) \text{ if } c_0 = 0 \end{cases}. \tag{1}$$

Our main objective is to analyze the *ASG-embedding* probability that is according to [4] defined as the conditional probability

$$P_n(Z^n) = \Pr\{(X_0^n, Y_0^n) \,|\, (\exists C_0^{n-1})\, \text{ASG}(X_0^n, Y_0^n, C_0^{n-1}) = Z^n\} \tag{2}$$

in the probabilistic model in which X and Y are assumed to be mutually independent sequences of independent uniformly distributed binary random variables. In this model,

$$P_n(Z^n) = \frac{1}{2^{2(n+1)}} |\{(X_0^n, Y_0^n) : (\exists C_0^{n-1})\, \text{ASG}(X_0^n, Y_0^n, C_0^{n-1}) = Z^n\}|. \tag{3}$$

We similarly define the *interleaving probability* as

$$p_n(W^n) = \frac{1}{2^{2n}} |\{(U^n, V^n) : (\exists C^n)\, \text{INT}(U^n, V^n, C^n) = W^n\}|. \tag{4}$$

Both probabilities are invariant under complementation, that is,

$$P_n(\overline{Z}^n) = P_n(Z^n) \tag{5}$$

$$p_n(\overline{W}^n) = p_n(W^n). \tag{6}$$

We are particularly interested in deriving the maximal and minimal values of the two probabilities over Z^n and W^n, respectively. They are denoted as $P_n^{\max}$, $p_n^{\max}$, $P_n^{\min}$, and $p_n^{\min}$, respectively. The empirical estimates from [4] are $P_n^{\max} \approx 0.72 \cdot 0.915^n$ and $P_n^{\min} \approx 2.7 \cdot 0.562^n$.

To this end, we introduce the decimation operation by $U^k = \text{DEC}(W^n, C^n)$ where w_i is taken to the output if $c_i = 1$ and discarded if $c_i = 0$, and $k = h(C^n)$ is the Hamming weight of C^n (for $k = 0$, U^0 is empty). Let

$$D_k(W^n) = \{U^k : (\exists C^n)\, \text{DEC}(W^n, C^n) = U^k\}, \quad 0 \leq k \leq n \tag{7}$$

$$\nu_n(W^n) = \frac{1}{2^n} \sum_{k=0}^{n} |D_k(W^n)|. \tag{8}$$

Clearly, $|D_k(W^n)| \geq 1$ and $|D_0(W^n)| = |D_n(W^n)| = 1$. Accordingly, $\nu_1(W^1) = 1$ and

$$(n+1)2^{-n} \leq \nu_n(W^n) \leq 1. \tag{9}$$

Since $\sum_{k=0}^{n} |D_k(W^n)|$ is the number of sequences, of various lengths, that can be obtained by decimating W^n, we can call $\nu_n(W^n)$ the *decimation probability* . Like $p_n(W^n)$, $\nu_n(W^n)$ is also invariant under complementation (see (6)). One can analogously define its maximal and minimal values, respectively.

3 Basic Relations

Lemma 1, based on the characterization (1), determines the relation between P_n and p_{n-1}. Lemma 2 specifies a basic relation between the interleaving probability p_n and the decimation probability ν_n. *Throughout the paper, in all the mathematical results stated, it is assumed that the unspeci□ed quantities take arbitrary values* (e.g., n and Z^n in Lemma 1).

Lemma 1.

$$\frac{3}{4} p_{n-1}(\dot{Z}^{n-1}) \leq P_n(Z^n) \leq p_{n-1}(\dot{Z}^{n-1}). \tag{10}$$

The same inequalities hold for the maximal and minimal values, respectively.

Proof The set $\{(X_0^n, Y_0^n) : (\exists C_0^{n-1})\, \mathrm{ASG}(X_0^n, Y_0^n, C_0^{n-1}) = Z^n\}$ can be partitioned into three subsets according to $x_0 \oplus y_1 = z_1 \neq x_1 \oplus y_0$, $x_0 \oplus y_1 = \overline{z}_1 \neq x_1 \oplus y_0$, and $x_0 \oplus y_1 = x_1 \oplus y_0 = z_1$. In the first two subsets (X_0^n, Y_0^n) uniquely determines c_0, whereas in the third subset this is not true. In view of (1), we first get

$$\begin{aligned}
&|\{(X_0^n, Y_0^n) : x_0 \oplus y_1 = z_1 \neq x_1 \oplus y_0, (\exists C_0^{n-1})\, \mathrm{ASG}(X_0^n, Y_0^n, C_0^{n-1}) = Z^n\}| \\
&\quad = |\{(X_0^n, Y_0^n) : x_0 \oplus y_1 = z_1 \neq x_1 \oplus y_0, \\
&\qquad\qquad (\exists C_1^{n-1})\, \mathrm{INT}(\dot{X}_0^{n-2}, \dot{Y}_1^{n-1}, C_1^{n-1}) = \dot{Z}^{n-1}\}| \\
&\quad = 4\, |\{(\dot{X}_0^{n-2}, \dot{Y}_1^{n-1}) : (\exists C_1^{n-1})\, \mathrm{INT}(\dot{X}_0^{n-2}, \dot{Y}_1^{n-1}, C_1^{n-1}) = \dot{Z}^{n-1}\}|
\end{aligned} \tag{11}$$

since $c_0 = 0$ and both x_0 and x_n can take arbitrary values. Analogous equation holds if $x_0 \oplus y_1 = \overline{z}_1 \neq x_1 \oplus y_0$, in which case $c_0 = 1$ and y_0 and y_n can be arbitrary. Consequently, we get

$$\begin{aligned}
&|\{(X_0^n, Y_0^n) : x_0 \oplus y_1 \neq x_1 \oplus y_0, (\exists C_0^{n-1})\, \mathrm{ASG}(X_0^n, Y_0^n, C_0^{n-1}) = Z^n\}| \\
&\quad = 8\, |\{(U^{n-1}, V^{n-1}) : (\exists C^{n-1})\, \mathrm{INT}(U^{n-1}, V^{n-1}, C^{n-1}) = \dot{Z}^{n-1}\}|.
\end{aligned} \tag{12}$$

In the remaining case $x_0 \oplus y_1 = x_1 \oplus y_0 = z_1$, c_0 can take both values. For $c_0 = 0$, similarly as (11), we get

$$\begin{aligned} &|\{(X_0^n, Y_0^n) : x_0 \oplus y_1 = x_1 \oplus y_0 = z_1, \\ &\qquad (\exists C_0^{n-1})\,(c_0 = 0, \mathrm{ASG}(X_0^n, Y_0^n, C_0^{n-1}) = Z^n)\}| \\ &= |\{(X_0^n, Y_0^n) : x_0 \oplus y_1 = x_1 \oplus y_0 = z_1, \\ &\qquad (\exists C_1^{n-1})\,\mathrm{INT}(\dot{X}_0^{n-2}, \dot{Y}_1^{n-1}, C_1^{n-1}) = \dot{Z}^{n-1}\}| \\ &= 4\,|\{(\dot{X}_0^{n-2}, \dot{Y}_1^{n-1}) : (\exists C_1^{n-1})\,\mathrm{INT}(\dot{X}_0^{n-2}, \dot{Y}_1^{n-1}, C_1^{n-1}) = \dot{Z}^{n-1}\}|. \qquad (13) \end{aligned}$$

Analogous equation is obtained for $c_0 = 1$, but the two corresponding subsets are not necessarily disjoint. Accordingly, we get

$$\begin{aligned} &4\,|\{(U^{n-1}, V^{n-1}) : (\exists C^{n-1})\,\mathrm{INT}(U^{n-1}, V^{n-1}, C^{n-1}) = \dot{Z}^{n-1}\}| \\ &\le |\{(X_0^n, Y_0^n) : x_0 \oplus y_1 = x_1 \oplus y_0, (\exists C_0^{n-1})\,\mathrm{ASG}(X_0^n, Y_0^n, C_0^{n-1}) = Z^n\}| \\ &\le 8\,|\{(U^{n-1}, V^{n-1}) : (\exists C^{n-1})\,\mathrm{INT}(U^{n-1}, V^{n-1}, C^{n-1}) = \dot{Z}^{n-1}\}|. \qquad (14) \end{aligned}$$

Finally, (10) is a direct consequence of (3), (4), (12), and (14). □

Lemma 2.

$$2^{-n} \le p_n(W^n) \le \nu_n(W^n). \qquad (15)$$

The same inequalities hold for the maximal and minimal values, respectively.

Proof The inequalities directly follow from

$$p_n(W^n) = \frac{1}{2^{2n}}\,|\cup_{k=0}^{n}\{(U^n, V^n) : (\exists C^n)\,(h(C^n) = k, \mathrm{INT}(U^n, V^n, C^n) = W^n)\}| \qquad (16)$$

$$|\{(U^n, V^n) : (\exists C^n)\,(h(C^n) = k, \mathrm{INT}(U^n, V^n, C^n) = W^n)\}| = 2^n |D_k(W^n)|, \qquad (17)$$

and (17) follows from the fact that when $h(C^n) = k$, then $\mathrm{INT}(U^n, V^n, C^n) = W^n$ holds iff $U^k = \mathrm{DEC}(W^n, C^n)$ and $V^{n-k} = \mathrm{DEC}(W^n, \overline{C}^n)$, whereas the remaining n bits of (U^n, V^n) are arbitrary. □

4 Maximal Probabilities

Our approach consists of obtaining exponentially small upper bounds on the maximal ASG-embedding probability $P_n^{\max}$ by deriving appropriate upper bounds on the decimation probability ν_n. An analytical method for deriving an upper bound on ν_n is presented in Section 4.1 and is further refined in Section 4.3 to determine $\nu_n^{\max}$ and thus obtain the tightest upper bound in terms of the decimation probability. A method based on a concatenation lemma and direct counting is given in Section 4.2.

4.1 Analytical Upper Bound

A run in a binary sequence W is a maximal-length segment of W that consists of equal bits. A binary sequence W^n can uniquely be represented as a sequence of r runs and let $L^r = l_1, l_2, \cdots, l_r$ denote the positive integer sequence of the run lengths. Accordingly, $\sum_{i=1}^{r} l_i = n$. Clearly, the only two sequences with the same L^r are W^n and $\overline{W}^n$.

Our objective is to derive an upper bound on $\nu_n(W^n)$ that is strictly smaller than 1 for every r and then use it to obtain an exponentially small upper bound on $P_n^{\max}$ by applying Lemmas 1 and 2. Our most involved mathematical result is the following lemma, which uses the concept of minimal decimation sequences introduced in [3].

Lemma 3.

$$\nu_n(W^n) < \frac{1}{2^n}\,\frac{\sqrt{5}+2}{\sqrt{5}}\left(\frac{\sqrt{5}+1}{2}\right)^r \prod_{i=1}^{r} l_i \le \frac{1}{2^n}\,\frac{\sqrt{5}+2}{\sqrt{5}}\left(\frac{\sqrt{5}+1}{2}\right)^r \left(\frac{n}{r}\right)^r. \quad (18)$$

Proof Every decimation sequence C^n such that $h(C^n) = k \ge 1$ can uniquely be represented as an increasing sequence of positive integers $i_1, i_2, \cdots, i_k$ where i_j is the index of the jth 1 in C^n. Now, for given W^n and U^k, there may exist different C^n such that $U^k = \mathrm{DEC}(W^n, C^n)$. However, as observed in [3], for any W^n and each U^k that can be obtained by decimating W^n, there exists a unique decimation sequence $\tilde{C}^n$ such that $U^k = \mathrm{DEC}(W^n, \tilde{C}^n)$ and that either $k = 0$ or $\tilde{C}^n$ is minimal in the sense that, for each j, i_j is minimal on the set of all C^n such that $U^k = \mathrm{DEC}(W^n, C^n)$.

Such a decimation sequence is called the minimal decimation sequence and can be recursively constructed as follows: i_1 is the index of the first bit of W^n equal to u_1, and for each $j \ge 2$, i_j is the index of the first bit w_i, $i > i_{j-1}$, equal to u_j. The constructed sequence is the unique minimal decimation sequence, because if we suppose that there exists a sequence C'^n such that $i'_j < i_j$ for at least one value of j, then we get a contradiction. Namely, from the construction it then follows that $i'_{j'} < i_{j'}$ for every $j' < j$, which is impossible for $j' = 1$.

Since, for a given W^n, there is an 1-1 correspondence between the minimal decimation sequences and all possible U^k, $\sum_{k=0}^{n} |D_k(W^n)|$ is equal to the number of the minimal decimation sequences given W^n. Each $\tilde{C}^n$ can be characterized by an r-bit sequence $D^r = d_1, \cdots, d_r$ such that $d_i = 1$ iff at least one bit from the ith run of W^n is taken to the output as well as by the numbers of bits taken to the output from each of these s runs, where $s = h(D^r)$. The constraints stemming from the definition of minimal decimation sequences are that there can exist no two consecutive 0's in D^r except at the end and that if $d_i = 1$ and $d_{i+1} = 0$, then the number of bits taken to the output from the ith run is maximal possible, that is, l_i. Let M_s denote the number of all such D^r, $s = h(D^r)$, $0 \le s \le r$.

Consequently, we obtain

$$\sum_{k=0}^{n} |D_k(W^n)| \le \sum_{s=0}^{r} M_s \prod_{i=1}^{r} l_i \le \left(\frac{n}{r}\right)^r \sum_{s=0}^{r} M_s \quad (19)$$

where, to get the right-hand inequality, we used $\sum_{i=1}^{r} l_i = n$ and the well-known inequality relating the geometric and arithmetic means, for nonnegative real numbers x_i, $1 \leq i \leq r$,

$$(\prod_{i=1}^{r} x_i)^{1/r} \leq \frac{1}{r} \sum_{i=1}^{r} x_i. \tag{20}$$

It remains to determine $\sum_{s=0}^{r} M_s$, which is the total number of r-bit sequences that can contain consecutive 0's only at the end. It is convenient to represent this number as $\sum_{j=0}^{r} N_j$, where N_j is the number of such sequences with the additional property that j is the index of the last bit equal to 1 (where $j = 0$ means that there are no 1's at all). It follows that $N_0 = N_1 = 1$. Let $\mathcal{N}_j$ denote the set of all j-bit sequences with the jth bit equal to 1 and without consecutive 0's, $j \geq 1$. If $B^j = b_1, \cdots, b_j \in \mathcal{N}_j$, then b_{j-1} can be equal to 1 or 0. In the former case, $B^{j-1} \in \mathcal{N}_{j-1}$ and in the latter case, $B^{j-2} \in \mathcal{N}_{j-2}$. Accordingly, we get

$$N_j = N_{j-1} + N_{j-2}, \quad j \geq 2. \tag{21}$$

Therefore $N_0, N_1, N_2, \cdots$ is the Fibonacci sequence, so that $\sum_{j=0}^{r} N_j$ can be expressed as

$$\begin{aligned} \sum_{j=0}^{r} N_j &= \frac{\sqrt{5}+2}{\sqrt{5}} \left(\frac{\sqrt{5}+1}{2}\right)^r + \frac{\sqrt{5}-2}{\sqrt{5}} \left(\frac{1-\sqrt{5}}{2}\right)^r - 1 \\ &< \frac{\sqrt{5}+2}{\sqrt{5}} \left(\frac{\sqrt{5}+1}{2}\right)^r . \end{aligned} \tag{22}$$

Finally, (19), (22), and (8) result in (18). □

Theorem 1.

$$P_n^{\max} \leq p_{n-1}^{\max} \leq \nu_{n-1}^{\max} < \frac{\sqrt{5}+2}{\sqrt{5}} \left(\frac{1}{2} e^{\frac{\sqrt{5}+1}{2e}}\right)^{n-1} < 2.08929 \cdot 0.906735^n. \tag{23}$$

Proof Lemma 1 and Lemma 2 imply that $P_n^{\max} \leq p_{n-1}^{\max} \leq \nu_{n-1}^{\max}$. Let

$$\alpha = \frac{\sqrt{5}+1}{2}, \quad \beta = \frac{\alpha}{e}. \tag{24}$$

Equation (18) from Lemma 3 can be put into the form

$$\nu_n(W^n) < \frac{\sqrt{5}+2}{\sqrt{5}} \left(\frac{1}{2} e^{f(r/n)}\right)^n \tag{25}$$

where $f(\gamma) = \gamma \ln \alpha - \gamma \ln \gamma$, $\gamma = r/n$. Accordingly, we have

$$\nu_n^{\max} < \frac{\sqrt{5}+2}{\sqrt{5}} \left(\frac{1}{2} e^{f_{\max}}\right)^n \tag{26}$$

where $f_{\max}$ is the maximum of $f(\gamma)$ on $(0,1]$. It is easy to prove that f'' is negative and hence f is concave and has a unique maximum reached for $\gamma = \beta$. Consequently, we get (23). □

The upper bound in (23) is smaller than 1 for $n \geq 8$.

4.2 Concatenation Upper Bounds

It is interesting that direct counting by computer simulations can be used to obtain exponentially small upper bounds on $\nu_n^{\max}$ via the following concatenation lemma for the decimation probability ν_n. This lemma and the resulting theorem have counterparts pertaining to the embedding probability for an embedding correlation attack on irregularly clocked shift registers under a constraint on the maximal number of consecutive clocks (see [9] and [3]).

Lemma 4.

$$\nu_{m+n}(A^m B^n) \leq \nu_m(A^m)\nu_n(B^n). \tag{27}$$

The same inequality holds for the maximal and minimal values, respectively.

Proof According to the definition of the decimation operation, it follows that $\mathrm{DEC}(A^m B^n, C^{m+n}) = W^k$ is true iff there exist k_1 and k_2 such that $0 \leq k_1 \leq m$, $0 \leq k_2 \leq n$, $k_1 + k_2 = k$, $W^k = U^{k_1}V^{k_2}$, $\mathrm{DEC}(A^m, C^m) = U^{k_1}$, and $\mathrm{DEC}(B^n, C_{m+1}^{m+n}) = V^{k_2}$. This then implies that

$$|D_k(A^m B^n)| \leq \sum_{k_1,k_2} |D_{k_1}(A^m)||D_{k_2}(B^n)| \tag{28}$$

where the sum is over all the permitted values of k_1 and k_2. Therefore, we obtain

$$\sum_{k=0}^{m+n} |D_k(A^m B^n)| \leq \sum_{k_1=0}^{m} |D_{k_1}(A^m)| \sum_{k_2=0}^{n} |D_{k_2}(B^n)| \tag{29}$$

which in view of (8) directly yields (27). □

Theorem 2.

$$P_n^{\max} \leq p_{n-1}^{\max} \leq \nu_{n-1}^{\max} \leq \eta_m (\nu_m^{\max})^{n/m} \tag{30}$$

$$\eta_m = \frac{1}{(\nu_m^{\max})^{1/m}} \max_{0 \leq l \leq m-1} \frac{\nu_l^{\max}}{(\nu_m^{\max})^{l/m}}. \tag{31}$$

Proof Let $n - 1 = m\lfloor (n-1)/m \rfloor + l$, $0 \leq l \leq m-1$. As a direct consequence of Lemma 4, we get

$$\nu_{n-1}^{\max} \leq \nu_l^{\max} (\nu_m^{\max})^{\lfloor (n-1)/m \rfloor} \tag{32}$$

and then (30) and (31) easily follow in light of Lemmas 1 and 2. □

By using Theorem 2, exponentially small upper bounds can be obtained from any $\nu_m^{\max} < 1$. It follows that $\nu_1^{\max} = \nu_2^{\max} = 1$, but we find that $\nu_m^{\max} < 1$ already for $m = 3$. By direct counting one can compute $\nu_m^{\max}$ for $m \geq 3$ and thus obtain various exponentially small upper bounds. For $m \geq 6$, these bounds are sharper than the bound in (23).

4.3 Tight Upper Bound

Direct counting via computer simulations for moderately small values of n shows that $\nu_n^{\max}$ is achieved by alternating sequences. An analogous observation for $P_n^{\max}$ is made in [4]. It is then reasonable to expect that this holds for any n. If this is true and if we are able to determine $\nu_n(W^n)$ for an alternating sequence W^n, we can then obtain the tightest upper bound on $P_n^{\max}$ in terms of the decimation probability. Indeed, this is achieved by Lemmas 5 and 6 and Theorem 3.

Lemma 5. *If W^n is an alternating sequence, then*

$$\nu_n(W^n) = \frac{\sqrt{5}+2}{\sqrt{5}}\left(\frac{\sqrt{5}+1}{4}\right)^n + \frac{\sqrt{5}-2}{\sqrt{5}}\left(\frac{1-\sqrt{5}}{4}\right)^n - \frac{1}{2^n}$$
$$< \frac{\sqrt{5}+2}{\sqrt{5}}\left(\frac{\sqrt{5}+1}{4}\right)^n. \quad (33)$$

Proof If W^n is an alternating sequence, then $r = n$, so that Lemma 3 directly implies that $\nu_n(W^n)$ is upper-bounded as in (33). Moreover, (19) then holds with equalities and hence (22) implies the equality in (33). □

Lemma 6.

$$\nu_{n+1}(W^n w_n) < \nu_{n+1}(W^n \overline{w}_n). \quad (34)$$

Proof According to the proof of Lemma 3, $\nu_n(W^n)$ can be expressed in terms of minimal decimation sequences as

$$\nu_n(W^n) = \frac{1}{2^n}\sum_{i=0}^{n} K_i(W^n) \quad (35)$$

where $K_i(W^n)$ is the number of the minimal decimation sequences $\tilde{C}^n$ such that i is the index of the last bit of $\tilde{C}^n$ equal to 1 (if $\tilde{C}^n = 0^n$, then $i = 0$ and $K_0(W^n) = 1$). It follows that $K_i(W^n) \geq 1$, because the decimation sequence $\tilde{C}^n = 1^i0^{n-i}$ is always minimal. As $K_i(W^n) = K_i(W^m)$ for $m \geq n$, it suffices to compare only $K_{n+1}(W^n w_n)$ and $K_{n+1}(W^n \overline{w}_n)$.

To this end, we have to consider only the minimal decimation sequences $\tilde{C}^{n+1}$ such that $\tilde{c}_{n+1} = 1$. By virtue of the minimality of minimal decimation sequences, the first n bits of any such sequence also constitute a minimal decimation sequence.

Further, for $W^n w_n$, the last two bits are equal, so that the minimality of minimal decimation sequences implies that $\tilde{c}_n = 1$. Hence

$$K_{n+1}(W^n w_n) = K_n(W^n). \tag{36}$$

On the other hand, for $W^n \overline{w}_n$, the last bit is different from all the bits in the last run of W^n whose length is l_r. The minimality of minimal decimation sequences then implies that $\tilde{C}^{n+1}$ is minimal iff $\tilde{c}_{n+1} = 1$ and $\tilde{C}^n$ is a minimal decimation sequence such that the index, i, of the last bit of $\tilde{C}^n$ equal to 1 satisfies $n - l_r \leq i \leq n$. Consequently, in light of (36), we get

$$K_{n+1}(W^n \overline{w}_n) = \sum_{n-l_r}^{n} K_i(W^n) = K_{n-l_r}(W^n) + l_r K_n(W^n). \tag{37}$$

Now, as $l_r \geq 1$ and $K_{n-l_r} \geq 1$, (36) and (37) imply that $K_{n+1}(W^n w_n) < K_{n+1}(W^n \overline{w}_n)$, so that (35) then results in (34). □

Theorem 3.

$$\begin{aligned} P_n^{\max} &\leq p_{n-1}^{\max} \leq \nu_{n-1}^{\max} \\ &= \frac{\sqrt{5}+2}{\sqrt{5}} \left(\frac{\sqrt{5}+1}{4}\right)^{n-1} + \frac{\sqrt{5}-2}{\sqrt{5}} \left(\frac{1-\sqrt{5}}{4}\right)^{n-1} - \frac{1}{2^{n-1}} \\ &< \frac{\sqrt{5}+2}{\sqrt{5}} \left(\frac{\sqrt{5}+1}{4}\right)^{n-1} < 2.34165 \cdot 0.809017^n \end{aligned} \tag{38}$$

and $\nu_n(W^n) = \nu_n^{\max}$ *i* W^n *is an alternating sequence.*

Proof In view of Lemmas 5, 1, and 2, it suffices to prove that $\nu_n(W^n) < \nu_n(A^n)$ if W^n is different from an alternating sequence A^n. This is a consequence of Lemma 6, which directly implies that $\nu_n(W^n) \leq \nu_n(A^n)$ and that $\nu_n(W^n) = \nu_n(A^n)$ iff W^n is an alternating sequence. □

Theorem 3 is our strongest result as it gives the sharpest upper bound on $P_n^{\max}$. It is interesting to note that the recursions (36) and (37) from the proof of Lemma 6 enable the efficient computation of $\nu_n(W^n)$ with complexity $O(r)$ instead of $O(2^n)$.

If R is the total length of LFSR_X and LFSR_Y, then the expected number of false candidates for the initial states of LFSR_X and LFSR_Y can be upper-bounded by $2^R P_n^{\max}$. The criterion $2^R P_n^{\max} \leq 1$ then yields an approximate output segment length required for a successful embedding attack as

$$n \geq 3.27\, R. \tag{39}$$

5 Minimal Probabilities

Although any upper bound on $P_n^{\max}$ is also an upper bound on the minimal ASG-embedding probability $P_n^{\min}$, our main objective here is to obtain sharper upper bounds on $P_n^{\min}$. More precisely, sharp upper and lower bounds on $P_n^{\min}$ are obtained by deriving the minimal interleaving probability $p_n^{\min}$ and by applying Lemma 1.

Lemma 7.

$$p_n^{\min} = \left(\frac{n}{2} + 1\right) \frac{1}{2^n} \tag{40}$$

and $p_n(W^n) = p_n^{\min}$ *if* W^n *is a constant sequence,* 0^n *or* 1^n.

Proof Consider a set of sequences $S_i = W^{i-1}\overline{w}_i$, $1 \leq i \leq n+1$, where it is assumed that $S_1 = \overline{w}_1$ and $S_{n+1} = W^n$. Now, if S_i is a prefix of U^n and W_i^n is a prefix of V^n and the remaining bits of (U^n, V^n) are arbitrary (for $i = n+1$, V^n is arbitrary), then all such (U^n, V^n) are different and clearly $\mathrm{INT}(U^n, V^n, C^n) = W^n$ for $C^n = 1^{i-1}0^{n-i+1}$. The number of such (U^n, V^n) is $\sum_{i=1}^{n} 2^{n-1} + 2^n = n2^{n-1} + 2^n$, so that $p_n^{\min} \geq n2^{-n-1} + 2^{-n}$. Further, if W^n is a constant sequence, then there are no other (U^n, V^n) that can form W^n by interleaving, because the prefixes of U^n and V^n forming W^n are then also constant sequences. Therefore, the equality is achieved and (40) thus follows. □

The following bounds are a direct consequence of Lemmas 7 and 1. Since $\nu_n^{\min} = (n+1)2^{-n}$, where $\nu_n(W^n) = \nu_n^{\min}$ iff W^n is a constant sequence, the upper bound in (41) is sharper than the upper bound, $\nu_{n-1}^{\min}$, which is a direct consequence of Lemmas 1 and 2.

Theorem 4.

$$\frac{3}{4}(n+1)\frac{1}{2^n} = \frac{3}{4}p_{n-1}^{\min} \leq P_n^{\min} \leq p_{n-1}^{\min} = (n+1)\frac{1}{2^n}. \tag{41}$$

6 Conclusions

The problem [4] of analyzing the ASG-embedding probability, which is conditioned on the given segment of the ASG output sequence, is theoretically solved. Exponentially small upper bounds on the maximal ASG-embedding probability, including the tightest upper bound in terms of the decimation probability, as well as sharp upper and lower bounds on the minimal ASG-embedding probability are derived. Apart from their wider theoretical merits for the analysis of interleaving and decimation operations, the results prove that the embedding attack [4] on the ASG is successful if the length of the given output segment is sufficiently large and that this length depends on the total length of the two underlying LFSR's only linearly.

References

1. J. Dj. Golić and M. Mihaljević, "A generalized correlation attack on a class of stream ciphers based on the Levenshtein distance," *Journal of Cryptology*, vol. 3(3), pp. 201-212, 1991.
2. J. Dj. Golić and S. Petrović, "A generalized correlation attack with a probabilistic constrained edit distance," in Advances in Cryptology - EUROCRYPT '92, *Lecture Notes in Computer Science*, vol. 658, pp. 472-476, 1993.
3. J. Dj. Golić and L. O'Connor, "Embedding and probabilistic correlation attacks on clock-controlled shift registers," in Advances in Cryptology - EUROCRYPT '94, *Lecture Notes in Computer Science*, vol. 950, pp. 230-243, 1995.
4. J. Dj. Golić and R. Menicocci, "Edit distance correlation attack on the alternating step generator," in Advances in Cryptology - CRYPTO '97, *Lecture Notes in Computer Science*, vol. 1294, pp. 499-512, 1997.
5. J. Dj. Golić and R. Menicocci, "Edit probability correlation attack on the alternating step generator," in Sequences and their Applications - SETA '98, *Discrete Mathematics and Theoretical Computer Science*, C. Ding, T. Helleseth, and H. Niederreiter eds., Springer-Verlag, pp. 213-227, 1999.
6. C. G. Günther, "Alternating step generators controlled by de Bruijn sequences," in Advances in Cryptology - EUROCRYPT '87, *Lecture Notes in Computer Science*, vol. 304, pp. 5-14, 1988.
7. S. Jiang and G. Gong, "On edit distance attack to alternating step generator," unpublished manuscript.
8. T. Johansson, "Reduced complexity correlation attacks on two clock-controlled generators," in Advances in Cryptology - ASIACRYPT '98, *Lecture Notes in Computer Science*, vol. 1514, pp. 342-357, 1998.
9. M. Živković, "An algorithm for the initial state reconstruction of the clock-controlled shift register," *IEEE Trans. Information Theory*, vol. 37, pp. 1488-1490, Sept. 1991.

Additive Autocorrelation of Resilient Boolean Functions

Guang Gong[1] and Khoongming Khoo[2]

[1] Department of Electrical and Computer Engineering
University of Waterloo, Waterloo, Ontario N2L 3G1, Canada.
ggong@calliope.uwaterloo.ca
[2] Department of Combinatorics and Optimization
University of Waterloo, Waterloo, Ontario N2L 3G1, Canada.
kkhoo@math.uwaterloo.ca

Abstract. In this paper, we introduce a new notion called the *dual function* for studying Boolean functions. First, we discuss general properties of the dual function that are related to resiliency and additive autocorrelation. Second, we look at preferred functions which are Boolean functions with the lowest 3-valued spectrum. We prove that if a balanced preferred function has a dual function which is also preferred, then it is resilient, has high nonlinearity and optimal additive autocorrelation. We demonstrate four such constructions of optimal Boolean functions using the Kasami, Dillon-Dobbertin, Segre hyperoval and Welch-Gong Transformation functions. Third, we compute the additive autocorrelation of some known resilient preferred functions in the literature by using the dual function. We conclude that our construction yields highly nonlinear resilient functions with better additive autocorrelation than the Maiorana-McFarland functions. We also analysed the saturated functions, which are resilient functions with optimized algebraic degree and nonlinearity. We show that their additive autocorrelation have high peak values, and they become linear when we fix very few bits. These potential weaknesses have to be considered before we deploy them in applications.

1 Introduction

Resiliency and high nonlinearity are two of the most important prerequisites of Boolean functions when used as combiners in stream cipher systems. Resiliency ensures the cipher is not prone to correlation attack [22] while high nonlinearity offers protection against linear approximation attack [16]. Another criteria, studied in many recent papers, is low additive autocorrelation [23, 24, 25, 26]. This ensures that the output of the function is complemented with a probability close to 1/2 when any number of input bits are complemented. As a result, the cipher is not prone to differential-like cryptanalysis [1]. This is a more practical condition than the propagation criteria of order k which, in the case of high nonlinearity, may cause linear structures to occur (as pointed out in [24]).

M. Matsui and R. Zuccherato (Eds.): SAC 2003, LNCS 3006, pp. 275–290, 2004.

In this paper, we study the autocorrelation and resiliency properties of Boolean functions with 3-valued spectrum. This is an important class of functions with many applications in cryptography, for example see [2, 4, 5, 20, 27]. We give several new constructions of resilient Boolean functions with high nonlinearity and optimally low additive autocorrelation. Then we show that our construction yields functions with better additive autocorrelation than known highly nonlinear resilient functions. Our findings are summarized in the following paragraphs.

First, we introduce a new notion called the *dual function*, which is defined as the characteristic function of the Hadamard transform. This notion turns out to be a very useful tool for studying functions with 3-valued spectrum. For such functions, we show that propagation criteria of order k and correlation immunity of order k are dual concepts. From this, we deduce that a function with 3-valued spectrum is correlation immune of order 1 if and only if its dual function is not affine.

Second, we look at preferred functions which have the lowest 3-valued spectrum $0, \pm 2^{(n+1)/2}$. We prove that, if a balanced preferred function $f(x)$ has a dual function that is non-affine or preferred, then $f(x)$ has several optimal cryptographic properties like 1-resiliency, high nonlinearity and optimal additive autocorrelation. We present some functions used in the construction of certain Hadamard difference sets, which achieve these properties. They include the Kasami functions, the Dillon-Dobbertin functions, the Segre hyperoval functions and the Welch-Gong Transformation functions [7, 8, 9, 11]. Moreover, some of these functions have high algebraic degree (for algebraic complexity) and large linear span (which offers protection against an interpolation attack [13]).

Third, we compute the additive autocorrelation of some known resilient functions with high nonlinearity. We show that our constructed functions have better additive autocorrelation than resilient preferred functions based on the Maiorana-McFarland construction [3]. We also investigate an important class of functions with 3-valued spectrum: the saturated functions constructed in [20] (which are resilient functions optimizing Siegenthaler and Sarkar-Maitra inequality). We compute a lower bound for the additive autocorrelation which improves on a bound given in [23]. We show that they have very high additive autocorrelation close to 2^n. Moreover an n-bit saturated function becomes linear when we fix just very few bits ($\log_2(n)$ or less bits). Thus, although a saturated function satisfies some very strong cryptographic properties, it may lead to a rigid structure which causes other weaknesses to occur.

2 Definitions and Preliminaries

The trace function $Tr : GF(2^n) \to GF(2)$ is defined as $Tr(x) = \sum_{i=0}^{n-1} x^{2^i}$. It is a linear function and is basic to the representation of polynomial functions $f : GF(2^n) \to GF(2)$.

The *Hadamard Transform* of a polynomial function $f : GF(2^n) \to GF(2)$ is defined by $\hat{f}(\lambda) = \sum_{x \in GF(2^n)} (-1)^{Tr(\lambda x)+f(x)}$.

There is a natural correspondence between polynomial functions $f : GF(2^n) \to GF(2)$ and Boolean functions $g : GF(2)^n \to GF(2)$. Let $\{\alpha_0, \ldots, \alpha_{n-1}\}$ be a basis of $GF(2^n)$ and $g(\underline{x})$ be the Boolean function representation of $f(x)$, then this correspondence is given by

$$g(x_0, \ldots, x_{n-1}) = f(x_0\alpha_0 + \cdots + x_{n-1}\alpha_{n-1}).$$

The *Hadamard Transform* of a Boolean function $f : GF(2)^n \to GF(2)$ is $\hat{f}(w) = \sum_{x \in GF(2)^n} (-1)^{w \cdot x + f(x)}$. This is equivalent to the definition for the corresponding polynomial function over $GF(2^n)$ [17].

We say the function $f : GF(2)^n \to GF(2)$ has *3-valued spectrum* if its Hadamard Transform $\hat{f}(\lambda)$ only takes on the values $0, \pm 2^i$.

Definition 1 *Let n be odd and $f : GF(2)^n \to GF(2)$. If $\hat{f}(w)$ only takes on the values $0, \pm 2^{(n+1)/2}$, then we say f is* preferred.

Remark 1. It is desirable for a Boolean function to have low Hadamard transform. We deduce from Parseval's equation: $\sum_w \hat{f}(w)^2 = 2^{2n}$ that a preferred function has the lowest Hadamard transform among functions with 3-valued spectrum. That is the reason they are called preferred functions in [12].

The *nonlinearity* of a function $f : GF(2)^n \to GF(2)$ is defined as $N_f = min_{\{a \text{ affine function}\}} |\{x | f(x) \neq a(x)\}|$. A high nonlinearity is desirable as it offers protection against linear approximation based attacks [16, 22].

A Boolean function $f : GF(2)^n \to GF(2)$ is *kth order correlation immune* , denoted $CI(k)$, if $\hat{f}(w) = 0$ for all $1 \leq wt(w) \leq k$ where $wt(w)$ is the number of ones in the binary representation of w. Correlation immunity offers protection against correlation attack [22]. Furthermore, if f is balanced and $CI(k)$, we say f is resilient of order k.

The *additive autocorrelation at* a is defined as $\Delta_f(a) = \sum_x (-1)^{f(x)+f(x+a)}$. We say f satisfies the *propagation criteria of order* k, denoted $PC(k)$, if $\Delta_f(a) = 0$ for all $1 \leq wt(a) \leq k$. If $\Delta_f(a) = \pm 2^n$, then a is called a *linear structure* of f which is undesirable.

Definition 2 *The* additive autocorrelation *of f is* $\Delta_f := max_{a \neq 0} |\Delta_f(a)|$.

Remark 2. This value is also called the *maximum indicator* in [24]. For a balanced function f, we want Δ_f to be low so that any change in the input bits will complement the output with probability close to 1/2. It was conjectured by Zhang and Zheng in [24, Conjecture 1] that $\Delta_f \geq 2^{(n+1)/2}$ for a balanced function $f : GF(2)^n \to GF(2)$. Although this conjecture was later disproved by Clark et. al. when n is even (see [6, Table 3]), it still holds when n is odd. Thus, we make the following definition.

Definition 3 *Let n be odd and $f : GF(2)^n \to GF(2)$ be balanced. f has* optimal additive autocorrelation *if* $\Delta_f = 2^{(n+1)/2}$.

The *linear span*, denoted $LS(f)$, of a polynomial function $f(x) = \sum_i \beta_i x^{s_i}$, $\beta_i \in GF(2^n)$, is the number of monomials x^{s_i} in its polynomial representation. We want it to be high to defend against interpolation attacks [13]. The *algebraic degree*, denoted $deg(f)$, of the corresponding Boolean function is given by the maximum weight of the exponents $\max_i wt(s_i)$ (see [17]). We want it to be high so that algebraic analysis is complex.

3 Cryptographic Properties of the Dual Function

Definition 4 *Let* $f : GF(2)^n \to GF(2)$. *Its* dual function σ_f *is de*□*ned as*

$$\sigma_f(w) = \begin{cases} 0 \text{ if } \hat{f}(w) = 0 \\ 1 \text{ if } \hat{f}(w) \neq 0. \end{cases}$$

Remark 3. From Parseval's equation: $\sum_w \hat{f}(w)^2 = 2^{2n}$, we see that $\sigma_f(w)$ has weight $2^{2(n-i)}$ if f has 3-valued spectrum $0, \pm 2^i$.

Next, we show that the Hadamard transform of the dual function is proportional to the additive autocorrelation of a function with 3-valued spectrum. It can be applied to derive several useful results in the next few subsections.

Lemma 1. *If* $f : GF(2)^n \to GF(2)$ *is a Boolean function with 3-valued spectrum* $0, \pm 2^i$, *then for all* $a \neq 0$

$$\Delta_f(a) = -2^{2i-(n+1)}\widehat{\sigma_f}(a).$$

Proof. We make use of the well known Wiener-Khintchine theorem (e.g. see [2, Lemma 1]): $\hat{f}(w)^2 = \sum_a \Delta_f(a)(-1)^{a\cdot w}$. By applying inverse Hadamard transform[1], we have the equivalent formula:

$$\Delta_f(a) = 1/2^n \sum_w \hat{f}(w)^2(-1)^{a\cdot w}. \quad (1)$$

By definition, $\hat{f}(w)^2 = 2^{2i}\sigma_f(w)$. Substituting this in equation (1), we get

$$\Delta_f(a) = 2^{2i-n} \sum_w \sigma_f(w)(-1)^{a\cdot w}.$$

By noting that $2\sigma_f(w) = 1 - (-1)^{\sigma_f(w)}$, we get

$$\Delta_f(a) = 2^{2i-(n+1)} \left(\sum_w (-1)^{a\cdot w} - \sum_w (-1)^{\sigma_f(w)+a\cdot w} \right).$$

This is $-2^{2i-(n+1)}\widehat{\sigma_f}(a)$ when $a \neq 0$ and 2^n when $a = 0$. □

---

[1] The inverse Hadamard transform is the formula: $F(w) = \sum_x f(x)(-1)^{w\cdot x} \Longrightarrow f(x) = 1/2^n \sum_w F(w)(-1)^{w\cdot x}$.

3.1 Correlation Immunity and Non-Affine Dual Function

In this section, we derive several useful results on correlation immunity from Lemma 1.

Proposition 1 *Let* $f : GF(2)^n \to GF(2)$ *be a Boolean function with 3-valued spectrum* $0, \pm 2^i$. *Then* f *is* $PC(k)$ *if and only if* σ_f *is* $CI(k)$.

Proof. f is $PC(k)$ $\Longleftrightarrow$ $\Delta_f(a) = 0$ for $1 \leq wt(a) \leq k$ $\Longleftrightarrow$ $\widehat{\sigma_f}(a) = 0$ for $1 \leq wt(a) \leq k$ (by Lemma 1) $\Longleftrightarrow$ σ_f is $CI(k)$. □

We need the following result from [2] for proving correlation immunity of Boolean functions.

Proposition 2 *(Canteaut, Carlet, Charpin and Fontaine [2, Theorem 7]) Let* $f : GF(2^n) \to GF(2)$ *be a polynomial function with 3-valued spectrum* $0, \pm 2^i$. *Then there exists a basis of* $GF(2^n)$ *such that the Boolean representation of* f *is* $CI(1)$ *if and only if* f *is not* $PC(n-1)$ *under any basis representation.*

Remark 4. We stated Proposition 2 in a modified form (from the original in [2]) so that it applies to polynomial functions. From the proof of Proposition 2, we see that the set $\{\lambda | \hat{f}(\lambda) = 0\}$ contains n linearly independent vectors. Based on these n vectors, Gong and Youssef gave an algorithm to find a basis of $GF(2^n)$ such that the Boolean form of f is 1-resilient in [11]. Proposition 2 was proven in another form by Zheng and Zhang [27, Theorem 2]. A related result concerning resilient preferred functions can be found in [15, Section 3].

Theorem 1 is a corollary of Proposition 1 and 2. Some applications can be found in Section 4.

Theorem 1 *Let* $f : GF(2^n) \to GF(2)$ *be a polynomial function with 3-valued spectrum* $0, \pm 2^i$. *Then there exists a basis of* $GF(2^n)$ *such that the Boolean representation of* $f(x)$ *is* $CI(1)$ *if and only if* σ_f *is not ane.*

Proof. f is $CI(1)$ in some basis $\Longleftrightarrow$ f is not $PC(n-1)$ in any basis (by Proposition 2) $\Longleftrightarrow$ σ_f is not $CI(n-1)$ in any basis (by Proposition 1) $\Longleftrightarrow$ σ_f is not affine. □

3.2 Computing Additive Autocorrelation from the Dual Function

In this section, we derive formulas to compute the additive autocorrelation of functions with 3-valued spectrum.

Proposition 3 *Let* $f : GF(2)^n \to GF(2)$ *has 3-valued spectrum* $0, \pm 2^i$. *Then* $\Delta_f \leq 2^{2i-1} - 2^{2i-n} N_{\sigma_f}$. *Thus* N_{σ_f} *is high* $\Longrightarrow$ Δ_f *is low.*

Proof. By Lemma 1, we have $\widehat{\sigma_f}(a) = -2^{n+1-2i}\Delta_f(a)$ for $a \neq 0$. By substituting this in the formula $N_{\sigma_f} = 2^{n-1} - 1/2 \max_a |\widehat{\sigma_f}(a)|$, we see that Δ_f is

$$\max_{a \neq 0} |\Delta_f(a)| = 2^{2i-(n+1)} \max_{a \neq 0} |\widehat{\sigma_f}(a)| \leq 2^{2i-(n+1)} \max_{a} |\widehat{\sigma_f}(a)| = 2^{2i-1} - 2^{2i-n} N_{\sigma_f}.$$

□

Low additive autocorrelation, i.e. toggling any number of input bits will result in the output being complemented with probability close to 1/2, is a useful generalization of the propagation criteria of order k. The next theorem shows when low additive autocorrelation can be achieved. Some applications can be found in Section 4.

Theorem 2 *If $f : GF(2)^n \rightarrow GF(2)$ is a balanced preferred function and σ_f is preferred, then $\Delta_f = 2^{(n+1)/2}$ and $\Delta_f(a) = 0$ for $2^{n-1} - 1$ a's. That is, f has optimal additive autocorrelation.*

Proof. By Lemma 1, $\widehat{\sigma_f}(a) = -\Delta_f(a)$ for $a \neq 0$ when f is preferred. σ_f is preferred means $\widehat{\sigma_f}(a) = 0, \pm 2^{(n+1)/2}$ which implies $\Delta_f(a) = 0, \pm 2^{(n+1)/2}$ for all $a \neq 0$. Thus, $\Delta_f = 2^{(n+1)/2}$.

Let v be the number of elements a such that $\widehat{\sigma_f}(a) = 0$. By Parseval's equation and the fact that σ_f is preferred, we have

$$\sum_a \widehat{\sigma_f}(a)^2 = 2^{2n} \Longrightarrow (2^n - v)2^{n+1} = 2^{2n} \Longrightarrow v = 2^{n-1}.$$

From remark 3, $\widehat{\sigma_f}(0) = 0$ because σ_f is balanced (note that $\Delta_f(0) = 2^n$). Therefore $\widehat{\sigma_f}(a) = 0$ for $2^{n-1}-1$ non-zero a's. By Lemma 1, $\Delta_f(a) = 0$ for $2^{n-1}-1$ elements a's. □

3.3 Nonlinearity and Algebraic Degree

Proposition 4 follows easily from the following relation:

$$N_f = 2^{n-1} - 1/2 \max_w |\hat{f}(w)|. \tag{2}$$

Proposition 4 *A function $f : GF(2)^n \rightarrow GF(2)$ with 3-valued spectrum $0, \pm 2^i$ have nonlinearity $2^{n-1} - 2^{i-1}$. By remark 1, a preferred function has the highest nonlinearity $2^{n-1} - 2^{(n-1)/2}$ among functions with 3-valued spectrum.*

Remark 5. In Section 4 and 5.1, we will concentrate on resilient preferred functions. Their nonlinearity $2^{n-1} - 2^{(n-1)/2}$ is considered high among resilient functions according to Carlet [3]. Sarkar and Maitra constructed resilient functions with nonlinearity $> 2^{n-1} - 2^{(n-1)/2}$ [19, Theorem 6]. But their construction only works when $n \geq 41$ for 1-resilient functions and $n \geq 55$ for 2-resilient functions.

From [27], if $f : GF(2)^n \rightarrow GF(2)$ satisfies $\hat{f}(\lambda) \equiv 0 \pmod{2^i}$ for all λ, then $deg(f) \leq n - i + 1$. The following proposition follows easily.

Proposition 5 *A function with 3-valued spectrum $0, \pm 2^i$ satisfies $deg(f) \leq n - i + 1$. By remark 1, the preferred functions have maximal bound for algebraic degree: $deg(f) \leq (n+1)/2$ among functions with 3-valued spectrum.*

4 Construction of Resilient Highly Nonlinear Boolean Functions with Optimal Additive Autocorrelation

Our main result in this section is to construct four classes of Boolean functions with desirable cryptographic properties, from functions used in the construction of Hadamard difference sets. This is achieved by applying Theorem 3 and 4, which are corollaries of Theorem 1, Theorem 2 and Proposition 4.

Theorem 3 *If $f : GF(2^n) \rightarrow GF(2)$ is a balanced preferred function such that its dual σ_f is non-ane, then*

1. *f is resilient of order 1 for some basis conversion.*
2. *f has high nonlinearity $2^{n-1} - 2^{(n-1)/2}$.*

Theorem 4 *If $f : GF(2^n) \rightarrow GF(2)$ is a balanced preferred function such that its dual σ_f is preferred, then*

1. *f is resilient of order 1 for some basis conversion.*
2. *f has high nonlinearity $2^{n-1} - 2^{(n-1)/2}$.*
3. *f has optimal additive autocorrelation, i.e. $\Delta_f = 2^{(n+1)/2}$ and $\Delta_f(a) = 0$ for $2^{n-1} - 1$ a's.*

Our first construction is based on a class of Kasami functions whose Hadamard transform distribution is found by Dillon.

Lemma 2. *(Kasami-Dillon [7, 14]) Let n be odd, $\gcd(n, 3) = 1$ and $f : GF(2^n) \rightarrow GF(2)$ be de□ned by $f(x) = Tr(x^d)$ where $d = 2^{2k} - 2^k + 1$, $3k \equiv 1 \pmod{n}$. Then f is preferred and satis□es*

$$\hat{f}(\lambda) = \begin{cases} 0 & \text{if } Tr(\lambda^{2^k+1}) = 0 \\ \pm 2^{(n+1)/2} & \text{if } Tr(\lambda^{2^k+1}) = 1. \end{cases}$$

Theorem 5 *The Kasami function $f(x)$ in Lemma 2 is 1-resilient, $N_f = 2^{n-1} - 2^{(n-1)/2}$ and $\Delta_f = 2^{(n+1)/2}$. Moreover, the algebraic degree is $deg(f) = \lceil n/3 \rceil + 1$.*

Proof. By Lemma 2, f is balanced because $\hat{f}(0) = 0$. Also by Lemma 2, $\sigma_f(x) = Tr(x^{2^k+1})$ which is preferred by [10]. Therefore, we can apply Theorem 4 because f is balanced and both functions f, σ_f are preferred.

For any k, the degree of f is $wt(2^{2k} - 2^k + 1) = k + 1$ for $1 \leq k \leq (n-1)/2$ and $wt(2^{2k} - 2^k + 1) = (n-k) + 1$ when $(n-1)/2 \leq k \leq n-1$ [14]. When $3k \equiv 1 \pmod{n}$, $k \equiv \pm\lceil n/3 \rceil \pmod{n}$. Therefore $deg(f) = \lceil n/3 \rceil + 1$ in this case. □

Our next construction is based on a class of functions from the construction of cyclic Hadamard difference sets by Dillon and Dobbertin [8].

Lemma 3. *(Dillon-Dobbertin [8]) Let n be odd. Define $f : GF(2^n) \to GF(2)$ by*

$$f(x) = \begin{cases} 0 \text{ if } x^{2^k+1} \in Im(\Delta_k) \\ 1 \text{ if } x^{2^k+1} \notin Im(\Delta_k). \end{cases}$$

where $\Delta_k(x) = (x+1)^d + x^d + 1$, $d = 2^{2k} - 2^k + 1$ and $\gcd(k,n) = 1$. Then $f(x)$ is preferred and satisfies

$$\hat{f}(\lambda) = \begin{cases} 0 & \text{if } Tr(\lambda^{\frac{2^k+1}{3}}) = 0 \\ \pm 2^{(n+1)/2} & \text{if } Tr(\lambda^{\frac{2^k+1}{3}}) = 1. \end{cases}$$

Theorem 6 *Let $f(x)$ be the Dillon-Dobbertin function in Lemma 3*

1. *$f(x)$ is 1-resilient and $N_f = 2^{n-1} - 2^{(n-1)/2}$.*
2. *Furthermore, if $k = 3$ or $3k \equiv 1 \pmod n$, then $f(x)$ is 1-resilient, $N_f = 2^{n-1} - 2^{(n-1)/2}$ and $\Delta_f = 2^{(n+1)/2}$.*
3. *If $3k \equiv 1 \pmod n$, then $LS(f) = 5n$ where*

$$f(x) = Tr(x^3 + x^{2^k+1} + x^{2^{2k+1}+1} + x^{2^{2k}+2^{k+1}+1} + x^{2^{2k+1}+2^{k+1}+3}). \quad (3)$$

The algebraic degree satisfies $deg(f) = 4$ for $n \neq 5$. $deg(f) = 3$ for $n = 5$.

Proof. 1. By Lemma 3, f is balanced because $\hat{f}(0) = 0$. Also by Lemma 3, f is preferred and the dual function is $\sigma_f(x) = Tr(x^{(2^k+1)/3})$ which is not affine. Therefore, we can apply Theorem 3.

2. If $k = 3$, then $(2^k+1)/3 = 3$ and $\sigma_f(x) = Tr(x^3)$ which is preferred by [10]. If $3k \equiv 1 \pmod n$, then $2^{3k} + 1 \equiv 2 + 1 \equiv 3 \pmod{2^n - 1}$. Therefore

$$(2^k+1)/3 \equiv (2^k+1)/(2^{3k}+1) \equiv 1/(2^{2k} - 2^k + 1) \equiv d^{-1} \pmod{2^n - 1}.$$

where $d = 2^{2k} - 2^k + 1$. Therefore the dual function is $\sigma_f(x) = Tr(x^{d^{-1}})$ which is preferred by the following argument:
We define $g(x) := Tr(x^d)$ which is preferred from [14]. This implies $\sigma_f(x)$ is preferred from the following computation.

$$\widehat{\sigma_f}(\lambda) = \sum_x (-1)^{Tr(x^{d^{-1}}) + Tr(\lambda x)} = \sum_y (-1)^{Tr(\lambda^{-d^{-1}} y) + Tr(y^d)} = \hat{g}(\lambda^{-d^{-1}}).$$

where we let $x = \lambda^{-1} y^d$. Therefore, we can apply Theorem 4 because f is balanced and both functions f, σ_f are preferred.

3. $f(x)$ is a 2^k+1-decimation of the characteristic function $b_k(x)$ of the Hadamard difference set B_k in [8, 9], i.e. $f(x) = b_k(x^{2^k+1})$. When $3k \equiv 1 \pmod n$, the trace representation of $b_k(x)$ in [8, 9] is

$$b_k(x) = Tr(x^{2^{2k}+2^k+1} + x^{2^{2k}+2^k-1} + x^{2^{2k}-2^k+1} + x^{2^k+1} + x).$$

The exponents of $f(x)$ in Equation 3 are obtained by multiplying all the exponents of $b_k(x)$ by 2^k+1, and noting that $3k \equiv 1 \pmod n$ implies $2^{3k} \equiv$

2 modulo $2^n - 1$. When we expand the 5 trace terms of $f(x)$, we get $5n$ monomials, i.e. $LS(f) = 5n$.
The maximum weight of the exponents of $f(x)$ in Equation 3 is 4 which comes from the exponent $2^{2k+1} + 2^{k+1} + 3$ for $n > 5$. Thus, $deg(f) = 4$. For $n = 5$, we can verify $deg(f) = 3$.

□

Our final construction is based on the hyperoval functions in [7].

Lemma 4. *(Hyperoval [7]) Let n be odd. Define $f : GF(2^n) \to GF(2)$ by*

$$f(x) = \begin{cases} 0 \text{ if } x \in Im(D_k) \\ 1 \text{ if } x \notin Im(D_k) \end{cases}$$

where $D_k(x) = x + x^k$ is a 2-to-1 map on $GF(2^n)$. Then $f(x)$ satisfies $\hat{f}(\lambda) = \hat{g}(\lambda^{\frac{k-1}{k}})$ where $g(x) = Tr(x^k)$.

The known values of k for which $x + x^k$ is a 2-to-1 map are $k = 2$ (Singer), $k = 6$ (Segre) and two cases due to Glynn. We will consider the Segre case $k = 6$.

Theorem 7 *Let $f(x)$ be the Segre hyperoval function for $k = 6$ in Lemma 4. Then $f(x)$ is 1-resilient and $N_f = 2^{n-1} - 2^{(n-1)/2}$.*

Proof. We see from Lemma 4 that when $k = 6$, f is balanced because $\hat{f}(0) = \hat{g}(0) = 0$ where $g(x) = Tr(x^6) = Tr(x^3)$. f is preferred because g is preferred [10] and $\hat{f}(\lambda) = \hat{g}(\lambda^{5/6})$ by Lemma 4. By the distribution of $\hat{g}$ from [10] and Lemma 4,

$$\hat{f}(\lambda) = \hat{g}(\mu) = \begin{cases} 0 & \text{if } Tr(\mu) = 0 \\ \pm 2^{(n+1)/2} & \text{if } Tr(\mu) = 1 \end{cases}$$

where $\mu = \lambda^{5/6}$. Therefore, $\sigma_f(x) = Tr(x^{5/6})$ which is not affine. Thus, we can apply Theorem 3 because f is a balanced preferred function and σ_f is not affine.

□

The Welch-Gong Transformation functions also corresponds to optimal Boolean function with low additive autocorrelation in the following remark.

Remark 6. In [11], the Welch-Gong Transformation function was shown to have good cryptographic properties: 1-resiliency, high nonlinearity $2^{n-1} - 2^{(n-1)/2}$, high algebraic degree $deg(f) = \lceil n/3 \rceil + 1$ and large linear span $LS(f) = n(2^{\lceil n/3 \rceil} - 3)$. A description of the function can be found in [11, Section 2].

Here, we remark that the Welch-Gong function has the additional property of optimal additive autocorrelation. This is because the Welch-Gong Transformation function $f(x)$ is a balanced preferred function and its dual function is $\sigma_f(x) = Tr(x^{d^{-1}})$, $d = 2^{2k} - 2^k + 1$ where $3k \equiv 1 \pmod{n}$ [11, Lemma 2]. By the same reason as in Theorem 6 part (2), we can apply Theorem 4 because f is balanced and both f, σ_f are preferred.

We present Table 1 to summarize our results and example 1 to demonstrate our construction.

Table 1. Cryptographic Properties of Preferred Functions

Kasami* (Theorem 5)	Dillon-Dobbertin* (Theorem 6)	Segre hyperoval* (Theorem 7)	Welch-Gong* (Remark 6)
Balance	Balance	Balance	Balance
High Nonlinearity	High Nonlinearity	High Nonlinearity	High Nonlinearity
Resiliency	Resiliency	Resiliency	Resiliency
Optimal Additive Autocorrelation	Optimal Additive Autocorrelation	-	Optimal Additive Autocorrelation
For odd n, $3 \not| n$	For odd $n \geq 5$	For odd $n \geq 5$	For odd n, $3 \not| n$
$deg(f) = \lceil n/3 \rceil + 1$	$deg(f) = 3, 4$ when $k = 3^{-1}$	-	$deg(f) = \lceil n/3 \rceil + 1$ $LS(f) = n(2^{\lceil n/3 \rceil} - 3)$

***Remark:** All the functions listed in Table 1 satisfies 2-level (multiplicative) autocorrelation, i.e. $C_f(\lambda) = \sum_{x \in GF(2^n)} (-1)^{f(x)+f(\lambda x)} = 0$ for all $\lambda \neq 1$ [7, 8, 9], for applications in pseudorandom number generation and communication systems.

Example 1. Let $GF(2^7)^*$ be generated by the element α satisfying $\alpha^7 + \alpha + 1 = 0$. Define $f : GF(2^7) \rightarrow GF(2)$ by $f(x) = Tr_1^7(x^3 + x^5 + x^9 + x^{19} + x^{29})$, which is the Dillon-Dobbertin function of Theorem 6 with $3k \equiv 1 \mod 7$, i.e. $k = 5$ (we have reduced the exponents of f to their cyclotomic coset leaders). By applying Algorithm 1 of [11] with the 7 linearly independent vectors $\{\alpha^i | i = 1, 2, 3, 4, 5, 6, 13\}$ satisfying $\hat{f}(\alpha^i) = 0$, a 1-resilient Boolean form of f is given by

$$
\begin{aligned}
g(x_6, x_5, x_4, x_3, x_2, x_1, x_0) &= x_6 x_3 x_1 x_0 + x_5 x_4 x_1 x_0 + x_5 x_3 x_2 x_0 \\
&+ x_5 x_3 x_1 x_0 + x_4 x_3 x_2 x_1 + x_6 x_5 x_3 + x_6 x_5 x_0 + x_6 x_4 x_0 + x_6 x_2 x_1 + x_5 x_4 x_2 \\
&+ x_5 x_3 x_2 + x_5 x_1 x_0 + x_4 x_3 x_1 + x_4 x_2 x_1 + x_4 x_1 x_0 + x_3 x_2 x_0 + x_3 x_1 x_0 \\
&+ x_2 x_1 x_0 + x_5 x_4 + x_5 x_3 + x_5 x_2 + x_5 x_0 + x_4 x_3 + x_4 x_2 + x_4 x_0 + x_3 x_1 \\
&+ x_3 x_0 + x_2 x_1 + x_2 x_0 + x_1 x_0 + x_6 + x_4 + x_2 + x_1 + x_0 .
\end{aligned}
$$

g is a Boolean function with 7 input bits, is 1-resilient and has algebraic degree 4, which is highest among all preferred functions by Proposition 5. The nonlinearity is $2^6 - 2^3 = 56$ which is optimal among 7-bit Boolean functions, see [18]. The additve autocorrelation is optimal, given by $\Delta_f = 2^{(7+1)/2} = 16$.

5 Additive Autocorrelation of Known Resilient Functions with High Nonlinearity

5.1 Comparison with Known Resilient Preferred Functions

In the known literature, there were many constructions for resilient preferred functions. Some examples include [2, 3, 11, 21]. A common construction belong to the Maiorana-McFarland class, see [3] for a summary. We present in Proposition 6 a general construction for Maiorana-McFarland resilient preferred functions.

Proposition 6 *(Carlet [3, page 555]) Let n be odd and $f : GF(2)^n \to GF(2)$ be de*□*ned by*

$$f(x, y) = x \cdot \phi(y) + g(y), \; x \in GF(2)^{(n+1)/2}, y \in GF(2)^{(n-1)/2}. \tag{4}$$

where g is any $(n-1)/2$-bit Boolean function, and $\phi : GF(2)^{\frac{n-1}{2}} \to GF(2)^{\frac{n+1}{2}}$ is an injection such that $wt(\phi(y)) \geq k + 1$. Then f is a k-resilient function with nonlinearity $2^{n-1} - 2^{(n-1)/2}$.

The above construction is quite useful. When $n \equiv 1 \pmod 4$, we can construct $(n-1)/4$-resilient functions having nonlinearity $2^{n-1} - 2^{(n-1)/2}$ from it.

We will show that the function $f(x, y)$ in Proposition 6 is preferred, and deduce its dual function and additive autocorrelation in Theorem 8. We define the *characteristic function* $\chi_A(x)$ on a set A to be: $\chi_A(x) = 1$ if $x \in A$ and 0 otherwise. We also denote the image set of ϕ by $Im(\phi)$.

Theorem 8 *Let $f(x, y)$ be the function de*□*ned in Proposition 6. Then it is preferred with dual function $\sigma_f(x, y) = \chi_{Im(\phi)}(x)$. The additive autocorrelation of f satis*□*es $\Delta_f \geq 2^{(n-1)/2}\sqrt{2^{n+1}/(2^{(n+1)/2} - 1)}$ which is approximately $2^{3n/4} > 2^{(n+1)/2}$.*

Proof. From [3], the Hadamard transform of f is:

$$\hat{f}(a, b) = \sum_y (-1)^{g(y)+b\cdot y} \sum_x (-1)^{x\cdot(a+\phi(y))} = 2^{(n+1)/2} \sum_{y\in\phi^{-1}(a)} (-1)^{g(y)+b\cdot y}$$

$$= \begin{cases} 0 \text{ , if } a \notin Im(\phi), \\ \pm 2^{(n+1)/2} \text{ , if } a \in Im(\phi), \end{cases}$$

because ϕ is injective. Therefore, f is preferred and $\sigma_f(x, y) = \chi_{Im(\phi)}(x)$. To find the additive autocorrelation of f, we can compute $\widehat{\sigma_f}$:

$$\widehat{\sigma_f}(a, b) = \sum_{x,y} (-1)^{\chi_{Im(\phi)}(x)+a\cdot x+b\cdot y} = \sum_y (-1)^{b\cdot y} \sum_x (-1)^{\chi_{Im(\phi)}(x)+a\cdot x}$$

$$= \begin{cases} 0 \text{ , if } b \neq 0, \\ 2^{(n-1)/2}\widehat{\chi_{Im(\phi)}}(a) \text{ , if } b = 0. \end{cases}$$

Note that $\widehat{\chi_{Im(\phi)}}(0) = 0$ because $\chi_{Im(\phi)}$ is balanced. Therefore, by Parseval's equation: $\sum_{a\neq 0} \widehat{\chi_{Im(\phi)}}(a)^2 = 2^{n+1}$ and Lemma 1: $\Delta_f = max_{(a,b)\neq(0,0)}|\widehat{\sigma_f}(a,b)|$,

$$\Delta_f = 2^{(n-1)/2} \max_{a\neq 0} |\widehat{\chi_{Im(\phi)}}(a)| \geq 2^{(n-1)/2}\sqrt{2^{n+1}/(2^{(n+1)/2}-1)}.$$

This lower bound is approximately $2^{n/2} \times \sqrt{2^{n/2}} = 2^{3n/4}$. □

Remark 7. We note that for n odd, Canteaut et. al. [2, Corollary 3] constructed 1-resilient preferred functions that can achieve all algebraic degree between 2 and $(n+1)/2$ by restricting a Maiorana-McFarland bent function to a hyperplane. The dual function and additive autocorrelation can be computed by a method similar to the proof of Theorem 8.

By Theorem 8, we see that the Maiorana-McFarland construction of resilient preferred functions have higher (worse) additive autocorrelation than our constructed functions from Table 1. Moreover, the Maiorana-McFarland function in equation (4) becomes linear when we fix $(n-1)/2$ input bits y. Our construction can avoid this possible weakness:

Example 2. The construction of Proposition 6 for a 7-bit 1-resilient preferred function with nonlinearity 56 is

$$f(x,y) = x \cdot \phi(y) + g(y), \;\; x \in GF(2)^4, y \in GF(2)^3.$$

where $\phi : GF(2)^3 \to GF(2)^4$ is an injection such that $wt(\phi(y)) \geq 2$.

f becomes linear when we fix three bits $y = (y_0, y_1, y_2)$. In comparison, our 1-resilient preferred function in example 1 is not linear when we fix any three bits. By Theorem 8, we deduce that $\Delta_f \geq \lceil 2^3 \times \sqrt{2^8/(2^4-1)}\rceil = 34$ while the additive autocorrelation of our function in example 1 is 16.

5.2 Potential Weaknesses of Saturated Functions

In this section, we investigate an important class of Boolean functions with 3-valued spectrum. They are the saturated functions introduced by Sarkar and Maitra [20]. If an n-bit Boolean function f have algebraic degree d, then the maximal order of resiliency it can achieve is $k := n-1-d$ by Siegenthaler's inequality [22]. If the order of resiliency is k, then the maximal nonlinearity it can achieve is $2^{n-1} - 2^{k+1}$ by Sarkar-Maitra inequality [20, Theorem 2]. When both these conditions are achieved, we say f is a *saturated function* and it necessarily have 3-valued spectrum $0, \pm 2^{k+2}$ [20]. Fix $d \geq 2$, Sarkar and Maitra constructed an infinite class of saturated functions having algebraic degree d in [20]. They denoted their class of functions by $SS(d-2)$.

Proposition 7 *([20, Theorem 5] Sarkar and Maitra) Construction for functions in $SS(d-2)$. Fix $d \geq 2$, let $n = r+s+t$ where $r = 2^{d-1}-1$, $s = d-1$ and $t \geq 0$. De□ne $f : GF(2)^n \to GF(2)$ by*

$$f(x,y,z) = x \cdot \phi(y) + g(y) + z_0 + \cdots + z_{t-1}, \;\; x \in GF(2)^r, y \in GF(2)^s, z \in GF(2)^t. \quad (5)$$

where $g : GF(2)^s \to GF(2)$ *is any function and* $\phi : GF(2)^s \to GF(2)^r$ *is an injection such that* $wt(\phi(y)) \geq r-1$ *for all* $y \in GF(2)^s$. *Then* $deg(f) = d$, f *is k-resilient having nonlinearity* $2^{n-1} - 2^{k+1}$ *where* $k = n-1-d$. f *necessarily has 3-valued spectrum* $0, \pm 2^{k+2}$.

The Boolean functions in Proposition 7 achieve two very desirable properties, maximal resiliency and nonlinearity, for applications in stream cipher systems. However, we will see in Theorem 9 that they have certain weaknesses that have to be considered in applications.

A good lower bound for the additive autocorrelation of a general k-resilient function[2] is given by Tarannikov et. al. in [23, Theorem 4]. In Theorem 9, we give a better (sharper) bound for the function in Proposition 7.

Theorem 9 *Fix* $d \geq 2$, *let* $f(x, y, z)$ *be a function in* $SS(d-2)$ *as defined in Proposition 7.*

1. *When* $t = 0$, $\Delta_f \geq (1 - \frac{2}{n})2^n$. *This bound is sharper than a general bound obtained by [23, Theorem 4]. Thus* Δ_f *has an asymptotic linear structure:* $\Delta_f / 2^n \to 1$ *as* $n \to \infty$.
2. *When* $t \geq 1$, $\Delta_f = 2^n$ *and the function has linear structures at* $(0, 0, a)$ *for all* $a \in GF(2)^t$.

Furthermore, when we fix $log_2(n)$ *or less input bits,* f *becomes linear.*

Proof. 1. When $t = 0$, we do not have any z-terms in equation (5):

$$\begin{aligned}\Delta_f(a,b) &= \sum_{x,y} (-1)^{x\cdot\phi(y)+g(y)+(x+a)\cdot\phi(y+b)+g(y+b)} \\ &= \sum_y (-1)^{a\cdot\phi(y+b)+g(y)+g(y+b)} \sum_x (-1)^{x\cdot(\phi(y)+\phi(y+b))} \\ &= \begin{cases} 0 \text{ , if } b \neq 0, \\ 2^r \sum_y (-1)^{a\cdot\phi(y)} \text{ , if } b = 0. \end{cases}\end{aligned}$$

Note that $|\{x \in GF(2)^r | wt(x) \geq r-1\}| = r+1 = 2^s = |Im(\phi)|$. Therefore we necessarily have $Im(\phi) = \{x \in GF(2)^r | wt(x) \geq r-1\}$ and $\{100\ldots0 \cdot \phi(y) | y \in GF(2)^s\} = \{0, 1, 1, \ldots, 1, 1\}$. This implies

$$|\Delta_f(100\ldots0, 000\ldots0)| = 2^r \left|\sum_y (-1)^{100\ldots0\cdot\phi(y)}\right| = 2^n - 2^{n-s+1}.$$

Therefore, $\Delta_f \geq 2^n - 2^{n-s+1} \geq 2^n - 2^{n-\log_2(n)+1} = (1-2/n)2^n$. The last inequality is true because $n = r+s = 2^s - 1 + s \Longrightarrow 2^s \leq n \Longrightarrow s \leq \log_2(n)$.

[2] We note that such a lower bound was first given by Zheng and Zhang in [26, Theorem 2]. Later this bound was improved by Tarannikov et. al. in [23, Theorem 4] for functions with order of resiliency $\geq (n-3)/2$.

By [23, Theorem 4], $\Delta_f \geq \left(\frac{2k-n+3}{n+1}\right) 2^n = \left(1 - \frac{2(s+1)}{n+1}\right) 2^n$ where $k = r - 2$ is the order of resiliency of f. It is easy to see by elementary algebra that their lower bound $\left(1 - \frac{2(s+1)}{n+1}\right) 2^n$ is not as sharp as our bound $\left(1 - \frac{2}{n}\right) 2^n$.

2. When $t \geq 1$, $\Delta_f(0,0,a) = 2^{s+r} \sum_z (-1)^{11\ldots1\cdot z + 11\ldots1\cdot(z+a)} = \pm 2^{s+r+t} = \pm 2^n$.

It is easy to see that equation (5) becomes linear when we fix y which has $s \leq log_2(n)$ bits. □

Remark 8. We have used the direct approach for computing additive autocorrelation in Theorem 9 because it gives sharper bounds than by using dual functions.

The saturated functions constructed by Proposition 7 are 'nearly linear' because they become linear when we fix very few ($\leq log_2(n)$) bits. Moreover, they have linear structures or asymptotic linear structures for the case $t = 0$. We see that although the resilient functions in Proposition 7 optimize Siegenthaler [22] and Sarkar-Maitra [20, Theorem 2] inequality. These strong conditions may cause the function to have linear-like structure.

6 Conclusion

We have introduced the dual function as a useful concept in the study of functions with 3-valued spectrum and derived several useful results for such functions. Then we constructed highly nonlinear resilient Boolean functions with optimal additive autocorrelation from functions used in the construction of Hadamard difference sets. Finally, we showed that our constructions have better additive autocorrelation than known highly nonlinear resilient Boolean functions.

Acknowledgement

We would like to thank Shaoquan Jiang for proofreading this paper and his many useful suggestions. We would also like to thank Douglas R. Stinson for proofreading an earlier version of the paper. Finally, we would like to thank the referees for their helpful comments. Research for this paper is supported by NSERC grant RG-PIN 227700-00. Khoongming Khoo's research is supported by a postgraduate scholarship from DSO National Laboratories, Singapore.

References

[1] E. Biham, A. Shamir, "Differential Cryptanalysis of DES-like Cryptosystems", *Journal of Cryptology*, vol. 4, 1991. 275

[2] A. Canteaut, C. Carlet, P. Charpin and C. Fontaine, "Propagation Characteristics and Correlation-Immunity of Highly Nonlinear Boolean Functions", LNCS 1807, *Eurocrypt'2000*, pp. 507-522, Springer-Verlag, 2000. 276, 278, 279, 285, 286

[3] C. Carlet, "A Larger Class of Cryptographic Boolean Functions via a Study of the Moriana-McFarland Construction", LNCS 2442, *Crypto'2002*, pp. 549-564, Springer Verlag, 2002. 276, 280, 285

[4] C. Carlet and E. Prouff, "On Plateaued Functions and their Constructions", *Proceedings of FSE 2003*, Springer-Verlag, 2003. 276

[5] F. Chabaud and S. Vaudenay, "Links between differential and linear cryptanalysis", LNCS 950, *Eurocrypt'94*, pp.356-365, Springer-Verlag, 1995. 276

[6] J. Clark, J. Jacob, S. Stepney, S. Maitra and W. Millan, "Evolving Boolean Functions satisfying Multiple Criteria", LNCS 2551, *Indocrypt 2002*, pp. 246-259, Springer-Verlag, 2002. 277

[7] J. F. Dillon, "Multiplicative Difference Sets via Characters", *Designs, Codes and Cryptography*, vol. 17, pp. 225-235, 1999. 276, 281, 283, 284

[8] J. F. Dillon and H. Dobbertin, "Cyclic Difference Sets with Singer Parameters", preprint, 12 August 1999. 276, 281, 282, 284

[9] H. Dobbertin, "Kasami Power Functions, Permutation Polynomials and Cyclic Difference Sets", *N. A. T. O.-A. S. I. Workshop: Difference Sets, Sequences and their Correlation Properties*, Bad Windsheim, Aug 3-14, 1998. 276, 282, 284

[10] R. Gold, "Maximal Recursive Sequences with 3-valued Cross Correlation Functions", *IEEE Transactions on Information Theory*, vol. 14, pp. 154-156, 1968. 281, 282, 283

[11] G. Gong and A. M. Youssef, "Cryptographic Properties of the Welch-Gong Transformation Sequence Generators", *IEEE Trans. Inform. Theory*, vol.48 no.11, pp. 2837-2846, Nov 2002. 276, 279, 283, 284, 285

[12] T. Helleseth and P. V. Kumar, "Sequences with Low Correlation", Chapter in *Handbook of Coding Theory*, North-Holland, 1998. 277

[13] T. Jacobsen, L. Knudsen, "The Interpolation Attack on Block Ciphers", LNCS 1267, *Fast Software Encryption*, pp.28-40, Springer-Verlag, 1997. 276, 278

[14] T. Kasami, "The Weight Enumerators for several Classes of Subcodes of Second Order Binary Reed Muller Codes, *Information and Control* 18, pp. 369-394, 1971. 281, 282

[15] K. Khoo and G. Gong, "New Constructions for Highly Nonlinear and Resilient Boolean Functions", LNCS 2727, *ACISP 2003*, pp. 498-509, 2003. 279

[16] M. Matsui, "Linear cryptanalysis method for DES cipher", LNCS 765, *Eurocrypt'93*, pp. 386-397, 1994. 275, 277

[17] F. J. McWilliams and N. J. A. Sloane, *Theory of Error-Correcting Codes*, North-Holland, Amsterdam, 1977. 277, 278

[18] N.J Patterson and D. H. Wiedemann, "The Covering Radius of the $(2^{15}, 16)$ Reed-Muller Code is at least 16276", *IEEE Trans. Inform. Theory*, vol. 29 no. 3, pp. 354-356, May 1983. 284

[19] P. Sarkar and S. Maitra, "Construction of Nonlinear Boolean Functions with Important Cryptographic Properties", LNCS 1807, *Eurocrypt'2000*, pp. 485-506, Springer-Verlag, 2000. 280

[20] P. Sarkar and S. Maitra, "Nonlinearity Bounds and Constructions of Resilient Boolean Functions", LNCS 1880, *Crypto'2000*, pp. 515-532, Springer Verlag, 2000. 276, 286, 288

[21] J. Seberry, X. M. Zhang and Y. Zheng, "On Constructions and Nonlinearity of Correlation Immune Functions", LNCS 765, *Eurocrypt'93*, pp. 181-199, 1994. 285

[22] T. Siegenthaler, "Decrypting a Class of Stream Ciphers using Ciphertexts only", *IEEE Transactions on Computers*, vol. C34, no. 1, pp. 81-85, 1985. 275, 277, 286, 288

[23] Y. Tarannikov, P. Korolev and A. Botev, "Autocorrelation Coefficients and Correlation Immunity of Boolean Functions", LNCS 2248, *Asiacrypt 2001*, pp. 460-479, Springer-Verlag, 2001. 275, 276, 287, 288

[24] X. M. Zhang and Y. Zheng, "GAC - The Criterion for Global Avalanche Criteria of Cryptographic Functions", *Journal for Universal Computer Science*, vol. 1 no. 5, pp. 316-333, 1995. 275, 277

[25] X. M. Zhang and Y. Zheng, "Autocorrelations and New Bounds on the Nonlinearity of Boolean Functions", LNCS 1070, *Eurocrypt'96*, pp. 294-306, Springer-Verlag, 1996. 275

[26] Y. Zheng and X. M. Zhang, "New Results on Correlation Immune Functions", LNCS 2015, *ICISC 2000*, pp. 264-274, Springer-Verlag, 2001. 275, 287

[27] Y. Zheng and X. M. Zhang, "Relationships between Bent Functions and Complementary Plateaued Functions", LNCS 1787, *ICISC'99*, pp. 60-75, Springer-Verlag, 1999. 276, 279, 280

On a New Notion of Nonlinearity Relevant to Multi-output Pseudo-random Generators

Claude Carlet[1]* and Emmanuel Prouff[2]

[1] Claude Carlet, INRIA Projet CODES
BP 105 - 78153, Le Chesnay Cedex, France
claude.carlet@inria.fr

[2] INRIA Projet CODES and University of Paris 11
Laboratoire de Recherche en Informatique
15 rue Georges Clemenceau, 91405 Orsay Cedex, France
prouff@info.unicaen.fr

Abstract. Vectorial functions (i.e. mappings from $\mathbb{F}_2^n$ into $\mathbb{F}_2^m$, also called S-boxes) can be used in pseudo-random generators with multiple outputs. The notion of maximum correlation of these S-boxes to linear functions, introduced by Zhang and Chan, plays a central role in the resistance of the resulting stream ciphers to correlation attacks. It can be related to a notion of "unrestricted nonlinearity". We obtain a new lower bound on the overall maximum correlation to linear functions of vectorial functions which results in an upper bound on the unrestricted nonlinearity. We compare it with the known upper bounds on the nonlinearity (which are also valid for the unrestricted nonlinearity of balanced functions). We study its tightness and we exhibit a class of balanced functions whose nonlinearity and unrestricted nonlinearity are high relatively to the upper-bounds.

1 Introduction

Let n and m be two positive integers. We focus in this paper on the mappings from $\mathbb{F}_2^n$ to $\mathbb{F}_2^m$, called (n, m)-functions or S-boxes. These mappings play a central role in block ciphers. In stream ciphers as well, it would be natural to use S-boxes in order to combine the outputs of n linear feedback shift registers (LFSR) or to filter the contents of a single LFSR, and then to generate m bits at each clock-cycle instead of a single one. This would result in a speed up of the encryption and of the decryption. But the robustness of such pseudo-random generators has to be studied and compared with the single-output ones.

A fundamental principle introduced by Shannon [23] for the design of conventional cryptographic systems is *confusion*, which aims at concealing any algebraic structure. Concerning S-boxes involved in the system, their adequacy with this principle must be quantified, so that we have a precise criterion for choosing

* Also member of GREYC-Caen and of the University of Paris 8

M. Matsui and R. Zuccherato (Eds.): SAC 2003, LNCS 3006, pp. 291–305, 2004.

these S-boxes. In the case of a Boolean function ($m = 1$), the main characteristic quantifying some kind of confusion induced into the system by the function is the *nonlinearity* . As shown in [3, 4, 18], this characteristic is related to the resistance to the *fast correlation attacks* on single-output stream ciphers introduced by Meier and Staffelbach [17].

In [7, 21] is studied a generalization of the nonlinearity of Boolean functions to S-boxes. This generalization is closely related to the *linear attack* of block ciphers introduced by Matsui [16]. A second generalization of the nonlinearity of Boolean functions to S-boxes, called *unrestricted nonlinearity* , can be related to their *maximum correlation* coefficients introduced by Zhang and Chan in [26], which quantify a certain type of correlation between an S-box and linear functions. Given a multi-output combining function in a combination generator or a multi-output filtering function in a nonlinear filtering generator, these coefficients must be as low as possible to make difficult correlation attacks (see [26]). So, we are interested in the maximum possible value of the maximum correlation coefficients (let us call it the *overall maximum correlation to linear functions*) which leads to the notion of unrestricted nonlinearity. Having low overall maximum correlation to linear functions is equivalent, for an S-box, to have high unrestricted nonlinearity. Zhang and Chan give only an upper bound on the maximum correlations of any S-box to linear functions (this upper-bound has been improved by the authors for perfect nonlinear S-boxes and, more recently, by Gong and Khoo [15] for some balanced S-boxes), which results in a lower bound on their unrestricted nonlinearity. This bound does not permit to know what is a reasonably high unrestricted nonlinearity. In this paper we study upper-bounds on the unrestricted nonlinearity and we exhibit S-boxes approaching them.

The paper is organized as follows. In Section 2, we recall the basic facts about the nonlinearity of functions (Boolean or vectorial). In Section 3, we recall how the notion of nonlinearity is relevant to fast correlation attacks on nonlinear filtering generators or on combination generators, and we recall the background on the maximum correlation to linear functions. We conclude this section by introducing the new notion of unrestricted nonlinearity. When the S-box $F : \mathbb{F}_2^n \mapsto \mathbb{F}_2^m$ is *balanced*, i.e. when it takes every value in $\mathbb{F}_2^m$ the same number 2^{n-m} of times, then its unrestricted nonlinearity is always lower than or equal to its nonlinearity and when $n = m$, it is null. In section 4, we exhibit a new general upper bound on the unrestricted nonlinearity of balanced S-boxes (equivalent to a lower bound on the overall maximum correlation to linear functions). We show that this bound is more precise than the upper bound $2^{n-1} - 2^{n/2-1}$ if and only if $n/2 < m$. To settle the remaining case $m \leq n/2$, we exhibit a class of balanced (n, m)-functions whose nonlinearity and unrestricted nonlinearity equal $2^{n-1} - 2^{n/2}$, which can be considered as high with respect to the introduced upper-bounds.

Length constraints do not permit us to give all proofs in details. They can be found in [6].

2 Preliminaries

2.1 Nonlinearity of Vectorial Functions

For every Boolean function f on $\mathbb{F}_2^n$, the set $\{x \in \mathbb{F}_2^n;\ f(x) = 1\}$, denoted by *Supp* f, is called the *support* of f. The cardinality of *Supp* f is called the *Hamming weight* of f and is denoted by $\omega_H(f)$. The *Hamming distance* between f and another function g, denoted by $d_H(f,g)$, being defined as the size of the set $\{x \in \mathbb{F}_2^n \mid f(x) \neq g(x)\}$, the nonlinearity N_f of f is the minimum Hamming distance between f and all affine functions $\ell(x) = a_1x_1 + \cdots + a_nx_n + a_0 = a \cdot x + a_0$ (where $a = (a_1, \cdots, a_n)$ ranges over $\mathbb{F}_2^n$ and a_0 ranges over $\mathbb{F}_2$). The value $a \cdot x$ in $\mathbb{F}_2$ is the usual inner product between a and x. Since the Hamming distance between two Boolean functions f_1 and f_2 equals $2^{n-1} - \frac{1}{2} \sum_{x \in \mathbb{F}_2^n} (-1)^{f_1(x)+f_2(x)}$, the nonlinearity N_f equals $2^{n-1} - \frac{1}{2} \max_{\ell \in R(1,n)} \sum_{x \in \mathbb{F}_2^n} (-1)^{f(x)+\ell(x)}$, where $R(1,n)$ denotes the set of all affine functions. Equivalently, we have

$$N_f = 2^{n-1} - \frac{1}{2} \max_{u \in \mathbb{F}_2^n} \Big| \sum_{x \in \mathbb{F}_2^n} (-1)^{f(x)+u \cdot x} \Big|. \tag{1}$$

The set of (n,m)-functions shall be denoted by $\mathcal{B}_{n,m}$ (if $m = 1$, we will denote it by $\mathcal{B}_n$, instead of $\mathcal{B}_{n,1}$). To every (n,m)-function F, we associate the m-tuple $(f_1, \cdots, f_m)$ of its coordinate Boolean functions such that $F(x) = (f_1(x), \cdots, f_m(x))$. In [7, 21] is studied a generalization of the nonlinearity of Boolean functions to S-boxes: the nonlinearity of an (n,m)-function F, denoted by N_F, is the minimum nonlinearity of all the Boolean functions $x \mapsto v \cdot F(x)$, $v \in \mathbb{F}_2^m$, $v \neq 0$, which implies

$$N_F = 2^{n-1} - \frac{1}{2} \max_{v \in \mathbb{F}_2^{m\,*},\ u \in \mathbb{F}_2^n} \left| \sum_{x \in \mathbb{F}_2^n} (-1)^{v \cdot F(x)+u \cdot x} \right|. \tag{2}$$

In other words, N_F equals $\min_{\ell \in R(1,m)^*} \min_{u \in \mathbb{F}_2^n} d_H(\ell \circ F, \ell_u)$, where ℓ_u denotes the linear Boolean function $x \in \mathbb{F}_2^n \mapsto u \cdot x$ and where $R(1,m)^*$ denotes the set of non-constant affine Boolean functions on $\mathbb{F}_2^m$. Notice that the nonlinearity, N_F, can be rewritten $2^{n-1} - 2^{n-1} \max_{u \in \mathbb{F}_2^n} c_F(u)$, where $c_F(u)$ is called the *linear correlation to the linear function* ℓ_u and is defined by

$$c_F(u) = \frac{1}{2^n} \max_{\ell \in R(1,m)^*} \sum_{x \in \mathbb{F}_2^n} (-1)^{\ell \circ F(x)+u \cdot x} = \frac{1}{2^n} \max_{v \in \mathbb{F}_2^{m\,*}} \left| \sum_{x \in \mathbb{F}_2^n} (-1)^{v \cdot F(x)+u \cdot x} \right| .$$

Relation (2) relates the nonlinearity of F to the Fourier transform of the so-called *sign* function, $\chi_F(x,v) = (-1)^{v \cdot F(x)}$, of F. This transform, that we shall call *Walsh transform* , is defined by the formula

$$\widehat{\chi_F}(u,v) = \sum_{x \in \mathbb{F}_2^n} (-1)^{v \cdot F(x)+u \cdot x} .$$

More generally, the Fourier transform of an integer-valued function φ on $\mathbb{F}_2^n$ is defined by $\widehat{\varphi}(u) = \sum_{x\in\mathbb{F}_2^n} \varphi(x)(-1)^{u\cdot x}$, $u \in \mathbb{F}_2^n$.

Using the Walsh transform, one can rewrite Relations (1) and (2) respecively as $N_f = 2^{n-1} - \frac{1}{2}\max_{u\in\mathbb{F}_2^n} |\widehat{\chi_f}(u)|$ and

$$N_F = 2^{n-1} - \frac{1}{2}\max_{v\in\mathbb{F}_2^{m\,*},u\in\mathbb{F}_2^n} |\widehat{\chi_F}(u,v)|. \tag{3}$$

For any (n,m)-function F, let φ_z denote the indicator function of the set $F^{-1}(z)$ (φ_z is defined by $\varphi_z(x) = 1$ if $F(x) = z$ and $\varphi_z(x) = 0$ otherwise), then we have

$$\widehat{\chi_F}(u,v) = \sum_{z\in\mathbb{F}_2^m} \widehat{\varphi_z}(u)(-1)^{v\cdot z} \tag{4}$$

(note that, $c_F(u)$, $u \in \mathbb{F}_2^n$, equals $1/2^n \max_{v\in\mathbb{F}_2^{m\,*}} |\sum_{z\in\mathbb{F}_2^m} \widehat{\varphi_z}(u)(-1)^{v\cdot z}|$).

We recall that every numerical function φ defined on $\mathbb{F}_2^n$ satisfies Parseval's relation,

$$\sum_{u\in\mathbb{F}_2^n} \widehat{\varphi}^2(u) = 2^n \sum_{x\in\mathbb{F}_2^n} \varphi^2(x), \tag{5}$$

and the inverse Fourier formula

$$\widehat{\widehat{\varphi}} = 2^n\varphi. \tag{6}$$

In the case of the Walsh transform of an (n,m)-function F, Relation (5) shows that $\sum_{u\in\mathbb{F}_2^n} \widehat{\chi_F}^2(u,v) = 2^{2n}$, for every $v \in \mathbb{F}_2^m$, which implies that N_F is upper bounded by $2^{n-1} - 2^{n/2-1}$ for every (n,m)-function F. If n is even and $m \le \frac{n}{2}$, then this bound is tight [20]. The functions achieving it are called *bent*. Chabaud and Vaudenay proved in [7] that the nonlinearity N_F also satisfies $N_F \le 2^{n-1} - \frac{1}{2}\sqrt{3\times 2^n - 2 - 2\frac{(2^n-1)(2^{n-1}-1)}{2^m-1}}$. This bound equals $2^{n-1} - 2^{n/2-1}$ if and only if $m = n-1$ and it is better than $2^{n-1} - 2^{n/2-1}$ if and only if $m \ge n$. When $m = n$, then Chabaud-Vaudenay's bound implies that the maximum possible nonlinearity of any (n,n)-function is upper bounded by $2^{n-1} - 2^{\frac{n-1}{2}}$. The functions achieving this nonlinearity are called *almost bent* [7] and exist only when n is odd. In the other cases (when $m = n$ and n is even or when $m < n < 2m$), the maximum values achieved by the nonlinearity are unknown.

2.2 Resilient Functions

A *combination generator* consists of several linear feedback shift registers whose output sequences are combined by a nonlinear Boolean - or vectorial - function (called a *nonlinear combining function* or a *combining function*). Let F be an (n,m)-function, used as combining function, and let t be a positive integer smaller than n. We know (see [2, 24]) that a stream cipher using F as combining function opposes a maximum resistance to correlation attacks involving at most t LFSRs, if and only if F is *t-th order correlation immune* i.e. if and only if its output distribution probability is unchanged when t - or at most t - of its input bits are kept constant. A function F is *t-resilient* if it is balanced and t-th order correlation immune. Clearly, an (n, m)-function F is t-th order correlation immune if and only if all the Boolean functions φ_z $(z \in \mathbb{F}_2^m)$ defined before Equation (4) are t-th order correlation immune and it is t-resilient if and only if all the Boolean functions φ_z $(z \in \mathbb{F}_2^m)$ have Hamming weight 2^{n-m} and are t-th order correlation immune. The property of t-th order correlation immunity (resp. the property of t-resiliency) can also be characterized (see [25, 2]) by the fact that $\widehat{\chi_F}(u, v)$ is null for every nonzero vector $v \in \mathbb{F}_2^m$ and for every vector $u \in \mathbb{F}_2^n$ such that $1 \leq w_H(u) \leq t$ (resp. such that $0 \leq w_H(u) \leq t$). Thus, an S-box F is t-th order correlation immune if and only if all the functions $v \cdot F$ $(v \in \mathbb{F}_2^{m*})$ are t-th order correlation immune and it is t-resilient if and only if all the functions $v \cdot F$ $(v \in \mathbb{F}_2^{m*})$ are t-resilient. Equivalently, an (n, m)-function F is t-th order correlation immune if and only if all the functions $g \circ F$ are t-th order correlation immune when g ranges over the set, $\mathcal{B}_m$, of m-variables Boolean functions (see [24]) and F is t-resilient if and only if all the functions $g \circ F$ are t-resilient when g ranges over the set of m-variables balanced Boolean functions.

Sarkar and Maitra proved in [22] that the values of the Walsh transforms of t-th order correlation immune (resp. t-resilient) Boolean functions on $\mathbb{F}_2^n$ are all divisible by 2^{t+1} (resp. 2^{t+2}). Obviously, according to the observations above, this property can be extended to S-boxes. This divisibility resulted in upper bounds (partially also obtained by Tarannikov and Zheng and Zhang) on the nonlinearities of t-th order correlation immune Boolean functions and t-resilient Boolean functions (see [22]), which are still valid for vectorial functions (see more in [6]).

3 Maximum Correlation and Unrestricted Nonlinearity

A *nonlinear filtering generator* consists of a single LFSR which is filtered by a nonlinear function. More precisely, the output sequence of a nonlinear filtering generator corresponds to the output, during a number of clock cycles, of a nonlinear function whose input bits are taken from some stages of the LFSR. To make a stream cipher with nonlinear filtering generator resistant against fast correlation attacks (see [1, 12, 13, 14, 17, 19]), the Boolean filtering function must be highly nonlinear. In the case of stream ciphers with a Boolean combining t-resilient functions f as well, Canteaut and Trabbia [4] and Canteaut [3] show that fast correlation attacks are as unefficient as possible if the coefficients $\widehat{\chi_f}(u)$ are small for every vector u of Hamming weight higher than, but close to, t and this condition is satisfied by highly nonlinear Boolean t-resilient functions. Since every known attack on a Boolean combining - or filtering - function can be applied to a Boolean function taking the form $v \cdot F$, where F is an (n, m)-function and v is a nonzero vector in $\mathbb{F}_2^m$, a vectorial combining - or filtering - function must be highly nonlinear (this ensures, by definition of the nonlinearity, that every nonzero linear combination $v \cdot F$ has also a high nonlinearity) and must also admit, in the case of stream ciphers with combination generator, a high resiliency order (ensuring then, as showed in section 2.2, that all the nonzero linear combinations $v \cdot F$ have also a high resiliency order). But, as observed by Zhang and Chan in [26], a correlation attack on stream ciphers involving a vectorial function F can still be made by considering all the non-constant Boolean combinations, $g \circ F$, instead of only the non-zero linear ones. As we recalled in section 2.2, the high-resiliency of an (n,m)-function F implies the high correlation immunity of the Boolean functions $g \circ F$. However, as mentioned by Zhang and Chan (see [26]) the high nonlinearity of F does not imply the high nonlinearity of the functions $g \circ F$.

3.1 Maximum Correlation of Vectorial Functions

The *maximum correlation* of a vectorial (n,m)-function F to the linear function $x \mapsto u \cdot x$, denoted $\mathcal{C}_F(u)$, has been defined by Zhang and Chan as $\mathcal{C}_F(u) = \frac{1}{2^n} \max_{g \in \mathcal{B}_m} \sum_{x \in \mathbb{F}_2^n} (-1)^{g(F(x))+u \cdot x}$.

We shall exclude henceforth the case $g = cst$ in the definition of the maximum correlation during our study of the coefficients of $\mathcal{C}_F$, since composing F by a constant function g has no cryptographic relevance. Notice that this changes only the value of $\mathcal{C}_F(0)$, since the summation $\sum_{x \in \mathbb{F}_2^n} (-1)^{g \circ F(x)+u \cdot x}$ is null for every constant function g and every nonzero vector $u \in \mathbb{F}_2^n$. So we define

$$\mathcal{C}_F(u) = 2^{-n} \max_{g \in \mathcal{B}_m^*} \sum_{x \in \mathbb{F}_2^n} (-1)^{g(F(x))+u \cdot x}; \; u \in \mathbb{F}_2^n, \tag{7}$$

where $\mathcal{B}_m^*$ denotes the set of all non constant Boolean functions defined on $\mathbb{F}_2^m$. The restriction on g (being not constant) makes $\mathcal{C}_F(0)$ an indicator of the balancedness of F whereas the definition of $\mathcal{C}_F(0)$ by Zhang-Chan (i.e. without this restriction) makes it always equal to 1.

Remark 1. The maximum correlation of the S-box to the null function is not of the same type as its maximum correlation to the nonzero linear functions. Indeed, the value $\mathcal{C}_F(0)$ gives statistic information about the system whereas the other coefficients are directly related to correlation attacks. Recall that an S-box gives no statistic information to the attacker if it is balanced. If F is an (n,m)-function, then we have

$$\mathcal{C}_F(0) \geq 1 - 2^{-m+1}, \tag{8}$$

the bound being tight if and only if F is balanced. Indeed, there always exists $z_0 \in \mathbb{F}_2^m$ such that $\#F^{-1}(z_0) \leq 2^{n-m}$ and choosing g equal to the indicator of the singleton $\{z_0\}$ in (7), shows Relation (8). The case of equality is easy to prove. Relation (8) shows that, for every function F, the coefficient $\mathcal{C}_F(0)$ takes a value near 1 (if m is large enough) whereas we shall see that, for a highly nonlinear (n,m)-function, the other coefficients are close to zero (see Remark 2). $\diamond$

It is shown in [26] that

$$\mathcal{C}_F(u) = \frac{1}{2^n} \sum_{z \in \mathbb{F}_2^m} \left| \sum_{x \in F^{-1}(z)} (-1)^{u \cdot x} \right| = \frac{1}{2^n} \sum_{z \in \mathbb{F}_2^m} |\widehat{\varphi_z}(u)| \ . \tag{9}$$

This implies, as shown in [26], the following relation between the maximum correlation to non-zero linear functions and the Walsh transform:

$$\forall u \in \mathbb{F}_2^{n*},\ \mathcal{C}_F(u) = \frac{1}{2^{m+n}} \sum_{z \in \mathbb{F}_2^m} \left| \sum_{v \in \mathbb{F}_2^m} \widehat{\chi_F}(u,v)(-1)^{v \cdot z} \right|. \tag{10}$$

Relation (9) and the facts recalled at Subsection 2.2 imply:

Proposition 1. *A balanced (n,m)-function F is t-resilient if and only if, for every vector $u \in \mathbb{F}_2^n$ such that $1 \leq w_H(u) \leq t$, one of the two following conditions is satis□ed :*
1. $c_F(u) = 0$,
2. $\mathcal{C}_F(u) = 0$,
that is, if and only if, for every vector $z \in \mathbb{F}_2^m$,
3. the Boolean function φ_z is t-th order correlation immune.

We recall now the following theorem giving an upper bound on the maximum correlation coefficients and which can be deduced straightforwardly from Relation (10).

Theorem 1. *[26] Let F be an (n,m)-function. For any nonzero vector $u \in \mathbb{F}_2^n$, we have*

$$\mathcal{C}_F(u) \leq 2^{m/2}(1 - 2^{-n+1} N_F). \tag{11}$$

Remark 2. If an (n,m)-function F (m small compared to n) has a high nonlinearity, say $N_F \geq 2^{n-1} - c \times 2^{n/2-1}$, where c is any constant value close to 1, then a first consequence of this theorem, is that, for $u \in \mathbb{F}_2^{n*}$, the maximum correlation coefficients to linear functions, $\mathcal{C}_F(u)$, are close to zero since according to Relation (11), we have $\mathcal{C}_F(u) \leq c \times 2^{m/2-n/2}$. $\diamond$

3.2 A New Notion of Nonlinearity of Vectorial Functions: The Unrestricted Nonlinearity

We introduce, now, a generalization of the nonlinearity of Boolean functions to S-boxes, which is directly related to the maximum correlation coefficients to linear functions.

Definition 1. *Let F be an (n,m)-function. We call* unrestricted nonlinearity *of F and we denote by UN_F the minimum Hamming distance between all Boolean functions $g \circ F$ ($g \in \mathcal{B}_m{}^*$) and all* non-constant *ane functions ℓ on $\mathbb{F}_2^n$, that is, the minimum distance of the functions $g \circ F$ to $R(1,n)^*$.*

According to Relations (1) and (7), we have

$$UN_F = 2^{n-1} - 2^{n-1} \max_{u \in \mathbb{F}_2^{n*}} \mathcal{C}_F(u). \tag{12}$$

For $m > 1$, we are obliged to exclude the case ℓ constant in Definition 1 (that is to exclude $u = 0$ in Relation (12)). If we did not, then, according to Remark 2, for all S-boxes F with reasonably high nonlinearities, we would have $UN_F = 2^{n-1} - 2^{n-1}\mathcal{C}_F(0)$ and UN_F would only quantify the balancedness of F. Note that $g \in \mathcal{B}_m{}^*$ can then be replaced by $g \in \mathcal{B}_m$ in Definition 1.

We shall call *overall maximum correlation* of an (n,m)-function F to non-zero linear functions, the value $\max_{u \in \mathbb{F}_2^{n*}} \mathcal{C}_F(u)$.

Relation (12) and Relation (9), for every $u \in \mathbb{F}_2^{n*}$, imply

$$UN_F = 2^{n-1} - \frac{1}{2} \max_{u \in \mathbb{F}_2^{n*}} \sum_{z \in \mathbb{F}_2^m} |\widehat{\varphi_z}(u)|. \tag{13}$$

According to Theorem 1 and to Relations (11) and (12), the unrestricted nonlinearity, UN_F, of any (n,m)-function F satisfies

$$2^{n-1} - 2^{m/2}(2^{n-1} - N_F) \leq UN_F. \tag{14}$$

Remark 3. If F is balanced, then $\widehat{\chi_F}(0,v) = 0$, for every $v \in \mathbb{F}_2^{m*}$, and we have then $N_F = 2^{n-1} - \frac{1}{2}\max_{u \neq 0, v \neq 0} |\widehat{\chi_F}(u,v)|$ that is $N_F = \min_{\ell \in R(1,m)^*} \min_{u \in \mathbb{F}_2^{n*}} d_H(\ell \circ F, \ell_u)$, which implies:

$$UN_F \leq N_F \leq 2^{n-1} - 2^{n/2-1}. \tag{15}$$

◇

This implies that the unrestricted nonlinearity of a surjective linear mapping L is null, since the inequality $0 \leq UN_L \leq N_L \leq 0$ holds.

The nonlinearity UN_F is actually "unrestricted" only for balanced functions F; for these functions, the condition $\ell \neq cst$ (that is, $u \neq 0$) does not make UN_F greater than N_F.

Since $R(1,n)^*$ is invariant under the right action of an affine invertible mapping, we deduce that, for any balanced (n,m)-function F, the unrestricted nonlinearity of F is unchanged when F is right-composed with such a mapping. Moreover, if A is a surjective linear (or affine) function from $\mathbb{F}_2^p$ into $\mathbb{F}_2^n$, then we have $UN_{F \circ A} = 2^{p-n} UN_F$.

Proposition 2. *Let F be an (n,m)-function and let p be any integer, then, for every (m,p)-function ϕ, we have $UN_{\phi \circ F} \geq UN_F$. If ϕ is a permutation on $\mathbb{F}_2^m$, then we have $UN_{\phi \circ F} = UN_F$.*

Remark 4. If F is a surjective (that is, balanced) affine function from $\mathbb{F}_2^n$ into $\mathbb{F}_2^m$, then we showed that $UN_F = 0$. Thus, the relation $UN_{\phi \circ F} = UN_F$, valid for every permutation ϕ, implies that, for every surjective affine (n,m)-function A and for every permutation ϕ on $\mathbb{F}_2^m$, the unrestricted nonlinearity of the (n,m)-function $\phi \circ A$ is null. ◇

The classical nonlinearity N_F corresponds, for balanced functions, to a version of UN_F in which g is chosen in the set of non-constant affine functions and not in the whole set $\mathcal{B}_m^*$ (cf. Remark 3). It is well known that the low nonlinearity of a function F permits a linear attack on block ciphers using this function as S-box. This attack is based on the fact that there exists at least one linear combination of the outputs of an S-box whose Hamming distance to the set of affine functions is small. Due to the iterative structure of a block cipher, the knowledge of a combination of the outputs of F with a low nonlinearity does not make more efficient the linear attack if the combination is not a linear one. But the knowledge of a nonlinear combination of the outputs of F with a low nonlinearity does make more efficient the correlation attacks in the case of stream ciphers. Indeed, as explained in [26], the maximum correlation to linear functions is relevant to stream ciphers because, when an S-box is used to combine n LFSR's or a single one (as filtering function), all of the m binary sequences it produces can be combined by a linear, or nonlinear, function g to perform correlation attacks. From this point of view, the unrestricted nonlinearity of an S-box used as combining - or filtering - function plays the same role with respect to correlation attacks on stream ciphers as nonlinearity with respect to linear attacks on block ciphers.

4 Analysis of the Unrestricted Nonlinearity

We recalled that the nonlinearity of any (n,m)-function is upper bounded by $2^{n-1} - 2^{n/2-1}$ and by $2^{n-1} - 2^{\frac{n-1}{2}}$ if $m = n$. Since we considered not only the non-constant affine functions but all the Boolean functions in ${\mathcal{B}_m}^*$ to define the unrestricted nonlinearity, there may exist a better upper bound on UN_F than $2^{n-1} - 2^{n/2-1}$. We study now such a bound.

4.1 An Upper Bound on The Unrestricted Nonlinearity of S-Boxes

We shall derive for any balanced (n,m)-function F such that $m < n$, a lower bound on the overall maximum correlation to non-zero linear functions, that is, an upper bound on UN_F.

Theorem 2. *Let F be a balanced (n,m)-function, then its overall maximum correlation to non-zero linear functions satis*□*es* $\max_{u\in\mathbb{F}_2^{n*}} \mathcal{C}_F(u) \geq C_{n,m}$, *where* $C_{n,m}$ *is de*□*ned for every pair* (n,m) *by*

$$C_{n,m} = \frac{1}{2^n}\left(\frac{2^{2m}-2^m}{2^n-1} + \sqrt{\frac{2^{2n}-2^{2n-m}}{2^n-1} + \left(\frac{2^{2m}-2^m}{2^n-1}-1\right)^2} - 1\right),$$

and its unrestricted nonlinearity is upper bounded by

$$\min\left(2^{n-1}-2^{n/2-1}, 2^{n-1}-2^{n-1}C_{n,m}\right) .$$

To prove this Theorem, we need the following lemma:

Lemma 1. *Let S be a set and let $\lambda = \sum_{z\in S}\lambda_z$ be a sum of $\#S$ non-negative integers indexed by the elements of S. Let M and k be two integers such that $\sum_{z\in S}\lambda_z^2 \geq M$ and $0\leq \lambda_z \leq k$, for $z\in S$. Then we have*

$$\lambda \geq \frac{M}{2k^2} + \frac{1}{2}\sqrt{4M + \left(\frac{M}{k^2}-1\right)^2} - \frac{1}{2}. \qquad (16)$$

Proof. Since, for every vector $z\in S$ such that $\lambda_z \neq 0$, the value of λ_z is lower than or equal to k, we deduce that $M \leq \sum_{z\in S}\lambda_z^2 \leq \#\{z\in S;\ \lambda_z\neq 0\}\times k^2$ i.e.

$$\#\{z\in S;\ \lambda_z \neq 0\} \geq \frac{M}{k^2}. \qquad (17)$$

On the other hand, we have

$$\left(\sum_{z\in S}\lambda_z\right)^2 = \sum_{z\in S}\lambda_z^2 + \sum_{z,z'\in S, z\neq z'}\lambda_z\lambda_{z'} = \sum_{z\in S}\lambda_z^2 + \sum_{z\in S}\lambda_z[\sum_{z'\in S, z'\neq z}\lambda_{z'}].$$

According to Inequality (17), the summation $\sum_{z'\in S, z\neq z'}\lambda_{z'}$ contains at least $\frac{M}{k^2}-1$ nonzero terms (upper than or equal to 1). We deduce that

$$\lambda^2 \geq \sum_{z\in S}\lambda_z^2 + \left(\frac{M}{k^2}-1\right)\sum_{z\in S}\lambda_z \geq M + \lambda\left(\frac{M}{k^2}-1\right),$$

that is $\lambda^2 - \lambda\left(\frac{M}{k^2}-1\right) - M \geq 0$ and therefore $\lambda \geq \frac{1}{2}\left(\frac{M}{k^2}-1+\sqrt{\Delta}\right)$, where Δ equals $\left(\frac{M}{k^2}-1\right)^2 + 4M$ (since $\frac{M}{k^2}-1-\sqrt{\Delta}$ is negative).

Proof of Theorem 2.
Due to Parseval's Relation (5), for every $z\in\mathbb{F}_2^m$, we have $\sum_{u\in\mathbb{F}_2^n}\widehat{\varphi_z}^2(u) = 2^n\sum_{u\in\mathbb{F}_2^n}\varphi_z^2(u)$, which becomes $\sum_{u\in\mathbb{F}_2^n}\widehat{\varphi_z}^2(u) = 2^n\omega_H(\varphi_z)$ since φ_z is a Boolean function. Thus, for every $z\in\mathbb{F}_2^m$, we have

$$\sum_{u\in\mathbb{F}_2^{n*}}\widehat{\varphi_z}^2(u) = 2^n\omega_H(\varphi_z) - \widehat{\varphi_z}^2(0) = 2^n\omega_H(\varphi_z) - \omega_H^2(\varphi_z),$$

that is $\sum_{u\in\mathbb{F}_2^{n*}}\widehat{\varphi_z}^2(u)=2^n(2^{n-m})-2^{2(n-m)}$, since F is assumed to be balanced. After summing up over $z\in\mathbb{F}_2^m$, we get

$$\sum_{u\in\mathbb{F}_2^{n*}}\sum_{z\in\mathbb{F}_2^m}\widehat{\varphi_z}^2(u)=2^{2n}-2^{2n-m}, \tag{18}$$

which implies

$$\max_{u\in\mathbb{F}_2^{n*}}\sum_{z\in\mathbb{F}_2^m}\widehat{\varphi_z}^2(u)\geq\frac{2^{2n}-2^{2n-m}}{2^n-1}. \tag{19}$$

On the other hand, for every $z\in\mathbb{F}_2^m$ and for every $u\in\mathbb{F}_2^{n*}$, the value of $|\widehat{\varphi_z}(u)|$ is upper bounded by $\omega_H(\varphi_z)=2^{n-m}$, since we have $|\widehat{\varphi_z}(u)|=|\sum_{x\in\mathbb{F}_2^n}\varphi_z(x)(-1)^{u\cdot x}|\leq\sum_{x\in\mathbb{F}_2^n}|\varphi_z(x)|=\omega_H(\varphi_z)$ and since F is balanced. Moreover, F being balanced and m being strictly lower than n, the number $\widehat{\varphi_z}(u)=\sum_{x\in\mathbb{F}_2^n}\varphi_z(x)(-1)^{u\cdot x}$ is a summation of an even number of ±1's and thus, $\widehat{\varphi_z}(u)$ is even. Then, due to Equations (18) and (19), one can apply Lemma 1 to

$$(S,\lambda,M,k)=(\mathbb{F}_2^m,\max_{u\in\mathbb{F}_2^{n*}}\sum_{z\in\mathbb{F}_2^m}\frac{|\widehat{\varphi_z}(u)|}{2},\frac{2^{2n}-2^{2n-m}}{4(2^n-1)},2^{n-m-1}),$$

and Relation (13) easily completes the proof. ◇

When the resiliency order t of a balanced (n,m)-function is strictly positive, then it is possible to improve the upper bound given in Theorem 2 by applying the divisibility property of Sarkar and Maitra and Relations (15), (12) and (7).

Proposition 3. *Let F be a t-resilient (n,m)-function. Then its unrestricted nonlinearity UN_F is upper bounded by the highest multiple of 2^{t+1} which is smaller than or equal to $2^{n-1}-2^{n/2-1}$, and to the highest multiple of 2^t which is smaller than or equal to*

$$2^{n-1}+\frac{1}{2}-\frac{2^{2m}-2^m}{2(2^n-1)}-\frac{1}{2}\sqrt{\frac{2^{2n}-2^{2n-m}}{2^n-1}+\left(\frac{2^{2m}-2^m}{2^n-1}-1\right)^2}.$$

Remark 5. If the degrees of the functions φ_z are all upper bounded by some integer $d<n-t-1$, then the bounds above can be slightly improved if $n-m\geq t+1+\left\lfloor\frac{n-t-1}{d}\right\rfloor$: according to the proof of [5, Theorem 6] and since all the functions φ_z have weight 2^{n-m}, the values of the Fourier transforms of the functions φ_z are then divisible by $2^{t+1+\left\lfloor\frac{n-t-1}{d}\right\rfloor}$ and UN_F is then upper bounded by the highest multiple of $2^{t+\left\lfloor\frac{n-t-1}{d}\right\rfloor}$ which is smaller than or equal to $2^{n-1}+\frac{1}{2}-\frac{2^{2m}-2^m}{2(2^n-1)}-\frac{1}{2}\sqrt{\frac{2^{2n}-2^{2n-m}}{2^n-1}+\left(\frac{2^{2m}-2^m}{2^n-1}-1\right)^2}$. ◇

We checked that Theorem 2 gives better information than the general upper bound $2^{n-1}-2^{n/2-1}$ if and only if $m\geq n/2+1$.

4.2 Construction of Balanced Vectorial Functions with High Nonlinearity and High Unrestricted Nonlinearity

Since the upper bound on the unrestricted nonlinearity of balanced (n, m)-functions given in Theorem 2 does not improve the general bound $2^{n-1} - 2^{n/2-1}$, when m is lower than or equal to $n/2$, we can try to find $(n, n/2)$-functions whose unrestricted nonlinearities approach $2^{n-1} - 2^{n/2-1}$. This will give a lower bound on the maximal possible value achieved by the unrestricted nonlinearity of the (n, m)-functions such that $m \leq n/2$.

In his Phd Thesis [9], Dillon introduces and studies a function, that we shall call *Dillon's function* , defined on the product of two finite fields of order $2^{n/2}$ by $F(x, y) = xy^{2^{n/2}-2}$, $(x, y) \in \mathbb{F}_{2^{n/2}} \times \mathbb{F}_{2^{n/2}}$, or equivalently:

$$F(x, y) = \begin{cases} \frac{x}{y} & \text{if } y \neq 0 \\ 0 & \text{if } y = 0 \end{cases} \tag{20}$$

One can check that, for a given even integer n, this Dillon's function admits an unrestricted nonlinearity equal to $2^{n-1} - 2^{n/2} + 1$. However, being bent, this function cannot be balanced and hence, does not satisfy an essential cryptographic criterion. One can modify the definition of Dillon to obtain balanced functions which still have high unrestricted nonlinearities (recall that the idea of modifying bent functions was that of Dobbertin in [10] to design highly nonlinear balanced Boolean functions). For a given even integer n, we shall call *modified Dillon's function* the function F defined on the product of two finite fields of order $2^{n/2}$ as:

$$F(x, y) = \begin{cases} \frac{x}{y} & \text{if } y \neq 0 \\ x & \text{if } y = 0 \end{cases} \tag{21}$$

One can easily check that this kind of function is balanced.

Proposition 4. *Let F be the modified Dillon's function defined on* $\mathbb{F}_{2^{n/2}} \times \mathbb{F}_{2^{n/2}}$, *then its unrestricted nonlinearity equals* $2^{n-1} - 2^{n/2}$.

Proof. For every pair $(x, y) \in \mathbb{F}_{2^{n/2}} \times \mathbb{F}_{2^{n/2}}$ and for every $z \in \mathbb{F}_{2^{n/2}}$, we have

$$\varphi_z(x, y) = 1 \iff \begin{cases} x = 0 & , \text{ if } z = 0 \\ (x = yz \text{ and } y \neq 0) \text{ or } (x = z \text{ and } y = 0) & , \text{ if } z \neq 0 \end{cases}$$

We deduce that

$$\varphi_z = \begin{cases} 1_{\{0\} \times \mathbb{F}_{2^{n/2}}} & , \text{ if } z = 0 \\ 1_{\mathbb{F}_{2^{n/2}} \times (z,1)} - \delta_{(0,0)} + \delta_{(z,0)} & , \text{ if } z \neq 0 \end{cases}$$

where $\mathbb{F}_{2^{n/2}} \times (z, 1)$ denotes the set $\{(uz, u);\ u \in \mathbb{F}_{2^{n/2}}\}$. So we have $\varphi_z = 1_{\mathbb{F}_{2^{n/2}} \times (z,1)} - \delta_{(0,0)} + \delta_{(z,0)}$ for every z. Then, for every element $z \in \mathbb{F}_{2^{n/2}}$ and every nonzero pair $(u, u') \in \mathbb{F}_{2^{n/2}} \times \mathbb{F}_{2^{n/2}}$, the value of $\widehat{\varphi_z}(u, u')$ equals:

$$\sum_{(x,y)\in\mathbb{F}_{2^{n/2}}\times\mathbb{F}_{2^{n/2}}} [\mathbb{1}_{\mathbb{F}_{2^{n/2}}\times(z,1)} - \delta_{(0,0)} + \delta_{(z,0)}](x,y)(-1)^{tr(ux)+tr(u'y)}$$
$$= \sum_{(x,y)\in\mathbb{F}_{2^{n/2}}\times(z,1)} (-1)^{tr(ux)+tr(u'y)} - 1 + (-1)^{tr(uz)}.$$

The summation $\sum_{(x,y)\in\mathbb{F}_{2^{n/2}}\times(z,1)}(-1)^{tr(ux)+tr(u'y)}$ equals

$$\sum_{y\in\mathbb{F}_{2^{n/2}}} (-1)^{tr(uyz)+tr(u'y)} = \sum_{y\in\mathbb{F}_{2^{n/2}}} (-1)^{tr(y(uz+u'))}.$$

The right-hand side equals $2^{n/2}$ if $uz = u'$ i.e. if (u, u') belongs to $\mathbb{F}_{2^{n/2}} \times (1, z)$ and equals 0 otherwise. Thus, we have

$$\widehat{\varphi_z}(u, u') = 2^{n/2}\mathbb{1}_{\mathbb{F}_{2^{n/2}}\times(1,z)}(u, u') - 1 + (-1)^{tr(uz)}, \quad (22)$$

and the result follows from Relation (13).

Remark 6. When the parameters m and n satisfy $m \leq n/2$, then one can apply Proposition 2 to modified Dillon's functions to establish that every (n, m)-function $\phi \circ F$, where ϕ is an $(m, n/2)$-function and where F is a modified Dillon's $(n, n/2)$-function, has an unrestricted nonlinearity greater than or equal to $2^{n-1} - 2^{n/2}$. If ϕ is balanced, then $\phi \circ F$ is balanced. ◇

According to Proposition 4, modified Dillon's function is an example of balanced function having a high unrestricted nonlinearity. Thus, for $m \leq n/2$, an upper bound on the unrestricted nonlinearity of the (n, m)-functions cannot lie below $2^{n-1} - 2^{n/2}$.

Note that the nonlinearity of modified Dillon's $(n, n/2)$-function equals $2^{n-1} - 2^{n/2}$. Indeed, due to Equation (4), for every pair $(u, u') \in \mathbb{F}_{2^{n/2}} \times \mathbb{F}_{2^{n/2}}$ and every element $v \in \mathbb{F}^*_{2^{n/2}}$, the number $\widehat{\chi_F}((u, u'), v)$ equals $\sum_{z\in\mathbb{F}_{2^{n/2}}} \widehat{\varphi_z}(u, u')(-1)^{tr(vz)}$ and the result can thus easily be deduced from Relation (22).

Modified Dillon's functions seem to satisfy all the criteria needed to be used as a filtering function in a nonlinear filtering registor. However, a new kind of attacks, called *algebraic attacks* , has been introduced against cryptosystems involving S-boxes as cryptographic primitives. The best such attacks have been led by Faugere and Ars or Courtois (see [8, 11]) against stream ciphers. Also, further work has to be done to define criteria, others than the algebraic degree, on Boolean or vectorial functions related to algebraic attacks (the algebraic degree has been pointed out as a relevant criterion but other criteria are needed; the classical criteria as resiliency and nonlinearity seem to be irrelevant to quantify the resistance of an S-box against this kind of cryptanalysis).

As it can be easily check, the resiliency of modified Dillon's functions cannot be greater than 0 and, thus, it is still an open problem to define resilient vectorial functions having a high unrestricted nonlinearity and being, then, good combining functions for a multi-output stream cipher with combination generator.

References

[1] R. Anderson. Searching of the optimum correlation attack. In *Fast Software Encryption: Second International Workshop. Leuven, Belgium, 14-16 December 1994, Proceedings*, volume 1008 of *Lecture Notes in Computer Science*. Springer, 1995. 295

[2] P. Camion and A. Canteaut. Generalization of Siegenthaler inequality and Schnorr-Vaudenay multipermutations. In *Advances in cryptology—CRYPTO '96 (Santa Barbara, CA)*, volume 1109 of *Lecture Notes in Comput. Sci.*, pages 372–386. Springer, Berlin, 1996. 294, 295

[3] A. Canteaut. On the correlations between a combining function and functions of fewer variables. In *IEEE Information Theory Workshop 2002*, 2002. 292, 295

[4] A. Canteaut and M. Trabbia. Improved fast correlation attacks using parity-check equations of weight 4 and 5. In B. Preneel, editor, *Advances in Cryptology - EUROCRYPT 2000*, volume 1807 of *Lecture Notes in Computer Science*, pages 573–588. Springer, 2000. 292, 295

[5] C. Carlet. On the coset weight divisibility and nonlinearity of resilient and correlation-immune functions. In *Sequences and their applications (Bergen, 2001)*, Discrete Math. Theor. Comput. Sci. (Lond.), pages 131–144. Springer, London, 2002. 301

[6] C. Carlet and E. Prouff. On the unrestricted nonlinearity. Rapport de recherche, INRIA, 2003. To appear, available at http:\\www-rocq.inria.fr/codes/Claude.Carlet/Conf/UNFSAC2003.ps. 292, 295

[7] F. Chabaud and S. Vaudenay. Links between differential and linear cryptanalysis. In *Advances in cryptology—EUROCRYPT '94 (Perugia)*, volume 950 of *Lecture Notes in Comput. Sci.*, pages 356–365. Springer, Berlin, 1995. 292, 293, 294

[8] N. Courtois. Fast algebraic attacks on stream ciphers with linear feedback. In *Advances in cryptology—CRYPTO 2003 (Santa Barbara, CA)*, volume 2729 of *Lecture Notes in Computer Science*, pages 177–194. Springer, Berlin, 2003. 303

[9] J. F. Dillon. *Elementary Hadamard Difference sets.* PhD thesis, University of Maryland, 1974. 302

[10] H. Dobbertin. Construction of bent functions and balanced boolean functions with high nonlinearity. In *Fast Software Encryption*, volume 1008 of *Lecture Notes in Computer Science*, pages 61–74. Springer-Verlag, 1994. 302

[11] J.-C. Faugère and G. Ars. An algebraic cryptanalysis of nonlinear filter generators using gröbner bases. Rapport de Recherche 4739, INRIA, february 2003. 303

[12] R. Forré. A fast correlation attack on nonlinearly feedforward filtered shift register sequences. In *Advances in cryptology—EUROCRYPT '89 (Brighton, 1991)*, volume 434 of *Lecture Notes in Comput. Sci.*, pages 586–595. Springer, Berlin, 1990. 295

[13] J. D. Golić, M. Salmasizadeh, L. Simpson, and E. Dawson. Fast correlation attacks on nonlinear filter generators. *Inform. Process. Lett.*, 64(1):37–42, 1997. 295

[14] T. Johansson and F. Jönsson. Improved fast correlation attacks on stream ciphers via convolutional codes. In M. Wiener, editor, *Advances in Cryptology — CRYPTO '99*, volume 1666 of *Lecture Notes in Computer Science*, pages 181–197. Springer-Verlag, 1999. 295

[15] K. Khoo and G. Gong. Highly nonlinear sboxes with reduced bound on maximum correlation. In *Proceedings of IEEE International Symposium on Information Theory*, page 254, 2003. 292

[16] M. Matsui. Linear cryptanalysis method for DES cipher. In *Advances in Cryptology - EUROCRYPT'93*, volume 765 of *Lecture Notes in Computer Science*, pages 386–397. Springer-Verlag, 1994. 292

[17] W. Meier and O. Staffelbach. Fast correlation attacks on certain stream ciphers. *J. Cryptology*, 1(3):159–176, 1989. 292, 295

[18] W. Meier and O. Staffelbach. Nonlinearity criteria for cryptographic functions. In *Advances in cryptology—EUROCRYPT '89 (Houthalen, 1989)*, volume 434 of *Lecture Notes in Comput. Sci.*, pages 549–562. Springer, Berlin, 1990. 292

[19] M. J. Mihaljević and J. D. Golić. Convergence of a Bayesian iterative error-correction procedure on a noisy shift register sequence. In *Advances in cryptology—EUROCRYPT '92 (Balatonfüred, 1992)*, volume 658 of *Lecture Notes in Comput. Sci.*, pages 124–137. Springer, Berlin, 1993. 295

[20] K. Nyberg. Perfect nonlinear S-boxes. In *Advances in cryptology—EUROCRYPT '91 (Brighton, 1991)*, volume 547 of *Lecture Notes in Comput. Sci.*, pages 378–386. Springer, Berlin, 1991. 294

[21] K. Nyberg. On the construction of highly nonlinear permutations. In *Advances in cryptology—EUROCRYPT '92 (Balatonfüred, 1992)*, volume 658 of *Lecture Notes in Comput. Sci.*, pages 92–98. Springer, Berlin, 1993. 292, 293

[22] P. Sarkar and S. Maitra. Nonlinearity bounds and constructions of resilient Boolean functions. In *Advances in cryptology—CRYPTO 2000 (Santa Barbara, CA)*, volume 1880 of *Lecture Notes in Comput. Sci.*, pages 515–532. Springer, Berlin, 2000. 295

[23] C. E. Shannon. Communication theory of secrecy systems. *Bell System Tech. J.*, 28:656–715, 1949. 291

[24] T. Siegenthaler. Correlation-immunity of nonlinear combining functions for cryptographic applications. *IEEE Trans. Inform. Theory*, 30(5):776–780, 1984. 294, 295

[25] G.-Z. Xiao and J. Massey. A spectral characterization of correlation-immune combining functions. In *IEEE Transactions on Information Theory*, volume IT 34, pages 569–571, May 1988. 295

[26] M. Zhang and A. Chan. Maximum correlation analysis of nonlinear S-boxes in stream ciphers. In *Advances in cryptology—CRYPTO 2000 (Santa Barbara, CA)*, volume 1880 of *Lecture Notes in Comput. Sci.*, pages 501–514. Springer, Berlin, 2000. 292, 296, 297, 299

Alternative Digit Sets for Nonadjacent Representations

James A. Muir[1*] and Douglas R. Stinson[2**]

[1] Department of Combinatorics and Optimization
[2] School of Computer Science
University of Waterloo
Waterloo, Ontario, Canada N2L 3G1
{jamuir,dstinson}@uwaterloo.ca

Abstract. It is known that every positive integer n can be represented as a finite sum of the form $n = \sum a_i 2^i$, where $a_i \in \{0, 1, -1\}$ for all i, and no two consecutive a_i's are non-zero. Such sums are called *nonadjacent representations*. Nonadjacent representations are useful in efficiently implementing elliptic curve arithmetic for cryptographic applications. In this paper, we investigate if other digit sets of the form $\{0, 1, x\}$, where x is an integer, provide each positive integer with a nonadjacent representation. If a digit set has this property we call it a *nonadjacent digit set* (NADS). We present an algorithm to determine if $\{0, 1, x\}$ is a NADS; and if it is, we present an algorithm to efficiently determine the nonadjacent representation of any positive integer. We also present some necessary and sufficient conditions for $\{0, 1, x\}$ to be a NADS. These conditions are used to exhibit infinite families of integers x such that $\{0, 1, x\}$ is a NADS, as well as infinite families of x such that $\{0, 1, x\}$ is not a NADS.

1 Introduction and History

In a base 2 (or *radix* 2) positional number system, representations of integers are converted into integers via the rule

$$(\ldots a_3 a_2 a_1 a_0)_2 = \cdots + a_3 2^3 + a_2 2^2 + a_1 2^1 + a_0 \ .$$

Each of the a_i's is called a *digit*. In the usual radix 2 positional number system the digits have the property that $a_i \in \{0, 1\}$, for all i. If we let $D = \{0, 1\}$ then we say that D is the *digit set* for this number system.

It is often advantageous to employ alternate digit sets. The digit set $D = \{0, 1, \bar{1}\}$, where $\bar{1}$ stands for -1, was studied as early as 1951 by Booth. In [1], Booth presents a technique whereby a binary computer can calculate a representation of the product of two integers without any extra steps to correct for its sign. His method is implicitly based on replacing one of the operands in the

* Supported in part by an NSERC Postgraduate Scholarship.
** Supported by NSERC grant RGPIN 203114-02.

M. Matsui and R. Zuccherato (Eds.): SAC 2003, LNCS 3006, pp. 306–319, 2004.

multiplication with a $\{0, 1, \bar{1}\}$ radix 2 representation. Later, in 1960, through his investigations on how to reduce the number of additions and subtractions used in binary multiplication and division, Reitwiesner [7] gave a constructive proof that every integer has a canonical $\{0, 1, \bar{1}\}$ radix 2 representation with a *minimal* number of nonzero digits.

Reitwiesner's canonical representations have a simple description. A $\{0, 1, \bar{1}\}$ radix 2 representation of an integer is in Reitwiesner's canonical form if and only if it satisfies the following property:

NA-1 *Of any two adjacent digits, at least one is zero* .

Said another way, for such representations, nonzero digits are nonadjacent. These representations have come to be called *nonadjacent forms* (NAFs).

Cryptographers came to be interested in NAFs through a study of exponentiation. Jedwab and Mitchell [3] noticed that it is possible to reduce the number of multiplications used in the square-and-multiply algorithm for exponentiation if a $\{0, 1, \bar{1}\}$ radix 2 representation of the exponent is used. This led them to an independent discovery of the NAF. However, in multiplicative groups, like those used for RSA and DSA, using the digit $\bar{1}$ requires the computation of an inverse which is more costly than a multiplication.

In elliptic curve groups this is not a problem since inverses can be computed essentially for free. Morain and Olivos [6] observed that in these groups the operation analogous to exponentiation could be made more efficient using $\{0, 1, \bar{1}\}$ representations. They give two algorithms for performing scalar-multiplication using addition and subtraction. The $\{0, 1, \bar{1}\}$ radix 2 representations upon which their algorithms are based are in fact the same ones that Booth and Reitwiesner studied. In the quest for efficient implementations of elliptic curve cryptosystems, NAFs and representations like them have become an important device; Gordon [2] and Solinas [9, 10] make this point quite convincingly.

If a finite length radix 2 representation has digit set D and satisfies **NA-1**, we call it a *D-nonadjacent form* (D-NAF). In this paper, we consider the question of which sets D provide nonadjacent forms for *every positive* integer. If D is such a digit set then we call it a *nonadjacent digit set* (NADS).

As a first investigation into this topic, we examine digit sets of the form $\{0, 1, x\}$ with $x \in \mathbb{Z}$. It is known that letting $x = \bar{1}$ gives a NADS, but it is somewhat surprising that there are many values of x with this property; for example, $x = \bar{5}$, $\overline{13}$, $\overline{1145}$ (note $\bar{5}$ means -5, etc.).

We give an infinite family of x's for which $\{0, 1, x\}$ is a NADS, and we also give an infinite family of x's for which $\{0, 1, x\}$ is not a NADS. We also give some results on the necessary conditions D must satisfy in order to be a NADS. The algorithms we present and analyze for computing D-NAFs might be of some interest as well.

2 Preliminaries

We start by introducing some definitions and notation which will facilitate our discussions.

If n is an integer and we write $n = (\ldots a_2 a_1 a_0)_2$ then we are expressing n as the sum of an *in nite* series. If there is some ℓ such that $a_i = 0$ for all $i \geq \ell$ then n is the sum of a *nite* series and we indicate this by writing $n = (a_{\ell-1} \ldots a_2 a_1 a_0)_2$. If, in addition, $a_{\ell-1} \neq 0$ we say this representation has *length* ℓ.

Definition 1. *The* length *of a representation* $(\ldots a_2 a_1 a_0)_2$ *is the largest integer* ℓ *such that* $a_{\ell-1} \neq 0$ *but* $a_i = 0$ *for all* $i \geq \ell$. *The length of the all zero representation is de ned to be zero.*

We will always use D to denote a digit set. The set of all *strings* of digits from D is denoted by D^*. The empty string is in D^* and is denoted by ϵ. Now, if D is the digit set for $(a_{\ell-1} \ldots a_1 a_0)_2$, then $a_{\ell-1} \ldots a_1 a_0$ is a string in D^*. Conversely, any string $\alpha \in D^*$ corresponds to a radix 2 representation with digit set D, namely $(\alpha)_2$. If $\alpha, \beta \in D^*$ then we denote their *concatenation* by $\alpha || \beta$.

We apply some of our terminology for representations to strings. If $0 \in D$ and a finite string $\alpha \in D^*$ satisfies the property **NA-1**, then we call α a D-NAF. If in addition, $(\alpha)_2 = n$ we say α is a D-NAF for n. Notice that if α is a D-NAF for n then α with any leading zeros removed is also a D-NAF for n. We denote the string formed by deleting the leading zeros from α by $\widehat{\alpha}$.

Given a digit set D and an integer n, we define a map

$$R_D(n) := \begin{cases} \widehat{\alpha} & \text{where } \alpha \in D^* \text{ is a } D\text{-NAF for } n\text{, if one exists} \\ \bot & \text{otherwise.} \end{cases}$$

Here, $\bot$ is just some symbol not in D. If $R_D(n)$ evaluates to a D-NAF for n, then by definition that string has no leading zeros. For example, if $D = \{0, 1, \overline{9}\}$ then $R_D(7)$ might evaluate to $1000\overline{9}$ since $1000\overline{9}$ is a D-NAF, has no leading zeros, and $(1000\overline{9})_2 = 1 \cdot 2^4 + 0 \cdot 2^3 + 0 \cdot 2^2 + 0 \cdot 2^1 + \overline{9} \cdot 2^0 = 7$. If there is more than one string in D which is a D-NAF for n and has no leading zeros then $R_D(n)$ might evaluate to any one of these strings. Later on we will prove that 3 does not have a D-NAF, hence $R_D(3) = \bot$.

We are interested in determining which integers have D-NAFs, so we define the set

$$\mathrm{NAF}(D) := \{n \in \mathbb{Z} : R_D(n) \neq \bot\} .$$

From our example with $D = \{0, 1, \overline{9}\}$ we see $7 \in \mathrm{NAF}(D)$ but $3 \notin \mathrm{NAF}(D)$. Using this notation, our definition of a nonadjacent digit set is as follows:

Definition 2. *D is a* nonadjacent digit set *if* $\mathbb{Z}^+ \subseteq \mathrm{NAF}(D)$.

3 Necessary Conditions for $\{0, 1, x\}$ to be a NADS

If we suppose $D = \{0, 1, x\}$ is a nonadjacent digit set then we can deduce necessary conditions on x.

Theorem 1. *Let* $D = \{0, 1, x\}$. *If there exists* $n \in \mathrm{NAF}(D)$ *with* $n \equiv 3 \pmod 4$, *then* $x \equiv 3 \pmod 4$.

Proof. Take $n \in \mathrm{NAF}(D)$ with $n \equiv 3 \pmod 4$. For some particular D-NAF, say $(\dots a_2 a_1 a_0)_2$, we have

$$\begin{aligned}(\dots a_2 a_1 a_0)_2 &= n \\ \Longrightarrow a_0 &\equiv 1 \pmod 2 \\ \Longrightarrow a_0 &\neq 0\ .\end{aligned}$$

Since a_0 is nonzero and the representation is nonadjacent we have $a_1 = 0$. Thus

$$\begin{aligned}(\dots a_2 0 a_0)_2 &= n \\ \Longrightarrow a_0 &\equiv 3 \pmod 4 \\ \Longrightarrow a_0 &\neq 1 \\ \Longrightarrow a_0 &= x\ .\end{aligned}$$

So $x = a_0 \equiv 3 \pmod 4$.

If $D = \{0, 1, x\}$ is a NADS then $3 \in \mathrm{NAF}(D)$, and by the previous result $x \equiv 3 \pmod 4$. So, if we are trying to find a value of x that makes $\{0, 1, x\}$ a NADS we need only consider those values congruent to 3 modulo 4.

3.1 The Case $x > 0$

If we restrict x to be a positive integer, then we can give a complete characterization of all values which make $D = \{0, 1, x\}$ a NADS. It is well known that $x = 3$ is such a value, and this is remarked by Solinas [8]. We give a proof of this fact and then show that no other positive value of x makes $\{0, 1, x\}$ a NADS.

Theorem 2. *The only NADS of the form* $\{0, 1, x\}$ *with* $x > 0$ *is* $\{0, 1, 3\}$.

Proof. Let n be any positive integer. We want to show that n has a $\{0, 1, 3\}$-NAF. Let $(\dots a_2 a_1 a_0)_2$ be the usual $\{0, 1\}$-radix 2 representation of n. If this representation satisfies **NA-1** there is nothing to prove, so suppose it does not. Let i be the smallest integer for which $a_{i+1} = a_i = 1$. Replace digits a_{i+1} and a_i by 0 and 3, respectively. Since $2^{i+1} + 2^i = 0 \cdot 2^{i+1} + 3 \cdot 2^i$, the resulting representation stands for the same integer.

By working from right to left, repeating this substitution as necessary, we transform $(\dots a_2 a_1 a_0)_2$ into a $\{0, 1, 3\}$-NAF. This proves that $\{0, 1, 3\}$ is a NADS.

Now consider x with $x > 3$. We show $n = 3$ does not have a $\{0, 1, x\}$-NAF. Suppose to the contrary that for some $\{0, 1, x\}$-NAF we have $(\dots a_2 a_1 a_0)_2 = 3$. Since 3 is odd, $a_0 \neq 0$ and so $a_1 = 0$. Now $a_0 \equiv 3 \pmod 4$ so it must be that $a_0 = x$. However, since each of the digits in $\{0, 1, x\}$ is nonnegative we have

$$3 = (\dots a_2 0 x)_2 = \dots + a_2 2^2 + 0 \cdot 2^1 + x \geq x > 3\ ,$$

which is a contradiction. So, 3 does not have a $\{0, 1, x\}$-NAF when $x > 3$.

An example helps illustrate the construction used in the above proof. Suppose $n = 237$. To find a $\{0,1,3\}$-NAF for 237 we start with its usual binary representation and then, working from right to left, replace any occurrences of the digits 11 with 03:

$$237 = (11101101)_2 = (10300301)_2 \ .$$

A natural question to ask is if this is the only $\{0,1,3\}$-NAF for 237. We give the answer in the next section.

3.2 Uniqueness

We show that every integer, not only just the positive ones, has at most one $\{0,1,x\}$-NAF where $x \equiv 3 \pmod 4$.

Theorem 3. *If $x \equiv 3 \pmod 4$, then any integer has at most one* ﬁ*nite length $\{0,1,x\}$-nonadjacent form.*

Proof. Let $D = \{0,1,x\}$ and suppose the result is false. Then it must be that

$$(a_{\ell-1}\dots a_2a_1a_0)_2 = (b_{\ell'-1}\dots b_2b_1b_0)_2$$

where $(a_{\ell-1}\dots a_2a_1a_0)_2$ and $(b_{\ell'-1}\dots b_2b_1b_0)_2$ are two different D-NAFs with lengths ℓ and ℓ' respectively. These representations stand for the same integer, call it n. We can assume that ℓ is as small as possible.

If $a_0 = b_0$, then

$$(a_{\ell-1}\dots a_2a_1)_2 = (b_{\ell'-1}\dots b_2b_1)_2 \ ,$$

and so we have two different, and shorter, D-NAFs which stand for the same integer, contrary to the minimality of ℓ. So it must be that $a_0 \neq b_0$.

If one of a_0 or b_0 is 0, then n is even, and so both a_0 and b_0 are 0. But a_0 and b_0 are different so it must be that a_0 is equal to 1 or x. Without loss of generality, we can assume the representations have the form

$$(a_{\ell-1}\dots a_2 0 x)_2 = (b_{\ell'-1}\dots b_2 01)_2 \ .$$

This implies $x \equiv 1 \pmod 4$, contrary to our hypothesis that $x \equiv 3 \pmod 4$. Thus every integer has at most one D-NAF.

4 Recognizing NADS of The Form $\{0,1,x\}$

From now on we fix $D = \{0,1,x\}$ with $x \equiv 3 \pmod 4$. In this section we work towards a method of deciding if $\{0,1,x\}$ is a NADS. By Theorem 2, this is easy when $x > 0$, so we will assume $x < 0$.

Recall that $R_D(n)$ either evaluates to the symbol $\perp$ or a finite string, with no leading zeros, that is a D-NAF for n. Theorem 3 tells us that any n has at most one D-NAF, so in the second case, the string returned by $R_D(n)$ is unique. Thus, $R_D(n)$ is well defined (i.e., for every input n there is exactly one output.).

The ability to evaluate $R_D(n)$ can be useful in deciding if D is a NADS. If we can find $n \in \mathbb{Z}^+$ such that $R_D(n) = \perp$ then we know that D is not a NADS. Also, if we have an algorithmic description of $R_D(n)$, we might be able to analyze this algorithm and show that for any $n \in \mathbb{Z}^+$, $R_D(n) \neq \perp$, thus proving that D is a NADS.

We show that $R_D(n)$ can be computed recursively and give an algorithm which evaluates $R_D(n)$ in this manner. We begin with some lemmas:

Lemma 1. *If* $n \equiv 0 \pmod 4$ *then* $n \in \mathrm{NAF}(D)$ *if and only if* $n/4 \in \mathrm{NAF}(D)$. *Further, if* $n \in \mathrm{NAF}(D)$ *then* $R_D(n) = R_D(n/4)||00$.

Proof. Since $n \equiv 0 \pmod 4$, the definition of the digit set D implies that any D-NAF for n is of the form $(a_{\ell-1}\dots a_3a_200)_2$, where $a_{\ell-1} \neq 0$. Now,

$$\begin{aligned} n \in \mathrm{NAF}(D) &\iff n \text{ has a } D\text{-NAF of the form } (a_{\ell-1}\dots a_3a_200)_2 \\ &\iff n/4 \text{ has a } D\text{-NAF of the form } (a_{\ell-1}\dots a_3a_2)_2 \\ &\iff n/4 \in \mathrm{NAF}(D) , \end{aligned}$$

which proves the first part of the lemma. If $n \in \mathrm{NAF}(D)$ then

$$R_D(n) = a_{\ell-1}\dots a_3a_200 = a_{\ell-1}\dots a_3a_2||00 = R_D(n/4)||00 ,$$

which proves the second part of the lemma.

We omit the proofs of the next three lemmas since they can be established by making only minor changes to the proof of Lemma 1.

Lemma 2. *If* $n \equiv 1 \pmod 4$ *then* $n \in \mathrm{NAF}(D)$ *if and only if* $(n-1)/4 \in \mathrm{NAF}(D)$. *Further, if* $n \in \mathrm{NAF}(D)$ *then* $R_D(n) = R_D(\frac{n-1}{4})||01$.

Lemma 3. *If* $n \equiv 2 \pmod 4$ *then* $n \in \mathrm{NAF}(D)$ *if and only if* $n/2 \in \mathrm{NAF}(D)$. *Further, if* $n \in \mathrm{NAF}(D)$ *then* $R_D(n) = R_D(n/2)||0$.

Lemma 4. *If* $n \equiv 3 \pmod 4$ *then* $n \in \mathrm{NAF}(D)$ *if and only if* $(n-x)/4 \in \mathrm{NAF}(D)$. *Further, if* $n \in \mathrm{NAF}(D)$ *then* $R_D(n) = R_D(\frac{n-x}{4})||0x$.

Given an integer n, if we somehow know that $n \in \mathrm{NAF}(D)$ then Lemmas 1–4 suggest a recursive procedure that we can use to evaluate $R_D(n)$. To illustrate suppose $D = \{0, 1, \overline{9}\}$. It was shown in an earlier example that $7 \in \mathrm{NAF}(D)$. Using these lemmas, we have:

$$R_D(7) = R_D(4)||0\overline{9} = R_D(1)||00||0\overline{9} = 1||00||0\overline{9} = 1000\overline{9} .$$

To describe the general procedure for computing $R_D(n)$, given that $n \in \mathrm{NAF}(D)$, we use the following two functions:

$$f_D(n) := \begin{cases} n/4 & \text{if } n \equiv 0 \pmod 4 \\ (n-1)/4 & \text{if } n \equiv 1 \pmod 4 \\ n/2 & \text{if } n \equiv 2 \pmod 4 \\ (n-x)/4 & \text{if } n \equiv 3 \pmod 4 , \end{cases} \qquad (1)$$

$$g_D(n) := \begin{cases} 00 & \text{if } n \equiv 0 \pmod 4 \\ 01 & \text{if } n \equiv 1 \pmod 4 \\ 0 & \text{if } n \equiv 2 \pmod 4 \\ 0x & \text{if } n \equiv 3 \pmod 4 . \end{cases} \tag{2}$$

Note that f_D returns an integer, and g_D returns a string. Here is the procedure described in pseudocode:

Procedure 4: EVAL$_\alpha$-$R_D(n)$

$\alpha \leftarrow \epsilon$
while $n \neq 0$
do $\begin{cases} \alpha \leftarrow g_D(n) \mid\mid \alpha \\ n \leftarrow f_D(n) \end{cases}$
return $\widehat{\alpha}$

Procedure 4 terminates on input n if and only if ${f_D}^i(n) = 0$ for some positive integer i. An easy calculation shows that, for $D = \{0, 1, \overline{9}\}$, ${f_D}^3(7) = 0$, and so the procedure terminates on input $n = 7$. However, $f_D(3) = 3$ and so ${f_D}^i(3) = 3 \neq 0$ for all i, thus the procedure does not terminate on input $n = 3$.

Using the previous lemmas, we can show Procedure 4 terminates on input n if and only if $n \in \mathrm{NAF}(D)$. Instead of making use of the lemmas individually, it is more convenient to summarize them as follows:

Lemma 5. *For all $n \in \mathbb{Z}$, $n \in \mathrm{NAF}(D)$ if and only if $f_D(n) \in \mathrm{NAF}(D)$. Further, if $n \in \mathrm{NAF}(D)$ then $R_D(n) = R_D(f_D(n)) || g_D(n)$.*

Now, suppose $n \in \mathrm{NAF}(D)$. Then the finite string $R_D(n)$ can be computed with a finite number of recursive steps. This implies that there is some positive integer i such that ${f_D}^i(n) = 0$, which in turn implies that the procedure terminates. Conversely, suppose the procedure terminates. Then ${f_D}^i(n) = 0$ for some i, and clearly $0 \in \mathrm{NAF}(D)$. Thus, ${f_D}^i(n) \in \mathrm{NAF}(D)$, and by the lemma $n \in \mathrm{NAF}(D)$.

Procedure 4 is named EVAL$_\alpha$-$R_D(n)$. We justify this name by noting that if the procedure terminates, it returns a string with no leading zeros (i.e., $\widehat{\alpha}$) equal to $R_D(n)$. We are not able to evaluate $R_D(n)$ for all values of n using this procedure because we have not yet described a way to recognize when $R_D(n) = \perp$. We proceed to do this now.

To decide if $D = \{0, 1, x\}$ is a NADS, it suffices to determine if there are any $n \in \mathbb{Z}^+$ for which Procedure 4 fails to terminate. We can determine if the procedure will terminate by examining the iterates of f_D.

Let n be a positive integer. Observe that, for $n \not\equiv 3 \pmod 4$, we have that

$$n > f_D(n) \geq 0 , \tag{3}$$

and, for $n \equiv 3 \pmod 4$, that

$$n > f_D(n) \iff n > \frac{-x}{3} \tag{4}$$

$$f_D(n) \geq 0 \iff n \geq x \ . \tag{5}$$

Since x is negative, we see that any iterate of the function f_D, on input n, always results in a nonnegative integer. Consider the graph G_n having directed edges

$$n \to f_D(n) \to {f_D}^2(n) \to {f_D}^3(n) \to \cdots \ .$$

The vertices of G_n are nonnegative integers. Inequalities (3) and (4) tell us that there must be some vertex of G_n that is less than $\frac{-x}{3}$. Suppose ${f_D}^i(n) < \frac{-x}{3}$. We claim ${f_D}^{i+1}(n) < \frac{-x}{3}$ as well. This is clearly true if ${f_D}^i(n) \equiv 0, 1, 2 \pmod 4$. If ${f_D}^i(n) \equiv 3 \pmod 4$ then

$$\begin{aligned} {f_D}^i(n) < \frac{-x}{3} &\implies \frac{{f_D}^i(n) - x}{4} < \frac{\frac{-x}{3} - x}{4} \\ &\implies {f_D}^{i+1}(n) < \frac{-x - 3x}{12} = \frac{-x}{3} \ , \end{aligned}$$

and so the claim is true. The claim also tells us that if ${f_D}^i(n) < \frac{-x}{3}$, then any subsequent iterate of f_D must be less than $\frac{-x}{3}$.

From the preceding discussion it is clear that for a positive integer n, either:

1. G_n is a path terminating at 0, or
2. G_n contains a directed cycle of integers in the interval $\{1, 2, \ldots, \lfloor \frac{-x}{3} \rfloor\}$.

If we can detect a directed cycle in G_n then we can determine whether or not Procedure 4 will terminate on input n. To do this we need to compute and store some of the vertices of G_n. However, as Procedure 4 executes, it computes all the vertices of G_n, so we might as well modify the procedure to detect a directed cycle in G_n on its own. This modification is described as Algorithm 5.

Algorithm 5: EVAL-$R_D(n)$

$\alpha \leftarrow \epsilon$
while $n > \frac{-x}{3}$
  do $\begin{cases} \alpha \leftarrow g_D(n) \,||\, \alpha \\ n \leftarrow f_D(n) \end{cases}$
$\mathcal{S} \leftarrow \varnothing$
while $n \neq 0$
  do $\begin{cases} \textbf{if } n \in \mathcal{S} \\ \quad \textbf{then return } \perp \\ \mathcal{S} \leftarrow \mathcal{S} \cup \{n\} \\ \alpha \leftarrow g_D(n) \,||\, \alpha \\ n \leftarrow f_D(n) \end{cases}$
return $\widehat{\alpha}$

Now we can use the title "Algorithm" rather than "Procedure", because EVAL-$R_D(n)$ terminates for every $n \in \mathbb{Z}^+$. (For some positive integers, it was shown that EVAL$_\alpha$-$R_D(n)$ fails to terminate, which is why it cannot technically be called an algorithm.) As its name suggests, Algorithm 5 evaluates $R_D(n)$ for any $n \in \mathbb{Z}^+$. It is possible to show that the running time of EVAL-$R_D(n)$ is $O(\lg n + |x|)$.

Returning to our main task of recognizing when $\{0, 1, x\}$ is a NADS, Algorithm 5 and the preceding analysis are very helpful since they lead us to the following result:

Theorem 6. *Suppose* x *is a negative integer and* $x \equiv 3 \pmod 4$. *If every element in the set* $\{n \in \mathbb{Z}^+ : n \leq \lfloor -x/3 \rfloor\}$ *has a* $\{0, 1, x\}$*-NAF, then* $\{0, 1, x\}$ *is a NADS.*

Proof. From inspection of Algorithm 5 this result is almost immediate, however we can give a formal argument using the graph G_n.

Suppose the hypothesis is true. We must argue that $\{0, 1, x\}$ is a NADS. Take any $n \in \mathbb{Z}^+$ and consider the graph G_n. Suppose G_n contains a directed cycle. Let n_0 be a vertex in this cycle. Then $1 \leq n_0 \leq \lfloor -x/3 \rfloor$, and G_{n_0} must contain the same directed cycle. This implies that n_0 does not have a $\{0, 1, x\}$-NAF, contrary to our hypothesis. So, G_n is a path terminating at 0, and thus n has a $\{0, 1, x\}$-NAF.

Theorem 6 suggests a computational method of determining if $\{0, 1, x\}$ is a NADS. For each $n \in \mathbb{Z}^+, n \leq \lfloor -x/3 \rfloor$, compute EVAL-$R_D(n)$. If all of these values have $\{0, 1, x\}$-NAFs then $\{0, 1, x\}$ is a NADS; otherwise, we find a value which does not have a $\{0, 1, x\}$-NAF which proves that $\{0, 1, x\}$ is not a NADS. To recognize a NADS, this method requires $\lfloor -x/3 \rfloor$ calls to EVAL-$R_D(n)$. However, we can decrease this number, as the next result shows.

Corollary 1. *Suppose* x *is a negative integer and* $x \equiv 3 \pmod 4$. *If every element in the set* $\{n \in \mathbb{Z}^+ : n \leq \lfloor -x/3 \rfloor, n \equiv 3 \pmod 4\}$ *has a* $\{0, 1, x\}$*-NAF, then* $\{0, 1, x\}$ *is a NADS.*

Proof. If $\{0, 1, x\}$ is not a NADS then choose the smallest integer $n_0 \in \mathbb{Z}^+$ such that G_{n_0} contains a directed cycle. By Theorem 6 it must be that $n_0 \leq \lfloor -x/3 \rfloor$. Let $n_1 = f_D(n_0)$, then (n_0, n_1) is an arc of G_n. If $n_0 \not\equiv 3 \pmod 4$ then $n_1 < n_0$ and G_{n_1} contains the same directed cycle, contrary to the choice of n_0. Thus, it must be that $n_0 \equiv 3 \pmod 4$. So, if the hypothesis is true, there can be no smallest positive integer which does not have a $\{0, 1, x\}$-NAF. Hence $\{0, 1, x\}$ is a NADS.

Now we can detect a NADS of the form $\{0, 1, x\}$ with $\lfloor -x/12 \rfloor$ calls to EVAL-$R_D(n)$. We have used this approach to find all the values of x greater than -10^6 such that $\{0, 1, x\}$ is a NADS. The Appendix lists all the negative values of x greater than -10^4 such that $\{0, 1, x\}$ is a NADS.

5 Some Infinite Families of NADS and non-NADS

Again, we fix $D = \{0, 1, x\}$ where $x < 0$ and $x \equiv 3 \pmod 4$. In this section, we give an infinite family of values for x which makes D a NADS. We also give some infinite families of values for x for which D is not a NADS.

If n is a nonnegative integer, $w(n)$ denotes the number of ones in the usual $\{0, 1\}$-radix 2 representation of n (i.e., the Hamming weight of n). We use the function $w(n)$ to describe our first infinite family.

Theorem 7. *Let x be a negative integer with $x \equiv 3 \pmod 4$. If $w\left(\frac{3-x}{4}\right) = 1$, then $\{0, 1, x\}$ is a NADS.*

Proof. Suppose $\{0, 1, x\}$ is not a NADS. Then there is some $n \in \mathbb{Z}^+$ for which the graph G_n contains a directed cycle. We can assume n is a vertex of this cycle. Let t be the number of vertices in the cycle, then

$$n \to f_D(n) \to {f_D}^2(n) \to \cdots \to {f_D}^{t-1}(n) \to n \ .$$

Let $n' = f_D(n)$. We want to relate $w(n')$ to $w(n)$. There are four possible residues of n modulo 4, and for the residues $0, 1, 2$ we can determine $w(n')$ exactly:

$n \bmod 4$	n'	$w(n')$
0	$\frac{n}{4}$	$w(n)$
1	$\frac{n-1}{4}$	$w(n) - 1$
2	$\frac{n}{2}$	$w(n)$

If $n \equiv 3 \pmod 4$, we have

$$n' = \frac{n-x}{4} = \frac{n-3}{4} + \frac{3-x}{4} \ .$$

By hypothesis $w\left(\frac{3-x}{4}\right) = 1$, and so

$$\begin{aligned} w(n') &= w\left(\frac{n-3}{4} + \frac{3-x}{4}\right) \\ &\le w\left(\frac{n-3}{4}\right) + w\left(\frac{3-x}{4}\right) \\ &= w(n) - 2 + 1 \\ &= w(n) - 1 \ . \end{aligned}$$

So, in any case, $w(n') \le w(n)$, but if n is odd then we have the strict inequality $w(n') < w(n)$. Applying this inequality to the integers in the cycle of G_n we see

$$w(n) \ge w(f_D(n)) \ge w({f_D}^2(n)) \ge \cdots \ge w({f_D}^{t-1}(n)) \ge w(n) \ .$$

However, some vertex in this cycle must be congruent to 3 modulo 4. If not, then the iterates of f_D are strictly decreasing on this cycle and we get

$$n > f_D(n) > {f_D}^2(n) > \cdots > {f_D}^{t-1}(n) > n \ ,$$

which is a contradiction. So, there is some odd vertex in the cycle which means one of the inequalities relating the Hamming weights of adjacent vertices is strict. This implies that $w(n) > w(n)$, which is a contradiction.

So, G_n cannot contain a directed cycle, and hence $\{0, 1, x\}$ is a NADS.

When x is negative, $w(\frac{3-x}{4}) = 1$ if and only if $\frac{3-x}{4} = 2^t$, $t \geq 0$. Letting $t = 0, 1, 2, 3, 4, \ldots$ we see that Theorem 7 asserts that $x = \overline{1}, \overline{5}, \overline{13}, \overline{29}, \overline{61}, \ldots$ all yield NADS. We now present an infinite family of integers x such that $\{0, 1, x\}$ is not a NADS.

Theorem 8. *Let x be a negative integer with $x \equiv 3 \pmod 4$. If $(2^s - 1) | x$ for any $s \geq 2$, then $\{0, 1, x\}$ is not a NADS.*

Proof. Let $n = -x/(2^s - 1)$. We show G_n contains a directed cycle. We have

$$\begin{aligned} n(2^s - 1) &\equiv -x \pmod 4 \\ \Longrightarrow n(0 - 1) &\equiv -3 \pmod 4 \\ \Longrightarrow n &\equiv 3 \pmod 4 \ . \end{aligned}$$

Note that,

$$n - x = \frac{-x}{2^s - 1} - x = \frac{-x - x\, 2^s + x}{2^s - 1} = 2^s \frac{-x}{2^s - 1} = 2^s n \ .$$

Now,

$$f_D(n) = \frac{n - x}{4} = 2^{s-2} n$$

Subsequent iterates of f_D will cancel out the factor 2^{s-2}. Thus, for some i, ${f_D}^i(n) = n$ and so G_n contains a directed cycle.

Theorem 8 says that many sets $\{0, 1, x\}$ are not NADS. In particular, it rules out values of x that are divisible by 3, 7, 31, etc.

Theorem 9. *If $x = 3 - 11 \cdot 2^i$, where $i \geq 2$, then $\{0, 1, x\}$ is not a NADS.*

Proof. We show that G_3 contains a directed cycle, and hence 3 does not have a $\{0, 1, x\}$-NAF. Let $y = \frac{3-x}{4} = 11 \cdot 2^{i-2}$. Note that, if $n \equiv 3 \pmod 4$, then

$$f_D(n) = \frac{n - x}{4} = \frac{n - 3}{4} + \frac{3 - x}{4} = \frac{n - 3}{4} + y \ .$$

Now, consider the iterates of f_D on input 3. We have

$$\begin{aligned} f_D(3) &= 11 \cdot 2^{i-2} \\ {f_D}^2(3) &= 11 \cdot 2^{i-4} \\ &\vdots \\ {f_D}^j(3) &= 11, \text{ for some } j \\ {f_D}^{j+1}(3) &= 2 + y \ . \end{aligned}$$

We proceed using case analysis.

Case $i \geq 5$: We have $2 + y = 2 + 11 \cdot 2^{i-2} = (10110\ldots010)_2$, and subsequent iterates of f_D will effectively strip off the nonadjacent representation $(0\ldots010)_2$ at the right of $2 + y$, and will return to the value $(1011)_2 = 11$. Hence, 11 is in a directed cycle of G_3.

Case $i = 4$: Here $y = 44$, and so $2 + y = 46$. By iterating f_D we see that in G_3 we have:

$$46 \to 23 \to 49 \to 12 \to 3 \; .$$

So, an iterate of f_D returns to the vertex 3 in G_3. Thus we have a directed cycle.

Case $i = 3$: Here $y = 22$, and so $2+y = 24$. The iterates of f_D are as follows:

$$24 \to 6 \to 3 \; .$$

So, we see G_3 contains a directed cycle.

Case $i = 2$: Here $y = 11$, and so $2+y = 13$. The iterates of f_D are as follows:

$$24 \to 6 \to 3 \; .$$

So, we see G_3 contains a directed cycle.

In all the above cases, G_3 contains a directed cycle, and $\{0, 1, x\}$ is not an NADS.

Theorem 10. *Let* $x = 3 - 7 \cdot 2^i$, *where* $i \geq 2$. *Then* $\{0, 1, x\}$ *is an NADS if and only if* $i \in \{2, 3\}$.

Proof. When $i = 2$, $x = \overline{25}$, and when $i = 3$, $x = \overline{53}$. We first show that both $\{0, 1, \overline{25}\}$ and $\{0, 1, \overline{53}\}$ are NADSs.

For $x = \overline{25}$, we have $\lfloor -x/3 \rfloor = 8$. By Corollary 1, it is sufficient to check that 3 and 7 have $\{0, 1, \overline{25}\}$-NAFs. Consider the graph G_3. Iterating f_D on input $n = 3$ we see G_3 is equal to:

$$3 \to 7 \to 8 \to 2 \to 1 \to 0 \; .$$

Notice that 7 is a vertex of G_3, and so G_7 is contained in G_3. Both G_3 and G_7 are paths terminating at 0, and hence both 3 and 7 have $\{0, 1, \overline{25}\}$-NAFs. Thus $\{0, 1, \overline{25}\}$ is a NADS.

For $x = \overline{53}$, we have $\lfloor -x/3 \rfloor = 17$. Arguing as before, we see that it is sufficient to demonstrate that G_n, where $n = 3, 7, 11, 15$, consists of a path. By iterating f_D on input $n = 3$ we see G_3 is equal to:

$$3 \to 14 \to 7 \to 15 \to 17 \to 4 \to 1 \to 0$$

This takes care of G_3, G_7 and G_{15}. Consider G_{11}:

$$11 \to 16 \to 4 \to 1 \to 0$$

Thus $\{0, 1, \overline{53}\}$ is an NADS.

Now, when $i \geq 4$ we must show that $\{0,1,x\}$ is not an NADS. We do so by showing G_7 contains directed cycle. Let $y = \frac{3-x}{4} = 7 \cdot 2^{i-2}$. We have

$$f_D(7) = \frac{7-3}{4} + y = 1 + y \ .$$

Since $i \geq 4$ we have $1 + y = (1110\ldots001)_2$. Subsequent iterates of f_D will effectively right shift $1+y$, leaving the representation $(111)_2 = 7$. So, we see that 7 is in a directed cycle.

6 Further Work

It is an interesting question if there exists a simply stated set of necessary and sufficient conditions for $\{0,1,x\}$ to be a NADS; the discovery of other infinite families of NADS and non-NADS may help us develop an answer.

The following result describes another infinite family (a proof will appear in an extended version of this paper):

Theorem 11. *Let* x *be a negative integer with* $x \equiv 3 \pmod 4$. *If* $w\left(\frac{3-x}{4}\right) = 2$ *and* $2^s - 1$ *does not divide* x *for any* $s \in \mathbb{Z}^+$, $s \geq 2$, *then* $\{0,1,x\}$ *is a NADS.*

In [4], Matula defines and investigates *basic* digit sets. Some of our results appear to have analogs for basic digit sets, so it is possible that the techniques used in Matula's theory may be applicable to nonadjacent digit sets.

References

[1] A.D. Booth. A Signed Binary Multiplication Technique, *Quarterly Journal of Mechanics and Applied Mathematics* **4** (1951), 236–240. 306

[2] D.M. Gordon. A Survey of Fast Exponentiation Methods, *Journal of Algorithms* **27** (1998), 129–146. 307

[3] J. Jedwab and C.J. Mitchell. Minimum Weight Modified Signed-Digit Representations and Fast Exponentiation, *Electronic Letters* **25** (1989), 1171–1172. 307

[4] D.W. Matula. Basic Digit Sets for Radix Representation, *Journal of the Association for Computing Machinery* , **29** (1982), 1131–1143. 318

[5] A.J. Menezes, P.C. van Oorschot, and S.A. Vanstone. *Handbook of Applied Cryptography*, CRC Press, 1996.

[6] F. Morain and J. Olivos. Speeding up the Computations on an Elliptic Curve using Addition-Subtraction Chains, *RAIRO Theoretical Informatics and Applications* **24** (1990), 531–543. 307

[7] G.W. Reitwiesner. Binary Arithmetic, In *Advances in Computers, Vol. 1*, Academic Press, 1960, pp. 231–308. 307

[8] J.A. Solinas. Low-Weight Binary Representations for Pairs of Integers. Technical Report CORR 2001-41, Centre for Applied Cryptographic Research. Available from `http://www.cacr.math.uwaterloo.ca/-techreports/2001/corr2001-41.ps`. 309

[9] J. A. Solinas. An Improved Algorithm for Arithmetic on a Family of Elliptic Curves. In "Advances in Cryptology – CRYPTO '97", *Lecture Notes in Computer Science* **1294** (1997), 357–371. An extended version of the paper is available from `http://www.cacr.math.uwaterloo.ca/techreports/1999/corr99-46.ps`. 307

[10] J. A. Solinas. Efficient arithmetic on Koblitz curves. *Designs, Codes and Cryptography* **19** (2000), 195–249. 307

Appendix

We list the all values of x from -1 to -10000 for which $\{0, 1, x\}$ is a NADS:

-1	-5	-13	-17	-25	-29	-37	-53	-61	-65
-113	-121	-125	-137	-145	-149	-157	-233	-241	-253
-257	-265	-269	-277	-281	-305	-317	-325	-437	-481
-485	-493	-505	-509	-517	-521	-533	-541	-557	-565
-601	-605	-613	-629	-641	-653	-673	-821	-869	-913
-937	-977	-989	-1013	-1021	-1025	-1033	-1037	-1045	-1061
-1073	-1081	-1097	-1117	-1133	-1145	-1165	-1265	-1273	-1277
-1289	-1297	-1325	-1345	-1349	-1357	-1621	-1637	-1733	-1745
-1765	-1885	-1933	-1949	-1985	-1993	-2017	-2021	-2033	-2041
-2045	-2053	-2069	-2101	-2105	-2113	-2129	-2137	-2141	-2153
-2161	-2165	-2173	-2185	-2189	-2197	-2237	-2273	-2285	-2293
-2297	-2321	-2353	-2365	-2369	-2381	-2393	-2405	-2425	-2497
-2525	-2533	-2557	-2593	-2609	-2621	-2641	-2645	-2669	-2677
-2693	-3245	-3265	-3337	-3385	-3421	-3509	-3541	-3557	-3629
-3653	-3673	-3761	-3797	-3853	-3877	-3881	-3917	-3925	-3929
-3961	-4001	-4033	-4037	-4085	-4093	-4097	-4105	-4117	-4121
-4133	-4141	-4145	-4153	-4157	-4201	-4205	-4217	-4253	-4261
-4273	-4285	-4297	-4337	-4345	-4349	-4373	-4393	-4397	-4469
-4537	-4541	-4573	-4589	-4597	-4601	-4621	-4633	-4645	-4649
-4661	-4693	-4777	-4801	-5021	-5077	-5093	-5101	-5105	-5113
-5129	-5137	-5153	-5165	-5189	-5197	-5213	-5273	-5281	-5365
-5377	-5381	-5393	-5405	-5437	-5441	-6565	-6613	-6773	-6805
-6929	-6973	-7033	-7277	-7333	-7345	-7381	-7393	-7397	-7465
-7477	-7561	-7597	-7613	-7621	-7649	-7741	-7817	-7865	-7877
-7901	-7949	-8045	-8053	-8065	-8069	-8081	-8093	-8101	-8117
-8129	-8165	-8173	-8177	-8185	-8189	-8201	-8213	-8221	-8233
-8237	-8297	-8305	-8317	-8333	-8341	-8369	-8417	-8429	-8437
-8441	-8453	-8485	-8497	-8501	-8573	-8581	-8593	-8597	-8665
-8669	-8681	-8693	-8717	-8725	-8741	-8753	-8789	-8797	-8825
-8837	-8921	-8977	-9089	-9101	-9133	-9157	-9161	-9181	-9209
-9221	-9245	-9341	-9353	-9421	-9425	-9433	-9461	-9473	-9497
-9505	-9509	-9581	-9665	-9673	-9677	-9697	-9761	-9925	-9997

Generic Efficient Arithmetic Algorithms for PAFFs (Processor Adequate Finite Fields) and Related Algebraic Structures
(Extended Abstract)

Roberto Maria Avanzi[1*] and Preda Mihăilescu[2]

[1] Institut für Experimentelle Mathematik, University of Duisburg-Essen
Ellernstrasse 29, D-45326 Essen
mocenigo@exp-math.uni-essen.de
[2] Universität Paderborn
FB 17, D-33095 Paderborn.
preda@upb.de

Abstract. In the past years several authors have considered finite fields extensions of odd characteristic optimised for a given architecture to obtain performance gains. The considered fields were however very specific. We define a *Processor Adequate Finite Field* (PAFF) as a field of odd characteristic $p < 2^w$ where w is a CPU related *word length*. PAFFs have several attractive properties for cryptography. In this paper we concentrate on arithmetic aspects. We present some algorithms usually providing better performance in PAFFs than in prime fields and in previously proposed instances of extension fields of comparable size.

Keywords: Finite extension fields, exponentiation algorithms, modular reduction, discrete logarithm systems.

1 Introduction

Most public key cryptosystems are based on the difficulty of the discrete logarithm (DL) problem: *If g is a generator of a group G and $h \in G$, ﬁnd an integer n with $g^n = h$*. Commonly used groups are: the *multiplicative group* of a finite field, the rational point group of an elliptic curve [13, 23] over a finite field or the group of rational divisor classes of an hyperelliptic curve [14]. *Binary ﬁelds*, i.e. fields of characteristic 2, and *prime ﬁelds*, i.e. $\mathbb{F}_p \cong \mathbb{Z}/p\mathbb{Z}$, are the most commonly used finite fields, but in principle *any* finite field can be used. Hence, one may choose the best field to optimize the *performance* on a target architecture, provided that the security prerequisites are satisfied.

In a cryptosystem designed around the multiplicative group of a finite field, the fundamental computation is the *exponentiation* : We present several algorithms to perform it in rather general extension fields.

---

* Partially supported by the Commission of the European Communities through the Fifth Framework Programme under Contract IST-2001-32613.

M. Matsui and R. Zuccherato (Eds.): SAC 2003, LNCS 3006, pp. 320–334, 2004.

One of our motivations for doing the present work was the lack of a comprehensive study of exponentiation algorithms for the type and size of fields we are interested in. Some of the methods which we present are much faster than those which are usually deployed. The techniques can be applied *mutatis mutandis* to compute scalar products in elliptic curves, in Jacobians of hyperelliptic curves having efficiently computable endomorphisms, or trace zero varieties [17, 3]: see § 3.5.

The DL problem in large enough finite fields seems hard [1, 25, 30] (see also [35, § 5]). DL based cryptographic schemes have been recently standardized also over generic finite fields. Fields other than prime and binary are already being considered by the industrial community: For example the XTR cryptosystem [35], which uses an extension of degree 6 of a prime field. The usage of more general extension fields $\mathbb{F}_{p^{6m}}$ is mentioned in [35], and investigated in [19], where however the structure of the extension field $\mathbb{F}_{p^{6m}}$ is not exploited to speed up the operations over the original system: the prime field $\mathbb{F}_p$ is merely replaced by $\mathbb{F}_{p^m}$. The methods presented here, together with the approach taken in [33], can be used to deliver fast XTR-like systems over the fields $\mathbb{F}_{p^{6m}}$. With the present contribution we hope to stimulate further research.

The structure of the paper is the following. In the next section we give a general introduction to finite extension field arithmetic and review some previous work. The exponentiation techniques are presented in Section 3. Section 4 is devoted to modular reduction. In Section 5, implementation data and benchmarks show that PAFFs can deliver up to 20 times better performance than prime fields of comparable size.

2 General Setting

Let p be an odd prime. It is known that for any $m \geq 1$, there is up to isomorphism exactly one finite field $\mathbb{F}_{p^m}$ with p^m elements. If $f(X) \in \mathbb{F}_p[X]$ is an irreducible polynomial of degree m, then $\mathbb{F}_{p^m} \cong \mathbb{F}_p[X]/(f(X))$. A *model* of $\mathbb{F}_{p^m}$ is given by a choice of $f(X)$ together with a *basis* of $\mathbb{F}_{p^m}$ as an $\mathbb{F}_p$-vector space. The *Frobenius automorphism* $\varphi : \mathbb{F}_{p^m} \longrightarrow \mathbb{F}_{p^m}$ given by $x \mapsto x^p$ is an $\mathbb{F}_p$-linear map. With respect to the chosen basis φ may be represented by a $m \times m$ matrix with entries in $\mathbb{F}_p$.

Let $x = X \bmod f(X)$ and assume that $\mathbb{F}_{p^m}$ has a power basis, i.e. any element $g \in \mathbb{F}_{p^m}$ can be written as $g = \sum_{i=0}^{m-1} g_i x^i$ with the $g_i \in \mathbb{F}_p$. Let $n \in \mathbb{N}$ be an exponent of the size of p^m and

$$n = \sum_{i=0}^{m-1} n_i \, p^i, \quad \text{with} \quad 0 \leq n_i < p \tag{1}$$

be its p-adic expansion. The exponentiation can be rewritten as

$$g^n = \prod_{i=0}^{m-1} (g^{n_i})^{p^i} = \prod_{i=0}^{m-1} \varphi^i(g^{n_i}), \tag{2}$$

thus reducing the problem to that of computing the powers g^{n_i}. It is usually much faster to compute m powers of the same base g to different u-bit exponents than only one power to a mu-bit exponent, as many common computations can be done only once. (Also, on a parallel device several units can compute many powers g^{n_i} simultaneously, but we are not concerned here with this situation.)

The model of the field $\mathbb{F}_{p^m}$ is of the utmost importance, since it influences the performance of the system. In particular we wish that:

A. Reduction modulo the defining polynomial $f(X)$ be *easy*.
B. The Frobenius matrix be sparse.
C. Modular reduction in the base field be particularly fast.

A. Lenstra proposed in [18] a model based on irreducible cyclotomic polynomials $f(X) = (X^{m+1} - 1)/(X - 1) \bmod p$, with $m + 1$ a prime. This leads to so called optimal normal bases of type I, on which the Frobenius maps act like permutation matrices. These fields are very practical, yet quite *scarce* because of the restrictions that $\ell = m + 1$ be a prime and that p be *primitive* modulo ℓ.

Bailey and Paar [4], following Mihăilescu [22], observed that taking $f(X)$ of the form $f(X) = X^m - b$ – a *binomial* – gives a much larger choice of fields while still fulfilling properties **A** and **B**. The corresponding power basis is called a *binomial basis* . The only restriction is that $\mathbb{F}_p$ must contain some m–th root of unity, i.e. $m|(p-1)$. An element b such that $X^m - b$ is irreducible is quickly found. The Frobenius map is still relatively efficient, even though less than for optimal normal bases. All one has to do is to precompute first c_1 and J such that $X^p \bmod (X^m - b) = c_1 X^J$, then c_1^t for $1 < t < m$. Then $\varphi(x) = c_1 x^J$ and $\varphi(x^t) = c_1^t x^{Jt \bmod m}$. The matrix of φ is the product of a permutation matrix and of a diagonal one. A Frobenius operation in $\mathbb{F}_{p^m}$ costs m multiplications in $\mathbb{F}_p$.

For efficient implementation in restricted environments, Bailey and Paar restricted the characteristic p to be of the form $2^k - c$ for $c \ll 2^{k/2}$, i.e. a *quasi Mersenne prime* , to adopt the reduction algorithm from [20, §14.3.4]. Extension fields defined by irreducible binomials and of quasi Mersenne characteristic are usually called *optimal extension* ﬁ*elds* (OEF).

Definition. *A* Processor Adequate Finite Field *(PAFF) is* ﬁ*eld of odd characteristic* $p < 2^w$ *were* w *is some processor related* word length.

The algorithms in Section 4 show that the gains achieved in modular reduction by means of OEFs can essentially be obtained for all PAFFs.

3 Exponentiation Algorithms

Let G be the multiplicative group of the field $\mathbb{F}_q$ where $q = p^m$, p a prime and $m > 1$. For $g \in G$ and $n \in \mathbb{N}$ we want to compute g^n. Just a few of the methods which can be used are: square and multiply [16] with the usual binary development or with the non-adjacent form (NAF, see [28]); unsigned sliding windows [20]; sliding windows across NAFs [2]; and the wNAF [32], which is called also *signed sliding windows* . These algorithms assume only that group multiplication and in some cases also inversion are available. In their basic forms, they do not take advantage of the Frobenius φ. This is what we are going to do.

In the next two Subsections we shall assume that φ can be computed in a reasonable time – i.e. of the order of one multiplication in G – but we do not require its cost to be negligible. Thus the requirement **B** of Section 2 is not stringent. If $\mathbb{F}_{p^m}$ is represented by a non binomial polynomial basis, in general the Frobenius will act on the basis like a non-sparse $m \times m$ matrix, and applying it costs like a schoolbook multiplication.

Based upon (2), the Horner scheme for the evaluation of g^n is

$$g^n = \prod_{i=0}^{m-1} \varphi^i(g^{n_i}) = \varphi(\cdots\varphi(\varphi(g^{n_{m-1}}) \cdot g^{n_{m-2}})\cdots g^{n_1}) \cdot g^{n_0} \tag{3}$$

and requires $m - 1$ multiplications and Frobenius evaluations.

3.1 Right-to-Left Square-and-Multiply

This algorithm was suggested in [18] and uses m temporary variables $x_0, \ldots, x_{m-1}$, which are initially set to 1. The elements g, g^2, $g^4, \ldots, g^{2^u}$ are computed by repeated squarings. When g^{2^j} is computed, for each i, $0 \le i \le m-1$, if the j-th bit of n_i is equal to 1 then x_i is multiplied by g^{2^j}. At the end $x_i = g^{n_i}$ and g^n is recovered by means of (3).

This method requires $u - 1$ squarings, on average $m(u/2 - 1)$ multiplications (for each variable x_i the first multiplication can be replaced by an assignment) and $m - 1$ Frobenius operations. This deceptively simple algorithm performs very well.

A. Lenstra [18] claims that the exponentiation method of Yao [36] as improved by Knuth [16] is 20% faster. Our implementations confirm this for fields of about 500 to 2000 bits. In the next two Subsections we shall describe even faster methods.

3.2 Baby-Windows, Giant-Windows

We consider again (3). We call the representation in base p the subdivision of n in *giant windows* , as the exponent is first read through windows of size $\log_2 p$, and then each n_i will be scanned by smaller windows. The exponents n_i are limited by a (relatively) small power of 2 and we must calculate all the g^{n_i}. A first approach would consist in precomputing all powers g^{2^j} for $2^j \le \max\{n_i\}$; Then, for each i, we obtain g^{n_i} by multiplying together the g^{2^j} where j runs through the bits of n_i equal to one. This is the core idea of the *baby windows*, which read the exponents in a radix 2^ℓ, for some integer $\ell \ge 1$.

Fix a small integer ℓ – the *width* of the baby windows. Let u be the bit-length of p, so $2^u > p > 2^{u-1}$ and write $u = K\ell + R$, with $R < \ell$. A 2^u-bit word will be subdivided in K' baby windows, with $K' = K$ if $R = 0$ and $K' = K + 1$ otherwise.

Upon developing the exponents n_i in base 2^ℓ, i.e. $n_i = \sum_{j=0}^{K'-1} n_{ij} 2^{j\ell}$ where all $n_{ij} \in \{0, 1, \dots, 2^\ell - 1\}$, we have

$$g^{n_i} = \prod_{\substack{0 \le j < K' \\ n_{ij} \ne 0}} g^{n_{ij} 2^{j\ell}}. \tag{4}$$

If the values $g^{t\,2^{j\ell}}$ for $0 \le j < K'$ and $1 \le t \le 2^\ell - 1$ are given, then each g^{n_i} can be computed with just $K' - 1$ multiplications. In fact, if $R \ne 0$, for $j = K$ we shall only need the values with $1 \le i \le 2^R - 1$ for $j = K$, so the last window is smaller. A similar approach is described in [9] for fields of even characteristic.

After ℓ has been selected (this is discussed later) one precomputes the set $\Im = \{g^{i\,2^{j\ell}} : 0 \le j < K'; 1 \le i \le 2^\ell - 1\}$. Then one computes all the values g^{n_i}, each by at most $K' - 1$ multiplications of elements of $\Im$. Last, g^n is obtained by (3).

Algorithm 1: ***Baby–windows giant–windows exponentiation***

---

1. Expand n p-adically: $n = \sum_{i=0}^{m-1} n_i p^i$ with $0 \le n_i < p$ (if not already given in that form).

2. Compute (or retrieve from a storage) the set
$\Im = \{g^{i\,2^{j\ell}} : 0 \le j < K'; 1 \le i \le 2^\ell - 1\}$.

3. Compute g^n by means of formula (3) where $g^{n_{d-1}}, \dots .g^{n_0}$ are computed using (4) by multiplying together elements of $\Im$.

The algorithm just described can be seen as a particular case of Pippenger's exponentiation algorithm: see Stam's Ph.D. Thesis for an accessible description of the latter [34].

To choose the optimal value of ℓ note that the cardinality of $\Im$ is $v := K(2^\ell - 1) + (2^R - 1) - 1$ so $(v-1)/2$ squarings and $(v+1)/2$ multiplications are required in Step 2. Step 3 uses $(K-1)m$ or Km multiplications, according to $R = 0$ or $R \ne 0$. One of the factors in (4) is $1 = g^0$ with probability $1/2^\ell$ (with probability $1/2^R$ in the last baby–window if $R \ne 0$). Therefore the total cost of the algorithm is roughly

$$f(\ell) = \big(K(2^\ell - 1) + (2^R - 1)\big)\frac{\tau_M + \tau_S}{2} - \tau_S + mK\Big(1 - \frac{1}{2^\ell}\Big)\tau_M + (m-1)\tau_\varphi$$

where τ_M, τ_S, and τ_φ denote the timings for a multiplication, a squaring and a Frobenius. It is tempting to optimize analytically the baby-window size by determining the minimum of $f(\ell)$: however this would require the evaluation of trascendental functions. In the applications the sizes of the exponents are bounded, and only few integer values of ℓ are admissible. Hence the best strategy to pick the optimal baby-window size consists in counting the amount of average operations required for several consecutive values of ℓ until a minimum is found. Many examples of this strategy are found in Table 1.

3.3 Abusing the Frobenius

We return to the problem of evaluating g^n in $\mathbb{F}_{p^m}$, but this time we require that computing the Frobenius is fast. We begin again by writing $n = \sum_{i=0}^{m-1} n_i p^i$, with $0 \le n_i < p$, and $n_i = \sum_{j=0}^{K'-1} n_{ij} 2^{j\ell}$, for some window size $\ell \ll u = \lceil \log_2 p \rceil$. Put $K = \lceil u/\ell \rceil$. While writing down the expansion of g^x we immediately change the order of the operations:

$$g^n = \prod_{i=0}^{m-1} \varphi^i(g^{n_i}) = \prod_{i=0}^{m-1} \prod_{j=0}^{K-1} g^{n_{ij} 2^{j\ell} p^i} = \prod_{j=0}^{K-1} \left(\prod_{i=0}^{m-1} g^{n_{ij} p^i} \right)^{2^{j\ell}} . \qquad (5)$$

Then for $j = 0, 1, \ldots, K-1$ we define the quantities

$$\Pi_j := \prod_{i=0}^{m-1} g^{n_{ij} p^i} = \prod_{i=0}^{m-1} \varphi^i(g^{n_{ij}})$$

which can be evaluated by a Horner scheme in φ, so that a second Horner scheme (in the guise of a square-ℓ-times-and-multiply loop) yields $g^n = (\cdots(\Pi_{K-1}^{2^\ell} \cdot \Pi_{K-2})^{2^\ell} \cdots \Pi_1)^{2^\ell} \cdot \Pi_0$.

Algorithm 2: *Frobenius-abusing exponentiation*

INPUT: An element g of $\mathbb{F}_{p^m}$, an exponent $n = \sum_{i=0}^{m-1} n_i p^i$ with $0 \le n_i < p$, and a window length ℓ.
OUTPUT: g^n.

---

1. Compute (or retrieve) $g^2, \ldots, g^{2^\ell - 1}$.
   Set $u \leftarrow \lceil \log_2 p \rceil$ and $K \leftarrow \lceil u/\ell \rceil$.
   Write $n_i = \sum_{j=0}^{K-1} n_{ij} 2^{j\ell}$ for $0 \le i < m$, with $0 \le n_{ij} < 2^\ell$.
   Set $x \leftarrow 1$.
   `for` $j = K-1$ `down to 0 do` {
2. $\quad\Pi \leftarrow 1$
   $\quad$`for` $i = m-1$ `down to 0 do` {
3. $\quad\quad\Pi \leftarrow \Pi \cdot g^{n_{ij}}$
4. $\quad\quad$`if` $i \ne 0$ `then` $\Pi \leftarrow \varphi(\Pi)$ }
5. $\quad x \leftarrow x \cdot \Pi$
6. $\quad$`if` $j \ne 0$ `then` $x \leftarrow x^{2^\ell}$ }
7. `return` (x)

We now write down the operation count. In Step 1, $2^{\ell-1}$ multiplications and $2^{\ell-1} - 1$ squarings are required. In Steps 3 and 4, an expected amount $mK(1-2^{-\ell})$ of multiplications and, respectively, $(m-1)K$ Frobenius operations are performed. In Step 6 $(K-1)\ell$ squarings are done. Hence the total is $\big(2^{\ell-1} + mK(1-2^{-\ell})\big)M + (2^{\ell-1} - 1 + (K-1)\ell)S + (m-1)K\varphi$. This algorithm bears

Table 1. Operation counts for one exponentiation in $\mathbb{F}_{4086122041^m}$

m	Ratios		Simple (§ 3.1)		Algorithm 1				Algorithm 2			
	$\frac{\tau_S}{\tau_M}$	$\frac{\tau_\varphi}{\tau_M}$	M/S/φ	Cost	ℓ	$\#\Im$	M/S/φ	Cost	ℓ	$\#\Im$	M/S/φ	Cost
4	.83	.42	60 31 3	87.95	1	31	63 31 3	90.95	4	15	33.4 32 20.5	69.70
6	.76	.25	90 31 5	114.83	2	47	87 31 5	111.83	4	15	47 32 34.2	80.30
8	.80	.24	120 31 7	146.48	2	47	111 31 7	137.48	5	31	60.2 32 40.4	95.53
16	.68	.15	240 31 15	264.30	3	72	182 41 15	213.34	5	31	106.4 32 86.7	143.27
32	.57	.12	480 31 31	501.07	4	119	295 63 31	334.88	6	63	190.7 32 155.6	223.75
64	.63	.06	960 31 63	983.67	5	188	510 97 63	576.25	7	127	347 32 280.5	384.00
128	.65	.04	1920 31 127	1943.15	6	317	881 161 127	985.86	7	127	632 32 565.5	668.43

the name "Frobenius-abusing exponentiation" because of the large amount of applications of φ, whereas the amount of other group operations is much smaller than with Algorithm 1.

Remark 1. If a binomial basis is used computing a power of φ is as costly as computing φ. All it takes is to precompute the constants and permutation map associated to φ^a: If $\varphi(x) = c_1 x^J$ then $\varphi^a(x) = c_1^a x^{J^a \bmod m}$. Hence if some $n_{ij} = 0$ in Step 3 the application of the Frobenius to Π can be delayed until a nonzero coefficient is found or $i = 0$. This non-trivial optimisation is most effective if ℓ is small.

3.4 Comparing the Exponentiation Algorithms

Table 1 contains the expected operations counts and costs of the three above exponentiation algorithms in a typical set of examples. We take $p = 4086122041$ so that $u = \lceil \log_2 p \rceil = 32$, and let m vary. $\mathbb{F}_{p^m}$ is, roughly, a $32\,m$-bit field. All the fields have been represented by binomial bases. The labels $\Im$, M, S, φ denote the number of memory registers used, and the amount of multiplications, squarings and Frobenius operations required. The relative speed ratios of squarings and Frobenius operations with respect to multiplications have been taken from our highly optimised library `MGFez`, which uses also the other arithmetic improvements described in this paper, by timing it on an Intel Pentium processor. For each value of m, in Algorithms 1 and 2 the optimal choice of ℓ for speed is used. Total costs are given relative to a multiplication. The results are then compared in Table 2 to the simple square-and-multiply algorithm and the sliding window method (using the optimal window size). The costs are computed with the same weights as before.

Table 2. Comparison with other exponentiation algorithms

m ($u = 32$)	4	6	8	16	32	64	128
Square and Multiply	169.41	241.16	332.00	603.48	1095.11	2313.61	4709.75
Sliding Windows	144.73 ($\ell = 4$)	197.24 ($\ell = 4$)	269.40 ($\ell = 4$)	459.36 ($\ell = 5$)	778.23 ($\ell = 5$)	1633.77 ($\ell = 6$)	3278.05 ($\ell = 7$)
Lenstra's Method Subsection 3.1	87.95	114.83	146.48	264.30	501.07	983.67	1943.15
Algorithm 1	90.95 ($\ell = 1$)	111.83 ($\ell = 2$)	137.48 ($\ell = 2$)	213.34 ($\ell = 3$)	334.88 ($\ell = 4$)	576.25 ($\ell = 5$)	985.86 ($\ell = 6$)
Algorithm 2	69.70 ($\ell = 4$)	80.30 ($\ell = 4$)	95.53 ($\ell = 5$)	143.27 ($\ell = 5$)	223.75 ($\ell = 6$)	384.00 ($\ell = 7$)	668.43 ($\ell = 7$)

For a 1024-bit field ($m = 32$) Algorithm 2 is 24% faster than Algorithm 1. However, if the ratios are different, then Algorithm 2 can be slower. This is the case, for example, if a generic (non binomial) polynomial basis is used: For $m = 32$, in this case we observed $\frac{\tau_S}{\tau_M} = 0.86$ and $\frac{\tau_\varphi}{\tau_M} = 2.13$ – then the cost of Algorithm 1 is $366.95M$ and that of Algorithm 2 is $505.83M$.

Even though the estimates apply to speci□c examples of □nite □elds, the advantages of the methods presented here in general for PAFFs should be obvious.

3.5 On Curves

Algorithms 1 and 2 can easily be adapted to compute scalar products in elliptic curves or in Jacobians of hyperelliptic curves with an efficiently computable endomorphism φ. For *sub□eld curves* – i.e. curves defined over $\mathbb{F}_{p^r}$ but considered over $\mathbb{F}_{p^m}$ with $r|m$ – this endomorphism is induced by the Frobenius automorphism of the field extension $\mathbb{F}_{p^m}/\mathbb{F}_{p^r}$. To perform an exponentiation in the chosen subgroup G, one uses in conjunction with φ the so-called τ-adic expansion of the exponent, where τ is a complex root of the characteristic polynomial of φ [15, 32], or exponent splitting techniques such as those by Gallant, Lambert and Vanstone [10], Müller [24], and Sica, Ciet and Quisquater [31]. Efficient ad-hoc exponent splitting techniques exist for trace zero varieties [17, 3].

For brevity, we skip further details. We just point out that little needs to be done other than changing the notation from multiplicative to additive. On curves and Jacobians the speed ratios of the operations (addition, doubling, endomorphism) differ greatly from the finite field case. Hence the optimal algorithm must be determined for every case.

4 Polynomial Arithmetic and Mixed Modular Reduction

Multiplication in extension fields is based on two types of modular reduction: reduction modulo the irreducible polynomial $f(X)$ and reduction of integers modulo the characteristic p.

The first one is a well investigated problem: we consider here only the case $f(X) = X^m - b$, which makes the Frobenius easy to compute and thus allows the use of Algorithm 2. If $X^m - b$ is irreducible and $x = X \bmod f(X)$, like in Section 2, we consider $\mathbb{F}_{p^m}$ as a $\mathbb{F}_p$-vector space with basis $[1, x, \ldots, x^{p-1}]$. Every element of $\mathbb{F}_{p^m}$ is represented uniquely as a polynomial in x of degree at most $m-1$ over $\mathbb{F}_p$. Addition is performed componentwise. The multiplication in $\mathbb{F}_{p^m}$ under this representation is induced from the polynomial multiplication in $\mathbb{F}_p[X]$, with the relation $x^m = b$: Write $\alpha = \sum_{i=0}^{m-1} a_i x^i$ and $\beta = \sum_{i=0}^{m-1} b_i x^i$. Then

$$\alpha\beta = \sum_{i=0}^{2m-2} c_i x^i = c_{m-1}x^{m-1} + \sum_{i=0}^{m-2} (c_i + bc_{i+m})\, x^i \; textwhere \; c_j = \sum_{\substack{j+k=i \\ 0\leq j,k<m}} a_j b_k .$$

In what follows w *denotes the bit-length of the integer registers of a given computing architecture (for example* 32 *or* 64*).*

The quantities c_j are computed modulo p: In a straightforward implementation the biggest part of the computation time is spent performing modulo p reductions. To speed up the multiplication in $\mathbb{F}_{p^d}$ we can:

(i) Speed up modulo p reduction.
(ii) Reduce modulo p less often while doing the polynomial arithmetic.

Instance (i) can be addressed in many ways, not equally satisfactory:

- Using the division-with-remainder operations of the CPU or some software macros to that effect [20, §14.3.1]. This solution is very slow [7].
- Barrett ([5] and [20, §14.3.3]) or Quisquater reduction [26, 27]. These methods are fast only for large inputs. See also [7].
- Use quasi-Mersenne primes, which are of the form $2^b \pm c$ with $c \leq 2^{b/2}$ (see [20, Algorithm 14.47]).
- Montgomery reduction [21]. Very efficient [7], but employs an alternate representation of the integers. See [20, §14.3.2].
- Modular reduction for generalized Mersenne primes according to [8].

Instance (ii) can be addressed in a simple way for small enough p, i.e. $m \cdot p^2 < 2^{2w}$: in this case several products can be added together and only the final result reduced – the application to schoolbook multiplication is obvious. Another solution is to allow triple precision intermediate operands, but efficient modular reduction for the accumulated result can only be done for specific types of primes (e.g. quasi-Mersenne). The Montgomery and Barrett algorithms cannot be used to reduce triple precision operands modulo a single precision prime, unless one *increases* the precision of all operands – resulting in a big performance penalty.

We shall provide more satisfactory answers to both problems.

4.1 A Modulo p Reduction Algorithm

In this Subsection we descrive a fast application of Barret's [5] modular reduction algorithm to the single precision case, which can be used as an alternative to Montgomery's [21]. The quantity to be reduced modulo p will be denoted by x and shall satisfy $x < p2^w$.

Barret's algorithm in single precision approximates the quotient q of $\lfloor x/p \rfloor$ by the formula $\lfloor \frac{x}{p} \rfloor \approx \lfloor (\lfloor \frac{2^{2w}}{p} \rfloor \cdot x/2^{2w} \rfloor$, then computes a remainder $r = x - qp$ and decrements it by p until it is $\leq p$: this adjustment needs to be done at most twice. Often a further approximation is done by truncating x, i.e. $\lfloor \frac{x}{p} \rfloor \approx \lfloor (\lfloor \frac{2^{2w}}{p} \rfloor \cdot \lfloor \frac{x}{2^w} \rfloor)/2^w \rfloor$ with 3 single precision multiplications, whereas the adjustment loop is repeated at most 3 times.

We observe that, when $\lceil \log_2(p) \rceil = w$, we have $\mu = 2^w + \mu_0$ with $0 < \mu_0 < 2^w$ and $q < 2^w$. By this the second approximation of $\lfloor x/p \rfloor$ is calculated by just one multiplication and and one addition. The complexity of the resulting method is comparable to that of Montgomery's.

By adjusting the parameters to the bit-size of the modulus we can perform such a cheap reduction modulo *all* primes, and not only to those with maximal bit length fitting in a word. If $u = \lceil \log_2(p) \rceil$, we replace 2^{2w} by 2^{w+u}. The following approximation of the quotient is used:

$$\left\lfloor \frac{x}{p} \right\rfloor \approx \left\lfloor \left(\left\lfloor \frac{2^{w+u}}{p} \right\rfloor \cdot x \right) / 2^{w+u} \right\rfloor \approx \left\lfloor \left(\left\lfloor \frac{2^{w+u}}{p} \right\rfloor \cdot \left\lfloor \frac{x}{2^u} \right\rfloor \right) / 2^w \right\rfloor .$$

We obtain the following algorithm:

Algorithm 3: *Modular reduction*

INPUT: p prime $\leq 2^w$; x an integer with $x \leq p \cdot 2^w$
OUTPUT: $x \bmod p$ (optional: x div p)

Assume u *and* μ_0 *known, where:* u *is s.t.* $2^u > p > 2^{u-1}$, *and*
$\mu_0 \leftarrow \lfloor 2^{w+u}/p \rfloor - 2^w = \lfloor 2^w(2^u - p)/p \rfloor$

---

1. $x_1 \leftarrow \lfloor x/2^b \rfloor$
2. $q \leftarrow x_1 + \left\lfloor \frac{x_1 \cdot \mu_0}{2^w} \right\rfloor$ [note that $q = \lfloor \frac{x_1 \cdot \mu}{2^w} \rfloor$]
3. $r \leftarrow x - q \cdot p$
4. `while` $r \geq p$ `do` { $r \leftarrow r - p$ (optional: $q \leftarrow q + 1$) }
5. `return` r (and optionally also q)

The correctness is obvious. Step 4 is iterated at most 3 times and, practice, it is repeated only 0.5–1.5 times, depending on the prime.

Only Mersenne-type moduli with very small coefficients allow a sensibly faster reduction, such as those of the form $2^m \pm 1$. Note, however, that multiplication in PAFFs is less sensitive to further improvements in modular reduction than multiplication in other algebraic structures, because of incomplete reduction, described in the next Subsection.

4.2 Incomplete Reduction

We return to the problem of computing the sum $\sum_{i=0}^{d-1} a_i b_i \mod p$ given a_i and b_i with $0 \le a_i, b_i < p$, where as always p is a prime smaller than 2^w, w being the single precision word size.

To use Algorithm 3 or Montgomery's reduction procedure [21] at the *end* of the summation, we just have to make sure that all partial sums of $\sum a_i b_i$ are smaller than $p\,2^w$: the number obtained by removing the least significant w bits should stay reduced modulo p. Hence, we add the double precision products a_i, b_i together in succession and we check if there has been an overflow or if the most significant word of the intermediate sum is $\ge p$: if so we subtract p. This requires as many operations as allowing intermediate results in triple precision, but either less memory accesses are needed, or less registers have to be allocated.

Furthermore, at the end we have to reduce a possibly smaller number, making the modular reduction faster than in the case with triple precision intermediate sums and, as already remarked, allowing a bigger choice of algorithms and primes.

Algorithm 4: ***Incomplete reduction***

INPUT: p (and μ_0), a_i and b_i for $i = 0, \ldots, t$,
OUTPUT: x with $x \equiv \sum_{i=0}^{t} a_i b_i \mod p2^w$ and $0 \le x \le p2^w$
NOTATION: $x = (x_{\mathrm{hi}}, x_{\mathrm{lo}})$ is a double precision variable.

1. `Initialise` $x \leftarrow a_0 b_0$
   `for` $i = 1$ `to` t `do` {
2. $\quad x \leftarrow x + a_i b_i$
3. $\quad$ `if carry or` $x_{\mathrm{hi}} \ge p$ `then` $x_{\mathrm{hi}} \leftarrow x_{\mathrm{hi}} - p$ }
4. `return` x

4.3 Fast Convolutions

Like in the case of long integer arithmetic, fast and nested convolution techniques [29, 6] can be used for additional speed-ups. We illustrate the methodology, and the issues, with two examples.

To multiply two degree m polynomials we can use a Karatsuba [12] step to reduce the problem to three multiplications of degree $\lceil m/2 \rceil$ polynomials. It is very well known that this leads to an $O(m^{\log_2 3})$ algorithm. For m small, say $m < 10$ or $m < 30$ depending on the implementation, schoolbook multiplication is faster.

Similar algorithms split their inputs in three or more parts, as the k-points Toom-Cook algorithm (cfr. [16, § 4.4.3]). Its time complexity is $O(m^{\log_k (k+1)})$, but in practice it gives gains only for input sizes steeply increasing with k. Karatsuba's method is the particular case $k = 2$.

Different types of convolutions can be nested, always choosing the optimal one for a given operand size. Since the schoolbook method is the fastest for small operands, it is always used at the bottom level of the recursion, called the *socle*. For many applications the only effective "short convolution" will be the shortest one, i.e. Karatsuba.

Care is required for the decision to keep which intermediate results in double precision. In fact, even if we save modular reductions by doing so, the number of memory accesses will increase and divisions by small constants will have to operate on double precision operands instead of on single precision ones. There are two basic partially delayed modular reduction variants:

- In the first one, all results are kept in double precision and the full modular reduction is done only at the very end.
- In the second variant the modular reduction is always done in the schoolbook socle. The convolutions above the socle operate only on single precision integers.

The first variant uses less CPU multiplications but more memory accesses, hence it is the approach of choice on workstations with large memory bandwidth. The second solution seems the best one on a PC.

5 A Software Experiment

We implemented the algorithms of Sections 3 and 4 in the software library `MGFez` (a quasi-acronym for Middle Galois Field Extensions), previously known as `PAFFlib`. For large extension degrees `MGFez` uses simple convolutions and recognizes automatically small primes, so that even without incomplete reduction the accumulated sums do not exceed 2^{2w}. The current version of `MGFez` works only with $w = 32$ and can be compiled on Pentium, Alpha and POWER processors.

For several values of a parameter B we compare the timings required by `gmp` version 4.0 to perform $a^n \bmod b$ where a, b and n are B-bit numbers, against the time required by `MGFez` to compute g^n, where g is an element of a finite extension field with about 2^B elements and $n \approx 2^B$. The manual of `gmp` describes all algorithms employed. For operands of the sizes which we tested, 3 points Toom-Cook convolutions and exact division algorithms are used.

Table 3 contains some sample timings in milliseconds on a 400 Mhz Pentium III. We explain the meanings of the captions:

- Inline asm = `gmp-4.0` compiled only using the C version with inline assembler macros for some double precision operations. *This is the same kind of optimization used in* `MGFez`.
- Asm kernel = `gmp-4.0` linked with aggressively optimised assembler portions, exploiting MMX operations for a bigger speed-up. This is the stardard installation.
- Large prime = the prime 4086122041 was used, close to 2^{32} but *not* of special form. Incomplete reduction (Algorithm 4) is used.
- Small prime = the prime 637116481 was used (29 bit). In this case no incomplete reduction is required in the schoolbook socle.

Table 3. *Some Timings.*

Bits	gmp-4.0		MGFez	
(B)	inline asm	asm kernel	large prime	small prime
128	0.5		0.11	
192	1.75		0.37	
256	3.5		0.52	
512	22	7	2.8	2.1
1024	160	45	13.2	9.4
2048	1158	340	68.2	49.4

Even though such comparisons must be taken *cum granum salis* , it is worth noting that an implementation of our algorithms with just a few assembler macros shows the performance advantages of PAFFs over prime fields - even when the latter are aggressively optimized.

6 Conclusions

We have presented techniques for arithmetic in PAFFs. The first are two exponentiation algorithms which make heavy use of the structure induced by the automorphism of the group. We illustrated them in detail in the case of the Frobenius of the multiplicative group of a field extension. The other techniques reduce the cost of a field reduction involved in a multiplication in $\mathbb{F}_{p^m}$, i.e. in typical field operations.

We implemented these techniques in a relatively portable software library. The run times compared to the fastest general purpose long integer arithmetic library `gmp`, version 4.0, display a speed up ranging between 10 and 20 over prime fields of cryptographically relevant sizes. Our exponentiation algorithms outperform also the previously used methods for the particular instances of the extension fields which we consider.

Acknowledgements

The authors wish to express their gratitude to Alessandro Baldaccini and to the anonymous referees for their valuable comments and suggestions.

References

[1] L. M. Adleman and J. DeMarrais. *A subexponential algorithm for discrete logarithms over all finite fields.* Advances in Cryptology: CRYPTO'93, Douglas R. Stinson, ed., LNCS, **773**, pp. 147–158. Springer, 1994. 321

[2] R. Avanzi. *On multi-exponentiation in cryptography.* Preprint. 2002. Available from `http://eprint.iacr.org` Newer version: *On the complexity of certain multi-exponentiation techniques in cryptography.* Submitted. 322

[3] R. Avanzi and T. Lange. *Cryptographic Applications of Trace Zero Varieties.* Preprint. 321, 327

[4] D. V. Bailey and C. Paar. *Efficient Arithmetic in Finite Field Extensions with Applications in Elliptic Curve Cryptography.* Journal of Cryptography **14**, No. 3, 2001, pp. 153-176. 322

[5] P. Barrett. *Implementing the Rivest Shamir and Adleman public key encryption algorithm on a standard digital signal processor*, In: Advances in Cryptology–Proceedings of crypto'86, LNCS vol. 263, pp. 311–323. Springer, 1987. 328, 329

[6] R. Blahut. *Fast Algorithm for Digital Signal Processing.* Addison Wesley, (1987). 330

[7] A. Bosselaers, R. Govaerts and J. Vandewalle. *Comparison of three modular reduction functions.* In: *Advances in cryptology: CRYPTO '93*, D. R. Stinson (editor). LNCS vol. 773, pp. 175–186. Springer, 1994. 328

[8] J. Chung and A. Hasan. *More generalized Mersenne Numbers (Extended Abstract).* This volume. 328

[9] J. von zur Gathen and M.Nöcker. *Exponentiation in finite fields: theory and practice.* Proceedings of AAECC–12, LNCS, vol. 1255, pp. 88–133. Springer, 1997, 324

[10] R. P. Gallant, R. J. Lambert, S. A. Vanstone. *Faster Point Multiplication on Elliptic Curves with Efficient Endomorphisms* In *Advances in Cryptology - CRYPTO 2001 Proceedings*, pp. 190–200. Springer, 2001. 327

[11] T. Grandlund. GMP. A software library for arbitrary precision integers. Available from `http://www.swox.com/gmp/`

[12] A. Karatsuba and Yu. Ofman. *Multiplication of multidigit numbers on automata.* Soviet Physics-Doklady **7** (1963), pp. 595–596. 330

[13] N. Koblitz. *Elliptic curve cryptosystems*, Math. Comp. **48** (177), pp. 203–209, (1987). 320

[14] N. Koblitz. *Hyperelliptic cryptosystems*, J. of Cryptology **1**, pp. 139–150, (1989). 320

[15] N. Koblitz. *CM-Curves with good Cryptographic Properties.* In: Advances in Cryptology - CRYPTO '91, LNCS vol. 576, pp. 279–287. Springer, 1992. 327

[16] D. E. Knuth. *The art of computer programming. Vol. 2, Seminumerical algorithms*, third ed., *Addison-Wesley Series in Computer Science and Information Processing.* Addison-Wesley, 1997. 322, 323, 330

[17] T. Lange. *Trace Zero Subvariety for Cryptosystems.* Submitted. 321, 327

[18] A.K. Lenstra. *Using Cyclotomic Polynomials to Construct Efficient Discrete Logarithm Cryptosystems over Finite Fields.* In: Proceedings ACISP'97, LNCS vol. 1270, pp. 127-138. Springer, 1997. 322, 323

[19] S. Lim, S. Kim, I. Yie, J. Kim and H. Lee. *XTR Extended to $GF(p^{6m})$.* In: Proceedings of *SAC 2001.* LNCS 2259, pp. 301–312. Springer, 2001. 321

[20] A. Menezes, P. van Oorschot and S. Vanstone. *Handbook of Applied Cryptography*, CRC Press (1997). 322, 328

[21] P. L. Montgomery. *Modular multiplication without trial division*, Math. Comp. **44** (170), pp. 519–521 (1985). 328, 329, 330

[22] P. Mihăilescu. *Optimal Galois Field Bases which are not Normal.* Recent Results Session, Fast Software Encryption Symposium, Haifa (1997). 322

[23] V. S. Miller. *Use of elliptic curves in cryptography*, In: Advances in cryptology—crypto '85, LNCS vol. 218, pp. 417–426. Springer, 1986. 320

[24] V. Müller. *Efficient Point Multiplication for Elliptic Curves over Special Optimal Extension Fields.* In "Public-Key Cryptography and Computational Number Theory", September 11-15, 2000, Warschau, pp. 197–207. De Gruyter, 2001. 327

[25] A. Odlyzko. *Discrete Logarithms: The past and the future*, Designs, Codes and Cryptography **19** (2000), pp. 129–145. 321

[26] J.-J. Quisquater. *Procédé de Codage selon la Methode dite RSA, par un Microcontrôleur et Dispositifs Utilisant ce Procédé.* Demande de brevet Français. (Dépôt numéro: 90 02274), February 1990. 328

[27] J.-J. Quisquater. *Encoding System According to the So-called RSA Method, by Means of a Microcontroller and Arrangement Implementing this System.* U. S. Patent 5,166,978, November 1992. 328

[28] G. W. Reitwiesner. *Binary arithmetic.* Advances in Computers **1**, pp. 231–308 (1960). 322

[29] A. Schönhage and V. Strassen. *Schnelle Multiplikation großer Zahlen*, Computing **7**, pp. 281-292. 330

[30] O. Schirokauer. *Using number fields to compute logarithms in finite fields*, Math. Comp. **69** (2000), pp. 1267–1283. 321

[31] F. Sica, M. Ciet and J.-J. Quisquater. *Analysis of the Gallant-Lambert-Vanstone Method based on Efficient Endomorphisms: Elliptic and Hyperelliptic Curves.* In: *Selected Areas of Cryptography 2002.* LNCS 2595. pp. 21–36. Springer 2002. 327

[32] J. A. Solinas. *An improved algorithm for arithmetic on a family of elliptic curves.* In: B. S. Kaliski, Jr. (Ed.), *Advances in Cryptology – CRYPTO '97.* LNCS vol. 1294, pp. 357–371. Springer, 1997. 322, 327

[33] M. Stam and A. K. Lenstra, *Efficient subgroup exponentiation in quadratic and sixth degree extensions.* In *Proceedings of Workshop on Cryptographic Hardware and Embedded Systems – CHES 2002.* LNCS 2523, pp. 318–332. Springer, 2003. 321

[34] M. Stam. *Speeding up Subgroup Cryptosystems.* Ph.D. Thesis, Technical University of Eindhoven, 2003. ISBN 90-386-0692-3. 324

[35] E. R. Verheul and A. K. Lenstra. *The XTR public key system.* In *Advances in Cryptography – Crypto '00*, M. Bellare, ed., LNCS vol. 1880, pp. 1–19. Springer, 2000. 321

[36] Andrew C. Yao. *On the evaluation of powers.* SIAM Journal on Computing **5** (1976), pp. 100–103. 323

More Generalized Mersenne Numbers
(Extended Abstract)

Jaewook Chung* and Anwar Hasan

Centre for Applied Cryptographic Research
University of Waterloo, Ontario, Canada
j4chung@uwaterloo.ca
ahasan@ece.uwaterloo.ca

Abstract. In 1999, Jerome Solinas introduced families of moduli called the generalized Mersenne numbers [8]. The generalized Mersenne numbers are expressed in a polynomial form, $p = f(t)$, where t is a power of 2. It is shown that such p's lead to fast modular reduction methods which use only a few integer additions and subtractions. We further generalize this idea by allowing any integer for t. We show that more generalized Mersenne numbers still lead to a significant improvement over well-known modular multiplication techniques. While each generalized Mersenne number requires a dedicated implementation, more generalized Mersenne numbers allow flexible implementations that work for more than one modulus. We also show that it is possible to perform long integer modular arithmetic without using multiple precision operations when t is chosen properly. Moreover, based on our results, we propose efficient arithmetic methods for XTR cryptosystem.

Keywords: Generalized Mersenne Numbers, RSA, XTR, Montgomery, Karatsuba-Ofman, Modular Reduction

1 Introduction

Many cryptosystems such as RSA, XTR, and elliptic curve cryptosystems (ECC) based on prime field involve significant use of modular multiplications and squaring operations. Hence it is very important to implement efficient modular multiplication and squaring operations in implementing such cryptosystems.

There are many well-known techniques for efficient implementation of modular arithmetic operations [5, 3]. The Montgomery algorithm is the most popular choice since it is very efficient and it works for any modulus. RSA cryptosystems are usually implemented using the Montgomery algorithm and ECC defined over prime field and XTR cryptosystems can also benefit from the Montgomery algorithm.

* This research was funded in part by Natural Sciences and Engineering Research Council of Canada (NSERC) through Post Graduate Scholarship – B (PGS-B) and in part by Canadian Wireless Telecommunications Association (CWTA) Scholarship.

M. Matsui and R. Zuccherato (Eds.): SAC 2003, LNCS 3006, pp. 335–347, 2004.

There are techniques that take advantage of special form of modulus. The Mersenne numbers $m = 2^k - 1$ [3] are well-known examples. However Mersenne numbers are never primes and thus they are not cryptographically useful. Due to Richard Crandall [2], the Mersenne numbers are generalized to the form $2^k - c$ where c is a small integer. Such families of integers are known as pseudo-Mersenne numbers. Modular reductions by pseudo-Mersenne numbers are very efficiently done using a few constant multiplications by a small integer c. However pseudo-Mersenne numbers are often avoided due to the patent issue [2].

In 1999, Jerome Solinas introduced families of moduli called the generalized Mersenne numbers [8]. The generalized Mersenne numbers are expressed in a polynomial form $p = f(t)$ where t is a power of 2. Such representations lead to fast modular reduction which uses only a few integer additions and subtractions. It is well-known that all 5 NIST-recommended curves [7, 6] defined over prime fields are based on the generalized Mersenne numbers.

However the generalized Mersenne numbers have a significant limitation: there could be only one number for a given bit length of p and a fixed $f(t)$. Hence, if $p = f(t)$ is not a desired number, we have to change either the bit length of p or $f(t)$. It follows that each generalized Mersenne number requires a dedicated implementation for that number. In some applications, this property makes the generalized Mersenne numbers less useful.

In this paper, we further extend the idea of generalized Mersenne numbers by removing the restriction that t must be a power of 2. Surprisingly, it will be shown that modular arithmetic based on such integers could lead to much faster modular arithmetic than the classical and the Montgomery modular arithmetic methods. We give criteria for choosing good $f(t)$'s and show further improvements are possible by choosing pseudo-Mersenne numbers for t or by choosing t whose bit length is a few bits shorter than processor's word size. The latter technique is quite useful in practice, since it makes possible to implement long integer modular arithmetic without using multiple precision operations. We also apply our methods and principles to the arithmetic operations required in XTR cryptosystems. We begin with a simple example.

2 An Example

We use the same polynomial $f(t) = t^3 - t + 1$ used in [8]. We generalize the ideas from [8] by removing the restriction that t must be a power of 2. Hence we assume that t could be any positive integer.

Let p be in the form $p = f(t) = t^3 - t + 1$ where t can be any positive integer. Note that any integers x and y, where $0 \leq x,\, y < p$, can be expressed in the form of the second degree polynomial in $\mathbb{Z}[t]$,

$$\begin{aligned} x &= x_2 t^2 + x_1 t + x_0 \ , \\ y &= y_2 t^2 + y_1 t + y_0 \ , \end{aligned} \tag{1}$$

where $|x_i|$, $|y_i| < t$ for $i = 0, 1, 2$. Using simple polynomial multiplication and reduction, the modular multiplication of x and y is done as follows,

$$\begin{aligned} xy \equiv & (x_2y_0 + x_1y_1 + x_0y_2 + x_2y_2)t^2 \\ & + (x_1y_0 + x_0y_1 - x_2y_2 + x_2y_1 + x_1y_2)t \\ & + x_0y_0 - x_2y_1 - x_1y_2 \pmod{t^3 - t + 1} \ . \end{aligned} \tag{2}$$

If the school-book method is used in computing (2), 9 multiplications are required. However, when multiplying two second degree polynomials, it is advantageous to use the 3-segment Karatsuba-Ofman Algorithm (KOA) [1]. We first compute 6 intermediate values, D_0 through D_5, using 6 multiplications (or 6 squarings when $x = y$). Note that the normal application of KOA would require 7 multiplications (or 7 squarings when $x = y$).

$$\begin{aligned} D_0 &= x_0y_0 \ , \\ D_1 &= x_1y_1 \ , \\ D_2 &= x_2y_2 \ , \\ D_3 &= (x_0 + x_1)(y_0 + y_1) \ , \\ D_4 &= (x_0 + x_2)(y_0 + y_2) \ , \\ D_5 &= (x_1 + x_2)(y_1 + y_2) \ . \end{aligned} \tag{3}$$

Then the modular multiplication of x and y is done in $\mathbb{Z}[t]/f(t)$ as follows.

$$xy \equiv c_2t^2 + c_1t + c_0 \pmod{t^3 - t + 1} \ , \tag{4}$$

where,

$$\begin{aligned} c_2 &= D_4 - D_0 + D_1 \ , \\ c_1 &= D_3 - (D_0 - D_5) - 2(D_1 + D_2) \ , \\ c_0 &= (D_0 - D_5) + (D_1 + D_2) \ . \end{aligned} \tag{5}$$

Note that, at this stage, modular reduction is partially done by a polynomial reduction which uses simple integer additions and subtractions only. Since the bit lengths of c_i's are about twice as large as that of t, c_i's must be reduced before further modular multiplication or squaring operations are performed. We express c_i's in the form of the first degree polynomial in $\mathbb{Z}[t]$ as follows,

$$\begin{aligned} c_2 &= c_{21}t + c_{20} \ , \\ c_1 &= c_{11}t + c_{10} \ , \\ c_0 &= c_{01}t + c_{00} \ , \end{aligned} \tag{6}$$

where $|c_{i0}| < t$ for $0 \le i \le 2$. To compute (6), 3 integer divisions are required. Then it follows that,

$$xy \equiv (c_{11} + c_{20})t^2 + (c_{01} + c_{10} + c_{21})t + c_{00} - c_{21} \pmod{f(t)} \ . \tag{7}$$

We repeatedly apply this reduction process until the absolute values of the resulting coefficients are all less than t.

2.1 Analysis

We assume that the modular multiplication is implemented in software. Note that microprocessors usually deal with the units of data known as words. Hence we analyze our modular arithmetic method in terms of word length.

Let t_m and t_d respectively denote the time required for a microprocessor to compute word level multiplication and division operations. According to [5], the running times required to compute long integer multiplication, squaring and division are given as follows,

$$\begin{aligned} M(a) &= a^2 t_m \ , \\ S(a) &= \frac{a^2+a}{2} t_m \ , \\ D(a,b) &= (a-b)(b+2)t_m + (a-b)t_d \ , \end{aligned} \tag{8}$$

where $M(a)$ and $S(a)$ are the running times for a long integer multiplication and a long integer squaring respectively, when multiplicands are both a words long. $D(a,b)$ is the running time for a long integer division when the dividend is a words long and the divisor is b words long.

Now, let n be the number of words required to store t. Suppose that t is fully occupying the n word blocks. Then the word length of $p = t^3 - t + 1$ should be about $3n$.

For simplicity, we do not consider the time required for additions and subtractions in our analysis. In (3), we need 6 integer multiplications ($6M(n)$). In (5), there are only additions and subtractions. For the first application of (7), we need 3 integer divisions ($3D(2n,n)$). Note that, after this first reduction, the size of coefficients should be about the same size as t. Therefore, we only need integer additions and subtractions in the subsequent applications of (7). Hence the total running time, $T_m(n)$ where n is the word length of t, of modular multiplication is,

$$\begin{aligned} T_m(n) &= 6M(n) + 3D(2n,n) \\ &= (9n^2 + 6n)t_m + 3nt_d \ . \end{aligned} \tag{9}$$

Similarly, the total running time, $T_s(n)$, for modular squaring is,

$$\begin{aligned} T_s(n) &= 6S(n) + 3D(2n,n) \\ &= (6n^2 + 9n)t_m + 3nt_d \ . \end{aligned} \tag{10}$$

In Table 1, we compare these results with the running times required for the classical methods and the Montgomery methods.

In Table 1, we see huge advantage of our modular multiplication and squaring methods over the classical algorithms. Our methods also should be usually faster than the Montgomery methods, since it is unlikely that there exists a microprocessor in which computing $9n^2$ multiplications is faster than computing $3n$ divisions.

Table 1. Running Time Comparison

	Modular Multiplication	Modular Squaring
Classical	$(18n^2 + 6n)t_m + 3nt_d$	$(13.5n^2 + 7.5n)t_m + 3nt_d$
Montgomery	$(18n^2 + 6n)t_m$	$(13.5n^2 + 7.5n)t_m$
Our methods	$(9n^2 + 6n)t_m + 3nt_d$	$(6n^2 + 9n)t_m + 3nt_d$
Our methods (no KOA)	$(12n^2 + 6n)t_m + 3nt_d$	$(7.5n^2 + 10.5n)t_m + 3nt_d$

In Table 1, we used the 3-segment KOA in the analyses of our methods, but we did not do the same in the analyses of the classical and the Montgomery algorithms. Note that typical software implementation of KOA leads to only 10%–20% improvement in the running time of long integer multiplications. Moreover such a noticeable improvement is expected only when the program is written very carefully and the operand size is very long (typically $>$ 32 blocks). However, in our method, it is easy to see that the running time for computing (4) is directly proportional to the required number of integer multiplications. For fair comparisons, in the last row in Table 1, we also provide the analysis results for our method assuming no 3-segment KOA is used in (3). Even without the KOA, our methods are still faster than the classical and the Montgomery algorithms.

3 The Ideas

In section 2, we have seen that efficient modular arithmetic is possible even though t is not a power of two. In this section, we discuss how the method shown in section 2 leads to fast modular arithmetic.

The proposed modular arithmetic is done in 3 steps as follows.

1. Polynomial multiplication (polynomials in $\mathbb{Z}[t]$)
2. Polynomial reduction by $f(t)$
3. Coefficient reduction (divisions by t)

It is clear that applying the KOA in polynomial multiplication step leads to a slight speed-up. Note that there could be similar *theoretical* improvements in the running times of the classical algorithms by applying the KOA. However, *in practice* , the KOA has significantly greater impact when it is applied to polynomial multiplications than when it is applied to integer multiplications.

The main source of speed-up is in the two reduction steps. Our method effectively splits one modular reduction into two steps: polynomial reduction step and coefficient reduction step. In polynomial reduction step, modular reduction is partially done using only a few integer additions and subtractions which are considered trivial. The rest of the reduction is done in coefficient reduction step. In that step, divisions are still unavoidable but many multiplications are saved.

The main idea of proposed modular arithmetic method is best described by Proposition 1.

Proposition 1. *Computing one long integer division takes more time than performing k short integer divisions where operands are shortened by the factor of k.*

Proof. We need to prove the following inequality.

$$D(a, b) > k \cdot D(\frac{a}{k}, \frac{b}{k}) \ , \tag{11}$$

where $a > b$ and $k > 1$. For simplicity, we assume that $k|a$ and $k|b$. Now it is easy to verify that,

$$D(a, b) - k \cdot D\left(\frac{a}{k}, \frac{b}{k}\right) = b(a-b)\frac{k-1}{k}t_m > 0 \ , \tag{12}$$

for $a > b$ and $k > 1$. □

What Proposition 1 says is that we can save about $b(a-b)(k-1)/k$ multiplications if we can break a long integer division into a number of short integer divisions. In practice, a should be about $2b$. Therefore the proposed modular arithmetic method saves about $b^2(k-1)/k$ multiplications, where k is the degree of $f(t)$ and b is the word length of p. In our example in section 2, the word length of p is $3n$ and $k = 3$. Hence, $6n^2$ multiplications are saved in reduction steps. Note that the number of saved multiplications increases as k increases. For large k, the number of saved multiplications gets close to b^2.

As shown in Proposition 1, now it appears to be clear that the proposed method is faster than the classical algorithms, since our method saves about $b^2(k-1)/k$ multiplications. Then, is the proposed method faster than the Montgomery algorithm? Note that the Montgomery algorithm uses the same number of multiplication as the classical algorithm but it does not use any division. If p is b words long, then the Montgomery algorithm saves b division instructions. Therefore, if $b^2(k-1)/k \cdot t_m > b \cdot t_d$, our method should be superior to the Montgomery algorithm. In our example in section 2, $b = 3n$ and $k = 3$. In such a case, if $2n$ multiplications take more time than single division, the proposed method should be faster than the Montgomery algorithm.

4 Desirable Properties of $f(t)$

We discuss which polynomials $f(t)$ are advantageous in our modular arithmetic method. The following is a list of desirable properties for good $f(t)$'s.

1. High degree polynomials.
   We have seen in section 3 that the efficiency of modular arithmetic increases as the degree of $f(t)$ increases. Hence it is advantageous to make the degree of $f(t)$ as high as possible. However using $f(t)$ of degree much higher than the word length of p should be avoided since it will increase the total number

of multiplications and divisions. In fact, it is best to choose the degree of $f(t)$ such that the following conditions are satisfied.

$$\begin{aligned} \frac{\text{word}(p)}{\deg(f)} &\approx l \cdot w \ , \\ \text{word}(t) \cdot \deg(f) &\approx \text{word}(p) \ , \end{aligned} \tag{13}$$

where word$(\cdot)$ denotes the word length of an integer, w is the processor's word size and $l > 0$ is an arbitrary positive integer. If the conditions (13) are not satisfied, the proposed modular arithmetic method could be slower than the classical algorithms.

2. Avoid using coefficients greater than 1.
   If any coefficient in $f(t)$ is greater than 1, it will introduce some constant multiplications by that coefficient value in polynomial reduction step.
3. Polynomials with small number of terms.
   It is easy to see that the number of terms in $f(t)$ has direct effect on the performance of polynomial reduction step. Suppose that degree k polynomial $f(t)$ has l terms. Then the number of additions or subtractions required to reduce polynomial of degree $2k-2$ is $(l-1)(k-1)$. Hence it is advantageous to choose $f(t)$ which has smaller number of terms.
4. Irreducible polynomials.
   For prime number generation, $f(t)$ should be chosen to be an irreducible polynomial. However, irreducible $f(t)$ does not guarantee the primality of $p = f(t)$.

It seems that choosing binomial $f(t) = t^k + 1$ is a good choice for most applications. Note that, for prime number generation, we have to choose k such that $f(t) = t^k + 1$ is irreducible. For example, $f(t) = t^3 + 1$ should not be used for prime generation since $f(t)$ is not an irreducible polynomial. In case $f(t) = t^k + 1$ is not irreducible, either choose a small integer $c \neq 0, 1$ which makes $f(t) = t^k + c$ irreducible or use polynomials other than binomials.

It should be noted that t in $f(t) = t^k + 1$ must be limited to even numbers in prime generation, since otherwise $p = f(t)$ is never a prime. This restriction does not occur in polynomials with odd number of terms (trinomial, pentanomial, *etc.*), provided that all coefficients are either 0 or 1. Thus such polynomials have a better chance to generate prime numbers.

5 Improvements

5.1 Improvement by Using $t = 2^n - c$ for Small c

In our method, we require k divisions by t in the coefficient reduction step. Note that division is an expensive operation in most microprocessors. However, for some special form of t, division can be avoided.

It is well-known that pseudo-Mersenne numbers $t = 2^n - c$, where c is a small (preferably positive) integer, lead to fast modular reduction methods [2, 5]. Here we derive an efficient algorithm which computes both remainder and quotient when $t = 2^n - c$.

Suppose an integer x is to be divided by t. Define $q_0 = \lfloor x/2^n \rfloor$ and $r_0 = (x \bmod 2^n) + c \cdot q_0$. Define q_i's and r_i's for $i > 1$,

$$\begin{aligned} q_i &= \left\lfloor \frac{r_{i-1}}{2^n} \right\rfloor \ , \\ r_i &= (r_{i-1} \bmod 2^n) + c \cdot q_i \ . \end{aligned} \tag{14}$$

Then we can write x as follows,

$$\begin{aligned} x &= q_0 \cdot t + r_0 \\ &= q_0 \cdot t + q_1 \cdot t + r_1 \\ &\ \vdots \\ &= \left(\sum_{i=0}^{s} q_i \right) \cdot t + r_s \ . \end{aligned} \tag{15}$$

Observe that the inequality,

$$r_{i-1} = r_i + t \cdot q_i > r_i \ , \tag{16}$$

where $i > 0$, must hold since q_i's are non-negative integers. Since r_i is a strictly decreasing sequence, there exists an integer s such that $r_s < t$. If $r_s < t$, the quotient is $\sum_{i=0}^{s} q_i$ and the remainder is r_s. Algorithm 1 is a formal description of the division method when $t = 2^n - c$. Note that the size of c has no effect on the performance of Algorithm 1 as long as the word length of c is fixed. Therefore it is easy to observe that the running time of Algorithm 1 is $O(n)$, assuming that c is a small, fixed integer.

Algorithm 1. Integer Division by $t = 2^n - c$

INPUT: Dividend $x \geq 0$.
OUTPUT: q and rem, such that $x = q \cdot t + rem$ and $0 \leq rem < t$.

1. $rem \leftarrow x$, $q \leftarrow 0$.
2. While $rem > t$ do:
   - 2.1 $A \leftarrow \lfloor rem/2^n \rfloor$.
   - 2.2 $q \leftarrow q + A$.
   - 2.3 $rem \leftarrow rem \bmod 2^n + c \cdot A$.
3. Return q and rem.

5.2 Avoiding Multiple Precision Operations

We propose using t whose bit length is a few bits shorter than processor's word size. In such a case, we could avoid multiple precision operations in modular arithmetic.

Suppose t is only a few bits shorter than a processor's word size. Then, when operands are expressed as polynomials in $\mathbb{Z}[t]$, all the coefficients are one word long. Therefore, in polynomial multiplication step, we only require processor's multiplication instructions, not the multiple precision multiplications. Since the bit length of t is slightly less than the word size, the results of the coefficient multiplications are stored in at most two words. Note that this does not cause problems, since many currently available processors support double word registers and instructions for simple arithmetic between double word operands. The results of coefficient multiplications should have enough bit margin in double word registers to prevent overflows and underflows during polynomial multiplication and polynomial reduction steps. The divisions in coefficient reduction step can also be implemented efficiently, since division instructions in most processors support dividing a double word dividend by a single word divisor.

We give a practical example. Suppose modular arithmetic operations are implemented on a processor where the word size is 32 bits long and the modulus p is about 160 bits long. Suppose 2-bit margin for t is required to prevent overflows and underflows during the modular arithmetic. Then t should be at most 30 bits long. It follows that the degree of $f(t)$ should be $\lceil 160/30 \rceil = 6$. Therefore we have to choose $\lceil 160/6 \rceil = 27$ bit t. In such a case, $p = f(t)$ will be about 162 bits long.

One drawback of this method is that it may increase the number of words required to store operands. In the above example, our method requires 6 word blocks, but originally only 5 words are sufficient. The increased word length may result in performance degradation. However, if the increment is not too large, this is not a serious issue. Usually there is a lot of unavoidable redundancy in the implementations of multiple precision arithmetic operations. In some cases when operand size is not too large, such redundancy overwhelms the running time of multiple precision operations. Hence, if the operand sizes are not too large, it is better to avoid multiple precision arithmetic, even though the increased word length may cause a slight drop in performance.

6 Advantages of Our Proposed Method

Note that one big issue for the generalized Mersenne numbers proposed in [8] is that there could be only one p for a given bit length and a polynomial $f(t)$. If $f(t)$ for some $t = 2^n$ is not useful, then we have no choice but to choose other polynomial $f(t)$ or change the bit length n of t. However our methods do not impose this kind of constraints. For a fixed $f(t)$, one can find many prime numbers $p = f(t)$ of the same bit length.

This makes significant difference in implementation. Note that there could be no general implementation for the generalized Mersenne numbers. In other words, each generalized Mersenne number requires a dedicated implementation. On the other hand, general implementation is possible in our case. If one implements modular arithmetic operations based on a pre-determined $f(t)$, then that implementation will work for any value of t. Even though $f(t)$ is not predetermined, it is still easy to implement a software that works for any $f(t)$.

Since parameter generation is not simple, it is a usual practice in ECC to share a set of pre-determined parameters among domain users. In this case, one implementation will benefit the entire domain which shares common parameters, and hence general implementation may not be needed. In fact, there are only 5 NIST (National Institute of Standards and Technology)-recommended curves based on prime fields and they all use the generalized Mersenne primes [7, 6].

However every user has to generate their own parameters in RSA cryptosystem and it is recommended that users generate their own parameters in XTR cryptosystem [4]. The generalized Mersenne numbers are not advantageous in such cases. On the other hand, the proposed method given in this paper is highly suitable for RSA and XTR cryptosystems, since it is easy to implement a software that works for all possible choices of $f(t)$ and t. Note that the more generalized Mersenne numbers are characterized by only $f(t)$ and t. Hence we can reduce the storage requirement for the modulus $p = f(t)$.

Our more generalized Mersenne numbers are also advantageous due to the efficiency of modular arithmetic. As shown in section 2, our modular multiplication and squaring methods are much faster than the classical and the Montgomery arithmetic methods. Moreover, further speed-up is possible by using special form of $t = 2^n - c$ for small integer c or using t whose bit length is a few bits shorter than the word size.

7 Efficient Arithmetic for XTR Cryptosystem

In this section, we apply our methods to the modular arithmetic operations required in XTR cryptosystems. Algorithm 2 is the simplest and fastest algorithm for generating two essential parameters p and q for use in XTR cryptosystem.

Algorithm 2. Selection of q and p [4]

OUTPUT: XTR parameters q and p such that both are primes and $q|(p^2 - p + 1)$.

1. $r \in_R \mathbb{Z}$ such that $q = r^2 - r + 1$ is a prime.
2. $k \in_R \mathbb{Z}$ such that $p = r + kq = kr^2 + (1 - k)r + k$ is a prime and is $2 \pmod 3$.

The prime $p = kr^2 + (1 - k)r + k$, generated by Algorithm 2, has special structure. In [4], it is stated that such p results in fast GF(p) arithmetic. However they did not show details on how to achieve efficient arithmetic using such p. Here we show detailed methods and analysis for efficient arithmetic in GF(p).

7.1 Efficient Arithmetic in GF(p) When $k = 1$

When $k = 1$, p takes its simplest form, $p = r^2 + 1$. We express elements x, $y \in$ GF(p) as polynomials in $\mathbb{Z}[r]$.

$$\begin{aligned} x &\equiv x_1 r + x_0 \pmod{r^2 + 1} \ , \\ y &\equiv y_1 r + y_0 \pmod{r^2 + 1} \ , \end{aligned} \tag{17}$$

where $|x_i|$, $|y_i| < r$ for $i = 0, 1$.

Then the modular multiplication is computed as follows,

$$xy \equiv z_1 r + z_0 \pmod{r^2+1} , \tag{18}$$

where,

$$\begin{aligned} z_1 &= C - A - B , \\ z_0 &= A - B , \\ A &= x_0 y_0 , \\ B &= x_1 y_1 , \\ C &= (x_0 + x_1)(y_0 + y_1) . \end{aligned} \tag{19}$$

Since the bit lengths of x_i's and y_i's are about half the bit length of p, we need 3 half-length integer multiplications to compute (18). However the bit lengths of two resulting coefficients in (18), z_1 and z_0, can be about twice the bit length of t. They must be reduced before further multiplication or squaring operations in GF(p) are performed, since otherwise the size of the multiplication result will keep growing. Using two divisions by r, we represent z_1 and z_0 in the following form,

$$z_1 = z_{11} r + z_{10} , \quad z_0 = z_{01} r + z_{00} , \tag{20}$$

where $|z_{10}|$, $|z_{00}| < r$. Then it follows that,

$$\begin{aligned} xy &\equiv (z_{11} r + z_{10}) r + z_{01} r + z_{00} \pmod{r^2+1} \\ &\equiv (z_{10} + z_{01}) r + z_{00} - z_{11} \pmod{r^2+1} . \end{aligned} \tag{21}$$

Note that $|z_{10} + z_{01}|$ and $|z_{00} - z_{11}|$ could be greater than r. In such a case, we repeatedly apply (21) until the desired results are obtained. However after the first application of (21), the resulting coefficients have almost equal lengths with r. Thus, we only need additions and subtractions instead of expensive integer divisions.

7.2 Efficient Arithmetic in GF(p) When $k \neq 1$

When $k \neq 1$, $p = kr^2 + (1-k)r + k$. Note that the coefficients are not all 1. Then we have to express x and y as polynomials in $\mathbb{Z}[kr]$.

$$\begin{aligned} x &\equiv x_1(kr) + x_0 \pmod{kr^2 + (1-k)r + k} , \\ y &\equiv y_1(kr) + y_0 \pmod{kr^2 + (1-k)r + k} , \end{aligned} \tag{22}$$

where $|x_i|$, $|y_i| < kr$ for $i = 0, 1$. The modular multiplication is computed as follows,

$$xy \equiv z_1 \cdot (kr) + z_0 \pmod{f(r)} , \tag{23}$$

where,

Table 2. Running Time Comparison of Modular Arithmetic Methods

	Modular Multiplication	Modular Squaring
Our Method ($k = 1$)	$(5n^2 + 4n)t_m + 2nt_d$	$(4n^2 + 4n)t_m + 2nt_d$
Our Method ($k \neq 1$)	$(5n^2 + 4n)t_m + 2nt_d + 4t_c$	$(4n^2 + 4n)t_m + 2nt_d + 3t_c$
Classical	$(8n^2 + 4n)t_m + 2nt_d$	$(6n^2 + 5n)t_m + 2nt_d$
Montgomery	$(8n^2 + 4n)t_m$	$(6n^2 + 5n)t_m$

$$\begin{aligned} z_1 &= C - A - 2B + D \ , \\ z_0 &= A - E \ , \\ A &= x_0 y_0 \ , \\ B &= x_1 y_1 \ , \\ C &= (x_1 + x_0)(y_1 + y_0) \ , \\ D &= Bk \ , \\ E &= Dk \ . \end{aligned} \tag{24}$$

Since z_1 and z_0 are not reduced, we express them as follows using two divisions,

$$z_1 = z_{11} \cdot (kr) + z_{10} \ , \quad z_0 = z_{01} \cdot (kr) + z_{00} \ , \tag{25}$$

where $|z_{10}|$, $|z_{00}| < r$. Then it follows that,

$$xy \equiv (z_{10} - z_{11} + z_{01} + kz_{11}) \cdot (kr) - k^2 z_{11} + z_{00} \pmod{f(r)} \ . \tag{26}$$

We repeatedly apply (26) until the desired result is obtained.

7.3 Analysis

We assume that r is stored in n word blocks. Then $p = kr^2 + (1 - k)r + k$ should be about $2n$ words long. Let t_c denote the time required to compute the constant multiplication by k. We use the same analysis technique from section 2 and the results are shown in Table 2. Table 2 also compares our methods with the classical and the Montgomery algorithms.

It is clearly seen in Table 2 that our methods save $3n^2$ and $2n^2$ multiplications for modular multiplication and modular squaring, respectively. Hence our methods are faster than the classical algorithms. Note that constant multiplications can be done efficiently if k is a very small integer or it has a low Hamming weight. Even though our methods use additional $2n$ divisions over the Montgomery algorithm, our modular multiplication methods should be faster if $3n^2$ multiplications are more expensive than $2n$ divisions. Similarly, if $2n^2$ multiplications are more expensive than $2n$ divisions, our modular squaring methods should be faster than the Montgomery algorithm.

8 Conclusions

In this paper, we further extended the generalized Mersenne numbers proposed in [8]. The generalized Mersenne numbers are expressed in polynomial form, $p = f(t)$ where t is a power of 2. However our generalization allows any integer for t. We have shown that efficient modular arithmetic is still possible even though t is not a power of 2. In our analysis, we have shown that our methods are much faster than the classical algorithm. We have also shown strong evidences that our methods are faster than the Montgomery algorithm. We have presented some criteria for good $f(t)$'s which lead to fast modular arithmetic.

Moreover, we have provided techniques for improving the modular arithmetic methods based on more generalized Mersenne numbers. One is using special form of $t = 2^n - c$ where c is a small integer. If such t is used, we can perform coefficient reduction steps using only constant multiplications. Another technique is using t whose bit length is slightly shorter than word size. In this case, the long integer modular arithmetic does not require multiple precision operations.

We have also shown efficient techniques for modular operations in XTR cryptosystem based on our results. Our analysis results show that the proposed methods should be faster than the classical and the Montgomery algorithms.

References

[1] Daniel V. Bailey and Christof Paar. Efficient arithmetic in finite field extensions with application in elliptic curve cryptography. *Journal of Cryptology*, 14(3):153–176, 2001. 337

[2] Richard E. Crandall. Method and apparatus for public key exchange in a cryptographic system (oct. 27, 1992). U.S. Paent # 5,159,632. 336, 341

[3] Donald E. Knuth. *Seminumerical Algorithms*. Addison-Wesley, 1981. 335, 336

[4] Arjen K. Lenstra and Eric R. Verheul. The XTR public key system. In *Advances in Cryptology - CRYPTO 2000*, LNCS 1880, pages 1–19. Springer-Verlag, 2000. 344

[5] Alfred J. Menezes, Paul C. van Oorschot, and Scott A. Vanstone. *Handbook of Applied Cryptography*. CRC Press, 1997. 335, 338, 341

[6] National Institute of Standards and Technology. Digital signature standard (DSS). FIPS Publication 186-2, February, 2000. 336, 344

[7] National Institute of Standards and Technology. Recommended elliptic curves for federal government use, July, 1999. 336, 344

[8] Jerome A. Solinas. Generalized Mersenne numbers. Technical Report CORR 99-39, Centre for Applied Cryptographic Research, University of Waterloo, 1999. http://cacr.uwaterloo.ca/techreports/1999/corr99-39.ps. 335, 336, 343, 347

Lower Bound on Linear Authenticated Encryption

Charanjit S. Jutla

IBM T. J. Watson Research Center,
Yorktown Heights, NY 10598, USA

Abstract. We show that any scheme to encrypt m blocks of size n bits each, which assures message integrity, is linear in $(GF2)^n$, uses $m + k$ invocations of random functions (from n bits to n bits) and vn bits of randomness, must have $k + v$ at least $\Omega(\log m)$. This lower bound is proved in a very general model which rules out many promising linear modes of operations for encryption with message integrity. This lower bound is tight as in an earlier paper "Encryption Models with Almost Free Message Integrity", Proc. Eurocrypt 2001, we show a linear scheme to encrypt m blocks while assuring message integrity by using only $m + 2 + \log m$ invocations of random permutations.

1 Introduction

Recently, new modes of operation for block ciphers (IAPM, IACBC, XCBC-XOR) were described in [9] and [5], which in addition to assuring confidentiality of the plaintext, also assure message integrity. Prior to this, two separate passes were required; first to compute a cryptographic MAC (e.g. CBC-MAC [2]) and then to encrypt the plaintext with the MAC appended to the plaintext (e.g. using CBC [18]). Following up on works of [9], and [5], another authenticated encryption mode (OCB) was described in [20].

Before the modes in [9] and [5] many unsuccessful attempts were made to do authenticated encryption in one pass (e.g. [4]). Most of these attempts try to use a simple checksum instead of a cryptographic MAC, as the tag appended to the plaintext before encryption. Other attempts try to do additional chaining, on top of the cipher block chaining in CBC (see figure 2 for one such mode called MPCBC [11] [12] - modified plaintext ciphertext block chaining). In essence, all these proposed modes try to do authenticated encryption by using only exclusive-or operations (i.e. operations linear in $(GF2)^n$, where n is the block cipher size), and without generating any extra randomness using the block cipher or some pseudo-random function. A successful mode for authenticated encryption was described in [10], however it increased the length of the ciphertext by a constant factor.

One of the modes in [9] is proven to be secure for both encryption and authentication even though it only uses operations linear in $(GF2)^n$ (apart from block cipher invocations), but it actually generates $\log m$ extra blocks of randomness

M. Matsui and R. Zuccherato (Eds.): SAC 2003, LNCS 3006, pp. 348–360, 2004.

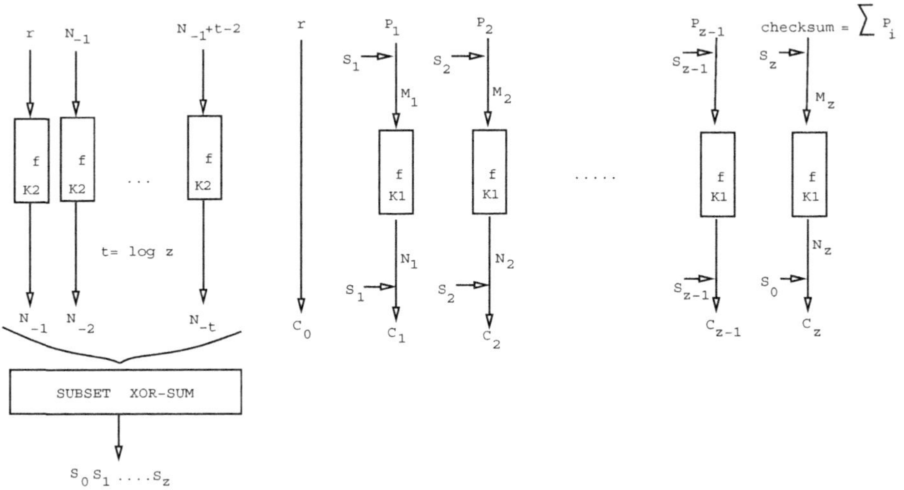

Fig. 1. Authenticated Encryption Mode IAPM

(where m is the number of blocks to be encrypted) by $\log m$ extra block cipher invocations.

In this paper we show a matching lower bound to the construction in [9] (see Figure 1). In other words, we show that the $\log m$ additional cryptographic operations in IAPM/IACBC scheme are essentially the least one has to do to assure message integrity along with message secrecy in any scheme linear in $(GF2)^n$.

We prove our lower bound in a very general model. We assume that the block cipher is modeled as a length preserving random function on n bits. Any invocation of such a random function constitutes one application of a cryptographic function. The only other operations allowed are linear operations over $(GF2)^n$ (i.e. n-bit exclusive-or), or testing an n bit quantity for zero. There is no other restriction on the scheme, apart from it being one to one (i.e. no two plaintexts generate the same ciphertext). There is no assumption about whether the scheme is actually invertible (which is the surprising part). The scheme is also allowed to be probabilistic with v blocks of randomness. For example, the v blocks of randomness could be v blocks of shared keys.

As our main result, we prove that any such linear scheme which encrypts m blocks of plaintext while assuring message integrity, using v blocks of randomness, and only $m+k$ cryptographic operations, must have $k+v$ at least $\Omega(\log m)$.

We use a well known theorem from linear algebra, and other techniques from linear algebra to prove our lower bound. Specifically we analyze the ranks of matrices and solution spaces of linear system of equations to prove the lower bound. Linear algebra techniques like analysis of rank of matrices have been used previously by [14] to show attacks on a whole class of schemes (double

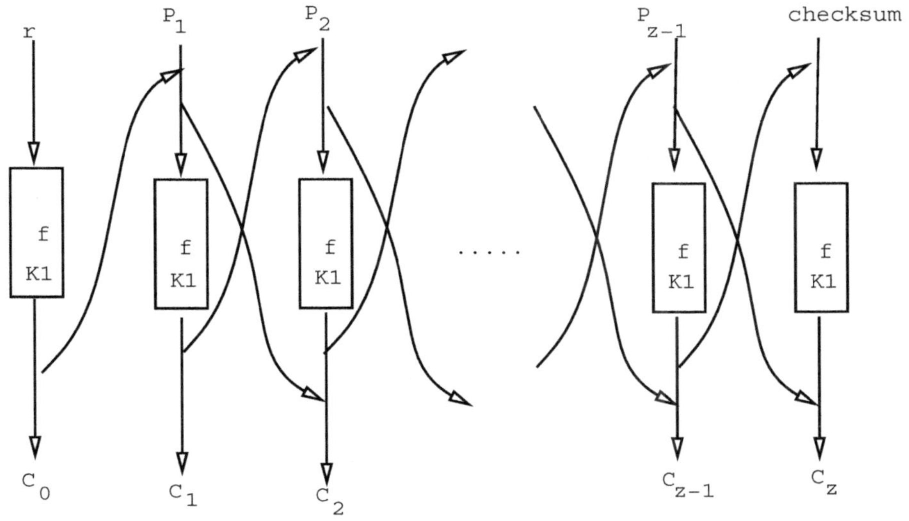

Fig. 2. Encryption Mode MPCBC

block length hash functions), although the matrices involved in [14] were of constant ranks (three or four).

We again emphasize that our lower bound is a very general result, as it rules out many potential schemes for authenticated encryption by just an inspection of the number of cryptographic operations, and the mixing operations used (i.e. regardless of the structure of the scheme). Figures 3 and 4 (in addition to Figure 2) describe some other modes which by this lower bound turn out to be insecure for authenticated encryption. The mode in Figure 3 tries to use the structure of both the counter mode[17], and the CBC mode. All mixing operations in Figures 1 to 4 are n-bit exclusive-or operations.

Note that there are versions of IAPM/IACBC in [9], and modes for authenticated encryption in [5],[20] which are proven secure while using only one or two extra cryptographic operations. This does not contradict our lower bound as these schemes are not linear in $(GF2)^n$. In fact, the main theorem in [9] shows that authenticated encryption can be achieved by generating and using (linearly) a sequence of random numbers which are only pairwise -differentially uniform (or XOR-universal, a property slightly weaker than pairwise independence). Such a sequence can be generated by only one additional cryptographic operation if operations in GFp or $GF(2^n)$ are allowed, but such a sequence does indeed require $\log m$ extra cryptographic operations, if only linear in $(GF2)^n$ operations are allowed.

It is worth noting that schemes which use $GF(2^n)$ to generate the XOR-universal whitening sequence are linear in $GF2$, and hence by the discussion in

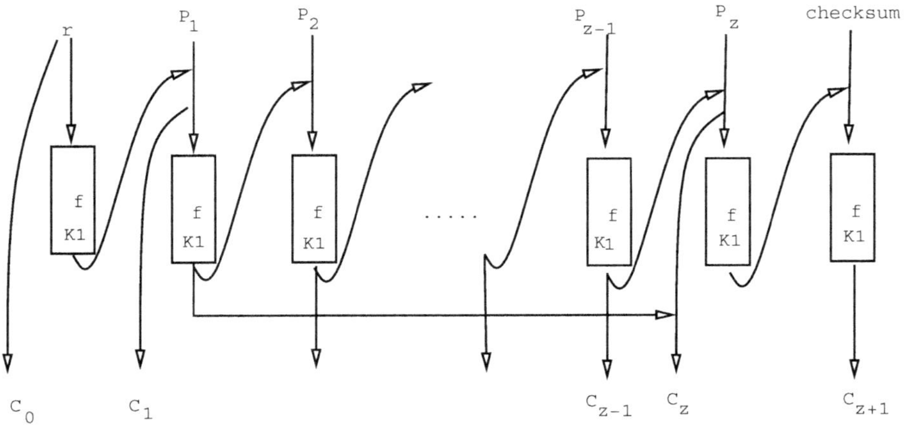

Fig. 3. Erroneous Mode 2

the previous paragraph, there cannot be a similar lower bound for schemes linear in $GF2$.

The rest of the paper is organized as follows. In section 2 we state some lemma from linear algebra which are used in proving the main theorem. In section 3 we describe the model of authenticated encryption. In section 4 we prove the main lower bound theorem.

2 Linear Algebra Basics

The first lemma is basic, and the second is a key theorem in linear algebra [13].

Lemma 2.1: Let

$$[X_1 ... X_q] \cdot \mathbf{A} = [Y_1 ... Y_m]$$

where $\mathbf{A}$ is a $q \times m$ binary matrix of rank m, and all the variables represent elements of $(GF2)^n$. If for some subset $\mathbf{B}$ of rows of $\mathbf{A}$, rank($\mathbf{B}$) $< m$, then there is a non-trivial linear (over GF2) relation between the variables $Y_1 ... Y_m$, and variables $\{X_i | i \in [1..q]$, and i not index of some row in $\mathbf{B}\}$.

Proof: Since $\mathbf{B}$ has rank less than m, there exists a non-zero vector x such that $\mathbf{B} \cdot x = 0$. In fact, the set of such vectors are of dimension $m-$rank($\mathbf{B}$) (see the next lemma). The following equation then yields the required linear relation:

$$[X_1 ... X_q] \cdot \mathbf{A} \cdot x = [Y_1 ... Y_m] \cdot x$$

Lemma 2.2: Let

$$[X_1 ... X_q] \cdot \mathbf{A} = [Y_1 ... Y_m]$$

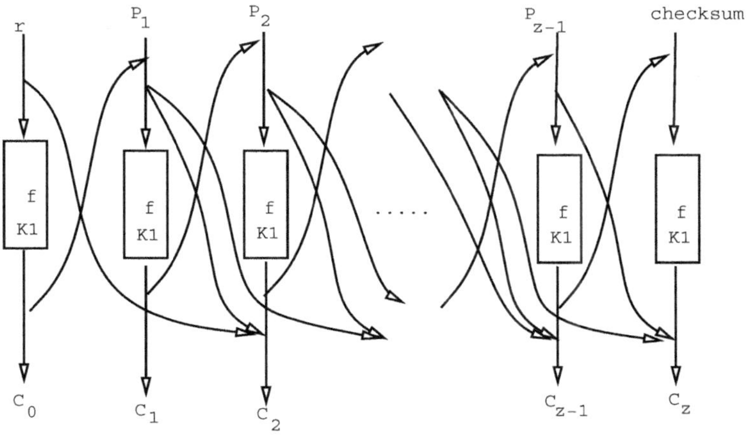

Fig. 4. Erroneous Mode 3

where **A** is a $q \times m$ binary matrix of rank $m' \leq m$, and $m \leq q$, and all the variables represent elements from $(GF2)^n$. Then for a fixed $Y = [Y_1...Y_m]$, which allows for at least one solution in $[X_1...X_q]$ of the above equations, the solution space of $[X_1...X_q]$ is a $q - m'$ dimensional affine space, namely

$$[X_1...X_q] = [< f(Y) >] + \alpha_1 \cdot V_1 + ... + \alpha_{q-m'} \cdot V_{q-m'}$$

where $< f(Y) >$ is a row of q linear functions determined by **A**, each of $\alpha_1...\alpha_{q-m'}$ is a scalar ranging over all elements in $(GF2)^n$, and $V_1...V_{q-m'}$ are $q - m'$ linearly independent binary row vectors determined by **A**.

The vectors $V_1...V_{q-m'}$ constitute a basis of the *null space* of **A**.

3 Linear in $(\mathbf{GF2})^n$ Authenticated Encryption Model

We consider the following model. We assume a fixed block size n for a block cipher (or random permutations or length preserving random functions). Any application of one of these will constitute one application of a cryptographic operation. From now on we will assume that the block cipher is modeled as a length preserving n bit random function. The only other operations allowed are linear operations over $(\mathrm{GF2})^n$, i.e. bit-wise exclusive-or. Of course, operations of testing whether an n bit quantity is zero is also allowed. Since, the scheme could be probabilistic, as IACBC/IAPM [9] is, we also allow v blocks of randomness, $r_1, ..., r_v$. These blocks of randomness could be shared beforehand as keys.

Let the message P to be encrypted be of size m blocks, i.e. mn bits (as we will see later, we only need to model a single message encryption). Call the input blocks $P_1, ..., P_m$. Let there be $m + k$ invocations of random functions, and let the inputs to these functions be $M_1, M_2, ..., M_{m+k}$. Similarly, let the outputs of these random functions be $N_1, N_2, ..., N_{m+k}$. Let, $C = C_1, C_2, ...C_{m+t}$ be linear functions of P's, r's, and N's. Here, $t \geq 0$. Similarly, each M_i is a linear combination of P, r and N.

Thus let,

$$[P_1...P_m r_1...r_v N_1...N_{m+k}\ 1] \cdot \mathbf{B} = [C_1...C_{m+t}]$$

$$[P_1...P_m r_1...r_v N_1...N_{m+k}\ 1] \cdot \mathbf{E} = [M_1...M_{m+k}]$$

where each of $\mathbf{B}$ and $\mathbf{E}$ is a binary matrix except for the last row in which each entry can have arbitrary elements in $(GF2)^n$.

We have not addressed the question of invertibility of this scheme. It will turn out, that for the purpose of proving our lower bound, it is not important whether the scheme is invertible or not. However, we do require the scheme to be one-to-one. More precisely, a scheme is *one-to-one* if it is not the case that there are two different plaintext messages P^1 and P^2, and a random string r, such that $\langle r, P^1 \rangle$ generates ciphertext C, and $\langle r, P^2 \rangle$ generates the same ciphertext C (as r could be part of the shared key, two different r's on different plaintexts are allowed to generate the same ciphertext).

Our aim is to show that either the scheme is not secrecy secure, or it is not message integrity secure, or it is not one to one (not just not invertible), or $k + v = \Omega(\log m)$. We now define each of these terms formally.

The scheme is not *secrecy secure* if an adversary can correctly predict a non-trivial linear combination of the plaintext blocks, given the corresponding ciphertext, with probability more than $1 - O(2^{-n})$, in time polynomial in m and n. Note that we do not need an epsilon-delta definition of security, as we will always be able to demonstrate attacks which work with high probability. Also our attacks will not need to see many ciphertexts before predicting the plaintext. Thus, we have a weak adversarial model.

For *message integrity* , let there be $u > 0$ MDC (manipulation detection code) functions $\mu_1, ..., \mu_u$, each a linear function of P's, M's, N's, and r's. Without loss of generality assume that they are linearly independent. During encryption of plaintext P, using randomness r, each μ_i is computed as a linear combination of P's, M's, N's, and r's. During decryption of the corresponding ciphertext C, another set of functions $\mu'_1, ..., \mu'_u$ is computed as a function of C's, M's, and N's. The decryption process passes the message integrity test if for all i, $\mu_i = \mu'_i$. For example in IAPM (fig 1), $\mu_1 = \Sigma\, P$, and $\mu'_1 = M_z \oplus S_z$, where S_z is some linear combination of $N_{-1}...N_{-t}$. Now, define $D_i = \mu_i \oplus \mu'_i$, a linear function of P,M,N,r, and C. Since C can be written as a linear combination of P, N, and r, each D_i is a linear function of P,M,N, and r. On a valid decryption all the D_i should evaluate to zero.

A scheme is not message integrity secure, if for a fixed r, and given P and corresponding C, an adversary can produce a $C' \neq C$ in time polynomial in m and n, such that on inversion, all the functions D_i evaluate to zero. Once again, our attacks do not require many plaintext, ciphertext combinations before a forged ciphertext is demonstrated. Note that the notion of message integrity here is that of ciphertext forgery in the known plaintext, known ciphertext model. Clearly, the lower bound holds as well for the chosen plaintext attacks.

Let

$$[M_1...M_{m+k}P_1...P_m r_1...r_v N_1...N_{m+k}\ 1]\cdot \mathbf{F} \;=\; [D_1...D_u]$$

We combine these three systems of equations to write a big system as follows:

$$[M_1...M_{m+k}P_1...P_m r_1...r_v N_1...N_{m+k}\ 1]\cdot \mathbf{G} \;=\; [C_1...C_{m+t}D_1...D_u\ 0...0]$$

where there are $m+k$ 0's in the R.H.S vector corresponding to the matrix $\mathbf{E}$ (i.e. second system of equations). More precisely,

$$\mathbf{G} \;=\; \underbrace{\begin{bmatrix}\mathbf{0} \\ \mathbf{B}\end{bmatrix}}_{m+t}\underbrace{\mathbf{F}}_{u}\underbrace{\begin{bmatrix}\mathbf{I} \\ \mathbf{E}\end{bmatrix}}_{m+k} \quad \begin{matrix}\}m+k \\ \}m+v+m+k+1\end{matrix}$$

We will refer to a given *authenticated encryption scheme* by the matrix $\mathbf{G}$.

4 Lower Bound

Theorem 1: If the scheme $\mathbf{G}$ is secrecy secure, message integrity secure, and one-to-one, then $k+v$ is at least $\Omega(\log m)$.

We first give an informal description of the proof technique, followed by lemmas and their formal proof, finally followed by the formal proof of this theorem.

We first prove that the number of extra encryptions (including the randomness used) is at least the number of extra ciphertexts and the number of checksum blocks minus one, or else the secrecy is compromised. This is far from obvious, and is proven formally in lemma 1 below. Informally, it is reasonable to assume that each extra ciphertext requires an extra encryption. However, the fact that each checksum block requires an extra encryption is a bit tricky. The main idea is that the checksum blocks in a valid decryption evaluate to zero, and being linearly independent of each other, they must not be just linear combinations of ciphertexts and plaintexts.

The scheme G maybe generating some or all of its ciphertext blocks in a manner similar to the counter mode. In other words, some ciphertext block C_i may just be the plaintext block P_i xor'ed with the encryption of a counter. We next prove that each such block of ciphertext which is generated using the "counter mode", requires its own checksum (MDC) block. This is proven formally in lemma 2.

We say that N_i and N_j *resolve* if $N_i \oplus N_j$ can be written as a linear combination of only the C's and P's. Similarly, we say that M_i and M_j resolve if $M_i \oplus M_j$ can be written as a linear combination of only the C's and P's.

Informally, if N_i and N_j resolve, an adversary can calculate the change required in the given ciphertext so that all the checksums come out correct. Thus, in lemma 3 we prove that if there exists a pair i, j, $i \neq j$, such that N_i and N_j resolve, M_i and M_j resolve, and N_i and N_j (similarly M_i and M_j) contribute identically to each MDC D, then that leads to the scheme being compromised for message integrity.

We show in lemma 4 that if the scheme is secrecy secure, and if the total number of extra encryptions (taking into account the bounds of lemma 1 and 2) is not at least $\log m$, then the conditions in the previous paragraph (i.e. the antecedent in lemma 3) are met.

Informally, that proves theorem 1. Now, to the formal proofs of the four lemmas.

Lemma 1: Either the scheme $\mathbf{G}$ is not secrecy secure or $k + v \geq t + u - 1$

Proof: Use the identity matrix in the top right corner of $\mathbf{G}$ to zero out the first $m + k$ rows of the the first $m + t + u$ columns. We call this new matrix $\mathbf{G}'$. We now write the columns corresponding to D as $[\mathbf{0}\ \mathbf{F}'^{\top}]^{\top}$. Thus,

$$\mathbf{G}' = \underbrace{\begin{bmatrix} \mathbf{0} \\ \mathbf{B} \end{bmatrix}}_{m+t}\!\!\underbrace{\begin{matrix} \mathbf{0} \\ \mathbf{F}' \end{matrix}}_{u}\!\!\underbrace{\begin{bmatrix} \mathbf{I} \\ \mathbf{E} \end{bmatrix}}_{m+k} \begin{matrix} \}m+k \\ \}m+v+m+k+1 \end{matrix}$$

We first show that w.l.o.g. we can assume that the rank of the matrix $\mathbf{G}'$ is at least $m + t + u$. Suppose the rank of the matrix $\mathbf{G}'$ is $m' < m + t + u$. Clearly the columns corresponding to D are linearly independent, as we assumed earlier. Thus, there are $m + t + u - m'$ columns corresponding to C which are linear combinations of the other columns corresponding to C, and the columns corresponding to D. However, on a valid encryption all the D_i are zero. This means, that these $m + t + u - m'$ C_i's corresponding to the columns mentioned can be computed as a linear combination of the other $m + t - (m + t + u - m') = m' - u$ C_i's. Thus, there need only be $m' - u$ C_is, in the big equation above. Thus, we can assume w.l.o.g that the rank of the matrix $\mathbf{G}'$ is at least $m + t + u$.

In fact by the above argument, the rank of the sub-matrix of $\mathbf{G}'$ consisting of the first $m + t + u$ columns is $m + t + u$.

Now, let's focus on the matrix $\mathbf{G}''$ comprising of only the first $m + t + u$ columns of $\mathbf{G}'$ and the rows of $\mathbf{G}'$ excluding the rows corresponding to P. If the rank of the sub-matrix $\mathbf{G}''$ is less than $m + t + u$, then there is a non-trivial linear relationship between C's, D's, and P. Once again, since on a valid encryption D's are zero, we would get a non-trivial linear relation between P's and C's, contradicting that the scheme is secrecy-secure. Since the $m + k$ rows of the first $m+t+u$ columns of $\mathbf{G}''$ are zero, we have that $(v+(m+k)+1) \geq m+t+u$, or $k + v \geq t + u - 1$.

Going back to $\mathbf{G}$, it is useful to reduce the rows corresponding to P in $\mathbf{B}$ and $\mathbf{F}$ to zero, if possible. In other words, we would like to express P in terms of M, N, and r, if possible (else such blocks are encrypted as in "counter mode"). So, by doing column operations, let the rows in $[\mathbf{I}\,\mathbf{E}^{\top}]^{\top}$ corresponding to P be reduced to

$$\begin{pmatrix} 0 & X \\ 0 & \mathbf{I} \end{pmatrix}$$

where the identity matrix is of size w, $0 \leq w \leq m$, resulting in the new equation

$$[M_1...M_{m+k}P_1...P_m r_1...r_v N_1...N_{m+k}\ 1] \cdot \begin{bmatrix} \mathbf{0} \\ \mathbf{B} \end{bmatrix} \mathbf{F}\ \mathbf{E}' \Bigg] = [C_1...C_{m+t}D_1...D_u\ 0...0]$$

Consequently we can assume, w.l.o.g., that the bottom w rows corresponding to P in $\mathbf{F}$ are zero. Let the resulting big matrix be $\mathbf{H}$.

We now have the system of equations

$$[M_1...M_{m+k}P_1...P_m r_1...r_v N_1...N_{m+k}\ 1] \cdot \mathbf{H} = [C_1...C_{m+t}D_1...D_u\ 0...0]$$

where in $\mathbf{H}$ the bottom w rows corresponding to P are zero in the columns corresponding to D.

Lemma 2: Either the scheme $\mathbf{G}$ is not message integrity secure or not one-to-one, or $u \geq (m - w)$

Proof: Let c be a ciphertext which is computed based on a given p and r. Consider the sub-matrix of $\mathbf{H}$ which consists of the first $m - w$ rows corresponding to the P's and the u columns corresponding to D. If this sub-matrix has rank less than $m - w$, then there is a $p' \neq p$ (with p' different from p only in the first $m - w$ indices (blocks)), such that D's remain same, i.e. zero. Because, of the identity matrix in $\mathbf{E}'$ we can arrive at a p'', which is identical to p' in the first $m - w$ blocks, but possibly different in the remaining w blocks, so that none of the M's and N's are affected (i.e. p'' is consistent with same Ms and Ns as computed from p). The new p'' still keeps all the Ds zero (as the bottom w rows corresponding to P were zeroed out in $\mathbf{F}$). This new p'' results in a new c'' which is different from c (as the scheme is 1-1). Thus, we have a different c''. Note that, $p'' \oplus p$, does not depend on p; and similarly, $c'' \oplus c$ does not depend on p (and not even c). Thus, an adversary with access to a valid c, can come up with a c'' which on decryption leads to all the D's being zero. Thus, $u \geq m - w$.

We will need yet another combination of equations to prove the next lemma. This time, using the identity matrix in $\mathbf{E}'$ corresponding to the P rows, we now also zero out the corresponding entries in $\mathbf{B}$ and let the new matrix be $\mathbf{H}'$. Thus, $\mathbf{H}'$ is different from $\mathbf{H}$ in only the columns corresponding to C.

Using $\mathbf{H}'$ (or $\mathbf{H}$) let's rewrite the equations for D more conveniently:

For $i = 1..u$, let

$$D_i = \sum_{j=1}^{m+k}(a^i_j \cdot M_j) \oplus \sum_{j=1}^{m+k}(b^i_j \cdot N_j) \oplus \sum_{j=1}^{v}(c^i_j \cdot r_j) \oplus \sum_{j=1}^{m-w}(d^i_j \cdot P_j)$$

In the matrix $\mathbf{E}'$, the first $(m - w)$ columns have the rows corresponding to P equal to zero. In a way these columns also work as hidden integrity checks, though not always. So, for $i = u+1..u+m-w$ define D'_i similar to above, using the $(m - w)$ columns of $\mathbf{E}'$ or $\mathbf{H}$.

$$D'_i = \sum_{j=1}^{m+k}(a^i_j \cdot M_j) \oplus \sum_{j=1}^{m+k}(b^i_j \cdot N_j) \oplus \sum_{j=1}^{v}(c^i_j \cdot r_j)$$

We say that N_i and N_j *resolve* if $N_i \oplus N_j$ can be written as a linear combination of only the C's and P's. Similarly, we say that M_i and M_j resolve if $M_i \oplus M_j$ can be written as a linear combination of only the C's and P's.

We will later show that there exists a pair $i, j, i \neq j, i, j \in [1..m+k]$ such that

1. N_i and N_j resolve
2. M_i and M_j resolve
3. For all $x \in [1..u+m-w]$, $a_i^x \oplus a_j^x = 0$, and $b_i^x \oplus b_j^x = 0$
4. There exists $y \in [1..m+t]$, $\mathbf{H'}_{2m+k+v+i,y} \oplus \mathbf{H'}_{2m+k+v+j,y} = 1$

In item (4), $\mathbf{H'}_{2m+k+v+i,y}$ is the entry in $\mathbf{H'}$ in row corresponding to N_i and in column corresponding to C_y. Essentially, it says that the rows corresponding to N_i and N_j are not identical (for the first $m+t$ columns).

In the next lemma we show that if such a pair exists with the above four conditions holding then the scheme $\mathbf{G}$ is not message integrity secure.

Lemma 3: If there exists a pair $i, j, i \neq j, i, j \in [1..m+k]$ such that the above four conditions hold, then the scheme $\mathbf{G}$ is not message integrity secure.

Proof: We will show that with probability greater then $1 - O(2^{-n})$ there exists a c' (different from a given c) which can easily be computed (given c and the corresponding p) such that

- $N_i' = N_j$
- $N_j' = N_i$
- for z different from i, j, $N_z' = N_z$
- the first $m-w$ blocks of P remain same

We have a similar set of relations for M, and hence given (3), all the D functions would evaluate to zero, leading to $\mathbf{G}$ being insecure for message integrity.

To demonstrate such a c', using $\mathbf{H'}$, we evaluate Δc, for ΔN and ΔM, where

- $\Delta N_j = \Delta N_i = N_i \oplus N_j$
- $\Delta M_j = \Delta M_i = M_i \oplus M_j$

Because of (3) all the D' remain zero, which means there is no change in any other N or M. Moreover the changes above in M and N do not cause any change in the first $m-w$ plaintext blocks (all the changes can be incorporated in the lower w blocks because of the identity matrix in $\mathbf{E'}$). Since the rows corresponding to the bottom w rows of P in $\mathbf{B}$ were zeroed out, these changes in the plaintext do not affect Δc.

Now, ΔN_j is non-zero with probability $1 - 2^{-n}$ (at least). Since M_i is related to N_i by a random function, the probability that ΔM cancels out ΔN in computing Δc is at most 2^{-n}. This leads to a non-zero Δc because of (4) above with probability at least $1 - O(2^{-n})$.

Since conditions (1) and (2) hold as well, an adversary can compute such a c' from c and p.

Lemma 4: Either $k+v+u+m-w$ is $\Omega(\log m)$, or the scheme $\mathbf{G}$ is not secrecy secure, or there exists a pair i, j satisfying (1),(2), (3) and (4)

Proof: Recall that,

$$[P_1 ... P_m r_1 ... r_v N_1 ... N_{m+k}\ 1] \cdot \mathbf{B} \ = \ [C_1 ... C_{m+t}]$$

The rank of the matrix $\mathbf{B}$ is at least m, say m'. Now, we call a pair of rows from the rows corresponding to N in $\mathbf{B}$ dependent if one row can be expressed linearly in terms of other using the bottom w rows corresponding to P. This is clearly an equivalence relation. From each such pairwise dependent set (including sets with only one row), pick only one row, and push the remaining rows to the bottom. Let q be the number of rows so picked. The rank of the top $m+v+q$ rows is still at least m'.

Now if we also ignore the top m rows (corresponding to P), the rank of the remaining $v+q$ rows is still m', for otherwise we have a non-trivial linear relationship between C and P, and hence the scheme is not secrecy secure.

This implies (by lemma 2.2) that

$$[r_1 ... r_v N_1 ... N_q] \ = \ [< f(C,P) >] + (\mathrm{GF2})^n \cdot V_1 + ... + (\mathrm{GF2})^n \cdot V_{q+v-m'}$$

where $< f(C,P) >$ is a set of linear functions of C and P, and V_i are linearly-independent binary row-vectors. For a subset of N's with indices a set $J \subseteq [1..q]$ to be pair-wise "non-resolving" thus requires $q+v-m' \geq \log |J|$. In other words, there exists $i, j \in J, i \neq j$, N_i and N_j resolve if $q+v-m' < \log |J|$. Stated differently, there is a set $J1$ of size $|J1| = (q)/2^{q+v-m'}$ in which all pairs of N's resolve with each other.

Now each M_i can be written as a linear combination of r, N and P (using matrix $\mathbf{E}$). Once again (using lemma 2.2) we have

$$[r_1 ... r_v N_1 ... N_{m+k}] \ = \ [< f'(C,P) >] + (\mathrm{GF2})^n \cdot V'_1 + ... + (\mathrm{GF2})^n \cdot V'_{m+k+v-m'}$$

where $V'_1 ... V'_{m+k+v-m'}$ are linearly-independent binary row vectors. Thus, for any set of indices $J' \subseteq [1..m+k]$, there is a a set $J'' \subseteq J'$ of size $|J''|$ at least $|J'|/2^{m+k+v-m'}$, such that all pairs of Ms in this set J'' resolve with each other.

Using $J1$ for J', thus there is a set $J2$ of size $q/2^{q+v-m'+m+k+v-m'}$ such that for all $i, j \in J2$, M_i and M_j resolve, and so do N_i and N_j.

Similarly, there is a set $J3$ of size $|J3| = |J2|/2^{u+m-w}$ such that

$$\forall k \in [1..u+m-w],\ \forall i, j \in J3: \ a_i^k \oplus a_j^k = 0$$

Thus, there exists a pair satisfying (1), (2) ,(3) and (4) if $2^{m+k+q+2v-2m'+u+m-w} < q$. Now, $q+v \geq m' \geq m$. Thus, either v is $\Omega(\log m)$ in which case we are done, or q is at least $\Omega(m)$. Thus, there exists a pair satisfying (1..4) if $m+k+q+2v-2m'+u+m-w < O(\log m)$. Since, $q-m < k$, the previous inequality is implied by $2(k+v)+u+m-w < O(\log m)+2(m'-m)$, which in turn is implied by $2(k+v)+2(u+m-w) < O(\log m)$. Thus, either there exists a pair with (1..4) holding or, $k+v+u+m-w$ is $\Omega(\log m)$.

Finally, we are ready to prove the main theorem.

Proof (**Theorem 1**): By Lemma 3, since the scheme **G** is message integrity secure, there does not exist a pair with conditions (1..4) holding. Thus, by lemma 4, and the fact that **G** is secrecy secure, we have $k + v + u + m - w > \Omega(\log m)$. By lemma 1 and 2 it follows that $k + v$ is at least $\Omega(\log m)$.

4.1 Block Ciphers as Random Permutation Generators

In section 3, and the corresponding theorem in section 4, the block cipher was modeled as a random permutation (or random function). However, it is plausible that the block cipher may be keyed differently to encrypt different blocks (particularly, since we allow v blocks of randomness which could be used as key materials).

It can be shown that the previous theorem generalizes to block ciphers modeled as functions from $2n$ bits to n bits (which is even more general than random function generators [8]) with only a factor of two cut in the lower bound. Essentially, the only change occurs in lemma 4, where we estimate the size of the set $J2$.

References

[1] ANSI X3.106, "American National Standard for Information Systems – Data Encryption Algorithm – Modes of Operation", American National Standards Institute, 1983.

[2] M. Bellare, J. Kilian, P. Rogaway, "The Security of Cipher Block Chaining", CRYPTO 94, LNCS 839, 1994 348

[3] M. Bellare, C. Namprempre, "Authenticated Encryption: Relations among notions and analysis of the generic composition paradigm", Proc. Asiacrypt 2000, T. Okamoto ed., Springer Verlag 2000

[4] V. D. Gligor, P.Donescu, "Integrity Aware PCBC Encryption Schemes", 7th Intl. Workshop on Security Protocols, Cambridge, LNCS, 1999 348

[5] V. D. Gligor, P. Donescu, "Fast Encryption Authentication: XCBC Encryption and XECB Authentication Modes", Proc. Fast Software Encryption 2001. 348, 350

[6] ISO 8372, "Information processing – Modes of operation for a 64-bit block cipher algorithm", International Organization for Standardization, Geneva, Switzerland, 1987

[7] ISO/IEC 9797, "Data cryptographic techniques – Data integrity mechanism using a cryptographic check function employing a block cipher algorithm", 1989

[8] M. Luby, "Pseudorandomness and Cryptographic Applications", Princeton Computer Science Notes, 1996. 359

[9] C. S. Jutla, "Encryption Modes with Almost Free Message Integrity", Proc. Eurocrypt 2001, LNCS 2045. 348, 349, 350, 352

[10] J. Katz and M. Yung, "Unforgeable Encryption and Adaptively Secure Modes of Operation", Proc. Fast Software Encryption 2000. 348

[11] Modified PCBC for DES, `http://diswww.mit.edu:8008/menelaus.mit.edu/kprot/23` 348

[12] Adam Black, Anton Stiglic, "Free-Mac Mode", sci.crypt Newsgroup, 2000/03/07 348

[13] Saunders MacLane, "Algebra", New York : Macmillan (1967) 351

[14] L. R. Knudsen, X. Lai, B. Preneel, "Attacks on Fasst Double Block Length Hash Functions", Journal of Cryptology, Vol 11, No. 1, Winter 1998 349, 350

[15] Hugo Krawczyk, "LFSR-based Hashing and Authentication", Proc. Crypto 94. LNCS 839, 1994

[16] C. H. Meyer, S. M. Matyas, "Cryptography: A New Dimension in Computer Data Security", John Wiley and Sons, New York, 1982

[17] National Institute of Standards and Technology, "Recommendation for Block Cipher Modes of Operation", SP 800-38A, `http://csrc.nist.gov/publications/nistpubs/index.html` 350

[18] National Bureau of Standards, NBS FIPS PUB 81, "DES modes of operation", U.S. Department of Commerce, 1980. 348

[19] RFC 1510,"The Kerberos network authentication service (V5)", J. Kohl and B. C. Neuman, Sept 1993

[20] Phillip Rogaway, Mihir Bellare, John Black, and Ted Krovetz, "OCB: A Block-Cipher Mode of Operation for Efficient Authenticated Encryption", Eighth ACM Conference on Computer and Communications Security (CCS-8), ACM Press, pp. 196-205, 2001. 348, 350

Author Index

Lecture Notes in Computer Science

For information about Vols. 1–2888

please contact your bookseller or Springer-Verlag

Vol. 3009: F. Bomarius, H. Iida (Eds.), Product Focused Software Process Improvement. XIV, 584 pages. 2004.

Vol. 3006: M. Matsui, R. Zuccherato (Eds.), Selected Areas in Cryptography. XI, 361 pages. 2004.

Vol. 3005: G.R. Raidl, S. Cagnoni, J. Branke, D.W. Corne, R. Drechsler, Y. Jin, C.G. Johnson, P. Machado, E. Marchiori, F. Rothlauf, G.D. Smith, G. Squillero (Eds.), Applications of Evolutionary Computing. XVII, 562 pages. 2004.

Vol. 3004: J. Gottlieb, G.R. Raidl (Eds.), Evolutionary Computation in Combinatorial Optimization. X, 241 pages. 2004.

Vol. 3003: M. Keijzer, U.-M. O'Reilly, S.M. Lucas, E. Costa, T. Soule (Eds.), Genetic Programming. XI, 410 pages. 2004.

Vol. 2999: E.A. Boiten, J. Derrick, G. Smith (Eds.), Integrated Formal Methods. XI, 541 pages. 2004.

Vol. 2998: Y. Kameyama, P.J. Stuckey (Eds.), Functional and Logic Programming. X, 307 pages. 2004.

Vol. 2997: S. McDonald, J. Tait (Eds.), Advances in Information Retrieval. XIII, 427 pages. 2004.

Vol. 2996: V. Diekert, M. Habib (Eds.), STACS 2004. XVI, 658 pages. 2004.

Vol. 2995: C. Jensen, S. Poslad, T. Dimitrakos (Eds.), Trust Management. XIII, 377 pages. 2004.

Vol. 2994: E. Rahm (Ed.), Data Integration in the Life Sciences. X, 221 pages. 2004. (Subseries LNBI).

Vol. 2993: R. Alur, G.J. Pappas (Eds.), Hybrid Systems: Computation and Control. XII, 674 pages. 2004.

Vol. 2992: E. Bertino, S. Christodoulakis, D. Plexousakis, V. Christophides, M. Koubarakis, K. Böhm, E. Ferrari (Eds.), Advances in Database Technology - EDBT 2004. XVIII, 877 pages. 2004.

Vol. 2991: R. Alt, A. Frommer, R.B. Kearfott, W. Luther (Eds.), Numerical Software with Result Verification. X, 315 pages. 2004.

Vol. 2989: S. Graf, L. Mounier (Eds.), Model Checking Software. X, 309 pages. 2004.

Vol. 2988: K. Jensen, A. Podelski (Eds.), Tools and Algorithms for the Construction and Analysis of Systems. XIV, 608 pages. 2004.

Vol. 2987: I. Walukiewicz (Ed.), Foundations of Software Science and Computation Structures. XIII, 529 pages. 2004.

Vol. 2986: D. Schmidt (Ed.), Programming Languages and Systems. XII, 417 pages. 2004.

Vol. 2985: E. Duesterwald (Ed.), Compiler Construction. X, 313 pages. 2004.

Vol. 2984: M. Wermelinger, T. Margaria-Steffen (Eds.), Fundamental Approaches to Software Engineering. XII, 389 pages. 2004.

Vol. 2983: S. Istrail, M.S. Waterman, A. Clark (Eds.), Computational Methods for SNPs and Haplotype Inference. IX, 153 pages. 2004. (Subseries LNBI).

Vol. 2982: N. Wakamiya, M. Solarski, J. Sterbenz (Eds.), Active Networks. XI, 308 pages. 2004.

Vol. 2981: C. Müller-Schloer, T. Ungerer, B. Bauer (Eds.), Organic and Pervasive Computing – ARCS 2004. XI, 339 pages. 2004.

Vol. 2980: A. Blackwell, K. Marriott, A. Shimojima (Eds.), Diagrammatic Representation and Inference. XV, 448 pages. 2004. (Subseries LNAI).

Vol. 2978: R. Groz, R.M. Hierons (Eds.), Testing of Communicating Systems. XII, 225 pages. 2004.

Vol. 2977: G. Di Marzo Serugendo, A. Karageorgos, O.F. Rana, F. Zambonelli (Eds.), Engineering Self-Organising Systems. X, 299 pages. 2004. (Subseries LNAI).

Vol. 2976: M. Farach-Colton (Ed.), LATIN 2004: Theoretical Informatics. XV, 626 pages. 2004.

Vol. 2973: Y. Lee, J. Li, K.-Y. Whang, D. Lee (Eds.), Database Systems for Advanced Applications. XXIV, 925 pages. 2004.

Vol. 2972: R. Monroy, G. Arroyo-Figueroa, L.E. Sucar, H. Sossa (Eds.), MICAI 2004: Advances in Artificial Intelligence. XVII, 923 pages. 2004.

Vol. 2971: J.I. Lim, D.H. Lee (Eds.), Information Security and Cryptology -ICISC 2003. XI, 458 pages. 2004.

Vol. 2970: F. Fernández Rivera, M. Bubak, A. Gómez Tato, R. Doallo (Eds.), Grid Computing. XI, 328 pages. 2004.

Vol. 2964: T. Okamoto (Ed.), Topics in Cryptology – CT-RSA 2004. XI, 387 pages. 2004.

Vol. 2963: R. Sharp, Higher Level Hardware Synthesis. XVI, 195 pages. 2004.

Vol. 2962: S. Bistarelli, Semirings for Soft Constraint Solving and Programming. XII, 279 pages. 2004.

Vol. 2961: P. Eklund (Ed.), Concept Lattices. IX, 411 pages. 2004. (Subseries LNAI).

Vol. 2960: P.D. Mosses (Ed.), CASL Reference Manual. XVII, 528 pages. 2004.

Vol. 2958: L. Rauchwerger (Ed.), Languages and Compilers for Parallel Computing. XI, 556 pages. 2004.

Vol. 2957: P. Langendoerfer, M. Liu, I. Matta, V. Tsaoussidis (Eds.), Wired/Wireless Internet Communications. XI, 307 pages. 2004.

Vol. 2954: F. Crestani, M. Dunlop, S. Mizzaro (Eds.), Mobile and Ubiquitous Information Access. X, 299 pages. 2004.

Vol. 2953: K. Konrad, Model Generation for Natural Language Interpretation and Analysis. XIII, 166 pages. 2004. (Subseries LNAI).

Vol. 2952: N. Guelfi, E. Astesiano, G. Reggio (Eds.), Scientific Engineering of Distributed Java Applications. X, 157 pages. 2004.

Vol. 2951: M. Naor (Ed.), Theory of Cryptography. XI, 523 pages. 2004.

Vol. 2949: R. De Nicola, G. Ferrari, G. Meredith (Eds.), Coordination Models and Languages. X, 323 pages. 2004.

Vol. 2948: G.L. Mullen, A. Poli, H. Stichtenoth (Eds.), Finite Fields and Applications. VIII, 263 pages. 2004.

Vol. 2947: F. Bao, R. Deng, J. Zhou (Eds.), Public Key Cryptography – PKC 2004. XI, 455 pages. 2004.

Vol. 2946: R. Focardi, R. Gorrieri (Eds.), Foundations of Security Analysis and Design II. VII, 267 pages. 2004.

Vol. 2943: J. Chen, J. Reif (Eds.), DNA Computing. X, 225 pages. 2004.

Vol. 2941: M. Wirsing, A. Knapp, S. Balsamo (Eds.), Radical Innovations of Software and Systems Engineering in the Future. X, 359 pages. 2004.

Vol. 2940: C. Lucena, A. Garcia, A. Romanovsky, J. Castro, P.S. Alencar (Eds.), Software Engineering for Multi-Agent Systems II. XII, 279 pages. 2004.

Vol. 2939: T. Kalker, I.J. Cox, Y.M. Ro (Eds.), Digital Watermarking. XII, 602 pages. 2004.

Vol. 2937: B. Steffen, G. Levi (Eds.), Verification, Model Checking, and Abstract Interpretation. XI, 325 pages. 2004.

Vol. 2934: G. Lindemann, D. Moldt, M. Paolucci (Eds.), Regulated Agent-Based Social Systems. X, 301 pages. 2004. (Subseries LNAI).

Vol. 2930: F. Winkler (Ed.), Automated Deduction in Geometry. VII, 231 pages. 2004. (Subseries LNAI).

Vol. 2929: H. de Swart, E. Orlowska, G. Schmidt, M. Roubens (Eds.), Theory and Applications of Relational Structures as Knowledge Instruments. VII, 273 pages. 2003.

Vol. 2926: L. van Elst, V. Dignum, A. Abecker (Eds.), Agent-Mediated Knowledge Management. XI, 428 pages. 2004. (Subseries LNAI).

Vol. 2923: V. Lifschitz, I. Niemelä (Eds.), Logic Programming and Nonmonotonic Reasoning. IX, 365 pages. 2004. (Subseries LNAI).

Vol. 2919: E. Giunchiglia, A. Tacchella (Eds.), Theory and Applications of Satisfiability Testing. XI, 530 pages. 2004.

Vol. 2917: E. Quintarelli, Model-Checking Based Data Retrieval. XVI, 134 pages. 2004.

Vol. 2916: C. Palamidessi (Ed.), Logic Programming. XII, 520 pages. 2003.

Vol. 2915: A. Camurri, G. Volpe (Eds.), Gesture-Based Communication in Human-Computer Interaction. XIII, 558 pages. 2004. (Subseries LNAI).

Vol. 2914: P.K. Pandya, J. Radhakrishnan (Eds.), FST TCS 2003: Foundations of Software Technology and Theoretical Computer Science. XIII, 446 pages. 2003.

Vol. 2913: T.M. Pinkston, V.K. Prasanna (Eds.), High Performance Computing - HiPC 2003. XX, 512 pages. 2003. (Subseries LNAI).

Vol. 2911: T.M.T. Sembok, H.B. Zaman, H. Chen, S.R. Urs, S.H. Myaeng (Eds.), Digital Libraries: Technology and Management of Indigenous Knowledge for Global Access. XX, 703 pages. 2003.

Vol. 2910: M.E. Orlowska, S. Weerawarana, M.M.P. Papazoglou, J. Yang (Eds.), Service-Oriented Computing - ICSOC 2003. XIV, 576 pages. 2003.

Vol. 2909: R. Solis-Oba, K. Jansen (Eds.), Approximation and Online Algorithms. VIII, 269 pages. 2004.

Vol. 2908: K. Chae, M. Yung (Eds.), Information Security Applications. XII, 506 pages. 2004.

Vol. 2907: I. Lirkov, S. Margenov, J. Wasniewski, P. Yalamov (Eds.), Large-Scale Scientific Computing. XI, 490 pages. 2004.

Vol. 2906: T. Ibaraki, N. Katoh, H. Ono (Eds.), Algorithms and Computation. XVII, 748 pages. 2003.

Vol. 2905: A. Sanfeliu, J. Ruiz-Shulcloper (Eds.), Progress in Pattern Recognition, Speech and Image Analysis. XVII, 693 pages. 2003.

Vol. 2904: T. Johansson, S. Maitra (Eds.), Progress in Cryptology - INDOCRYPT 2003. XI, 431 pages. 2003.

Vol. 2903: T.D. Gedeon, L.C.C. Fung (Eds.), AI 2003: Advances in Artificial Intelligence. XVI, 1075 pages. 2003. (Subseries LNAI).

Vol. 2902: F.M. Pires, S.P. Abreu (Eds.), Progress in Artificial Intelligence. XV, 504 pages. 2003. (Subseries LNAI).

Vol. 2901: F. Bry, N. Henze, J. Ma luszyński (Eds.), Principles and Practice of Semantic Web Reasoning. X, 209 pages. 2003.

Vol. 2900: M. Bidoit, P.D. Mosses (Eds.), Casl User Manual. XIII, 240 pages. 2004.

Vol. 2899: G. Ventre, R. Canonico (Eds.), Interactive Multimedia on Next Generation Networks. XIV, 420 pages. 2003.

Vol. 2898: K.G. Paterson (Ed.), Cryptography and Coding. IX, 385 pages. 2003.

Vol. 2897: O. Balet, G. Subsol, P. Torguet (Eds.), Virtual Storytelling. XI, 240 pages. 2003.

Vol. 2896: V.A. Saraswat (Ed.), Advances in Computing Science – ASIAN 2003. VIII, 305 pages. 2003.

Vol. 2895: A. Ohori (Ed.), Programming Languages and Systems. XIII, 427 pages. 2003.

Vol. 2894: C.S. Laih (Ed.), Advances in Cryptology - ASIACRYPT 2003. XIII, 543 pages. 2003.

Vol. 2893: J.-B. Stefani, I. Demeure, D. Hagimont (Eds.), Distributed Applications and Interoperable Systems. XIII, 311 pages. 2003.

Vol. 2892: F. Dau, The Logic System of Concept Graphs with Negation. XI, 213 pages. 2003. (Subseries LNAI).

Vol. 2891: J. Lee, M. Barley (Eds.), Intelligent Agents and Multi-Agent Systems. X, 215 pages. 2003. (Subseries LNAI).

Vol. 2890: M. Broy, A.V. Zamulin (Eds.), Perspectives of System Informatics. XV, 572 pages. 2003.

Vol. 2889: R. Meersman, Z. Tari (Eds.), On The Move to Meaningful Internet Systems 2003: OTM 2003 Workshops. XIX, 1071 pages. 2003.

GPSR Compliance

The European Union's (EU) General Product Safety Regulation (GPSR) is a set of rules that requires consumer products to be safe and our obligations to ensure this.

If you have any concerns about our products, you can contact us on ProductSafety@springernature.com

In case Publisher is established outside the EU, the EU authorized representative is:

Springer Nature Customer Service Center GmbH
Europaplatz 3
69115 Heidelberg, Germany

Batch number: 10844669

Printed by Printforce, the Netherlands